LAKE WINNIPEG

BLOODVEIN

MANITOBA

DAUPHIN LAKE

AUPHIN

RIDING MOUNTAIN
NATIONAL PARK

LAKE MANITOBA

WINNIPEG

BRANDON

Valley of the Birdtail

VALLEY
OF THE
BIRDTAIL

An Indian Reserve, a White Town,
and the Road to Reconciliation

ANDREW STOBO SNIDERMAN &
DOUGLAS SANDERSON (AMO BINASHII)

HarperCollins*Publishers*Ltd

Published by HarperCollins Publishers Ltd

First edition

HarperCollins Publishers Ltd
Bay Adelaide Centre, East Tower
22 Adelaide Street West, 41st Floor
Toronto, Ontario, Canada
M5H 4E3

www.harpercollins.ca

Endpaper map by Scott B. Henderson.

Library and Archives Canada Cataloguing in Publication

Title: Valley of the Birdtail : an Indian reserve, a white town, and the road to reconciliation /
Andrew Stobo Sniderman and Douglas Sanderson (Amo Binashii).
Names: Sniderman, Andrew Michael Stobo, 1983- author. |
Sanderson, Douglas, 1971- author.
Description: Includes bibliographical references and index.
Identifiers: Canadiana (print) 20220171122 | Canadiana (ebook) 20220172420 | ISBN
9781443466301 (hardcover) | ISBN 9781443466318 (ebook)
Subjects: LCSH: Rossburn (Man.)—Social conditions. | LCSH: Rossburn (Man.)—
Economic conditions. | LCSH: Manitoba—Race relations—History. | LCSH: Manitoba—
Ethnic relations—History. | CSH: First Nations—Manitoba—Social conditions. |
CSH: First Nations—Manitoba—Economic conditions.
Classification: LCC HN110.M35 S65 2022 | DDC 301.097127/3—dc23

Printed and bound in the United States of America

23 24 25 26 27 LBC 6 5 4 3 2

For Mom and Dad, best of parents,
and Mariella, mon tesoro.
A.S.

For my grandmothers and grandfathers,
and for all of us still wrestling with the legacy of the
Indian residential school system.
D.S. (Amo Binashii)

CONTENTS

LIST OF PEOPLE

Waywayseecappo First Nation

Maureen Twovoice (*Binesi Ikwe*)	(1991–)	Student
Linda Jandrew	(1959–)	Maureen's mother
Michael Twovoice (*Niizhwaandem*)	(1920–1987)	Maureen's grandfather
Jim Cote (*Makade Makwa*)	(1941–)	Elder
Hugh McKay	(1919–1997)	Jim's stepfather

Town of Rossburn

Troy Luhowy	(1971–)	Gym teacher
Nelson Luhowy	(1943–)	Troy's father
Dick Yaskiw	(1888–1944)	Troy's great-grandfather
Maksym Yaskiw	(1851–1911)	Troy's great-great-grandfather
Dorota Yaskiw	(1855–1942)	Troy's great-great-grandmother

Government of Canada

Alexander Morris	(1826–1889)	Treaty negotiator
Hayter Reed	(1849–1936)	Indian agent
Clifford Sifton	(1861–1929)	Minister of the Interior

AUTHORS' NOTE

THIS IS A TRUE STORY, OR AS TRUE AS IMPERFECT MEMORIES and incomplete records allow.

In Canada, 330,000 people live on reserves, the tiny remainder of vast lands Indigenous Peoples once governed. Of those living on reserves, 120,000 are children; one in two grows up in poverty, which is triple the national average, and only four in ten graduate from high school, which is half the national average.[1] A child growing up on a reserve is more likely to end up in a jail cell than a university classroom.

Though these problems are vast, we opted to investigate them with a microscope. We looked for explanations in two neighbouring communities, in the lives of two families. We also looked inside government archives, where the dead continue to whisper their secrets. We examined thousands of records, catalogued by department and date, name and volume, box and file. It turns out there is nothing accidental or inevitable about poverty in Indigenous communities.

"We," Andrew and Douglas, didn't start this project as a co-author team. The book began as an article for *Maclean's* magazine written by Andrew in the summer of 2012, while he was a law student at the University of Toronto. A few years later, he wrote a follow-up piece. Both times, he reported over the phone, from thousands of kilometres away. Haunted by what he had learned and determined to dig deeper, he booked a one-way flight to Manitoba in the fall of 2017 and first laid eyes on the valley of the Birdtail.

It became obvious to Andrew—a second-generation Canadian raised in Montreal with grandparents from Russia, Poland, and Wales—that he alone couldn't do justice to this story. So he reached out to Douglas, his former law professor.

Douglas grew up all over Western Canada—an Indian kid in cowboy towns. Later, at law school, he was asked why he wanted to pursue legal studies. He answered, "I want to know how the red man is being kept down."

Our paths first crossed in a classroom, with Andrew as a student in Douglas's property law seminar. In an early assignment, Andrew wrote that an Indigenous community had "roamed" an area of British Columbia. Douglas circled the word and added in the margin, "We could use all kinds of words to describe this: 'travelled,' 'crossed,' 'commuted,' 'perambulated.' Why 'ROAMED'?" Which was a polite way of saying: *Roaming is what animals do.*

With this unlikely beginning, an enduring friendship was born.

We wrote this book because schools on reserves have been grossly underfunded for decades. To reckon with this appalling fact is to discard the comforting notion that discrimination against Indigenous Canadians occurred in the distant past, perpetrated by strangers who are long dead. Rather, the combination of less funding and worse outcomes for Indigenous students persisted in our time, under Liberal and Conservative prime ministers. This book explains why, and shows how to ensure Indigenous children and their communities are given a fair chance.

We also address the fundamental question: How can Indigenous and non-Indigenous Canadians live side by side, as equals?

Together, we have tried to see the past more clearly, and to imagine a better future. The result is a story of villains and heroes, irony and idealism, racism and reconciliation. The story happens to take place in Canada, but if you listen carefully you can hear echoes of events in the United States, Australia, and throughout the Commonwealth.

Reconciliation is a process, and that process must begin with an honest assessment of our history. As Murray Sinclair, the former chair of Canada's Truth and Reconciliation Commission, has said:

"The truth will set you free. But first it's going to piss you off."

A NOTE ON TERMINOLOGY

Words used to refer to the earliest inhabitants in Canada—including "Indian," "Native," "First Nations," "Aboriginal," and "Indigenous"—have shifted over time. Words like "white," "non-Indigenous," and "settler" have their own upsides and shortcomings. The text of this book reflects language from primary sources and otherwise seeks to use terminology most fitting to a given context. This is easier said than done.

"THE VALLEY OF THE BIRDTAIL"

PEOPLE SAY MANITOBA IS SO FLAT THAT YOU CAN WATCH a dog run away for days. Not here, though—here, there is a valley, the parting gift of a retreating glacier. Along the floor of this valley winds the Birdtail River. It is not the mightiest of rivers; some maps acknowledge a mere creek. Still, the current was once strong enough to drown a boy. That's how the Birdtail River got its name, or so an old story goes.[1]

Sioux Indians on a buffalo hunt had set up teepees beside the river. The sun was high and bright when the Chief's son, a toddler, noticed an enchanting bird over the water. Its feathers were turquoise, except for its breast, which was as red as a raspberry. Transfixed, the boy walked to the edge of the river. As the boy watched, a hawk swooped from above to attack the colourful bird, which narrowly dodged the predator's talons with a sudden contortion. The movement dislodged from the bird's tail a single blue feather, which floated slowly downward, twirling in the breeze. It was falling close to the boy—so close that he reached out to grasp it. But he leaned too far and fell into the river.

Later, too late, the boy's body was recovered downstream, bobbing like driftwood. One of his tiny hands was balled into a fist. Inside was the bird's bright blue feather.

After the drowning, the river was called the Bird's Tail, which became, in time, the Birdtail. In 1877, federal surveyors marked out an Indian reserve near the river's western bank. The community assumed the name of its leader, Waywayseecappo, which means "The Man Proud of Standing Upright."

Two years later, a group of settlers decided to plant a crop of potatoes on the other side of the river. They called their new town Rossburn, in honour of the man who built its first school, Richard Ross. According to a local history written in 1951, "Nowhere in Manitoba is there a finer sight than the valley of the Birdtail, just west of the present town of Rossburn. It must have grieved the early settlers to find it set aside as an Indian Reserve."[2]

Waywayseecappo and Rossburn have been neighbours nearly as long as Canada has been a country. The town and the reserve are divided by a valley, a river, and almost 150 years of racism.

Today, the average family income in Rossburn is near the national average, and more than a third of adults have graduated from university. By contrast, the average family in Waywayseecappo lives below the national poverty line, and less than a third of adults have graduated from high school.[3]

This book is about how these two communities became separate and unequal, and what it means for the rest of us. The story of Waywayseecappo and Rossburn reflects much of what has gone wrong in relations between Indigenous Peoples and non-Indigenous Canadians. It also offers, in the end, an uncommon measure of hope.

Waywayseecappo, February 2006

Maureen Twovoice's alarm first buzzed at 7:00 a.m., but she kept swatting the snooze button every five minutes. Eventually, her mom, Linda, got annoyed. "Maureen, come on," Linda called out. "It's time to get up!" Maureen grumbled, then farted in defiance. If the sun wasn't up yet, why should she be? A cool draft wandered through the house. Maureen was not keen to put her warm feet on the tile floor.

"It's *seven twenty*!" Linda yelled, her voice sharper now. "The bus is coming in fifteen minutes. I don't know why you say you want to stay in school if you're not willing to get up and go." This was enough to get Maureen out of bed and into the bathroom.

First, she washed her face, then she cupped hot water in each hand and ran it along her upper arms, just to heat them up a bit. Maureen showered at night, to save time in the morning, so before school she was content to sprinkle her wavy hair and brush it a few times to avoid the appearance of a full-blown nest.

She hurried to put together an outfit—colour-coordinated, as usual, with shiny bracelets and earrings—but she didn't have time to eat breakfast. On her way out the front door, she asked her mom for a single rolled cigarette to go. Linda picked her battles, and this was not one of them. Maureen put the cigarette in her pants pocket, hoping it would make the journey more or less intact.

Maureen lived near the corner of Cloud Road and Shingoose Road—not that there were any actual road signs on the reserve. She attended high school across the river, in Rossburn, ten minutes due east on Cloud Road, if you drove directly. But Linda didn't own a car, so Maureen had to settle for two separate school buses, which took more than an hour because they had to collect kids from homes scattered all over the one hundred square kilometres of the reserve.

Maureen Twovoice (Courtesy of Maureen Twovoice)

The first bus picked Maureen up right outside her front door, then headed north on Shingoose Road. Maureen propped her backpack against the window and rested her head on it. She would have loved a nap, but the bus shuddered and shook on the gravel road. Even at this hour in the morning, in the interlude without moon or sun, she could make out bluffs of poplar and the occasional house. She knew these roads as well as anyone. Maureen and her friends had made a habit of "borrowing" her grandmother's car keys so that they could drive around, even though none of them had a licence yet. It was amazing how much driving you could do around the reserve with just five or ten bucks for gas. The important thing was to keep the windows rolled up, to avoid getting all that dust from the gravel roads in your hair.

Maureen's empty stomach was rumbling by the time the bus dropped her off at JJ's, the gas station at the corner of Shingoose Road and a road that didn't really have a name, unless you counted something like "that road where Jess and Germaine Clearsky live." JJ's was where Maureen and the other students from the initial pickup route waited while the driver picked up another group elsewhere on the reserve. Maureen used these spare twenty minutes to pop into the store and buy her breakfast/lunch: a six-inch bun filled with pepperoni, cheese, and tomato sauce, plus a can of Pepsi. She also had time to smoke the crumpled cigarette in her pocket. Even in the middle of winter, she was too cool to wear a hat or gloves, so she smoked with one hand in her coat pocket, alternating hands between drags.

Around eight thirty, Maureen boarded her second bus, which took Shingoose Road to Highway 45, the only paved road on the reserve. By now the sun had climbed over the horizon and sparkled in the snow-encrusted trees. When the bus reached the edge of the Birdtail valley, Maureen sat up in her seat to get a better view. This was her favourite moment on the ride, when the whole landscape unfurled before her. The bus picked up speed as it rolled down the slope. She could feel the descent in her stomach.

Off to the left stood the hockey arena where the Waywayseecappo Wolverines, a team in the Manitoba Junior Hockey League, played for boisterous crowds of nearly a thousand people. Whenever Maureen attended a game, she imagined how it might feel to score a goal. Her father had been a good hockey player, good enough to earn the nickname "Fast." Family friends used to call Maureen "Little Fast," but she didn't see much of her father and never really learned to skate. Her household had been too chaotic to get her to and from all those practices and games, plus the equipment had always been too expensive. Maureen had friends just as poor who somehow ended up with their own skates, but they were all boys.

As the bus approached the bottom of the valley, Maureen assembled her mental armour for the upcoming day in Rossburn. Waywayseecappo had its own school for children living on the reserve, but it only went up to Grade 8, so kids had to head across the river for high school. Nine of Maureen's Grade 9 classmates rode with her on the bus from the reserve, but most of the students at the school were pale, fair-haired teens from Rossburn with Ukrainian names full of *y*'s and *k*'s: Lysychin, Trynchuk, Olynyk. As far as Maureen could tell, there weren't really friendships between kids from Waywayseecappo and Rossburn. The boys from town barely even acknowledged her presence. "They probably thought we were all troubled," Maureen later said.

The average student from Waywayseecappo starting at Rossburn Collegiate was two to four years behind academically. Most ended up dropping out. Maureen got a reminder of the attrition rate during her morning bus commute: the number of students in each grade decreased the closer they got to Grade 12. None of Maureen's three older siblings had made it beyond Grade 11. Neither had her parents, who didn't study beyond Grade 10.

Maureen wanted something more for herself—what exactly that was, she couldn't say, but she was certain that she didn't want to spend the rest of her life eating crappy welfare dinners like fried baloney and Kraft Dinner, waiting for a biweekly government cheque that didn't buy much. *If I can get through high school,* she thought, *I can get a job. And if I can get a job, I can find another way.*

The bus engine groaned as they headed up the other side of the valley. To her right was the Birdtail River, frozen solid enough to walk on. For a brief moment, she could see a long stretch where the serpentine river split the valley, marking the line where Waywayseecappo ended and Rossburn began. Maureen crossed that line every day to get to high school.

ROSSBURN, SEPTEMBER 2006

Troy Luhowy woke up at 7:00 a.m., the same time Maureen's buzzer was going off on the other side of the Birdtail. But Troy was not a snooze button kind of guy. He didn't even bother with an alarm. He just woke up on time, battery charged, ready to roll. After a quick shower, he put on the work clothes he had laid out the night before: a monochrome tracksuit, black or blue, with a collared golf shirt and running shoes. A perfectly respectable outfit for a gym teacher.

Breakfast was a bowl of cereal—Vector, the healthy option, or Frosted Mini-Wheats, the usual. Then he made a cup of instant coffee, fastened the lid on his travel mug, and was out the door of his mobile home and into his Ford Explorer by seven thirty.

Troy could count on a quick drive to work. He didn't have to worry about traffic, or even traffic lights. The whole town fit within a single square kilometre. The tallest building was the grain elevator, which loomed next to rusting tracks that hadn't borne a train in a decade. At this time in the morning, there were never more than a few vehicles on the road. Students wouldn't be dropped off at school for another hour or so, plus the streets these days were quieter than they used to be. The town's population had peaked at 694 a quarter century before, when Troy was ten years old.

Troy drove past the modest houses lining his residential street, then turned right on Main Street. Up ahead and to the left stood the town hall where his parents had held their wedding reception. And there, just beyond, was the post office. He had mailed some letters there a few days before.

"Troy, good to see you," the postmaster had said. "I hear you've moved back."

"Yeah, I'm working in Wayway now."

"Oh," the postmaster said, pausing an extra beat. "Good luck straightening that out!"

Troy usually let that kind of comment go. He had heard far worse about Waywayseecappo from friends and family. "Ah, it's not bad," he said this time. "It's, you know, they're just kids."

The building after the post office was the hardware store. When Troy was growing up, a group of men from the reserve used to hang out there, carrying bottles in paper bags and flashing uneven smiles. People in town called them "the Veterans." Troy could tell by looking at them that they were sleeping outdoors. Sometimes they slept in rusting cars that sat abandoned at the edge of town, or in the small park next to the train stop. Other times they made it no farther than bushes outside the Rossburn Hotel bar, around the corner from the hardware store.

"Fucking Indians," Troy heard neighbours complain. "They shouldn't be allowed here."

When Troy was older, close enough to the legal drinking age, he would spend his Friday nights at the hotel bar. It was the most racially mixed place in town—"Moccasin Square Gardens" is what he and his friends sometimes called it. Inside, wooden beams running along the ceiling were covered with paper money in various denominations, signed by patrons looking to buy a little piece of immortality. Troy had left a two-dollar bill, signed with his nickname, Heavy. (This was a joke, as his limited mass had been the primary defect in an otherwise promising hockey career.) Nearby, a $100 bill had "FUCK U" written on it. In this bar, as in others, the odd punch was clumsily thrown for forgettable reasons. Sometimes, it was enough that "you're Indian and I'm not," as Troy later put it, though on such occasions he considered himself more of a peacemaker than a main combatant.

Troy sipped his coffee as he kept driving along Main Street, which was lined on each side with a single file of elm and oak trees. As he approached the corner of Main and Cheddar Avenue, he checked to see if his dad's lights were on, which would mean he was getting ready for work. Nelson still lived in the two-storey house where Troy grew up as an only child. The family's religion had ostensibly been Catholic, but mostly Troy was expected to worship the Montreal Canadiens.

At thirty-five, Troy was not quite the formidable hockey player he once was. His knees bore the scars of nine surgeries. For a time, he had thought his hockey days were over, but recently a few old friends coaxed him out of retirement. Now he was playing twice a week, and he'd never had more fun, with none of the pressures of old. His pre-game routine just needed a couple of adjustments: he popped two or three Advils, lathered stiff joints with a balm that made his skin tingle, and slid on knee braces he rarely washed. Troy still loved the way locker rooms everywhere stank the same.

A few short blocks after his dad's place, he passed by Rossburn Collegiate, his old high school. In its library sat a copy of the 1990 yearbook, which contained a picture of him in his senior year, along with an assessment by his peers: "Troy Luhowy—We don't know what he's on, but we all want some." The boy in the yearbook, with his fresh face and plentiful hair, looked more like a stranger with each passing year. But Troy hadn't lost that way about him, that aura of undaunted, infectious energy. It made him nearly impossible to dislike.

Troy Luhowy (Courtesy of Troy Luhowy)

The drive through town was over in less than a minute. Troy didn't encounter a stop sign until he reached Highway 45, which was lined on both sides by farms. The last crop standing was canola, now fast approaching the shade of radioactive yellow that would signal harvest time.

Troy didn't have long on the highway before he turned onto Cemetery Road to take a shortcut to work. On his left, a small clearing contained rows of tombstones, many with names obscured by moss or rubbed out with the passage of time. The cemetery held no special significance for Troy, as he didn't have family there. This was a resting place for the town's old Anglo-Saxon stock. The Ukrainians, Troy's people, were buried elsewhere.

Just beyond the last row of tombstones, the road plunged sharply into the valley's steepest parabola. Some people called this descent Cemetery Hill; others called it Suicide Hill. Troy rode the brakes all the way down. This was where the lid on his mug came in particularly handy. To his right, the morning sun lit up a bend in the Birdtail River.

Down then up Troy went, until he reached the far edge of the valley. Had he continued straight ahead, along Cloud Road, he would have ended up at Maureen Twovoice's house, but at this point Troy still hadn't met Maureen, who was spending her days at school in Rossburn. He instead turned left, toward the Waywayseecappo Community School, which had a green metal roof and brick walls painted an earthy brown.

Troy enjoyed spending his days with kids, but he wasn't really planning on sticking around as a teacher in Waywayseecappo. The pay was lousy, and he had too many classes with thirty-five or so students. Typically a few students in each class had fetal alcohol syndrome, and an uncomfortably large number of students arrived at school hungry and wearing the same clothes as the days before. All this made teaching on the reserve particularly challenging, so when teachers got the chance to relocate, they almost always did. The students noticed, of course. They came to understand that their school was something to be endured and escaped.

All told, Troy's drive to work took six minutes. Each morning and afternoon, he and Maureen criss-crossed the Birdtail valley from opposite directions, with destinations less than five kilometres apart. It felt a lot farther than that.

PART I

"MASTERS OF THEIR OWN DESTINY"

I

"DEAR DIARY"

ER MOM GAVE HER A DAY TO PACK. MAUREEN, AGED ten, wanted to stay in Winnipeg, but Linda was tired of raising kids alone in a jagged corner of the city. Maureen knew better than to ask too many questions. She grabbed a camo-patterned duffle bag and filled it with a few of her favourite books and a disproportionately red wardrobe. The last item she packed was her teddy bear, a Christmas gift from recent foster parents. It was white, soft, and huggable, with a crimson hat and matching suit. One of her sisters used to have the same bear from the same foster parents, until her brother ripped its head off.

Maureen's favourite thing about Winnipeg was her public school, Greenway Elementary, where she wrote rhyming poems in the quiet library and had a quirky teacher who wore a jean dress backwards during Spirit Week. Maureen liked school so much that she tagged along when her younger sister, Samantha, had been forced to attend summer classes.

One day after school, Maureen was running in a park, through a row of trees, figure-eight style. She raced with arms outstretched, enjoying the whoosh in her ears. "I'm Pocahontas!" she shouted to her older sister, Jacinda. Maureen had just seen the Disney film, so nothing was cooler than being like Pocahontas. Jacinda laughed and said, "You know that's what we are, right?" Actually, *no*. Until that moment, Maureen had never thought of herself as Indigenous.

Now her mom was moving them to the reserve, whatever that meant.

"Mom, what is a reserve?" Maureen asked.

"It's where our family lives."

Maureen had already been there once, when she was seven, to spend time with a stranger named Maurice whom her mom had introduced as Maureen's dad. He had picked her up in Winnipeg and then they drove to Waywayseecappo, just the two of them. He let Maureen sit in the front seat. As he spotted cows in the fields, he shouted, "Hamburger! Hamburger!" Maureen was relieved to have something to laugh about.

When they arrived at her dad's home, she was struck by the quiet. Compared with the cacophony of downtown Winnipeg, everything felt impossibly calm and spread out. She spent a lot of time playing alone among the trees, all those willows and poplars, and caught dark green lizards that felt cold to the touch. Under a canopy of branches, she came across a pocket knife, half-buried in the ground. It was sharp and rusty. She took it back to show her dad, who gently folded the blade into the handle and set it aside.

After that trip, Maureen started writing her father elaborately decorated holiday cards. "Merry Xmas dad, I love you!" Maureen pictured her dad sticking the cards on his fridge, smiling at the thought of his brilliant daughter. But Maureen never actually mailed anything to him. She was too scared that he wouldn't write back.

Three years after that first visit, Maureen was returning to the reserve with her mom, sisters, and teddy bear, this time to stay.

The drive from Winnipeg to Waywayseecappo takes about three and a half hours by car, but Linda didn't own a car, so it took closer to six on a Greyhound bus. Maureen sat alone in a separate row and stared out the window, lost in whys and whats and wheres. The flatness, which extended all the way to the horizon, left even more room for the sky. The bus travelled north and mostly west, through farmland frosted by snow.

Linda tapped Maureen on the shoulder. "We're getting close." The bus stopped with a hiss. "Ross-BURN," the driver announced. Maureen watched a few passengers get off in a town that looked like little more than a main street. "Next stop, Way-way-see-CAPPO."

Just beyond the outskirts of Rossburn, the bus dipped into a valley, giving Maureen a momentary flutter in her belly. Soon, the bus dropped them off in front of a strip of low-slung buildings at the side of the highway. Linda headed to a payphone to call her father, Alvin, for a ride. Maureen was sitting on her camo bag when her grandfather pulled up in a yellow Oldsmobile. It was so low to the ground it reminded Maureen of a boat.

Before long, they arrived at a three-bedroom house made of wood and painted brown and white. Alvin had vacated it to give Linda and the kids a place to stay. Inside, the house smelled older than it looked. A film of dust covered nearly everything except the rocking chair and its green cushion. The walls were bare.

On the upside, Maureen and Samantha each got their own room, which was definitely a step up from their smaller apartment in Winnipeg. And Maureen liked that she couldn't see any neighbours. She could go outside to sit on the front steps and just listen to the stillness. At night, far from city lights, Maureen could not believe how bright the moon looked. Sometimes it felt like the moon was parked directly above the house, shining a spotlight on them.

THE HARDEST PART of the move for Maureen was changing schools. Her mom knew it wasn't ideal to switch halfway through the year, but she hoped Maureen would fit in easily among other Native children. For her first day, Maureen wore her favourite outfit: black sweatpants and a red V-neck sweater, plus lip gloss that tasted like watermelon. Her classmates thought the new girl looked like a tomboy.

For the first time in her life, Maureen found herself surrounded by hundreds of students who shared her skin colour and dark hair. "There are lots of kids that look like me," she recalls thinking. "I was just, like, looking at people. They were probably wondering why."

Inside the classroom, Maureen was in for an even bigger adjustment. In math class, a girl sitting next to her whispered, "This is so hard. I can't do it." Maureen did not know what to say: she found the material almost laughably easy. It didn't take long for her Grade 5 teacher, Tammy McCullough, to realize that Maureen was far advanced compared with her peers. When McCullough took Maureen to a quiet corner of the classroom to perform a standardized reading and spelling assessment, it became obvious that Maureen was well above her grade level. That year, she would average 98 percent on her spelling tests.

Even the way Maureen carried herself stood out: standing tall, shoulders back, confident. McCullough recalls the way Maureen smiled when she put up her hand to show she had completed an assignment first: "Some kids can be rude, like, 'I'm done first, yay for me.' Maureen wasn't that type of kid. She wanted extra assignments." Maureen was also quick to raise her hand whenever McCullough asked a question. "Anytime I called on her, she was always right," McCullough says. Sometimes McCullough pretended not to see Maureen's raised hand, just to give other students a chance.

Maureen read ahead, which left her even more bored in class. "I could see how behind they were," Maureen says. "I kept thinking: this is weird, why are we relearning what I already know?" She passed the time by helping other students with their homework or doodling increasingly elaborate renditions of her name.

"I just kept waiting to learn," Maureen says. "I felt like an alien."

At home, Maureen faced other challenges.

When her mom was drinking, Maureen tried to hide in her room, though this didn't work particularly well because there was no lock on her door. Linda would wobble in and sit on Maureen's bed, crying and muttering about times she had been humiliated and abused as a girl at residential school. Maureen could see the hurt in her mom, could see it in the shadows that darkened her face. Still, Maureen thought: *Mom, come back sober. I shouldn't have to listen to this.*

"I remember feeling so lonely," Maureen says, "and sometimes wished I had a different, loving family." She could not remember her mom ever saying the words "I love you."

Sometimes Maureen came home from school, took one glance at her mother's unsteady lean, then went right back outside for a long walk. Her cousin Tamara lived within walking distance, and Maureen visited so often she wore a path through the field of waist-high prairie grass that separated their homes.

Maureen went to Tamara's place when things were particularly rough at home. It got to the point where Maureen didn't even have to ask Tamara's parents if she could sleep over. "I just went over," Maureen says. "'Camping.' That's the word we used. They'd say, 'Are you going to camp here tonight?'"

Maureen poured her frustrations into a diary. She would sit on the couch with her legs folded into her chest and the purple notebook resting on her knees. She had been keeping a detailed record of her thoughts ever since she had read Anne Frank's diary while she was living in Winnipeg. Maureen imagined that one day people would pore over her every word, so she took the time to write in her best handwriting. Every day she wrote, in bubbly cursive, about her frustrations at school and at home. A typical entry posed a question and then tried to answer it. "Dear Diary," she always began.

"Why is life like this?"

"How come schoolwork is so easy?"

"Why does my mom have to drink all the time?"

"Why is there nothing on the walls?"

MAUREEN'S REPORT CARDS document a slow and steady slide. In Grade 6, her second year in Waywayseecappo, a teacher wrote that Maureen had "started showing little enthusiasm." Back when she lived in Winnipeg, she had loved school. Increasingly, it was a source of boredom. In Grade 7, Maureen concluded that middle school most definitely sucked. Just getting out of bed in the morning felt daunting. On days when she was really not feeling it, which was more and more often, she tried to sweet-talk her mom into letting her stay home. Occasionally Linda caved and called the school to report that Maureen was feeling sick. Usually, though, Linda did her best to nag Maureen into submission. "Why, Maureen? *Why* don't you want to go to school?" Even while Linda was herself struggling, she never stopped encouraging Maureen to go to school.

When Maureen did show up, her favourite activity became hanging out in the girls' bathroom with one of her cousins. They squeezed into a stall together, sharing the toilet as a seat. They talked about teenage stuff: notably, boys, and, before long, the cousin's pregnancy. Sometimes they worried that a teacher would bust them for skipping class, but they always got away with it. Maureen liked to stand up on the toilet to doodle on the ceiling. A typical entry memorialized a crush. "Maureen & Craig: forever and always," she wrote, framing the words with a heart.

One of Maureen's various schemes to skip class involved complaints that she needed glasses. She had perfect vision but pretended the whiteboards appeared blurry to her. The closest ophthalmologist was in the town of Brandon, 150 kilometres away and a veritable metropolis compared to other towns closer to the reserve. Brandon was Maureen's favourite place to shop for clothes. She was also vaguely aware that her mom had once attended a school there, and that she had never made it beyond Grade 8.

For a time, it was not clear whether Maureen would make it past Grade 7. Homework was easy, but she didn't bother to do it. Trying to fit in better, she became a half-hearted badass. She was one of those teenagers who knew what she *ought* to do but did the opposite to get attention. She talked back to teachers, missed too much class, fought at recess. An evaluation in Grade 7 showed that she had fallen below the standard reading level—a sign either that she didn't take the test seriously or that she was indeed falling behind.

In November 2003, Maureen was suspended for three days for fighting. She was also caught smoking, and the principal sent a letter to Linda emphasizing the school's zero-tolerance policy. In January, Linda received another letter from the principal, saying that Maureen was harassing a student and threatening to fight her. "Watch your back," Maureen had reportedly told another girl, who was so scared that she stopped going to school. "If this doesn't stop immediately," the principal wrote, "I will be informing the RCMP"—the Royal Canadian Mounted Police.

That spring, after another fight, Maureen received an indefinite suspension. "Dear Diary," she wrote. "Am I going to graduate?"

Maureen doesn't remember much about what she did next. She chilled a lot. At some point near the end of the school year, she belatedly realized she was facing the prospect of repeating Grade 7 in the same class as her younger sister, Samantha. Maureen begged the school to let her write the final exams in English, math, science, and social studies. After the school agreed, Maureen barely studied but still managed to pass. For her, this was a stark reminder of just how far ahead she had been when she arrived on the reserve a couple of years before.

In Grade 8, though, Maureen's behaviour, attendance, and grades didn't get any better. Her first report card showed her failing seven of her nine classes, with an attendance rate of about 50 percent. In their comments, teachers made copious use of exclamation marks. "Poor attendance and participation!" "Many assignments were not handed in!" "More effort required!" "Does not use class time wisely!" "Poor attendance / Poor achievement!"

Seeing Maureen struggle pained Linda, and she tried to offer encouragement. "I know I drink," she told Maureen. "I know it's hard. But you have to go to school. Look at me, I only made it to

Grade 8. You've still got a chance." Maureen tuned her out, thinking, *If it's that important, Mom, why didn't you finish?*

Maureen listened more carefully to her grandfather, Alvin, who was less inclined to tell her what to do. "He wasn't one to go on a big lecture about life," Maureen says. They spent the most time together during the winter, when he would drive her to the local hockey arena to watch the Waywayseecappo Wolverines play. Alvin would describe life on the reserve when he was young. Mostly, he talked about what the land used to look like. There were more trees, for one thing, and plenty of elk, moose, ducks, and partridges. During the car rides, Alvin made a point of asking Maureen how she was doing at school. He himself had only made it to Grade 5, he told her. When Maureen confided that, actually, things weren't going great, Alvin tried to give her a boost. "You can make it," he would say. "You can do something, you can be somebody." She wanted to believe him. When she was alone, in her darkest moments, Alvin's words glowed like fireflies. *Do something*, she told herself. *Be somebody.*

Maureen kept writing in her diary, day after day, month after month. Over time, she accumulated a pile of booklets. Whenever she flipped through the pages and reviewed old entries, the level of detail in her catalogue of disappointments amazed her. Writing made her feel better, but reading her own words made her feel worse. Sometimes she started a new notebook even when plenty of blank pages remained in an older one. "I changed notebooks because what was inside was so ugly," she recalls. "I thought maybe if I started over it would be better."

Maureen also found other, more destructive ways to deal with her feelings. When they were thirteen, Maureen and her best friend, Amanda, started drinking regularly. Getting their hands on a bottle wasn't particularly hard, even though the reserve was officially dry. That just meant people bought their booze in Rossburn. That same year, Maureen registered her first email account: chug4life666@hotmail.com.

When Maureen and Amanda found themselves particularly bored and despondent on weekends, they took turns choking each other. They would sit facing each other on the couch, then Amanda would put both her hands around Maureen's throat and squeeze. When Maureen felt sufficiently dizzy, she gave Amanda a tap. It was a good feeling, that whirling in her head. *Yeah*, they thought, *this is the shit!* Sometimes one of them blacked out, but it never lasted long enough to really scare them. Even as they hurt each other, they took comfort in being together.

Maureen also started cutting herself when she was alone. She sliced near her wrists and hid the scabs and scars with long sleeves. She found a kind of grim satisfaction in her own pain. One night in her room, she used a piece of glass she'd recovered from a smashed bottle. She accidentally cut deeper than usual and was scared by all the blood—more gush than dribble. She wanted to scream but stayed mute, paralyzed, while she bled. Fortunately, her uncle Matthew picked that moment to open the door to say hello. "Maureen, *what* are you doing!" he exclaimed, loudly but not angrily. He rushed to get a tea towel and pressed it firmly on her arm. Maureen just sobbed.

The next morning, Maureen found her mother seated at the dining table, waiting for her. She asked Maureen to sit down. "You know," Linda said, "when people take their lives they don't go anywhere. Their spirit just stays on the earth, wandering, sticking around until the time they were actually supposed to go." As she said this, she remained perfectly calm. Linda had a habit, when she was in a really deep conversation, of making a fist and wrapping the other hand around it as though she was going to crack her knuckles. This is what she was doing now. "If you chose to do that to yourself," Linda said, "your spirit wouldn't be at peace." Maureen began to cry.

Linda talked about how sad she would be if she lost Maureen, and then she talked about Maureen's siblings and nieces and nephews. How would they feel? What would Linda tell them? Maureen stayed quiet, her cheeks wet with tears. Part of her appreciated that her mother was showing how much she cared. Another part of her wanted to say, "Mom, you're part of the reason why." Maureen hated coming home and wondering whether her mom was going to be drunk. But Maureen didn't mention that, and after Linda was done talking, the two of them hugged for a long time in silence. Linda didn't tell Maureen she loved her—it just wasn't something she did in those days—but Maureen could feel love in that hug.

After a particularly taxing stretch in Grade 8, Maureen decided to burn her diaries, hoping that would give her the fresh start she needed. That afternoon, her mom's partner, Earl, had lit a fire in the backyard to burn leaves and garbage, as he often did. A towering spruce tree stood a few paces away from the firepit, close enough that the smoke curled through the outstretched branches. Earl was poking the fire with a stick when he saw Maureen come out the back door carrying a large wooden chest she had made at school. The industrial arts teacher had asked his students to create a hope chest where they could store their most prized possessions. Building that chest was probably the highlight of Grade 7 for Maureen. She had painted it blue and black and decorated it with a few squiggly red flourishes. Inside, she had stacked her diaries.

Maureen put the chest down next to the fire. She fished out the purple diary, her first one ever, then ripped out a few pages.

With what she imagined was a dramatic flourish, she tossed the pages into the fire. She was close enough to the flames to feel their warmth on her face. It felt quite good, actually. Earl watched on with a look that said, *Really?* But he said nothing. Maureen proceeded to burn the diaries one at a time, oldest to newest. She thought, *Now I can let go of what I wrote.* And so what if future generations never read her beautiful cursive. She cherished a rare wave of relief as she looked at the ashes, a growing heap of grey streaked with dancing orange. She burned to forget.

Maureen kept no more diaries after that.

IN GRADE 8, after repeatedly talking back to teachers and getting caught smoking and fighting, Maureen was expelled and told there was no way back. She enrolled in a "transition program" for students on the reserve who were not coping with the regular school. Maureen felt she had really messed up this time. She became convinced she wasn't where she was supposed to be. This made her feel dumb, though deep down she suspected she was smart. She heard her grandfather urging her on. *Do something. Be somebody.*

A teacher in the program recommended that Maureen try to publish an article in *Say Magazine*, a national publication looking for submissions from Indigenous youth. Maureen decided to give it a try. To her surprise, the magazine accepted her submission and published it in the Winter 2006 issue. "I'm Maureen Lynn Twovoice," she began, "a fourteen-year-old Anishinaabe from the Waywayseecappo First Nation in Manitoba. I'm finishing up Grade 8 in a Co-Op Program." She wrote about her favourite music (powwow) and her "huge mistake" (giving up on school). She described her volunteer work at a home for the elderly in

Rossburn, which was a mandatory part of her program. She was helping with baking, hairstyling, and nail painting. She had even learned how to make perogies, a beloved Ukrainian dish. "I talk and listen to what they have to say and I tell you they have lots to say," Maureen wrote. "Some people just don't take the time to listen."

She also wrote warmly about her mom, who had encouraged Maureen "to finish school so I could be successful" and taught her "not to judge someone by his or her looks." Maureen felt happy to write about her mom like that. She knew that Linda, for all her faults, had been trying. "My mom was a single parent who raised me without my dad," Maureen recalls. "This was a way to acknowledge her."

A copy of the magazine arrived shortly after Maureen started Grade 9 in Rossburn. Linda was so proud that she cut out Maureen's article and framed it on the wall. In the final sentence of the essay, Maureen wrote, "I want to be an inspiration to other youth."

LINDA'S SHOES

AS A LITTLE GIRL GROWING UP IN WAYWAYSEECAPPO, Linda Jandrew bathed in the Birdtail River, which was so clear she could count the minnows darting along the bottom. Her kokom—"grandmother" in Ojibway—kept a close watch from the shore, even though the water came up only to Linda's belly button. The current was gentle, a caress.

Every August, Linda joined her kokom for berry-picking around the reserve. "*Naadinaan mskomnak jimiijyan,*" her kokom said. "Get the berries to eat." As Linda went from one bush to the next, she had to watch out for thorns, which could cut right through the thin rubber soles of her shoes. She carried a plastic bucket to put the raspberries in. "*N-ji kenndaam wedodamaan kinaawin. Kaayi memech gda mamaa jibaayaat zaam minitwe pane,*" her kokom said. "We know what to do ourselves. It is not necessary that your mother come along. She drinks too much, all the time."

Linda lived with her grandparents, parents, and older brother, Matthew, in a three-bedroom house on the reserve. On the back door, her mooshum (grandfather) hung his traditional medicine bag and skin drum, which he took along to Sun Dances.

When Linda's parents were drinking and yelling and fighting, which was too often, her grandparents took her and her brother to a special hiding place, a tent made of tan-coloured canvas within walking distance of home. Sometimes they spent days at a time out there, but they never wanted for food. Her mooshum would disappear for a few hours and return with a snared rabbit. Her kokom would cut off its head and paws, then skin and gut it. Some of the meat was sliced into ribbons and hung on a branch to dry just beyond the reach of their bounding dog. The rest of the meat went into a soup, which slowly boiled in a large pot on an open fire. For dessert, Linda's favourite was bannock sprinkled with sugar. At dusk, they burned sage to ward off the mosquitoes. This was a time for stories, told in Ojibway.

Linda fondly remembers one night in particular. Inside the tent, her kokom laid down a thin blanket that she had stitched together out of purple and black squares. Linda could still feel the ground through the blanket, but she didn't mind. She was resting back-to-back with her kokom, who wore a one-piece cotton dress in a flowery pattern. They whispered to each other as all around them frogs croaked and crickets chirped and owls called. Then, in the distance, wolves began howling.

"Shhh," her kokom said. "Do you hear them?" Linda and her brother went perfectly still and they all lay there, listening. The howls lingered as they cascaded through the valley. Linda loved the way her back pressed up against her kokom's when they inhaled deeply at the same time.

This was one of the last times in Linda's life she felt truly safe.

★ ★ ★

IN THE FALL of 1965, Linda was told that she had to go to boarding school. She didn't understand why, and when an unfamiliar bus full of other children from Waywayseecappo came to pick her up, no one mentioned that the destination was 150 kilometres away, near the town of Brandon. Linda was six years old.

The Brandon Indian Residential School, an imposing brick structure with limestone trim, loomed on a hillside, visible from the main road into town. It looked so grand, so modern, so impressive that it awed many who drove by. To the students inside, however, it felt like prison.

The Brandon Indian Residential School, circa 1910 ("Brandon Industrial Institute," United Church of Canada Archives, 93.049P/1396)

When Linda arrived, she was instructed to remove her clothes and given a bath. Then her long, dark hair was cut into a short pageboy style, which is the way mandatory trims would keep it for years to come. After the haircut, a full bottle of anti-lice mix was poured on her scalp and roughly kneaded in. Even after a cold shower, a foul chemical taste lingered in her mouth for hours, and in her memory forever.

Linda slept with dozens of other girls in a large dormitory with single beds arranged in a grid several rows deep. Her bedsheets smelled like mothballs. If a girl had the misfortune to wet her bed at night, she would be punished in front of the others with a strap on the hand or across the backside. Yet somehow this regime of terror did not have the desired deterrent effect on the girls' bladders.

The atmosphere at the school was severe and oppressive. As Linda later put it, "Not often, we were allowed to laugh." Students had to obey all kinds of rules and orders, which was particularly challenging for Linda at first, because she did not understand English well. When a supervisor heard her speaking Ojibway, he slapped her across the mouth. "I couldn't speak my language," she recalls. Her older brother, Matthew, was already at the school when Linda arrived, but they rarely saw each other because most activities were organized by age. The school did not even permit siblings to hug.

For breakfast, they were served porridge, always porridge, which Linda grew to loathe. She ate as much as she could get anyway, because she was hungry all the time. There was never enough food.[1] The exceptions were the few occasions when family members were permitted to visit, such as on Thanksgiving, Christmas, and Easter, when the school served heaping portions of ham and potato salad. "They would try to impress the people visiting us, so they didn't think we were getting starved," Linda says. "That's the only time we really got to eat." On these occasions, her lone visitor was her aunt.

And the shoes. Linda will never forget the shoes: black oxfords, which all the students had to wear. They were a mandatory part of the school uniform, affixed to the feet of every Indian child on the assembly line to Anglo-Saxon respectability. Their heaviness surprised Linda; they felt clunky at the end of her spindly legs. She was made to shine them until she could see her face in the leather. And, most important of all, she was not allowed to leave her dormitory without them. Civilized people wore shoes. Don't ever forget them, the students were warned.

BY THE TIME Linda arrived, the Brandon Indian Residential School had been operating for seventy years. Its doors opened in 1895 as one of many residential schools funded by the Canadian government and run by churches. Their purpose was to sever the link between Indigenous children and their culture, in order to assimilate Indians into the Euro-Christian mainstream. The government sought to keep its costs low by partnering with churches, which were more interested in souls than salaries. Between the opening of the first such school in 1880 until the closing of the last one in 1996, more than 150,000 Indigenous children attended such institutions, including both of Maureen's parents and all four of her grandparents.[2]

In the beginning, many Indigenous communities welcomed government promises to provide education, believing new schools could offer a bridge to a better future. Treaty agreements with Indigenous Peoples often specified that these schools would be situated in Indigenous communities. Nevertheless, churches and the government favoured more distant locations, because they believed children could be more easily reformed if kept away from the supposedly malign influence of their parents. As Prime

Minister John A. Macdonald put it, "When the school is on the reserve, the child lives with its parents, who are savages, and though he may learn to read and write, his habits and training mode of thought are Indian. He is simply a savage who can read and write."[3]

The case of the Brandon school was typical. In the late 1880s, Methodists petitioned the federal government to start a school and insisted on avoiding "the serious disadvantage of having such an institution in or near an Indian Reserve."[4] For its part, the city council of Brandon warmly welcomed the opportunity to host a federal school, notably because it would bring more government investment into the area.[5]

Chief Jacob Berens (Nauwigizigweas in Ojibway) was the leader of a reserve in northern Manitoba and a pious Methodist himself. When he heard about the plans for a new school in Brandon, he expressed his opposition in a letter to the secretary of the Methodist Mission Society in Toronto, Reverend Sutherland. Though Chief Berens and his community welcomed a new school, Brandon was too far away: "Our hearts are sad for one cannot think of sending our children away such a long distance from their people & homes. No, we love our children like the white man & are pleased to have them near us."[6] Reverend Sutherland wrote a condescending response in which he expressed doubt that Chief Berens was the real author of the letter written in his name, and opined that Berens had in fact written "at the suggestion of others" who were hostile to the church.[7]

Chief Berens replied that the reverend's letter was "very ungenerous and unchristianlike" and criticized him for presuming to know the best interests of the community "without consulting our views."[8] Berens also wrote a letter to the federal government to argue against putting the school in Brandon: "We cannot really think of ever sending any of our children so far away from our reserves even for the purpose of getting an education."[9]

Nauwigizigweas (Chief Jacob Berens) (Archives of Manitoba, 1909, Item Number 1, Coloured Negative 117, Still Images Collection, Personalities Collection)

In the end, Berens's forceful protestations were ignored. Brandon it would be.

The school's first principal, Reverend J. Semmens, doggedly travelled around Manitoba seeking prospective students. In his personal journal, he described the territory around Lake Winnipeg as his "recruiting field." He reached many communities by canoe, portaging between "stormy lakes," and at times he found "the mosquitoes intolerable."[10] But his greatest obstacle by far was skeptical parents. The reverend recorded the questions they asked him after he made his sales pitch:

> *"Will the Government keep this promise or break it as they have others made in like beautiful language?"*
>
> *"Can the children return at their own wish or at the wish of the parents before the term at School expires?"*
>
> *"Is it the purpose to enslave our children and make money out of them?"*
>
> *"Is it the object of the Gov't to destroy our language and our tribal life?"*[11]

It is unclear what, if anything, Semmens said in response, but the truth would have confirmed their worst fears.

Reverend Semmens wrote to the Department of Indian Affairs to report the widespread reluctance he was encountering. In response, an official recommended that Semmens remind parents of "the powers vested in the Department," which would compel attendance if parents did not "evince their willingness to have their children educated."[12] Under the Indian Act of 1894, parents who refused could be jailed.

For years, parents in Waywayseecappo, as those in other communities, resisted sending their children to faraway schools. A government official overseeing Waywayseecappo (one of the so-called "Indian agents" who was in charge of enforcing federal policy on reserves) reported in 1907, "I am quite safe in saying that very few parents voluntarily bring their children to school."[13]

One reason was surely the mortality rate. In 1902, for example, at least six students died at the Brandon residential school. The following year, nine more died, which prompted a statistically minded government official to note: "a larger percentage than the average number of deaths has occurred."[14]

Carpentry class at the Brandon Indian Residential School, circa 1910 (United Church of Canada Archives, 93.049P/1368N)

Heavy farming equipment crushed at least one student during field labour, but mostly the killers were preventable diseases such as scarlet fever, pneumonia, tuberculosis, and typhoid, abetted by a crowded building that incubated illness. "From time to time sickness came," wrote Reverend Semmens in his journal. "It was sad beyond measure when we had to bury a pupil so far away from home and friends. Distress keen and trying was felt when in hours of extreme illness the dear children longed for their dusky mothers and their humble wigwam homes."[15] Of course, it was the reverend who had separated the children from their families in the first place.

A recruiter of students wrote to a Methodist leader in 1907 to say that parents in Manitoba had become "dumb to entreaties" to send their children to the Brandon school. The student deaths "completely knock the attempts re: Brandon . . . in the head. They just sit right down on a fellow. And one must shut up because there is at least a degree of justice on their side."[16]

Across Canada, thousands of students died at residential schools. It is hard to say with much precision how many, because of shoddy record keeping and unmarked graves, but the number is at least 4,400 and possibly many multiples of that.[17] They died from disease, from malnutrition, from neglect. Duncan Campbell Scott, a bureaucrat who oversaw the residential school system for two decades, wrote in 1913: "It is quite within the mark to say that fifty per cent of the children who passed through these schools did not live to benefit from the education which they had received therein."[18] Scott added, a few years later: "It is readily acknowledged that Indian children lose their natural resistance to illness by habituating so closely in the residential schools and that they die at a much higher rate than in their villages. But this does not justify a change in the policy of this Department which is geared towards a final solution of our Indian Problem."[19] (This invocation of a "final solution" predates its use by the Nazis, but Scott's words reveal the lengths to which the government was willing to go, with the churches as their accomplices.) The second principal at the Brandon school, Reverend Doyle, kept a portrait of Campbell Scott hanging in his office.

As the years went on, more and more students from Waywayseecappo attended residential schools in the towns of Brandon and Birtle, largely as a result of unrelenting pressure by zealous missionaries and Indian agents. In a characteristically patronizing report, a federal inspector noted in 1914, "Education now occupies a prominent place in their minds, and it is now the desire of the band that their children shall receive an education not inferior to the average education of the white child. Slowly the light of civilization is penetrating and the marks of progress are apparent."[20]

The United Church took over the Brandon school from the Methodists in 1925 and oversaw a major renovation to the main building, including adding a limestone trim to the facade. In 1930, the revamped school published a promotional pamphlet saying that its students were being trained "to become happy, successful, and useful citizens when they go out to take their place in life."[21] According to the then principal Reverend Doyle, "a wholesome and balanced diet is being followed."[22]

Students and their concerned parents reported otherwise. In 1935, a mother with a child at the Brandon school wrote to the Department of Indian Affairs to report that students were so hungry that they were resorting to shoplifting in town stores. She accused the principal of "training the children to be thieves" by leaving them with no choice but "to steal to fill their empty bodys." A student who attended the school in the 1940s later detailed the experience he and hundreds of others endured: they ate food that was "prepared in the crudest of ways" and "served in very unsanitary conditions," including "milk that had manure in the bottom of the cans and homemade porridge that had grasshopper legs and bird droppings in it." The students also faced "cruel disciplinary measures . . . such as being tied to a flag pole, sent to bed with no food, literally beaten and slapped by staff."[23] Under these conditions, it is not surprising that so many students tried to escape.

A RELIABLE GAUGE of student abuse at the Brandon school was the steady stream of runaways. In 1942, twelve children between the ages of ten and fifteen fled the school. The problem worsened when Reverend Oliver Strapp became principal in 1944. Previously, Strapp had been principal at a residential school in Ontario, where the year before he faced complaints of "improper conduct" with female students.[24] There was no formal investigation, and the United Church shuttled him to Brandon. An Indian agent described Strapp as "an aggressive type" and a "strict disciplinarian."[25] Jim Cote, a former student from Waywayseecappo, recalls Strapp's fondness for corporal punishment with a leather belt: "He certainly earned his name."

Reverend Oliver Strapp (Manitoba Historical Society,
"Memorable Manitobans: Oliver Bailey Strapp," Courtesy of Gayle Strank)

39

There were so many runaways during Strapp's time that the problem came to the attention of Tommy Douglas—preacher of gospel, pioneer of medicare, and premier of Saskatchewan. On September 23, 1946, RCMP officers forcefully removed Clifford Shepherd, thirteen, and his sister Verna from a day school on the Moose Mountain Reserve, in Saskatchewan, against the wishes of their parents. The two children were transported two hundred kilometres away to the Brandon residential school. A few days later, Premier Douglas sent a telegram to the federal minister of Indian affairs:

CLIFFORD AND VERNA CHILDREN OF JOHN SHEPHERD OF MOOSE MOUNTAIN RESERVE AT CARLYLE WERE FORCIBLY REMOVED FROM DAY SCHOOL LAST MONDAY BY RCMP AND SENT TO BRANDON INDIAN SCHOOL –STOP– FATHER AND MEMBERS OF BAND HAVE PROTESTED ARBITRARY ACTION [. . .] –STOP– SCHOOL PRINCIPAL AND OSTRANDER REFUSE TO TAKE ACTION TO RESTORE CHILDREN TO RESERVE ALTHOUGH DAY SCHOOL AFFORDS ADEQUATE ACCOMMODATION AND INSTRUCTION –STOP– THIS MATTER REQUIRES YOUR IMMEDIATE ATTENTION FOR WHICH I THANK YOU –STOP–[26]

On October 9, Clifford ran away from the school when students were let outside to play. Two days later, the RCMP tracked him down in the town of Redvers, Saskatchewan, 150 kilometres southwest of the school and most of the way home. He was taken into custody and dropped off at the Brandon school at three thirty in the morning of October 12.

Three weeks later, Clifford escaped again. This time, he made it all the way home, travelling most of the distance by stowing himself in a boxcar of a freight train. The RCMP eventually located him on his reserve. When apprehended, Clifford was wearing a tweed cap, an air force jacket, and a grey-and-blue shirt with matching overalls. Once again, the officers drove him back to the Brandon school.

In early December, Clifford escaped a third time, along with two other boys from the same reserve, aged nine and eleven. Principal Strapp himself set off in pursuit, driving his car along the highway headed west, asking farmers about errant children. Later that day, Strapp and RCMP officers found Clifford and the other two boys walking along the Canadian Pacific rail line, twelve kilometres west of the school, where they were "successfully apprehended," according to an RCMP report. The boys were then driven back. "Just as we entered the school," Strapp later wrote, "Clifford made an attempt to run away again and put up quite a fight." During the struggle, Clifford managed to land a kick to Strapp's groin—a fact that Strapp himself did not acknowledge, though an RCMP report did. "I was compelled," Strapp said, "to use considerable force to remove him to the dormitory." The principal pinned Clifford to a bed and sent another student to retrieve a strap.

After inflicting corporal punishment, Strapp asked Clifford to give his word that he would not attempt another escape. Clifford refused. Strapp then decided to lock Clifford into a room alone and without clothes. In the days that followed, Clifford remained in confinement, naked, with meals delivered at regular intervals. According to an RCMP report, Clifford "threatens openly that he will leave the minute his clothes are returned to him."

Shortly thereafter, Tommy Douglas once again wrote to the minister of Indian affairs to demand that something be done to remedy the situation. Douglas had heard that "the boy, Clifford, has again run away from the Brandon Residential School and returned home by hitch hiking and on foot. I understand that he travelled through a severe blizzard and returned home ill-clothed and in a weakened condition." And Douglas had heard of others running away, too. "These incidents," he wrote, "have caused grave concerns among the Indians of the district," who worried that "the children in the Brandon Residential School are not properly cared for, that they do not receive sufficient supervision or training, and that the food is inadequate." Douglas urged the minister to reconsider the possibility of "returning these children to their parents" and sending them to a nearby day school.

A copy of the premier's letter found its way to Reverend G. Dorey of the United Church, which was then responsible for administering the school. The reverend joked to a colleague that if Premier Douglas accepted allegations of Indians "at their face value . . . all I can say is that he will have plenty to do looking after the Indians . . . without being able to give much time to his duties as Premier."[27]

On January 6, 1947, Douglas wrote directly to Principal Strapp to emphasize that "neither [Clifford] nor his parents desire that he continue as a student of your school." Douglas added, "I do think that it is improper to coerce a lad of fourteen years into remaining at your school by locking him in his room and depriving him of his clothing. I am certain you will agree with me on this score."

Clifford was allowed to return home three weeks later. When questioned by the RCMP, Strapp blamed Clifford's escapes on encouragement from the boy's parents and relatives. As for the federal minister of Indian affairs, he assured Douglas that the school was well run and providing a "satisfactory" diet. Of course, this wasn't true—not then or long after.[28]

STRAPP STAYED. MORE students fled. Bleak reports about the Brandon school continued piling up. In 1951, a visiting nurse observed, "The overall picture of the institution is pretty grim."[29] That same year, a regional supervisor for Indian Affairs wrote, "There is certainly something wrong as children are running away most of the time. . . . The sooner we make a change the better."[30]

One of the runaways was Jim Cote, a boy from Waywayseecappo. Jim was twelve when he arrived at the Brandon school in 1953, having been expelled from the residential school in Birtle for refusing to let a teacher inflict corporal punishment on him. Jim had dared to snatch the strap out of his teacher's hand and chase the teacher around the room with it.

As a student in Brandon, Jim spent half his days doing physical labour, cleaning the barn and milking a cow he nicknamed Elsey. Jim talked to Elsey while he pumped her udders, hoping she didn't kick. "Hey Elsey," he said. "How are you doing today?" He milked her at dawn and dusk. Elsey provided more milk than the other cows, but the school officials didn't know that because Jim was sneaking in a full cup in the barn twice a day, a supplement to the school's otherwise execrable diet.

At night in the dormitory, Jim listened to boys sniffling and crying, talking about their homes. "We suffered humiliation, physical abuse, sexual abuse," he recalls. It wasn't long before he resolved to escape. The fact that the school was 150 kilometres from his home in Waywayseecappo did not deter him. "I didn't tell anyone I was going to run away," he says. "I was afraid of a snitch."

One morning, he ran out of the building and kept running. "I just ran, I was happy, I was headed home to see my mom and dad and that gave me the strength to go. I was running far from that damn school and barn, away from Elsey!"

Jim stayed away from the main roads to avoid capture. When it became too cloudy to orient himself by the sun, he carefully examined trees because he knew moss grows best on the north side of the trunks. At night, he found a quiet spot in a wooded area and sheltered himself from the wind with branches he gathered. As Jim listened to coyotes howl in the dark, he imagined his family's dog, Sparkie, lying in a nearby bush to protect him.

Jim fed himself by sneaking into the gardens of "white folks" and stuffing as many potatoes, beets, carrots, and turnips into his pockets as he could run with. "I ate potatoes like apples," he says. He recalls that one pilfered carrot was a good seven inches long—"I never ate a carrot that tasted so good." He also gorged on dark saskatoon berries and rosy-red chokecherries, which were so tart his lips puckered.

After three days of flight, entirely on foot, Jim finally made it back to Waywayseecappo. He had covered more than the distance of a marathon each day. "I was a tough little bugger," he says. When Jim arrived home—exhausted, triumphant—his mother gave him a big hug. Then she told him to brush his teeth, which were blackened by all the berries.

It wasn't long until his father, Hugh, said, "You know you're going to have to go back, right?" Since truancy remained a federal offence for which Hugh's parents could be sent to jail, the family had no meaningful choice.[31] When Waywayseecappo's Indian agent found out that Jim was with his parents, he promptly drove him back to Brandon. Jim's three-day escape was undone by three hours in the back of a flatbed truck.

Strapp was finally removed as principal in 1955. Jim recalls that when students heard the news, they let out a loud cheer. "It was like we got rid of a devil." Incredibly—or, perhaps, not too surprisingly—the United Church then appointed Strapp principal at another school, this one in Alberta. He was reprimanded five years later by a government official for the "poor diet" his students were receiving.[32] Strapp retired the following year, at the age of sixty-nine, and lived peaceably into his late eighties.

Problems at the Brandon school persisted after Strapp's departure. A senior government official told a colleague in 1956 that he was "disturbed about the serious danger of the adverse publicity which is likely to arise from the unsatisfactory operation of the Brandon school"—as if the prospect of bad publicity was the most disturbing thing.[33]

DURING THE YEARS Linda walked the school hallways in her black oxfords, the principal, Ford Bond, regimented the school like an army barracks. They recited prayers four times a day: after breakfast, before class, after supper, and before bed.

In the evening, the students were lined up for showers, counted, and given half a teaspoon of baking soda to wash their teeth with. Supervisors counted the children multiple times a day to make sure nobody had strayed or run away. Linda's brother, Matthew, once made a daring escape by tying a makeshift rope with bedsheets and lowering himself from the third-floor window of the boys' dormitory. He was caught by the road, along with two other fugitive students, and welcomed back with an exemplary strapping.

The school's assistant administrator was the hawk-eyed Mrs. McKay, who was known to stalk the halls with a long ruler in her right hand. She had worked her way up from head of the sewing room and was now in charge of all the female students. "We had to go by what she said," Linda later said. "She was kinda—well, the boss." When the students lined up outside the dining room for a head count before every mealtime, Mrs. McKay insisted on absolute silence. She used to say that she wanted "to be able to hear a needle drop."

FIFTY YEARS LATER, Linda says she would prefer to forget about her four years at the Brandon school, but she can't. "No matter what I went through, I always remembered," she says. "Ha ha ha!"

Linda's laugh takes some getting used to. She often says unfunny things, then bursts into joyless laughter, typically in spurts of three with enough force to empty her lungs. It is a smoker's laugh, raspy, as close to a cough as a laugh can be. "We all cope in different ways," she says, speaking of residential school Survivors. "Some become alcoholics, some don't. I chose to drink my life away, ha ha ha!"

Linda has repeatedly sought help for her addiction. She checked herself into treatment centres five times: in 1974, 1986, 1995, 2001, and 2005. In her fifties, she developed cirrhosis, a disease often caused by a liver drowning in booze. Her doctor told her she would die if she didn't stop drinking. Linda's mother, who also attended a residential school, developed the same condition sooner in life. She died at forty-two. Linda is sober now, except on the worst days.

Her favourite activity is spending time with her grandchildren. She makes a point of speaking to them in Ojibway and saying she loves them—two things she had rarely done with her own children.

Linda never says "residential school." She says, simply, "residential"—as in, "after residential, I felt guilty for years anytime I grew out my hair." She has tried to push the memories away, but they might as well be nailed into her. She remembers her loneliness. She remembers her fear. She remembers that her mother never visited. "Mom was always drunk, ha ha ha!"

Linda speaks little and softly. In conversation, she angles her face slightly to the left as she listens. That's because she's deaf in her left ear.

One day, Mrs. McKay rang the bell for dinnertime. Linda was six years old, and had been at the school for only two months. Fifteen minutes were allotted for supper, and students had mere seconds to form a straight, orderly line outside the dining room, which was in the basement of the school building. "As soon as the bell would go, there was no time," Linda says.

As Linda found a place in the queue, she realized that she had forgotten her shoes. She had rushed from the dormitory upstairs, belly growling with hunger, without realizing her mistake. Now Mrs. McKay was standing at the entrance of the dining room, counting each student she let in, and there was no time for Linda to do anything except look guilty. Sure enough, when Linda's turn came, Mrs. McKay noticed she was in her socks and asked where her shoes were. At first Linda didn't respond, frozen with fear and unsure of her English, but then she tried to explain she had forgotten them. Mrs. McKay stepped toward Linda, cocking her right arm as she approached. With an open palm, she struck Linda hard on the left side of her head. Linda staggered, then began to cry. Mrs. McKay told her to retrieve her shoes.

"I remember crying and holding my left ear and running upstairs to get my shoes," Linda later said in sworn testimony. After finding them, she sat down on the edge of her bed and put her hands over her ears—the ringing in her head was overpowering. By the time she returned to the dining room wearing her black oxfords, the only food left to put on her plate was a piece of bread.

After that, Linda always remembered her shoes. And she never heard with her left ear again.

Ha, ha, ha.

3

"AN INDIAN THINKS"

ICHAEL TWOVOICE, MAUREEN'S PATERNAL GRAND-
father, was born in 1920. He came to be seen as one
of Waywayseecappo's greatest minds and orators.
"He could out-talk any white man," his friend Jim Cote fondly
remembers. According to family lore, the name Twovoice comes
from the sounds that follow a nearby lightning bolt: first a boom,
then a rumble.

Michael loved words. He read constantly—newspapers,
magazines, books, whatever he could get his hands on. He even
liked to carry around a dictionary, just in case. One time, after
he spotted a cougar prowling the reserve, friends asked him to
describe it. To Michael, the animal wasn't "fast" or "quick" but,
rather, "fleet-footed."

Michael's way with words made him Waywayseecappo's go-to
MC for holiday parties and charity events. He chaired community
meetings. He occasionally preached in the reserve's Presbyterian
church, though he wasn't the pastor, or even a Presbyterian. He
was a Catholic, but that didn't seem to bother anyone because

he sure knew his Bible. Beside his bed, he kept a copy with an Ojibway translation.

Michael Twovoice (Courtesy of Maureen Twovoice)

Michael walked with a limp, slightly stooped over to his left side. As a young man, he had lost a lung to tuberculosis, so strenuous activity left him huffing and puffing. He did not own a car, and when walking from the reserve to Rossburn he needed to take breaks. Sometimes, while he caught his breath, he lit a cigarette. You could hear the phlegm in his voice.

Michael, his wife, and their children lived on the reserve in a modest two-bedroom house with little insulation. When it was cold in the winter, Michael kept the fire going all night. On particularly hot summer days, he went shirtless. That's when his children could see the six-inch scar below his left armpit that looked like a zipper.

A dedicated writer, Michael often worked at a small brown desk in the corner of the living room. His daughter, Hazel, could

always tell when he was thinking deeply about something, searching for just the right words: he would prop his elbows on the
desk, look out the window, and chain-smoke. He couldn't afford
a typewriter, so he wrote by hand, his letters looping and elegant,
his glasses slipping halfway down his nose. He kept his papers
neatly ordered in the desk's six drawers to protect them from the
entropy of his children. "Don't touch my paperwork," he gently
reminded them. "There's important stuff in there."

In 1951, Michael published an essay in the *Rossburn Review*
titled "An Indian Thinks."[1] It begins like this: "It often amuses
me, when I am among white strangers, to have them look at me
intently, quite unaware that I am observing them. As they gaze at
my expressionless and impassive features, I know they are wondering what goes on in an Indian's mind. What does go on in an
Indian's mind? I shall attempt to answer this question in part."

For Michael, as for others, the answer was complicated.

MICHAEL DEVOTED MUCH of his life to politics. As one of the few
Indians of his generation to get his high school diploma, he tended
to be thrust into roles that involved writing. After serving in the
Canadian military during the Second World War, Michael worked
as the secretary to Waywayseecappo's Chief, Prince Astakeesic. He
then became the secretary for the Manitoba Indian Association,
an organization that dedicated itself to reforming the Indian Act,
the federal law that set out rules that applied only to Indians and
detailed the many ways in which bureaucrats were empowered to
micromanage them.

At a fundamental level, Michael believed that Indians needed
more control over their own lives. "Things will never change," he
told his son Maurice, "as long as those guys over there are calling

the shots." His finger wagged vaguely towards Ottawa and the Department of Indian Affairs. "We will progress more as Native people when we can govern ourselves," he said.

Michael insisted that his children "never, ever look down on anybody or judge anybody by the colour of their skin, whether they're black, Chinese, or white." Michael didn't mention any of his own experiences with discrimination. "He went to residential school," Hazel says. "Maybe that's where he learned about racism."

In 1951, the Indian Act was amended. Michael welcomed some of the changes: restrictions on Indian ceremonies and dancing were removed, as were limitations on hiring lawyers. But Michael thought that more drastic change was still urgently required. He applauded Indians who continued "appealing for justice to the Canadian government." They were "right in fighting for their security and other humanitarian rights which, at this date, are not given.... It is only just and fair that the Parliament of Canada should heed their plea." Real progress would not occur, he wrote, unless "barriers which are hedging in the Indian of today, in matters of handling their own affairs, are broken down."

At the time, federal Indian agents still enjoyed immense, and virtually unchecked, power over life on reserves. For example, an Indian on reserve could not sell their produce or cattle off reserve without the specific permission of an Indian agent. This was typical of the kind of paternalistic government that Michael despised. "We can't just obey anymore," he said. "Let's do things on our own. We don't need any help from the Indian agent."

IN 1952, A new Indian agent, Fred Clarke, arrived in Waywayseecappo, along with his wife, Lillian. Fred wore his pants high, well above his hips, which did not so much obscure his considerable belly as make his upper body look compressed. While Fred worked as the Indian agent, his wife worked in the community as a nurse. The Clarkes went on to spend five years in Waywayseecappo, until Fred was rotated to another reserve in 1957. Upon their departure, Lillian published a letter reflecting upon their experience. "The years we spent on Wayway were very happy ones," she wrote. "We had a comfortable four bedroom home but no telephone, electricity and no water!" Mrs. Clarke was probably not aware that people on the reserve used to sardonically refer to her home as "God's house."

"Most of the Indian people," Mrs. Clarke wrote, "are very reserved and withdrawn until a white person proves himself to them and gains their respect and trust. They always seem to expect persons in authority to treat them as an inferior class." Perhaps Mrs. Clarke had some sense why. In any case, she believed she and her husband were different: "Our friends on Wayway soon found out that they were to be treated as equals."[2]

She did not mention the fact that her "equals" were still not allowed to vote in federal elections, a right they wouldn't receive until 1960, the same year Premier Tommy Douglas observed that Canada was still treating the Indian as "a second-class citizen." "We are going to have to make up our minds," Douglas said, "whether we are going to keep the Indian bottled up in a sort of Canadian Apartheid."[3]

Fred Clarke served as Waywayseecappo's Indian agent during a time when many of the community's children were being hauled off to residential schools. One of them was Jim Cote. When Jim escaped from the Brandon Indian Residential School and ran 150 kilometres to give his parents a hug at home in Waywayseecappo, Fred Clarke was the Indian agent who promptly drove him all the way back.

* * *

ON JANUARY 17, 1957, residents of Rossburn gathered at the town hall to fete the Clarkes before their departure. The evening featured songs and hymns, an accordion solo, a piano-accordion duet, and a tap dance. The next day, another goodbye ceremony was held in Waywayseecappo. There, a local man rose "on behalf of all the members of the Waywayseecappo Reserve" to thank the Clarkes. He said news of their departure had left the people of Waywayseecappo "with heavy hearts." The Clarkes had arrived soon after new revisions to the Indian Act. "We needed someone to guide us and lead us through it all. Then through God's holy providence you were sent to us."

"Although you were vested with much authority over us," the speaker continued, "you met us on our level. You were not prejudiced because our colors were different, you thereby gave us a chance to cast aside our cloaks of inferiority complex." In time, the community had "learned to love and appreciate you."[4] In concluding, he bade the Clarkes farewell and offered a pair of lamps as a gift.

A reporter from the *Rossburn Review* was so impressed by the speech that he typed up the whole thing for publication in the following week's paper. The speech concluded with these words:

> *Thank you for what you have done for us and please forgive us*
> *if we haven't done too much for you.*
> > *On behalf of my people, I am*
> > *Michael Twovoice*

Indeed, it was Michael Twovoice, dedicated opponent of the Indian Act, who so effusively praised an Indian agent. Was this simply a tactical curtsy to power, or a sign of something else? What *was* going on in Michael's mind?

MICHAEL LEFT BEHIND his published words, fossils of a vibrant mind. Unfortunately, his personal papers, which he had scrupulously ordered and archived, were lost in a fire after his death. The remaining fragments do not resolve his paradoxes but deepen them.

In 1959, two years after his speech in honour of the Clarkes, Michael published a short and telling history of Waywayseecappo in the *Rossburn Review*.[5] He started back at the beginning, when Waywayseecappo and his braves roamed in peace over a "vast tract of land" that was "rich in game, fowl and fur." Then "the Great Queen Victoria's representatives [came] to stipulate lasting treaties with the Indians across the breadth of the Prairies to the Rocky Mountains." After Chief Waywayseecappo signed a treaty and his band moved to the reserve, the "only enemy" that remained was "the onslaught of the deep-freeze of winter." Michael commended the government for being "benevolent" to Chief Waywayseecappo "and his braves."

The government should be "given full credit" for improving "the Welfare of the people" and "steering them in the things of life that are good," Michael wrote. "The Indians of Waywayseecappo feel forever grateful for this, as they have been well cared for from the earliest times." These are hardly the words of a revolutionary.

Michael went on to praise the "unceasing labor in the spiritual welfare of the people" by the Presbyterian and Catholic missionaries. "Much can be said of both churches in administering to the Indians," he wrote. They established the first schools on the reserve, though these were "given up when Residential Schools were built in centrally located places to serve a greater number of Reserves." Michael's history included no criticism of these residential schools.

In 1960, Michael did appear before Waywayseecappo's band council to address a concern he had about residential schools. The concern was this: Michael wanted to ensure that Roman Catholic children had access to Roman Catholic instruction.[6] The next year, Michael was asked by the band council to personally escort a child to the Brandon Indian Residential School, because the parents did not seem to be providing adequate care at home. Michael drove along the same roads that Agent Fred Clarke had taken when driving Jim Cote back after his escape.[7]

When it came time for Michael's own children to be sent to residential schools, his daughter Hazel recalls, "There was sadness. But he never said, 'You aren't going to go.' You had to accept it. They just took us."

MICHAEL TWOVOICE WROTE in his 1951 essay that, for Indians, "it is one of their greatest ambitions to be assimilated generally into all phases of Canadian life—social, political and economical."

Assimilate. That was a word the government of Canada had been using for a long time. Prime Minister John A. Macdonald said, "The great aim of our legislation has been to do away with the tribal system and assimilate the Indian people in all respects with the other inhabitants of the Dominion, as speedily as they are fit for the change."[8] For the Canadian government, assimilation was both means and end.

Did Michael Twovoice embody Macdonald's grand plans? As a child, Michael attended the Qu'Appelle Indian Industrial

School in Saskatchewan, also known as the Lebret Residential School. A history of the school, published in 1955, was dedicated to "the great missionary pioneers, men and women, who spent their lives . . . for the civilization and the Christianization of the Indian Nation."[9] No doubt Michael's time at this school left a lasting mark. As Jim Cote puts it, "Mike was a smart man, educated. He was well taught at residential school."

Unlike many of his contemporaries, Michael cultivated ties in Rossburn. In 1952, he posted an ad in the Classified section of the *Rossburn Review*: "POSITION WANTED—Desire job as assistant in any town establishment. Have qualified Junior Matriculation. Nationality – Indian. Steady employment preferable. Contact Michael Twovoice."[10]

The fact that Michael felt the need to disclose his Indian "nationality" says a lot about the norms of the time, and his willingness to abide by them. In any case, he got what he wanted: his ad landed him a job . . . working at the *Rossburn Review*, as an assistant editor. Years later, after a fire damaged his family's home, Michael received gifts of clothing and supplies from people in town. Afterwards, he published a letter in the newspaper on behalf of his family: "We would like to extend our thanks to our friends in Rossburn."[11] On another occasion, Michael was the one receiving public thanks in the paper for his contribution to a charity bake sale in Rossburn.

Michael's daughter, Hazel, remembers trips to Rossburn's butcher shop with her dad, who took pleasure in bantering with the staff. Hazel saw that her dad wasn't afraid when he spoke to white people. She loved that about him.

"See," Michael told his daughter, "that's why you go to school. So you can talk with these people." Michael always insisted that she stay in school, no matter how frustrated she got. "You have to learn," he told her. "You have to learn the white man's ways to survive. We're living in their world." The point of all this, as far as Hazel could tell, was that her dad wanted her to have access to everything Canada had to offer. "That's why education was so important to him," Hazel says. "So we could communicate with all kinds of people, so we could work with them." Michael knew there was a system restricting the social mobility of Indians, and he wanted his children to have a pass.

In 1951, MICHAEL was thirty-one years old, father to three children, and infected with tuberculosis, which had destroyed his left lung and threatened his life. He went to a sanatorium in Brandon, where a surgeon removed a rib and the infected lung. Michael penned his essay "An Indian Thinks" during his convalescence— his side aching, his fresh stitches itching, and the site of the surgery still just a patched wound, not yet a scar. Michael had just sacrificed one lung to protect the other. Now he was asking himself what he was willing to concede to survive in Canada.

Michael refused to renounce his culture. "I, for one, am proud to have been born an Indian," he wrote. "I take pride in our traditions and heritage as Canada's own children of nature." Michael spoke Cree and Ojibway fluently. With his children, he stuck mostly to Ojibway. And he attended local Sun Dances, though not as often as some others. In a photo taken at a Sun Dance, Michael is seen standing alongside his wife, Annie, as a spectator, not participating as a dancer in regalia. He is present and supportive, yet somehow apart.

At the same time, he served as an informal intermediary between the government and Waywayseecappo. One of his friends on the reserve, Norbert Tanner, saw him as a bridge. On many occasions, when a government official visited Waywayseecappo, community members would ask Michael to speak on their behalf. He was tasked with explaining to Indian agents like Fred Clarke the concerns of his community. In turn, Michael often appeared before Waywayseecappo's band council to explain in Ojibway what the government was trying to do. "He talked to both sides, to make sure everyone had a clearer understanding of what was going on," Tanner says. "Mike was an interpreter." To help his community as best he could, and to survive the challenges he had faced in his own life, Michael Twovoice had learned to speak with two voices.

Despite everything Michael had seen and endured, he was still convinced that the government meant well, that Canada could change, that the future could brighten—if not in time for him, at least for the generations to follow. "In this country, with its democratic principles and its great opportunities for achievement," Michael wrote, he hoped for a future in which Indians "shall not be discriminated against or retarded in any way." Michael wanted to believe in Canada's promise, even though Canada had always relegated him to second-class status. The residential school where he had learned to write was premised on the idea that his culture was backwards and worthless. As of 1951, when Michael wrote his essay, Canada still did not trust him enough to cast a vote or buy a beer. The Brandon Sanatorium where he was receiving treatment for tuberculosis was a segregated facility. Indian patients were not allowed to mix with white patients, even though they were all suffering from the same disease.

Michael knew what it was to be separate and unequal, and that's not what he wanted for his children. He believed they would have to adapt, as he had, as he would continue to do. He thought that the best hope for his children was "a good education."

From his bed in the sanatorium, he concluded his essay: "It gladdens my Indian heart to visualize the future in which I see my people working side by side with their palefaced brothers, making of this wonderful country a still greater Canada. I think of the inevitable day when I shall have reached with my children the parting of the ways.... As they stand proudly on the threshold of their futures, I shall say to them, 'Children, there lies your Canada, yours by heritage. Make use of its vast opportunities.'"

As early as 1948, the federal government could see that residential schools were failing.[12] At that time, there were seventy-two residential schools in operation, educating 9,368 children, but the attitude in the Department of Indian Affairs, according to one history, "was that the sooner the residential schools were done away with the better."[13]

Economic considerations drove the government's about-face. The population of Indian students was rapidly increasing, and bureaucrats wanted to avoid building and maintaining yet more costly residential facilities. The first alternative was opening more day schools on reserves, where students could be educated while living at home. An analysis by the Department of Indian Affairs determined that the cost per student at a residential school was nearly four times more than the cost at a day school.[14] A senior bureaucrat argued that "the education requirements of the great majority of the Indians could be met by day schools to the decided benefit of the Indians and to the financial benefit of the taxpayer."[15] Schools on reserves also happened to be what treaties between the government and Indigenous leaders in the nineteenth century had explicitly called for, though this did not seem to be a factor in the policy shift.

In a total reversal, the government came to doubt the wisdom of educating children away from their parents after all. In the new era of "educational services," according to one government memo following the change, "everything possible will be done to enable families to stay together so children will not have to be separated from their parents needlessly."[16] In Waywayseecappo, the result of the shift was the opening of two day schools in the 1950s. A majority of students from Waywayseecappo, including Linda Jandrew and Jim Cote, continued to be sent away to residential schools in Brandon and Birtle. But more and more were being educated on the reserve, close to their homes and families. (It would still take almost five decades to close all these schools, largely because of staunch resistance from the churches running them.[17] That is why Linda could still be put on a bus to the Brandon residential school in 1965.)

Meanwhile, the federal government was also developing another option that it preferred most of all: the integration of Indian students into provincial public schools. Again, the prospect of lowering expenditures weighed heavily. The cost of integrated education "would in the end be substantially less" than the cost of running a separate school system, federal bureaucrats concluded.[18] The Department of Indian Affairs became "convinced that where possible, Indian children should be educated in association with children of other racial groups."[19]

In the United States, a parallel movement was taking place to integrate Black children into public schools. "Separate educational facilities are inherently unequal," the United States Supreme Court ruled in a ground-breaking judgment in 1954, Brown v. Board of Education. "To separate [Black children] from others of similar age and qualifications solely because of their race generates a feeling of inferiority as to their status in the community that may affect their hearts and minds in a way unlikely ever to be undone."[20] This argument—that racial separation was necessarily harmful—gained traction in Ottawa as well. The Canadian government came to believe that racial integration in public schools was the best recipe for equality. By passing more time with white peers, officials noted, Indians could "quicken and give meaning to the acculturative process through which they are passing."[21] Which is to say: the method was changing, from segregated to integrated schools, but the goal remained assimilation.

By the late 1950s, the Department of Indian Affairs was pressuring Waywayseecappo to send its children to study in Rossburn and selling Rossburn on the merits of opening its schools to students from the reserve. The incentive for public school boards to accept Indigenous children was simple: more funding. The federal government paid school boards for every Indian pupil attending a public school and also promised to invest in upgrades to elementary and secondary school buildings. In exchange, school boards had to agree that "there will be no segregation in the schools by reason of race or colour."[22]

On March 30, 1961, Rossburn's school board agreed to accept students from the reserve. The only remaining hurdle was approval by Waywayseecappo's elected band council, which scheduled a meeting on April 11 to debate the measure. The question was whether it would be better for their children to receive a segregated federal education, on the reserve and at residential schools, or an integrated education in the provincial public school system.

Four days before the band council meeting, a teacher at Waywayseecappo's day school, C.M. King, wrote to the federal government to express doubts about integrated education in Rossburn. King was "deeply agitated" because he doubted children from the reserve would "cope with the troubles that a minority group meets in an integrated situation." He did not think that Rossburn's teachers were aware of the distinct needs of Indian children or would "take the time to give . . . the extra consideration" these students might need. Instead, he worried that Rossburn was just allowing Indian students to enrol to "reap the harvest of many more dollars to pay for their new school expenditures." He added: "I feel that integration of all children is the coming thing, but I also feel that it is not yet time for total integration. . . . It looks to me that Rossburn School has more to gain than the Indian child."[23] None of these prescient warnings were heeded.

When Waywayseecappo's Chief and four band councillors met on April 11, they voted unanimously to close the day schools on the reserve and send their students into Rossburn. One of these councillors was Michael Twovoice, then serving in his first term as an elected member of the council. He signed the resolution in his refined cursive.[24]

Michael, a product of residential school, helped usher in the era of integrated education. "Children, there lies your Canada, yours by heritage," Michael had written hopefully a decade before. "Make use of its vast opportunities." For too many children in Waywayseecappo, and on reserves across Canada, it didn't work out that way.

4

"WHITEWASH"

B Y THE TIME THE BRANDON INDIAN RESIDENTIAL
School fully closed in 1970, about half of all Native students across Canada were attending provincial public
schools. Linda had left Brandon the previous year, after finishing Grade 4. She was "discharged," as the Department of Indian
Affairs records put it, as if she were leaving a prison or a hospital.
Linda returned home to live with her aunt and enrolled in Grade 5
at Rossburn Elementary, where the experiment in integration
had been under way for a decade. Linda found herself among 160
students from Waywayseecappo studying in town.

Linda was glad to escape the horrors of Brandon, but now
she had to deal with white classmates in Rossburn calling her
a "wagon burner." The expression never made any sense to her,
but apparently Indians were known to torch cowboy wagons in
Hollywood movies. "Dirty Indian" was another favourite, along
with "savage," the classic. As a girl, Linda could expect to be called
a "squaw." "The teachers didn't really stop the white students
from saying these things," Linda remembers. "On the playground,

white students stood in little groups of four or five and called me names. They thought they were smart. They weren't. I tried to ignore them. It hurt."

Linda had struggled as a student ever since Mrs. McKay had struck her in the ear. The assault shattered her trust in authority figures like teachers. She took to sitting at the back of class, where her impaired hearing made it even more difficult for her to follow lessons. She also avoided raising her hand. "I was scared to ask anything after I got hit."

In Rossburn, Linda often felt like white students were laughing at her, but she never really understood why. And she didn't find the teachers, all of whom were white, much better. "I always felt unwanted," she says. "The teachers couldn't care less if we were there or not. They were always yelling at us. They were more on the white side." Linda retreated behind the thickest shell she could muster and kept to the company of other students from Waywayseecappo whenever possible. "I stayed away from whites as much as I could," she says. "I felt unsafe all the time. I wanted to get away from there. We could have gotten hurt on the playground and teachers wouldn't have done anything about it. They didn't give a shit, ha ha ha."

Linda made her own lunch every morning: two fried eggs, which she placed in a plastic sandwich bag before embarking on her thirty-minute walk to school. The school also provided a small carton of chocolate milk at noon to all the students from the reserve, paid for by Waywayseecappo's band council. Still, Linda had to fight to protect her lunch from hungry students who tried to take her cold fried eggs. "I felt bad for kids who had no lunch," she says. "But I thought, it's not my fault. I wasn't going to walk home on an empty stomach."

Former teachers from this period attest to difficult conditions facing many of their students from Waywayseecappo. One teacher says she kept spare towels and soap in the classroom, so that her students from the reserve could slip away as discreetly as possible for a hot shower, something that was often not available in their homes. A former principal, Con Erickson, recalls that during the bitter cold of the winter, many students showed up at school without hats and mittens, so a group of his teachers collected winter gear so that every student could safely go outside during recess.

One of the school's greatest challenges was regular attendance. "In order for a kid to get to school," Erickson says, "the kid has to get up, get dressed, eat if there is anything to eat, and be on the bus at eight in the morning. And if mom and dad are not helping, that's a pretty hard thing." Erickson recalls spotting children from the reserve hanging around town late at night because they had to wait for the adults to finish up at the bar.

Linda was living with her aunt, whose place was a thirty-minute walk from school, and Linda relied on her own legs to get to school and back. But when she was a little girl, before she was sent off to Brandon, she had once been one of those children, waiting outside the Rossburn Hotel in the dark, just wanting to go home.

IN 1969, PRIME Minister Pierre Trudeau's government unveiled a plan to deal with the separateness and inequality of Native peoples once and for all.[1] This proposal became enduringly known as "the White Paper." As the policy was unveiled, Minister of Indian Affairs Jean Chrétien said, "This government believes in equality." The central premise of the White Paper was that the best way to improve the living conditions of Indians was to treat them exactly like everyone else: "The separate legal status of Indians and the policies which have flowed from it have kept the Indian people apart from and behind other Canadians.... The treatment resulting from their different status has been often worse, sometimes equal and occasionally better than that accorded to their fellow citizens. What matters is that it has been different."

The White Paper approach was consistent with Trudeau's view of Quebec, which he insisted should be a province like the others, without distinct status or powers. For Indians, as for Quebec, Trudeau saw different treatment as fundamentally at odds with the ideal of equality. As long as Indians were treated differently and kept separate, the White Paper argued, they would not become equal. The reserve system should accordingly be abolished, and services like education should be administered wholly by the provinces, not the federal government. The ongoing integration of Indian students into public schools would be just one aspect of a larger process of integration. "The traditional method of providing separate services to Indians must be ended," the White Paper continued. "The legal and administrative discrimination in the treatment of Indian people has not given them an equal chance of success.... Discrimination breeds discrimination by example, and the separateness of Indian people has affected the attitudes of other Canadians towards them." Here, the document might as well have invoked the attitude of many people in Rossburn, who harboured suspicions that the federal government, in dealing with Indians separately, was according them preferential treatment.

At this time, a man named Arnold Minish was superintendent of the Pelly Trail School Division, which included Rossburn's schools. Minish had become chair of the school division in 1968 and quickly earned the respect of Rossburn's high school principal, who described him as "young, dynamic, knowledgeable, aggressive and well-organized."[2] Minish was six foot four, with a booming voice. A former colleague remembers Minish as someone who "pushed his view forward as hard as he could. He was a little bullish."

On April 22, 1970, Minish mailed a letter to Minister Chrétien. "Dear Sir," Minish wrote,

> The Pelly Trail School Division . . . wishes to bring to your attention the utterly deplorable conditions on the Waywayseecappo Indian Band living on the Lizard Point Indian Reserve located at Rossburn, Manitoba.
>
> Indian students integrated into the Rossburn Elementary and High School systems . . . come from homes where work opportunities are nil, where moral standards are nonexistent, and where drunkenness and debauchery are the order of the day.
>
> The Pelly Trail School Division Board would like you to appear at a meeting to be held at Rossburn at your convenience to discuss ways and means of launching a frontal attack on the conditions of this reserve before they spill out into the surrounding community to a greater extent than they do now and destroy the surrounding civilization and particularly the school system.[3]

Chrétien's assistant replied that the minister was "sorry" to hear about the "problems" but believed "that this situation may be remedied with the cooperation of all involved."[4] Representatives from Waywayseecappo, the school board, and the federal government assembled in Rossburn in late June. The most senior federal official present was J.R. Wright, the district superintendent of education for Indian Affairs, who took extensive notes.[5]

Minish started the meeting with a lengthy presentation about the problems with Indian students in Rossburn's schools: their attendance was terrible and getting "progressively worse"; teachers expended disproportionate time and resources on them; their "general health and cleanliness" was questionable; many were too old for their grade; they were passive and showed "little interest" in their courses. Minish was also troubled that "Indian children were robbing lunch pails of non-Indian children." There were only a few thieves, he said, but they were disrupting the entire school. The underlying problem seemed to be children from Waywayseecappo arriving at school without lunch and having eaten no breakfast. As far as Minish was concerned, integration of Waywayseecappo's students into Rossburn's schools was not working. He "stressed that the climate in the school was getting worse and worse each year as the problems seem to mount rather than diminish."

The meeting then turned to a video recording of Dan George, a former Chief of the Tsleil-Waututh Nation in British Columbia, who discussed the challenges of integrated education from a Native point of view. (That same year, George starred alongside Dustin Hoffman in a Hollywood film called *Little Big Man*, for which he received an Oscar nomination.) In his recorded speech, George said:

> *You talk big words of integration in the schools. Does it really exist? . . . Unless there is integration of hearts and minds you have only a physical presence and the walls are as high as the mountain range. Come with me to the playgrounds of an integrated high school. . . . Over here is a group of white students and see over there near the fence a group of Native students . . . and a great chasm seems to be opening up between the two groups.*[6]

According to the meeting notes taken by J.R. Wright, several people then argued that the deeper issue "was a Waywayseecappo–Rossburn problem, that any lasting and useful solution would have to be the result of day-by-day communication between the people of Rossburn and the people of Waywayseecappo. Until such communication was in effect there would be hostilities between the two communities."

Wright concluded his report of the meeting with his own assessment:

> *The people on the Waywayseecappo Reserve must come to understand that they are masters of their own destiny and that the effectiveness of the education program for their children depends to a large extent on their willingness to create an environment on the reserve which will promote good learning habits on the part of the students. . . .*
>
> *Just as the band members at Waywayseecappo must take action . . . so must the community around Waywayseecappo reassess their historical attitudes towards the Indian people in the area and must come to respect them as people having rights and privileges as do all the other people in the area, as people who are to be respected and treated with respect and trust by their neighbours in the larger community. There has been many, many years of mistrust and it can therefore be assumed that this change in attitude will require several years.*

In the months that followed, Minish and Wright continued exchanging cordial letters, one superintendent to another, about the unfolding disaster. "The attendance of the Indian children in the Rossburn school is not good," Minish wrote on October 23, 1970.[7] For years, he had been trying to hire a truancy officer to help get more students from Waywayseecappo to school. Waywayseecappo's band council had even passed a resolution in 1968 approving the idea. But Minish had been unable to hire anyone because, he wrote, "the white people refuse to take the job of going onto the reserve to bring the Indian students to school." Minish settled for asking local RCMP officers to keep an eye out for students skipping class.

"I think it is indeed unfortunate," Wright replied five days later, "that no one in the Rossburn area will go on to the reserve for the purpose of enforcing school attendance, but this is perhaps understandable when one realises the hostility that has existed between the people at Rossburn and Waywayseecappo over the last many years."[8] It is not clear whether either man considered hiring someone from Waywayseecappo to perform the role.

At the end of 1971, Minish again wrote to Minister Jean Chrétien, this time to plead for additional federal funding.[9] He explained that providing remedial services for Indian students required resources that the school board could not afford. He acknowledged that the school board could, in theory, raise additional funds with "a special levy to help educate these children," but that would amount to an extra tax on families in the school district, and that was not going to happen. "We are in a dilemma," Minish explained, "as the Pelly Trail Board has established policy whereby they refuse to further subsidize the education of Indian children." Rural taxpayers felt they were carrying an unfair burden, and they'd had enough.[10] In years to come, this was to be a recurring theme in relations between Waywayseecappo and Rossburn.

In February 1972, Wright wrote a long and heartfelt letter to encourage Minish to make changes to help Indian students succeed:

71

I think all of us who are involved in implementing joint school projects were quite naive at the time as to the implication of the action that we were proposing. The result was that in many cases our joint school project was simply an exercise in which Indian children attended a provincial school, but where no real tangible changes in the Provincial school program were put into effect in order to meet the educational needs of the Indian children. The result has been that in almost every Division we have still large numbers of drop outs. . . . Almost all the students go through the system without really gaining a pride in themselves or their heritage, two things which are essential if people are to live a happy life.[11]

Around that time, only 4 percent of Indian students across Canada were graduating from high school.[12] Wright offered a series of concrete suggestions: offering Ojibway language classes; changing the name of the school to the Rossburn-Waywayseecappo School; and teaching all students, not just Indian students, more about Native history and culture. "By this," Wright wrote, "I do not mean Indian culture that comes from the stereotype image that many people have gained about Indian people, but a real attempt on the part of the teaching staff and students to learn about Indian people in their area." Above all, he asked Minish to "insist that all education officials are committed to the fact that Indian children have the same basic intelligence as other children" and "can learn." If Minish did these things, he could create "really joint schools in fact as well as in name."

Minish did not stick around long enough to try. Later that year, he transferred to another school division.

By then, Linda had also left Rossburn after only one year in the elementary school. At the end of Grade 5, she was removed from her home by Manitoba's child welfare agency. Over the course of the next six years, she would live with nine white foster families, in places all over Manitoba. This was possible only because of a 1951 law that authorized provincial child welfare agencies to apprehend Indian children. Over the following three decades, more than twenty thousand Indian, Métis, and Inuit children were taken from their homes and sent out for adoption to primarily white families across Canada and the United States. Those not adopted outright were placed into foster homes. This widespread removal of Indian children from their homes is sometimes called the Sixties Scoop, but the practice was common through the 1980s.[13]

The United Way was the organization charged with arranging Linda's foster placements. At one point—Linda doesn't remember exactly which year—the United Way sent a photographer to take her portrait. In this photo, Linda is holding a rose. It is an image she vividly remembers because it ended up on the cover of a widely distributed pamphlet about adoption. In subsequent years, whenever Linda came across any of these pamphlets, she would pick them up, crush them inside her fist, and throw them into the closest garbage can.

As ARTHUR MINISH and J.R. Wright swapped letters about Waywayseecappo's students in Rossburn, Indigenous opponents of integrated education were mobilizing. Trudeau and Chrétien's White Paper had been resoundingly opposed by Native peoples. Cree leader Harold Cardinal described the government's policy as a "thinly disguised programme of extermination through assimilation" and ridiculed the government for trying to solve the "Indian problem" through "gallons of white paint liberally applied."[14]

The Manitoba Indian Brotherhood, an organization representing Manitoban Chiefs, gathered in 1971 to articulate a new
vision for relations between Indians and non-Indians. Among
those gathered was Hugh McKay, a friend of Michael Twovoice,
who was then serving a two-year term as Waywayseecappo's
elected Chief. The assembled leaders produced a manifesto called
Wahbung: Our Tomorrows. It began with a declaration of "confidence in the integrity and goodwill of the majority of the people
of Canada."[15] It also demanded an end to integrated education.

Wahbung called on the federal government to "recognize the
total failure of the present education system for Indian people."
Integrated education, the Chiefs believed, was just the latest
iteration of education without "relevance to the Indian reality."
The architects of integration had sought to bring Indians into
the Canadian mainstream, and not without a measure of good
intentions. But in the end, the new policy amounted to another
"invitation to participate in the annihilation of our culture and
our way of life. The government had simply rephrased this long
standing invitation." Indian students continued to feel like strangers in the classroom, in schools that offered no instruction of
Native cultures and languages. "Many non-Indians believe that
we have failed education," *Wahbung* stated, "but the truth of the
matter is that education has failed us." Across the country, Indian
communities were protesting against integrated education in
public schools.

The following year, another watershed document, titled
"Indian Control of Indian Education," was released by the
National Indian Brotherhood, or NIB. "Until now, decisions on
the education of Indian children have been made by anyone and
everyone, except Indian parents," the document declared. "This
must stop." The NIB proposed locally controlled education

aimed at two primary goals: first, to "reinforce . . . Indian identity," and, second, to prepare students to make "a good living in modern society." Twenty years earlier, Michael Twovoice might have advocated for similar objectives, but he had believed integrated education was compatible with them. Increasingly, Indian leaders and parents like Hugh McKay were convinced otherwise. Instead of empowering Indian students, integration had too often left them experiencing feelings of "inferiority, alienation, rejection, hostility."[16]

In response, Minister Chrétien, erstwhile champion of the White Paper, acknowledged that public education for Indigenous students continued to be "a whitewash" that equipped students "with white values, goals, language, skills needed to succeed in the dominant society," but with "very little recognition of the importance of cultural heritage in the learning process."[17] Instead, these schools were offering a "cookie-cutter education" in order "to turn out functional and identical Canadians." Chrétien admitted that this approach was not working. An integrated school "of the whitewash variety" could "serve no purpose in a child's world. Rather it alienates him from his own people." Under heavy political pressure, Chrétien conceded the proposition that Indian communities should have a greater say over schooling their own children. It would take some years yet to implement, but the shift was clear, and fundamental.

IN 1980, MAUREEN Twovoice's uncle, Lyle Longclaws, was elected president of the Manitoba Indian Brotherhood on the third ballot of a closely contested election.[18] He was only twenty-five years old and his winning campaign focused on education. "Indian schools should be controlled by Indians because our children receive a poorer quality of education than the average Canadian," he said. "We're tired of seeing taxpayers' dollars funneled into a solution that won't work," he added, shrewdly undermining the stereotype that Indians heedlessly devoured public resources.[19]

The numbers in Waywayseecappo told a dismal story. In the two decades that followed Michael Twovoice's 1961 vote for integrated education in Rossburn, 80 percent of students from Waywayseecappo dropped out of school by Grade 8. From 1965 to 1982, only a single student graduated from Grade 12.[20] The proportion of students completing Grade 10 and beyond actually diminished between 1954 and 1983.[21] In most cases, students who continued beyond Grade 8 in Rossburn were funnelled into a special program called the Occupational Entrance Course, commonly known as OEC. This was a euphemism for "dummy classrooms" where students learned little and had no route to a high school diploma, according to Waywayseecappo Elder Bryan Cloud. *Our kids aren't dumb*, parents and community leaders thought as their children struggled in Rossburn's schools. *This can't be right.*

Meanwhile, Waywayseecappo's band council was paying the public school division full year's tuition, even for students who often dropped out before Christmas. Tuition was paid out based on the "nominal roll," which was calculated in October, the second month of the school year. "They were glad to take our bucks but weren't interested in helping our children," Bryan Cloud recalls. "So we said, 'Screw that.'"[22]

In the spring of 1982, Waywayseecappo's band council announced that all of the community's 155 students in Rossburn's schools would be withdrawn the following academic year. For the public school board, this meant a loss of about $300,000 in revenue, which led to staff layoffs. Despite the financial loss, the reaction of many in Rossburn was, to a great extent, *good riddance.* The chair of the public school board insisted, "We have done everything within our power to accommodate them."[23] It is difficult to take this assertion seriously, given how little was done to create an environment where Native students and their culture were respected. Notably, none of J.R. Wright's suggestions to create "joint schools in fact as well as in name," outlined a decade before, had been implemented.

For Waywayseecappo, the most pressing challenge became finding an alternative place to educate their children. The best option, as it happened, was the hockey arena. The federal government had financed an indoor hockey rink on the reserve in 1978, but it turned out that the water available from nearby wells contained so much zinc and salt that forming ice was almost impossible. In the four years following the arena's construction, no one had skated in it. In order to finance the construction to convert the useless arena into a school, Waywayseecappo received a federal grant. The band council also took out a $400,000 loan from the Rossburn Credit Union, with an interest rate of 18.5 percent (the prime lending rate plus 1.5 percent).[24] Waywayseecappo was evidently willing to pay a high price to establish their own school. By the end of summer, fourteen extra-large classrooms had taken shape inside the hockey arena, and this still left plenty of room for a colossal gym.

In September 1982, Waywayseecappo became the twentieth reserve in Manitoba to establish and manage its own school. The community greeted the opening with euphoria. There would finally be formal Ojibway language instruction, and even adults who had been out of school for years decided to return to classrooms that smelled like freshly cut wood. In the school's first three years, attendance rose to 85 percent, about double the previous attendance rate in Rossburn. "If the Indian People of the

Waywayseecappo Band are to survive," Chief Robert Shingoose wrote in the first school yearbook, "we must develop and control our own education. Education has always been seen by our Indian Leaders as one of the major tools that would help us strike off the shackles of poverty." In the same yearbook, Grade 2 student Kevin Mecas wrote, "I like Wayway school because . . . the teachers here are better friends than the other teachers in Rossburn school. I like learning Ojibway best."[25] The school's first Ojibway teacher was Jim Cote, Hugh McKay's stepson.

In Waywayseecappo, the new school became a symbol of renewal. One community member, Ron Rattlesnake, wrote that "the transformation of the arena into a school in my opinion has been the greatest accomplishment in the history of Waywayseecappo."[26]

The federal government was less impressed. Since the school construction was done with plywood and with great speed, the building had become a certifiable fire hazard. An internal memo of the Department of Indian Affairs noted, "The school facility was built . . . generally to unacceptable standards, and fire, health and physical safety deficiencies are major concerns." (It is not clear what, if anything, was done to mitigate these risks.)

A new body called the Waywayseecappo Education Authority was created to oversee the school. Hugh McKay became its first chairman, eleven years after calling for the end of integrated education. In one of his first letters to the federal government in his new role, he wrote, "We want it clearly understood that the Waywayseecappo Education Authority is in control of the situation." And this is how he signed off: "Yours in Recognition of Total Control of Indian Education, Hugh McKay."[27]

Two decades after Michael Twovoice voted for integration, his friend Hugh McKay's vision of separation prevailed. For

Hugh, a separate school was not an end in itself—it was a way to give Waywayseecappo's children an opportunity to grow up with dignity, in a country that had long sought to impose a choice between being Canadian and being Indian. Michael had been more willing to celebrate Canada's abstract ideals, more generous in his assessment of Canada's ability to change. But it was Indigenous students who had been asked to make all the concessions, in exchange for a so-called "good education."

Hugh McKay and Michael Twovoice were contemporaries, born a year apart. They both attended residential schools. They both served in Canada's armed forces and heard the same grandiloquent speeches about Canada's contribution to the global fight for freedom. Each still professed loyalty to Canada—in 1967, they marched, side by side, as representatives of Waywayseecappo in a parade held in the nearby town of Russell marking Canada's centenary. But Hugh and Michael had different notions of what Canada really was, and they reached different conclusions about how Indians could flourish within it. Hugh held the more pessimistic view, and in his lifetime he seemed to have the more accurate understanding of Canada's enduring racism. Unlike Michael, Hugh never had a good word to say about assimilation. By 1982, most parents in Waywayseecappo shared his belief that a separate school for their children was a better way to secure equality. Even Michael had become disillusioned by how Native children were faring in Rossburn, and came to support the idea of a school on the reserve.

Within the span of a few decades, Waywayseecappo's students had gone from involuntary racial segregation (in Indian residential schools), to racial integration (in provincial public schools), to voluntary separation (in a school on the reserve). The hope was to be separate *and* equal.

It did not take long for a dispute to arise between Waywayseecappo and the federal government about funding for the new school. Waywayseecappo had achieved more local control but still relied on federal money, a paradox that continues to plague most reserves. "There is a need for more financial assistance," Waywayseecappo's Chief wrote to the Indian Affairs Department in 1983, "and we feel that there should be identical rules . . . for all—rules that take a realistic look at what Indian people are trying to accomplish."[28] Jim Manly, the member of Parliament for the area, contributed his vocal support of the reserve's educational efforts. "The entire system is stacked against Indian control of Indian education," he wrote in a letter to the minister of Indian affairs, Jim Munro. "Please take action to enable these people to control their own educational institution without being completely starved for funds."[29]

Munro's response was by turns frank and evasive. "You are no doubt aware that my Department, as is the case with all Government departments, is under extreme resource constraints," he wrote. (At the time, the federal government was running a deficit.) He also noted that it was "fair" and "appropriate" to compare the costs of the Waywayseecappo school with the costs of neighbouring provincial schools, but insisted that Waywayseecappo's school was not receiving less.[30] This claim—that students on reserves like Waywayseecappo were receiving fair and equal treatment—would become more and more difficult to sustain as time wore on.

AFTER FOUR YEARS of educating all its students in elementary and secondary grades, Waywayseecappo concluded in 1986 that it did not have enough students to justify its own high school program. The closest provincial high school was in Rossburn, just down the road, but community leaders and parents preferred to send students to a particularly well regarded public high school in Dauphin, a hundred kilometres away, even if it meant that students would have to live in residences away from home. That is how desperate the parents of Waywayseecappo were for quality, non-discriminatory education for their children, and how convinced they were that no such education was to be found in Rossburn.

Waywayseecappo asked the Department of Indian Affairs for reimbursement of the lodging costs in Dauphin, but they were turned down on the basis that there were perfectly good public schools nearby, notably in Rossburn.[31] Waywayseecappo's director of education replied to explain that Waywayseecappo had "deliberately" removed its students from Rossburn a few years before and that it would be "ridiculous" to send them back to a place where their students had underachieved for two decades.[32] Their experience in Rossburn had been too disappointing and the acrimony between the communities ran too deep.

Yet federal officials would not budge, which infuriated Robert Shingoose, Waywayseecappo's Chief. In a letter to the government, he asked, "Where in the hell is this so called Local Control?"[33] In the end, Waywayseecappo opted to bus its high school students to and from the town of Russell, twenty-five kilometres away.

In the fall of 1990, six students from the reserve decided to enrol in Rossburn's high school—partly because of mixed experiences in Russell, and partly because of the shorter commute. It had been eight years since Waywayseecappo removed all its students from Rossburn.

Almost as soon as the six students arrived, things went badly. They were called the same old names and reportedly told to "go to your own damn school."[34] Julia Mecas, aunt of one of the six students, promptly drove to Rossburn to share her concerns with the principal. During this meeting, a few students from Rossburn snuck out to the parking lot and propped nails behind one of Julia's tires. When she later backed out of her parking spot, her tire went flat with a hiss. She and the six students were furious, and the students promptly decided to collectively withdraw from the school. They had been attending classes for less than a week.

Outraged family members published a letter in the *Rossburn Review* in which they decried discrimination against Native students just like in "years gone by." They concluded:

> *It's sad to say that racism and prejudice is still so evident in Rossburn; to our way of thinking racism is a learned thing. It is passed from one generation to the next. It is instilled in children when they are very young. The intent here is not to stereotype all the white society as being racist against Natives. Those people who have been a party to racist teachings know who they are. Are these the same "Good Christians" who appear in church on Sunday mornings and teach each other to "Love thy Neighbour?"*[35]

One of the concerned parents, Norbert Tanner, told a *Brandon Sun* reporter that nothing seemed to have changed since Waywayseecappo pulled out all its students almost a decade before. "We had hoped there was a better understanding and a better acceptance. . . . You feel it when you go to town. Nobody talks to you. It is as if they are ashamed of standing beside a native. . . . They have got to accept us. We are here. We are here forever."[36]

Rossburn's student council hastily composed an apology letter and sent it to Waywayseecappo's band council. "We hope you do not condemn our whole staff and student body for the actions of a small minority," they wrote. "It is unfortunate that we did not have the opportunity to become friends." One of the letter's young authors told a reporter from the *Winnipeg Free Press*, "We were sort of disappointed they didn't give us a second chance." Presumably, this teenager knew little about all the prior chances that had come and gone.

Rossburn's principal blamed separation for the persistent racial discord. "The real problem," he said, "is that during the developmental period in their lives, the kids have no contact with each other. So they never have the opportunity to mix and learn and see other people in the educational system. As a result, our kids, the image they get of native people comes from the few they see who spend the afternoon in the hotel." The principal ignored the not-so-distant failure of integrated education less than a decade before. For so many, for so long, mere proximity between Waywayseecappo and Rossburn had not led to greater understanding. Rather, in the absence of respect, contact tended to provoke yet more discord.

One of the six students from Waywayseecappo, Carolyne Longclaws, spoke to the same *Winnipeg Free Press* reporter. "I just hope they can change," she said about people in Rossburn. "They probably won't change inside, but they might change outside. The way they really feel about us inside, I don't think that will change."[37]

PART II

"THE CUNNING OF THE WHITE MAN"

5

"LET US LIVE HERE LIKE BROTHERS"

W HAT I HAVE TO TALK ABOUT CONCERNS YOU, YOUR children, and their children, who are yet unborn," the treaty negotiator Alexander Morris said to hundreds of Cree and Ojibway Indians gathered inside a cavernous tent three hundred kilometres northwest of Winnipeg. "What I want is for you to take the Queen's hand, through mine, and shake hands with her forever."[1]

The year was 1874, and Canada was seven years old. Politicians in faraway Ottawa dreamed of a railway stretching from the east coast to the Pacific Ocean bearing goods and settlers. With this spine of iron, Canada could stand up to the United States. But a major obstacle was blocking this grand plan: Indigenous Peoples claimed to own the land over which these trains would run. So the government sent Morris, a lawyer and politician with a gift for metaphor, to make a series of deals.

Morris arrived with two armed battalions dressed in Her Majesty's signature red coats—113 men in all, along with a two-hundred-pound cannon. Indians made up the majority in the prairies, and Morris estimated that they could field as many as five thousand warriors for battle, if it came to that.[2] But he did not want a fight. The federal government had neither the will nor the means to conquer the West with soldiers and bullets.[3] Ottawa preferred to avoid the kind of bloody, drawn-out "Indian wars" that were then roiling the American Midwest. Prime Minister Alexander Mackenzie instructed Morris that "our true policy was to make friends of [the Indians] even at a considerable cost."[4]

At these treaty talks in the fall of 1874, Morris was charged with securing control of 120,000 square kilometres without firing a shot. Negotiations began on September 8, just as the landscape was darkening from green to brown following the first overnight frosts. The soldiers accompanying Morris had erected a marquee tent on the shore of Lac Qu'Appelle—the "Calling Lake," named for its echoes. At dawn, a layer of mist covered the water, but the white veil lifted as the sun climbed. Morris dispatched a bugler to announce the start of the first meeting. The blasts from the brass horn rolled across the water.

Like other statesmen of his day, Alexander Morris was an unabashed imperialist. He hoped "Christianity and civilization" would replace "heathenism and paganism among the Indian tribes."[5] Yet he did recognize what he called the "natural title of the Indians to the lands," as had Canada's first prime minister, John A. Macdonald, who characterized Indians as "the original owners of the soil."[6] Morris's job was to settle their claims.

The year before, in 1873, Morris had received a letter from a group of Chiefs in the prairies who had spotted white surveyors marking off land. The Chiefs wished to "inform your Honor that we have never been a party to any Treaty . . . made to extinguish our title to Land which we claim as ours . . . and therefore can not understand why this land should be surveyed." One of the Chiefs was identified as Wahwashecaboo, an early spelling of Waywayseecappo.[7]

Alexander Morris (Library and Archives Canada, Topley Studio fonds/a025468)

Cree and Ojibway negotiators knew their long-standing ties to the land and ongoing presence gave them some leverage, but they also understood that their bargaining position had been deteriorating. Recent smallpox epidemics in the prairies had subjected each

Native life to a coin toss: one in two died.[8] And the buffalo that had provided them with food, clothing, and shelter were depleted, owing in part to a concerted American campaign to slaughter the herds. ("Every buffalo dead is an Indian gone," a U.S. Army colonel once boasted.)[9] Indians on the prairies were in acute need of new livelihoods.

They also sensed that trickles of white settlers augured a flood. As one Cree leader put it, Indians could not "stop the power of the white man from spreading over the land like the grasshoppers that cloud the sky and then fall to consume every blade of grass and every leaf on the trees in their path."[10]

Another threat lay to the south: American traders who crossed the border were showing no qualms about killing Indians who got in their way. Morris referred to these incidents as the "constant eruptions of American desperadoes."[11] During one incursion of heavily armed traders across the Canadian border in the summer of 1873, more than twenty Indians were killed in what came to be known as the Cypress Hills Massacre.[12] And the cavalry of the United States Army was feared even more—Indians referred to them as the "long knives."[13] For the Cree and Ojibway Indians who gathered at Lac Qu'Appelle, a deal with the Queen's redcoats seemed like a safer bet than the alternatives.

Morris, a seasoned negotiator, knew which strings to pluck. "We are here to talk with you about the land," he said to those gathered in the marquee tent. "The Queen knows that you are poor. . . . She knows that the winters are cold, and your children are often hungry. She has always cared for her red children as much as for her white. Out of her generous heart and liberal hand she wants to do something for you, so that when the buffalo get scarcer, and they are scarce enough now, you may be able to do something for yourselves."[14]

In response, two Cree Chiefs, Kakushiway and Kawacatoose, sought to unnerve Morris. They arranged for bags full of soil to be carried into the tent and laid at Morris's feet. Kawacatoose asked Morris how much money he had brought, because for each sack of dirt Morris would need a full sack of money. Then Kawacatoose said, "This country is not for sale."[15]

One of the main Ojibway spokespeople was Otakaonan (translated to English as "The Gambler"). He belonged to the band led by Chief Waywayseecappo, who had not himself travelled to Lac Qu'Appelle for reasons lost to history.

Otakaonan, "The Gambler" (Provincial Archives of Saskatchewan, R-11962, photo by Edgar C. Rossie)

Speaking through a translator, Otakaonan opened by recalling how his people had welcomed European settlers to the plains. "When the white skin comes here from far away I love him all the same," he said to Morris.[16] Yet Otakaonan objected to the way the government had recognized land rights claimed by the Hudson's Bay Company, a British trading group that had been operating in the area. Four years before, in 1870, the federal government had paid £300,000 to the company to purchase these supposed land rights.[17] Otakaonan did not think the Hudson's Bay Company should have been paid for territory it did not rightfully own.

"When one Indian takes anything from another we call it stealing," Otakaonan said.

"What did the Company steal from you?" Morris asked.

"The earth, trees, grass, stones, all that which I see with my eyes."

Morris was unmoved. "Who made the earth, the grass, the stone and the wood?" he asked. "The Great Spirit. He made them for all his children to use, and it is not stealing to use the gift of the Great Spirit." Morris pointed out that the Ojibway had themselves arrived on the prairies only a few generations before, after migrating west from the Great Lakes region in the eighteenth century. (Morris left unspoken the fact that aggressive Euro-Canadian settlement was a cause of the Ojibway migration.) "We won't say [the Ojibway] stole the land and the stones and the trees," Morris continued. "No . . . the land is wide . . . it is big enough for us both, let us live here like brothers."[18]

This sentiment met with approval from an Indian named Pahtahkaywenin, who agreed on the need for cooperation: "God gives us land in different places and when we meet together as friends, we ask from each other and do not quarrel as we do so."[19] To reach a deal, Morris offered one-time cash gifts, annual payments, and hunting rights on land that remained unsettled. He promised 640 acres for every family of five on "reserves," land that would be protected from encroachment by settlers. The government would also provide agricultural assistance so that, in time, farms on reserves would provide the livelihood that buffalo no longer could. And the government pledged to build schools on the reserves and send teachers, so that Indians might "learn the cunning of the white man."[20]

"We won't deceive you with smooth words," Morris insisted. "We have no object but your good at heart."

"Is it true you are bringing the Queen's kindness?" a Chief asked.

"Yes, to those who are here and those who are absent," Morris replied.

"Is it true that my child will not be troubled for what you are bringing him?"

"The Queen's power will be around him."[21]

AFTER SIX DAYS of negotiations, a document titled "Treaty No. 4" was finalized on September 17, 1874. Morris had likely arrived at Lac Qu'Appelle with a pre-drafted template that left only a few blank spaces for dates, names, territorial limits, and payment amounts.[22] The final text of Treaty 4 was virtually indistinguishable from another treaty Morris had negotiated the year before ("Treaty No. 3"), which applied to another massive expanse of territory in Ontario and Manitoba. Morris would ultimately negotiate four similar treaties dealing with land between the Great Lakes and the Rocky Mountains.

It is highly doubtful that government and Indian negotiators shared the same understanding of what Treaty 4 meant.

The text was written in English, which the Indian negotiators could not read. When Morris instructed a translator to read the document out loud before the parties formally signed, a white observer found it "immensely amusing" to watch the translator's "look of dismay and consternation" as he attempted to hold the "bulky-looking document" and convert the English into Cree and Ojibway.[23]

According to oral history, the Chiefs believed that the treaty represented a partnership that bonded Indians and settlers into one family, with a commitment to share the land and bring mutual aid.[24] The government would take a more narrow view, relying heavily on the legalese affirming, among other things, that with their signatures the Chiefs agreed to "cede, release, surrender and yield up . . . all their rights, titles and privileges whatsoever, to the lands."[25] (This provision became known as the "surrender clause.") Morris would later describe the terms of the treaty as "fair and just."[26] One hundred years later, a group of Indigenous leaders in Manitoba would describe Treaty 4, and other treaties like it, as "one of the outstanding swindles of all time."[27]

After a signing ceremony,[28] Morris travelled two hundred kilometres east to Fort Ellice, where he was to meet with more Indian leaders who had not been present at the Lac Qu'Appelle negotiations. Among them was Chief Waywayseecappo, who was then around fifty years old.[29]

At least as far back as 1859, Waywayseecappo had been trading furs at the Hudson's Bay Company outpost in Fort Ellice, in exchange for cloth, flints, knives, tobacco, and ammunition.[30] A company trader described Waywayseecappo as "a giant in size and ancient in days and devilment."[31] Morris wanted Waywayseecappo to sign Treaty 4 on behalf of the fifty families in his band, which Otakaonan had not had the authority to do at Lac Qu'Appelle.

"What we offer will be for your good," said Morris. "I think you are not wiser than your brothers."[32]

A witness to the meeting sketched Waywayseecappo's profile with a lump of charcoal, leaving his only surviving likeness.

Chief Waywayseecappo
(Library and Archives Canada, Sydney Prior Hall fonds/e010999415)

Chief Waywayseecappo, who could not read or write English, signed the treaty with an "X." His name, transcribed as "Way-wa-se-ca-pow," was translated as "the Man proud of standing upright."[33]

It is difficult to say what Chief Waywayseecappo thought about the treaty, but shortly after signing it he demonstrated his good faith. Reports reached him that a Métis man named McIver had killed a white settler near Fort Ellice. After hearing this, Waywayseecappo picked four of his ablest men to join him in a hunt for the killer. They successfully captured McIver and brought him to the nearest detachment of Mounted Police. (McIver was convicted of murder the following year.) Canada's governor general, Lord Dufferin, was so impressed when he heard what Waywayseecappo had done that he sent a message to the Chief expressing "great appreciation of his conduct, and that of his 'braves,' in having given so practical a proof of their desire to assist the government in carrying out the laws of the country."[34] This would not be the last time Chief Waywayseecappo showed his loyalty to Canada.

It was not long, however, before the federal government turned its laws against Indians. In 1876, two years after the signing of Treaty 4, Parliament passed the first incarnation of the Indian Act, a law that defined who would be counted as Indian and detailed how they would be controlled. First Nations were to be treated not as equal partners but as wayward children. As the minister of Indian affairs said, "Our Indian legislation generally rests on the principle, that the aborigines are to be kept in a condition of tutelage and treated as wards or children of the State"—until, that is, the government could successfully lift Indians into a state of "higher civilization."[35] The long-term goal of the Indian Act was to assimilate Native peoples into the Euro-Canadian mainstream, building on a prior law that was more revealingly called the Gradual Civilization Act.

Parliament assumed it had the power to pass a law like the Indian Act because Canada's 1867 Constitution had granted the federal government exclusive control over "Indians and lands reserved for the Indians." The Fathers of Confederation did so, of course, without consulting any actual Indians. The "overall effect" of the Indian Act, as the Royal Commission on Aboriginal Peoples would later note, "was ultimately to subject reserves to the almost unfettered rule of federal bureaucrats."[36]

THE WAYWAYSEECAPPO RESERVE and the town of Rossburn were created within two years of each other, and not by coincidence.

After signing Treaty 4, Chief Waywayseecappo requested reserve land in an area where his band had planted its summer gardens since the early 1800s, inside a far larger Traditional Territory where they had lived, hunted, and traded for the previous century.[37] The reserve was formally established in 1877, and some two hundred people moved there. Among them were families named Longclaws, Keewaytincappo, and Jandrew—names that later featured in some of the thickest branches of Maureen Twovoice's family tree. For a time, the government referred to the community as Lizard Point, a name inspired by the dark green salamanders that were ubiquitous in the area after extended periods of rain. An early map of the reserve—formally known as Indian Reserve #62—shows that it is bordered on the east by the Birdtail River.[38]

Treaty 4 simultaneously authorized the creation of reserves and declared "that it is the desire of Her Majesty to open up [land] for settlement, immigration, trade and such other purposes." And so it was that a mere two years after the Waywayseecappo reserve was established, a wave of settlers made their way to the valley of the Birdtail, just as Her Majesty Queen Victoria had supposedly desired. Among them was Richard Rose Ross, whose family had come to Manitoba by way of Scotland, Manhattan, and Ontario.

In 1879, Ross set off from Winnipeg along with a small group of men wheeling a half-dozen carts. They dreamed of a fertile new home with enough hills to protect crops from flash floods. They headed north as far as the town of Portage, then continued west through sleet and storm and a "sea of mud."[39] "Foremost in their minds," according to a chronicle of the trip, "was the thought of owning land which extended for hundreds of miles, large tracts inhabited only by Indians."[40] Thanks to Alexander Morris, these Indians were no longer considered much of an obstacle.

After walking 221 kilometres from Portage, Ross and his companions found what they were looking for. Near the banks of a gurgling river, they planted their first potatoes. They claimed the land as squatters.[41] Later, each man applied under Manitoban law for a homestead of 160 acres. In exchange, they paid a modest fee of ten dollars (the equivalent of about $325 today) and promised to build a house and cultivate twenty acres of land within three years. It was not long until "old Mr. Ross," as he was affectionately known, helped build a school, store, and post office.

Early relations between the new town and the reserve appear to have been largely friendly. Indians from Waywayseecappo visited Rossburn to trade moccasins, baskets, and rugs. They also sold tanned moosehides, dried elk meat, and fish from the largest lake on the reserve. Some settlers in Rossburn were given Ojibway names: one elderly man was called Wapawayap—"white eyebrow." A few of Ross's sons even learned to speak Ojibway. A Rossburn resident later remembered "what fine men some of the braves were when the settlers first came in, big strapping healthy fellows—ideal pictures of Indians."[42] According to an 1882 report by a federal official, "These Indians are all very well disposed towards the settlers, and whenever trouble has arisen it has, on all occasions which I have investigated, been directly attributable to the settlers, who dislike to see the Indians in possession of desirable locations."[43]

Chief Waywayseecappo himself developed friendships in town. Toward the end of his life, though the old Chief had gone blind, he continued to travel by foot with the assistance of his wife, who held out a stick to guide him. One day, Waywayseecappo walked with his wife all the way to Rossburn, grasping the guiding stick with one hand and holding a gun with the other. He was looking for one settler in particular. When he found him, Waywayseecappo greeted his white friend warmly and handed him the gun, as a gift.[44]

It is possible to imagine how the relationship between Waywayseecappo and Rossburn might have deepened over time, built on respect, trade, and friendship. But that is not how things turned out—not at this time, not in Canada.

The overwhelming majority of people living in Waywayseecappo continued to regularly travel far beyond the borders of the reserve. In December 1881, when a federal agent recorded census data, 190 of 220 band members were off reserve, hunting in the Riding Mountain area to the northeast.[45] This was part of the long-standing seasonal rhythm of the community: they hunted goose and duck in the spring, deer in the summer, and elk, moose, and prairie chicken in the fall.[46] Yet big game was growing scarcer, and the arrival of ever more settlers was restricting traditional hunting. Band members had established a wide network of trails to hunt in land around the reserve, but with the arrival of more settlers around Rossburn, the reserve's border was slowly becoming more meaningful. "As the valley became more thickly populated," one settler recalled, "the Indians frequented the valley less and less. . . . Their old trails finally disappeared as fields were plowed and fences erected [by settlers]."[47]

One particular incident seems to capture a shift in the relationship between the two communities. In 1884, two settlers built a stone grist mill with a water wheel along the Birdtail River. The purpose of the mill was to produce flour, but one of its effects was to block fish from making their way up the river to the reserve. That year, Waywayseecappo's residents "complained of starvation" to a federal official, in part because of the effect of the mill on their access to fish.[48] At the time, the federal Indian agent responsible for the area was Lawrence Herchmer, who showed little sympathy. Rather, Herchmer believed hunger would motivate more industrious farming, which he saw as a necessary step in the civilizing of Indians. "A little starvation will do them good," he wrote.[49]

Just as families in Waywayseecappo struggled with an abrupt and painful transition from traditional livelihoods, so did many other communities that had been abruptly transplanted to reserves. To make matters worse, aberrant weather caused widespread crop failures in 1883 and 1884. Across the prairies, the overwhelming majority of Indians were depending on government food rations of bacon and flour to survive.[50] It was called "the Time of the Great Hunger."[51]

In the summer of 1884, within a decade of Alexander Morris's grand pronouncement during treaty negotiations, a group of two thousand Cree Indians assembled near Duck Lake (in present-day Saskatchewan). They discussed fears of being "cheated" by a government that had made "sweet promises" in order to "get their country from them." They claimed that the government had not been living up to its treaty commitments, including the promises of agricultural support and supplies, and said that Indians had been "reduced to absolute and complete dependence upon what relief is extended to them." They told a federal official that "it is almost too hard for them to bear the treatment received at the hands of the government," yet they were "glad the young men have not resorted to violent measures."[52]

The peace did not last another year.

6

"IRON HEART"

ONE OF THE 113 SOLDIERS WHO ACCOMPANIED Alexander Morris to the Treaty 4 negotiations in 1874 was a young man named Hayter Reed, who had a wispy moustache and mutton chops venturing well below his jawline. Hayter marched forty-five kilometres a day, for a total of almost five hundred kilometres, to get from his military base at Fort Garry (near present-day Winnipeg) to Lac Qu'Appelle. There, he "came in close touch with the Redman," as he later put it.[1] Hayter was struck by the "picturesqueness" of the Indians, with their painted faces, multicoloured beads, and ceremonial feathers.[2] This was the beginning of Hayter's lifelong fascination with Indians, whom he described as a "human creature that sickens beneath our civilization, and dies midst our prosperity."[3]

Born in 1849 and raised in Toronto, Hayter turned eighteen the same year that Confederation made Canada a country. By then, Hayter was already barking orders as a drill instructor for the Kingston Rifle Battalion. He later said that marching with his regiment to the tune of a brass band was the highlight of his young life.[4] At the age of twenty-two, he jumped at a chance to join a battalion deploying to the North-West, which at that time referred to all of Canada west of Ontario and east of British Columbia. In time, this is where Hayter would attain fame, and infamy.

Hayter Reed (McCord Museum of Canadian History, portrait 53878, 1880, Notman & Sandham)

But first, young Hayter had to actually get to the North-West, which was no small undertaking in the days before a national railroad. Hayter's battalion of four hundred men headed westward in the final months of 1871, just as winter's white blanket was snuffing out the last embers of fall. Their final destination, Fort Garry, was two thousand kilometres away, almost exactly midway between the Atlantic and Pacific oceans. A steamship carried them as far as the western shore of Lake Superior, where the harder work began. The troops were divided into groups of two dozen and assigned to small boats they would have to row through hundreds of kilometres of rivers, streams, and lakes. As they traversed this "immense volume of water," Hayter later wrote, they encountered "every kind of waterfall, from chutes to cataracts."

Hayter had headed west looking for adventure, and it didn't take long for him to find something to boast about. "To shoot the many Falls or the numerous Rapids, to lift and haul the boats from the whirling rush of water and launch them by the edge of a whirlpool—all had more or less a spice of danger."[5]

The battalion avoided the most perilous stretches of water by making overland portages as long as six kilometres, over which the men had to haul their boats along roughly cut trails featuring occasional inclines of sixty degrees. Each man carried a backpack with fifty kilograms of equipment and rations. Hayter came to resent the "heavy military tents," "cumbersome iron camp kettles," and "iron shovels without number" that had been assigned by clueless officers at faraway headquarters.

Travel by boat was no less strenuous. Sometimes a waterway would start to freeze as the men rowed and they would use their oars to stab at the ice and cut a way forward. As the weeks wore on, Hayter wrote, "the blades were entirely worn off the oars so that we were towards the end of the journey driven in some instances to the use of shovels for paddling—the only use we ever found for these shovels by the way."

Finally, after twenty-six days of rowing and portaging, the men reached what is now the town of Kenora, near Ontario's border with Manitoba, where they left their boats behind. The last stretch to Fort Garry was a 175-kilometre march "through deep and fine dry snow, making it very much like heavy loose sand to walk in," Hayter recalled. With thermometers reading minus fifteen degrees Celsius, the men reached the fort "in the pink of health, though rugged, ragged and torn." Of all those who had undertaken the journey, "there was not one who had a pair of trowsers [sic] reaching below the knee—the bottoms having been torn and cut off."

With Fort Garry as its base of operations, Hayter's battalion fended off cross-border raids by armed groups from the United States that had "the idea they could snatch Canada . . . away from the British Empire," Hayter wrote.[6] (Strange as it sounds today, the threat arose from Irish revolutionaries called Fenians, whose roundabout plan to support Irish secession from the United Kingdom involved attacks in North America).[7]

During his military service, Hayter also found time to pursue legal studies, an early sign of his uncommon drive and ambition. Within a year of his arrival in Manitoba, he was called to the bar. He became only the sixteenth person in the province to be recognized as a lawyer there. He swore two oaths: an oath of allegiance and an oath of attorney. First, to "Her Majesty Queen Victoria," he pledged to "defend Her to the utmost of my power against all traitorous conspiracies." Second, he swore to act "honestly" as a lawyer, "according to my best knowledge and ability. So help me God."[8] In the years to come, he proved more adept at punishing perceived traitors than acting honestly.

Hayter's military unit was disbanded in 1880, and he left the military as a major. He then worked briefly as a land guide for settlers, directing them to their new homes in the North-West.[9] Hayter was the first point of contact for every prospective settler who passed through Winnipeg. It is entirely possible that he sang the praises of a promising settlement along the Birdtail River, which had a view of the most beautiful valley in Manitoba. Yet his job as a land guide was only part-time, and he kept looking for work that was more suited to his talents.

Then, in 1881, Hayter embarked on a path that would transform his life for the better—and the lives of countless others for the worse—when he was appointed Indian agent with the federal Department of Indian Affairs.[10] His job was to enforce federal law and policy regarding the Native population in the Battleford region of Saskatchewan, a role that infused Hayter with considerable power over the daily lives of more than a thousand Indians.[11] Hayter's predecessor in the Battleford region had left the job because he feared the Indians he sought to govern, but Hayter was undaunted. He embraced "the labourious and often dangerous work of transforming Bands of Savages into peaceable agricultural labourers," as he put it.[12] To civilize, he was willing to die, and even, it later became clear, to kill.

Hayter described the life of a federal Indian agent as "a state of practical exile," in which the agent is "debarred from all the pleasures of the world, from society, from civilization."[13] Hayter oversaw a sprawling area of more than twenty-two thousand square kilometres, which he traversed on horseback and by dogsled, in the "heat of summer and extreme cold of winter," sometimes travelling eighty or even a hundred kilometres a day.[14] During his arduous travels, he would be overcome by "strange weird feelings" when he looked at "the unending vision of sky and prairie," he wrote. "I very doubt if it be possible to place before your mental vision anything like a true picture of the loneliness of endless space."

As Hayter travelled the plains, he spent many nights in Indian encampments, where he was welcomed as a guest. He watched as men danced naked "without surprise or comment," though women appeared to be "more decently clothed." "Many and many a time," he wrote, he was kept up all night "by the revels of the young Indians, in which the tom tom or Indian drum was incessantly beaten."[15] Hayter's notes of such encounters evince only a limited understanding of what was happening around him and the cultural significance it might have held.

Hayter claimed to have witnessed Indian bands preparing to launch attacks on one another. "I saw them perform their dances and sing their war songs and go through the different rites and ceremonies preparatory to such expeditions," he wrote, "resulting in either the taking of scalps, or stealing of horses or both." He rode along on a few such "marauding undertakings," to watch as much as possible before slipping away in advance of any fighting. He said he was never directly involved in any of these skirmishes, though "in one or two instances I was closer to them than I fancied, as upon one occasion a young brave rode up to me where I was encamped on the plains, and held up a scalp from which the blood was still running, and offered it to me as a present." Hayter accepted the gift and went on to keep the scalp for decades as a memento. (He eventually donated it to McGill University, along with his vast collection of "Indian relics," though the item has since gone missing.)[16]

Such intimate experiences with Indians—and, no doubt, Hayter's colourful recounting of them—earned him a reputation within the government as an expert. His boss, Edgar Dewdney, commended him for "having a knowledge of the Indian character possessed by few in the country."[17] Indeed, during his time on the plains, Hayter claimed to have identified the "great difference between the Indian and the Civilized people." It was not their degree of intelligence or their brand of religion, he insisted.

Rather, it was morality: Indians had none. As far as Hayter could tell, the concepts of right and wrong had no meaning for an Indian, who "remained a savage simply from a lack of a code of morals." Instead, "all was Right that he wished to do, all was wrong that opposed him."[18]

Hayter concluded that allowing "an ignorant savage to determine his own course for himself" was as foolish as allowing children to raise themselves.[19] Rather, "what the Indian requires to have brought to bear upon him are the influences of Christian civilization." Amazingly, Hayter acknowledged that if the "advantages of civilization" were only offered rather than imposed, "the Indian may not covet them for himself, or for his children." That is why consulting Indians was pointless.

The Royal Commission on Aboriginal Peoples would later describe some Indian agents as "petty despots who seemed to enjoy wielding enormous power over the remnants of once powerful Aboriginal nations."[20] Hayter Reed, it seems, was of this type. The sudden disappearance of the buffalo and the abrupt transition to life on reserves had left thousands of Cree, Ojibway, Lakota, Assiniboine, and Blackfoot Indians on the prairies reliant on government food rations. Within the area he purported to administer and control, Hayter established a simple rule: "If a man would not work, he would not eat."[21] Rations would be denied to the idle. This policy, which was soon emulated by other Indian agents, won praise from the Department of Indian Affairs.

Of course, Indian agents were the ones who dictated what counted as real work. Typically, this meant farming, which the government saw as the Indians' surest path to civilization. Hayter insisted that his firm approach was best in the long run, both for Canada and for Indians themselves, and he resented critics who portrayed Indian agents as dishonest tyrants. Hayter said he was willing to endure a stream of complaints from Indians, though from time to time he felt the need to retreat from his office "in order to obviate the constant nagging, noise and stench."[22] He once warned a superior who was planning a visit to the area that he would probably "be greeted on setting foot in this Agency, with sorrowful tales of my hardheartedness."[23]

Hayter proved so inflexibly harsh that he earned the nickname "Iron Heart" from Indians under his supervision.[24] As for Hayter, he described some of his charges as "the scum of the Plains."[25] Nevertheless, Hayter's superiors viewed him as a model Indian agent. He was praised for being "very faithful" and "an indefatigable worker."[26] In 1882, the highest-ranking Indian Affairs official in the prairies reported to the prime minister that Hayter had "been of good service, his legal training being of much assistance."[27] Hayter would soon receive a succession of rapid promotions, giving him ever more power over yet more people.

Those who witnessed Hayter's work on the ground were more skeptical. A colleague described him as "entirely lacking in sympathetic understanding of the Indians" and attributed "much of the unrest existing amongst the different bands" to Hayter's "management or mismanagement."[28] A settler in Battleford accused Hayter of "immoral behaviour" with two Indian women and of fathering an illegitimate child, calling Hayter "a libertine" with "no respect for the virtue of women."[29] Hayter denied everything and escaped the episode without official censure.

Hayter distinguished himself by helping create the first government-sponsored residential schools, which he embraced as a "solution of the Indian problem."[30] He later bragged that "the Indian Industrial Schools, from Winnipeg to the Pacific, were all established by me."[31] He fiercely advocated for the suppression of Indigenous languages at the schools. He wrote: "Use of the native tongue in the schools, for any purpose whatsoever, is one which I feel convinced should on no accounts be allowed."[32] Tellingly, he refers to the students at residential schools as "inmates."[33] After opening one school in Saskatchewan, in 1882, Hayter insisted on personally giving an Indian boy his first bath, which Hayter claimed to have caused "great amusement." Who exactly was so greatly amused he does not specify, though perhaps no one more than Hayter.

Hayter also helped establish the Qu'Appelle Indian Industrial School in Saskatchewan, which Michael Twovoice later attended. The school's principal, Father Hugonard, once wrote to Hayter to thank him for helping to get police to pick up "our fugitives"— that is, students who had fled the school.[34] Hayter also personally reviewed and modified the architectural drawings for the building that would become the Brandon Indian Residential School, where Linda Jandrew was later sent.

In 1883, Hayter faced his greatest challenge yet. Thousands of Cree and Assiniboine had gathered in Treaty 4 territory, in the Cypress Hills near the U.S. border. (Hayter estimated their number at eight thousand, though his boss put the number closer to three thousand—an indication of Hayter's unreliability as a narrator.)[35] The encampment was led by two Cree Chiefs, Payipwat (Piapot) and Mistahimaskwa (Big Bear), both fierce skeptics of the treaties negotiated by Alexander Morris. Piapot and Big Bear were particularly unhappy with how the scattered reserves stranded their people on small pockets of undesirable land they called *iskonikan*, "leftovers."[36] The Chiefs wanted to consolidate reserve land into a larger, contiguous territory with more autonomy.[37]

Of course, spreading out bands to weaken their collective power was a key aspect of government policy. "The Canadian system of band reserves has a tendency to diminish the offensive strength of the Indian tribes,"[38] Morris had noted. Likewise, Hayter praised the government for having the "wisdom" to avoid establishing "large Reservations," so giving Indians "less opportunity for hatching mischief."[39] He had previously reported that "Big Bear and his followers were loath to settle on a Reserve," and he anticipated that they would gather to "test their powers with the authorities."[40] For the Canadian government, this would not do. Hayter was dispatched to defuse the situation and get the Indians back on their assigned reserves.

Hayter's first move was to cut off the provision of government rations—he would starve Big Bear, Piapot, and their followers into submission. After three months of watching their children wither to skin and bone, the Cree dropped their demands and agreed to return to their reserves without violence. Hayter, never one to overlook his own ingenuity and daring, attributed his success to months of "hard work," with "not a little risk of life."[41] To get the Indians moving, Hayter's men "pulled tents down."[42] Hayter described the scene as thousands decamped and headed northward:

> *The wild cavalcade stretching out for a mile or so in length and some hundreds of yards in width that wended away with its paint and war-plumes fluttering, trophies and savage embroidery. . . . Old squaws mounted on shaggy meagre looking ponies with perhaps one or two painted children seated behind them clinging to their tattered blankets. Young squaws with faces of various colors, red, green, white and yellow with necklaces of brass or other beads, gaudy colored earrings of shells or metal. . . . Tall, lank, young men on their best ponies with a defiant air leading the way. . . . Some carrying long lances, some with guns and rifles, most with bows and arrows at their backs, all headed by Chiefs*

Piapot and Big Bear . . . with their war bonnets and bearing their shields which fluttered with eagle feathers. This will never be seen again.[43]

Perhaps what comes out most clearly in this description, despite Hayter's florid efforts to characterize it otherwise, is the dignity displayed in the darkest of times by Piapot, Big Bear, and those who accompanied them.

The following spring, in April 1884, Hayter wrote a memo warning of possible new attempts by Indians to "congregate in large numbers." To "prevent these gatherings," Hayter advised, "if the slightest pretext offers, to arrest some of the ringleaders before the Indians have assembled—the law might have to be strained a little to meet a particular case, but in the interests of the country at large as well as the Indians themselves such a course would I think be advisable."[44] This was an early sign of government tactics still to come.

As INDIAN RESENTMENT of the federal government festered on the prairies, about fifteen hundred Métis living along the Saskatchewan River were coming to see that they too were under threat. The Métis were the descendants of Euro-Canadians and Indians who had intermarried. Since the end of the eighteenth century, they had forged a distinct identity, with their own customs and laws. Many referred to them as "half-breeds." One Protestant missionary, similarly keen on descriptions based on fractions, characterized the Métis as "one-and-a-half men"—that is, "half Indian, half white and half devil."[45] The prime minister, John A. Macdonald, referred to them simply as "those wild people."[46] The federal government was controlled at the time by Anglo-Saxon Protestants, and the Saskatchewan River Métis were largely French-speaking and Catholic. This meant they had "three strikes" against them, as Jean Teillet notes in her history of the Métis Nation. They were "too Indian, too Catholic and too French."[47]

By the spring of 1884, the Métis living along the Saskatchewan River felt squeezed, and the pressure kept mounting. Euro-Canadian settlers were coming from Ontario and claiming land that the Métis had occupied for at least a generation. Métis custom was to divide land abutting the river into "rangs"—long, skinny rectangles that ran along the water for eight hundred feet and stretched away from the river for two miles. This arrangement gave more families direct access to the water, which they relied on for irrigation as well as transportation. But the federal government would only recognize settlement on square plots and was quick to credit claims made by Euro-Canadian newcomers.

Back in 1874, Alexander Morris had excluded Métis from formal Treaty 4 negotiations but insisted at the time that the Queen would "deal generously and justly with them" in due course.[48] Instead, their claims continued to be ignored. Starting in 1878, the Métis community started sending petitions to Ottawa in an effort to have their land rights recognized. In 1882, for example, they wrote to Prime Minister Macdonald: "We appeal to your sense of justice . . . and beg you to reassure us speedily, by directing that we shall not be disturbed on our lands" occupied in "good faith."[49] This petition, like dozens of others, received no response.

The Métis eventually turned to the one person they thought might be able to get the federal government's attention, a man many Métis considered their "national apostle": Louis Riel.[50]

Louis Riel (Provincial Archives of Manitoba, N-5733)

In 1869–70, Louis Riel had led a Métis resistance against a federal plan to annex what is now Manitoba without any regard for the rights and customs of eight thousand Métis who constituted the majority of the people living there. Prime Minister Macdonald believed the "impulsive half-breeds . . . must be kept down by a strong hand until they are swamped by the influx of settlers."[51] Yet Riel, then aged twenty-six, emerged as the leader of his people and the Métis took up arms to seize control of the territory. They sought a negotiated settlement with the federal government, which ultimately made some grudging concessions.[52] Yet despite assurances of amnesty for those who had participated in the Métis resistance, a warrant was issued for Riel's arrest. Even as an outlaw, Riel managed to be elected to Parliament twice, in 1873 and 1874, though he was never allowed to take his seat in Ottawa. He eventually accepted an amnesty deal in 1875, in exchange for five years of exile. He settled down across the U.S. border in Montana, where he worked as a teacher and lived with his wife and two children. This is where, in the spring of 1884, a Métis delegation seeking his help found him. Riel agreed to come and serve his people as best he could.

In the months after his return from Montana, Riel pursued a peaceful strategy, putting his faith in persuasion and yet more petitions. He sought a more representative local government and recognition of valid land claims, including those of recent settlers. Riel also sought to make common cause with Indians. "When I came to the North West in July [1884]," Riel would later say, "I found the Indians suffering."[53] Government agents noted with alarm that Riel spent two days in August 1884 in talks with the Cree Chief Big Bear, who had disbanded the mass gathering at the Cypress Hills only a year before.[54] Riel became increasingly convinced that Indians, like the Métis, were being denied their true rights to land, and references to Indian interests made their way into his petitions. By February 1885, Hayter Reed warned the prime minister that Indians "were beginning to look up to [Riel] as the one who will be the means of curing all their ills and of obtaining all their demands."[55]

Still, Ottawa continued to ignore Riel and the Métis petitions. On March 3, 1885, Riel wrote in his diary, "O my Métis people! You complain that your lands have been stolen. Why, how can it be that you have not yet recovered them? You hold all the cards, you are strong enough."[56] The following week, Riel and a council of Métis leaders assembled near the town of Prince Albert to draft a Revolutionary Bill of Rights. Most of the demands related directly to the Métis, but the seventh item urged that "better provision be made for the Indians."[57] Riel ensured that a copy of this latest petition reached the local member of Parliament, Lawrence Clarke, with an urgent request to get it to the prime minister. This was the eighty-fourth petition the Métis had sent to Ottawa since 1878. It would be Riel's last.

While the Métis waited for a response, Major Lief Crozier of the North-West Mounted Police telegrammed his superiors with an assessment of a growing threat: "Halfbreed rebellion likely to break out any moment. If Halfbreeds rise Indians will join them."[58]

On March 18, the Métis received an unofficial message from Ottawa via Clarke, who said the latest petition would be "answered by powder and bullet."[59] Clarke also claimed that a detachment of police was on its way to arrest Riel. As it happens, this was not true, but the lie escalated an already tense situation.[60] The next day, Riel and a few hundred of his followers, mostly Métis and some Cree, declared a provisional government and overran the town of Batoche.

As Riel and his men seized control of the Saint-Antoine de Padoue Catholic Church, the resident priest said, "I protest your touching the church." Even in this fateful hour, Riel did not miss a chance to indulge his love of puns. "Look at him," Riel said, pointing with amusement at the priest. "He is a protestant!" Then Riel, a Catholic, added, "We are protesting against the Canadian Government, he is protesting against us. We are two protestants in our own ways."[61]

Riel was by now convinced that the federal government had "usurped the title of the Aboriginal Halfbreeds to the soil" and that "we are justified before God and men to arm ourselves, to try to defend our existence rather [than] to see it crushed."[62] Riel expected to rally support among Indians disgruntled with their treatment in the aftermath of the treaties. "I hear the voice of the Indian," he wrote. "He comes to join me. . . . He is in the mood for war."[63] Riel's greatest hope—that an alliance between the Métis and the Plains Indians would emerge—was the government's greatest fear.

On March 26, Major Crozier led ninety-nine men outfitted in red coats, a mix of mounted police and volunteer militia, to confront Riel. The two forces faced off near the town of Duck Lake, some five hundred kilometres northwest of Waywayseecappo and Rossburn.

Major Crozier and a translator met two Métis at the midpoint between the front lines. But the talks went badly and a scuffle broke out, culminating in one of the Métis negotiators being shot in the head. Crozier ran back toward his men, yelling, "Fire away, boys!" As the first bullets started to whistle and whine, Riel surveyed the scene from a hollow to the north. He sat atop his horse to get a better view, even though this left him exposed within gunshot range. He was armed with only a crucifix.

Riel's men had Crozier outflanked. They had also secured higher ground and taken positions among willow trees and dense brush. Sharpshooters flung blankets on the snow, lay down on their stomachs and started firing their Winchester rifles at the redcoats down below. Another group of Métis found cover in a nearby log cabin and shot from the windows.

Crozier's men, by contrast, were badly exposed. The luckier ones crouched behind their sleighs that were loaded with supplies, and some even resorted to placing their cooking stoves on top to secure a few extra inches of protection. Many had no cover at all and made easy targets as they lumbered through a metre of snow crusted with ice. Crozier did have command of a 224-pound brass cannon, which was their only chance against the Métis snipers in the log cabin. The first four cannon shots sailed beyond their mark, but got closer each time. Then a jittery soldier mistakenly loaded a fifth shell before inserting powder, which rendered the cannon useless.

Sensing that the battle was lost, Crozier ordered a retreat. There was no time to collect the dead, though the major ensured the disabled cannon got dragged along. The wounded left behind a bloody trail in the snow, crimson blots on a white canvas. Riel opted against pressing his advantage and ordered his men not to pursue. "For the love of God," he said, "don't kill any more. There's too much blood spilled already."[64] Notwithstanding Riel's display of mercy, a haunted police officer recalled, "The Indians were all painted like demons."

In thirty minutes of fighting, Riel had lost four men, Crozier twelve.[65] Hayter "Iron Heart" Reed, a man whose career had prepared him for exactly this kind of crisis, reported, "It is probable that an Indian war is on our hands."[66]

WHEN NEWS OF the battle at Duck Lake reached Ottawa, the government urgently summoned a company of infantry from Toronto and two companies of field artillery from Kingston and Quebec City. Most of the call-ups were not full-time soldiers. In Toronto, a colonel barked, "I don't care who a man is, or what he is doing, but I want every man in the regiment to be under arms and ready!"[67] Departure was delayed by a full day because the Toronto City Council needed more time to collect enough underwear, boots, and mufflers to keep the departing troops warm.[68] They would be travelling in open railcars through territory still under the dominion of winter. When the militiamen finally pulled out of the train station, they were cheered on by a raucous crowd of thousands caught up in a patriotic delirium. They sang, "We'll hang Louis Riel on a sour-apple tree."[69]

The train ride west was less thrilling. For days, the troops caught no sight of the sun or moon; the sky offered only snow and sleet. They ate rations of salted pork and biscuits smeared with rancid butter. "There were fifty of us to a car, piled one on top of each other, drenched by the rain which fell on our backs in torrents," a soldier wrote. "For the first time, we really knew what misery was."[70] Along the way, one man died from exposure.

In Rossburn, reports of Riel's resistance spurred settlers to volunteer for the front lines. Among them were James Stitt, Alex Brown, and James McBride.[71] The trio headed 120 kilometres southwest to the nearest recruiting station, in Moosomin. When they arrived, primed for action, military officials were still working out logistics. So Stitt, Brown, and McBride had to endure a few days of boredom. During this languid period, a measure of doubt crept in. McBride thought of his wife and children. He decided that maybe his country wasn't worth his life after all, then mounted his horse and headed back to Rossburn. Brown, too, lost his passion for the fight. According to Stitt, Brown was "looking forward to the choice of several blondes who had come into the district." Off Brown went, chasing greater glories.

That left Stitt, who decided to stick it out. Only a few hours after his friends departed, he received orders to head farther west. Each man received ten bullets and a rifle. The weapons were so rusty that it seemed to Stitt that they "had not been used since the battle of Waterloo, I am sure, and were much more dangerous than an Indian skirmish."

Louis Riel, too, was working to rally more support to his cause, following his victory at Duck Lake. Runners carried his letters to Métis communities and Indian reserves across

Saskatchewan and Manitoba. Riel predicted that "the struggle will grow, Indians will come in from all quarters."[72] This would turn out to be wishful thinking.

In the next few weeks, the forces Riel did manage to assemble seized control of two government forts. At Frog Lake, a group of Cree Indians in Chief Big Bear's band killed two priests, five white settlers, and two federal officials, one of them an Indian agent who, in the mould of Hayter Reed, had denied rations to the starving. A few of the dead bodies were mutilated and two white women were taken hostage.[73] Newspaper headlines announced the "Frog Lake Massacre."[73] Big Bear had actually tried to prevent the killings, but he ultimately could not control his more militant warriors. "It was as if they were trying to lash out against years of abusive deprivation, abuse and wounded pride," write historians Blair Stonechild and Bill Waiser.[74]

With a wider war looming, the mood in Rossburn darkened. The town's residents heard that a Native uprising was under way in Saskatchewan, led by that rascal Riel, and now the Indians in Waywayseecappo seemed to be behaving suspiciously. "Fear of the Indians was a constant worry," a settler recalled. "They would come with their paint and feathers requesting food or simply staring about in their silent way. . . . The uncertainty of what they would do next . . . was ever present."[75] Others recalled how "some of the young bloods in the reserve here became truculent in manner" and "asked questions about the ownership of stock. We thought that they were sizing up the possibility of owning them soon."

From the edge of the valley just west of town, a large encampment of Indians on reserve land was visible. "There were so many tents it looked like the area was covered with giant puffballs," one settler said.[76] "We were, you might say, surrounded by the Indians," said another.[77]

A town councillor, Robert Carson, hosted a group of men at his home to discuss how to prepare for an Indian attack. They considered digging an underground hideaway but ultimately decided against it because their children probably wouldn't keep quiet enough. The meeting adjourned without a plan.[78]

The next day, Carson passed anxious hours whittling a fallen branch into a tool called a double tree, used to connect horses to a wagon. By dusk, his handiwork still just looked like a big stick. He went home for supper and rested his work-in-progress outside the entrance. It was a windy night. After supper, Carson and his wife tucked their children into bed and went to sleep. But a loud thud on the front door startled the family awake. A gust of frigid air whistled through the house, which could only mean that the front door was ajar. Carson was "sure the Indians were upon us" and rushed from his bedroom to confront the invaders.

What he saw was this: The front door wide open, and his whittled branch lay on the floor. Carson laughed nervously. It was just the wind, just a stick. The Indians had not attacked. Yet.

ALL TOLD, THE Canadian government mobilized eight thousand troops to face Louis Riel, who had mustered only a few hundred fighters to his cause. Hayter Reed was assigned to advise General Middleton, the man in charge of Canada's military efforts. Within two months, Riel's resistance was overcome. Roughly one hundred people lost their lives in the fighting; hundreds more were wounded. Stitt, the brave bachelor from Rossburn, never even fired his rusty rifle, while the Métis defended their stronghold of Batoche until they ran out of bullets.

Government troops overtook Batoche on May 12, and Riel turned himself in three days later. A central factor in his defeat was the refusal of the vast majority of Indians in the North-West to assist him. Once signed, the treaties signalled a commitment to peace, and the Indians took that seriously. According to a history written by Maureen Twovoice's grandfather Michael, Chief Waywayseecappo "staunchly sided his sympathies with the Government" during the "unrest" of 1885. The Chief "counselled his braves for peace and ensured that they kept it."[79] Yet again, Chief Waywayseecappo provided a clear demonstration of his loyalty to Canada, his treaty partner.

The local Indian agent, Lawrence Herchmer, gave himself most of the credit for keeping the peace. "The outbreak of the rebellion naturally greatly excited my Indians," he wrote in a memo to headquarters. "I am happy to report, however, that I had no difficulty during that trying time in managing [them]."[80]

In Rossburn, settlers soon began to regain their optimism. "Riel had been crushed and the fear of the Indian rebellion removed," one resident recalled. "Now the West was on its way."[81] Another settler admitted that their anxieties had been overblown: "As a matter of fact, the Indians were never dangerous to any but mental well-being. . . . There was a certain fear of the Indians, although no single story of harm from them was ever told."[82]

But even as Rossburn's fears dissipated, the government was intent on making sure the Natives could never cause so much trouble again. The West needed to be made safe for settlement, once and for all. It fell to Hayter Reed to devise a plan. "I have a few radical changes to suggest," he wrote to his superior.[83]

On July 20, 1885, Hayter delivered a document entitled "Memorandum on the Future Management of Indians." Among other draconian measures, his plan proposed a "pass" system to keep "rebel Indians" on their reserves unless they received signed permission to leave. "The dangers of complications with white men will thus be lessened," he reasoned.[84]

Hayter also prepared a list of Indian bands in Canada, accompanied by notes on the extent of each band's loyalty during the recent violence. He deemed the Ojibway of Keeseekoownin "Loyal" and the Sioux of Standing Buffalo "Very Loyal." The Chippewas of Kinoosayo were among the "Disloyal." And for the Cree of Okemasis, near Duck Lake, Hayter simply wrote, "Ditto."

Waywayseecappo received a more ambiguous assessment:

Way-way-se-cappo, Salteaux (Ojibway)
Bird Tail & Lizard Pt.   *A few became impudent*

Altogether, twenty-eight bands were deemed outright disloyal. Hayter recommended a pass system for these treacherous Indians. Prime Minister Macdonald agreed but proposed to extend the measure to *all* reserves. "As to disloyal bands," Macdonald instructed, the pass system "should be carried out as the consequence of their disloyalty." Then the prime minister added, fatefully: "The system should be introduced in the loyal bands as well and the advantage of the changes pressed upon them."[85]

The pass system was born.

MEANWHILE, LOUIS RIEL was charged with high treason, punishable by death. According to government prosecutors, Riel "most wickedly, maliciously and traitorously, did levy and make war against our said Lady, the Queen." By contrast, Riel believed that all his actions could be justified—that he was a patriot, not a rebel. "I have the honour to answer the court that I am not guilty," he said at the beginning of his trial.[86] "I have acted reasonably and in self-defence."[87]

His lawyers submitted a defence of insanity, despite Riel's forceful objections. Even though it was probably his best chance to avoid execution, Riel was not interested in procuring his survival at the expense of his dignity. "Here I have to defend myself against the accusation of high treason, or I have to consent to the animal life of an asylum. I don't care much about animal life, if I am not allowed to carry with it the moral existence of an intellectual being," he wrote.[88] He went on to undermine his lawyers' insanity argument by defending himself with two cogent speeches in English, his second language. Rather than rely on a claim that he was himself mad, Riel insisted that he had been "contending with an insane and irresponsible government."[89]

An all-white, all-anglophone, all-Protestant jury found Riel guilty. The jury recommended clemency, but the judge sentenced him to "be hanged by the neck till you are dead." Two subsequent appeals came to nothing, and his hanging was eventually scheduled for November 15, 1885. Shortly before his execution, Riel wrote: "I have devoted my life to my country. If it is necessary for the happiness of my country that I should now soon cease to live, I leave it to the Providence of my God."[90] He was hanged shortly after eight in the morning.

Eighty-one Indians were also formally charged with taking up arms against the government, of which fifty-five were convicted. Eight Cree Indians received death sentences, the largest collective death penalty in Canadian history. Hayter Reed expressed hope that public executions would cause those who supported Riel to "meditate for many a day" on their "sound thrashing."[91] Prime Minister Macdonald said, "The execution of Riel and of the Indians will, I hope, have a good effect on the Metis and convince the Indians that the white man governs."[92]

On the day of the scheduled mass hanging, before a crowd of Indians and settlers, the eight condemned men remained defiant. Standing atop the scaffold, their ankles tied together and their heads shaved by their captors, they spoke their final words. Among them was Big Bear's son, Imasees (Little Bear). According to an eyewitness, Little Bear "told the Indian onlookers to remember how the whites had treated him—to make no peace with them." Another of the condemned urged Indians "to show their contempt for the punishment the government was about to inflict on them."[93] Then the executioners drew black caps over the prisoners' faces and bound their hands. With the pull of a lever, the scene came to a macabre end.

THE FOLLOWING YEAR, 1886, Indian agents across Canada received their first batch of blank pass booklets. Any Indian who wanted to leave a reserve would first have to obtain an official pass specifying the purpose and duration of the absence, duly signed by an Indian agent.

Valid reasons for granting passes included to "get married" (ten days), "go hunting" (twenty-one days), or "visit a daughter at school" (fifteen days).[94] Sometimes passes were granted only "until sunset." In some places, Indians needed to submit a letter of recommendation from another federal official before an agent would authorize a pass.[95] Hayter Reed once described passes as a "privilege," revocable if "abused."[96] Anyone caught off the reserve without a pass was liable to be arrested for vagrancy or trespass and forcibly returned. The system transformed every unauthorized traveller into a fugitive and every reserve into a holding pen.

The pass system was used to limit contact between parents and children who were attending residential schools. Hayter Reed boasted in an annual report, "I must not forget to notice the success attained in preventing Indian visitors banging about the schools, and so unsettling the minds of the children, as well as too often insisting upon carrying them off for visits to their homes, from which they would only be recovered with much difficulty if at all."[97] Limiting passes for parents was a key tool for attaining this "success."

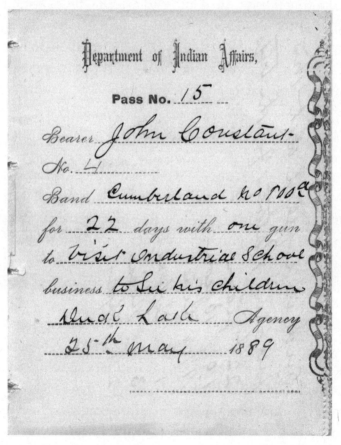

Pass issued in 1889 to John Constant so that he could travel "to see his children" who were attending an Indian residential school (PAS, S-E 19.35a)

In the decades to come, the cumulative effects of the pass system on Indigenous communities were devastating. It was a barrier to finding work, customers, or other opportunities off reserve. It also choked traditional education and culture by limiting opportunities to gather for ceremonies. By design, reserves became an archipelago of open-air prisons. A web of interconnected communities was cut into scattered threads.

Fears of another rebellion enabled the creation of the pass system, but other motives sustained it. Passes were justified on the dual grounds of protecting whites and civilizing Indians, though proponents of the system did not hesitate to obscure the true reasons behind false pretexts.

Canada was struggling to attract immigrants to settle the West, and Riel's uprising had given prospective settlers further pause. At the time, Indigenous Peoples constituted about half of the population of the North-West.[98] Indian hunters made farmers nervous about their cattle, if not their lives. The government hoped the new constraints on Indian movement would reassure settlers that their expansion would not be contested.

Keeping Indians on the reserves was also defended as a more effective means of reforming them. The Department of Indian Affairs wanted Indians to hunt less and farm more, and surely they would tend more to their crops on reserve if it was impossible for them to go anywhere else. Hayter adopted the paradoxical view that Indians had to be segregated before they could be integrated. He wanted Indians to become "imbued with the white man's spirit and impregnated by his ideas."[99] But first they had to remain physically separate for a little while longer: "It seems better to keep them together for the purpose of training them for mergence with the whites, than to disperse them unprotected among communities where they could not hold their own, and would speedily be downtrodden and debauched." Indians were apparently so vulnerable to corruption by white society's vices that they could not be trusted to travel freely. If they had a choice, Hayter thought, they would choose poorly, particularly when it came to alcohol.[100] Reserves were officially dry, and Hayter speculated that a further prohibition on movement was the best way to keep Indians sober. The pass system would keep Indians separate and, supposedly, protected.

INCREDIBLY, FROM THE very beginning, the architects of the pass system recognized its flagrant illegality. Even Indians were entitled to the freedom of movement. The treaties negotiated with Alexander Morris had explicitly guaranteed the right to hunt and trap off reserve.[101] Privately, the prime minister acknowledged as much.[102] Even Hayter Reed, an attorney, said the Indians had "the law on their side,"[103] though that fact did not seem to particularly bother him. "I am adopting the system of keeping the Indians on their respective Reserves and not allowing any leave them without passes," Hayter wrote. "I know this is hardly supportable by any legal enactment but we must do many things which can only be supported by common sense and by what may be for the general good."[104] Hayter penned those words on August 18, 1885. Only a few weeks before, he had been appointed a justice of the peace, tasked with upholding the law in the North-West Territories.

Many Indians "refused to tolerate the [pass] system and were often aggressive in demanding their rights," the scholar F. Laurie Barron writes.[105] As it happened, they had an unlikely ally in Lawrence Herchmer, who had risen from his position as Waywayseecappo's Indian agent to become the commissioner of the North-West Mounted Police. It was not the harshness of the pass system that disturbed Herchmer, a man who had previously said that starvation could do Indians some good. Rather, he was concerned that the system put his officers in an untenable position of enforcing a non-existent rule. As one police officer noted, Indians without passes were sent back to their reserves "on every possible occasion, but seeing that the Police have no right to do anything of the kind, it behooves one to be very careful."[106] In 1892, Herchmer sought advice from judges and government legal counsel, who told him that the pass system was unambiguously illegal. The next year, Herchmer ordered his officers to stop enforcing it.[107]

Hayter Reed, who had risen considerably in the government's hierarchy in the eight years since he had drafted the original memo proposing passes, expressed "extreme regret" in response to Herchmer's decision.[108] Hayter directed his Indian agents to keep enforcing the pass system anyway, notwithstanding the squeamishness of the Mounted Police. He acknowledged once again that "there has never been any legal authority for compelling Indians who leave their Reserve to return to them, but it has always been felt that it would be a great mistake for this matter to stand too strictly in the letter of the law. So long as this course is followed in the interests of the Indians themselves, a benefit rather than a wrong is done them. . . . All we can endeavor to do is to keep the true position from the Indians as long as possible."[109]

In the end, Hayter's view prevailed: the Mounted Police resumed enforcing the pass system in 1904, after Herchmer was no longer commissioner.[110] In certain places, the system was enforced until 1941, more than half a century after the first passes were issued.[111]

★ ★ ★

HAYTER MOVED TO Ottawa in 1893 after receiving yet another promotion; he was now deputy superintendent of Indians Affairs, the department's top bureaucrat. He had come a long way since his first encounter with "the Redman" at Lac Qu'Appelle as a young soldier two decades before. Gone were his musket and red coat and mutton chops—now Hayter wore ties and smoked cigars and signed memos. He had traded adventure on the plains for an office in the nation's capital, where it didn't take long for him to distinguish himself as "the crack polo player of Ottawa."[112]

Hayter Reed (McCord Museum of Canadian History, McGill University/11-10654, 1894)

At the age of forty-four, Hayter "Iron Heart" Reed married Kate Armour, a widow with a talent for interior design and an expansive social network in Ottawa. They built a magnificent stone house next to the Rideau River, within walking distance of Parliament Hill. Their hallway entrance featured the stuffed head of a buffalo.

7

"THE YOUNG NAPOLEON OF THE WEST"

A T THE END OF THE NINETEENTH CENTURY, WHILE MEN
like Hayter Reed fulfilled their frontier fantasies, it was
still far from clear whether Canada was a viable country. For decades, more people had been emigrating *from* Canada
than were immigrating *to* Canada.[1] The colossus to the south, the
United States, was pulling one family after another into its orbit.
Canada had an abundance of arable land but a shortage of willing
farmers. Then came the general election of 1896 and the Liberal
government of Wilfrid Laurier, who promised more immigrants
and put a thirty-five-year-old Manitoban named Clifford Sifton
in charge of finding them.

Sifton arrived in Ottawa with a bushy moustache that was not
altogether successful in conferring the air of a statesman on his
youthful face. He was six feet tall, five inches taller than the average man of the time. The *Globe and Mail* described Sifton as "a
Canadian of Canadians, a Liberal of the Liberals . . . a young man
with every faculty at command in the full exercise of its powers,
with a clean record, with high ideals and aspirations—what may

not Canada reasonably expect from him?"[2] He would go on to redeem and betray such lofty expectations.

Clifford Sifton (Library and Archives Canada, "Hon. Clifford Sifton (Minister of the Interior)," Topley Studio fonds/a027943)

Sifton's grandparents were Irish Protestants who had crossed the Atlantic Ocean in the 1830s and settled in Ontario. His father was the first member of the family to head west after being awarded contracts to extend a telegraph line and railway tracks in Manitoba toward Saskatchewan. The contract for the telegraph line, which ran over a portion of Treaty 4 territory, was tendered less than a month after Chief Waywayseecappo signed with his "X."

When Sifton was a child, a bout of scarlet fever left him partially deaf. For the rest of his life he compensated by outworking his peers. He graduated at the top of his law class, though he didn't consider himself the best or the brightest of his cohort. Rather, "I worked harder than they did and I got the reward."[3]

For a time, Sifton had imagined his future might carry him away from Canada. A few months in England as a teenager had given him the ambition to join the British civil service and help administer India (where actual "Indians" lived). In the end, though, he opted to follow his father west after completing his legal training. In 1882, he and his brother moved to Brandon, a frontier town two hundred kilometres due west of Winnipeg that was booming because of a new railway connection. They established a law firm, Sifton & Sifton, where Clifford specialized in land and homestead law, which was the main preoccupation of new settlers. In his spare time, he excelled at lacrosse, a sport invented by the Iroquois and known at the time as Canada's national game.

During the Riel scare of 1885, Sifton joined a home guard militia scouring Brandon for rebels. He patrolled the streets for four nights in succession with a shotgun in his hands and a "6-shooter" handgun on his hip.[4] For all his ardour, he never found an occasion to shoot.

Three years later, at the age of twenty-seven, Sifton won his first election to the provincial legislature against a heavily favoured Conservative candidate. He prevailed by only forty-two votes. Sifton, a teetotaller and the son of a prohibitionist, brushed off accusations that he plied prospective voters with whiskey. The next election, he won again, and his Liberal Party captured a majority in the legislature. He earned the nickname "Young Napoleon of the West" for his tactical brilliance during electoral campaigns.[5] He later boasted that if you gave him the name of a voter in North Brandon, he could tell you the colour of that person's hair.[6] Sifton became Manitoba's attorney general in 1891 and developed a reputation as the finest orator in the legislature.

When Laurier became prime minister in 1896, he recruited Sifton to his cabinet as minister of the interior and gave him a wide mandate to settle the prairies. The mayor of Brandon hailed the appointment: "Mr. Sifton possessed within him abilities equaled by few and surpassed by none."[7] Sifton was now in charge of Canada's immigration policy, and he vowed to create a nation of farmers.

In a memo to the prime minister, Sifton said that "the object which is constantly kept in view" was "development of natural resources and the increase of production of wealth from these resources."[8] He was convinced that Canada would progress only through agriculture, which in turn depended on the recruitment of a hardier breed of settlers: "the possession of a preponderating rural population having the virtues and strength of character, bred only among those who follow agricultural life, is the only sure guarantee of our national future."[9] Unless Canada settled its vast territory and exploited its natural wealth, he argued, the country would not reach its full potential. Immigration would make Canada great.

The question was where to find more able bodies. Sifton opposed an influx of Asians on the supposed grounds that they made bad farmers, and he doubled the head tax on prospective Chinese immigrants. The agricultural prowess of Jews was similarly suspect. To lure Americans, Sifton sent samples of wheat to South Dakota and Indiana, "to prove to people there that it could be grown in Manitoba."[10] Still, there weren't enough Americans or Brits willing to give Canada a try—harsh winters were something of a deterrent. For a time, Sifton even considered banning the publication of the daily temperature in Manitoba.[11]

Sifton was looking for people "to fight the battle of the pioneer's life," which required "the toughest fibre that can be found."[12] He set his sights on eastern Europeans, particularly Ukrainians. That such people lived half a world away did not impede Sifton's ambition. He saw in Catholic Ukrainians singular talents for tireless farming and prolific babymaking. His ideal migrant was "a stalwart peasant in a sheep-skin coat, born on the soil, whose forefathers have been farmers for ten generations, with a stout wife and a half-dozen children."[13] Cheap, plentiful labour was what he wanted. "I do not care what language a man speaks, or what religion he professes," Sifton said. "If he will go on the land and make a living for himself and family, he is a desirable settler for the Dominion of Canada."[14] In time, he was confident that they would "assimilate with Canadians."[15]

IN EUROPE, THE Ukrainians were a conquered people, their territory carved up and controlled by Austria-Hungary and Russia. Landlords called Ukrainians pigs and shut down their schools. Ukrainian peasants had to bow when they came within one hundred metres of their landlord's mansion. They were not even allowed to marry without permission. Russia-controlled Ukraine had been renamed Little Russia, and the words "Ukraine" and "Ukrainians" were forbidden.[16] In 1863, Russia barred the use of the Ukrainian language altogether. Meanwhile, Russian authorities demanded crops for taxation and men for military service. Under such conditions, Ukrainians dulled their misery by consuming astounding amounts of hard liquor: twenty-six litres per year per person, if you included every man, woman, and child.[17]

When Ukrainians spoke of "land," the word was often married with another: "problem." For a growing family on a modest farm, the "land problem" meant that a family's property could be divided among grown children only so many times. Subsistence farms became too small, and then smaller still. In the late nineteenth century, the average Ukrainian family farm had only four acres.[18] For the children of such families, immigration was more an imperative than a choice. As the poet Alexander Kolessa-Khodovitsky later wrote:

Perhaps a river deep
We shall cross
But in our native land
We shall perish.[19]

Word spread that a country called Canada was doling out plots of 160 acres, for free! That fact alone made a strong case for migration, but Clifford Sifton also enlisted the power of profit and propaganda. He reached an agreement to pay a Hamburg-based shipping outfit, the North Atlantic Trading Company, for every Ukrainian peasant it brought to Canada: five dollars per male head of a family, plus two dollars for a wife and each additional child. Sifton also made sure his immigration agents were no longer paid on salary but instead received a commission, per migrant they recruited.

Sifton saw himself as a salesman, with the Canadian dream as his commodity. He dispatched thousands of agents to Europe to distribute hundreds of thousands of pamphlets, promising "Free land is waiting for you" and "Canada will give you land."[20] He authored a brochure claiming that the prairie soil was so rich it "stands more cropping without manure, than any other surface known to agriculture."[21] In August on the prairies, he wrote, "it is harvest time, and the wheat fields are like a sea of gold."[22] A 1904 pamphlet proclaimed that "there are no castes or classes in this country, all are equal," and that "all religious denominations, whether Christian or otherwise, enjoy equal rights." The schools were said to be "equal to any on the continent," and the prairie land was described as "the best poor man's country between the Atlantic and the Pacific oceans." Another pamphlet described Canada simply as the "land of promise."[23]

FREE FARMS

FOR MILLIONS.

.❦ .❦ .❦

200 MILLION ACRES

Wheat and Grazing Lands for Settlement in Manitoba and the Canadian North-West.

.❦ .❦ .❦

Advertisement in the *Nor-West Farmer*, June 1897 (Archives of Manitoba/N11695)

Russian and Austria-Hungarian authorities became increasingly alarmed that emigration might deplete Ukraine's (exploited) labour force, and they took measures to stop it. In one case, a man named Iwan Pillipiw visited Manitoba to see for himself whether it was worth uprooting his family. He decided it was. When he returned home to sell his property and urge others to join him on the journey, he was arrested, charged with criminal propaganda, and sentenced to a month in jail.[24] After his release, he and his family promptly packed up and left for Canada.[25]

To stem the outflow of migrants, the authorities deployed more armed guards at the border. Ukrainian priests were ordered to preach against emigration and to emphasize the prospect of starvation in Canada.[26] Yet migrants sought and found ways out, in large and growing numbers. In 1896, 2,576 Ukrainians arrived in Canada. The following year, as Sifton's propaganda campaign was revving up, the number grew to 4,999,[27] and by 1902 it was 10,309. The next year, 17,418 more came. Many read the words of Ivan Drohomereski in his poem "Exodus From the Old Country":

> *I once was in my native land,*
> *And I often thought:*
> *Why should I be suffering*
> *In unhappiness?*
> *I shall go into the wide world,*
> *Where there's neither oppression nor lord*
> ....
> *Oh, to Canada I'll go,*
> *To the new land,*
> *And where, as they say,*
> *It is a free country.*[28]

Pushed by fear and pulled by hope, in 1899, Ukrainians coming to Canada outnumbered the total number of American and British immigrants for the first time.[29] Among these Ukrainian migrants were Troy Luhowy's great-great-grandparents, Maksym and Dorota Yaskiw. They took their four children, who were between the ages of six and thirteen, and left the Ukrainian province of Galicia to journey across the Atlantic to Canada.

The trip took them a month. The train heading to Hamburg journeyed via the Austria border town Oswiecim (which later became infamous by its German name, "Auschwitz"). The fortunate travellers sat on narrow benches along the sides of the railcars; the rest perched crookedly on their bags in the aisles. At each stop, border agents, doctors, and merchants—along with plenty of scammers—did their best to extract whatever meagre savings the travellers had stashed in their luggage and underwear.

In Hamburg, then Europe's busiest port, Canadian agents were on the lookout for the right kind of immigrant. "If one should examine twenty people who turn up at Hamburg to emigrate," Sifton said, "he might find one escaped murderer, three or four wasters and ne'er-do-wells, some very poor shop-keepers, artisans or laborers and there might be one or two stout, hardy peasants in sheep-skin coats. Obviously the peasants are the men that are wanted here."[30] Sifton was content "letting the riff-raff go on to the United States and to South America."[31]

Maksym and Dorota were among the chosen ones. From Hamburg, the boat ride to Halifax on Canada's eastern shore took two weeks or so, depending on the whims of the ocean. The migrants stayed below water level in steerage, packed into bunk beds lining stuffy compartments. The seasick were plied with garlic and whiskey to calm stormy stomachs. The travellers whispered to one another about the *vilni zemli*, "free land," that awaited them.

Their boat, the coal-powered S.S. *Phoenicia*, carried 1,308 passengers. This ship was among the more comfortable vessels carrying migrants across the seas in those days, because it was actually designed to transport humans. Often, immigrants travelled on cargo ships that had carried cattle, pigs, or grain from North America to Europe. The passengers of such ships arrived in their new country smelling like the animals that had preceded them.

The Yaskiws landed in Halifax on May 21, 1899. The wooden dock was lined with sheds full to bursting with coal. After passing a medical screening, the family was ushered into a train, where they sat on bare wooden boards. Bold letters inscribed on the trains read "COLONIST CARS."[32] The words meant nothing to Maksym and Dorota, who didn't know a word of English. Thanks to Minister Sifton, there was no fare to pay.

The train rumbled westward. To farmers from the Ukraine, the rough terrain of western Ontario, with its never-ending parade of cliffs, rocks, and forests, hardly seemed like an agricultural paradise. A ripple of panic spread through the train—perhaps they had been dreaming a lie, after all.[33] But once they reached the unrelenting flatness of Manitoba, their worst fears receded. Then, after 3,500 kilometres by rail, their train pulled into Winnipeg's central station.

From there, the Yaskiws took yet another train, which took them north to the town of Shoal Lake, where they were handed tents, axes, pots, utensils, flour, and sugar. Then the family hitched a wagon to their final destination, some place called Rossburn. Later that summer, Maksym and Dorota completed paperwork to receive a 160-acre government-issued homestead for a mere ten dollars.

In 1896, the year Sifton became minister of the interior, the government granted 1,861 homesteads to newcomers. By 1904, that number had skyrocketed by almost twenty times, to 32,684.[34] Each one anchored a family determined to rewrite its destiny.

For some, the journey ended in tragedy. In the spring of 1899, an outbreak of scarlet fever engulfed a group of new arrivals to

Manitoba. Four hundred people were quarantined a few kilometres from Rossburn and housed in makeshift tents. In May, just
weeks before Maksym and Dorota arrived, a freak spring snow-
storm proved too much for the most vulnerable to endure. Three
adults and forty-two children died.

However, the overwhelming majority of new arrivals settled
safely and set about fulfilling Sifton's lofty expectations of productivity. While Sifton was minister, new immigrants helped triple the number of acres under cultivation in Canada, to more
than three million, and production of wheat quadrupled.[35] Sifton
exulted over such figures. In a speech in 1902, he boasted about
the transformation of the prairies. Before, he said, the Canadian
West had been described "as a land of large promise but somewhat slow and poor performance, as a land of illimitable possibility but limited realities, a land generally described, indeed, with a
fine flow of rhetoric." But, thanks to the influx of settlers, Sifton
said, "stagnation has given way to abounding activity . . . and the
whole situation has undergone an alternation that is little short
of phenomenal."[36]

Still, Sifton remained driven by an anxiety that "just as soon
as you stop advertising and missionary work, the movement is
going to stop."[37] He maintained a frenetic pace, habitually working fourteen to sixteen hours a day.[38] Even after plowing through
mounds of paperwork late into the night, he was known to be
back at the office before the rest of his staff arrived the next morning. "The burden of carrying the affairs of the West is a heavy
one," he confided in a colleague.[39] "I am worked out," he wrote to
another. "I wish some of the damn fools who are grumbling had
my job for a week. They would quit it wiser and sadder men."[40]

During the summer of 1898, he collapsed from exhaustion.[41] After resting for a few weeks and regaining his strength,

he resumed the same manic work habits as before, perfectly in keeping with his lifelong scorn for idleness. To Sifton, a wasted work hour in Ottawa was as unforgivable as an uncultivated acre in Manitoba.

The results of his dogged efforts were indisputable. On Sifton's watch, more than one million people came to Canada, boosting the country's population by about 20 percent.[42] Yet what Sifton viewed as a historic achievement did not immediately receive the rapturous praise he thought it deserved. "I find some ground for wonder," he told a friend in 1902, "in the lack of appreciation of what is going on in the West where we have turned dismal failure into magnificent success."[43]

On the contrary, the new wave of immigration had sparked a nativist backlash. The Ukrainians in particular, though they constituted only a fraction of the new arrivals, tended to attract the most malignant scrutiny from newspapers and Sifton's political opponents. The year of the Yaskiws' arrival, newspapers in nearby Brandon, the town Sifton represented in Parliament, labelled the incoming Ukrainians as "barbarians," "pampered paupers," and "ignorant and vicious foreign scum."[44] According to one editorial, "Importing such creatures into our country is about as sensible as deliberately bringing vermin into a new house." The premier of Manitoba, Sir Edward Roblin, called the immigrants "foreign trash."[45]

A newspaper in Winnipeg labelled Ukrainians as "probably the least promising material that could be selected for nation-building." The next year, the same paper wrote with even less subtlety: "It cannot be too emphatically repeated that the people of Manitoba want no such 'settlers' as these 'Galicians.'"[46] (Like the Yaskiws, many of the immigrants were from the province of Galicia.) The article continued: the "dumping of these filthy, penniless and ignorant foreigners into progressive and intelligent communities is a serious hardship to these communities. . . . These people bring with them disease . . . and dirty habits." Though the federal government welcomed the Ukrainians, evidently many Canadians did not.

When a Ukrainian was suspected of shooting and killing an Anglo-Saxon woman in Winnipeg in 1899, the *Winnipeg Telegram* ran a headline calling it "Another Siftonian Tragedy."[47] Shortly thereafter, an Anglo-Saxon woman named Hilda Blake confessed to the crime, though the reflex to scapegoat Ukrainians far outlived this particular incident. It was a time for scornful epithets: "European freaks and hoboes,"[48] "scum of Europe," "herds of half-civilized Galicians."[49] Established Euro-Canadians, usually Protestants, sneered at the Eastern Catholic strangers pouring into the countryside. Like Maksym and Dorota, the newcomers were often poor and poorly educated. Most were illiterate. Critics derided them as "Sifton's pets."[50]

Undeterred, Minister Sifton remained their bugle and their shield. In 1899, Conservative Party member Edward Prior attacked the new immigrants during a speech in Parliament. Prior called the Galicians a "menace to our well-being and prosperity." He added, "The worst of it is, that these men are not coming in solely of their own accord, but they are coming in with the assistance of the government."

Across the parliamentary chamber, Sifton rose and spoke, loudly and proudly, in defence of the strangers he had helped bring to Canada. "So far as the Galicians are concerned, the attacks that have been made upon them, in my judgment, are most unfair and most ungenerous. If we are ever going to have the North-west populated, we shall not succeed in doing it by standing on our boundary with a club or putting the microscope on every man who wishes to come into the country."[51] Sifton insisted that all Canadians would benefit from the industry of these hardy settlers who were willing to toil "from daylight to dark."[52] Across the aisle, Prior remained unconvinced, though he eventually conceded, "I have never been in company with . . . a Galician . . . that I know of, but I have heard a great deal about them."

In 1899, Sifton told a skeptical crowd in Winnipeg that he "was willing to stake his reputation as a member of Parliament and a minister of the Crown that in five years' time there would not be found a business man who would say that the policy pursued was not a wise one."[53]

Privately, Sifton was blunter. "The cry against the . . . Galicians is the most absolutely ignorant and absurd thing that I have ever known in political life," he told a friend. "There is simply no question in regard to the advantage of these people, and I do not think there is anyone in the North West who is so stupid as not to know it. . . . The policy adopted of exciting racial prejudice is the most contemptible possible policy because it is one that does not depend upon reason. . . . All you have to do is keep hammering away and appealing to their prejudices, and in the course of time you will work up an excitement, but a more ignorant and unpatriotic policy could not be imagined."[54]

Sifton faced opposition from both sides of the political aisle on this issue. A fellow Liberal member of Parliament, Frank Oliver, said "these people" would be "a drag on our civilization and our progress," even if they did contribute economically. He recognized they were adept at working the soil, but to be worthy of living in Canada "it is not enough to produce wheat out of the ground."[55] They were an "alien race" with "alien ideas," and their presence would deter immigrants "of a superior class."[56] Likewise,

Hugh John Macdonald, the leader of the Conservative Party and son of Sir John A., declared that he did "not want a mongrel breed" coming to Canada. Instead, he "wanted white men."[57] At this time in Canadian history, Maksym and Dorota, for all their pallor, did not qualify as white.

Yet Sifton never wavered. When the general election of 1900 rolled around, Sifton eagerly courted the votes of the new arrivals who had received their naturalization papers. He helped create and distribute a political pamphlet that described how Galicians had been "neglected and in a miserable condition and that immediately after I took office they were looked after and work found for them."[58] The Liberals won another majority, and Sifton remained at the helm of the Department of the Interior.

Immigrants kept coming by the tens of thousands, clearing land, enduring winters, and, over time, thriving. With his mission largely accomplished, Sifton resigned from his post in 1905, after nearly a decade in the job. He retired altogether from politics in 1911, having unalterably changed the course of his country. Some 180,000 Ukrainians made their way to Canada in the two decades between 1895 and 1914, by which point Ukrainians outnumbered Indigenous Peoples.

After his retirement, Sifton's legacy was widely celebrated. His critics had been proved wrong. Prime Minister Robert Borden said of Sifton, "He was inspired with a sincere patriotism, and no Canadian had a broader outlook or a higher optimism as to the future of our country."[59] The London Advertiser wrote, "A new Canada emerged with the twentieth century, and Clifford Sifton's name is written imperishably in this inspiring chapter of Canadian history."[60]

And yet there is another side, less well known and certainly less inspiring, to the story of Clifford Sifton.

★ ★ ★

DURING THE YEARS Sifton was minister of the interior, he was *also* the superintendent of Indian affairs. This put him in charge of both Canada's newest arrivals and its first inhabitants. His twin missions were to welcome immigrants and civilize Indians. The logic of this dual mandate was simple: clear the path for settlers.

When Sifton assumed the leadership of the Department of Indian Affairs, his top bureaucrat was Hayter "Iron Heart" Reed. The two men shared the basic view that Indians could not be trusted to govern their own lives. "Our position with reference to the Indians is this," Sifton said, speaking on behalf of the government. "We have them with us, and we have to deal with them as wards of the country."[61]

Sifton began his tenure with a promise to limit spending on Indians as much as possible. Over the course of his decade as superintendent, funding for the Department of Indian Affairs would increase by a relatively modest 30 percent.[62] During the same period, the overall budget of the Department of the Interior, of which Indian Affairs was a part, increased by 400 percent. "Immigration we must have," Clifford Sifton once told his top official stationed in Europe. "You will have all the money that may be necessary."[63] Indians were a far lower priority.

In the longer term, Sifton saw government-funded education as the most viable way "to bring the Indians into a state of civilization or comparative civilization," and to reduce "any chance of them becoming a disturbing factor in the community."[64] Which was not to say that he expected too much from them. "I have no hesitation in saying, we may as well be frank, that the Indian cannot go out from a school, making his own way and compete with the white man."[65] As compared to white Canadians, an Indian "has neither the physical, mental or moral get-up to compete. He cannot do it."

Under Sifton's leadership, the number of Indian children receiving a state-sponsored education rose to ten thousand. Meanwhile, he insisted that "the expenditure upon Indians, and particularly upon Indian education, has reached a high water mark, and we must now look to reducing rather than increasing it in any way."[66]

In order to trim the budget while still maintaining the project of civilizing Indians through education, Sifton approved a gradual shift away from attempts to teach them trades at so-called industrial schools. Rather, he proposed "a less elaborate system of what we call boarding schools where a larger number of children can for a shorter time be educated, more economically and generally more effectively."[67] In time, Canada would come to call these institutions residential schools. To Sifton, it was crucial that these schools would be far from reserves, so that Indian children would be "removed from the surroundings which tend to keep them in a state of more or less degradation."[68]

Along with Hayter Reed, Sifton had a direct hand in establishing the residential schools that Maureen's mother Linda and grandfather Michael later attended. In 1897, Hayter wrote a memo to Sifton recommending a per student grant of $110 to the Brandon Indian Residential School, to get the school up and running. Sifton approved.[69]

In 1904, after a fire destroyed the Qu'Appelle Indian Industrial School in Saskatchewan, Sifton personally intervened to have it rebuilt.[70] The new building was where Michael Twovoice learned to read and write, and where missionaries trumpeted the virtues of assimilation.

Tragically, during Sifton's time as superintendent of Indian affairs, some residential schools had mortality rates of *50 percent*. In 1907, a government-appointed inspector called the mistreatment of Indigenous children at these institutions a "national crime."[71] At the Brandon residential school alone, at least forty-one students died on Sifton's watch.[72]

In 1899, Sifton approved Treaty 8 to solidify government control over 850,000 square kilometres of land in parts of what are now Alberta, Saskatchewan, British Columbia, and the Northwest Territories. Like other treaties signed in the same era, Treaty 8 was a document riddled with arcane legal jargon, negotiated with people who could not read it and who left with a completely different understanding of what it meant. To Sifton, the purpose of the treaty was "to pacify and keep pacified the North-West territories" and to avoid "having an Indian trouble on our hands."[73] There was a gold rush under way in northern Canada, and Sifton wanted to make sure the Natives were no impediment.

As well, he oversaw the work of Indian agents across the country, who were vested with pervasive power over Indians on reserves. Yet Sifton insisted that Indian agents tread softly in at least one respect: "It is absolutely essential that Indian Agents should scrupulously refrain from interfering directly or indirectly with the Missionaries upon Indian Reserves."[74] Indians were wards; missionaries were untouchable.

Looking back on his record as a government minister, Sifton was proud of what he had accomplished. "I shall be content, when the history of this country shall be written, to have the history of the last eight or nine years, so far as western administration is concerned, entered opposite my name," he said.[75] To Sifton, his most important mission had been increasing immigration.[76] He viewed Indians, his "wards," as a liability to be managed and minimized.

Meanwhile, he celebrated immigrants, his "pets," as the guarantors of Canada's future prosperity. And since the material progress of new arrivals like Maksym and Dorota Yaskiw was the best advertisement for others to follow, Sifton did everything in his considerable power to ensure that they got the favourable start they needed. Compared to a place like Rossburn, Waywayseecappo was an afterthought.

Years later, an early Ukrainian settler to Rossburn wrote a poem that began,

> *Many came from distant lands*
> *Unaware what the future held,*
> *To settle on unknown Canadian virgin lands*
> *A new life, in a new land to weld.*[77]

Virgin land, but for those Indians across the Birdtail.

8

"ONE LOAD OF BARLEY"

IN 1889, 153 INDIANS LIVED ON THE WAYWAYSEECAPPO reserve. About half had been categorized by the government as "pagans," but the determined efforts of Christian missionaries had been steadily increasing the number of Roman Catholics and Presbyterians among them. There was also more farming on the reserve. A federal inspector with the Department of Indian Affairs noted with satisfaction that 182 acres of crops—wheat, oats, barley, rye, potatoes, turnips, carrots, and onions—had been sown in the reserve's heavy black loam soil, up from 50 acres the previous year. Slightly more than twenty of these acres were overseen by Otakaonan ("the Gambler"), now more than a decade removed from his speeches at Treaty 4 negotiations. "Some of the young men have begun farming for the first time this year," the inspector noted approvingly.[1] The federal government continued to profess that farming was the surest route to progress for Indians.

In October that year, after the fall harvest, the Department of Indian Affairs announced a radical new approach to agriculture on reserves. Henceforth, labour-saving machinery would be banned. Although farming technology was improving rapidly at the time, Indian agents would require farmers on reserves to seed by hand, harvest with scythes and hoes, and grind grain with hand mills. Furthermore, Indians would be required to manufacture these most basic of tools themselves. On some reserves, even nails were not permitted.[2] In other cases, Indian agents banned lanterns.[3] So at the same time the government was forcing Indians into agriculture in the name of productivity, it was banning the most productive tools.

The mastermind of this new policy was none other than Hayter Reed, avid proponent of the pass system. "The general principle," Hayter explained, "is not to allow machinery to save [Indians] work that they should do with hands available on Reserves."[4] Indians would have "to cut and sow their grain in the most crude manner possible."[5] With less technology and less efficiency, the thinking went, more Indians would work harder, and thereby experience the redemptive power of industry, thrift, and self-sufficiency. What's more, officials saw little point in letting Indians invest in technology they could not afford, because they were viewed as too feeble-minded to manage debt.[6] Bands that tried to pool their resources to buy expensive machinery were to be stopped.[7] "Great discretion has to be used relating to the kind of investments the Indian is allowed to make," Hayter wrote.[8]

Hayter believed new machinery could be justified only when manual labour was scarce, which he didn't think was the case on reserves. It did not seem to occur to him that coerced inefficiency was a powerful incentive to do less.

In 1893, a group of Cree and Ojibway Indians on Treaty 4 territory petitioned Parliament to permit them to purchase a mechanical binder, a machine that cut stalks of grain and bound them into bundles. An official in the Department of Indian Affairs, they wrote, had "objected to us buying a Binder as he said it would make the young men lazy. . . . This has completely discouraged us, as our old implements are worn out . . . [and] many of the fields we used to farm are now all grown over with grass."[9] Even some federal officials conceded how counterproductive the policy was. "Personally," one Indian agent observed, "I do not see how any band of Indians in this district can ever raise sufficient grain or cattle to become self-supporting as long as they have to work with sickles and scythes only."[10]

Meanwhile, farmers in Rossburn had collectively organized themselves to purchase a threshing machine.[11] Such a machine could do in one afternoon what ten men did by hand in two weeks. Surely people in Waywayseecappo were aware of this, and even Hayter acknowledged that Indians "see white men in the possession of self-binders and other costly inventions for saving labor" and "think that they should have such implements."[12] But he believed that the use of such tools by Indians would "leave them little more to do than to sit by and smoke their pipes, while work is being done for them without exertion on their part." Hayter embraced the racist idea, then prevalent, that races progressed in fixed, progressive stages, and, therefore, Indians should not be permitted to "emulate in a day what white men have become fitted for through the slow progress of generations." The Indians could have better technology when they were civilized enough to deserve it.

Under Hayter Reed's fastidious watch, the Department of Indian Affairs enforced these restrictions on farming technology from 1889 until 1897, the year Hayter retired from government. During that span, per capita acreage under cultivation on reserves across the prairies fell by about half.[13] Farmers on Waywayseecappo fared even worse. In 1889, they cultivated 182 acres, but nine years later, that number had fallen to a mere 8.[14]

IN ADDITION TO restrictions on technology, Waywayseecappo also had to contend with what was known as the "permit system," created in 1882 by an amendment to the Indian Act. Without signed permission from an Indian agent, Indians living on reserves were not allowed to sell food they grew or animals they raised to anybody off reserve.[15] Unlike the pass system, which was enforced despite its manifest illegality, the permit system was spelled out in legislation that made it perfectly legal. In principle, the freedom of contract was sacrosanct in Canadian common law, but this liberty was suspended for Indians, whom the state accorded the legal status of children.

The federal government sought to justify the permit system on the basis that it would protect Indians from fraud. Without benevolent supervision, Hayter Reed explained, Indians would first "part with hay while their cattle were left to starve" and trade away "grain and roots which they require for sustenance," then "squander the proceeds" and ultimately "come on the Government for support."[16] Prime Minister John A. Macdonald made a similar assessment: "If the Indians had the power of unrestricted sale, they would dispose of their products to the first trader or whiskey dealer who came along, and the consequence would be that the Indians would be pensioners on the Government during the next winter."[17] The government argued that the permit system would instead promote self-sufficiency and thereby stave off future federal expenditures.

In practice, the permit system hamstrung farmers on reserves. As a group of Cree and Ojibway Indians on Treaty 4 territory noted in an 1893 petition: "Whenever we have a chance to sell anything and make some money the Agent or [Farming] Instructor steps in between us and the party who wants to buy, and says we have no power to sell: if this is to continue how will we be able to make a living and support ourselves? We are not even allowed to sell cattle that we raise ourselves."[18]

Even some settlers publicly condemned the unfairness of the permit system. The *Virden Chronicle*, a newspaper based in a small town a hundred kilometres south of Waywayseecappo, ran an article titled "Indian Grievances" on January 11, 1894. Indians on reserve were "very dissatisfied" with the permit system, the newspaper reported. "They farm their own land, work hard all summer, and through the obnoxious order are not allowed the full benefit of the fruit of their own labour. They are thus placed at a disadvantage in competition with their white and more highly civilized neighbours." Rather than celebrating this disadvantage, the *Virden Chronicle* heaped scorn upon it, because the permit system was creating grievances that could "assume serious proportions and we do not want another rebellion." Louis Riel's shadow still loomed.

Not only were Indians being restricted from selling their goods, the article explained, but Indian agents were fining or threatening white buyers for making purchases without permits. As a result, "The grain dealers have almost concluded not to purchase any more grain from the Indians, except at very low rate, as they are entirely at the mercy of the Indian Agent. . . . An Indian's wheat is just as good as a white man's, but the dealers claim that if they are by purchasing it, making themselves liable to prosecution, they must protect their own interests." The *Virden Chronicle* demanded an investigation into Indian complaints and an end to the permit system.[19] Yet nothing changed, in Waywayseecappo or elsewhere.[20]

Between the technology restrictions and the permit system, Indians were not permitted to farm efficiently or to sell their products freely. Meanwhile, the arrival of a (heavily government subsidized) railway connection in Rossburn in 1905 gave Waywayseecappo's white neighbours the incalculable benefit of access to distant markets.

In short, the government repeatedly declared that it wanted Indians to farm in order to become more civilized, but it made it nearly impossible for farming on reserves to be successful.[21]

At best, federal policies for reserves were the result of disastrously misguided paternalism, though the historian Sarah Carter advances a more damning interpretation. She argues that the federal government was in fact trying to "protect and maintain the incomes of white farmers" by insulating them from on-reserve competition.[22] In 1888, for example, a group of settlers in Saskatchewan wrote to their member of Parliament to complain that "the Indians are raising so much grain and farm produce that they are taking away the market from the white settlers."[23]

Of course, it remained all too easy to attribute blame to Indians themselves. One of Waywayseecappo's Indian agents criticized the reserve's "not very good farmers" for being "easily discouraged."[24] A federal inspector described Waywayseecappo's inhabitants as "unprogressive, morose, and unwilling to be guided by officials. Their inordinate pride appears to be the greatest obstacle to their advancement."[25] Across the valley of the Birdtail, settlers in Rossburn looked on—and drew similar conclusions.

This was part of a broader pattern: the government orchestrated failure on reserves, then Indians who suffered the consequences got blamed.

★ ★ ★

Though Hayter Reed's technology restrictions stopped being enforced in 1897, the permit system lasted far longer. Half a century later, in February 1942, a federal official caught two men from Waywayseecappo selling wood at $1.50 per load to a white farmer without authorization. One of the men, Joe Mentuck, later told the RCMP, "I did not have a permit to sell, I know I should have one and meant to get one but left it too long."[26] Mentuck had hoped to exchange the wood for a dozen chickens, an overcoat, and a sweater. His family was hungry, and the winter was frigid.

The local Indian agent, A.G. Smith, was slated to review the incident in Rossburn on March 6, at which point he could lay formal charges for the violation of the Indian Act. (In such cases, Indian agents assumed the role of magistrates.) Smith was sufficiently troubled by the circumstances of the case to write his superior in Ottawa to ask whether he had discretion to waive fines, especially when he thought an Indian was not particularly blameworthy. The purchaser and seller were each subject to a $20 fine, even if the load of wood was worth only $1.50. "The white man can probably pay the fine with ease," Smith wrote, "but the Indian may have to deprive his family of some of the necessities of life to pay his fine, or go to prison."[27]

There is no surviving record of what Agent Smith ultimately decided.[28] Yet he and his successors would be tasked with enforcing the permit system for decades to come. As late as 1969, the Department of Indian Affairs and Northern Development issued a permit to allow the sale of a heifer.[29] And the provision of the Indian Act that made it illegal for Indians to sell to non-Indians was not repealed until 2014.[30]

★ ★ ★

ON THE MORNING of Sunday, October 17, 1943, the pews of Waywayseecappo's Presbyterian church were packed for an event about the ongoing World War. Seen from the outside, the white paint on the wooden building gave it a ghostly pallor among the sharpening colours of autumn. To ward off the chill, volunteers periodically shovelled coal into the basement furnace.

Waywayseecappo's Chief at the time was Prince Astakeesic, the grandson of Waywayseecappo, and he addressed the congregants first. He spoke in Ojibway, but a local translated into English. According to a report published in the *Rossburn Review*, the Chief "spoke very feelingly and patriotically of the young men and the cause for which they volunteered to work and fight. He spoke of the Blessing of Freedom and was convinced that the British would see the war through to a grand Victory and Freedom for all."

Chief Astakeesic concluded by unveiling the Honour Roll, a plaque listing the names of men from the reserve who had already signed up. The names were bordered by stylized maple leaves, painted green and yellow, alongside the flags of Great Britain and Canada. The name of the Chief's son, George Astakeesic, was printed near the top of the alphabetical list. George was deployed with the 1st Canadian Infantry Division, which was then facing off against German tanks in the deserts of North Africa.

Next, a recruiter from the Canadian military made his way to the podium. He praised "the splendid attitude of men coming forward and ready, if need be, to pay the supreme sacrifice, not only for loved ones at home and for country and Empire, but for the unfortunate peoples being so basely and cruelly treated in the War Zones."

The local Presbyterian missionary spoke last. He pointed to the Union Jack and marvelled at the way it was "honoured by peoples of all classes, colours, creeds and languages, and how, at the sound of distress and pain from Europe, the men had rallied together from Continents and Isles of the Sea." Thanks to so many brave men, "the oppressors were feeling the weight and power of the Soldiers of Truth and Righteousness."[31] The service concluded with the singing of the hymn "Onward, Christian Soldiers":

> *Like a mighty army*
> *Moves the Church of God:*
> *Brothers, we are treading*
> *Where the Saints have trod.*
> *We are not divided;*
> *All one body we:*
> *One in hope and doctrine,*
> *One in charity.*

Michael Twovoice, Maureen's grandfather, was among those listed on the Honour Roll, though he was never shipped overseas on account of his tuberculosis infection. Michael's friend Hugh McKay was also on the Honour Roll and had already been serving in Europe for months at the time of the October ceremony in the Presbyterian church. After basic training, Private McKay shipped overseas in December 1942 as a machine gunner in the Royal Canadian Artillery. He would go on to serve in the Army for forty-four months and was abroad for three years. A month after D-Day, he helped liberate the French town of Caen from Nazi control. Hugh fought in France, Belgium, Holland, and finally Germany, where he was wounded in combat.

McKay was discharged on February 19, 1946, six months after the Japanese joined the Germans in unconditional surrender. He received enough medals to crowd the left breast of his uniform, including the War Medal 1939–1945, the France and Germany Star, the Defence Medal, and the Canadian Volunteer Service Medal and clasp. His military records indicate he was five feet eight inches tall, with brown hair and black eyes. His complexion is listed as "dark."

Pte. Hugh McKay (Courtesy of Jim Cote)

After returning from Europe, McKay settled back home in Waywayseecappo. Soon after, he received a letter dated July 31, 1946, from the Department of National Defence. "This Certificate is forwarded you with the sincere congratulations of this Headquarters," a brigadier wrote. The document recognized McKay for his "bravery in action" and was signed by Canada's secretary of state for war "to record His Majesty's high appreciation" for McKay's "distinguished service." Hugh framed the certificate and hung it on his wall.

Like many veterans, McKay seldom talked about the war, even with his son Jim. But what he did share Jim remembers, including a story about a time McKay approached his commanding officer seeking deployment to the front lines. The officer liked the young private enough to discourage him from putting himself in even greater danger. "If you go to the front," he told McKay, "you will see things you'll never forget for the rest of your life, terrible things. And that's *if* you come back."

Driven by a sense of duty, McKay persisted, and got his wish. He later told his son, "That officer was right." For years after returning home, McKay experienced debilitating flashbacks when airplanes rumbled overhead or when storms popped and flashed. His wife would try to bring him back into the present by slapping him in the face and yelling, "Hugh! Hugh!"

While he was an active member of the Army, McKay had visited bars across Canada in uniform and was served without question. After he returned home in 1946 as a civilian, he visited the bar in the Rossburn Hotel, expecting nothing different. When he entered, though, the patrons turned their heads in unison. They looked like a group of cows distracted from their cud.

"Hey, you," the bartender said. "Get lost."

"I'm a veteran, I served," Hugh said.

"I don't care what you did, get the hell out."

In the Canada of 1946, the bartender was following the law. Beer parlours could not legally admit Indians, even those who had risked their lives fighting Nazis. "There was something patently ridiculous," the historian James Gray writes, "in a system which permitted an Indian to risk his life for his country but denied him access to a bottle of beer."[32] Like many thousands of other Native veterans, McKay had to confront the painful dissonance between Canada's wartime rhetoric about freedom and the harsh reality of his racist neighbours in a racist nation.

MCKAY NEVER FORGOT nor forgave his expulsion from the Rossburn Hotel and made a point of avoiding town as much as possible afterwards. (Years later, he would relish Waywayseecappo's establishment of its own separate school.) After the war, he worked to earn his living as a farmer. Still, he could not escape further indignities, including the demands of the permit system.

Permit to sell a load of barley (Courtesy of Jim Cote)

On November 25, 1947, McKay received permit no. 49539, which authorized him to sell "one load of barley" for $65.20. McKay was "permitted to sell" only because he and a buyer had first obtained the express permission of the local Indian agent. A freedom fighter abroad, Hugh McKay was still treated as a ward at home.

Jim recalls an occasion in the 1950s when his father tried to sell a cow. "I nursed that calf!" McKay yelled. "I pulled it out of its mother with my hands. I fed it, I raised it. It's my cow! I should be able to sell it."

His request for a permit had been denied.

9

"REASONABLE AMUSEMENT"

O N THE EVENING OF FEBRUARY 17, 1896, THE TEMPER-
ature in Ottawa plunged to minus thirty-five Celsius.
This did nothing to deter the guests of the Historical
Fancy Dress Ball, who kept warm under fur blankets as they
glided along Wellington Street in horse-drawn sleighs.

The ball was organized by the governor general's wife, Lady
Aberdeen, who was thrilled to have the chance to host a lavish
event for the rich and powerful of the nation's capital. "To tell the
honest truth," she confessed to her diary, "we started this idea of
having a Ball representing the outstanding periods of Canadian
history with the hope that it might lead young people to reading
up a bit & that it might divert Ottawa gossip at least into past
times, away from . . . the everlasting discussion of hockey and winter sports varied with Ottawa society scandal."[1] Among those to
receive a coveted party invitation was Hayter Reed, on account
of his wife Kate's friendship with Lady Aberdeen.

The Senate Chamber of Parliament was cleared of its chairs
and desks to make way for a temporary white pine dance floor.

Banners of blue silk garlanded the sixteen marble pillars lining the walls. With the seated galleries full and the chamber packed to standing-room capacity, one thousand people managed a snug fit.

At nine o'clock, the crowd hushed as an orchestra started playing "God Save the Queen." This was the cue for the governor general and Lady Aberdeen to enter in a procession through the middle of the chamber. Lady Aberdeen wore a purple satin dress featuring a bodice of darker velvet, along with a coronet of sparkling diamonds that held her veil in place. Her two youngest boys trailed immediately behind, wearing powdered wigs and carrying the train of their mother's dress. Once the viceregal couple reached the dais at the far end of the room, they sat down on a pair of thrones. Then Lady Aberdeen gave a nod, and trumpets announced the start of the first dance. "From the first moment," she later wrote, "one could not help feeling that the thing was 'going.'"

The Aberdeens' fancy dress ball in the Senate Chamber (Library and Archives Canada/Samuel J. Jarvis fonds/c010108)

The entertainment kicked off with a series of dance performances representing nine periods in Canada's history, from Viking
incursions in the 1100s to the arrival of the Loyalists in 1779.
From the galleries overlooking the chamber, the view was posi-
tively kaleidoscopic. "The floor beneath resembled a mosaic, with
men and women, garbed in vari-hued apparel, as the pieces that
made up the whole," an onlooker noted. "Every conceivable tint
was in evidence. . . . Wander as the eye might, it was always met by
a spectacle of colored loveliness."[2]

After the final dance performance, the guests briefly resumed
their mix-and-mingle before they were interrupted by a series of
lurid whoops and cries. A group of people dressed up as Indians
sprang from the four corners of the room, pantomiming toma-
hawk chops in their best impressions of noble savages. They soon
converged in front of the governor general and Lady Aberdeen.
The group's leader wore a wig with braided ponytails, along with
a feathered headdress that hung from his head to his heels. He
carried an eight-foot-long wooden staff adorned with feathers.
His fringed buckskin and shirt were a haphazard mix of Cree and
Blackfoot styles.

Kate Armour Reed was among the few to recognize the man
in the costume: it was her husband, Hayter, thoroughly enjoying
himself, his pale face smudged with reddish-brown paint. He was
joined by his stepson Jack, also dressed up for the occasion. Hayter
had provided many of the outfits for the performance from clothing he had collected during his fifteen years with the Department
of Indian Affairs. (Hayter's collection was so extensive that he had
loaned many items from it a few years earlier for an exhibition at
the Chicago World's Fair.) "Their striking costumes added a pic-
turesque effect to the brilliant scene," *Lounger Magazine* reported.
"They would have delighted the heart of a genuine son of the

forest if he could have seen them."[3] Of course, there was no actual Indian present at the party to test that proposition.

Hayter Reed and his stepson Jack (Library and Archives Canada, Topley Studio fonds/a139841)

"Tenth Historic Group: Indian Group," with Hayter standing fourth from the right (Library and Archives Canada, Mrs. K. Stephen collection/ICON14103)

Hayter was playing the character of Donnacona, an Iroquois Chief whom French explorer Jacques Cartier had encountered on his first transatlantic trip, in 1534. When Cartier first set foot in North America, he declared possession of the territory and planted a thirty-foot cross with an engraving in French: "Vive le roi de France." But Donnacona objected. According to Cartier, the Chief approached in a canoe, "then he pointed to the land all around us, as if to say that all the land was his, and that we should not have planted the cross without his leave."[4] To avoid a confrontation, Cartier pretended that the cross was innocuous, a mere navigational landmark. The following year, when Cartier returned, he kidnapped Donnacona and took him to France, where the Iroquois Chief was paraded before the French king as exotic proof of the New World. Donnacona ended up dying in France, far from home.

Now, three and a half centuries later, Hayter was addressing the governor general and Lady Aberdeen in broken Cree, doing his best Donnacona impression in the wrong language.[5] He expressed the "love of his Indians" for Canada's head of state.[6] As Hayter spoke, the other members of his party whooped and grunted in approval. Then, after Hayter finished his address, he presented the governor general and Lady Aberdeen with a peace pipe. As absurd as this whole display was, the audience found it utterly compelling. Here in Ottawa, Hayter was the undisputed voice of Native peoples.

Hayter and his band of ersatz Indians had stolen the show. "The whole proceeding was well managed," a historian later wrote, "and certainly unique in the Senate chamber, which has never before been invaded by the Indian aborigines, in real or mimic guise."[7] After the performances, dinner was served in the cavernous rotunda of the main Parliament building, where guests "chatted in the gay and happy spirit characteristic of the evening," one observer said.[8] A member of Hayter's group felt sufficiently emboldened to (falsely) boast to partygoers that he was wearing moccasins made with human scalps.

"The history of our own country is too little known," a journalist noted, "and the historical pageant had the effect of bringing it before the society of the capital in a most striking and effective manner."[9] The event forced even "the careless student of our history to recognize its great charm and varied interest," another wrote, "and to feel a deeper pride in this 'Canada of ours.'"[10]

The glowing reviews delighted Lady Aberdeen. She had only one regret, which she expressed repeatedly over the course of the evening: if only she had thought to request an Indian war dance.[11]

MEANWHILE, IN WAYWAYSEECAPPO, federal agents were intensifying their long-standing efforts to suppress Native dancing ceremonies, which the government viewed as obstacles to the civilizing process. Hayter Reed himself had long championed these draconian restrictions.

Back in 1884, Parliament amended the Indian Act to criminalize "giveaways," rituals involving gifts, which were a common feature of many Indigenous ceremonies.[12] Hayter supported banning this "very objectionable" practice because it was "occasion for an interchange of presents and the giving away of property, even to outsiders. In many instances Indians are known to have dispossessed themselves of everything they owned."[13] Hayter described Indians on the plains as "the only perfect socialist in the world."[14] In time, the government hoped to transform them into straight-thinking individualists.[15]

After Hayter became the top bureaucrat in the Department

of Indian Affairs, he supported a further legislative amendment in 1895 that prohibited any ceremony involving "wounding or mutilation."[16] This amendment aimed to suppress the Sun Dance, widely practised in the prairies, which involved feats of physical endurance, including, in some cases, skin piercing.

Technically, only events involving "giveaways," "wounding," or "mutilation" were illegal—but, just as with the pass system, Indian agents were encouraged to operate beyond the strict letter of the law. Claiming legislative authority, agents worked to quash all sorts of ceremonies nationwide. Those who defied the prohibition faced the prospect of months in jail.

In Waywayseecappo, the annual Sun Dance was the community's most sacred traditional ceremony, and participants from other reserves travelled long distances to attend. The dance took place in an encampment formed of teepees arranged in a circle, with a round ceremonial lodge at its centre. The circular shape affirmed a sense of coming together and unity. Inside the central lodge, there was singing, drumming, and dancing. Those who had pledged to dance continued intermittently for multiple days and nights, during which time they neither ate nor drank. "The dancing was a fulfilment of personal vows," Waywayseecappo Elder Jim Cote says. "It was dancing for the wellness of all family members and the community. That's what those dances were for."[17]

A Sun Dance ceremony often lasted four days, but it could go on for as long as eight. The Sun Dance was a time to feast, to pray, to give thanks, to renew bonds within and between communities. It was a place where traditional teachings were passed along from one generation to the next. Elders led the proceedings, while the young watched, listened, and learned. Inside the circle, participants feasted together on soup, meat, berries, and bannock. Many gifts were exchanged, including clothing and blankets and even horses and wagons. These were ways to affirm the importance of caring for each other and sharing the bounty of the land.

"It is these annual acts of renewal and spiritual and community refurbishment," Harold Cardinal and Walter Hildebrandt write, "that enabled . . . First Nations to retain their inner strength, cohesion, and spiritual integrity."[18] And it was precisely because of the immense cultural importance of these Sun Dances that the Canadian government was so hostile to them.

In Rossburn, the annual Sun Dance in Waywayseecappo was a source of terror. One Rossburn family, the McKees, recalled watching with trepidation every summer as "tribes gathered from all over the country." Rhythmic booms from the steady drumming cascaded through the valley. "The noise of the tom-toms was terrifying," the McKees said. It came as a great relief when another settler "warned the government and these things were stopped."[19]

In 1896, the Indian agent overseeing the Waywayseecappo reserve was J.A. Markle, whom Minister Clifford Sifton later described as "one of the best Agents in our service and a man of sound judgment and high character."[20] His office was in the town of Birtle, some thirty kilometres from the Waywayseecappo reserve. In June, about four months after Hayter and his pantomiming Indians dazzled the Historical Ball in Ottawa, Agent Markle received a tip about an impending Sun Dance in Waywayseecappo. Markle promptly summoned the Chief for a meeting in Birtle. At this time, the Chief was Waywayseecappo's son, Astakeesic—"Sky Is Crossing" in Ojibway—who was described in a government report as "temperate but not at all enterprising [and] is too influenced by his old father who still clings to pagan customs."[21]

According to Markle's account of his conversation with Chief Astakeesic, Markle read out loud the dancing provisions in the Indian Act and said he was prepared to enforce the law as necessary, but "appealed to [Astakeesic] not to jeopardize our present friendly relationship after he had been kindly and fairly warned." Markle reported that Astakeesic "could not at first see how it would be possible to cancel the dance and ask the invited friends to return home." Eventually, though, the Chief promised that if any dancing occurred, it would be kept short, and would not have a "torture, give away or fasting feature." He also assured Markle that he would turn back any visitors from other communities.

In the same report, Markle also described a subsequent meeting with a group of Indians from the Crooked Lake reserve who were travelling to attend Waywayseecappo's Sun Dance. Markle warned them that if they participated in a dance, "I certainly would give them trouble." According to Markle, "after a long talk," the group's leader eventually "promised to return home, and that he would not take part in any dance on the Waywayseecappo's Reserve." For his part, Markle "consented to allow him to visit the Reserve and camp one night to see his friends." The pass system made that consent necessary.

Three days later, Markle filed a follow-up report. He noted that visitors from three other reserves had indeed converged in Waywayseecappo, but they had quickly dispersed without dancing. "I am glad to be able to report that I persuaded the Indians not to hold a Sun Dance," he wrote. Then he added, "All the Indians present are unquestionably a sorrowful lot, and gave up the dance very reluctantly, but they did it without one angry word being spoken on either side."[22]

It is hard to imagine that angry words were not spoken once Markle left.

★ ★ ★

IN 1898, THE Department of Indian Affairs' most senior official in the prairies, Commissioner Amédée Forget, advised an Indian agent that a given dance could technically not be stopped if the specific banned features were not present. Forget warned against "ascribing to the [Indian] Act a scope which it does not possess."[23] Even so, agents were encouraged to use other methods at their disposal: namely, withdrawing rations from those who participated in dancing and refusing travel passes to Indians who wanted to attend dances on other reserves.

That year, eighty-two-year-old Cree Chief Piapot was arrested, convicted, and imprisoned for taking part in a Sun Dance. Fifteen years earlier, faced with the starvation tactics of Hayter Reed, Piapot had joined Big Bear in leading the dignified procession of thousands who decamped from the Cypress Hills. Now Forget invited Chief Piapot to his office to discourage him from supporting dancing in his community. A translator named Peter Hourie mediated the conversation, which reportedly went as follows:

> FORGET: *Ask him, Peter, why, when he knew that it was contrary to the policy of the Department, he allowed a Sun Dance to be held.*

> PIAPOT: *When the Commissioner gets up in the morning he has many varieties of food placed before him, and if he doesn't like what is in one dish, he has a number of others from which to choose. He does not know what it is to have an empty belly. My people, however, are often hungry and when they cannot get food, they pray to God to give it, and their way of praying is to make a Sun Dance.*

FORGET: *He has an argument there. Tell him, Peter, that we are two big chiefs here together. I ask him as one big chief speaking to another, not to make any more Sun Dances.*

PIAPOT: *Very well, I will agree not to pray to my God in my way, if you will promise not to pray to your God . . . in your way.*

FORGET: *By Jove, he has me there. The old rascal should have been a lawyer.*[24]

Banter aside, the government made no concessions, opting instead to invoke powers under the Indian Act to unilaterally remove Piapot as his community's Chief.

Across Canada, federal restrictions on traditional ceremonies continued to provoke deep resentment among Indians. In British Columbia, intense opposition convinced the provincial government to formally appeal to Minister Sifton in 1898 to ease restrictions affecting the potlatch, a ritual involving so-called giveaways. The potlatch occurs in a feast hall and is the principal meeting place among the West Coast tribes featuring gift giving, feasting, and dancing. It is a time to celebrate marriages, confer names, confirm social status, settle land disputes, and gather clans for collective decision-making.

Sifton rejected the request on the grounds that such ceremonies had a "most demoralizing effect upon the Indians who participate."[25] (By "demoralizing," he was referring to a supposed negative effect on morality, not on morale.) Sifton added that "the repeal of the law now . . . would be viewed by the Indians as an evidence on the part of the Government of weakness and vacillation and would produce disrespect and want of confidence in the source from which it emanates." Sifton stayed the course, as did his successors, who went on to legislate yet more restrictions.

In 1902, eighty-six-year-old Piapot met with the governor general, Lord Minto, and persuaded him that the limitations on dancing were misguided. Yet Minto, in turn, could not persuade the government to change its approach.[26]

Decades passed. Still, the Indians danced.

In 1913, Duncan Campbell Scott became the head bureaucrat in the Department of Indian Affairs, a position he held for nearly twenty years. Scott exhibited a singular disdain for what he called the "senseless drumming and dancing" of the Indians.[27] On December 15, 1921, he circulated a letter to his agents across the country:

Sir,--

It is observed with alarm that the holding of dances by the Indians on their reserves is on the increase. . . .

I have, therefore, to direct you to use your utmost to dissuade the Indians from excessive indulgence in the practice of dancing. You should suppress any dance which cause waste of time, interfere with the occupations of the Indians, unsettle them for serious work, injure their health or encourage them in sloth and idleness. You should also dissuade, and, if possible, prevent them from leaving their reserves for the purpose of attending fairs, exhibitions, etc., when their absence would result in their own farming and other interests being neglected. It is realized that reasonable amusement and recreation should be enjoyed by Indians, but they should not be allowed to dissipate their energies and abandon themselves to demoralizing amusements. By the use of tact and firmness you can obtain control and keep it, and this obstacle to continued progress will then disappear.[28]

In 1925, Percy Lazenby was the Indian agent for the Rolling River, Swan Lake, and Waywayseecappo reserves. In one of his reports about Waywayseecappo, Lazenby described the "moral status" of its Indians as "deplorable."[29]

In June of that year, after Lazenby refused to allow a Sun Dance to be held at Rolling River, he received a letter from a lawyer representing the residents of that reserve. "As far as I can see," the lawyer wrote, "the holding of the sun dance is not contrary to the law."[30] He was referring to the fact that the Indian Act did not ban all dancing, but only criminalized dances if they contained the prohibited features.

A few days later, another lawyer, this time representing the Swan Lake reserve, wrote a similar letter to Lazenby. This lawyer contended that his clients should be allowed to hold a Sun Dance in a form that did not break the law. Swan Lake even invited a Christian missionary, an Indian agent, and a Mounted Policeman—the ultimate trifecta of officialdom—to witness their dance and verify that nothing unlawful transpired. "Everyone has a celebration of some sort," the lawyer wrote, and Canada's "earliest inhabitants should be entitled to their own, particularly when they are not doing anyone any harm."[31] The Indians of Swan Lake, their lawyer wrote, "would be pleased to know if the Ottawa authorities in whose fairness they have great faith will . . . allow them to hold this Sun Dance."

This faith was sorely misplaced. Earlier that year, the most senior Indian Affairs official in the prairies, Indian Commissioner W.M. Graham, had instructed Agent Lazenby that "even though the dances might not actually be illegal, they should be discouraged."[32] Agent Lazenby subsequently received explicit instructions from his superiors to prevent Rolling River's proposed Sun Dance, in any form.[33]

Lazenby knew full well that he was acting beyond the scope of the law—incredibly, he acknowledged as much in one of his own reports: "I realise that if the Indians refrain from doing anything forbidden in . . . the Indian Act, they cannot legally be stopped from having a dance." And yet he still stopped them, as instructed. "We met the Chief on the road just outside of the reserve, and talked with him about the dance, and told him that instructions had been received from the Commissioner's office, that the dance must not be put on." Before signing off, Lazenby added, "I am expecting that the Waywayseecappo Indians will be requesting permission to hold a Sun Dance shorn of it's [sic] illegal aspects, and I would be glad if the Department would advise me just what attitude to take when these requests are made."[34]

As it happened, Waywayseecappo was planning a Medicine Dance, not a Sun Dance, [35] but the dances all looked the same to settlers, who had come to fear the sound of Indian drums. Agent Lazenby dutifully called a Mounted Policeman, Sergeant Mann, to help break it up. Mann rushed to meet Lazenby in Rossburn, and together the men headed across the Birdtail River. They found that the Medicine Lodge, the epicentre of the ceremony, had already been dismantled in response to an order by another official from the Department of Indian Affairs that the dance be stopped. "Although the Indians acted and spoke in a very respectful manner to us," Sergeant Mann later reported, "I could see that there was an undercurrent of feeling amongst them, as it appears that they cannot understand why the Dept. would not let them hold the dance as they had broken no law in so doing, but that as they had received orders to stop, they had stopped."[36] Once again, there is no record of the Indian point of view.

Sergeant Mann was sufficiently troubled by the incident that he filed a separate, "Confidential" report to his commanding officer, outlining his concerns:

1. There are only two dances that are unlawful. The Sun Dance with the old mutilation and wounding included, and the "Give Away Dance." . . .

2. It is becoming apparent that many of the Indians are aware of the above fact.

3. It is becoming apparent that the Indians especially the oldtimers cannot see why at their annual reunions that they cannot hold and take part in some of the oldtime ceremonies, of course leaving out the objectionable portions. In connection with this they know that religious thought both Christian and heathen is a personal matter and not restricted by law.

That summer, Sergeant Mann wrote, he had been called upon to stop "dances which were according to the [Indian] Act quite legal"—first at Rolling River, and now at Waywayseecappo. In the future, he expected trouble if officers had to enforce rules that both police and Indians knew did not exist.[37]

Around the same time, the two most senior officials in the Department of Indian Affairs—Deputy Superintendent Scott and Commissioner Graham—were discussing the best way to address the ongoing scourge of Native dancing. Their exchange had been provoked by the two lawyers who had the audacity to insist that their Indian clients could lawfully dance.

"The matter of these aboriginal dances and celebrations of the Indians is a vexed question," Scott wrote. "So much valuable time is squandered that ought to be devoted to farm work, that the department has set its face against them. At the same time we do not wish to deprive the Indians of reasonable amusements." In the end Scott concluded, "The time has gone by for the sun dance."[38]

For his part, Commissioner Graham wrote that "nothing in the nature of aboriginal dances will be tolerated." He fretted that even graduates of residential schools "dress up like old time Indians and are the laughing stock of the white community around." Graham thought the continued dancing made the work of converting Indians into farmers more difficult. "Unless a firm stand is taken by the Department," Graham concluded, "we are not going to get far."[39]

Two years later, in 1927, the Indian Act was amended to make it nearly impossible for Indians to hire lawyers. It became a crime for lawyers to receive payment in pursuit of a legal claim "for the benefit" of an "Indian tribe or band"—unless, that is, the federal government gave its written permission.[40]

ON SEPTEMBER 21, 1936, Canada's governor general, Lord Tweedsmuir, travelled to the town of Fraserwood, Manitoba, 250 kilometres due east of Rossburn. He was there to address a crowd of 1,500 Ukrainian Canadians, "from babes in arms to aged patriarchs," according to a report by the *Winnipeg Free Press*.

A local Ukrainian Canadian politician spoke first (in Ukrainian, but translated to English). He praised Canada for having welcomed so many of his kin as immigrants: "Here they have found liberty, freedom of thought and speech and great opportunities for themselves and their children."[41]

The governor general spoke next. "The Ukrainian element is a very valuable contribution to our new Canada," he said, articulating an early version of what later came to be called multiculturalism. "I wish to say one thing to you. You have accepted the duties and loyalties as you have acquired the privileges of Canadians citizens, but I want you also to remember your old Ukrainian traditions—

your beautiful handicrafts, your folksongs and dances and your folk legends. I do not believe that any people can be strong unless they remember and keep in touch with all their past. Your traditions are all valuable contributions toward our Canadian culture which cannot be a copy of any old thing—it must be a new thing created by the contributions of all the elements."[42]

A troupe of Ukrainian youth celebrated Tweedsmuir's visit with a series of performances in "richly-colored native costumes." A photographer from the *Winnipeg Tribune* took a picture of the governor general watching the ceremony. The caption in the newspaper reads, "His Excellency smiles with evident pleasure as he watches tiny tots mincing through their folk dances."[43]

It would remain illegal for Indigenous Peoples to dance and hold ceremonies in Canada for another fifteen years.

THERE IS NO better embodiment of the dissonance between the federal government's embrace of immigrants and oppression of Indians than the career of Clifford Sifton, the Young Napoleon of the West. If Hayter Reed is the undisputed villain of this story, Clifford Sifton is its greatest hypocrite.

"I have an almost fanatical opposition to any legislation which interferes with contractual rights," Sifton once said.[44] Yet he didn't seem to mind that the Indian Act placed onerous restrictions on a simple contract for a load of barley. As minister of the interior, he sponsored the global journey of downtrodden immigrants, but as superintendent of Indian affairs, he presided over unlawful confinement of Indians to reserves. Sifton helped tens of thousands of settlers receive 160-acre plots for a pittance, but the Indian Act made Indians ineligible for homesteads.[45] Canada made room for

Catholic Ukrainians, but not for "pagan" Indians. And there was never such a thing as the Ukrainian Act.

In 1927, Sifton gave a graduation speech at Queen's University, which was awarding him an honorary doctorate. He was sixty-five years old, long retired from politics, and just two years away from a heart attack that would end his life. "Few, I think, have had occasion to see more of Canada and Canadian conditions than I have," he told the graduating students.

"You are Canadians. What does that call to your mind? That you are one of nine million people to whom Providence has committed perhaps the greatest heritage that has ever been given to an equal number of people." Sifton paused, then added, "Nine millions of white people."

Sifton argued that Canada was particularly blessed because it did not have to contend with the usual litany of obstacles facing other countries. "No negro problem; no yellow problem; no slum problem, because our climate does not favour, and in fact, does not permit the existence of large slum populations." (He did not even bother mentioning the "Indian problem," as some of his peers did.) "You are part of these nine million people," he continued, knowing his audience, "and by your academic training and your intellectual equipment, you are called upon to lead them. The resources of Canada are before you. It is the part of these nine million to determine how these resources shall be employed—in short, to make or mar Canada. Do your part, and the future of the country will take care of itself."[46]

Sifton himself had already done as much as anyone, both making and marring Canada.

PART III

"SIFTON'S PETS"

10

"NEVER FORGET"

I T DIDN'T TAKE LONG, AFTER CLIFFORD SIFTON'S RETIRE-
ment from politics in 1911, for Canada to turn on the immigrants he had fought so hard to welcome. Many Canadians
continued to view the recent arrivals as unwelcome strangers
despite their undeniable usefulness. In wartime, they came to be
seen as a threat.

In 1914, the assassination of the archduke of Austria in
Sarajevo set off a cascade of ever-larger dominoes that ultimately
provoked the First World War. Canada, still an appendage of the
British Empire, was dragged into the fighting. This, in turn, set off
another destructive chain of events at home.

In Rossburn, an effigy of the German kaiser Wilhelm II was
set alight on Main Street.[1] Suspicions grew about the Ukrainian
immigrants who had formerly lived in the Austro-Hungarian
Empire, now among Canada's avowed enemies. The federal government required immigrants who had not yet received Canadian
citizenship to register as "enemy aliens" and regularly report their
whereabouts. Parliament also passed the Wartime Elections Act,

which stripped the right to vote from Ukrainian Canadians who had been naturalized as citizens after 1902. "Sifton's pets" no longer had a powerful guardian.

The RCMP attempted to assuage unfounded fears. The Ukrainians caused "little trouble" despite "wild rumours," the RCMP insisted. "No fear need be entertained."[2]

"Enemy aliens" behind barbed wire near Vernon, British Columbia (Image E-06412 courtesy of the Royal BC Museum)

Incredibly, even though the "enemy aliens" who had come to Canada from the Ukraine were formally barred from enlisting in the Canadian armed forces, thousands did so anyway by lying about their birthplaces. Yet such displays of fealty did not quell widespread suspicions of treachery. Employers caved to popular pressure to fire their Ukrainian employees. Thousands lost their jobs. Before long, municipalities resented the growing burden imposed by the recently unemployed, many of whom were young Ukrainian men. To avoid the expense of covering their basic welfare needs, municipalities encouraged the federal government to arrest and detain them.[3] In time, as many as 5,954 Ukrainians were detained in makeshift penal camps. Of 950 internees held at a squalid detention centre in the town of Brandon in 1915, for example, the overwhelming majority (820) were Ukrainian.[4] The men were forced into hard manual labour and paid twenty-five cents a day, a fraction of the prevailing market wage.

A prisoner inside an internment camp in British Columbia, Mr. N. Olynyk, wrote a letter to his family in which he said, "We are not getting enough to eat—we are hungry as dogs . . . and we are very weak. Things are not good. . . . We get up at 5 o'clock in the morning and work until 10 o'clock at night. Such conditions we have here in Canada, I will never forget."[5]

In Alberta, detainees built much of the infrastructure of Banff National Park. Among them was seventeen-year-old John Kondro, otherwise known as "Prisoner of War 224."[6] On February 8, 1916, his father, Jacob, wrote a letter to the government seeking his release: "I did not think that Canada would take their own people and put them in prison in an internment camp. I am naturalized as a citizen of the Dominion of Canada. Please let him go." It seems that even citizenship was an inadequate defence against wartime xenophobia.

In Parliament, a few lonely voices dissented from the government's heavy-handed measures. Wilfrid Laurier, who had once stood shoulder to shoulder with his trusted minister Clifford Sifton, was no longer prime minister and his Liberal Party was out of power. But he was still a member of Parliament, and he used a speech in the House of Commons in 1917 to denounce the treatment of immigrants: "Do you believe that when Canadian immigration agents will go . . . among [eastern Europeans], that these different races will be disposed to come to this country when they know that Canada has not kept its pledges and promises to the people from foreign countries who have settled in our midst? ... I believe we shall be judged some day by our actions here."[7]

By the end of 1917, most Ukrainian detainees had been released, though not on account of Laurier's advocacy. Rather, the war had caused an acute shortage of manpower in the private sector, and, with most other able-bodied men fighting abroad, employers needed Ukrainians to fill the gap. Ironically, they then earned higher than normal wages because of ongoing labour scarcity. This, in turn, triggered yet more resentment. A bitter observer wrote in 1918: "You can see the country being cleaned out of our fine, Anglo-Saxon stock and the alien left to fatten on war prosperity."[8] The war came to an end later that year, but antagonism between Ukrainians and Anglo-Saxons would endure for a long time to come.

VLADIMIR YASKIW, TROY Luhowy's great-grandfather, was eleven years old when he accompanied his parents Maksym and Dorota on their trip from the Ukraine to Canada in 1899.[9] It wasn't long before Vladimir changed his name to Dick, and as soon as he became eligible for his own homestead at the age of eighteen, he applied for one just south of his father's.

The First World War broke out when Dick was twenty-six, but he was among the lucky ones who managed to avoid internment. Instead, he found decent-paying jobs laying railway tracks and drilling oil wells. In 1919, he became the first Ukrainian settler in Manitoba to own a Ford Model T. Nevertheless, his growing family remained in an economically precarious position. Dick and his wife, Lucia, bought their first house with the help of a bank loan, but they soon fell on harder times and were evicted after missing a series of payments. By 1925, Dick and Lucia were raising ten children in a two-room house made of mud and brick. There was so little space and warmth that the smaller children slept at the foot of each bed, perpendicular to the others. Then Lucia gave birth to twins. On the most frigid days of winter, the children were forced to skip school because they didn't have adequate clothing.

In the early decades of the twentieth century, the "pioneer" years, resilience was the most highly prized virtue. Parents told their children a proverb from the old country: "*De nema boliu tam nema i zhyttia*" (Without pain, there is no life). Hectare by hectare, they cleared the land: adults chopped trees, horses uprooted stumps, toddlers picked pebbles. For many, home was a building called a *budda*: a cramped, tent-shaped structure made of mud and hay with a thatched roof, built in the Old World style. The floor was of packed earth, and children often kept warm by sleeping on top of mud stoves. In the evening, families sang folk songs:

We toiled and we suffered
That better times should come
That others may prosper.

In the meantime, children found fun where they could. Wrapping from store purchases became colouring paper; whittled willow branches made the best slingshots; horse turds became passable hockey pucks.

In those days, the town of Rossburn was populated mostly by Anglo-Saxons, and Ukrainians lived on farms in the surrounding countryside. Outside of planting and harvesting seasons, Ukrainians sought wages wherever they could, and Anglo-Saxons were all too happy to have cheap labour to clean their houses and staff their businesses. As a sympathetic poet in Rossburn wrote:

These sturdy peasants from o'er the sea,
in silence and in pain
Slaved at all the menial jobs,
a piece of bread to gain[10]

Parents wanted better for their children, yet lack of access to quality education remained a major barrier to economic advancement. The rural schools attended by Ukrainian children rarely attracted qualified teachers, who were loath to venture into "foreign" districts that were considered backwards.

"Hardship was a way of life," said Troy's great-grandfather Bill Derlago, who arrived in Rossburn as a child in 1906. "It took a great deal of courage and tenacity to survive. . . . But I sincerely believe that the hardships we endured made us strong, endowed us with a capacity for endurance which sustained us to this day, and I'm sure will sustain us in the days ahead." This sentiment was typical of the pioneer mentality, seared into one generation after the next.

TROY'S FATHER, NELSON Luhowy, was born in 1943. When he was three years old, a young sociologist from Toronto named P.J. Giffen spent a few weeks in Rossburn. This is how he described a Saturday night on Main Street:

Throngs of people come and go on the street and from the lighted
cafés and stores. Several vans with steaming horses stand in the
street, and a large number without horses are lined up in front
of the livery stable. The sound of music comes from the large
community hall where a dance is being held. . . . The atmosphere
is one of the rough hustle and bustle of a frontier community.[11]

To Giffen, the most striking thing about Rossburn was "the existence side by side of two social systems." There was, he wrote, an "almost complete cleavage between the two groups at the level of informal interaction." They did not share tables at Rossburn's café, let alone eat dinner in one another's homes. Local dances were widely attended but even under the cover of music and merriment there was little mixing. A man from Rossburn said, "Their men are jealous as anything if one of their girls" crossed the dance floor, which made them "get mad and want to start a fight."[12] Intermarriage was almost unheard of. Giffen could identify only a single couple that had dared.

The fact that the two groups lived apart, one in town and the other in "the bush," increased the social disconnect. "I don't like . . . the way they always stick to themselves," complained a Rossburn resident. "They don't seem to want to mix, no matter how hard you try to make them welcome." Another said, "They still live like pigs with their huge families," "always jabbering away in their own language."[13]

"They just don't live like white people," a Rossburn resident said. Another added, "They're great ones for making bootleg liquor," and a typical wedding was "a real drunken brawl."[14]

These were descriptions of Ukrainians, not Indians. By the 1940s, the fair-skinned immigrants still weren't considered white enough by Anglo-Saxons, and deep antagonism against the newcomers remained.

The business of hiring, buying, and selling did bring the Anglo-Saxons and Ukrainians into regular and close contact, though there was often a stark imbalance in economic power. "As is usual in the case where two antagonistic groups live side by side," Giffen observed, "a modus vivendi has been achieved which enables the community to function with a minimum of overt conflict."[15] Yet the way people treated one another during such "necessary contacts" gave "no clue to the bitterness that would be expressed to the sympathetic listener in private conversation by members of either group."[16]

In response to feeling discriminated against, many Ukrainians wished to live and thrive separately. "English people won't accept us as equals," one Ukrainian said, "so if we lose our culture we are nothing." Another told Giffen, "The British people made it plain they thought they were better than Ukrainians and didn't want us, so [we] said 'to hell with you, we can get on by ourselves.'"[17] Decades later, leaders in Waywayseecappo would strike similar notes when they withdrew their students from Rossburn.

As Giffen surveyed the situation in Rossburn in 1946, he was skeptical that the Ukrainians could resist assimilation over time. American ballroom dance was replacing traditional Ukrainian dances. Daughters were not learning from their mothers the painstaking craftwork that had been practised for generations. "Loss of the ethnic culture appears to be inevitable in the long run," Giffen concluded.[18] "Assimilation is taking place," slowly, surely—just as Clifford Sifton had once hoped.[19]

NELSON LUHOWY GREW up on a farm fifteen kilometres south of Rossburn. He was the fifth boy of six—Clifford Sifton would have approved of Mrs. Luhowy's brood of a half-dozen.

When Nelson was born, the municipality was three-quarters Ukrainian and their proportion was still growing. Anglo-Saxons resented what they called an "invasion."[20] Still, Rossburn itself remained largely Anglo-Saxon, with Ukrainian families like Nelson's mostly living on homesteads outside of town.

Nelson's childhood fit squarely within the pioneer narrative of struggle and overcoming—even more so, perhaps, than most. One day, when Nelson was six years old, he developed a severe headache during a trip with his parents to Rossburn's grocery store. By the time they returned home, he was flushed with fever and dripping sweat. His mother gently placed cold cabbage leaves on his forehead while he lay down. He felt himself go limp, from boy to abandoned marionette. He lost feeling in his arms and legs. A doctor confirmed the worst: Nelson had polio.

Nelson Luhowy *(front row, right)* (Courtesy of Nelson Luhowy)

His parents took him by train to Winnipeg, where he was admitted into a children's hospital. Doctors stuck long needles into his legs and nurses placed hot yellow towels on his arms. He remained in hospital for six months, fearing the periodic jabs from giant needles. He was kept in a big ward with fifty or sixty other children afflicted with polio, each confined to a single bed with white sheets.

When Nelson was eventually discharged, the hospital refused to send him away with crutches. Walking would be hard, the staff said, but he needed to grow stronger. At home, though, a sympathetic older brother could not bear the sight of Nelson wincing and wobbling, so he made him a pair of crutches out of plywood two-by-fours. When the crutches broke a few months later, Nelson pleaded for another pair. This time his brother was less merciful. "No," he told Nelson, "you have to start walking on your own."

At the dinner table, Nelson's parents grumbled about the arrogance of the "English," who looked down on Ukrainians. But the Luhowys were going to make it, whatever it took. Industriousness and thrift were both mantra and necessity. Every child constantly had to earn his keep; even polio was no excuse for idleness. In harvest season, while his brothers baled hay, Nelson made himself useful by driving the tractor, swinging his whole body to change gears with the stick shift. Many of the nearby farms hired Indians to help out during the harvest, but Nelson's parents were able to make do with the help of their sons. Nelson did get a pass from milking the cows, even though the family relied on weekly income from selling cans of cream. If a cow stood up and kicked, he wasn't agile enough to get out of the way.

The only way for the boys to get pocket change of their own was trapping muskrat, mink, and beaver and selling the fur. Nelson was put in charge of the skinning in the barn. Somehow there was never quite as much blood as he expected. After making a few incisions down to the bone, he held the hind legs with one hand and with the other tugged the skin away from his chest. It was like pulling off a sock.

For as many years as he could get away with it, Nelson leaned on his mother when they walked together, arms linked at the elbow. Eventually, mostly thanks to hours of biking around the farm, his legs strengthened enough for him to play sports with his friends. Hockey was his favourite game, and Maurice "Rocket" Richard of the Montreal Canadiens was his favourite player. The Rocket didn't back down from anything. Nelson listened to Habs games on the radio, and on Saturday nights in the 1950s he visited an uncle's house to watch *Hockey Night in Canada* on the black-and-white TV. Though he liked to imagine himself scoring just like the Rocket, he never quite managed to skate. His ankles just weren't strong enough. He settled for playing goalie in boots.

Baseball became Nelson's second-favourite sport, even though he wasn't able to run. When he hit a pitch, another boy would bolt toward first base in his place. It was on the way to a baseball game in the nearby town of Birtle that Nelson saw an Indian residential school for the first time. The large building was visible from the road, just outside the town. His parents told him it was the school for the Indians. As far as Nelson could tell, the Indians seemed to have a comfortable place to live and sleep, and he was sure they were getting a better education than he was. At the time, Nelson's school had only a single room, which all the students in Grades 1 through 8 shared. "When I looked at the big building there, I didn't say: 'Look at that awful place,'" he recalls. "I never thought people were being mistreated. I thought they were lucky to have that big building, to have that yard and garden. It looked state-of-the-art. Compared to their school, mine was nothing." The sight of the residential school actually made Nelson jealous.

Nelson's ideas about Indians developed in the absence of any direct contact with them. He can't remember having a single conversation with an Indian while he was growing up, though he used to see some from time to time near his family's farm. They trapped muskrats in the sloughs along the roads. Indians also came up in conversation at home. On occasions when Nelson neglected his clothing or didn't do a chore, his parents would say, "You're just like an Indian." Because Indians, he was made to understand, were careless, lazy, and reliant on constant handouts—in short, the opposite of hardened, industrious pioneers.

Nelson's dad warned him early on to be wary of Indians. The message stuck after an incident involving one of Nelson's older brothers. One day, an Indian walking down the road bordering the farm asked the brother for help: he was stranded and his car had run out of gas—could he borrow some? He promised he'd pay it back. Nelson's brother agreed to help, but after borrowing the gas, the visitor never returned. *Of course*, scoffed Nelson's father when he found out that his son had been had. "You can't trust Indians."

On Saturdays, the whole family would drive into town to collect their mail, shop for groceries, and visit friends. Businesses stayed open until ten, and Rossburn's Main Street swelled with cars. Nelson's favourite place in town was the movie theatre. A quarter from his parents was enough to buy french fries, a drink, and a movie ticket. In those days, many of the movies had to do with cowboys and Indians. "The Indians lost in every movie," Nelson remembers. "Their Chief would be killed in battle, and we'd get the land. They were always losers." Sometimes Nelson would spot a real-life Indian in the theatre with him. He didn't object but he was surprised. He expected them to be too intimidated to sit with everyone else.

Nelson recalls seeing drunken men from Waywayseecappo staggering along Rossburn's sidewalks. (It wasn't until much later that he came to understand that Indians were drinking in alleys because they weren't allowed to enter the bar.) A few times, Nelson witnessed brawls among them. Whenever fights broke out, groups of passersby gathered to gawk and sneer. Nothing Nelson saw or heard in Rossburn challenged his assumption that Indians belonged on the lowest social rung. Ukrainians might not have been rich, but they took comfort in not being Indian. "The English looked at us the way we looked at Wayway," Nelson says.

NELSON, HIS PARENTS' fifth son, was the first in the family to graduate from high school. His four older brothers had all dropped out to work, but Nelson's physical disability gave him more leeway to stay in school. Then, with encouragement from one of his teachers, he decided to train to become a teacher himself. He only needed one year at teachers' college, which he completed in Winnipeg before starting his teaching career in 1964. The school was in the town of Solsgirth, thirty-five kilometres from Rossburn.

Within a few years, Nelson married a fellow Ukrainian Canadian, Anne Kozun, and, after saving up a down payment, the young couple bought a two-storey house in Rossburn. The only way Nelson and Anne could afford the house was with the help of a twenty-five-year mortgage. Getting the loan from a bank didn't seem like a particularly remarkable thing to Nelson—this was what most people buying houses did. This is what his parents had once done and, before that, what his grandparents Dick and

Dorota Yaskiw had done. It would have surprised Nelson to learn that it was nearly impossible for anyone in Waywayseecappo to get a bank loan, whether to purchase a home or to start a business. This was because banks were not allowed to seize property on reserves, as a consequence of the unique legal status of reserve land, and, therefore, Indians living on reserve had no access to the collateral necessary to obtain loans. As far as Nelson was concerned, "The Ukrainians got 160 acres and that was it." In reality, this land *also* gave them access to capital, which made all the difference between economic progress and stagnation.

To help make ends meet, Anne landed a job at the local credit union. Whereas Nelson had a half-hour drive to work, Anne just had to walk down the street. Their new home was located on Main Street, two blocks down from Pioneer Avenue.

PEOPLE LIKE NELSON Luhowy were raised to see themselves as part of a heroic story, which went something like this: Ukrainian immigrants arrived in Canada without English, without education, without wealth. But they strived and endured and, over time, prospered. Because the Ukrainians escaped poverty and withstood racism, they knew it was possible. "We had to make it on our own," Nelson says. "We struggled, but we all worked. There was never too much work." For a Ukrainian who went from a childhood in a mud house to having grandchildren comfortably in the middle class, it was hard not to conclude that the Ukrainian immigrants earned and deserved their success. And they *had* worked hard. Who could deny it?

The Indians across the Birdtail started poor, just like the Ukrainians, but they stayed poor. "They were given land, too," Nelson says, "but they didn't make anything of it." Looking at this situation, many Ukrainian Canadians concluded: We are doing something right, and the Indians must be doing something wrong. If we succeeded and they failed, surely people were getting what they deserved.

And what was it, exactly, that was holding the Indians back? Laziness, surely! Meanwhile, the federal government was trying so hard, spending so much, decade after decade, to fix Waywayseecappo's problems. And everyone knew the Indians on the reserves were paying lower taxes. They had it easier yet somehow still did worse . . . or at least that's how it looked from across the valley.

This story, built on stereotypes, is the kind of story that explains *and* justifies. For someone like Nelson, the inequality between the two sides of the Birdtail, stark and long-standing, was a fact of life. The Indians' poverty was expected. It was normal. Just being Indian explained the poverty.

Nelson did what most people instinctively do when confronted with a disparity between groups: he blamed individuals. The decades of government policies that had held reserves back were largely invisible to outsiders, while the shortcomings of particular Indians were on clear display. As Ibram Kendi, a scholar of racism, observes, "Racial inequity is a problem of bad policy, not bad people."[21] Yet too often we conclude the opposite. The stereotyping that Ukrainians had themselves endured did not inoculate them against the same kind of thinking. Ironically, their own bitter experiences with racism tended to further distance them from Indians. After all, Ukrainians had overcome their challenges, so why couldn't the Indians?

During Clifford Sifton's tenure and well beyond, the federal government had constricted technology, goods, and people on reserves, with disastrous and enduring results. The effects of these policies compounded over time, year after year, generation by generation. Meanwhile, people in Rossburn largely saw their neighbours as the authors of their own misfortune.

We might call this racism. We might also call it intimate familiarity with only one side of a long and tragic story.

11

FACEOFF

WHEN TROY LUHOWY WAS A TODDLER, HIS FATHER, Nelson, put a hockey stick into his hands and insisted that he treat it henceforth like an appendage. Troy's childhood orbited the town's indoor hockey rink, just a few minutes' walk from his home. This was where Nelson came to fetch him most winter nights before bedtime. Troy loved skating so much that the only way his dad could get his son off the ice was by shutting off all the lights.

Troy's modest size didn't stop him from becoming the star of his Eight and Under team. In one game, as Troy streaked down the ice on yet another breakaway, a man stood up in the stands and shouted, "Kill the little bastard!" During hockey season, Troy's heroics were featured in almost every issue of the *Rossburn Review*. His mom diligently scissored out each story and stored them in a blue binder. On December 10, 1979, the paper reported that Troy's team had managed a 4–4 tie against the nearby town of Shoal Lake: "Scoring for Rossburn was Troy Luhowy, with all 4 goals." The following week, the team beat archnemesis Birtle

11–6. "Scoring for Rossburn was Troy Luhowy, with 10 goals and one assist." And so on, game after game, with the news clippings slowly filling up the two-inch binder.

Troy Luhowy, aged eight (Courtesy of Troy Luhowy)

Troy attended Rossburn Elementary, which had never bothered to change its name to include "Waywayseecappo." The school offered second-language classes in French and Ukrainian, but not Ojibway. By the time Troy started Grade 1, in 1976, the school had been racially integrated for fifteen years. This seemed normal to Troy, whose hockey team included two players from Waywayseecappo.

The one downside to having teammates from the reserve was their erratic attendance. Troy remembers hearing adults asking, in the minutes before games started, "Think the Indians will show?" The main obstacle was that families in Waywayseecappo often didn't own cars, which made reliable transport difficult, and parents from Rossburn rarely offered rides to make up for this. Troy's dad certainly didn't.

At school, Troy's small size left him vulnerable to enemies that he made with his big mouth. Luckily for him, he also became friends with a boy from Waywayseecappo who sat immediately behind him in class. As Troy recalls it, on the very first day of Grade 4, Lionel leaned forward and offered a warm hello. As time went on and they became closer friends, Lionel made a point of checking whether anyone was bothering Troy—if so, he would gladly straighten it out. Lionel had long black hair and wore a jean jacket with studs, a good look for intimidating the people who might give Troy a hard time. This worked well for Troy, except that Lionel was showing up to school only a couple of times a week. During his absences, assignments piled up on his desk. When he did attend class, Troy helped him sort through the stack. "Don't worry about this one," Troy would say. "And this one is just some busywork you don't have to hand in. But try this one, and that one." Still, Lionel ended up further and further behind.

Two girls from Waywayseecappo, Joyce Shingoose and Belina Oudie, also took a liking to Troy. They were both a bit older and, by Grade 5, about a foot taller. One time, Troy bragged a tad too gleefully about some of his hockey heroics, which drew unwanted attention from two bullies from Rossburn—"heavies," as Troy later described them. But then Joyce and Belina materialized, inserting themselves between Troy and his assailants. "Leave him alone," Belina said. And just like that, the heavies backed off. "If someone tried to bother any of the non-Natives and they were our friends," Belina recalls, "Joyce and I would stick up for them. Troy was friendly, easy to get along with, and every once in a while I think I asked him for a bit of help with a math question."

When Troy started school, he hadn't noticed anything particularly different about students from Waywayseecappo. "They weren't the Wayway kids to me," he recalls. "They were just kids." As time passed, though, he noticed that teachers weren't investing quite as much time in students from Waywayseecappo and that more and more of them were being held back to repeat grades. The older students were often "quite a bit bigger than the rest of us," Troy says. Lionel was among them, and Troy could tell how uncomfortable this made him. He recalls Lionel asking him, "What do I have to do to pass?" Troy wasn't sure what to say. He didn't develop any real understanding of why Lionel and other students from Waywayseecappo had such irregular attendance, or what might be holding them back. "I just assumed everyone had a house like mine," he says. "I assumed they all had parents like I did, a mom and dad who would help with schoolwork."

Troy had more contact with students from Waywayseecappo than most Rossburn kids had, but he rarely saw them outside of school and hockey. He never once visited the home of a friend on the reserve, which made it easier for him to maintain his assumptions. "I never said, 'Hey, you want to come over?' and they didn't say, 'Hey, do you want to come over?'" Troy recalls. "Back then, nobody really did that." Besides, Troy's dad would not have allowed it. Nelson pictured his only child going into a decrepit house on the reserve, creeping with mice and who knows what diseases, and being fed a sandwich with mouldy bread—no way.

In the summer of 1982, Waywayseecappo withdrew all its students from Rossburn. When Troy returned to start Grade 6 after the summer vacation, Joyce, Belina, and Lionel were gone, along with the rest of the students from the reserve. For Troy, the change was most obvious during recess. "I didn't have my muscle anymore," he recalls, "so I learned pretty quickly to keep my mouth shut." The era of integration with Waywayseecappo had come to an abrupt end.

Troy lost touch with friends from Waywayseecappo—the relationships were too shallow to survive separation. Still, he kept seeing people from Waywayseecappo in town. The reserve had relatively few shops of its own and did not permit the sale of alcohol, so people came to Rossburn for restaurants, shopping, and drinking. Troy could tell the hotel bar was busy when he spotted unaccompanied children from Waywayseecappo hanging around nearby, waiting for adults to take them home. The racial dynamic that he witnessed in town was similar to what his father had seen a generation earlier.

Every now and then, Troy would run into a former classmate from the reserve, such as the time he was bicycling past the hotel and noticed a dark-haired boy named Derek sitting in a parked car. The window was down. Derek looked bored. Troy slowed down and waved.

"Hi, Troy," Derek said.

"Hi, Derek," Troy replied, before pedalling away.

Neither had anything more to say.

★ ★ ★

HOCKEY WAS THE axis of Troy's adolescence. He was a solid student, but he only really tested his limits on the ice. He relished being the smaller guy who worked harder. More often than not, he was chosen to be team captain. Coaches trusted him during crunch time, to nurse leads or kill penalties. Troy spent a lot of time in the "dirtier" areas on the ice, places that more delicate and sane players avoided, like the corners, where he charged in heedlessly to fetch pucks, his opponents trailing by inches, or near the net, where he wormed and slashed to hold his ground against thicker defencemen. Troy never topped 160 pounds in high school, and his game relied to a worrisome degree on his kamikaze certainty that he was the kinetic equal of two-hundred-pound opponents.

When Troy was fifteen years old, he was recruited by Rossburn's adult hockey team, which travelled around the province for games. His job was to prolong the glory days of beer-bellied veterans in their thirties and forties. That year, the Rossburn team made it to the league finals, a best-of-seven series. The opposing team was from the Sioux Valley reserve, an hour's drive south of Rossburn. One game in particular stands out in Troy's memory. It was late in the series, on neutral territory, and featured four or five hundred fans in the stands—two-thirds Native, one-third white, many drunk. Bad blood had been brewing between the teams from the start of the series.

A behemoth defenceman named Frank was the most feared player on the Sioux Valley team. He was so big that he didn't even bother with shoulder pads. During warm-ups, Frank skated over to one of Troy's teammates, Kevin, who was stretching on the ice. Frank pointed his stick at Kevin's head and said, "I'm going to tear out your fucking eyeballs tonight." Kevin kept stretching for a few more moments, thinking it over, and then he returned to the locker room to take off his uniform. He had decided to sit out the game. "You know," he said to his teammates, "this is senior hockey. It's just not worth it."

Rossburn's coach then had the brilliant idea of pairing Troy with Frank during the game, an assignment Troy embraced. He had to wear a full face mask because he was a minor—as far as he was concerned, this made him invincible.

At faceoff, Troy lined up opposite Frank and looked over at a man more than twice his age. Frank was chewing gum. Sweat dripped off his stubbly chin, and his jersey tightened over the beginnings of a gut. Frank glared back at fresh-faced Troy, with his full mask, and stopped chewing.

"Get out of your cage, Tweety Bird!" Frank said.

"Fuck you, Indian!" Troy replied.

Troy had known Frank's name, but in that moment he reached for a cruder instrument. "I wasn't thinking," he says, decades later. "It just came out. At the time, that's what I heard in the dressing room, that's what I heard on the bench—'fucking Indians.' The older guys, they didn't say, 'You shouldn't be saying stuff like that.' More like: 'Right on, give it to them!' My dad was no different. I heard what he and others were yelling in the stands."

Rossburn went on to lose the game. In the stands, heated arguments broke out along racial lines. It seemed like worse was still to come, so someone decided to call the police. Troy was taken aback when two squads of RCMP officers entered the locker room to escort his team out of the arena. They took the fire exit, just in case the national pastime degenerated into something more akin to civil war.

The next year, while Troy was in Grade 11, he joined a regional team with players his own age in the Manitoba Midget "AAA" Hockey League. Troy was the team's second-highest scorer that season, with twenty-nine goals and thirty-six assists. The team was called the Yellowhead Chiefs, and its logo was a ripoff from the Chicago Blackhawks: a stereotypical Indian in profile, with feathers in his hair.

There was not a single Native player on the team.

TROY SUSPECTED HE wouldn't make it as a pro hockey player but he kept striving anyway. He proved good enough on the ice and clever enough in the classroom to get offered an athletic scholarship to attend Brown University, an Ivy League school in the United States. It wasn't the NHL, but it was still a ticket to a wider world. Unfortunately for Troy, in a game he played shortly after receiving the offer from Brown, his right skate got stuck in a rut at precisely the wrong split second, long enough for a player from the opposing team to collide with him. Troy heard ligaments in his knee pop. It sounded like wet wood in a fire.

Troy told Brown's hockey coach about the injury but insisted that he could recover in time to play for the university. He completed every step of the recommended rehab and counted the days until he could play again. In his first game back, nine months and two days after his injury, he wore a knee brace, just in case. Back on the ice, he felt like he had wings again. Then, just a few shifts in, an opposing player blindsided Troy. He felt the exact same ligaments snap.

Disconsolate, he called Brown's hockey coach and said, "It happened again. I tore everything again." Troy's competitive hockey career was over, along with any dreams of the Ivy League. There would be no more news clippings for his mom's blue binder.

In time, Troy settled on a new plan. After a miserable summer laying highway asphalt, he decided to become a teacher, just like his dad. He studied physical education at the University of Manitoba in Winnipeg, then moved to Brandon in the fall of 1994 to study for his teacher's certification at Brandon University.

DURING TROY'S FIRST autumn in Brandon, Halloween fell on a Sunday. Troy started the night at a house party, drinking Coors Light with a group of classmates. Normally they would have gone to a bar, but bars were closed on Sundays. Someone suggested a trip to "the old Indian school," the closest thing Brandon had to a haunted house. Troy and a few others had heard that students had died out there a long time ago, but no one knew how or why. "If there are any ghosts," one of Troy's friends said, half-drunk, half-joking, "this is, like, the perfect time to check it out." *Yeah,* Troy thought, *let's do it.*

They piled into two trucks and drove west from the city, along Grand Valley Road, and before long they spotted the silhouette of the abandoned school at the top of a hill. It looked just as spooky as they had hoped. The trucks followed a bumpy gravel driveway that led to the rear of the main building. They arrived around midnight, with a generous slice of moon overhead.

Troy and his companions headed for the main entrance. They were far from the first visitors to the derelict school, which was surrounded by broken beer bottles. Previous revellers had long since kicked down the flimsy plywood that had once sealed off the entrance. Troy ambled in with a can of beer in his right hand and a second can bulging in his jacket pocket.

Inside, bits of plaster and chunks of concrete littered the floor. Each step crunched. "There was a lot of damage in there, a lot of smashed walls, a lot of smashed windows," Troy recalls. Moonlight illuminated parts of the building, but otherwise he and his friends found their way using lighters, the flames casting dancing shadows. As they explored, some of the guys started telling scary stories. "I heard someone died in *this* room," one said, eyeing a small, windowless chamber. "And the basement, that's where they put the morgue. That's where they kept the dead bodies."

The group decided to split up and then try to scare each other. Troy headed off alone, squinting as he slowly picked his way through the debris. He paused when he found a room with a gaping hole in the wall, which seemed like a perfect place to stage an ambush. He picked up a piece of concrete from the ground and waited, sipping his beer. When he finally heard a few of his friends approaching, he selected just the right moment to toss his projectile toward them through the hole. The concrete landed with a crash, and his friends yelped like puppies.

The rooms and hallways Troy wandered that night were the same rooms and hallways where Principal Strapp locked Clifford Shepherd without clothes, where Jim Cote plotted his escape, where Linda Jandrew lined up without her shoes. To Troy, though, it was just a creepy old building, a place that time and everyone else had forgotten. With the past muted, all he heard was the crunching underfoot and the occasional screams and peals of laughter when one friend sprung out and shouted, "Boo!"

Troy cannot recall the topic of residential schools ever coming up during the two years he spent at Brandon University's teachers' college. The year he graduated, 1996, was the same year that the last Indian residential school in Canada closed.

12

BLOODVEIN

IN THE FALL OF 1999, TROY'S FIRST FULL-TIME TEACHING job brought him to the Bloodvein First Nation reserve, in northern Manitoba. He had never heard of the place. "It's only 236 kilometres from Winnipeg!" the man recruiting Troy exclaimed. "There are lots of young teachers up here. It's good!" Troy would fill the shoes of a gym teacher who was leaving partway through the school year. He planned on getting some experience on a reserve up north, as many new teachers did, then moving on to a "normal" job in a provincial public school.

The Bloodvein reserve spans sixteen square kilometres, but most of its roughly one thousand inhabitants live near the shore of the mighty Bloodvein River, which flows into Lake Winnipeg. The river was reportedly named by Christian missionaries in the aftermath of a battle between Ojibway bands in the eighteenth century, when gore stained the water pink. Troy didn't hear that story until later, so at first he thought the name came from the crimson streaks on the stones that lined the riverbanks. The bright lines looked like arteries.

In warmer months, the trip to the reserve required a ferry or an airplane to cross Lake Winnipeg.[1] Since Troy was arriving in early March, though, he was told he could make it all the way in his truck, as long as he was willing to brave a stretch of winter road over the frozen lake. On his drive in, he was distressed to find himself going through occasional patches of slush. He wondered, *What the hell am I doing here?*

Like the other teachers who were not from the community, Troy lived in a compound of apartments called the teacherage, which, as a bastion of relative affluence, was the target of frequent break-ins. The windows were smashed often enough by thieves that the teachers eventually boarded them up with plywood and sacrificed sunlight for safety. The lock on Troy's door made him think of a bank safe. It took a forceful heave of an arm to move the heavy steel bolt, which turned with a thunk.

Most teachers didn't last long in Bloodvein. Some were there only a few months, and almost nobody stayed more than a few years. They found the reserve too remote, the work too hard, the pay too low. And there were always the ones who came thinking that by teaching on a reserve they were going to save the world. Troy got to know the type. They didn't last either. "They gave it their all for two months, then they left," he says. "They couldn't handle the place. They got frustrated. They thought they weren't making a difference. They saw no hope for the kids, basically."

As far as Troy was concerned, though, teaching gym was a blast. His abiding mission was to keep all his students engaged for the entire class. Nothing irked Troy like a kid who never got off the bench. But ordering a student to just get out there and play was not his style. Instead, he invented games that involved everyone, including those who didn't like sports. Since most of his students spoke Ojibway as their first language, he looked for fun ways to build their English vocabulary. To win a game, a team might have to bounce a ball, score a basket, and complete ten jumping jacks, but also spell a challenging word, like "December," or write down, say, two rules of soccer. "The kids who could read well would be embraced because each team needed them, too," Troy says. "Maybe they couldn't kick a ball, but they could spell." He estimates that three-quarters of his Grade 7 students could not compose full grammatical sentences in English.

Sometimes Troy insisted that a goal would not count unless a team member solved a multiplication problem. On a chalkboard along the wall, he would write out something like "$5 \times 6 = ?$" That might stump half the Grade 7 class, Troy recalls. Other times, he opted for an impressive-looking subtraction, something like "$12,687,249 - 6 = ?$" "One of those would just blow them away," he says. No more than a few could figure it out. Troy was aware that this was not normal, this was not good, but he tried not to dwell on it.

Troy was facing the same challenges as the other teachers, of course. Students who arrived at school with empty stomachs were irritable. Those without running water at home were seldom clean. Over time, Troy was astonished to learn how many children from the community were living with foster parents. "But I didn't feel sorry for the kids or anything," he recalls. "They were just kids. A lot of them, when you see what they have going on in their families and at home, you're amazed by how resilient they are."

Troy's students especially appreciated that he would come back to the school at night to open up the gym for a few hours, just to give them an indoor space to play in. It wasn't long before the students started calling him "Coach" instead of "Mr. Luhowy." That's when he knew he was in.

Within a few months of his arrival, Troy received an invitation from community members to go moose hunting. Troy knew a little about shooting but nothing about hunting. "You'll learn," people told him. After a few hours of trekking on foot into the bush, Troy spotted a moose within firing range. He aimed his rifle at the massive animal. "I can get him," he said excitedly. "Wait," his companions urged. "Not yet."

But Troy had a clear shot, so he pulled the trigger. The butt of the rifle slammed into his shoulder. Up ahead, the moose recoiled, shuddered for two heartbeats, and collapsed with a wet thud. Troy's companions scolded him. "Good luck carrying that out by yourself," they said. The plan, which everyone but Troy had understood, had been to kill a moose closer to the river, so the dead animal could be floated home. Instead, Troy was forced to carry the awful weight of the moose's severed, bloody haunches. "I couldn't carry it all, but they made me carry the most," he recalls. "So I learned."

BACK IN ROSSBURN, Nelson officially retired in 2001, two years after Troy moved to Bloodvein. He was fifty-eight years old and had been teaching in provincial public schools for almost four decades. That summer, Waywayseecappo happened to be looking for an instructor to teach mature students working toward their high school diplomas. Nelson received an unexpected call: Would he consider teaching in Waywayseecappo for a few months? "It was the last thing in the world I figured I'd do," he recalls. But his wife was still working full-time as a bank teller, and he didn't have anything else to keep himself busy. After checking whether taking the job would affect his pension (it would not), he decided he had no excuse. He was willing to give it a try.

Classes were held at the old hockey rink that had been converted into a school in 1982. (A new kindergarten to Grade 8 school, the one Maureen Twovoice would later attend, was built in 1992.) The building was run down, Nelson recalls, with peeling plaster and broken urinals. None of this really bothered him, although he did struggle with the staircase he had to walk up every day to get to his classroom. He used a cane and leaned heavily on the railing. "Once I got up there," Nelson says, "I didn't go down until the end of the day."

At this point, Nelson knew nothing about treaties, nor why reserves existed. He had never heard about anything bad happening at Indian residential schools, which he still regarded as superior to the schools he had attended as a child. Because of where he had taught during his thirty-eight years in the provincial school system, he'd had only a handful of Native students, all of them living with white adoptive families. After spending virtually his entire life within a few kilometres of a reserve, Nelson had never developed a real friendship with an Indigenous person. Of course, this had not prevented him from forming judgments based on the little he had seen and heard. His whole life, he'd been hearing family and friends saying things like "they're not paying taxes," "they're on welfare," "their houses are built for them."

Nelson wasn't quite sure what to expect in his new job, but he arrived with his guard up and his expectations low. Some of his students would be fresh out of prison, sent to his classroom by court order. Others would be grandparents who were older than he was. But since this was a paying job, and a job he had agreed to do, he resolved to teach to the best of his ability. Going in, Nelson says, "I didn't know if I could trust them. Not that I had any experience—I never had anything to do with them."

Before long, one student in particular came to stand out.

Her name was Elizabeth Shingoose, and she went by Tizz. When Nelson met her, she was in her early thirties. Nelson later learned that she had dropped out of high school after getting pregnant when she was in Grade 10. On Nelson's route to work, he sometimes noticed Tizz walking up a steep hill that led to the school. Even as fall turned to winter, with snow piling up deeper and deeper at the side of the road, Tizz kept walking to school up that hill and always showed up on time. One week, she got sick with a bad cold, but that didn't stop her from coming to class. She arrived wearing a face mask, to protect others from getting sick. Nelson was impressed.

Tizz also happened to be exceptionally bright. When Nelson asked a question of the class, she was usually the first to volunteer an answer. She had grown up mostly in the city of Brandon and attended provincial public schools. She once joked to her classmates that she knew all the answers because "I didn't go to the Wayway school."

"Well," another student shot back, "if you're so smart, how come you never graduated?"

Tizz paused, searching for the right comeback. "Because I fell in love!"

Sometimes Nelson asked Tizz to translate words into Ojibway for the benefit of the class. He joked, "Tizz, those aren't swear words, are they?" She laughed and said, "I wouldn't do that to you, Mr. Luhowy."

Nelson had been apprehensive when he started the job, but it wasn't long before that feeling "went away completely," he recalls. "They were so dedicated. They wanted to learn. Before I would have said, 'they didn't want to work.'"

Nelson was getting occasional glimpses into the lives of his students, often from reading personal essays he assigned for homework. "One wrote about looking forward to the night when she could have a warm shower and sleep in clean sheets," he says. "Quite a few wrote about growing up with kokum. I didn't even know what a kokum was—eventually I figured out they were talking about a grandmother, because their parents had been out of action."

He noticed that many of his students were showing up to class hungry, or kept wearing the same jacket even as the seasons changed. Some couldn't afford to pitch in five dollars a month toward a shared coffee supply. If a student broke or misplaced their glasses, it was usually months before they managed to get a new pair. "In the meantime," Nelson says, "the only way they could read was by putting the paper two inches from their face."

At lunchtime, Nelson ate at his desk, and he liked to chat with students who came by to say hello. Bit by bit, these conversations helped him gain a better understanding of what it took for them just to attend classes. "There are so many issues that you don't realize unless you are there," Nelson says. "No food, no job, no car, no gas for the car, family issues, medical issues. It takes a lot of courage on their part to keep going and be successful. I could see them struggling, but they try and try."

THE JANITOR OF Bloodvein's school, Leslie, took a special liking to Troy. Leslie had grown up on the reserve and had lived there most of his life. It wasn't long before he introduced Troy to mackerel fishing along the Bloodvein River, which they explored together on Leslie's sixteen-foot boat. He taught Troy how to navigate the powerful currents by reading subtle wrinkles on the water's surface. Leslie had enormous, callused hands, and Troy marvelled at how deftly he tied and baited hooks.

Pictographs along the Bloodvein River (Courtesy of Hidehiro Otake)

Leslie spoke to Troy in Ojibway, teaching him one word at a time. He would point at objects or animals they could see from the boat. "*Ziibi.*" River. "*Migizi.*" Bald eagle. "*Makwa.*" Bear. In time, Troy's Ojibway outpaced his limited Ukrainian. He was feeling a deep need to adapt himself to his surroundings, in a way he never had before.

Mostly Leslie and Troy fished in silence, but every now and then Leslie would ask Troy a question.

"*Troy, aandi ezhaayan?*" ("Troy, where are you going?")

"Uh, I'm going fishing."

"No . . . I mean, where are you going? In life?"

"I don't know," a puzzled Troy said. "I'm here."

Leslie gave him a severe look. "I'm trying to teach you something here, Troy. Think about it. You have to know where you're headed."

Troy didn't have much of a plan, really. He had already been in Bloodvein far longer than most teachers and hadn't made any plans to leave. He had fallen in love with a redhead from Brandon named Michelle, whom he had gotten to know during weekends away from the reserve, and he had managed to persuade her to try living with him in Bloodvein ("It's only 236 kilometres from Winnipeg!" he found himself exclaiming.) "I think Leslie knew I wasn't going to be in Bloodvein forever," Troy says. "I think he had seen a lot of teachers go through there. I think his point was, 'As much as you like it, you're not from Bloodvein, you're far from your family.'" And there were practical matters, too—Troy wouldn't be able to have his own house in Bloodvein, since he wasn't a member of the First Nation. "I don't think he wanted me to get out of there. He just wanted me to think about what I would do, where I would be, later on."

ONE DAY, NELSON noticed that Tizz wasn't her usual gregarious self. She was quiet, brooding. Nelson invited her over to his desk during the lunch break and asked her what was wrong. "I'm pregnant," Tizz said. "And I'm not sure if I can keep coming to class."

Tizz was starting to put on weight from the pregnancy, and the walk to the school was becoming too demanding. She also had two other children to look after.

"I don't see you as a quitter," Nelson said.

"How can you tell?" Tizz asked.

"It's just the personality that comes out of you, your determination to get things done," Nelson told her. "How about I make a plan to pick you up and drive you to school?" It wasn't much of a detour from his regular route, and he recalled his own dad or brothers driving him to school every day. (It wasn't until later that he thought about all the times Troy's teammates from Waywayseecappo missed games because no one was willing to pick them up.)

Tizz said a ride would make a big difference, actually. She offered to pay Nelson him for the trouble, but he rejected the offer. "I don't want your money," he said. "I want you to graduate."

And so Nelson started picking up Tizz every morning at 8:45 a.m. sharp. This arrangement continued for months, until shortly before Tizz gave birth to a baby girl in a hospital in Brandon. By that time, she had reluctantly reached the conclusion that she wouldn't be able to keep attending school while she cared for her newborn.

Nelson decided to pay Tizz a visit in the hospital. He had caught wind of her plan to put her studies on hold and wanted to see how she was doing. As Tizz recalls it, when Nelson arrived unannounced in her hospital room, she was lying on the bed, cradling her daughter in her arms. Nelson looked at the baby and smiled. "Such a cute little sweetheart," he said. Still smiling, he looked at Tizz and deadpanned, "So, I hear you're going to quit!"

They both allowed themselves a laugh. Then Tizz admitted that, yes, she had real doubts about whether she could carry on with school. Nelson said, "Well, I'm sure we can work something out." He suggested that he could arrange a small room adjacent to the classroom with a computer, space for a cradle, and enough privacy for her to feel comfortable breastfeeding.

Tizz was surprised—shocked, really. She had never had a teacher support and encourage her like this. Her eyes filled with tears. "Okay," she said. "When I'm out of hospital, I'll come talk to you. I'm going to keep going."

About five months after Tizz returned to class, she received her high school diploma. Nelson arranged for a special graduation cap to be made for her daughter, complete with its own little tassel.

Nelson, flicking Tizz's tassel for good luck (Courtesy of Elizabeth Shingoose)

After the ceremony, Tizz gave Nelson a hug. "I thanked him for not giving up on me," she recalls, "and for not letting me give up on myself." Now it was Nelson's turn to cry.

Nelson had been hired to teach in Waywayseecappo for one year, but he decided to stick around. "People were taking courses to help get a job, to better themselves," he recalls. "Many were there to encourage their children or grandchildren, to show that education was important. It was a surprise to me. Before, I didn't know they cared so much. Their dedication made me want to try harder, too. It made me feel different toward them. I thought, if they can learn, maybe I can learn."

★ ★ ★

THE SPRING OF 2006, Troy and Michelle made plans to leave Bloodvein. Troy had taught there for seven years, far longer than outsiders usually stayed. The community held a ceremony to thank him for all his work, though Troy didn't think he had done anything special. "I just kept coming back," he says. If it weren't for falling in love with Michelle, he probably would have stayed longer. But now they wanted to start a family, and being closer to home would make that easier. Troy had heard about a job teaching gym in Waywayseecappo and applied. He got the job, at least partly because of the respect his dad had earned as a teacher there. Soon, both father and son would be teaching in Waywayseecappo.

At the end of the school year in Bloodvein, the time came to say goodbye. As Troy packed up his things, one of his students came by to ask: "Coach, is it true you're not coming back next year?" Before long, a group of current and former students assembled to help carry boxes to his truck. "Are you going to visit?" one asked. "Yeah, yeah, I'll come back," Troy said. He meant it, but he also wasn't sure what else to say.

Troy and Michelle drove to the main dock, where they would catch the ferry that could accommodate their car on its deck. A group of friends and students had gathered to send them off, Leslie among them. He shook Troy's hand, then they hugged. "I'll see you again," Troy said. "Yeah," Leslie replied, "I'll see you when you visit."

As the ferry left the shore, Troy waved to all those who had come to say farewell. He would miss them.

He regrets not returning since.

13

"THE WAY IT WORKS"

W HEN TROY LUHOWY BECAME WAYWAYSEECAPPO'S
gym teacher, in 2006, he taught every grade, from
kindergarten all the way to Grade 8. He was probably the only teacher who knew the name of every single student
in the school. Most of his classes had more than thirty students.
Some had as many as thirty-five. On the worst days, teaching felt
like crowd control, but even then Troy liked his job. He got to
play with kids all day.

Perhaps a third of Troy's students had been required to repeat
grades; a lot of Grade 7 or 8 students were old enough to be
in Grade 9 or 10. The wide age range in classes posed a challenge for the school's teachers, but it didn't take long for Troy to
spot an opportunity. As he saw it, students with a few extra years
of puberty were poised to become dominant athletes. Though
reserve schools were not officially part of the regular sports
leagues for provincial schools, Troy threw his considerable energy
into organizing matches and joining tournaments in towns near
and far.

For starters, he stacked a middle school soccer team with a lineup of "big boys," as he called them. They didn't have cleats or shin pads—neither the school nor their families could afford them—but they kept winning anyway. The Waywayseecappo team was so dominant, in fact, that it became hard for Troy to find anyone willing to play goalie. On this superteam, the goalie was little more than a spectator without a seat. In preparation for one regional tournament, Troy hoped to recruit a Waywayseecappo student named Darwin, a cherubic boy of questionable athletic ability. "Okay, boys," Troy told the team, "you have to be really nice to Darwin. We need him." Of course, nothing was to be said to Darwin about the position he would play. "Let's get him on the bus," Troy advised. "Don't say anything about goalie until we start rolling." Everything went according to plan: Darwin signed up to join the team. Then, safely aboard and en route to the tournament, Darwin took a long look at the hulks surrounding him and, the realization finally dawning on him, said, "I'm going to end up in net, won't I?"

During the entire tournament, Darwin didn't allow any goals. It helped that he didn't face a single shot.

Troy developed a knack for producing champions. Once, he spotted a Grade 8 student named Everett who had what it took to become a track-and-field star. The only real barrier to glory was Everett's choppy school attendance. Before a competition, Troy would remind him, "Everett, no matter how late you get to bed, or whatever, you're coming to this race. No matter what!" If Everett still didn't show up on time, Troy would commandeer the school van and go to his house to get him.

In one track-and-field competition for their provincial school division, Troy signed Everett up for every possible event: 100 metres, 200 metres, 400 metres, 1500 metres, long jump, high jump—you name it. By the end of the meet, Everett was pea-cocking for photographs, his chest festooned with blue first-place ribbons. Troy looked on, grinning as widely as Everett.

"I wanted kids that maybe weren't the best students to have something they could excel at," Troy says. "My goal was to give them a little bit of a boost. It was also for all the students in Wayway, to make them feel, 'We can do this, we're as good as the other schools.'"

The competition was less thrilled, and Troy got the feeling that other schools took a special dislike to losing to Waywayseecappo. The following year, the provincial schools started insisting on new age limits for athletic competitions, and the brief era of Troy's superstars came to a close.

TROY ENJOYED TEACHING in Waywayseecappo, just as he had in Bloodvein, but he wasn't particularly surprised when col-leagues didn't stick around. Of twenty or so teachers on staff, a third to half left every year. A central reason was money: Waywayseecappo's teachers received far less than their peers in nearby provincial schools—as much as $20,000 less, depending on seniority. On top of that, the teachers in Waywayseecappo had to deal with packed classrooms and an especially large share of students with special needs of one sort or another. During one particularly bad year, a Grade 4 class cycled through four separate teachers.

A general lack of resources also made teaching at Wayway-seecappo challenging. When Troy started, the school had long since given up on providing textbooks to each student. Instead, teachers handed out photocopies or just used overhead projectors. There was also a regular shortage of basics like pens, pencils, crayons, glue, and markers—items the school tried to provide because so many parents couldn't afford them. Veteran teachers knew that the week before the school year started was the best time to visit the supply room and stock up; supplies usually ran out well before the end of the year. On at least one occasion, the principal called a staff meeting to remind teachers to take only what they absolutely needed from the supply room. According to Jim Cote's niece, Marellia Cote, who had grown up in Waywayseecappo and been working at the school since 1997, the most committed teachers came to accept that paying for some basic materials was part of the job.

Recruiting qualified staff to Waywayseecappo was an annual nightmare, and the school often had no choice but to hire less-than-stellar candidates. The school mostly hired inexperienced teachers fresh out of university or retired provincial school teachers looking for extra income. The school would commonly find itself without a full roster of qualified teachers in the last week of August, right before classes started. "By that time, you're really scraping the bottom of the barrel," a senior administrator recalls. If a teacher didn't have a job by then, there was often a good reason for their unemployment.

The truth is, Troy didn't plan on sticking around long term either. After two years in Waywayseecappo, he applied for a position at Rossburn High School, which was looking for someone to teach physical education and basic computer programming. The job paid $12,000 more than what he made on the reserve. Troy and Michelle had just welcomed their first child and they were planning on a second. Their two-bedroom mobile home was only sixteen feet wide. With the extra money, they could find a bigger place. The only hitch was that Troy knew approximately nothing about computer programming, so he wasn't shocked when he didn't get called back. But he knew there would be more openings. It was just a matter of time.

DURING TROY'S FIRST four years teaching in Waywayseecappo, the school churned through three principals. The third one didn't even last a summer: she quit without notice or explanation the day before classes were set to begin in September 2010. That left the school even more desperate than usual. Still, Troy was surprised to be asked to take the reins as principal. His first thought was: *I like the gym, leave me alone.* On reflection, though, he decided to give it his best shot. He was pretty sure he could do no worse than the previous principal. Plus, there were ten new teachers that year. "I figured they wouldn't really be able to tell if I didn't know what the hell I was doing," he says.

His first order of business as principal was to take a close look at the school's budget. Jackie McKee, the school's no-nonsense finance director, walked him through a series of grim spreadsheets. She told him money was so tight that the school was chronically late on its electricity bill.

"Jackie," Troy said, "how are we supposed to make this work?"

"We have to make it work. This is what we get."

Jackie explained that Waywayseecappo's band council received about $7,300 per student from the federal government to cover education expenses. By comparison, she told him, the public school in Rossburn, just down the road, received about $10,500 per student from the Manitoba government—over 40 percent more.

"That's crazy," Troy said.

"Well, that's the way it is."

"But it makes no sense."

"That's how it works, Troy. We do the best we can."

By this time, Troy had been working at reserve schools for more than a decade. He knew that these schools were funded by the federal government and that regular public schools were funded by provincial governments. He also knew that he had always been paid less than his counterparts in provincial public schools, even though many people in Rossburn assumed he was paid more. But this was the first time it had really dawned on him that, year after year, reserve schools across the country were receiving far less money than provincial schools. "They were all getting funded like that," Troy says. "I had been in First Nations education for a long time, ten years, and I had no clue. I was naive."

Then Jackie explained another crucial, unpleasant fact about students from Waywayseecappo who were attending school off reserve. Waywayseecappo's school went up only to Grade 8, so students had to leave the reserve for high school. When a student like Maureen Twovoice crossed the Birdtail to attend Grade 9 in Rossburn, the federal government continued to provide $7,300 to the Waywayseecappo band council to cover the cost of educating that student. But—and here was the rub—the Rossburn school board charged Waywayseecappo $10,500, the annual cost of educating the student in its provincial school. The $3,200 difference had to come from somewhere, and Waywayseecappo had no choice but to siphon funding from its own school. Even though fewer than a quarter of Waywayseecappo's students were studying in provincial high schools in Rossburn and nearby Russell, those students were consuming more than a third of Waywayseecappo's overall education budget. So the amount of money actually available to spend on a student at the reserve school was not even the comparatively low $7,300, but closer to $6,300.

This diversion of resources from on-reserve education budgets to provincial schools was a common problem. In Ontario, according to an analysis by the federal parliamentary budget officer, federal funding for the education of students living on reserves increased by 1 percent per year between 2004 and 2015, but virtually all of that funding increase went toward paying provincial school tuition for students studying off reserve.[1] In other words, overall funding was modestly increasing, but support for schools on reserves was stagnant.

After his conversation with Jackie, Troy retreated to his office, where he sat in stunned silence. He pulled out a cheap solar calculator and subtracted 7,300 from 10,500, then multiplied that by 314, which was how many students he had in kindergarten through Grade 8. *Holy shit,* he thought, *that's a lot of money—* more than a million dollars. He could now see why the teachers were underpaid, why the classes were so big, why there never seemed to be enough crayons by April. He also knew what most people in Rossburn thought, which was that Waywayseecappo was receiving plenty of money from the federal government, as usual, but just wasn't using it right. Troy looked at his calculator again. It made no sense to him. If he tried to explain this back in town, he thought, people wouldn't believe him.

"There are so many people who automatically think that those reserve kids get more but never learn," Troy says. "People just don't know. They don't get it." And neither, for a long time, had Troy. "I just fit in with that perspective that they have all this money but they were blowing it. But they didn't, and they never did."

During Troy's drive home, down and up the valley, he thought of his son Reid, who would soon start Grade 1 in Rossburn. *What if Reid was the one being sent to a school that always got less?*

Over dinner with Michelle, Troy shared what he had learned that day. He said, "We're cheating these kids." He did not expect to play some heroic role in fixing the problem, but promised himself to do the best he could.

A few months later, Troy received the results of a reading test that had been given to Waywayseecappo's students. Of thirty students in Grade 4, only one was reading at grade level. In Grades 1, 2 and 3, none were.

Of course, people in Waywayseecappo with a knowledge of history found all of this less surprising than Troy did. In an interview with the *Winnipeg Free Press*, community Elder Bryan Cloud said, "Apartheid is alive and well in Canada."[2]

PART IV

PARTNERSHIP

14

"STARK AND OBVIOUS"

MAUREEN TWOVOICE STARTED HER DAILY COMMUTE across the Birdtail River in 2006, the same year Troy began teaching in Waywayseecappo. Maureen would later say of her time attending high school in Rossburn, "Damn, it was so hard."

By the time students from Waywayseecappo started Grade 9 in Rossburn, most were years behind the provincial curriculum. Many were stuck at what educators call a "frustrational reading level," which means: you are so far behind, and it is so obvious, that you'd rather slam your desk than turn the page. The principal at the time, Tammy McCullough, saw how many students from Waywayseecappo struggled to adapt to the "big shocker" of transitioning to a provincial high school. "I cared about all my students," McCullough says, "and it's heartbreaking to see where there's that gap. The opportunities just hadn't been there for them. It's sad. They just get gobbled up."

McCullough had been Maureen's Grade 5 teacher on the reserve before she accepted a teaching job in Rossburn, in part

233

because the move bumped up her salary by $11,000. Now, as principal, McCullough watched her former star pupil struggle. Maureen "had probably fallen behind a bit every year," she says. "Her spark was still in her, but it was not quite as bright."

In class, Maureen felt lost, disoriented. Beyond the challenge of schoolwork, she had to adapt to classrooms where most students weren't Indigenous and all her teachers were white. "I felt like there were less people on my side if anything were to happen," she says. In the beginning, math class was the only place where she ever raised her hand to ask a question, partly because math class was where she had the most friends from Waywayseecappo.

After years of hearing her mom tell dispiriting stories about attending school in Rossburn, Maureen came in expecting similar treatment. "It was almost like the negative experiences my mother had were mine too," she says. "I had this standoffish behaviour. If something was bothering me, I would just shut down instead of saying anything."

Still, she tried her best to focus on schoolwork. She realized how close she had come to dropping out altogether the year before, and she was not going to waste her second chance. "When I got the opportunity to get to Grade 9, there was no way I was messing it up," she says. "I wasn't interested in high school drama or making friends. I was just there to catch up and get out of there."

To her surprise, she started noticing that a number of her teachers seemed genuinely to care about her. Bit by bit, she warmed to them, and as the months went by she developed a habit of going to see these teachers after class. By the end of Grade 9, she was regularly raising her hand in all her classes.

Maureen caught up, and then she pulled ahead. In Grade 10, she made the honour roll. In report cards, her English teacher praised her as "an exceptional student showing determination and intelligence." Her science teacher described her as "a wonderful, dedicated and conscientious student." Her math teacher said she was "a joy to have in class." She hadn't received report cards like this in years.

During this time, Maureen didn't make a single close friend from Rossburn. She never endured racist taunts as her mother had, but there was always a social barrier that kept students from Rossburn and Waywayseecappo apart. "We exchanged words here and there, but not to create friendship," Maureen says. Bob Ploshynsky, the principal who succeeded Tammy McCullough, recalls that "prejudice was palpable in the building." Maureen tried not to dwell on it.

One incident, though, pierced her armour. It happened during a class in which Maureen happened to be the only student from Waywayseecappo. A teacher was talking about the early history of Manitoba when a boy with blond hair and blue eyes blurted out, "We were here first!" By "we," he meant Ukrainians. Maureen could not tell if he was joking. She thought, *Um, no you weren't*, but she wasn't quite sure how to respond. "I knew that what he said bothered me," she recalls, "but I felt like I didn't know enough of my own history to argue back without sounding like I was making it up." Instead, she stayed quiet, and her face flushed red with frustration.

Though this moment lingered with her, Maureen knew it wasn't much compared with what her mom had put up with. While Maureen was in Grade 11, Prime Minister Stephen Harper delivered a formal apology in the House of Commons for Canada's treatment of Indigenous children at residential schools. Maureen came across a printed copy of the speech and decided to take it home to show her mom. Linda took the document to her room to read it alone. "To the approximately 80,000 living former students and all family members and communities," the prime minister said,

> the Government of Canada now recognizes that it was wrong to forcibly remove children from their homes, and we apologize for having done this. We now recognize that it was wrong to separate children from rich and vibrant cultures and traditions, that it created a void in many lives and communities, and we apologize for having done this. We now recognize that in separating children from their families, we undermined the ability of many to adequately parent their own children and sowed the seeds for generations to follow, and we apologize for having done this. We now recognize that far too often these institutions gave rise to abuse or neglect and were inadequately controlled, and we apologize for failing to protect you. . . .
>
> The Government of Canada sincerely apologizes and asks the forgiveness of the aboriginal peoples of this country for failing them so profoundly.[1]

After Linda finished reading, she crumpled the paper and flung it into the hallway. "This won't bring back the hearing in my ear," she said.

THE FOLLOWING YEAR, 2009, Maureen graduated from high school.

On the morning of the ceremony, her younger sister, Samantha, devoted more than an hour to curling Maureen's wavy hair. "Oh my god," Samantha said, "I can't believe you did it!" Maureen put on a sky-blue dress she had picked for the occasion. The dress exposed her shoulders, which, to Maureen's annoyance, were spotted with acne. She solved the problem by using an elegant white scarf as a shawl. A pair of matching white sandals pinched her toes but completed the outfit perfectly. Maureen felt beautiful.

Of the ten other students from Waywayseecappo that had started high school in Rossburn with Maureen, only three were graduating with her. As Maureen watched her classmates being called up to receive their diplomas, she thought of her grandfather Michael, who had received his high school diploma almost sixty years before. Maureen had never met him—Michael died four years before she was born—but she had seen old pictures of him and grown up hearing stories about his way with words. One time, she had a particularly vivid dream in which she found herself walking into a home that was bubbling with voices and laughter. She saw her grandfather inside—all dressed up, with greased hair and a spiffy suit. He seemed to be hosting the event, some kind of community feast, and all of a sudden Maureen found herself seated near him at a table. He was talking to her animatedly. When Maureen woke up, she could still see her grandfather's face. But though she tried and tried she could not remember his words.

Twovoice was the last name called at the graduation ceremony. By that time, Maureen's curls had reverted to waves. She didn't really care—this was a moment she had been imagining for a long time, and here it was. As she headed up the aisle to collect her diploma, she made sure to locate her mom's face in the crowd. "Just her being there was a big thing," Maureen recalls. "Even after all the times we hadn't gotten along, she was there to experience the accomplishment with me." Linda was smiling, her face streaked with tears. Maureen felt a lump growing in her throat, and kept walking toward the stage.

★ ★ ★

MAUREEN TWOVOICE BEAT the odds. Between 2011 and 2016, only a quarter of students living on reserves in Canada graduated from high school in four years.[2] Most never do. The consequences of the staggering dropout rate are well documented: lower employment and higher incarceration; less political engagement and worse health; shorter lifespans and deeper poverty.

Today, some 120,000 school-age children live on reserves across Canada. All too often, their families are racked by high rates of intergenerational trauma, financial hardship, substance abuse, youth suicide, and sexual violence: aftershocks of Canada's legacy of residential schools and structural inequities. *In addition* to these imposing hurdles, the schools these children attend have been chronically underfunded, just like Maureen's school in Waywayseecappo.

Ninety percent of Canadians are educated in public schools that are funded and regulated by provinces. A signature feature of the provincial public education system is that it invests more, not less, in schools that have higher costs and greater needs: notably, schools that are geographically remote, or that have more low-income students or second-language learners. The rationale is to give every student, no matter where or who they are, a fair chance at success. Yet federally funded schools on reserves—which often have a disproportionately high number of students with acute needs—have systematically received less. For decades.

After communities such as Waywayseecappo recoiled from provincial public schools and established control over their own schools on reserve—a shift that began in the 1970s and was the norm by the 1980s[3]—it became ever clearer that the federal government was not matching the level of funding that provincial schools received. In 1984, teachers at the Waywayseecappo school wrote letters to Ottawa as part of a campaign for additional resources. "My children are the hope for the future in this reserve," teacher Lorana Chandler wrote. "I am not asking for the world, I am asking for the essentials that are enjoyed in *every* provincial school." Another teacher, Duncan Allen, wrote, "Is there a high school in the Public School system which does not have a library facility? Is there a high school in the Public School system in which science has to be taught without laboratory facilities? The answer to both these questions is obviously 'NO.' Why then I ask you, should the pupils at Waywayseecappo Community School be subjected to these unreasonable and unnecessary barriers to their education?"[4]

Waywayseecappo's appeals for fairer education funding continued after Brian Mulroney replaced Pierre Trudeau as prime minister in 1984. In response to a query about funding for education on reserves, the minister of Indian and northern affairs, David Crombie, wrote in 1986, "My department is concerned that funding for Indian schools should be equivalent to that provided by the provinces, and is making every effort to ensure that this will take place."[5] And yet, equivalent funding did not materialize.

On the contrary, by the late 1980s, the inequality was "stark and obvious," according to Harry Swain, the deputy minister of Indian and northern affairs (as the department was then called) between 1987 and 1992. Swain was the most senior bureaucrat in the department, nearly a hundred years after Hayter Reed occupied the same post with a different title. He recalls that the official department policy was to provide equal services on reserves.[6] In principle, that meant that students living on reserves were supposed to receive a quality of education comparable to what was available to a similarly situated non-Native community. "Reaching parity was our aspirational goal," Swain says, but the government did not invest enough to make it a reality. "By our calculations, we were spending fifteen to twenty-five percent less per capita than what provincial governments were spending, which led to predictably worse outcomes. Parity would have taken a hell of a lot more resources than we had."

The gap appalled Swain. Every year he was deputy minister, he says, he pushed for a bigger budget to improve services on reserves. One of his main arguments was that Canada was violating the constitutional guarantee, in section 15 of the Charter of Rights and Freedoms, to "equal protection and equal benefit of the law without discrimination." When Swain faced off against officials trying to slash budgets, he told them that the failure to provide equal services on reserves was an open invitation to a discrimination lawsuit. He says he used to warn his government colleagues, "We're going to get our asses sued off and we're going to lose."[7] In the end, Swain thinks his efforts had some effect—not in achieving equal funding, but in staving off an even bigger gap.

Meanwhile, Waywayseecappo and communities like it suffered the consequences. In January 1991, five members of the Waywayseecappo Education Authority wrote to the federal government about yet another dispute over funding:

> Why is it always nearly impossible for us native people to get what we need, when other races of people have no problem whatsoever in getting their needs fulfilled? Is it what we think it is, because if it is let us remind you that this is the 90's. The needs, aspirations and goals of our native children are the same as their neighbours just over the reserve boundaries.[8]

One of the authors of this letter was Jim Cote, Hugh McKay's son.

★ ★ ★

JEAN CHRÉTIEN WAS elected prime minister in 1993, more than two decades after he had belatedly acknowledged the failings of integrated education "of the whitewash variety." Chrétien inherited a federal government sinking into a quicksand of debt. His finance minister, Paul Martin, promised to tame the deficit come "hell or high water." As part of Martin's plan, a 2 percent cap was placed on annual spending increases for services on reserves, including education, even though a 2 percent annual increase was manifestly insufficient to keep up with the rates of inflation and population growth. The measure was said to be temporary, and other departments faced outright cuts to their budgets.

The deputy minister of Indian affairs at the time, Scott Serson, recalls calling Phil Fontaine, the national Chief of the Assembly of First Nations, to assure him that the spending cap would be removed as soon as the deficit was under control. In time, Serson became ashamed of that phone call. By 1998, the government was back to running budget surpluses, yet the 2 percent spending cap would remain in place for almost two more decades, until 2016. Michael Wernick, who served as deputy minister of Indian affairs between 2006 and 2014, observes, "Every single year, for close to twenty years, ministers of finance from the Chrétien government, the Martin government, and the Harper government had an opportunity to change it, but they didn't." Spending less was a *choice* that was made repeatedly, year after year.

At the time the cap was implemented, Scott Serson says he thought it was "about defeating the deficit, not holding a group of Canadian citizens at an insufficient level for 22 years." He went on to write that "it is only reasonable to conclude that the deliberate, but unstated, policy of the Canadian government is to maintain the vast majority of First Nations in poverty."[9] In a 2012 interview, Paul Martin said, "The cap was a mistake and there's no excuse for it."[10]

Meanwhile, Manitoba and other provinces ramped up their education spending. Between 1996 and 2015, provinces increased funding for public schools about twice as fast as the federal government increased funding for on-reserve education.[11] Over time, the two funding curves diverged, at first by a bit, eventually by a lot, until one day in 2010, Troy Luhowy looked at the numbers on his calculator and wondered how things had gone so terribly wrong. A gap had become a chasm.

The inequality between the two sides of the Birdtail was not an aberration. It was not some unfortunate, isolated case. It was, rather, perfectly in keeping with the norm for the five hundred schools on reserves across Canada. In 2012, Saskatchewan's minister of education, Russ Marchuk, estimated that in his province students on reserves were receiving as much as 40 percent less funding than students in public schools. "You observe the effects of a lack of resources first-hand," he said. "Lower graduation rates, children not school-ready, lower employment rates. These are the results of a lack of funding."[12] Yet again, Canada was making a mockery of Alexander Morris's assurance, all those years ago, that the Queen "always cared for her red children as much as for her white."

The disparity in funding has been mirrored by a disparity in outcomes. Canada's auditor general, the government's most credible number-cruncher, calculated in 1996 that the outcomes gap between Indigenous students living on reserves and the Canadian student population as a whole would close by 2019. But as time passed, things progressively worsened. In 2000, the auditor general estimated that the gap would persist until 2023.

In 2004, the projection extended to 2032. In 2011, the auditor general said it might take even longer than that, but declined to specify a date.[13]

Treaty 4, like other treaties, includes a promise from the government to maintain a school on each community's reserve ("Her Majesty agrees to maintain a school in the reserve"), but Indigenous communities have paid a steep price for invoking this right. Canada's underfunding has ensured that these separate schools would be unequal. Knowing this, Waywayseecappo and almost every other reserve community *still* chose to retain their own schools. That's how deep the wound was from residential and integrated schools. That's how deep the need was to have a meaningful say in the education of their children.

In 2012, politicians in Ottawa were sufficiently roused by activists and media scrutiny to formally recognize that there was a problem. The following non-binding resolution received unanimous support in the House of Commons: "That, in the opinion of the House, the government should" be "providing funding that will put reserve schools on par with non-reserve provincial schools."[14] After the resolution passed—once parliamentarians from all parties had uttered many fine words and patted one another on the back in a rare display of righteous unanimity—nothing much changed. Parliament had committed itself to an aspirational goal and then failed to implement a plan to make it a reality.[15] In 2016, the national funding gap between reserve schools and provincial public schools was reported to be approximately 30 percent, which amounted to a staggering shortfall of $665 million in that year alone.[16]

Beyond all the material constraints the chronic financial shortfall imposed, it also suggested to hundreds of thousands of Indigenous students that maybe they didn't really deserve any better. It was as though Canada was telling them, "You get less because you'll never amount to anything anyway."

"It's always been that way," says Waywayseecappo's long-time elected Chief, Murray Clearsky. "They don't want to educate the Indian, to put it mildly."

Which prompts the question: *Why?* Why did Canada under-fund education on reserves for so long? This is the query that first brought us to Waywayseecappo and Rossburn, to the valley they share and the river between them. If Canada is to meaningfully address this long-standing problem, we need a clear diagnosis of its causes.

15

"PEOPLE SAY WE'RE RACISTS"

IN CANADA'S EARLY YEARS, THE LIKES OF HAYTER REED and Clifford Sifton assumed that Indigenous Peoples were inherently inferior to whites, and said so openly. It is comforting to think that state-sanctioned racism is a thing of the distant past, perpetrated by villains in black-and-white photographs. And yet, *after* embracing a Charter of Rights and Freedoms in 1982 and formally apologizing for abuses at residential schools in 2008, modern Canada continued to systematically underfund students like Maureen Twovoice on reserves like Waywayseecappo. Successive federal governments, Liberal and Conservative, sustained this underfunding, with the tacit support of Canadians who elected them. Indeed, the contemporary mistreatment of Indigenous students is consistent with the broader historical pattern.[1] We have just replaced evil masterminds with cruel neglect. The villains today might be less readily identifiable, but Canada is still guilty.

Part of the explanation is the long half-life of racism, which endures in ever more insidious forms. Indigenous lives remain widely devalued—in our policies, in our politics, in our minds. The underfunding of Indigenous schools could continue because too few Canadians noticed, and, of those who did, too few cared. The fact of grossly unequal services on reserves may have been "stark and obvious" by the late 1980s, but by then Canadians had grown accustomed to the idea of failing Indigenous communities, failing reserve schools, failing Indigenous students. Too many Canadians came to see obviously worse outcomes on reserves as normal and Indigenous Peoples themselves as responsible. This explanation had the added attraction of skirting the ways settlers had benefited from the dispossession of Indigenous Peoples. Racism is a filter that renders the obvious invisible.

From the very outset, reserves were especially vulnerable to unequal treatment because they were separate from the rest of the country. This separation is not merely geographic—there are also constitutional and administrative dimensions. The document that accompanied Canada's birth as a confederation, the British North America Act of 1867, put provinces in charge of education and the federal government in charge of "Indians and lands reserved for the Indians." This original division of power is the reason why Manitoba is responsible for funding public schools in Rossburn and the federal government is responsible for funding Waywayseecappo's school just across the valley. As the anthropologist Harry Hawthorn once put it, reserves are "isolated federal islands surrounded by provincial territory."[2] This jurisdictional Swiss cheese enabled what followed: separate became, then remained, unequal.

People living on reserves constitute only about 1 percent of Canada's overall population, and, therefore, have extremely limited electoral clout. But to be few is one thing—to be few *and* separate raises further challenges. When a province alters funding to public schools, which over 90 percent of students attend, almost all students in the provincial system are affected. If funding decreases, everyone suffers; if funding increases, everyone benefits. Either way, there is a common outcome for most people, and, therefore, a common cause. But the situation is altogether different for students on reserves. Their schools do not benefit from increased provincial spending and, conversely, no child in provincial schools is affected by the underfunding of reserve schools. Non-Indigenous parents never have to contemplate the possibility that their own children could attend a chronically underfunded school, let alone a school on a reserve.

The geographic separateness of reserves only further accentuates their political isolation. Most Canadians have never set foot on a reserve, many of which are distant from urban centres and some of which are not even accessible by road. This makes it even easier for most voters and the politicians they elect to ignore reserve communities.

To make matters worse, the federal government did not feel bound by law to deliver basic services on reserves comparable to services provided by provinces (and still doesn't). Worse, starting in 2007, it engaged in slow and expensive litigation to defend the government's right to use its discretion to provide less.[3]

The issue is not simply that reserves are too easily overlooked—they are also widely *resented*. Ask Nelson Luhowy; he'll tell you. The prevailing view in Rossburn is that reserves like Waywayseecappo receive *too much* government money, not too little. Polling data show that many, if not most, Canadians agree with this sentiment.[4] Nelson hears about it all the time at the Rossburn Hotel over lunch. Whenever Waywayseecappo comes up, Nelson hears the same old stuff. Namely, that people on the reserve do not pay their fair share of taxes.

"Oh," Nelson says, "are people ever sore about the question of taxes." For purchases made in Waywayseecappo, as on other reserves, people who are officially recognized by the federal government as "Status Indians" do not pay federal or provincial sales taxes.[5] In addition, income earned on reserve by Status Indians is sometimes not subject to income tax. In Rossburn, as elsewhere, this seems wrong, unfair, a basic violation of the social contract.

"If I go to a store and I pay a dollar, then you pay a dollar and thirteen cents, that would bother you, wouldn't it?" Nelson says. "That communicates to people that it's not fair." When the federal government funds anything in Waywayseecappo, Nelson says, the first reaction over lunch in Rossburn is often, "Oh, guess that's more of our money going in to pay for it." *Our* money: Nelson hears a lot of that. As in, *our* tax dollars, to which *they* don't contribute. The fact that a disproportionate number of people in Waywayseecappo rely on government assistance only hardens the sense of grievance in Rossburn. "We're paying their welfare," Nelson hears at lunch. "They're getting a free ride." Despite support—or, many suspect, *because* of it—Waywayseecappo doesn't get its act together.

Federal politicians have long been aware of widespread hostility to government spending on reserves, and acted accordingly. "Putting it as bluntly as possible, no government ever won votes by spending money on Indians," long-time member of Parliament Charlie Angus writes.[6] In recent decades, whenever a federal politician in the governing party was asked a question about unequal services on reserves, the stock answer avoided the issue of inequality and instead emphasized how much the federal government was already spending. This sent a clear message to the (non-Indigenous) majority of voters: All this money we're spending, all those billions, that's *your* money—doesn't it sound like enough? As one Rossburn resident put it over lunch, "What is the Indian Affairs budget? It's, you know, billions of dollars. Where does that money come from? Even a dummy can figure that out. And yet, somehow, we're the assholes."

Beyond the taxation bugbear, many Canadians are also generally disinclined to support greater funding on reserves because of opposition to federal programs that seem to provide special benefits to Status Indians. For example, in Waywayseecappo, as on other reserves, Status Indians receive extended coverage for dental care and prescription drugs. To many, the existence of such programs undercuts claims that other services, such as primary and secondary education, are underfunded.

Brian Brown, who served as the mayor of Rossburn between 2014 and 2018, is the kind of person who prides himself on saying out loud what others only think. He is among the many who firmly believe that Status Indians should not receive any benefits not available to Rossburn's non-Native population. "I have a granddaughter," Brian said while he was still mayor. "How do I explain to her that when she goes to university, it will cost her twenty grand a year, but when her friend from the reserve goes, it will cost her absolutely nothing? To me, it's not right, and most of my constituents feel the same way. People say we're racists. I don't think I'm racist. I'd call it resentment. I just want everyone to be treated the same."

Like a majority of Canadians, Brown doesn't think that Indigenous Canadians should have any kind of special status.[7] This position is akin to the long-standing and widespread view that Quebec wrongly enjoys an exalted status among supposedly equal provinces. Brown is among the many who would still gladly embrace the approach Pierre Trudeau and Jean Chrétien once attempted with the White Paper of 1969: abolish Indian status and Indian reserves, along with any differential treatment that comes with them.

Brown's views stem in part from the conviction that Ukrainian Canadians never benefited from special treatment. "A lot of people here," he said, "their grandparents were immigrants. They know how rough it was." Yet people in Rossburn feel that they are being held responsible for Waywayseecappo's failures. "If something bad happens, we're the bad guy. Somehow it's our fault. I think they associate every white person with the past." And yet, Brian notes, he didn't have anything to do with residential schools.

Brown is also inherently suspicious, as many are, of anything that looks like an affirmative action program based on race rather than on economic need. "You and I may be different, with different nationalities, from different parts of the country, but in everything else we should be equal," Brown said. "But the reserve population is not." By which he means: the reserve population is treated differently, sometimes even preferentially. That so many people on reserves live in abject poverty does not seem to alter the enduring perception that Indians are receiving undeserved advantages.

BEFORE RESPONDING TO such views, as we must, it is important to recognize how widespread they are, and to take them seriously. We should not simply label the citizens of Rossburn as racist and then stop listening to what they have to say. We would do well, as a country, to linger with Nelson and Brian on Main Street, so that we may seek to understand, to reflect on where they are coming from. And empathize.

If we imagine ourselves in their shoes and hear the story they tell themselves, it is easier to recognize how utterly compelling it is. Rossburn's posture toward Waywayseecappo is inextricably linked to a larger story about immigrants who have struggled and endured, all the while feeling that the government has never done them any favours. The pioneer narrative of resilience, hard work, and self-reliance continues to inspire and enthrall.

Meanwhile, economic anxiety gnaws at rural communities like Rossburn. Wages are largely stagnant. As the town's population continues to fall, the tax base shrinks. The roof on the ice rink is leaking, and repairs will cost $50,000. There is also an unfinished, unkempt baseball diamond at the edge of town, still without a pitcher's mound. It has been that way for years, providing a daily reminder of decline.

It should not be surprising that many of the town's residents resent the reserve across the valley, which is seen to be benefiting from favourable tax rules and the federal government's largesse. Indeed, this phenomenon is not unique to Canada. Many American conservatives, as sociologist Arlie Hochschild notes, perceive a "rift between deserving taxpayers and undeserving tax money takers."[8] These conservatives, particularly in rural areas, profoundly resent that the government is "taking money from the workers and giving it to the idle," "taking from people of good character and giving to people of bad character." Those who benefit from the redistribution are seen to be "violating rules of fairness." Or, as Troy Luhowy often heard while he was growing up: Indians were "getting everything for nothing."

So the resentment is real, and it is deeply felt. Yet it is mostly anchored in assumptions and stereotypes that simply do not reflect reality. When it comes to taxation, for example, the views commonly heard in Rossburn are almost completely wrong.

There is a widely held misconception that Indigenous Peoples in Canada pay no taxes.[9] But this is patently false. Off reserve, Indians pay income tax, sales tax, property tax, provincial sales tax, federal sales tax, gas taxes, taxes levied on cigarettes and gasoline and alcohol—in other words, all the same taxes as non-Indians.

It is true that neither federal nor provincial sales tax is collected on goods purchased and used on reserves, but most reserve communities don't have enough retail merchants for the exemption to have much impact. Status Indians who work for their community are indeed exempt from paying income tax, but this exemption does not extend to commercial or non-governmental employment. And, because of this exemption, band councils often pay on-reserve employees 75 percent of what an off-reserve employee would earn doing the same job, reasoning that since the take-home pay will be roughly the same, no one should complain, and mostly no one does.

A virtually unusable sales tax exemption and an income tax exemption offset by low salaries are, at day's end, very slender benefits, if they are benefits at all.

There is nothing new in any of this. To the narrow extent that they exist, tax exemptions on "Indian lands" date back to before Confederation. In 1850, legislation in Upper and Lower Canada exempted reserves from taxation, and so did the first Indian Act of 1869.[10] During at least some treaty negotiations, the government seems to have promised that a treaty would "not open the way to the imposition of any tax."[11] As recently as 1990, the Supreme Court reviewed tax exemptions on reserves and held that they were still very much legal and legitimate.[12] People such as Brian Brown "don't understand the deal we had with the Queen," says Waywayseecappo's Chief Clearsky.

What's more, a high percentage of people on reserves are poor, which means, practically speaking, that most would not pay income taxes even if they were subjected to the exact same rules as everyone else. Reserves are simply not dragon dens where riches are hoarded to the detriment of Canada and the citizens of Rossburn. The average family in Waywayseecappo lives below the poverty line.

It is true that many First Nations communities invest in post-secondary education, providing tuition funds and sometimes living expenses for community members. But it is important to understand this arrangement for what it is: a local government choosing to invest in post-secondary education at the cost of using that same money to pay for other things such as road maintenance. Rather than asking why Indigenous communities do this, a better question might be why cities and towns focus on potholes and police rather than providing university tuition for their residents.

It is also true that the Indian Act lays out distinctive rules for Status Indians. This raises suspicions among those who equate equality with identical rules for all. Yet since its inception the Indian Act has been used to oppress Indigenous Peoples, not to privilege them. Any honest look at the history of the Department of Indian Affairs makes this clear.

And yet the idea that Indians have received and continue to receive unfair advantages persists. It is an idea rooted in ignorance and maintained by resentment. Only when people such as Nelson begin to spend time in reserve communities do they hear the stories, not of easy money, but of hard challenges and intergenerational trauma the likes of which they had never imagined.

Given Canada's wealth and Waywayseecappo's poverty, it is incredibly frustrating for people on the reserve—and Indigenous Canadians, generally—to hear about all the unfair benefits they are imagined to receive. Indeed, complaints by non-Indigenous Canadians about taxes and preferential treatment seem to altogether ignore Canada's long history of questionable dealings with Indigenous Peoples, particularly with respect to land. Whatever modest benefits Status Indians receive are tiny compared to the immense wealth Canada has extracted, and continues to extract, from Traditional Indigenous Territory—such as the $230 million the Province of Manitoba collected in 2019 from royalties on mineral mining, to pick but one example.

"Sure, we'll gladly pay more taxes," more than a few Indigenous Canadians have joked, "if you give us our land back."

As many in Waywayseecappo thought it was unfair for its primary and secondary students to receive lower government funding for education, so did many in Rossburn think it was unfair for Waywayseecappo to pay less tax or receive subsidized medications at the pharmacy. Canadians on either side of such arguments rarely convince each other. Mayor Brian Brown and Chief Murray Clearsky certainly haven't. Both sides invoke equality, but there is no basic agreement on what equality means or what fairness entails.

And this, it seems, is where Canada has been stuck for a long time. The resistance among non-Indigenous Canadians to further spending on reserves has never been specifically directed at the funding of primary and secondary education, nor at Native students themselves. Yet young people such as Maureen Twovoice have long been the collateral damage of deeper misunderstandings and disagreements between Indigenous and non-Indigenous Canadians.

For generations, Rossburn and Waywayseecappo were as stuck in this rut as any two communities could be. But then—incredibly, improbably—they found a way forward. In 2010, just a few months after Troy Luhowy became principal of the Waywayseecappo school, everything changed.

16

"KIDS ARE KIDS"

W AYWAYSEECAPPO AND ROSSBURN REMAINED emblematic of the national funding gap between Indigenous and non-Indigenous students until November 29, 2010. On that frigid day, which reached minus twenty-two Celsius with wind chill, something miraculous happened: a deal was reached to ensure that every student in Waywayseecappo would receive the exact same funding as a student in Rossburn. All of a sudden—literally, overnight—the federal government would match the provincial standard, dollar for dollar. With over three hundred students living on the reserve, that meant an infusion of more than a million dollars into Waywayseecappo's annual education budget.[1]

At this point, Troy Luhowy had been principal of the Waywayseecappo school for only three months and he had not been involved in the negotiations. Still, he could appreciate the significance of the moment. "After being behind all these years, now they were on a level playing field," he says. "It's amazing how difficult it was to get people to see the problem."

The new agreement was the product of more than two years of negotiations between representatives of Waywayseecappo, the federal government, the government of Manitoba, and the local provincial school division. It became known simply as "the partnership," and it launched a unique experiment to discover what would happen when students on a reserve received the same funding and services as students in provincial schools. Canada had never bothered to ask or answer that question.

THE AGREEMENT THAT equalized funding for Waywayseecappo began, as many changes do, with a person wondering: Why not?

In this case, that person was Colleen Clearsky, Waywayseecappo's long-time director of education. For years, she had been hearing about the "education gap" between Indigenous and non-Indigenous students. "Every time I went to a meeting someone mentioned it," she says. "My main goal was to try to close that gap, to do something for our students, but it was getting larger and larger." She and others in Waywayseecappo had been trying as best they could, with the limited resources the band council could offer, to "cover up all the cracks" that students were falling through. Colleen helped establish the adult education program for those who wanted another shot at a high school diploma, for which Nelson Luhowy would go on to teach; an "off-campus transition" program for teenagers, such as Maureen Twovoice, who were not coping with the regular classroom; and a kindergarten program, which first operated only for half days, and later was expanded to full days, five days a week.

All the while, Colleen was acutely aware of how much less the federal government was funding Waywayseecappo's students compared with students in provincial schools. "I looked at the funding we were getting here, and I looked at what they were getting in the provincial system, and I wanted to know: Why can't we just get the same funding as they were getting?"

Together with her colleague Jackie McKee, and with support from Waywayseecappo's elected leadership, Colleen started looking to partner with Park West School Division, the group of fourteen nearby provincial schools that included Rossburn's elementary and secondary schools. But what incentive might a group of provincial schools have to work more closely with a reserve school?

Stephen David was the assistant superintendent of Park West School Division when the partnership was launched, and he is the superintendent today. To hear David tell it, the partnership arose from a moment of moral reckoning. Before 2010, he says, "We had a school with 340 kids six kilometres from Rossburn, and so much disparity in terms of educational outcomes. The reality, when you coalesced it, is that it was about funding. You may hear people say it's not just about the money. Well, a lot of it was."

David insists that he and others felt a "moral imperative" to help close the funding gap—and, more importantly, the gap in outcomes—between students from Waywayseecappo and the rest of the students in his school division. He imagined his own daughter being sent to a chronically under-resourced school. "Of course I wouldn't want that, and neither would anyone else who could avoid it," he says. "There is no way to justify the way things were. I think if you try to think logically and rationally, there was no way to make sense of it. It was totally illogical, totally irrational. Beyond that—it was appalling. We have an obligation to people down the road. Kids are kids. They want to learn."

The man who became Park West's superintendent in 2012, Tim Mendel, emphasized other considerations in an interview with the *Winnipeg Free Press.* "It is in Park West's best interests that [the partnership] does well," Mendel said, because students from Waywayseecappo "will eventually come to our high schools."[2]

Yet even this kind of thinking, persuasive as it might seem in retrospect, did not capture the full extent of Park West's motivations. After all, students from Waywayseecappo had been underperforming in provincial high schools for generations, and this had not catalyzed any major changes before. Rather, the sense of urgency in 2010 came from another source: enrolment in the provincial school division had been steadily declining. For years, fewer students had been entering Grade 1 than were leaving Grade 12. This reflected the slow and steady depopulating of rural Manitoba: farms were increasingly larger and more mechanized, which meant fewer actual farmers with children to send to schools. Park West School Division's administrators had been watching the downward enrolment trend with alarm and increasing desperation.

If enrolment kept dropping, programs for students would be cut, teachers would lose their jobs, schools would close. Kids are kids, but they are also, from the perspective of school administrators, sources of revenue. And this is where Waywayseecappo, with its rapidly increasing population of school-age children, entered the equation. If Waywayseecappo's students could somehow be counted as part of the provincial school division, then Park West could solve its enrolment problem.

Colleen Clearsky had no illusions about why the provincial schools were suddenly eager to move forward with the partnership. "Their school population was declining, ours was rising. They needed our students, and we needed the funding. It went hand in hand. We both knew what we were doing, and why." Under the proposed terms of a partnership, every student at the Waywayseecappo school would be considered part of the provincial school division, and, crucially for Park West, Waywayseecappo would be required to use a portion of its increased federal funding to contribute to shared services. In this way, the partnership would directly benefit both Waywayseecappo *and* all the neighbouring public schools.

The partnership hinged, of course, on the federal government agreeing to dramatically increase Waywayseecappo's funding, for which the motivation is harder to explain. Didn't the provision of equal funding for Waywayseecappo represent a tacit admission of unequal funding for so many other communities? In the most bureaucratic way possible, an internal government memo conceded as much: "Although this arrangement would cost approximately $1 million more annually than the Waywayseecappo First Nation's current education-related funding, it would provide rapid alignment of First Nation and provincial school standards."[3] The very rationale for the partnership was an indictment of the federal approach to many other communities.

For years, the government of Stephen Harper had seemed strongly disinclined to spend a large amount of additional money on reserves. One of Harper's first acts as prime minister was to renege on a commitment by his predecessor, Paul Martin, to spend an additional $5 billion over five years to improve services on reserves. Harper reportedly told a senior aide, "If I had $5 billion to give away, I would give it to the farmers."[4] Reserves were simply not a political priority, and the government was generally skeptical that more money could improve outcomes without deeper (and controversial) reforms. However, Harper had delivered a seemingly heartfelt apology in 2008 for the federal government's role in supporting residential schools, which had the effect of bringing increased public attention to the deplorable educational outcomes for Indigenous students. According to Michael

Wernick, who was then the top civil servant in the Department of Indian and Northern Affairs, the Harper government was open to supporting locally driven initiatives that could make a strong case for improving results. The proposed Waywayseecappo partnership was exactly this kind of initiative.

Crucially, it was not particularly expensive for the federal government. As Wernick says: "You can find a million dollars in a seven-billion-dollar department. But if you had to find fifty million, that wouldn't have been possible. It was the small scale, the granularity, that made it possible."

Federal funding sealed the deal, but at its heart the partnership resulted from local actors seeing that investing more in students from the reserve was in everyone's best interests.

Canada as a whole was still failing to reach a similar conclusion.

AFTER RECEIVING THE new infusion of money, the first thing Waywayseecappo did was hire six more teachers. This nearly halved the average class size, to fewer than twenty students. Teachers also received raises to bring their salaries in line with those of their peers in Rossburn—for most, this meant an annual increase of between $13,000 and $18,000. And the school made long-deferred investments in textbooks and its library.

In exchange for additional funding, the federal government insisted on regular testing of students to track whether the partnership affected outcomes over time. Baseline results from 2010 showed that among all the school's Grade 1 to 4 students, only a single student was reading at grade level—one child out of 122. Six years later, half of students in Grades 1 to 4 were reading at grade level.[5]

"Half is still not acceptable," Troy said, "but we've come a long way. Things have gotten better in a hurry."

There were other signs of improvement, too. Overall student attendance improved, rising to 90 percent from 80 percent. Incident reports, which are written when a student does something sufficiently bad to warrant a trip to the principal's office, decreased 65 percent, from more than 2,500 a year to fewer than 900. In other words, students were doing a lot less fighting with each other or swearing at teachers.

It used to be common for the school to lose a third or more of its teachers every year. After the partnership began, though, turnover plummeted. By the 2016–17 academic year, Waywayseecappo had better teacher retention than the fourteen provincial schools in the division. "When a provincial school could offer teachers $15,000 more and classrooms that didn't have thirty-five kids, teachers left our school," Troy said. "Now, our students actually expect teachers to come back." A teaching vacancy at the Waywayseecappo school used to attract perhaps two or three applicants, and hardly the pick of the litter. These days, each opening receives hundreds of qualified applicants. In 2015, an experienced teacher from a provincial public school actually asked that she be transferred to Waywayseecappo. "I can guarantee you that never would have happened before," Troy said.

After a few spins around a virtuous circle, teachers and students allowed themselves higher expectations. Teachers started assigning more reading to be completed at home because they trusted that the students would actually do it and that loaned books would be returned. A 2015 survey of Waywayseecappo's Grade 8 students showed that 72 percent of them hoped to attend university, at a time the national high school graduation rate for students living on reserves was only about 40 percent.

Hope is not just a start—it is a necessary first step.

★ ★ ★

THE TANTALIZING TURNAROUND of Waywayseecappo's school can be attributed to equal access to services as much as equal money. With Waywayseecappo paying its share, the provincial school division began treating the school as a full member. That meant Waywayseecappo could take advantage of all the services available to the school division, including teacher training, student counselling, a speech pathologist, the latest teaching materials and curricula, maintenance crews, computer technicians, and all the sports leagues. (For Troy, there was no greater glory than the girls' basketball team winning the 2016 divisional championship.) At the same time, the Waywayseecappo school retained control over its hiring and curriculum, including the ability to teach culturally relevant subjects such as Ojibway language. Waywayseecappo has found a way to retain its autonomy while still benefiting from the economies of scale that came with being part of a larger unit. "I am not giving up much authority for the amount of good education we are getting," said Chief Murray Clearsky. "With more resources, the kids are already doing better."[6]

As part of the partnership, students from Rossburn now go to the Waywayseecappo school for opportunities that are not available in town, such as woodworking classes, where they churn out benches and shelves, and a cosmetology program, where budding hairstylists beautify their first clients. Sending provincial school students to attend any kind of class on a reserve was unheard of. For years, Waywayseecappo's students had crossed the valley to attend high school in Rossburn—now the flow of students runs both ways. As Colleen Clearsky says, "We wanted to give non-Aboriginal students a chance to see how it was when they came to our school. It was always us going out—why couldn't it be them coming to our school?"

Not all parents in Rossburn embraced the partnership. A member of Troy's extended family refused to allow his child to participate in the cosmetology program. "There's no way my daughter is going to school on the reserve," he allegedly told the Rossburn High School principal. But this kind of outspoken opposition was rare. There seemed to be a growing recognition that there might be things to learn on both sides of the Birdtail.

"Before, we were here, but it was like we were living on an island," said Marellia Cote, who grew up in Waywayseecappo and has taught at its school since 1997. "Now we are building bridges between the communities. We see each other more as people now."[7] For Chief Clearsky, this is a welcome development. "For so long our children never really mingled with off-reserve kids," he said. "I like seeing more of that. I don't want them to be assimilated, but in today's society we all have to get along." And Colleen Clearsky, who did so much to get the partnership under way, said it has resulted in a constant process of mutual learning. "They're teaching us and we're teaching them." She hoped that Waywayseecappo's students would learn to "walk in both worlds," as she put it. "I want them to be able to know where they come from, and to be comfortable in their own skin. And I want them to feel that way on the outside, off reserve, too."

The partnership also presented an opportunity for nearby provincial schools to adapt their practices to show a greater respect for Indigenous cultures—something the federal official J.R. Wright had advised, fruitlessly, half a century earlier, as had countless parents since. In 2017, Park West School Division advertised a position for an Indigenous coordinator to help infuse a

Native perspective into its schools. They hired a twenty-six-year-old by the name of Maureen Twovoice.

AFTER HIGH SCHOOL, Maureen attended the University of Winnipeg, where she studied the history of Indigenous Peoples in Canada. There, for the first time, she read widely about Indian residential schools.

During one class, as she sat in the third row listening to a professor talk about intergenerational trauma, it finally struck her: *So this is why my family is the way it is.* Picturing her mom at the Brandon residential school made Maureen feel sick to her stomach. She thought of all the times she had gotten mad at her mom for drinking, all the times she wished her mom would just get over it. *Maybe,* Maureen now thought, *maybe it's not really the kind of thing people get over.* Maureen's hands grew sweaty. *Breathe,* she told herself. *Breathe.* She hoped her professor wouldn't ask her a question, because she was sure she would burst into tears before she could utter a single word. Her panic continued to rise, until she decided to escape from the classroom. In the hallway, she found a water fountain, drank deeply, and paced.

In a paper she went on to write about residential schools, Maureen explored the ways "intergenerational effects continue to control Indigenous people's daily lives" by looking at her own family. "Both my mother and father attended Indian Residential Schools," an experience that "has taken a toll on them both, especially in terms of parenting." Maureen wrote, "My mother also suffers from alcoholism. . . . When you look into her eyes you can almost feel the pain and adversity she has overcome in her life. She is willing to share with anyone who cares enough to ask."

Maureen described her father as "smart, humorous and generous," though he did suffer from alcoholism for a long period in his life. He had not shown up to her high school graduation ceremony, an absence that had wounded her. But, in time, she had learned to let it go. "My father was not present all the time throughout my life," she wrote. "I did not blame him after learning and understanding where he was coming from as an Indigenous man who had been a part of Canada's cultural genocide."

Maureen graduated in 2016 with a bachelor of arts in Indigenous studies and history, then enrolled in a master's degree in Indigenous governance. She began to research the way Indigenous leaders had understood Treaty 4 when they signed it. By this time, she had also fallen in love and, after four years together, Maureen and her partner decided they wanted to start a family. At the age of twenty-seven, Maureen gave birth to a girl, Teagan. She promised to try to be the kind of person for her daughter that she herself had needed as a child. "I wanted to break the cycle," she says.

When Maureen heard about the job opening for an Indigenous coordinator with Park West, she thought it might be a good fit. She had always hoped to return to Waywayseecappo in a role connected to education. This was her chance, and she seized it.

By the time she was hired, in 2017, the education partnership had been in place for seven years. Maureen was excited that Waywayseecappo students were finally getting the same resources as students in Rossburn. At the same time, it angered her to think of all the years they hadn't. She thought of her friends who didn't make it through high school. "Looking back," Maureen says, "I am upset for those who didn't make it. The government gave us the bare minimum. Did they not believe we could succeed? We all can."

As part of her job, Maureen organized workshops in provincial public schools about Indigenous history and culture. She also spent a lot of time with students from Waywayseecappo who were attending high school in Rossburn or Russell. Every now and then, a student would glance knowingly at the scars on her arms. "I've been there," Maureen would tell them. "I know how it feels. You can do this."

Maureen's work took her to every school in the division, but her office was in the Waywayseecappo school. Troy's office was two doors down.

17

"BURY THE HATCHET"

T HE BRANDON INDIAN RESIDENTIAL SCHOOL WAS demolished in 2000—forty-seven years after Jim Cote's escape, thirty-one years after Linda's discharge, seven years after Troy's trespass. A vacant lot now occupies the top of the hill from which the school used to loom. All that remains of the old building are a few half-buried bits of brick and concrete. On a warm summer day, the air smells of sage. Yellow butterflies abound, applauding with their wings. You might describe the place as serene if you didn't know its sordid history.

Troy Luhowy didn't know. Linda Jandrew can't forget.

In recent years, former students have held annual meetings at the old school site to share stories and try to come to terms with their experiences. Linda has never attended any of these gatherings. She wants nothing to do with the place.

As part of a 2006 legal settlement with the federal government, former residential school students received financial compensation for harms they suffered at these institutions. Those who had spent a year at a residential school were entitled to $10,000 in damages, plus $3,000 per additional year in attendance. Linda was among eighty thousand people who received this monetary payment—a crude and modest remedy for lasting wounds.

Students who were victims of serious physical or sexual abuse were also eligible for more financial compensation if they successfully presented their case to a special tribunal. Linda reluctantly joined thirty-eight thousand others who took this additional step. The first part of the process to quantify damages involved a chart that awarded "points" for various types of abuse, according to severity. Fondling or kissing by school staff was worth five to ten points, while "repeated, persistent incidents of anal or vaginal intercourse" or "penetration with an object" counted for between forty-five and sixty points. Adjudicators were required to "draw out the full story from witnesses . . . and test the evidence," including by cross-examination. Despite efforts to make the process less adversarial than a courtroom trial, historian J.R. Miller concludes that "for most survivors . . . the experience was trying, and for some traumatic."[1]

Linda's hearing was held on July 20, 2009, a few weeks after Maureen graduated from high school. During the questioning, she broke down in tears. "You did a good job by crying," Linda recalls her lawyer telling her afterwards, as if she had staged it. The adjudicator, Helen Semaganis, went on to approve Linda's claim. Semaganis wrote, "I found Linda Jandrew to be a truthful person. She did not exaggerate the details of her abuse." Semaganis added that it had been "an honour and privilege" to meet Linda, who had shown "courage" and "inner strength" during the proceedings.

Linda Jandrew (Courtesy of Maureen Twovoice)

Linda received a typed transcript of what was said during her hearing. During a spring cleaning a few years later, she threw the papers into the garbage, for the same reason Maureen had once burned her diaries. She didn't want the reminder. "But the memories," she says, "I can't get rid of them."

JIM COTE, HUGH McKAY's son, is now one of Waywayseecappo's most respected Elders and refers to himself as "a young dinosaur." It has been more than six decades since he ran 120 kilometres from the Brandon residential school to his home in Waywayseecappo. He is a grandfather now, cherished for his wisdom and wit. Though he owns a truck, he jokes that he is still a "horse and buggy man." Like his father, Jim served many years as an elected representative on Waywayseecappo's band council.

Jim Cote (Courtesy of Jim Cote)

For decades after Jim's time at residential school, the mere sight of white people summoned images of his former torment-ors. "I would walk around Rossburn and see the faces of my old teachers who hit me for speaking my language or hugging my sister," Jim says. "It was something that was stuck in the back of my head. I had to fight it. As time went by, I tried to learn to black it out, to let it go."

These days, Jim is hopeful that relations between Waywayseecappo and Rossburn can improve. "We've never really had a buddy-buddy relationship," he says. "They used us—we spent our money there. But we always stayed in our own corners. I've always thought that wasn't right. If I was ever going to chair a meeting with people from Waywayseecappo and Rossburn, I would tell people to mingle." Jim still believes it is important and necessary for Waywayseecappo to have its own school, but he also tries to encourage young people on the reserve to be friendly when they're in town.

"When are we going to bury the hatchet?" Jim asks.[2] "And not in each other's backs."

ROSSBURN'S POPULATION HAS been declining since 1980. In April 1993, town residents chipped in $2,080 to buy full-page advertisements in Toronto newspapers that proclaimed "Lots for $1." A century had passed since Clifford Sifton lured faraway immigrants to the area with a promise of free land, and now Rossburn was desperately trying to recapture some of the old magic. A headline in the ad described Rossburn as a "GREAT PLACE TO LIVE!" Further exclamation marks followed in quick succession: "Clean air! Low crime rate! Wildlife!" For a time, at least, the gambit had the desired effect: the aggressive advertising and free lots attracted forty new residents within months. Yet it wasn't long before the town's population resumed its slow, inexorable decline.

In 2016, only 512 people lived in Rossburn, down 7 percent from five years before. In the same period, Waywayseecappo's population increased 12 percent, to 1,365.[3] The average age in Waywayseecappo today is twenty-six; in Rossburn, it is fifty. Rossburn's remaining businesses increasingly rely on customers from Waywayseecappo to survive, a fact that has shifted the perceived balance of power between the communities. "We need them," Nelson Luhowy says. "We'd be gone without them."

On July 10, 2018, after an incident at the laundromat in Rossburn, Jim Cote's niece, Gabrielle Cote, posted the following message on Facebook:

> *Old bastards in Rossburn, telling my sister "Wayway should have their own laundromat" . . . your town would DIE without WAYWAY, this is OUR laundromat lol!!! We shop here, WE*

have more people that spend here. THIS IS WAYWAY TOO 😊😊😊 *fuck sakes pissed off.*

Gabrielle's friends posted thirty-one comments, including:

"Shame on them!"

"Boycott 😊*"*

"Just ignorance is all"

"Everyone keep your heads up we are strong"

"we're not like that, we're welcoming to any stranger that enters our area! . . . WELCOME TO WAYWAY!"

Now, as ever, both communities continue to debate the merits of separation and cooperation. Divisions, real and imagined, still run deep.

In October 2019, one year after Brian Brown lost his bid for a second term as Rossburn's mayor, he published a letter in a local newspaper. The letter was prompted by a story about an Indigenous hockey player who had been called racial epithets, and Brian seized the opportunity to unload his opinions about racism, reserves, reconciliation, and residential schools.

"The racism card seems to be getting played on a regular basis," he wrote. "It seems that it is not racism unless it is directed by a white person toward a non-white person." Brown recognized there were sexual crimes committed at Indian residential schools, but he saw the bulk of the other physical abuse as resembling the severe discipline all children of that era endured. Brian suggested that the history of residential schools was being used as an excuse for contemporary problems on reserves and that Indigenous leadership was too corrupt to make necessary reforms: "What are they doing to get their people off welfare, off booze and off drugs?" he wrote. "Obviously not very much when you look at the living conditions on most reserves." Brown concluded with his grim assessment of the future: "Unfortunately for the rest of the people in Canada, we have a prime minister who would rather reconcile (pay them what they want) than make an attempt to change the status quo."[4]

Brown's letter disheartened Waywayseecappo Chief Murray Clearsky, who responded by publishing a letter of his own the following week. "This opinion, written by the former mayor of Rossburn no less, contained nothing but racist stereotyping, false equivalence, ignorance and misinformation." Chief Clearsky expressed hope that Brown's letter did not reflect widely held views in Rossburn, but acknowledged that the relationship in Canada between Indigenous Peoples and non-Indigenous peoples remained broken. He rejected the comparison between what generations of Indigenous children endured in residential schools to standard, old-fashioned discipline, writing, "Genocide was in fact Canadian policy." In response to the trope of corrupt Indigenous politicians, Chief Clearsky noted that "First Nations governments are not any more corrupt than other levels of government, whose scandals also become public, but never a stereotype." (He might have invoked the staggering levels of corruption in Quebec uncovered by the 2011 Charbonneau Commission, but he tactfully declined to point fingers.)

In conclusion, Clearsky wrote: "We are not weak. We are not lawless. We will not apologize for struggling to overcome what has been done to us, and we certainly recognize that there are those among us who are struggling profoundly. What certainly doesn't help are non-Aboriginal Canadians airing their uninformed, racist beliefs and opinions about our lives and communities."[5]

Rossburn's elected leadership joined Chief Clearsky in repudiating Brown's comments, and the town councillors committed themselves "to move forward in partnership with [Indigenous Peoples] in a spirit of reconciliation and collaboration."[6]

WHEN NELSON LUHOWY began teaching adult ed in Waywayseecappo, in 2001, he thought it would be a temporary gig. He ended up staying for eighteen years. In that span, some seven hundred students passed through his classroom. About 160 received their high school diplomas. Even though most didn't complete the program, Nelson saw how hard they tried. "Lots of them were so dedicated. They wanted to better themselves, one way or another. That's the most important thing I saw," Nelson says. "And they treated me well."

Some of Nelson's favourite moments as a teacher involve students who were older than sixty-five. "They wanted to impress their grandkids, to show that education was important, that it can be done."

In Nelson's final two years teaching in Waywayseecappo, one of his students was Linda Shingoose, the mother of his former student Tizz. "Nelson seemed different from other people from Rossburn," Linda Shingoose says. "It was like he didn't think of me as Native— he thought of me as a person. And that's how he treated a lot of people I knew. If I had a problem, he would listen and not interrupt. He said I was pretty smart. I said, 'Me, smart?' 'Yes, you are,' he said. 'And you'll be graduating next year.' I didn't believe him, but he was right." Seventeen years after her daughter completed the same program, Linda Shingoose, at the age of sixty-six, received her diploma in June 2019, just as Nelson was retiring. The following year, Tizz's daughter, Tori—who was born while Tizz was pursuing her diploma with Nelson—also graduated from high school.

It has now been two decades since Tizz met Nelson. "He's white and I'm Native," she says. "Our reserve and Rossburn are usually racist against each other. But he didn't treat us like that. He had confidence we could complete Grade 12. He's the best instructor I ever had, a very awesome guy. I'm glad I had him and still have him in my life."

At Waywayseecappo's annual summer feast later that summer, Nelson was honoured for his many years of teaching. Chief Clearsky presented him with a locally quilted star blanket, a rare honour and a sign of both acceptance and respect.

Nelson receiving a star blanket, with Verna Wilson (*left*), Evelyn Seaton, and Chief Murray Clearsky (Courtesy of Troy Luhowy)

The ceremony prompted Nelson to reflect on what he had learned during his years teaching on the reserve. "My opinions changed," he says. "I learned to have more patience, more tolerance, more understanding." If Nelson could, he would try to talk to his younger self. "I'd try to change the old Nelson. I would try to convince myself. I'd say, 'You know, give them a chance. Don't think they're all bad. They're as good as we are.'"

Nelson pauses, then adds: "Would I have listened? I don't think so. I was a racist. I likely still am."

AT THE WAYWAYSEECAPPO Community School, the day officially starts at 9:00 a.m., when a voice on the intercom announces, "Please stand for 'O Canada.'" By 9:03, the students have been reminded to *stannnnd on guarrrd* for their country.

The fall of 2019 marked Troy's tenth year as principal. On a wall in his office, he has pinned a printed message from one of his teachers: "Keep Calm and Let Troy Handle It." On the same wall there are pictures of his two kids, Addison and Reid, in full hockey gear, alongside another portrait of the whole family outfitted in Montreal Canadiens jerseys.

Troy and Michelle, with their children Reid and Addison
(Courtesy of Troy Luhowy)

It is still too soon to tell whether the partnership with Waywayseecappo will translate into higher graduation rates. Students who began kindergarten in 2010 with equal funding only recently entered high school in Rossburn. It will take even longer to determine the impact on outcomes such as employment, health, and well-being. Still, it is clear that, a decade in, things are headed in the right direction.

Yet Troy finds himself contending with expectations that by now Waywayseecappo's students should already be having the same outcomes as students from Rossburn. When the partnership was first announced, he recalls thinking: *They're finally on a level playing field.* He now recognizes it's not that simple.

Troy plans on sticking around for more of the journey. In 2018, there was a vacancy for the position of principal at Rossburn's elementary school. Once upon a time, it's a job he would have jumped at. But he didn't pursue it. "I didn't want to leave Wayway," Troy explains. "I like the programs we've got going on, and the partnership with the school division is going forward. And I like the kids the most. I didn't want to leave behind the relationships that I've built. I've been here long enough to see how lots of people would leave to go to another school. It wasn't fair to the kids or to the community." In 2019, there was another job opening in Rossburn, this time for principal at the high school. Troy didn't apply to that position, either.

That same year, Troy and Maureen attended an education conference together. One of the speakers talked about the legacy of residential schools, which prompted Troy to share with Maureen the story of how he and his friends had partied at the Brandon residential school on Halloween all those years ago, oblivious to all the suffering that had taken place there. "I didn't have a clue," Troy said. "Nobody told me and I never asked." As

Maureen listened, she found it hard not to get angry. Part of her was thinking, *How the fuck did you not know?* At the same time, she appreciated his honesty. "It takes a lot for someone to say he was wrong," Maureen says.

The two of them agreed that today's students needed to know better. "We need to make sure that the Rossburn kids know," Troy says. "That everybody knows. If we know what happened, maybe we'd understand a bit better what's going on now. Maybe we'd have more empathy. If kids learn about what happened, they won't be as fast or as harsh judging what's happening on the reserve two miles away."

In June 2019, Rossburn's elementary school invited Maureen to give a presentation about residential schools to a Grade 6 class. She knew this was where her mom had once endured incessant racist put-downs. Maureen hoped she could help improve the behaviour of the next generation.

During her talk, Maureen tried to convey the lasting consequences of residential schools by talking about the effects they'd had on her own family. She described how her parents were taken away from their families at a very young age, then asked the students to imagine what that might feel like. Maureen explained that even things that had happened a long time before she was born could still have a profound impact on her life. "Do your parents say that they love you?" Maureen asked the class. They nodded: *Of course.* "Well, my mom didn't say it to me out loud until I was in my early twenties."

After discussing how residential schools suppressed Native languages and culture, Maureen talked about her own journey as a mother, trying her best to pass along Ojibway traditions. She described the ceremony where her daughter Teagan, then aged one, had received her name in Ojibway. Maureen wrote it out on the chalkboard—Zaagaate Giizis—and invited the students to say it out loud. It was the first time they had heard or spoken words in Ojibway.

Sarah Saley, the class's teacher, recalls that she didn't have to quiet her students once while Maureen was giving her presentation. "Maureen spoke in such a tactful, kid-friendly manner," Saley says. "The kids were attentive, really focused—much more than if I had tried to share the same information with them. There's still so much prejudice, so many stereotypes. There are these things about our neighbours we assume are true, but aren't near true. I'll be honest—I've heard some of my students say these things. Some of my colleagues say things that are just awful. Being able to see Maureen come in and talk about these things so openly, so candidly, it for sure gave the students a lot of information. I don't know if they'll be disagreeing with their parents—I hope so—but at least they'll have a different perspective, a more open-minded perspective."

18

"A GRAND NOTION"

THE TROUBLED RELATIONSHIP BETWEEN INDIGENOUS Peoples and non-Indigenous Canadians sometimes snaps into focus: a young Indigenous woman who is supposed to be in protective care is abandoned in a motel and then found dead after being raped and thrown from a bridge;[1] a carload of Indigenous teens seeks help with a flat tire at a farmhouse and one of them is shot dead by a farmer who assumes they have come to rob him;[2] hospital workers taunt an Indigenous woman as she draws her final breath;[3] a patch of overgrown scrub yields up the bodies of hundreds of Indian children, long buried in unmarked graves—the horror of which had been whispered for decades.[4] But it is never long before the news cycle turns and saves us the trouble of having to look away. Outrage blurs once more into indifference.

It seems as though nothing has changed, and nothing ever will. First Nations remain poor, the Indian Act is still valid legislation, and violence stains the Indigenous landscape.

The reserve system has made interactions between Indigenous and non-Indigenous settler people less frequent than they otherwise might be. Poverty goes unseen, violence happens elsewhere, and inequality is a lot easier to stomach when you're not the one losing out. We just don't regard each other as neighbours.

But we *are* neighbours, just as Rossburn and Waywayseecappo have been for more than a century. Yet these two communities show the remarkable extent to which neighbours can remain strangers. Only recently, after all those years sharing the valley of the Birdtail, have they started to see each other differently and cooperate more. The change is limited. But it's a start.

Perhaps the most basic challenge is that Indigenous and non-Indigenous Canadians talk past each other. When we think about our history, Indigenous and settler narratives rarely intersect. The bigger picture, that we are all bound together, entangled in unexpected and uncomfortable ways, is too often obscured.

How many people in Rossburn have heard about the permits that for so long hamstrung Waywayseecappo's farmers? Not many, and perhaps as few as the number of people in Waywayseecappo who are familiar with the bigotry Ukrainians endured for multiple generations. It wasn't until Maureen was attending university that she first heard about the internment of Ukrainian Canadians during the First World War. It reminded her of the pass system that had confined Indians to reserves, and it got her thinking about other parallels she had never really considered. "Rossburn had its own history," Maureen says, "but I had never bothered to look into it."

Clifford Sifton once said that "the history of Canada is one of absorbing and romantic interest." By teaching Canadian history to Canada's students, he hoped the country would develop a sense of "national unity—a Canadian soul and Canadian outlook from coast to coast." He hoped that students would be taught about the contributions immigrants made to the prairies: "The epic story of Canadian pioneering, with the high courage of those whose faith moved mountains, properly told, will thrill our children."[5] And so it did—millions of Canadians such as Nelson Luhowy grew up within the soothing confines of this heroic narrative. But so long as we allow ourselves to be trapped inside narrow stories about the past, reconciliation can never truly begin. Here in the present, the relationship between Indigenous and non-Indigenous Canadians remains broken. The underfunding of reserve schools is merely one symptom of a much deeper sickness: profound inequalities in education, health, and wealth outcomes.

Listening to each other's stories is one way to stitch Canada back together. Reconciliation will require us, at the very least, to acknowledge each other's dignity.

Indigenous Peoples know that there's more to listening than letting a message wash over you. Listening activates our hearts, which allows us not simply to listen to one another but to really hear what is being said. There is a Haudenosaunee ceremony that is a prelude to any meeting between themselves and another Nation: participants begin with an act of compassion—wiping away each other's tears. The ceremony, sometimes called the Three Bare Words, both acknowledges a participant's humanity and underscores a key concept of Haudenosaunee philosophy: we all need help sometimes.

Of course, listening more is one thing, but acting differently— as individuals, as a country—is another. In recent years, Rossburn and Waywayseecappo have provided an example of what mean- ingful cooperation between Indigenous and non-Indigenous people can look like. Forced to see that each community needs the other, Rossburn and Waywayseecappo were able to imagine a shared future. There are lessons to be learned from their example, or, as might be said in Waywayseecappo, teachings to be heard.

THE INEQUALITY BETWEEN settler and Indigenous communities has been present since Confederation. What is true about on-reserve education is also true of other basic services, like access to health care and child welfare resources: far worse services on reserves are the norm. It is as though Canadians accept this inequality and go to bed each night untroubled by the lack of basic infrastructure in reserve communities. For now, equal outcomes remain beyond reach.

And yet Canadians view themselves as deeply committed to equality. The Constitution and provincial human rights codes enshrine equality rights. But what does it mean for an education system to treat children equally? The answer is more complicated than at first it may seem.

One way to think about the education partnership that began in 2010 is simply as an equalization of resources. With equal funding, the educational outcomes of children living on the reserve quickly improved. And so one might argue that increased spending in other Indigenous communities could work the same magic. To give credit where credit is due, since 2015, the Liberal government of Justin Trudeau has substantially increased spending on Indigenous children. "It is simply not right that young people in Indigenous communities don't have the same dollars spent on education that young people in provincial schools do," Trudeau has said.[6] The year 2021 marked the first time the federal government was providing students on reserves funding roughly comparable to that of students in provincially funded schools.[7]

But although this recent increase in federal investment will surely make a positive difference, there is no talk of making up for all the years of comparative underfunding.

We might use, as a basis for judging equality, the measuring stick of resources. Dollar for dollar, each child should receive the same spending on programs and services. But equal distribution of resources alone cannot address the structural inequalities between First Nations and settler communities. First Nations communities are often small and remote. So a small reserve school could receive, per student, the same funding as a provincial school in a larger school district, but would not have the benefit of increased efficiencies that come with a larger population. That is why, after Waywayseecappo's partnership with the nearby provincial schools, children on the reserve suddenly had access to a speech therapist. For a single school this was an unaffordable luxury, but shared between the fifteen schools in the district, a speech therapist was perfectly affordable.

Another method of measuring equality is to focus our concern not on equality of resources but on equality of outcomes. With respect to school funding, what would matter is not how much money is spent per child but, rather, whether enough money is spent so that children are achieving at roughly the same levels regardless of whether they live on or off reserve. Equality of outcomes allows us to focus on an endpoint of equality, and equality of this sort just costs what it costs.

But this outcomes-focused approach to equality also has shortcomings. We can identify a desired outcome as a marker of equality—for example, scores on standardized tests—but that outcome may not be the priority for First Nations communities.[8] Indigenous Peoples want quality education for their children, just as any parents do. But, also like other parents, Indigenous parents want a say in the contents of that education. They want schools that prepare children for success in the world while also nurturing ties to Indigenous knowledge and ways of being. To give merely the most obvious examples, communities might want to focus more heavily on teaching an Indigenous language or incorporating land-based learning.[9] Equality of outcomes only makes sense if we all value the same outcomes. This simply isn't the case when it comes to bringing standard Canadian education into Indigenous communities.

Back in 1996, the Royal Commission on Aboriginal Peoples described Canada as a "test case for a grand notion—the notion that dissimilar peoples can share lands, resources, power and dreams while respecting and sustaining their differences. The story of Canada is the story of many such peoples, trying and failing and trying again, to live together in peace and harmony."[10]

We are still failing. It is time to try a fundamentally different approach.

THE PRESENT-DAY INEQUALITIES between Indigenous and settler peoples are the inevitable result of governments of all stripes ignoring with impunity the needs of Indigenous Peoples: this is the root of the problem, and this is what must be addressed.

Indigenous Canadians are poorer, get imprisoned more often, attain lower levels of formal education, and have worse health outcomes than their settler neighbours. Hardship and unequal treatment have become endemic and routine. Poking away with new programs here and there and hoping for a brighter future will not meaningfully alter the economic and social outcomes of Indigenous Canadians.

To undertake fundamental change, we need to rethink our approach to two key mechanisms of government. The first is law-making: Who gets to make what kinds of law, and where? The second is financing: Where does the money come from to pay for roads and judges and schools and nurses?

With regard to jurisdiction, our Constitution gives the federal government exclusive authority over issues of national concern (such as banking, national defence, and "Indians and lands reserved for Indians"), while the provinces and territories have jurisdiction over issues of more local concern (such as property and civil rights). This is called the division of powers, and it is an arrangement from which First Nations communities are entirely excluded. First Nations governments have only limited decision-making authorities, as set out in the Indian Act, federal legislation that has dictated the nature of Indigenous government, its participants, and capacities for more than 150 years.[11] Band councils such as Waywayseecappo's have authority over such narrow matters as beekeeping and the regulation of trespassers, while other, more meaningful powers (policing, social welfare programs, game and wildlife, mining, forestry, and courts) are held by the provinces. But even if First Nations governments had legal authority to do more, it costs money to pay police, teachers, and nurses, just as it costs money to finance and regulate mining, forestry, and other industries.

Governments tax people and things to raise money, but First Nations have been left as bit players in this regard, with nearly all the powers of taxation taken up by the federal, provincial, and, to a lesser degree, municipal governments. First Nations can charge sales and property tax on their reserves, but reserve economies are so small that there is little revenue to be realized through these avenues.[12]

Because of the widespread myth that Indigenous Peoples in Canada pay no taxes, non-Indians believe that they are the ones holding the bag and subsidizing Indigenous communities. In fact, exactly the opposite is true. To explain how, we need to understand how taxation works, and why taxation has the potential to make Indigenous communities places where hope wins out over despair.

Taxation is the lifeblood of governance. Without tax revenue, there are no schools or any other kind of civic infrastructure. Without the capacity to raise funds, Indigenous communities cannot set and pursue ends of their own. Instead, the money for nearly every expense of an Indian band comes from another government, principally the federal government.[13] To state the obvious, the federal government could underfund on-reserve education only because it controlled the funding.

In an Indigenous community such as Waywayseecappo, there is a rapidly growing population and an extremely limited tax base, where virtually all incoming resources are transferred from the federal government. A community such as this has to make hard choices about what to do with that money: build a community centre or provide home care to elderly residents; fund primary education or repair roads; build additional housing or purchase a fire engine. Of course, all governments have to make similar choices, but non-Indian governments have the ability to raise or introduce taxes, a choice largely denied to First Nations communities. Rather than think about where to increase spending, Indigenous communities are usually only left with choices about what to cut.

★ ★ ★

GIVING FIRST NATION communities the power to tax an adequate land base would be a first step to empowering effective local government. To show what this might look like, we can look at a group of forty-three communities in northern Ontario that are far more remote than Waywayseecappo. Except during the coldest days of winter, when it is possible to construct ice roads, half of these communities are accessible only by air. There are very few signs of federal or provincial Crown presence: no government offices, no hospitals, no high schools, no courthouse. It is hard to understand why federal and provincial lawmakers should govern over places so removed from federal and provincial government services and legislatures.

If we were to take seriously the idea that these forty-three First Nations should be able to govern themselves, what would that mean? What sorts of resources and governmental powers would they need?

To start with, they would have to exercise jurisdiction over a much larger area of the province than the land that makes up reserves—the reserves are tiny compared with the vast expanse of government-owned Crown land in the north.[14] First Nations would need this enlarged territory in order to have sufficient land from which to extract resources for sale or on which to tax the extraction of those resources by others. With jurisdiction over this larger territory, these communities would have the financial resources to do the sorts of things that other local governments are expected to do: operate schools and a justice system, provide clean running water, fix roads, staff a fire department, and provide health services.

The lands of the north are rich. In recent years, the government of Ontario collected about $100 million annually in revenue from Crown timber fees from forestry activities, largely located in the northern parts of the province.[15] Those lands are the Traditional Territories of Cree and Ojibway people and for thousands of years provided Indigenous Peoples the means to live a good life—and they should do so again.

Were we to give Indigenous communities in northern Ontario the ability to govern themselves in this way, we could eliminate dependence on federal money. Some might argue that it is unfair to place Indigenous communities in the position of having to extract natural resources or to tax the extraction of natural resources from their Traditional Territories. But this is just what governments do: tax activities (such as forestry and mining) and people (via sales or income tax), and then spend that money on citizens, community infrastructure (schools, police, hospitals), and connections to other communities (highways, rail corridors). Indigenous governments should be no different, and they should be the ones making the difficult choices about what taxes to collect and which resources to extract.

So now we imagine forty-three First Nations communities in northern Ontario having jurisdiction over their Traditional Territories. It is probably not within the capacity of a small population to govern over such vast territories. Instead, small First Nations communities would need to work together in some form of confederacy to create viable governments capable of making complex land use and spending decisions.[16] The money raised from taxation could then be spent on building adequate schools and housing, paying teachers' salaries, and initiating environmental remediation in lakes and streams. Perhaps most important, Indigenous governments would surely prioritize what the federal government has long neglected: the well-being of Indigenous children.

But solutions to big problems are never cost-free. In the scenario we set out, the Province of Ontario would have a hole in its budget more or less exactly the same size as the revenue generated by Indigenous taxation of northern Ontario. And this provincial revenue loss would not be a minor concern. Across Canada, the vast majority of Crown lands are held provincially, not federally.[17] This means that any effort to redistribute territorial jurisdiction between provinces and First Nations will require not merely provincial cooperation but a willingness to give up territory to Indigenous governments. In other words, to the extent that the territorial jurisdiction of First Nations is enlarged, jurisdiction over provincial land is necessarily diminished.[18] Provincial coffers, likewise, will experience a considerable diminishment of revenues, because a great deal of provincial revenue is raised from taxing resource industries in the north.

We must come to accept that reconciliation between Indigenous and settler peoples will require a redistribution of access to wealth and to the mechanisms of governance. But the provinces will obviously be concerned about a plan requiring them to relinquish their most resource-rich areas. Provincial leadership, and Canadians in general, may be interested in reconciliation, but not at the cost of billions of dollars in annual tax revenue. And yet, to flourish, Indigenous Peoples will need to raise revenues through taxation, and so will require territory of sufficient size and wealth to invest in their communities. And that land will have to come from somewhere. The transfer of jurisdiction from provinces to First Nations may be seen—particularly by Indigenous Peoples themselves—as the righting of a historic wrong. Yet, at the same time, there is likely a large non-Indigenous southern population who would see the present-day transfer of land to First Nations as unfair.[19]

To reconcile these views, we must face a simple truth: the problem is distribution. Readjusting the borders of Indigenous territories means readjusting the borders of what would otherwise be provincial lands. And because the lands of northern Canada are rich in resources, redistribution of those territories is also a massive redistribution of wealth. So it seems that we are at a logjam: First Nations communities need land over which to govern, and the provinces require that same land in order to tax resource extraction.

To find a way through this conundrum, we need to see that the distribution problem we face is not of lands but of resources and wealth. Would residents of Toronto or Vancouver care who governed over their provinces' northern territories if it meant no material change to government services or the rate of taxation?[20] We think not. So, the question isn't who governs, but who benefits.   .

CANADA'S WEALTH IS not distributed equally among its provinces and territories; it varies based on factors such as population density and natural resources, and it fluctuates over time—with the collapse of a fishery, say, or a spike in oil prices.

Nevertheless, a key feature of Canadian federalism is the principle that every citizen, no matter where they live, should receive a similar level of government services. And, except on Indian reserves, Canada largely delivers on this commitment. The guarantee of equal government services at the provincial level is made possible through an economic program called equalization—which, for all its controversies, has enjoyed longstanding and widespread support among Canadians.[21] Through the equalization formula, regional disparities are smoothed out by a federally administered program that allocates federal revenue to provincial coffers. Redistribution levels the playing field among provinces. Whether you live in Newfoundland, Manitoba, or Quebec, equalization ensures that you receive comparable quality schooling and medical care. (In 2019–20, for example, Manitoba received an infusion of $2.25 billion.) Without equalization, smaller provinces such as Prince Edward Island simply could not generate enough tax revenue to provide similar services to those living in oil-rich Alberta. Yet no one ever asks whether Prince Edward Island deserves decent schools. It is a given. Prince Edward Island's citizens have decent elementary schools and clean running water, even if this requires redistribution of wealth. Equalization is how Canada balances our provincial and regional inequalities. Yet Indigenous communities neither contribute to nor benefit from equalization. First Nations do not share any part in the redistribution of national wealth. But imagine if this basic principle of equality were extended to Indigenous Peoples and communities.

Under the proposal we offer here, First Nations communities of northern Ontario might collect $1 billion in revenue from taxing resource extraction, the same $1 billion that once financed health care, policing, and education in Toronto, Windsor, and the like. The First Nations in northern Ontario could spend the tax money on community infrastructure to provide decent services for their citizens, and this would very likely cost considerably less than $1 billion annually. And we can then imagine the remaining funds being deposited into the equalization formula for redistribution to Ontario, thus somewhat ameliorating the budget shortfall that would otherwise occur.

In this way, First Nations communities would govern territories and tax resource extraction so as to make finally and abundantly clear that citizens in southern Canada are, and have been, subsidized by the north for at least 150 years. Under our proposal,

First Nations governments would be signing the cheques that underwrite their southern neighbours.

IN MANY REGIONS of the Canadian north, Indigenous Peoples are virtually the only human inhabitants, and always have been. In these areas in particular, it makes sense to think about recognizing a robust third order of government: Indigenous, in addition to federal and provincial. An Indigenous order of government would provide a way for Indigenous Peoples to finally be brought into the Canadian confederation as partners, not subjects. Communities such as these would also be better placed to consider the environmental effects of resource industries. After all, Indigenous Peoples have lived in these territories for thousands of years, and they intend to remain there for thousands more. This means it will be Indigenous Peoples, exercising jurisdiction over their territories, who will keep safe the watersheds and forests that provide southern Canadians with clean water to drink and fresh air to breathe.

Band councils like Waywayseecappo's are ostensibly governments in that they have some governmental powers, but in the absence of a meaningful capacity to tax resources and people, these band councils do not really govern—they merely spend money transferred to them by the federal and provincial governments. Indigenous governance of much larger Traditional Territories is an altogether different proposition, and should become a familiar feature of our political landscape. Crucially, because these communities would be self-governing, and self-financing, they would be immune from the financial vagaries of a federal government that has often not felt the need to treat all its citizens equally.

First Nations communities and Indian reserves are not all located in the north. Many bump right up against cities and towns like Rossburn and Vancouver. In these situations, we would need to consider the manner in which municipalities in the south raise tax revenues. In cities such as Toronto, the primary forms of government revenue are property and land-transfer taxes. To the extent that southern reserve communities were provided expanded territorial jurisdiction under our proposal, these communities would need to draw on the same resources as southern municipalities—namely, property taxes. This in turn means that some residents of southern Ontario might find themselves no longer living within settler-run municipalities but would instead be residents of a First Nations–led municipality. This would not, to be clear, affect who owns what land. Private landowners would simply find themselves paying taxes to a different order of government: an Indigenous municipal government instead of a settler municipal government.

Consider a 2020 U.S. Supreme Court case about an Indian reservation created by a nineteenth-century treaty between the Creek tribe of Indians and the U.S. government. The reservation had been in what was then Indian country, but as soon as oil was discovered, the newly formed state of Oklahoma assumed control of the territory. Oklahomans and the U.S. government acted as though the declaration of statehood was a sufficient legal act to extinguish the Creek Indian reservation. At issue was the question of whether the state diminishment of the Creek Indian reservation was legal. The majority judgment was written by Neil Gorsuch, a conservative judge appointed by Donald Trump:

> *How much easier it would be, after all, to let the State proceed as it has always assumed it might. But just imagine what it would*

*mean to indulge that path. A State exercises jurisdiction over
Native Americans with such persistence that the practice seems
normal. Indian landowners lose their titles by fraud or otherwise
in sufficient volume that no one remembers whose land it once
was. All this continues for long enough that a reservation that
was once beyond doubt becomes questionable, and then even far
fetched. Sprinkle in a few predictions here, some contestable commentary there, and the job is done, a reservation is disestablished.
None of these moves would be permitted in any other area of
statutory interpretation, and there is no reason why they should
be permitted here. That would be the rule of the strong, not the
rule of law.*[22]

As a result of the McGirt decision, the western half of Oklahoma,
including much of the city of Tulsa, is for some purposes once
again recognized as an Indian reservation. Gorsuch noted that
"many of [Oklahoma's] residents will be surprised to find out
they have been living in Indian country this whole time." The
U.S. Supreme Court is untroubled by the result (even if some
Oklahomans are indeed rattled) because the court can clearly
see that no transfer of property is taking place—borders have
changed, but nobody's land was taken.[23]

What happened in Oklahoma could happen in Canada.
Jurisdictions shift, politics adapt, and new relationships become
possible.

FOR MORE THAN 150 years, we have attempted to find a way to live
side by side as Indigenous and settler people, just as the citizens
of Waywayseecappo and Rossburn have lived side by side. What
has made all the difference to Rossburn and Waywayseecappo

295

has been the realization that they are better off working together rather than against each other. It is important to note that neither the citizens of Rossburn nor the citizens of Waywayseecappo agreed to the partnership out of generosity. Instead, each community understood the arrangement in terms of its own self-interest. And it is in our larger self-interest as Canadians to recognize that the relationship between Waywayseecappo and Rossburn is no different from the broader relationship between Indigenous and settler people. Keeping Indigenous Peoples poor is an expensive proposition for everyone else as well.

Consider the case of education. An estimated 70 percent of new jobs require some amount of post-secondary education, so an Indigenous person without a high school diploma is twice as likely to be unemployed. Lower rates of formal education are also linked to worse health outcomes and higher rates of incarceration. Beyond the direct toll on Indigenous Peoples themselves, the resulting costs to taxpayers are immense, including hundreds of millions in additional dollars spent on income support, health services, and prisons. In Manitoba, for example, 75 percent of persons admitted into custody are Indigenous, even though Indigenous Peoples account for only 15 percent of the province's population.[24] Keeping a single inmate in federal prison costs $125,000 each year. Compared to the alternatives, investing more in education for Indigenous Peoples is a bargain. And yet we haven't, opting instead for an approach that is both cruel and self-defeating.

What's more, because Indians raised on reserves receive cheap, subpar education, they usually don't go on to fill high-paying jobs, and so don't pay as much into the income tax system. Collectively, we also lose out on so much of the talent that they have to offer. It is expensive to keep Indians poor, and we would all benefit from *full access* to the economy, access which comes only with *full access* to education, health care, and clean running water.

Since the release, in 2015, of the Truth and Reconciliation Commission's report on the Indian residential school system, there have been attempts by churches, unions, school boards, and governments to respond meaningfully to calls for reconciliation. Some of the resulting changes, such as the now widespread invocation of the land acknowledgement at public events, will take a generation to bear fruit, as our children grow up in a world where they understand that we all live on Traditional Indigenous Territories and not merely land homesteaded by settlers. In the meantime, while we may acknowledge Traditional Territories, we do nothing to return their governance to Indigenous Nations.

Many Canadians fear or do not believe in the viability of an Indigenous order of government. But the proposals we are making here are based on principles our country knows and has long used: extending policies like the equalization formula to Indigenous communities is just to invite First Nations into Confederation on familiar terms. Reconciliation will require not only a common understanding of the jagged contours of our shared history, but also enacting a fair distribution of resources and the authority to make decisions about land use. To redraw jurisdictional borders and redistribute governmental powers of taxation is to recognize the dignity and equality of Indigenous Peoples.

All across this great land, Indigenous Peoples entered into treaties with the government of Canada. They understood these agreements as sacred: the land was sacred and so were the agreements for its sharing. More and more Canadians are beginning to understand that we are all treaty people. Indigenous Peoples and settlers alike are party to the treaties, and the treaties are not just historical documents—they set out a plan for sharing territory and providing the legal authority to do so. When entering into these agreements, Indigenous Peoples understood the Canadian government's promises to be honourable, good-faith efforts. For nearly three centuries before Confederation, in 1867, Indigenous Peoples worked alongside the British and French as military allies, trading partners, and family members.[25] But, after Confederation, the young Dominion government of Canada turned its back on the very idea that treaties should be honoured and that the land could be shared. First Nations were moved onto tiny reserves and governed as wards of the state. Indeed, settler Canadians have been the only beneficiaries of historic treaties with First Nations.

Pushed aside and given few resources, Indigenous Peoples have suffered an inequality that is more like abject poverty. Without the capacity to raise meaningful resources through taxation, First Nations have been left to eat from the hand of the federal Crown. It is easy to think that we might address these inequalities through increased funding for basic services in Indigenous communities, but that increased funding has rarely arrived, and Canada continues to under-service Indigenous communities.

In 2000, an outbreak of *E. coli* bacteria contaminated the water supply of Walkerton, Ontario. Six people died and more than two thousand people were infected. Almost immediately, a boil-water advisory was issued, and the town of Walkerton no longer had access to clean running water. Police began an investigation. Needless to say, once identified, the source of contamination was addressed and the taps were turned back on within days. A public inquiry was called, criminal charges were laid, elected officials were held to account.

In contrast, more than thirty First Nations communities have been living under boil-water advisories for more than a decade.[26] There has been no public inquiry, no one is held accountable, and day after day, year after year, the taps spill out contaminated water, undrinkable and unusable for laundry or bathing yourself or your newborn.

A feature of the pervasive racism toward First Nations people is the ability to so undervalue Indigenous lives that settler citizens sleep comfortably at night, safe in the knowledge that their water is clean and not caring, or even knowing, that First Nations communities have no such luxury. First Nations citizens are too few in number to effectively hold public officials accountable at the ballot box, and so beyond the obvious immorality of the situation, public officials have little incentive to act, and, for the most part, they have not. We are left with an uncomfortable truth: the inequality between settler and Indigenous Canadians results from politics, and, so far, not enough Canadians have been motivated to upend an unfair and unequal system.

In Waywayseecappo, as across Canada, Indians are short-changed, neglected, and impoverished. Even if Canadian citizens and politicians were to muster the political will to fund services in First Nations and settler communities equally, how long would it be before the inequalities began to creep back in, as governments struggled to determine how best to spend limited resources? If 150 years of history is anything to go by, it would be only a matter of time until we reverted to the discriminatory norm.

The Canadian commitment to equality was set out in the 1982 Charter of Rights and Freedoms. Section 15 states, "Every individual is equal before and under the law and has the right to equal protection and equal benefit of the law . . . without discrimination based on race, national or ethnic origin, colour, religion, sex, age or mental or physical disability." And yet, as we have seen, Indigenous Canadians have markedly unequal access to government services of all kinds. We do not think that it is too much to insist on changes that ensure Indigenous Peoples have access to services that are on par with what provinces provide to every other Canadian. The best way to do this is to give Indigenous Peoples the necessary power to ensure a fairer distribution of lands and resources.

The proposals we are making here may seem ambitious, extraordinary even, but Canadians have done this before. Modern-day land claim agreements—treaties—in the Yukon and in the James Bay region of Quebec provide extensive self-government arrangements.[27] There, and in other regions subject to modern-day treaties, First Nations governments exercise jurisdiction over broad territories and many areas of governance. These are no longer experiments: Indigenous-governed territories are now woven into the fabric of Canada. In other words, the future we propose is already a part of our present-day Canadian identity. The only difference is this: modern-day treaties are mostly in British Columbia and Yukon, where no treaties were previously signed. What we are proposing is to implement these same sort of arrangements—modern-day treaties—where it makes sense to do so, including in places like Manitoba where historical treaties negotiated by Alexander Morris have proved inadequate.

And we need look no further than Quebec to see that religious, linguistic, and even legal accommodation is possible. Provincial law in Quebec is governed by a civil code, a set of laws found nowhere else in Canada. Part of what makes Canada great has been our accommodation of difference. To form a country with two official languages, two official sets of laws, and two distinct peoples, was, in 1867, the product of profound imagination.

But just as Canada found a way to accommodate two founding European peoples, now we must find a way to afford Indigenous Peoples in Canada the equality and dignity they deserve.

To see First Nations governance as an integral part of our Canadian culture is not to stretch the imagination—it is to stretch our arms, and embrace each other as equal partners in a vast and complicated land. There is enough to share. Land, resources, wealth: there *is* enough for everyone, and there always has been.

Epilogue

"SHINING SUN"

August 2019

TRADITIONAL SONGS AND DANCES CONTINUE TO OCCUPY a special place in the hearts of many Ukrainian Canadians, including Nelson Luhowy's. That is why, during the first weekend of August, Nelson makes the seventy-minute drive from Rossburn to Dauphin for the National Ukrainian Festival. The event is Nelson's best opportunity each year to hear the beats and lyrics of his boyhood. "I like hearing the songs in Ukrainian," he says, "even though I don't really understand them. They just sound good."

The festival draws five thousand attendees and lasts all weekend, featuring buffets of Ukrainian cuisine, booths with traditional arts and crafts, shirtless and sun-burned men dancing while holding overflowing glasses of beer, and—of course—a perogy-eating contest. This year, the champion manages to hoover down a plate of twenty-four perogies within ninety-four seconds.

At night, Nelson stays with his brother Don in a mobile home parked in a sprawling campground infused at dinnertime with the aroma of sausage. During the day, Nelson explores the festival grounds on an electric scooter, his crutches jutting out the rear. At any given moment, there are two or three live performances taking place, some of them given by musicians who flew all the way from the old country. Nelson has plenty of time to watch a whole slew of traditional dances: the *hutzul*, the *poltava*, the *transcarpathian*, the *volyn*. On this weekend at least, the fiddle is king.

This year, Troy, Michelle, and their kids, Reid and Addison, didn't make the drive to the festival. The kids never expended much effort learning Ukrainian folk dances, unlike some of their cousins. "Learning the dances takes a lot of time," Nelson says. "But so does hockey." By August, Reid and Addison have already started their training camps for the upcoming hockey season, and they're just fine with eating perogies at home.

ON THE SAME weekend as the Ukrainian Festival, Waywayseecappo hosts a powwow. More than 350 dancers from across the Canadian prairies and the United States converge for the event. Hundreds more spectators pack the wooden stands. Among them are Linda, Maureen, and Teagan, seated a few rows back from a drum circle.

Teagan does not flinch, even though the drums are so loud her chest vibrates with a second heartbeat. This is her third time at the annual event, and she is not yet three years old. She is mesmerized by the dance circle, a shimmering swirl of movement and colour. The dancers orbit a central wooden pole, moving clockwise on a ring of grass. It is as if buckets of bright paint were being poured into a whirlpool, creating a churn of yellow and green, blue and red, purple and pink. Each dancer wears a distinctive combination of feathers, regalia, and animal skins—the sight would surely make Hayter Reed roll in his grave.

Teagan's own regalia is the work of many hands. Her father's aunt stitched her dress (mostly pink and floral), Maureen sewed beads into the belt (in the shape of yet more flowers), and Maureen's friend Grace made the moccasins (with red and pink beadwork). Like many of the women and girls in attendance, Teagan is wearing a "jingle dress" adorned with dozens of tiny bells that ring out whenever she moves. The dress is associated with a healing dance meant to repair wounds in a community.

Eighteen drumming groups take turns singing and setting the pace for the dancers. In between songs, a loquacious MC keeps up a steady stream of banter and uplift: "Through all the trials and tribulations, ladies and gentlemen, we're still here, we've always been here." More than a century has passed since Waywayseecappo's drums terrified residents in Rossburn. Two-year-old Teagan knows there's nothing to be frightened of, except maybe that man draped in a bear's skin.

The whole spectacle is enough to make Maureen tear up. Someone once told her that when she feels like crying while watching the powwow, that's her ancestors reaching out to her. Maureen likes to think of her ancestors continuing to dance through all those years when the government was trying to stop them.

Over the loudspeaker, the MC announces the Initiation Dance for first-timers: "New dancers, welcome to the dance circle. We're welcoming you to our big family circle. Welcome to the powwow family, for the rest of your lives. Parents, thank you for teaching the young ones." Teagan sits this one out because she was initiated last year, shortly after she started walking. Maureen had held her hand as she completed her first lap around the circle and received blessings from the community.

This year, Teagan's time to shine is the "Tiny Tots" dance. On cue, she joins dozens of toddlers in the dance circle, and the drumming begins anew. Teagan knows what to do: she puts her hands on her hips, grins widely, and starts bouncing. Around her, there is a range of skill. For the smallest dancers, it is an achievement to simply stay on their feet. Teagan clearly feels the music, though her little body can't quite keep up with the rhythm. As she gets older, she will add other elements, like waving a handkerchief or feather fan. For now, she knows the main thing is to keep her hands firmly on her hips while she twirls.

Watching Teagan dance makes Maureen feel like a good mom. "Traditional dancing was something I didn't know much about while I was growing up," she says. "As Teagan learns more, she'll be able to teach me, too."

Teagan will soon start attending kindergarten at Waywayseecappo Community School. Because of all the positive changes in recent years, Maureen is comfortable with this. "I want her school to be up to par, for her not to go through what I went through," she says. "I hope for her not to be behind. I hope that wherever she goes to school, in a city or on a reserve, that she receives a fair education."

The drums are still beating, the chants continue, the song goes on. Maureen leans forward, scanning the circle of diminutive dancers to locate her daughter. There is Teagan, still twirling in her jingle dress. Maureen's face softens, then brightens with a smile.

Zaagaate Giizis, Teagan's name in Ojibway, means "Shining Sun."

AFTERWORD

BY MAUREEN TWOVOICE, BINESI IKWE (THUNDERBIRD WOMAN)

O N JULY 1, 2021—CANADA DAY—I WOKE FIVE MIN-
utes before my alarm clock that I set for 5:30 a.m. I
put on my skirt, found my orange T-shirt that reads
"Every Child Matters," and packed my snacks and *nibi*. Before I
left I captured a mental photo of my sleeping husband and our
nidaanisag in our bed, then grabbed my decaf coffee and walked
out the door.

I drove through the valley, heading south along Highway 45.
I enjoy rides through the reserve. Appreciating the landscape,
mishoomis giizis, mitigoog, and the silence of *aki*. Imagining what
the community looked like when the gravel roads were dirt
wagon trails, when there was more bush. How beautiful *giizis*
looks when it peeks through *mitigoog*.

I arrived at my friend Marisa's kokom's home, our meeting
place before we started our day further southwest. Marisa has
been my friend since I was eleven years old, when I forged my
mother's signature to attend a week-long cultural camp located in

the valley that divides Wewezhigaabawing and Rossburn. Marisa was there and showed me kindness. We set up camp, working together to create a shelter in case it rained, making our beds, rummaging through our cooler full of food. I was gone for a week, and I felt safe.

Now we continued on the back roads until we reached the Birtle Indian Residential School. Waiting was the pipe carrier, eagle staff, and a gathering of people from First Nations across Manitoba. Ceremony began on the front lawn of the school. As I sat on the ground with my skirt and legs to one side, I looked up at the building: there was the front door, a few shorts steps from the driveway. All I could think was, *My grandparents were dropped off at schools like this, taken from my great-grandparents by law and left alone with hundreds of other children.* My heart started to hurt and my eyes filled with tears. I took a deep breath. This is where intergenerational trauma started for my family. Or maybe it was another generation before my grandparents, but that's a history search for another time.

After the pipe ceremony came the walk from the Birtle Residential School to Wewezhigaabawing. There were at least forty or more Anishinaabeg dedicating their day to walk. Marisa and I followed a group of four ladies as they walked from the school on the left side, through the back, through the tall grass, along the tree line, up to the old train tracks. I looked back and wondered if children running from the school had looked back as they fled into the night. *Giizis* was already getting hot. We walked for about thirty minutes on the gravel road. To the left of us in the pasture were maybe ten black stallions. They came and formed a semicircle facing us, and then they walked with us along the fence. I had a lump in my throat remembering the teaching I received about horses and the healing they bring. It was like they knew we needed healing that day. I am afraid of horses, but that day I embraced what they came to share.

I walked for my maternal mooshum Alvin Jandrew and kokom Thelma Ross, who both attended Birtle Residential School. I walked for my paternal mooshum Michael Twovoice, who attended the Lebret Residential School, and kokom Annie Keewatincappo, who also attended the Birtle school in the early forties. I walked for my mother Linda, who attended the Brandon Residential School, and my father Maurice, who attended Sandy Bay Residential School in the late fifties and early sixties. I also walked for all the other children from our community who attended residential school. I was told once that when you do something as little as walk in honour of someone, their spirit heals.

It was July 1, but I do not celebrate Canada Day. After learning about the atrocities Anishinaabeg across Turtle Island have endured, why would I celebrate a day that praises a country that attempted to assimilate my people? A country that attempted to strip from us Anishinaabemowin, ceremony, teachings, and traditional life skills, a country that set us up for failure through residential school education.

As an Anishinaabeikwe, I am relearning about *mashkiki*, which I was fortunate to identify alongside the road. A sense of pride ran through my body as I was able to identify and share other medicine plants with whoever was walking beside me. I wondered if the cultural disconnect was already present when children were running away from residential schools. One *mashkiki* was the root of bulrushes; one of its purposes is to give you energy if you do not have food. My friend Shirli taught me that while we were looking for *wekay* one summer. These were *mashkiki* my great-grandparents would have known and utilized for minor and major injuries. I was working to reclaim a traditional skill to revitalize my people's ways of knowing and understanding the world around us.

During the walk, I was surrounded by community members, who were exchanging stories. One community member said, "My grandparents went to Sandy Bay School." I shared, "My parents went to Brandon and Sandy Bay." Some wondered about the shoes children were issued—the shoes they wore as they stood in line for meals, the shoes they forgot beside their bed and were struck across the head for, the shoes they wore as they fled into the night. Another said, speaking of our walking today, "This is nothing compared to what our parents went through." And then it hit me again: this is why my family is the way it is. It wasn't just me, or my mom, or even my community. This was a reality for my people for generations.

There was a stretch when I was walking alone and I just cried. I could hear the birds singing in the distance. I could hear the footsteps of the walkers on the gravel road. I could hear laughter, even though we were all carrying a heavy heart that day. I could see all the beauty Mother Earth provides for us, *aki*, *mashkiki*, *noodin*, and *giizis*. I felt alone, walking, thinking of my family who have been deeply affected by residential schools and how directly connected I am to intergenerational trauma, whether I like it or not. I thought about being the first generation not to have attended residential school. I am now thirty years old.

Walking the whole way from the school to Wewezhigaabawing would have taken me eight and a half hours. But after six hours, I could not walk anymore. I developed blisters on the back of my ankles and my toes were throbbing. I imagined young children, alone, running, with whatever shoes that had been given to them. Children like Jim Cote, now one of our most respected Elders. I tried not to complain about my feet until the pain overrode my focus. I imagined how far from the road the children had to hide to continue their journey. How brave they were, how determined to get home. In most cases, they would be brought right back to the doorstep of a residential school when they were discovered by an Indian agent or church official.

I looked up ahead and was surprised to see farmers standing at the end of their driveways handing out freezies and bottles of *nibi*. "I am so glad you're doing this walk," a woman said with her hand placed across her heart. A man had driven from Birtle with his son and was stopping to hand out *nibi* to walkers.

A woman not from the reserve sat in her parked vehicle, holding a tissue as tears fell down her face. I could see she was hurt and showed compassion for the walkers and acknowledged the pain of our people.

Miigwech to those who showed empathy from the surrounding communities. Maybe next time they will walk with us.

I am most grateful for my parents, Linda Jandrew and Maurice Twovoice, for their resiliency during a period of history when the goal was to assimilate every Indigenous child. For all of my grandparents: Michael and Annie Twovoice (née Keewatincappo), and Alvin and Thelma Jandrew (née Ross). Without the generations before me, their strength and their determination, I would not be who I am today. And *gichii miigwech* to leadership from Waywayseecappo First Nation throughout the years who challenged the status quo for a better future.

Lastly, I walked for Zaagaate Giizis and Binesi, my daughters. With their names given through ceremony, they will both know the direction they are going in life. They will know the history of where they come from. They will be familiar with teachings. They will have the tools and knowledge about Anishinaabeg that my husband and I did not receive until later in life. These will help guide them to walk in two worlds, a talent our people require. I will show them how to teach those around them, in a kind way, so that they will be ready to advocate for Anishinaabeg rights for the next generations.

GLOSSARY

aki: earth; land
Anishinaabeg: Ojibway people
Anishinaabeikwe: Ojibway woman
Anishinaabemowin: Ojibway language
binesi: thunderbird
gichii miigwech: big thank you
giizis: sun
kokom: grandmother
mashkiki: medicine
miigwech: thank you
mishoomis giizis: grandfather sun
mitigoog: trees
mooshum: grandfather
nibi: water
nidaanisag: my daughters
noodin: wind
Turtle Island: according to a creation story shared among Anishinaabeg, Canada is part of the turtle's back
wekay: sweetflag/sweet calamus
Wewezhigaabawing: traditional pronunciation for Waywayseecappo
Zaagaate Giizis: shining sun

ACKNOWLEDGEMENTS

WE ARE, FIRST AND FOREMOST, GRATEFUL TO Maureen Twovoice, Linda Jandrew, Jim Cote, and Troy and Nelson Luhowy for their time and generosity of spirit. We have done our best to honour your trust by telling this story accurately and well.

We also wish to thank the many people in Waywayseecappo, Rossburn, and beyond who shared their thoughts and memories, including Norbert Tanner, Hazel Twovoice, Maurice Twovoice, Elizabeth "Tizz" Shingoose, Linda Shingoose, Jackie McKee, Colleen Clearsky, Brad Clearsky, Marellia Cote, Bryan Cloud, Raymond Clearsky, Amanda Cooke, Madaline Whitehawk, Murray Clearsky, Michelle Luhowy, Tammy McCullough, Stephen David, Bob Plachinski, Dennis Kaskiw, Joe Arruda, Brian Brown, Morley Luhowy, John Kostecki, Paulette and Jack Mann, Con Erikson, Larry Huston, Travis Laing, Russ Andrews, Harry Swain, Scott Serson, and Michael Wernick.

A special thanks goes to Lorena Fontaine, for her early support and insights. Esther Sanderson, Louise Garrow, and John Borrows aided us with Cree and Ojibway translations. Paul Williams assisted with the details of the Three Bare Words ceremony. We also appreciate those who provided invaluable feedback and encouragement along the way, including Jody Porter, Justin Ferbey, Sarah Prichard, Allan Sniderman, Anmol Tikoo, Arvind Nair, Raghu Karnad, Bob and Judith Rae, Scott McIntyre, Lea Nicholas-MacKenzie, Sara Robinson, Rosanna Nicol, Jane Gaskell, William Westphal, Julia Sande, Sarah Molinoff, Erin Freeland, Jessica Magonet, Emma Preston-Lanzinger, Sheila Sanderson, Amal Haddad, Elyse Decker, Tiffany Wong-Jones, Hayden Eastwood, Tom Brennan, Arthur Ripstein, Promise Holmes Skinner, John Bonin, Michael Walsh, Jason Baker, Barry Elkind, and Mayo Moran.

This book would not have been possible without the support of a number of institutions, including the University of Ottawa's Human Rights and Education Research Centre (with the unwavering enthusiasm of John Packer), the O'Brien Fellowship program at the McGill University Faculty of Law's Centre for Human Rights and Legal Pluralism (with special thanks to Nandini Ramanujam and Sharon Webb), and the Center for Human Rights and Global Justice at New York University's School of Law (with particular gratitude to Lauren Stackpoole and Philip Alston). Generous financial support from the Wesley M. Nicol Foundation made the initial research for this book possible. And, way back in 2012, Anne Marie Owens and Mark Stevenson at *Maclean's* gave the go-ahead to an intern to write a feature story—everything since flowed from there.

A number of research assistants made important contributions, in part thanks to funding from Swarthmore College and SSHRC. Hope Rumford, Shelisa Klassen, Shay Downey, Henry Lei, CeCe Li, Serene Falzone, and most especially Daniel Diamond: we appreciate your help.

In Winnipeg, Aaron Trachtenberg was always a warm and welcoming host. So too were Heather Dean and Philip Carter on their farm in Sainte-Anne-des-Chênes, where delicious meals and good cheer were in bountiful supply.

In November and December of 2018 and again in December 2019, Andrew had the privilege of being a fellow in the Logan Nonfiction program at the Carey Institute for Global Good in Rensselaerville, New York. Thanks to Carlie Willsie and Josh Friedman for believing in this project, and to Meg Kissinger, Pat Evangelista, and Susan Berfield for their advice and (much-needed) cheerleading.

We were lucky to have the assistance of competent archivists across the country. A most special thank-you goes to David Cuthbert, based at the Winnipeg branch of Library and Archives Canada, who went above and beyond the call of duty. Many thanks, too, to Library and Archives staff in Ottawa, particularly Naïka Monchery. This project also benefited from the assistance of Rob Phillipson at the Provincial Archives of Saskatchewan, Joan Sinclair at the Archives of Manitoba, and Heather McNabb and Jonathan Lainey at the McCord Museum in Montreal. We also wish to acknowledge the work of prior archival researchers, whose footnotes often showed us where to start our own detective work. The research of Sarah Carter, John S. Milloy, J.R. Miller, and Katherine Pettipas proved particularly valuable in this regard.

This book would not have reached its potential without the zealous advocacy of our agent, Michael Levine, at Westwood Creative Artists. We also benefited from early editorial advice from Dan Crissman and Andrea DenHoed. Thankfully, we found a happy home for this book at HarperCollins, and we are grateful to Iris Tupholme, publisher extraordinaire, and to our editor, Jim Gifford, for his wise counsel and deft touch. Copy editor Shaun

Oakey and production editor Canaan Chu also contributed with their considerable talents.

Most of all, we are indebted to our spouses, Mariella and Tanya, who turned pages and calmed nerves and never stopped believing.

ENDNOTES

Authors' Note

1. Natasha Beedie et al., "Towards Justice: Tackling Indigenous Child Poverty in Canada," Upstream and Canadian Centre for Policy Alternatives, 2019; "A Portrait of First Nations and Education," Assembly of First Nations, 2012; Barry Anderson and John Richards, "Students in Jeopardy: An Agenda for Improving Results in Band-Operated Schools," C.D. Howe Institute, Commentary No. 444 (2016), 4.

Prologue: "The Valley of the Birdtail"

1. Marion Abra, *A View of the Birdtail: A History of the Municipality of Birtle 1878–1974* (Altona: The History Committee of the Municipality of Birtle, 1974), 3–4. See also Nathan Hasselstrom, *Pivotal Events: Birtle's Significant Historical Themes and Events* (n.p.: n.p., 2018), 130. Hasselstrom references the alternative theory that "the name was derived from the original Native name which was descriptive of its shape, since branches of the creek at its source resemble a spreading bird's tail."

2. Reita Bambridge Sparling, *Reminiscences of the Rossburn Pioneers* (Rossburn: Rossburn Women's Institute, 1951), 70. For ease of reading, we have changed the original "No where" to "Nowhere" and added a comma after "Birdtail."

3. Statistics Canada, *Rossburn, Municipality, Census Profile*, 2016 Census; Statistics Canada, *Waywayseecappo First Nation, Indian Reserve, Census Profile*, 2016 Census. For the purposes of this paragraph, we use the word "family" to connote what Statistics Canada calls an "economic family." In 2016, the average family income in Rossburn was $58,880; in Waywayseecappo, it was $26,517.

2: Linda's Shoes

1. Ian Mosby, "Administering colonial science: Nutrition research and human bio-medical experimentation in Aboriginal communities and residential schools, 1942-1952," *Histoire sociale/Social history* 46, no. 1 (2013): 145-72. Lack of food for Indigenous children in residential schools was not only the result of neglect. Some children were intentionally starved in nutritional "experiments" without their knowledge or consent.

2. There were schools run by various Christian denominations prior to 1880. For example, the Mohawk Institute opened in Ontario in 1831 under the adminis-tration of the Anglican Church. The federal government did not formally assume control of educating Indian children until 1880.

3. House of Commons, Debates, 9 May 1883, 1107-8.

4. Correspondence from A. Sutherland, General Secretary, Mission Board, to Superintendent General of Indian Affairs, 18 January 1890, vol. 6255, file 576-1, part 1, RG10, LAC, Ottawa.

5. John S. Milloy, *A National Crime: The Canadian Government and the Residential School System, 1879 to 1986* (Winnipeg: University of Manitoba Press, 1999), 58-9.

6. Correspondence from Chief Berens to A. Sutherland, 12 August 1891, vol. 6255, file 576-1, part 1, RG10, LAC, Ottawa.

7. Correspondence from A. Sutherland to Chief Berens, 23 September 1891, vol. 6255, file 576-1, part 1, RG10, LAC, Ottawa.

8. Correspondence from Chief Berens to A. Sutherland, 8 January 1891, vol. 6255, file 576-1, part 1, RG10, LAC, Ottawa. Berens adds, "Notwithstanding your oppo-sition to and arguments against local . . . schools, my views on that point are unshaken and as firm as ever."

9. Correspondence from Chief Jacob Berens et al. to E. McColl, Inspector of Indian Agencies, 25 February 1892, vol. 6255, file 576-1, part 1, RG10, LAC, Ottawa.

10. John Semmens, "Notes on Personal History," 1915, Accession 85-28, I.D. 3460, loca-tion PP37, Rev. John Semmens fonds, United Church of Canada Archives, Manitoba Northwestern Ontario Conference and All Native Circle Conference, 94.

11. Correspondence from J. Semmens to McColl, 19 February 1895, vol. 6255, file 576-1, part 1, RG10, LAC, Ottawa.

12. Correspondence from Deputy Superintendent of Indian Affairs to E. McColl, 8 March 1895, vol. 6255, file 576-1, part 1, RG10, LAC, Ottawa.

13. G.H. Wheatley (Indian Agent), "Letter to the Superintendent General of Indian Affairs Re: North-west Superintendency, Birtle Agency," 22 April 1907, in Dominion of Canada, *Annual Report of the Department of Indian Affairs for the Year Ended March 31, 1907* (Ottawa, 1908). Wheatley is speaking generally about the Birtle Agency, which included Waywayseecappo.

14. Dominion of Canada, *Annual Report of the Department of Indian Affairs for the Year Ended June 30, 1903* (Ottawa, 1904); Katherine Lyndsay Nichols, "Investigation of unmarked graves and burial grounds at the Brandon Indian Residential School" (MA thesis, University of Manitoba, 2015), 249–50. The dead in 1903 included Allan Ross on 27 January, Mary Captain on 30 March, Victoria Trout on 11 May, John Hastings on 3 November, David Moar on 26 November, and Annebella Sinclair on 11 December.

15. Semmens, "Notes on Personal History," 97–8.

16. Correspondence from W.W. Shoup (Nelson House) to A. Sutherland, 17 March 1907, box 7, file 127, A. Sutherland Papers, United Church of Canada Archives, as quoted in J.R. Miller, *Shingwauk's Vision: A History of Native Residential Schools* (Toronto: University of Toronto Press, 1996), 349.

17. Kristy Kirkup, "Names of 2,800 children who died in residential schools documented in registry," *Globe and Mail*, 30 September 2019; "Murray Sinclair on the deaths of children in residential schools, and what must be done to help survivors," *The Current*, CBC Radio, 1 June 2021. The National Centre for Truth and Reconciliation has estimated that approximately 1,600 names of deceased students remain unknown. Murray Sinclair estimates that as many as 25,000 Indigenous children died while attending residential schools.

18. Truth and Reconciliation Commission of Canada, *Canada's Residential Schools: Missing Children and Unmarked Burials: The Final Report of the Truth and Reconciliation Commission of Canada*, vol. 4 (Kingston: McGill-Queen's University Press, 2015), 30.

19. Correspondence from Duncan Campbell Scott to B.C. Indian Agent Gen.-Major D. MacKay, 12 April 1910, as quoted in Georges Erasmus, "Reparations: Theory, Practice and Education," *Windsor Yearbook of Access to Justice* 22 (2003): 189, 192.

20. "Report of S.J. Jackson, Inspector for Lake Manitoba Inspectorate, Manitoba," in Dominion of Canada, *Annual Report of the Department of Indian Affairs for the Year Ended March 31, 1914* (Ottawa, 1914).

21. Correspondence from J.A. Doyle, "To Indian Agents, Missionaries, Teachers, and Parents or Guardians of Indian Children," 16 March 1931, vol. 6350, file 753-5, part 2, RG10, LAC, Ottawa.

22. Correspondence from J.A. Doyle, "To Indian Agents, Missionaries . . . ," 21 March 1932.

23. To Miss . . . , 16 February 1966, and attached correspondence, file 1/25-20-1, vol. 1, INAC, LAC, as quoted in Milloy, *National Crime*, 284. See also Miller, *Shingwauk's Vision*, 315.

24. Truth and Reconciliation Commission of Canada, "They Came For the Children: Canada, Aboriginal Peoples, and Residential Schools" (Winnipeg, 2012), 51–2;

Elizabeth Graham, *The Mush Hole: Life at Two Indian Residential Schools* (Waterloo: Heffle, 1997), 12, as cited in Milloy, *National Crime*, footnote 7 in the Foreword.

25. Agent's Report, J. Waite, Brandon School, 1950, vol. 7194, file 511/25-1-015, MR C 9700, RG10, LAC, Ottawa, as cited in Milloy, *National Crime*, 266.

26. The material relating to Clifford Shepherd, Tommy Douglas, and Oliver Strapp draws on the following sources: T.C. Douglas collection, R-33.1, file 7336, PAS, Regina; correspondence from T.C. Douglas to J.A. Glen, Canadian National Telegram, 28 September 1946, vol. 6259, file 576-10, part 15, RG10, LAC, Ottawa; correspondence from T.C. Douglas to J.A. Glen, 11 December 1946; correspondence from Minister Glen to T.C. Douglas, 2 January 1947, vol. 6259, file 576-10, part 16, RG10, LAC, Ottawa; Truth and Reconciliation Commission of Canada, *Canada's Residential Schools: The History, Part 2: 1939–2000* (Kingston: McGill-Queen's University Press, 2015), 372–3. The Department of Indian Affairs claimed that Clifford should not be staying with his mother on account of her ill health, but Douglas noted that he was informed that "at present" she was "in reasonably good health."

27. Correspondence from G. Dorey to C. Neary, 27 December 1946, vol. 6259, file 576-10, part 16, RG10, LAC, Ottawa. Years later, Rev. George Dorey would publish a book entitled *No Vanishing Race: The Canadian Indian Today* (Toronto: Committee on Missionary Education, United Church of Canada, 1955) in which he wrote: "Scarcely a century has passed since the Christian missionary, with selfless dedication and intrepid courage, first joined battle with the entrenched forces of savagery, paganism and superstition that held a race enthralled."

28. Canada, Royal Commission on Aboriginal Peoples, *Report of the Royal Commission on Aboriginal Peoples, Volume 1: Looking Forward, Looking Back* (Ottawa, 1996), 386. "The diet at Brandon school, which was condemned by nutritionists, was allowed to remain wholly inadequate for more than six years, from 1950 to 1957."

29. Correspondence from Mrs. A. Swaile to R.S. Davis, 6 October 1951, vol. 7194, file 511/25-1-015, MR C 9700, RG10, LAC, Ottawa, as quoted in Milloy, *National Crime*, 266.

30. Correspondence from R.S. Davis to P. Phelan, 1 November 1951, and R.S. Davis to Phelan, 25 October 1951, LAC, Ottawa, as quoted in Milloy, *National Crime*, 266.

31. Indian Act Amendment and Replacement Act S.C. 2014, c. 38. Truancy remained a punishable federal offence for Status Indians until 2014.

32. Milloy, *National Crime*, 268.

33. Correspondence from R.F. Davey to H. Jones, 12 December 1956, vol. 7194, file 511/25-1-015, MR C 9700, IRG10, LAC, Ottawa, quoted in Milloy, *National Crime*, 268.

3: "An Indian Thinks"

1. Michael Twovoice, "An Indian Thinks," *Rossburn Review*, 7 March 1951.

2. Rossburn History Club (hereafter RHC), *On the Sunny Slopes of the Riding Mountains: A History of Rossburn and District*, vol. 1 (Rossburn: RHC, 1984), 294.

3. Peter Lozinski, "Indigenous people of Saskatchewan get full liquor privileges," *Prince Albert Daily Herald*, 27 July 1960. The context that prompted Douglas's comment was the question of whether or not Indians should be admitted into beer parlours.

4. Michael Twovoice, "Farewell Address," *Rossburn Review*, 24 January 1957.

5. Michael Twovoice, "Brief History of Waywayseecappo Band," *Rossburn Review*, 12 November 1959.

6. Waywayseecappo Band, Band Management, Minutes of Council, 1959-01-01– 1964-04-30, BAN 2000-01600-6, Box 5, file 57713-6-11, part 1, stack 1, RG10, LAC.

7. Waywayseecappo Band, Band Management, Minutes of Council, 1959-01-01– 1964-04-30.

8. Canada, Sessional Papers, 6th Parliament, 1st Session, vol. 16, 3 January 1887. Decades later, Duncan Campbell Scott, who was serving as the government's top Indian education official, described the overarching purpose of the department's policies: "I want to get rid of the Indian problem. . . . Our objective is to continue until there is not a single Indian in Canada that has not been absorbed into the body politic, and there is no Indian question, and no Indian Department"; correspondence from Hayter Read to the Superintendent General, 15 January 1889, vol. 6255, file 576-1, part 1, RG10, LAC, Ottawa. In 1889, Hayter Reed used the term "assimilate" in his letter about the ideal location for the Brandon Residential School. Reed had hoped that situating Indian students near settlers would "assimilate them with the white population, and save them from relapsing into ignorance and barbarism."

9. Sister G. Marcoux, *History of the Qu'Appelle Indian School* (Lebret, Sask.: n.p., 1955).

10. Michael Twovoice, "Classifieds," *Rossburn Review*, 23 July 1952.

11. Michael Twovoice, "Thanks Extended For Assistance," *Rossburn Review*, 7 March 1968.

12. From 1946 to 1948, a joint committee of the House of Commons and Senate conducted an investigation into Canada's approach to Indians, and at public hearings the committee heard nearly unanimous denunciations of residential schools.

13. R. Davey's remarks, Regional School Inspectors' Conference, 10–11 April 1958, vol. 8576, file 1/1-2-21, MR C 14215, RG10, NAC, as cited in John S. Milloy, *A National Crime: The Canadian Government and the Residential School System, 1879 to 1986* (Winnipeg: University of Manitoba Press, 1999), 195.

14. Correspondence from T.A. Crerar to Rev. G. Dorsey, 20 October 1941, vol. 7185, file 1/25-1-7-3, part 1, RG10, NAC, as quoted in Milloy, *National Crime*, 193. The cost per capita at residential school was $159, while the cost of a day school student was $47.

15. Correspondence from H. McGill to Deputy Minister, 25 November 1942, vol. 6479, file 940-1 (1-2), MR C 8794, RG10, NAC, as quoted in Milloy, *National Crime*, 192.

16. Correspondence from D. Kogawa to R.L. Boulanger, 25 January 1973, file 301/25-13, vol. 4, RG10, NAC, as quoted in Milloy, *National Crime*, 200.

17. Milloy, *National Crime*, 211.

18. R.A. Hoey to the Deputy Minister, 7 June 1944, file 468-1, MR C 7937, vol. 6205, RG10, NAC, as quoted in Milloy, *National Crime*, 194.

19. Canada, Department of Indian and Northern Affairs, *A Survey of the Contemporary Indians of Canada: Economic, Political, Educational Needs and Policies – Part 2 [The Hawthorn Report]* (Ottawa, 1967).

20. Brown v. Board of Education, 347 U.S. 483 (1954). "Does segregation of children in public schools solely on the basis of race, even though the physical facilities and other 'tangible' factors may be equal, deprive the children of the minority group of equal educational opportunities? We believe that it does."

21. Statement Presented by Mr. R.F. Davey on Behalf of Indian Affairs Branch To the Standing Committee of Ministers of Education, 25 September 1963, file 6-2-21, vol. 3, INAC, LAC, as quoted in Milloy, *National Crime*, 196. By 1956, the view of the Department of Indian Affairs was that "the best hope of giving the Indians an equal chance with other Canadian citizens to improve their lot and to become fully self-respecting, is to educate their children in the same schools with other Canadian children."

22. "Memorandum of Agreement between Her Majesty the Queen and the Board of School Trustees of the Consolidated School District of Rossburn," March 1965, file 511/25-11-231, RG10, LAC, Winnipeg.

23. Correspondence from C.M. King to Mr. J. Slobodzian, 7 April 1961, "Rossburn Joint School: Feb 1961 – Dec 1971," file 501/25-11-231-01, vol. 005, RG10, LAC, Winnipeg.

24. Band Council Resolution, 11 April 1961, "Rossburn Joint School: Feb 1961 – Dec 1971," LAC, Winnipeg.

4: "Whitewash"

1. Canada, Department of Indian and Northern Affairs, "Statement of the Government of Canada on Indian Policy (The White Paper)" (Ottawa, 1969). Later published in *Aboriginal Policy Studies* 1, no. 1 (2011), 192–215.

2. W.E. Stefanuk, *One Room and Beyond* (Rossburn: n.p., n.d.) (available in the Rossburn Regional Library). Stefanuk described Minish as an educator with "progressive ideas and methods."

3. Correspondence from A.G. Minish to Jean Chrétien, 22 April 1970, "Rossburn Joint School: Feb 1961 – Dec 1971," file 501/25-11-231-01, BAN no. 2000-01170-5, RG10, LAC, Winnipeg.

4. Correspondence from William Mussell to A.G. Minish, 5 June 1970 "Rossburn Joint School: Feb 1961 – Dec 1971."

5. Memorandum to the Regional Superintendent of Education in Manitoba from J.R. Wright, District Superintendent of Education, Dauphin, 23 June 1970, "Rossburn Joint School: Feb 1961 – Dec 1971." Chief Lynn McKay and Hugh McKay represented the reserve at the meeting.

6. Chief Dan George, "A Talk to Teachers," Ottawa, Department of Indian and Northern Affairs, 1970. George was born with the name Geswanouth Slahoot; like many others, he received his English name at residential school. In a speech George delivered in 1967, entitled "A Lament for Confederation," he said: "But in the long hundred years since the white man came, I have seen my freedom disappear like the salmon going mysteriously out to sea. The white man's strange customs, which I could not understand, pressed down upon me until I could no longer breathe. When I fought to protect my land and my home, I was called a savage. When I neither understood nor welcomed his way of life, I was called lazy. When I tried to rule my people, I was stripped of my authority. My nation was ignored in your history textbooks—they were little more important in the history of Canada than the buffalo that ranged the plains."

7. Correspondence from A.G. Minish to J.R. Wright, 23 October 1970, "Rossburn Joint School: Feb 1961 – Dec 1971."

8. Correspondence from J.R. Wright to A.G. Minish, 28 October 1970, "Rossburn Joint School: Feb 1961 – Dec 1971."

9. Correspondence from A.G. Minish to Jean Chrétien, 21 December 1971, "Education G.S. – Indian Education – Joint Schools – Rossburn," file 501/25-11G/82, vol. 01, 1971-12-01 to 1974-12-31, RG10, LAC, Winnipeg.

10. Correspondence from Jean Chrétien to A.G. Minish, 1 February 1972, "Education G.S. – Indian Education – Joint Schools – Rossburn." Chrétien ultimately declined, but suggested Minish seek more provincial funding.

11. Correspondence from J.R. Wright to A.G. Minish, 10 February 1972, "Education G.S. – Indian Education – Joint Schools – Rossburn."

12. Canada, House of Commons, Report of the Standing Committee on Indian Affairs, 22 June 1971, as cited in Verna J. Kirkness, *Creating Space: My Life and Work in Indigenous Education* (Winnipeg: University of Manitoba Press, 2013), 79.

13. Indigenous Services Canada, "Reducing the Number of Indigenous Children in Care," 2021. Even today, Indigenous children make up more than one half of all children in foster care, even though they are only 8 percent of all children in Canada.

14. Harold Cardinal, *The Unjust Society: The Tragedy of Canada's Indians* (Edmonton: Hurtig, 1969), 90. Cardinal writes, "In spite of all government attempts to convince Indians to accept the white paper, their efforts will fail, because Indians understand that the path outlined by the Department of Indian Affairs through its mouthpiece, the Honourable Mr. Chrétien, leads directly to cultural genocide. We will not walk this path."

15. Indian Tribes of Manitoba, "Wahbung: Our Tomorrow" (Manitoba Indian Brotherhood, 1971), 1, 108, 109, 117.

16. National Indian Brotherhood, "Indian Control of Indian Education" (Ottawa: Assembly of First Nations, 1972), 25.

17. Minister's Address to the Council of Ministers of Education, 23 June 1972, file 501/25-1, vol. 9, RG10, LAC, as quoted in Milloy, *A National Crime: The Canadian Government and the Residential School System, 1879 to 1986* (Winnipeg: University of Manitoba Press, 1999), 199.

18. Bob Rowlands, "MIB presidential election sparks bitterness in ranks," *Winnipeg Tribune*, 24 July 1980.

19. George Stephenson, "Schools issues won't die: Indians," *Winnipeg Sun*, 29 March 1982. Longclaws predicted that many "non-Indian communities will be in trouble because education is a multi-million dollar industry."

20. "Waywayseecappo Education Authority Annual Report," "Education – General – Education Authority – Waywayseecappo First Nation Education Authority, 1983-08-01 to 1985-03-30," 1985, ACC: 2001-00966-6, vol./box 2, file WIN-E-4700-22-285-02, RG10, LAC, Winnipeg. Attendance of students from Waywayseecappo in the Rossburn schools ranged from 40 to 60 percent.

21. Irv Freitag, "Proposal for funding for an analysis and evaluation of educational trends and strategy development at Waywayseecappo," 28 March 1983, "Education – General – Education Authority, Waywayseecappo First Nation Education Authority, 1980-01-01 to 1983-07-30," ACC 2001-00924-0, vol. 13, file WIN-E-4700-22-285-01, RG10, LAC, Winnipeg.

22. "Education – General – Waywayseecappo First Nation, 1981-01-01 to 1982-12-31," ACC 2001-00939-9, vol./box 009, file WIN-E-4700-285-03, RG10, LAC, Winnipeg. On 7 April 1982, a Waywayseecappo band council resolution resolved to create an on-reserve school. The previous year, on 25 May 1981, another resolution had stated "That the Waywayseecappo feel that the children are not getting

the education that they need." The federal government recognized the resolution but said funding for a school on reserve would not be available until "some future year" (15 June 1981).

23. Laura Rance, "Indian Band Seeks Funding for Reserve School," *Brandon Sun*, 22 March 1982.

24. Correspondence from D.G. Biles to John Bagacki, 21 October 1982, "Education – General – Education Authority – Waywayseecappo First Nation Education Authority," ACC 2001-00924-0, vol. 13, file WIN-E-4700-22-285 01, RG10, LAC, Winnipeg; correspondence from Ron Hedley to John Bagacci [*sic*], 16 December 1982, "Education – General – Education Authority, Waywayseecappo First Nation Education Authority," 1980-01-01 to 1983-07-30; Waywayseecappo Band Council Resolution, 13 April 1982.

25. Waywayseecappo Community School, *Yearbook* (Waywayseecappo: 1983).

26. Waywayseecappo Community School, *Yearbook*.

27. Correspondence from Hugh McKay to Ron Penner, 10 November 1982, "Indian Education – Waywayseecappo," file 501/25-1-285-0, RG10, LAC, Winnipeg.

28. Correspondence from Hugh McKay and Robert Shingoose to Gary Maxwell, 5 May 1983, "Education – General – Education Authority, Waywayseecappo First Nation Education Authority, 1980-01-01 to 1983-07-30." Waywayseecappo claimed that it was not receiving sufficient funds to be successful, and that its school was receiving less funding than schools that were federally funded.

29. Correspondence from Jim Manly to John Munro, 23 June 1983, "Education – General – Education Authority, Waywayseecappo First Nation Education Authority, 1980-01-01 to 1983-07-30."

30. Correspondence from John Munro to Jim Manly, 4 November 1983, "Education – General – Education Authority – Waywayseecappo First Nation Education Authority, 1983-08-01 to 1985-03-30." An earlier draft of the letter, dated 2 September, was more frank: "The Department of Indian Affairs and Northern Development is under extreme resource constraints. The budgets passed on the band education authorities and band management units reflects the most equitable allocation of funds that could be devised in view of this restraint. Many of the decisions that had to be taken were as unpalatable to Regional officials as they were to the education authorities who presented them."

31. Correspondence from E. Korchinski to Brian Cloud, 23 April 1986, "Education – General – Waywayseecappo First Nation," WIN-E-4700-22-285 (E 26), Box 24, 1986-01-01 to 1987-12-31, 2001-00939-9, RG10, LAC, Winnipeg.

32. Correspondence from Bryan Cloud to Mr. Korchinski, 14 April 1986, "Education – General – Waywayseecappo First Nation."

33. Correspondence from Robert Shingoose to J. Bagacki, 29 July 1986, "Education – General – Waywayseecappo First Nation."

34. Dan Lett, "Racist slurs drive natives from Rossburn high school," *Winnipeg Free Press*, 16 September 1990.

35. Mr. and Mrs. Norbert Tanner et al., "Parents Comment on Racial Incident," *Rossburn Review*, 18 September 1990.

36. Lyndenn Behm, "Distraught band members disclose 10 years of racism in Rossburn," *Brandon Sun*, 14 September 1990.

37. Dan Lett, "Apology fails to halt switch," *Winnipeg Free Press*, 16 September 1990.

5: "Let Us Live Here Like Brothers"

1. Alexander Morris, *The Treaties of Canada with the Indians of Manitoba and the North-West Territories, including the Negotiations of Which They Were Based, and Other Information Relating Thereto* (Toronto, 1880; Project Gutenberg, 2004).

2. Correspondence from Morris to Alexander Campbell, 11 August 1873, "Correspondence, 1845–1911," Hetchison Collection, as quoted in Robert Talbot, *Negotiating the Numbered Treaties: An Intellectual and Political Biography of Alexander Morris* (Saskatoon: Purich, 2009).

3. David Treuer, *The Heartbeat of Wounded Knee: Native America from 1890 to the Present* (New York: Riverhead Books, 2019), 92. Treuer notes that in the United States, between 1850 and 1975 "it is estimated that at least twenty thousands Indians and eight thousand Anglo settlers and soldiers died in twenty-five years of warfare, although the figure for Indian deaths, based on U.S. Army records, almost certainly should be higher."

4. Correspondence from Alexander Mackenzie to Alexander Morris, 6 December 1873, "Correspondence, 1845–1911," Hetchison Collection, as quoted in Talbot, *Numbered Treaties*, 80–1.

5. Morris, *Treaties*.

6. Morris, *Treaties*; House of Commons, *Debates*, vol. 9, 5 May 1880. Macdonald said: "We must remember that they are the original owners of the soil, of which they have been dispossessed by the covetousness or ambition of our ancestors . . . the Indians have been great sufferers by the discovery of America and the transfer to it of a large white population."

7. Lyle Longclaws and Lawrence J. Barkwell, "The History of Waywayseecappo First Nation," in *History of the Plains-Ojibway and the Waywayseecappo First Nation* (Rossburn: Waywayseecappo First Nation, 1996). The letter was dated 11 October 1873. It is a mystery why the letter was written so formally, or who wrote it in English.

8. Sarah Carter, *Aboriginal People and Colonizers of Western Canada to* 1900 (Toronto: University of Toronto Press, 1999), 38. See also James Daschuk, *Clearing the Plains: Disease, Politics of Starvation, and the Loss of Aboriginal Life* (Regina: University of Regina Press, 2013), 96–8.

9. J.R. Miller, *Skyscrapers Hide the Heavens: A History of Native–Newcomer Relations in Canada*, 4th ed. (Toronto: University of Toronto Press, 2017), 186.

10. Peter Erasmus and Henry Thompson, *Buffalo Days and Nights* (Calgary: Fifth House Books, 1999), as quoted in J.R. Miller, *Compact, Contract, Covenant: Aboriginal Treaty-Making in Canada* (Toronto: University of Toronto Press, 2009), 4. These words were spoken in the context of subsequent 1876 Treaty 6 negotiations.

11. Talbot, *Numbered Treaties*, 79.

12. Philip Goldring, "Cypress Hills Massacre," *The Canadian Encyclopedia*, 4 March 2015.

13. Miller, *Compact, Contract, Covenant*, 159.

14. Morris, *Treaties*. Indigenous treaty discussions frequently employed family and kinship metaphors. By invoking the mother metaphor, Morris was using Indigenous ideas about relationships to propound a lie about what the Indigenous/settler relationships would be.

15. John S. Milloy, "Tipahamatoowin or Treaty 4: Speculations on Alternate Texts?" *Native Studies Review* 18, no. 1 (2009): 110. This story is derived from oral history.

16. Morris, *Treaties*.

17. Bill Waiser, *A World We Have Lost: Saskatchewan Before* 1905 (Markham: Fifth House, 2016), 5–6. These rights had been granted by the Crown to the Hudson's Bay Company in 1670.

18. Morris, *Treaties*.

19. F.L. Hunt, "Notes of the Qu'Appelle Treaty," *The Canadian Monthly and National Review*, March 1876, 180.

20. Danny Musqua, "Treaty Elders Forum," Office of the Treaty Commissioner, Saskatoon, 1997. In 1997, Saulteaux Elder Danny Musqua provided an account that was related to him by his grandfather, who was present at the negotiations as a young boy. An elderly Ojibway asked about a man taking notes for the Treaty Commissioners. On being told that this was a "learned man," the Ojibway man said, "That is what I want my children to have. That kind of education is what my children must have."

21. Morris, *Treaties*.

22. Sheldon Krasowski, "Mediating the numbered treaties: Eyewitness accounts of treaties between the Crown and Indigenous Peoples, 1871–1876" (doctoral thesis, University of Regina, 2011), 189. "The surrender clause was part of the template and was not changed."

23. Hunt, "Notes," 180.

24. Harold Cardinal and Walter Hildebrandt, *Treaty Elders of Saskatchewan: Our Dream Is That Our Peoples Will One Day Be Clearly Recognized as Nations* (Calgary: University of Calgary Press, 2000), 115. Oral histories of Treaty 4 stated that the Cree and Saulteaux did not surrender any of their rights or titles to land. They merely agreed to share the land "to the depth of a plow." As Elder Gordon Oakes states, "There were two nations that negotiated the treaty. You know, this country belongs to the Indian people; the Creator gave us this country. Then the treaties were taking place, that's what they gave up, a tip of the plough, so the people that came from elsewhere, different countries, they can farm, ranch, all that. We never gave up anything more than that."

25. Canada, "Treaty No. 4 between Her Majesty the Queen and the Cree and Saulteaux Tribes of Indians at the Qu'appelle and Fort Ellice." Handwritten copy available at "Correspondence and Report on the Indians in Treaty 4," October 1875, vol. 3625, file 5489, MIKAN 2060606, RG10, LAC, Ottawa.

26. Morris, *Treaties*.

27. Indian Tribes of Manitoba, "Wahbung: Our Tomorrow" (Manitoba Indian Brotherhood, 1971), xii.

28. Sheldon Krasowski, *No Surrender: The Land Remains Indigenous* (Regina: University of Regina Press, 2019), 155. There was a conspicuous absence of a pipe ceremony. By some accounts, the failure to invoke and participate in a pipe ceremony suggests that to the Indigenous signatories the deal was not yet done. A pipe ceremony typically accompanies treaty signings, and indicates a sacred solemnity to the agreement.

29. Longclaws and Barkwell, *History of the Plains-Ojibway and the Waywayseecappo First Nation*. According to Longclaws and Barkwell, Waywayseecappo was born around 1825 and died in 1902 or 1903.

30. Longclaws and Barkwell, *History of the Plains-Ojibway and the Waywayseecappo First Nation*, 18.

31. Heather Devine, "Les Desjarlais: The Development and Dispersion of a Proto-Métis Hunting Band, 1785–1870," in *From Rupert's Land to Canada*, ed. Theodore Binnema, Gerhard J. Ens, and R.C. MacLeod (Edmonton: University of Alberta Press, 2001), 149. It is not entirely clear that this is in reference to the correct person, referring to "Wah-ween-shee-cap-po." This individual was said to be "dreaded" for his knowledge of "Indian medicine and black art."

32. Morris, *Treaties*.

33. "Treaty No. 4," MIKAN 3974413, item 7, vol. 1846, RG10, LAC, Ottawa.

34. Correspondence from and written on behalf of the Earl of Dufferin (author's

name illegible) to the Minister of the Interior, 30 November 1875, vol. 3625, file 5617, RG10, LAC, Ottawa.

35. Dominion of Canada, *Annual Report of the Department of the Interior for the Year Ended 30th June, 1876* (Ottawa, 1877).

36. Canada, Royal Commission on Aboriginal Peoples, *Report of the Royal Commission on Aboriginal Peoples, Volume 1: Looking Forward, Looking Back* (Ottawa, 1996), 259.

37. Michael Twovoice, "Brief History of Waywayseecappo Band," *Rossburn Review*, 12 November 1959. Michael described the band's Traditional Territory as follows: "a vast tract of land extending from the source of Birdtail, south as far as where Birtle is situated and as far west as to the emptying of the Qu'Appelle River, into the Assiniboine River, north as far as the present townsite of Russell, along the banks of the Assiniboine."

38. Ian Froese, "Waywayseecappo reaches $288M settlement with Ottawa over forced surrender of their lands," *CBC News*, 17 July 2019. Originally, the Waywayseecappo reserve included land to the east of the Birdtail River. Under dubious circumstances, however, this land was "surrendered" by the Waywayseecappo band in 1881, for sale to a group of settlers. In 2012, the Waywayseecappo First Nation brought a legal claim alleging that this sale was improper, and in 2019 the federal government agreed to a $288-million settlement to compensate for the unlawful surrender. For more details about the claim, see documents for claim SCT-4001-12, available on the website of the Specific Claims Tribunal of Canada.

39. J.L. Swanson, *Our Ancestors Arrive in Manitoba* (Winnipeg: de Montfort Press, n.d.). The group waited a week until the ground was dry enough to bear the weight of their carts.

40. Rossburn History Club (hereafter RHC), *On the Sunny Slopes of the Riding Mountains: A History of Rossburn and District*, vol. 1 (Rossburn: RHC, 1984), 369.

41. RHC, *Sunny Slopes*, 2:1. "Samuel Warnock was the first to make a squatters claim."

42. Reita Bambridge Sparling, *Reminiscences of the Rossburn Pioneers* (Rossburn: Rossburn Women's Institute, 1951), 4.

43. Report of J.W. Herchmer (Indian Agent) to the Superintendent-General of Indian Affairs, Manitoba, Fort Ellice, Birtle, 24 October 1882, 42–3. Herchmer was based in Birtle and writing about the whole agency.

44. Sparling, *Reminiscences*, 5.

45. Dominion of Canada, *Annual Report of the Department of Indian Affairs for the Year Ended 31st December, 1881* (Ottawa, 1882).

46. HTFC Planning and Design, *"See What the Land Gave Us": Waywayseecappo First Nation Traditional Knowledge Study for the Birtle Transmission Line* (2017), 20.

47. RHC, *Sunny Slopes*, 1:24.

48. T.P. Wadsworth's report re: "Way-way-see-cappo's Band," in Dominion of Canada, *Annual Report of the Department of Indian Affairs for the Year Ended 31st December,* 1884 (Ottawa, 1885).

49. L.W. Herchmer, 13 August 1883, in Dominion of Canada, *Annual Report of the Department of Indian Affairs for the Year Ended 31 December,* 1883 (Ottawa, 1884).

50. Aidan McQuillan, "Creation of Canadian Reserves on the Canadian Prairies 1870–1885," *Geographical Review* 7, no. 4 (1980): 392. In 1884, "only 770 of a total of 20,230 Indians in the Territories were not reliant on government relief supplies."

51. Blair Stonechild, "The Indian View of the 1885 Uprising," in *Sweet Promises: A Reader on Indian-White Relations in Canada,* ed. J.R. Miller (Toronto: University of Toronto Press, 1991), 263.

52. Correspondence from J.A. MacRae to Dewdney, 25 August 1884, vol. 3697, file 15,423, RG10, LAC, Ottawa. An account of this meeting is given in Arthur J. Ray, Jim Miller, and Frank Tough, *Bounty and Benevolence: A History of Saskatchewan Treaties* (Montreal: McGill-Queen's University Press, 2002), 197–200. See also Dewdney to Macdonald, 9 February 1885, MG 26A, vol. 117, LAC, as cited in John L. Tobias, "Canada's Subjugation of the Plains Cree, 1879–1885," *Canadian Historical Review* 64, no. 4 (December 1983). The Cree at this meeting were signatories to Treaty 6, which was also negotiated by Alexander Morris. In February 1885, the most senior official in the Department of Indian Affairs, Edgar Dewdney, conceded that the government had violated the treaties.

6: Iron Heart

1. Hayter Reed, "Notes on my early days in the North-West" (1928), P056 (1815–1944), Box 1, Folder 11, Reed Family fonds, McCord Museum, Montreal, 12. The same folder contains two slightly different drafts of this speech.

2. Reed, "Notes on my early days," 31; David Laird, "North-West Indian Treaties," Manitoba Historical Society Transactions, Series 1, no. 67 (1905): "Most of these Indians which met us at Qu'Appelle in 1874 were wild, painted Indians, having buffalo robes or blankets around their shoulders, and a majority of men with only Nature's leggings"; Hayter Reed, "On the Aims of Government in Dealings with our Indians" (undated, but speech delivered in 1899, 1900, or 1901 based on its contents), P056 (1815–1944), Box 1, Folder 12, Reed Family fonds, McCord Museum, Montreal, 12. Hayter went on to observe that the treaties had been more than fair and had "extinguished on liberal terms" Indian land rights.

3. Reed, "Notes on my early days," 20.

4. Hayter Reed, untitled, undated short autobiography (evidently written late in his life), P056 (1815–1944), Box 1, Folder 16, Reed Family fonds, McCord Museum,

Montreal. At the top of the paper is printed: "White Star Line Mediterranean Cruise: On Board S.S. 'Adriatic.'"

5. Reed, "Notes on my early days," 7. A dash has been inserted after "whirlpool" here for clarity.

6. Reed, "Notes on my early days," 4.

7. The threat of violence was not remote or unfounded. A year earlier, in 1868, Thomas D'Arcy McGee, often termed "Canada's first nationalist," was assassinated by the Fenian operative Patrick J. Whelan.

8. "Minutes #1 – 309, September 16, 1870 to December 21, 1878," Executive Council Minutes, A 0070, GR 1659, Archives of Manitoba, Winnipeg.

9. Correspondence from Lindsay Russell to Hayter Reed, April 1880, vol. 245, file 23563, D-OO-1, part 1, RG15, LAC, Ottawa.

10. Correspondence from Augusta Draper to John Macdonald, 10 February 1880, microfilm CC-1748, MG 26A, LAC, Ottawa. Hayter got the job with the help of his aunt, who wrote to the prime minister, a family friend, on Hayter's behalf.

11. Aidan McQuillan, "Creation of Canadian Reserves on the Canadian Prairies 1870–1885," *Geographical Review* 7, no. 4. (1980): 391. There were about 1,300 Indians in the district in 1884.

12. Reed, "On the Aims of Government," 24.

13. Hayter Reed, undated memo (circa June 1892), Inspection of Agencies, 1885–1896, vol. 17, Reed Papers, LAC, as quoted in Brian E. Titley, "Hayter Reed and Indian Administration in the West," in *Swords and Ploughshares: War and Agriculture in Western Canada*, ed. R.C. Macleod (Edmonton: University of Alberta Press, 1993), 127.

14. Robert Irwin, "Indian Agents in Canada," *The Canadian Encyclopedia*, 25 October 2018. "The Battleford Indian Agency, situated west of North Battleford, Saskatchewan in the Treaty 6 region, consisted of Cree and Stoney reserves including the Moosomin, Poundmaker, Red Pheasant, Sweet Grass, Thunderchild, Little Pine, Mosquito, Grizzly Bear's Head, Lean Man, and Lucky Man reserves." Hayter wrote that he often travelled fifty or sixty miles a day.

15. Reed, "Notes on my early days," 16, 46, 43.

16. "Valuable Indian relics received," *Montreal Daily Star*, 21 July 1931.

17. Correspondence from E. Dewdney to J.A. Macdonald, 11 April 1884, vol. 212, p. 90065, Macdonald Papers, LAC, Ottawa, as quoted in Titley, "Hayter Reed and Indian Administration in the West," 116.

18. Reed, "Notes on my early days," 40–1. In a speech that Reed delivered some three decades before (see Reed, "On the Aims of Government," 4–5), he attributed this observation to Col. Richard Irving Dodge of the U.S. Army.

19. Reed, "On the Aims of Government," 9, 32–3. Hayter wrote: "True may it be that where the advantages of civilization are viewed in prospect, the Indian may not covet them for himself, or for his children, but suppose his feelings had been consulted in such regard, what would his fate have been today?"

20. Canada, Royal Commission on Aboriginal Peoples, *Report of the Royal Commission on Aboriginal Peoples, Volume 1: Looking Forward, Looking Back* (Ottawa, 1996), 242.

21. Reed, "On the Aims of Government" (bullet point notes attached to the main document). Hayter said that few knew "how often agents, faithful to the interests of the government and to the best interests of the Indians themselves, fairly refused to give supplies to the idle, although their lives were threatened for so doing, while they were being held up to the light of the public in the light of dishonest tyrants." He also handwrote the following bullet points: "No credit ever given to agents" and "Honest though great temptation."

22. Correspondence from Reed to E. Dewdney, 17 March 1883, vol. 3949, file 126886, RG10, LAC, Ottawa.

23. Correspondence from Reed to Indian Commissioner, 18 June 1881, vol. 3755, file 30961, RG10, LAC, Ottawa.

24. Reed to E. Dewdney, 18 June 1881; Headquarters to Assistant Commissioner E.T. Gait, 25 July 1881, vol. 3755, file 30961, RG10, LAC, as quoted in Titley, "Hayter Reed and Indian Administration in the West," 113.

25. Correspondence from, Reed to T.M. Daly, 1893, Hayter Reed fonds, Personnel A-G, vol. 18, LAC, Ottawa.

26. Titley, "Hayter Reed and Indian Administration in the West," 118.

27. Correspondence from E. Dewdney to J.A. Macdonald, 27 September 1883, vol. 211, p. 89923, John A. Macdonald Papers, MG 26A, LAC, as quoted in Macleod, *Swords and Ploughshares*, 113.

28. Harry Loucks, *Voice of the People* (n.p., n.d.), 129, as quoted in Sarah Carter, *Lost Harvests: Prairie Indian Reserve Farmers and Government Policy* (Montreal: McGill-Queen's University Press, 1990), 144.

29. Letter from William Donovan, 30 October 1886, vol. 3772, file 34938, MIKAN 2059746, RG10, LAC, Ottawa.

30. "Education," in Dominion of Canada, *Annual Report of the Department of Indian Affairs for the Year ended 30th June, 1892* (Ottawa, 1893).

31. Hayter Reed, "Notes on my early days in the North-West—Industrial Schools," P056 (1815–1944), Box 1, Folder 11, Reed Family fonds, McCord Museum, Montreal. In the same document, he refers to the students at the schools as "inmates."

32. "Education - General Remarks," in Dominion of Canada, *Annual Report of the Department of Indian Affairs for the Year Ended 31st December, 1889* (Ottawa, 1890), 354.

33. Reed, "Notes on my early days in the North-West—Industrial Schools."

34. Father Hugonard to Hayter Reed, 2 December 1887, Hayter Reed fonds, LAC, Ottawa. Hugonard is writing in French. He refers to "nos fugitifs" and their "desertions." A few years later, on Christmas Eve in 1889, a group of students at the school composed an eerie letter directly to Reed: "Considering you as a kind father to us all here, allow the Inmates of our Industrial school to wish you a merry merry Christmas and a thrice happy new year."

35. Reed, "Notes on my early days"; Brian E. Titley, *The Frontier World of Edgar Dewdney* (Vancouver: UBC Press, 1999), 51.

36. Jean Teillet, *The North-West Is Our Mother* (Toronto: HarperCollins, 2019), 386.

37. J.R. Miller, *Skyscrapers Hide the Heavens: A History of Native–Newcomer Relations in Canada*, 4th ed. (Toronto: University of Toronto Press, 2017), 187. In addition to contiguous reserves, they also wanted treaty revisions.

38. Alexander Morris, *The Treaties of Canada with the Indians of Manitoba and the North-West Territories, including the Negotiations of Which They Were Based, and Other Information Relating Thereto* (Toronto, 1880; Project Gutenberg, 2004).

39. Reed, "On the Aims of Government," 24.

40. H. Reed to the Indian commissioner, 28 December 1883, vol. 3668, file 10,644, MIKAN 2057930, 12, RG10, LAC, Ottawa.

41. Reed to T.M. Daly, 1893, Personnel A–G, vol. 18, Hayter Reed fonds, LAC, Ottawa; Titley, *The Frontier World of Edgar Dewdney*, 51. Hayter's tactical achievement thrilled his superior, Edgar Dewdney, who viewed the removal of thousands of Indians "and scattering them through the country as a solution to one of our main difficulties, as it was found impossible at times to have such control as was desirable over such a large number of worthless and lazy Indians, the concourse of malcontents and reckless Indians from all the bands in the Territories."

42. Reed, "Notes on my early days," 31. In handwriting on the typewritten page, Reed wrote: "To make them start pulled tents down."

43. Reed, "Notes on my early days."

44. Correspondence from Reed to the Superintendent General of Indian Affairs, 12 April 1884, vol. 3668, file 10,644, RG10, LAC, Ottawa.

45. Murray Dobbin, *The One-and-a-Half Men* (n.p., n.d.), attributed the quote to James Dreaver, as cited in Teillet, *North-West*, xxi.

46. A.S. Morton, *A History of the Canadian West to 1870–71* (Toronto: University of Toronto Press, 1973), 872, as cited in Teillet, *North-West*, 216.

47. Teillet, *North-West*, 204.

48. Morris, *Treaties*. Otakaonan said, "Now when you have come here, you see sitting out there a mixture of Half-breeds, Crees, Saulteaux and Stonies, all are one, and

you were slow in taking the hand of a Half-breed." Morris replied, "You may rest easy, you may leave the Half-breeds in the hands of the Queen who will deal generously and justly with them."

49. Teillet, *North-West*, 395.

50. Teillet, *North-West*, 400.

51. Teillet, *North-West*, 273.

52. Beverley McLachlin, "Louis Riel: Patriot Rebel," *Manitoba Law Journal* 35, no. 1 (2011): 4. Riel "had won Provincial status for Manitoba against persistent opposition and had secured linguistic and religious recognition for his people."

53. Louis Riel, "Final Statement of Louis Riel at his Trial in Regina," 31 July 1885.

54. Michele Filice, "Mistahimaskwa (Big Bear)," *The Canadian Encyclopedia*, 19 December 2006. Riel met with Big Bear on 17 August 1884.

55. Richard Gwyn, *Nation Maker: Sir John A. Macdonald: His Life, Our Times* (Toronto: Random House Canada, 2011), 433.

56. Bob Beal and Rod Macleod, *Prairie Fire: The 1885 North-West Rebellion* (Toronto: McClelland & Stewart, 1994), 134.

57. Keith D. Smith, ed., *Strange Visitors: Documents in Indigenous–Settler Relations in Canada from 1876* (Toronto: University of Toronto Press, 2014), 56.

58. Correspondence from Crozier to Dewdney, 13 March 1885, 1: 348–51, Dewdney Papers, LAC, Ottawa, as cited in Beal and Macleod, *Prairie Fire*, 137.

59. Patrice Fleury, "Reminiscences," Saskatchewan Archives Board, file A-515, 6.

60. In fact, the government had dispatched none other than Hayter Reed to negotiate with Riel. Hayter set off dutifully toward Duck Lake, but he didn't quite make it before fighting broke out. See "Trouble with Half-Breeds and the Abandoning of Fort Carlton" (undated), P056 (1815–1944), Box 1, Folder 17, Reed Family fonds, McCord Museum, Montreal.

61. Beal and Macleod, *Prairie Fire*, 12–3; Louis Riel, "Final Statement of Louis Riel at his Trial in Regina."

62. George F.G. Stanley, ed., *The Collected Writings of Louis Riel*, vol. 3 (Edmonton: University of Alberta Press, 1985), 60; Item 035, 1885/03/23.

63. Thomas Flanagan, *The Diaries of Louis Riel* (Edmonton: Hurtig Publishers, 1976), 66.

64. George Stanley, *The Birth of Western Canada* (Toronto: University of Toronto Press, 1961), 328. Original quotation in French: "Pour l'amour de Dieu de ne plus en tuer . . . il y a déjà trop de sang répandu."

65. Beal and Macleod, *Prairie Fire*, 156.

66. Charles Pelham Mulvaney, *The History of the North-West Rebellion* (Toronto: A.H. Hovey, 1886), 144. Hayter filed the report on 5 May.

67. Mulvaney, *North-West Rebellion*, 144. His name was Colonel Miller.

68. Desmond Morton, *The Last War Drum: The North West Campaign of* 1885 (Toronto: Hakkert, 1972), 34.

69. Teillet, *North-West*, 413. A hyphen has been added between "sour" and "apple" for clarity.

70. Morton, *Last War Drum*, 41.

71. Reita Bambridge Sparling, *Reminiscences of the Rossburn Pioneers* (Rossburn: Rossburn Women's Institute, 1951), 22–4.

72. Stanley, *The Collected Writings of Louis Riel*, vol. 3, letter 047. The letter is dated 29 March 1885. See also vol. 3, letter 048, and a sequence of letters dated 6–9 April 1885. In early April, Riel wrote his "Dear Relatives": "We have the pleasure to let you know that . . . God has given us a victory over the Mounted Police . . . be courageous. Do what you can. . . . Come and reinforce us."

73. Miller, *Skyscrapers*, 195: "The incident, essentially a bloody act of reprisal against unpopular officials, became unjustifiably known as the Frog Lake Massacre."

74. Blair Stonechild and Bill Waiser, *Loyal Till Death* (Markham: Fifth House, 2010), 117.

75. Sparling, *Reminiscences*, 107, 75, 68–9.

76. Rossburn History Club (hereafter RHC), *On the Sunny Slopes of the Riding Mountains: A History of Rossburn and District*, vol. 1 (Rossburn: RHC, 1984), 24.

77. Sparling, *Reminiscences*, 9.

78. Sparling, *Reminiscences*, 67–8; RHC, *Sunny Slopes*, 1:118.

79. Michael Twovoice, "Brief History of Waywayseecappo Band," *Rossburn Review*, 12 November 1959.

80. L.W. Herchmer to Superintendent-General of Indian Affairs, 4 October 1885, in *Annual Report of the Department of Indian Affairs for the Year Ended 31st December*, 1885 (Ottawa, 1886). Note that "[them]" is substituted for "my Indians."

81. RHC, *Sunny Slopes*, 2:33.

82. Sparling, *Reminiscences*, 39, 107.

83. Correspondence from Hayter Reed to Edgar Dewdney, C-4595, image 305, Northwest Rebellion, MG 27, IC4, vol. 5, Edgar Dewdney fonds, Glenbow Library and Archives.

84. Correspondence from Hayter Reed to Edgar Dewdney, 20 July 1885, vol. 3710, file 19,550-3, RG10, LAC, Ottawa. The assessment of Waywayseecappo occurs at MIKAN 2058918 (item 149).

85. Correspondence from E. Dewdney to J.A. Macdonald, 21 August 1885, vol. 3710, file 19,550-3, RG10, LAC, Ottawa. Macdonald made the additional comment in the margins of Hayter's July memo, which was passed along by Commissioner Dewdney.

86. Gwyn, *Nation Maker*, 458.

87. "Government Report of Riel Transcript 1886," 154, as cited in Martin L. Friedland, "Louis Riel and His Appeal to the Privy Council," *Criminal Law Quarterly* 69, no. 3 (August 2021): 9.

88. Canada, Parliament, Sessional Papers, 1886, Volume 12, No. 43, 143.

89. Gwyn, *Nation Maker*, 461.

90. Gwyn, *Nation Maker*, 474.

91. Correspondence from Reed to Dewdney, 6 September 1885, vol. 5, p. 1240, Dewdney Papers, LAC, Ottawa, as cited in Titley, "Hayter Reed and Indian Administration in the West," 117.

92. Gwyn, *Nation Maker*, 489. Future prime minister Wilfrid Laurier was outraged by the executions: "If I had been on the banks of the Saskatchewan [River], I too would have shouldered my musket to fight against the neglect of government and the greed of speculators."

93. William Cameron, *Blood Red the Sun* (Calgary: Kenway, 1950), 210–1.

94. Alex Williams, *The Pass System*, 2015, documentary film.

95. The letters of recommendations had to come from federal farm instructors.

96. Correspondence from Hayter Reed to Lawrence Herchmer, 16 February 1891, MG 29, E106, vol. 13, Hayter Reed fonds, LAC, Ottawa.

97. Hayter Reed, "Annual report for the fiscal year 1890–91," in Dominion of Canada, *Annual Report of the Department of Indian Affairs for the Year Ended 31st December,* 1891 (Ottawa, 1892).

98. David J. Hall, "North-West Territories (1870–1905)," *The Canadian Encyclopedia*, 7 February 2006: "The 1885 census of Assiniboia, Saskatchewan and Alberta reported a total population of 48,362. Of this, 20,170 people (41.7 per cent) were Status Indians."

99. Dominion of Canada, *Annual Report of the Department of Indian Affairs for the Year Ended 31st December,* 1889 (Ottawa, 1890).

100. Correspondence from Hayter Reed to Edgar Dewdney, 20 July 1885, vol. 3710, file 19, 550-3, RG10, LAC, Ottawa. "By preserving a knowledge of individual movements," Reed wrote, "any inclination to petty depredations may be checked."

101. Correspondence from Alexander Morris to the Minister of the Interior, 23 October 1875, vol. 3625, file 5489, RG10, LAC. In a conversation with Chief Waywayseecappo a year after he signed the treaty, Morris assured the Chief that "he had the same right of hunting as before."

102. Lawrence Vankoughnet to John A. Macdonald, 14 August 1885, vol. 3710, file 19, 550-3, RG10, LAC, Ottawa, as cited in Laurie F. Barron, "The Indian Pass System in the Canadian West, 1882–1935" in *Immigration and Settlement, 1870–1939*, ed.

Gregory P. Marchildon (Regina: University of Regina Press, 2009), 216. When Prime Minister Macdonald approved the pass system, he acknowledged that "no punishment for breaking bounds can be inflicted & in case of resistance on the grounds of Treaty rights [punishments] should not be insisted on."

103. Correspondence from Hayter Reed to Minister of the Interior, MG 29, EI06, vol. 14, file T.W. Day, RG10, LAC, Hayter Reed Papers, as cited in Barron, "Indian Pass System," 37. Reed, too, acknowledged that "it was especially stipulated . . . when [Indians] entered Treaty that they should not be tied down to their Reservations, and although I have often taken the responsibility of employing police to send them home, the greatest caution has to be exercised, for were they to offer resistance and conflict ensue, they have the law on their side."

104. Correspondence from Hayter Reed to Edgar Dewdney, 16 August 1885, MG 27, 2076-87, Dewdney Papers, North-West Rebellion, LAC, Ottawa, as cited in Barron, "Indian Pass System," 37. It is notable that they are implementing the system even before the prime minister approves the memo.

105. Barron, "Indian Pass System," 29.

106. Correspondence from Sergeant R. Burton Deane (Lethbridge, Alberta) to NWMP commissioner, 12 February 1891, MG 29, E106, vol. 12, file R. Burton, 1891, Hayter Reed fonds, LAC, Ottawa.

107. Barron, "Indian Pass System," 36.

108. Correspondence from Hayter Reed to Deputy Superintendent of Indian Affairs, 14 June 1893, vol. 6817, file 487-1-2, part 1, reel C-8539, RG10, LAC, Ottawa: "Unfortunately, however, the Police Department has become alarmed about the risk of assuming its share of responsibility. . . . I cannot refrain from an expression of extreme regret that such order should have been given. . . . Had the order been kept quiet, the Indians might have remained for some time in ignorance, but as I have already seen references to it in the public press, no expectation of withholding it from them need now be entertained."

109. Correspondence from Hayter Reed to Indian Agent in Carlton, Saskatchewan, 15 June 1893, vol. 1597, RG10, LAC, Ottawa. Document courtesy of Sarah Carter.

110. Sarah Carter, "Controlling Indian Movement: The Pass System," NeWest Review (May 1985); Miller, Skyscrapers, 212. Miller has written, "The pass system, however, was never very effective. It was not often enforced in the 1880s, and by 1893 was virtually a dead letter." Carter suggests otherwise, and indeed there is evidence of enforcement as late as in 1941.

111. Correspondence from Harold McGill to Inspectors of Indian Agencies and Indian Agents, 11 July 1941, and correspondence from Alfred G.B. Lewis to I Secretary, Indian Affairs Branch, 24 July 1941, "Correspondence regarding Indian Pass system,"

M3281, Harold and Emma McGill fonds, Glenbow Library and Archives. In 1941, more than half a century after the first passes were issued, McGill, an official in the Department of Indian Affairs, circulated a notice to staff across Canada:"There seems to be a misunderstanding in the minds of some Indian agents and other officials concerning the right of Indians to leave their reserves. Indians are not compelled to remain upon their reserves and are free to come and go in the same manner as other people. No law or regulation exists to the contrary. Please be guided accordingly."To help clear up the "misunderstanding," McGill requested that all remaining passbooks be sent to Ottawa to be destroyed. Two weeks later, an Alberta-based Indian agent named Alfred Lewis mailed a reply. He enclosed one partially used booklet of forms, along with eleven unused booklets. Lewis wrote,"The writer regrets that this action was found necessary as it will be now impossible to control our farming Indians."

112. Kate Armour Reed, *A Woman's Touch: Kate Reed and Canada's Grand Hotels* (Westmount: John Aylen Books, 2017), 87–9.

7: The Young Napoleon of the West

1. Richard Gwyn, *Nation Maker: Sir John A. Macdonald: His Life, Our Times* (Toronto: Random House Canada, 2011), 385.

2. "Sifton: Review of the Young Minister's Career," *Globe and Mail*, 18 November 1896.

3. "Speech Delivered on Receiving Degree of L.L.D. by Queen's University," 1927, vol. 313, Manuscript Group 27, series II D 15, Clifford Sifton fonds, LAC, Ottawa.

4. Clifford Sifton to [illegible], 5 March 1901, C-422, Clifford Sifton fonds, LAC, Ottawa.

5. D.J. Hall, *Clifford Sifton*, vol. 1, *The Young Napoleon, 1861–1900* (Vancouver: UBC Press, 1981), 294; Robert Russell, "The Young Napoleon of the West," *The Busy Man's Magazine*, June 1908; *Winnipeg Free Press*, 10 November 1900.

6. John Wesley Dafoe, *Clifford Sifton in relation to his times* (Toronto: Macmillan of Canada, 1931), 48.

7. D.J. Hall, *Clifford Sifton* (Don Mills, Ont.: Fitzhenry & Whiteside, 1976).

8. Mabel F. Timlin, "Canada's Immigration Policy, 1896–1910," *The Canadian Journal of Economics and Political Science* 26, no. 4 (November 1960), 518.

9. D.J. Hall, "Clifford Sifton and Canadian Indian Administration, 1896–1905," *Prairie Forum* 2, no. 2 (November 1977), 253.

10. Sifton, "The Immigrants Canada Wants," *Maclean's Magazine*, 1 April 1922.

11. Timlin, "Canada's Immigration Policy," 521–2. Sifton wanted to suppress publication of the temperatures but apparently was "dissuaded." Ultimately, he decided a cover-up was worse than the clime.

12. Sifton, "Immigrants Canada Wants"; Dafoe, *Clifford Sifton*. On another occasion, Sifton added: "If you are to settle the rough lands you have to settle them with these people, because the average young Canadians or American farmer will not do it."

13. Sifton, "Immigrants Canada Wants."

14. House of Commons, *Debates*, Fourth Session, 8th Parliament, vol. 1, 7 July 1899, 6859. Sifton added: "Any man . . . willing to till the soil, is a welcome addition to this Western country, and his arrival is a national blessing."

15. Bohdan S. Kordan and Lubomyr Y. Luciuk, *A Delicate and Difficult Question: Documents in the History of Ukrainians in Canada, 1899–1962* (Kingston: Limestone Press, 1986), 17. Sifton insisted that their "strongest desire is to assimilate with Canadians."

16. Paul Yuzyk, *The Ukrainians in Manitoba: A Social History* (Toronto: University of Toronto Press, 1953), 13.

17. Pierre Berton, *The Promised Land: Settling the West, 1896–1914* (Toronto: Anchor Canada, 2011), chap. 2, "The Sheepskin People," Part 1, "The long voyage," Kindle.

18. P.J. Giffen, *Adult Education in Relation to Rural Social Structure: A Comparative Study of Three Manitoba Communities* (Winnipeg, 1947), 110 (viewed at the Manitoba Legislative Library).

19. M.H. Marunchak, *The Ukrainian Canadians: A History* (Yorkton: Redeemer's Voice Press, 1970), 297.

20. Marunchak, *The Ukrainian Canadians*, 71.

21. D.J. Hall, "Clifford Sifton's Vision of the Prairie West," in *The Prairie West as Promised Land*, ed. R. Douglas Francis and Chris Kitzan (Calgary: University of Calgary Press, 2007), 83.

22. Clifford Sifton, *Geography of the Dominion of Canada and Atlas of Western Canada* (Ottawa: Department of the Interior, 1904), 10.

23. Hall, "Vision of the Prairie West," 85, 86; Yuzyk, *Ukrainians in Manitoba*, 30.

24. Michael Ewanchuk, *Pioneer Profiles: Ukrainian Settlers in Manitoba* (self-pub., 1981), 3.

25. William A. Czumer and Vasyl A. Chumer, *Recollections about the Life of the First Ukrainian Settlers in Canada* (Edmonton: Canadian Institution of Ukrainian Studies, 1981), 12–3.

26. Yuzyk, *Ukrainians in Manitoba*, 31.

27. Orest T. Martynowych, *Ukrainians in Canada: The Formative Period, 1891–1924* (Edmonton: University of Alberta Press, 1991), 46.

28. Elsie Lesyk, *Sifton Then and Now: A Reminiscence of the Pioneer Era* (Dauphin: self-pub., 1992), 4–9.

29. Martynowych, *Ukrainians in Canada*, 46; Hall, *Young Napoleon*, 262.

30. Sifton, "Immigrants Canada Wants."

31. D.J. Hall, *Clifford Sifton*, vol. 2, *A Lonely Eminence, 1901–1929* (Vancouver: UBC Press, 1985), 65.

32. Marunchak, *Ukrainian Canadians*, 80.

33. Jaroslav Petryshyn, *Peasants in the Promised Land: Canada and the Ukrainians, 1891–1914* (Toronto: Lorimer, 1985), 60.

34. Dafoe, *Clifford Sifton*, 323; Hall, *A Lonely Eminence*, 957. A total of 115,478 homesteads were issued during Sifton's nine-year tenure.

35. Dafoe, *Clifford Sifton*, 324. Canada went from a million acres producing 14,371,806 bushels of wheat to 3,141,537 acres producing 55,761,416 bushels of wheat.

36. Hall, "Clifford Sifton's Vision of the Prairie West," 77.

37. House of Commons, *Debates*, Fourth Session, 8th Parliament, 27 July 1899, 8655.

38. Dafoe, *Clifford Sifton*, 528.

39. Hall, *A Lonely Eminence*, 158.

40. Dafoe, *Clifford Sifton*, 11.

41. Hall, *The Young Napoleon*, 292.

42. Dafoe, *Clifford Sifton*, 316–7; Hall, *A Lonely Eminence*, 63. During his first full year as minister, in 1897, 16,835 immigrants arrived in Canada. That number rose to 141,465 in 1905, Sifton's last full year as minister.

43. Hall, *A Lonely Eminence*, 42.

44. Lubomyr Luciuk and Stella Hryniuk, eds., *Canada's Ukrainians: Negotiating an Identity* (Toronto: University of Toronto Press, 1991), 289; "scum" comment from the *Winnipeg Free Press*, 17 July 1899.

45. Luciuk and Hryniuk, *Canada's Ukrainians*, 289.

46. Marunchak, *Ukrainian Canadians*, 299, 74; *Winnipeg Daily Nor-Wester*, 23 December 1896.

47. *Winnipeg Telegram*, "Another Siftonian Tragedy," July 1899, as quoted in Berton, *Promised Land*, chap. 2, "The Sheepskin People," Part 2, "Dirty, ignorant Slavs."

48. Winnipeg Free Press, 22 October 1898.

49. O.W. Gerus and J.E. Rea, *The Ukrainians in Canada* (Ottawa: Canadian Historical Association, 2018), 9.

50. "Look out for it," *Winnipeg Tribune*, 22 October 1898.

51. House of Commons, *Debates*, Fourth Session, 8th Parliament, 7 July 1899, 6835.

52. Sifton, "Immigrants Canada Wants."

53. "Mr. Sifton at Winnipeg: Enthusiastic Audience Greets the Minister of the Interior," *Globe and Mail*, 28 October 1899.

54. Hall, *A Lonely Eminence*, 70 (citing a letter from Sifton to Dafoe, 11 November

1901). Sifton refers to "the cry against the Doukhobors and the Galicians." The Doukhobors were another ethnic group from eastern Europe.

55. House of Commons, *Debates*, 9th Parliament, 1st Session, 12 April 1901.

56. "Immigration Discussed," *Globe and Mail*, 13 April 1901.

57. Hall, *The Young Napoleon*, 264.

58. Berton, *The Promised Land*, chap. 1, "The Young Napoleon of the West," Part 4, "The spoils system."

59. Dafoe, *Clifford Sifton*, 547.

60. Dafoe, *Clifford Sifton*, 541.

61. Hall, "Clifford Sifton and Canadian Indian Administration," 192.

62. Hall, "Clifford Sifton and Canadian Indian Administration," 184. The total budget of the federal government doubled in that span.

63. Petryshyn, *Peasants in the Promised Land*, 22; W.T.R. Preston, *My Generation of Politics and Politicians* (Toronto: D.A. Rose, 1927), 215.

64. House of Commons, *Debates*, 1901, col. 2763, 10 April 1901.

65. House of Commons, *Debates*, 18 July 1904, 6946–56; House of Commons, *Debates*, 23 July 1903, cols. 7260–1. Punctuation has been moderately altered for clarity.

66. Hall, "Clifford Sifton and Canadian Indian Administration," 189. The comment was made by Sifton in 1897. Sifton later acknowledged the difficulty of recruiting qualified teachers for these boarding schools, as the department only offered half of the pay available in an urban public school where non-Native Canadians were being educated. House of Commons, *Debates*, 1902, cols. 3043–6, 18 April 1902.

67. Hall, "Clifford Sifton and Canadian Indian Administration," 191. Sifton said, "I have followed the policy of encouraging the establishment of boarding schools"; House of Commons, *Debates*, 1904, cols. 6946–56, 18 July 1904. Indian Affairs finally gave up the distinction between industrial and boarding schools in 1923, when both types of schools were amalgamated into a single category known as residential schools.

68. Hall, "Clifford Sifton and Canadian Indian Administration."

69. Hayter Reed, "Memorandum for the information of the Minister relative to application of the per capita grant system of maintenance to the Brandon Indian Industrial School," 28 January 1897, vol. 6255, file 576-1, part 1, RG10, LAC, Ottawa. Sifton's approval was contingent on "the official consent of the Church."

70. Sister G. Marcoux, *History of the Qu'Appelle Indian School* (n.p., 1955), 14–5. The cost of the rebuild was $125,000. This school was also known as the Lebret Residential School, and was situated close to where Alexander Morris had promised that Indian children would learn the "cunning of the white man" during Treaty 4 negotiations.

71. P.H. Bryce, *Report on the Indian Schools of Manitoba and the North-West Territories* (Ottawa: Government Printing Bureau, 1907).

72. Katherine Lyndsay Nichols, "Investigation of unmarked graves and burial grounds at the Brandon Indian Residential School" (MA thesis, University of Manitoba, 2015), 92.

73. Hall, *The Young Napoleon*, 273, 193. Sifton said "the main reason for making this arrangement is to pacify and keep pacified the North-West Territories" and to avoid "having an Indian trouble on our hands." The superintendent later wrote that he discounted most signed statements by Indians. "It is possible for persons to get the Indians to sign almost any kind of statements, if a little excitement and agitation be got up beforehand, and we are unable therefore to rely to any extent upon written statements that come in signed by Indians."

74. Correspondence from Clifford Sifton to J. Peuder, 13 March 1897, C-403, image 385, Clifford Sifton fonds, LAC, Ottawa.

75. Dafoe, *Clifford Sifton*, 305–6.

76. Sifton, "Immigrants Canada Wants": "While I had many other duties [as minister of the interior], I regarded my most important mission as connected with Immigration."

77. Mrs. J. Skavinski (Annie Danylyko), "The Early Pioneers" (undated), in Rossburn History Club, *On the Sunny Slopes of the Riding Mountains: A History of Rossburn and District*, vol. 1 (Rossburn: RHC, 1984), 299.

8: "One Load of Barley"

1. Dominion of Canada, *Annual Report of the Department of Indian Affairs for the Year Ended 31st December, 1889*, 7 October 1889 (Ottawa, 1890). A comma between "time" and "this" has been removed for added clarity.

2. Sarah Carter, *Lost Harvests: Prairie Indian Reserve Farmers and Government Policy* (Montreal: McGill-Queen's University Press, 1990), 212.

3. Sarah Carter, "Two Acres and a Cow: 'Peasant' Farming for the Indians of the Northwest, 1889–97," *Canadian Historical Review* 70, no. 1, (March 1989), 44–5. Indians said that lanterns would help them care for cattle after nightfall, but to no avail.

4. Reed to T.M. Daly, (date illegible) 1893, Personnel A-G, vol. 18, Hayter Reed fonds, LAC, Ottawa.

5. RG10, Deputy Superintendent General of Indian Affairs Letterbooks, vol. 1115, p. 220, Reed to Forget, 12 June 1894, as cited in Carter, *Lost Harvests*, 218.

6. Carter, "Two Acres and a Cow," 33.

7. Carter, "Two Acres and a Cow."

8. Hayter Reed, "On the Aims of Government in Dealings with our Indians," P056 (1815–1944), Box 1, Folder 12, Reed Family fonds, McCord Museum, Montreal, 28.

9. McGirr to Reed, MG29, vol. 13, no 960, Hayter Reed Papers, LAC, Ottawa, as cited in Carter, "Two Acres and a Cow," 48.

10. Correspondence from Chas. De Cases to Reed, 19 November 1896, vol. 3964, file 148,285, RG10, LAC, Ottawa. The quotation later continues: "Perhaps in the south where the seasons are longer the system would work successfully, but up here no whiteman attempts to do so."

11. The first threshing machine in Rossburn arrived in 1880.

12. Dominion of Canada, *Annual Report of the Department of Indian Affairs for the Year Ended 31st December,* 1889 (Ottawa, 1890).

13. Sarah Carter, "'We Must Farm to Enable us to Live': The Plains Cree and Agriculture to 1900," in *The Prairie West as Promised Land,* ed. R. Douglas Francis and Chris Kitzan (Calgary: University of Calgary Press, 2007), 122: "by the mid 1890s, per capita acreage under cultivation had fallen to about half of the 1889 level and many had given up farming altogether."

14.

Year	Total acres under crop	Year	Total Acres under crop
1882	76	1891	103 13/32
1883	66	1892	100
1884	70	1893	18 5/16
1885	(data not available)	1894	13 11/24
1886	96	1895	20.61
1887	29 1/4	1896	13
1888	50	1897	16
1889	182	1898	7.88
1890	66 23/48	Sources: Annual reports of the Department of Indian Affairs, 1882-98	

15. The Indian Act, R.S.C. 1886, c. 43, s. 30. The prohibition on selling livestock appears in 1930 revisions to the act, and the permit system was limited to Alberta, Manitoba, Saskatchewan, and the Territories.

16. Reed to T. Mayne Daly, 13 March 1893, Hayter Reed Archives, LAC, Ottawa.

17. House of Commons, *Debates,* 24 March 1884, at 1063, as cited in Carter, "Two Acres and a Cow," 37.

18. McGirr to Reed, 8 March 1893, Hayter Reed Papers, LAC, vol. 13, no 960, as cited in Carter, "Two Acres and a Cow," 48.

19. *Virden Chronicle,* 11 January 1894 (viewed at the Manitoba Legislative Library).

20. Correspondence from J.A. Markle to the Secretary, Department of Indian Affairs, "Timber: Waywayseecappo Reserve No. 62, Brandon District," 11 June 1900, file 577/20-7-11-62, vol. 7057, MIKAN 2047064, RG10, LAC, Ottawa; correspondence from J.D. Maclean to J.A. Markle, 18 June 1900. The restrictions even extended to trees cut for firewood. On 11 June 1900, Markle, Waywayseecappo's Indian agent, wrote his superior to ask "whether it is necessary for [an] Indian to procure a permit to cut and remove a single load of wood to procure food for himself and family." Maclean, a senior official, replied from Ottawa one week later. He told Markle that "no deviation can be made from previous instructions," which specified that "Indians have not the right to cut timber on their Reserves for sale . . . without the sanction of the Department." He added, by way of explanation: "If an Indian can, without permission, cut and sell one load of wood, he might urge this plea of necessity for continuous cutting and selling and there would be no control over his operations." A version of this restriction remains in Article 93 of the Indian Act as of January 2021.

21. Carter, *Lost Harvests*, ix.

22. Carter, *Lost Harvests*, 193.

23. House of Commons, *Debates*, 19 May 1880, 1610; Walter Hildebrandt, "From Dominion to Hegemony: A Cultural History of Fort Battleford" (unpublished manuscript, 1988), Department of Environment, Parks, Prairie Region, as cited in Carter, "Two Acres and a Cow," 36.

24. Annual report of G.H. Wheatley (Indian Agent) to the Superintendent General of Indian Affairs Re: North-west Superintendency, Birtle Agency, 10 July 1906, Dominion of Canada, *Annual Report of the Department of Indian Affairs for the Year Ended June 30, 1906* (Ottawa, 1907).

25. Inspector of Indian Agencies, Birtle Agency, Dominion of Canada, *Annual Report for the Department of Indian Affairs for the Year Ended March 31, 1908* (Ottawa, 1908).

26. RCMP Report re: "Joe MENTUCK et al. (Treaty Indians) Selling timber on reserve without permit," Timber–Waywaysucappo Reserve No. 62 from 1893 to 1989, C-12967, 4 March 1942, file 577/20-7-11-62, vol. 7057, RG10, LAC, Ottawa.

27. Correspondence from A.G. Smith to the Secretary, "Timber: Waywayseecappo Reserve No. 62, Brandon District," 13 March 1942, "Portage La Prairie Agency – Correspondence and reports concerning licence to cut timber; trespass, removal and illegal sale of timber on the Waywayseecappo (fishing station) and Lizard Point reserves," file 577/20-7-11-62, vol. 7057, RG 10, LAC, Ottawa.

28. Correspondence from T.R.L. MacInnes to A.G. Smith, "Timber: Waywayseecappo Reserve No. 62, Brandon District," 4 April 1942, "Portage La Prairie Agency."

Smith's superior (MacInnes) replied, "It is impossible to give any general directions on a subject of this kind," but each case should be decided based on "its merits and in accordance with your best discretion and judgment."

29. Alex Williams, *The Pass System*, 2015 (documentary film).

30. By the year of its repeal, the prohibition applied only to Indians in Alberta, Saskatchewan, and Manitoba.

31. "Waywayseecappo Reserve," *Rossburn Review*, 21 October 1943.

32. James H. Gray, *Bacchanalia Revisited: Western Canada's Boozy Skid to Social Disaster* (Saskatoon: Western Producer Prairie Books, 1982), 117.

9: Reasonable Amusement

1. Cynthia Cooper, *Magnificent Entertainments: Fancy Dress Balls of Canada's Governors General, 1876–1898* (Fredericton: Goose Lane Editions, 1997), 70.

2. Cooper, *Magnificent Entertainments*, 75.

3. *The Lounger*, July 1896.

4. Marcel Trudel, *The Beginnings of New France: 1524–1663*, Canadian Centenary Series (Toronto: McClelland and Stewart, 1973), 44.

5. That Cree was the language he spoke at the event is an educated guess. We know that he spoke what sounded like an Indigenous language to onlookers, and that he had picked up some language skills on the plains. The likely bet for the language is Cree, given that this was the predominant language in the Battleford region where he had first served as an Indian agent.

6. Cooper, *Magnificent Entertainments*, 89.

7. J.G. Bourinot, *Illustrations of the Historical Ball Given by Their Excellencies the Earl and Countess of Aberdeen in the Senate Chamber, Ottawa, 17th February, 1896* (Ottawa: John Durie, 1896).

8. *The Lounger*, July 1896.

9. Cooper, *Magnificent Entertainments*, 96.

10. Bourinot, *Illustrations of the Historical Ball*.

11. Cooper, *Magnificent Entertainments*, 88. "Even Lady Aberdeen repeatedly lamented not having thought of organizing a war dance."

12. Giveaways are a common feature of many Indigenous ceremonies. For example, witnesses to a naming ceremony receive small and useful items like tea towels or more personal items for close relations and friends. On the West Coast, the potlatch ceremony involves the distribution of vast numbers of goods, the purpose of which is both distributive and demonstrative of a Chief's ability to manage property in a productive manner. See also Katherine Pettipas, *Severing the Ties that Bind* (Winnipeg: University of Manitoba Press, 1994), 252–3. In 1903, a judge in

Saskatchewan ruled that the provision of tea and bannock at a dance was sufficient to make the ceremony illegal.

13. Hayter Reed, memo re: "suggested Amendments to the Indian Act," 20 December 1889, vol. 3832, file 64,009, MIKAN 2060836, RG10, LAC, Ottawa.

14. Hayter Reed, "Notes on my early days in the North-West," 1928, P056 (1815–1944), Box 1, Folder 11, Reed Family fonds, McCord Museum, Montreal, 29.

15. Hayter Reed, "On the Aims of Government in Dealings with our Indians," P056 (1815–1944), Box 1, Folder 12, Reed Family fonds, McCord Museum, Montreal, 25: "the inculcation of this spirit of individualism is one of the most strenuously marked features of the Department's Indian policy."

16. *An Act providing for the organisation of the Department of the Secretary of State of Canada and for the management of Indian and Ordnance Lands*, S.C. 1868, c. 42, s. 149.

17. HTFC Planning and Design, *"See What the Land Gave Us": Waywayseecappo First Nation Traditional Knowledge Study for the Birtle Transmission Line* (2017), 44.

18. Harold Cardinal and Walter Hildebrandt, *Treaty Elders of Saskatchewan: Our Dream Is That Our Peoples Will One Day Be Clearly Recognized as Nations* (Calgary: University of Calgary Press, 2000), 14.

19. Reita Bambridge Sparling, *Reminiscences of the Rossburn Pioneers* (Rossburn: Rossburn Women's Institute, 1951), 47.

20. Correspondence from Clifford Sifton to Bishop of Calgary and Saskatchewan, 28 January 1901, C-440, image 1276, Clifford Sifton fonds, LAC, Ottawa.

21. Names of Chiefs and Minor Chiefs in Canada, 1894, Box B-8-ak, vol. 12010, no. 5103711, RG10, LAC. Ottawa.

22. J.A. Markle to the Indian Commissioner, 13 June 1896 and 16 June 1896, vol. 3825, file 60,511-1, RG10. LAC, Ottawa.

23. Correspondence from Forget to Office of the Indian Agent, Blood Agency, 11 July 1898, vol. 3825, file 60,511-1, RG10, LAC, Ottawa. Forget invokes "material withdrawal of assistance." Regarding trespass, see letter of 9 June 1896 in the same file.

24. W.P. Stewart, *My Name is Piapot* (Maple Creek: Butterfly Books Limited, 1981), 103–4. The conversation took place in 1899.

25. Correspondence from Sifton to Governor General in Council, 18 January 1898, vol. 1121, C-9002, RG10, 399–400.

26. John L Tobias, "Payipwat (Piapot, Hole in the Sioux, Kisikawasan, Flash in the Sky)," *Dictionary of Canadian Biography*, vol. 13. "I have no doubt he has been too harshly dealt with," Lord Minto said of Piapot; D.J. Hall, *Clifford Sifton*, vol. 2, *A Lonely Eminence, 1901–1929* (Vancouver: UBC Press, 1985), 48. In 1902, Lord Minto said this of Clifford Sifton: "Speaking generally, while fully recognizing the great success of Canadian administration of Indian affairs, it has seemed to

me that there is a want in many cases of human sympathy between the white administrator and the Indian, and that possibly . . . somewhat narrow religious sentiments have not conduced to a sympathetic understanding of the Indian races."

27. Correspondence from Scott to Graham, 4 October 1921, vol. 3826, file 60, 511-4A, RG 10, LAC, Ottawa. See also Brian Titley, *A Narrow Vision: Duncan Campbell Scott and the Administration of Indian Affairs in Canada* (Vancouver: University of British Press, 1986), 177.

28. Stan Cuthand, "The Native Peoples of the Prairie Provinces in the 1920's and 1930's," in *Sweet Promises: A Reader on Indian-White Relations in Canada*, ed. J.R. Miller (Toronto: University of Toronto Press, 1991), 389–90.

29. Correspondence from Lazenby to Assistant Deputy and Secretary, July 1923, vol. 6609, file 4106-6P, 28, P.G., RG10, LAC, Ottawa: "If the Missionary would devote his entire time to his Missionary work, as he should do, there might be a better chance of improving the moral status of this band, which is, to say the least, at present deplorable."

30. Correspondence from C.L. St John to Department of Indian Affairs, 18 June 1925, vol. 3827, file 60,511-4B, RG10, LAC, Ottawa.

31. Correspondence from A.M. Messner to Minister of Interior, 20 June 1925.

32. Correspondence from P.G. Lazenby to Assistant Deputy and Secretary, Department of Indian Affairs, 29 June 1925.

33. In the same letter, Lazenby says he gets a call from Inspector Christianson: "instructions had been received from the Commissioner's office."

34. Correspondence from P.G. Lazenby to the Assistant Deputy and Secretary, Department of Indian Affairs, 29 June 1925.

35. Correspondence from Sergeant Mann to the Officer Commanding, "Re: Lizard Point I.R. – Rossburn, Man – Assistance to Indian Dept," 11 July 1925. Mann acted per instructions from Commissioner Graham.

36. Correspondence from Sergeant Mann to the Commissioner, RCMP, 11 July 1925, vol. 3827, file 60,511-4B, RG10, LAC, Ottawa. Mann added: "I stayed round the camp for some time that evening. . . . With regard to those Indians, they have . . . been very orderly and well behaved, this much credit is due to them."

37. Mann further added: "Now the main point I have in mind is that there is a possibility in the future of like circumstances reaching an impasse as many of the Indians know as far as the Act is concerned they are doing nothing unlawful, which is liable to bring about a delicate state of affairs as far as the police are concerned when called upon by the dept to stop these dances," Correspondence from Sergeant Mann to the Commissioner, RCMP.

38. Correspondence from Duncan Campbell Scott to A.M. Messner, 30 June 1925, vol. 3827, file 60,511-4B, RG10, LAC, Ottawa. This letter is directed at one of the lawyers. There was indeed an exchange of letters between Scott and Graham, but in this particular government file only Graham's side of the conversation was preserved.

39. Correspondence from W.M. Graham to D.C. Scott, 4 July 1925.

40. Indian Act, 1927, R.S. 1927, c. 98, s. 141: "Every person who, without the consent of the Superintendent General expressed in writing, receives, obtains, solicits or requests from any Indian any payment or contribution . . . for the prosecution of any claim . . . for the benefit of the said tribe or band, shall be guilty of an offence and liable upon summary conviction for each such offence to a penalty not exceeding two hundred dollars and not less than fifty dollars or to imprisonment for any term not exceeding two months."

41. "Lord Tweedsmuir Wins His Way Into Hearts of Interlake Folk," *Winnipeg Evening Tribune*, 22 September 1936.

42. Oleh W. Gerus and Denis Hlynka, eds., *The Honourable Member for Vegreville: The Memoirs and Diary of Anthony Hlynka, MP* (Calgary: University of Calgary Press, 2005), 160.

43. "Lord Tweedsmuir Wins His Way." Tweedsmuir wished the audience "health and prosperity" in Ukrainian.

44. Clifford Sifton, "The Immigrants Canada Wants," *Maclean's Magazine*, 1 April 1922. Sifton also said: "I am just as much opposed to interference with the rights of property as anybody alive."

45. Sarah Carter, *Lost Harvests: Prairie Indian Reserve Farmers and Government Policy* (Montreal: McGill-Queen's University Press, 1990), 162. Under clause 70 of the 1876 Indian Act, an Indian could not take up a homestead unless he was willing to give up Indian status.

46. "Speech Delivered on Receiving Degree of L.L.D. by Queen's University," vol. 313, Manuscript Group 27, series II D 15, Clifford Sifton fonds, LAC, Ottawa.

10: "Never Forget"

1. Rossburn History Club (hereafter RHC), *On the Sunny Slopes of the Riding Mountains: A History of Rossburn and District*, vol. 1 (Rossburn: RHC, 1984), 344.

2. Lubomyr Luciuk and Stella Hryniuk, eds., *Canada's Ukrainians: Negotiating an Identity* (Toronto: University of Toronto Press, 1991), 302.

3. Luciuk and Hryniuk, *Canada's Ukrainians*, 294.

4. Oleh W Gerus and J.E. Rea, *The Ukrainians in Canada* (Ottawa: Canadian Historical Association, 1985), 11; Orest T. Martynowych, *Ukrainians in Canada: The Formative Period, 1891–1924* (Edmonton: University of Alberta Press, 1991), 323.

5. Bohdan S. Kordan, *Enemy Aliens, Prisoners of War: Internment in Canada During the Great War* (Montreal: McGill-Queens University Press, 2002), 70. Kodro was in the Castle Internment camp.

6. Bohdan S. Kordan and Peter Melnycky, eds., *In the Shadow of the Rockies: Diary of the Castle Mountain Internment Camp, 1915–1917* (Edmonton: Canadian Institute of Ukrainian Studies Press, 1991), 6; Bohdan S. Kordan, *No Free Man: Canada, the Great War, and the Enemy Alien Experience* (Montreal: McGill-Queens University Press, 2016), 130 As his father continued to work for his release, John managed to escape by making a mad dash into the bush during a day of forced labour on a bridge.

7. House of Commons, *Debates*, 1917, 5889:"among [eastern Europeans]" substituted for "among the Galicians, Kukovians, and Rumanians."

8. Frances Swyripa and John Herd Thompson, eds., *Loyalties in Conflict: Ukrainians in Canada During the Great War* (Edmonton: Canadian Institute of Ukrainian Studies Press, 1983), 75.

9. Linda and Darcy Yaskiw, *Our Heritage: Vladimir (Dick) Yaskiw, Lucia Drewniak: A Collection of Data, Photographs and Stories Contributed by Their Descendants* (Canada, 2012).

10. Marge and Mike Sotas, "The Early Birdtail Valley Settlers (1879–1914)," in RHC, *Sunny Slopes*, vol. 2, 25.

11. P.J. Giffen, *Rural Life: Portraits of the Prairie Town, 1946* (Winnipeg: University of Manitoba Press, 2004), 71.

12. Giffen, *Rural Life*, 79, 119, 86.

13. Giffen, *Rural Life*, 86.

14. Giffen, *Rural Life*, 86, 87.

15. P.J. Giffen, "Adult Education in Relation to Rural Social Structure: A Comparative Study of Three Manitoba Rural Communities" (master's thesis, University of Toronto, 1947), 150 (viewed at the Manitoba Legislative Library).

16. Giffen, *Rural Life*, 84.

17. Giffen, *Rural Life*, 88, 83.

18. Giffen, *Rural Life*, 117.

19. Giffen, "Adult Education," 208.

20. Giffen, "Adult Education," 139.

21. Ibram X. Kendi, *How to Be an Antiracist* (New York: One World, 2019), 218.

12: Bloodvein

1. An all-weather road connecting the provincial highway to the reserve wouldn't come for another eighteen years.

13: "The Way It Works"

1.   Canada, Office of the Parliamentary Budget Officer, "Federal spending on Primary and Secondary Education on First Nations Reserves" (Ottawa, 2016), 2. The 1 percent figure is after inflation.

2.   Nick Martin, "Higher education: Funding puts reserve school on par with public system," *Winnipeg Free Press*, 19 May 2012.

14: "Stark and Obvious"

1.   Canada, *House of Commons Debates*, vol. 142, no. 110, 2nd Session, 39th Parliament, 11 June 2008.

2.   Canada, Office of the Auditor General of Canada, *Report 5—Socio-economic Gaps on First Nations Reserves*, Indigenous Services Canada, 2018. "Our calculations showed that, on average, only about one in four (24%) students actually completed high school within 4 years." The overall graduation rate, allowing for more years to complete high school, is about 40 percent. See also Matthew Calver, *Closing the Aboriginal Education Gap in Canada: Assessing Progress and Estimating the Economic Benefits*, CSLS Research Reports March 2015, Centre for the Study of Living Standards, 18, 19, 36.

3.   "How Stanley Redcrow and First Nations activists reclaimed the Blue Quills Residential School," *CBC News,* 10 May 2017.

4.   Correspondence, 5 November 1984, 2001-00966-6, 002, WIN-E-4700-22-285 0c, RG10, LAC, Winnipeg.

5.   Correspondence from David Crombie to Charles Mayer, 14 February 1986, E-4700-22-285, RG10, LAC, Winnipeg. Crombie also noted that funding was "equitable in the sense" that all bands received comparable funding, which is to say that when it came to education funding, all Indian bands were shortchanged by the same amount when compared with provincial schools.

6.   Michael Mendelson, "Improving Education on Reserves: A First Nations Education Authority Act" (Ottawa: Caledon Institute of Social Policy, 2008), 6–7. Federal policy was to deliver provincial-level education on reserves, though without guaranteeing comparable funding. Mendelson writes, "The harsh reality is that the Department's confidence in the parity of its funding is misplaced, since it simply does not know. There are no regular data collected to compare provincial and federal education funding levels, nor is there any mechanism in the budget-setting process for First Nations education to ensure that funding levels are indeed comparable to those in provinces."

7.   Harry Swain's prediction eventually came true. In 2006, the First Nations Children and Family Caring Society and the Assembly of First Nations brought a complaint

alleging that the federal government "discriminates in providing child and family services to First Nations on reserve and in the Yukon, on the basis of race and/or national or ethnic origin, by providing inequitable and insufficient funding for those services." After a ten-year legal battle, the Canadian Human Rights Tribunal found a *prima facie* case of discrimination against First Nations children and families. See First Nations Child and Family Caring Society of Canada et al. v. Attorney General of Canada (Representing the Minister of Indian Affairs and Northern Development Canada) 2016 CHRT 2, 6, 456.

8. "School Buildings – Waywayseecappo First Nation," 1986-02-01 to 1981-06-30, ACC: 2001 - 01057-5, vol./Box 4, file number WIN-E-4965-285 02, RG10, LAC, Winnipeg.

9. Scott Serson, "The Canadian Government Knowingly and Deliberately Maintains First Nations in a State of Poverty," Submission to the Special Rapporteur on the rights of Indigenous Peoples, 14 October 2013.

10. Andrew Stobo Sniderman, unpublished interview with Paul Martin, August 2012. Martin continued: "Let's say the cap was reasonably fair for four or five years because it was an increase at a time when other departments were getting cut. But then it stayed on for a number of years too long. The first thing that I did when I became [prime minister] was to move to eliminate the gap. That's what the [2005] Kelowna [Accord] money was all about. Did the cap last longer than it should have, and was a Liberal government in office when it did? Yes, the answer is yes."

11. Truth and Reconciliation Commission of Canada, *Executive Summary* (Kingston: McGill-Queen's University Press, 2015), 148. See also Canada, Office of the Parliamentary Budget Officer, "Federal Spending on Primary and Secondary Education on First Nations Reserves" (Ottawa, 2016), 1–2. Between 1996 and 2006, provincial funding to provincial schools increased annually by an average of 3.8 percent, while Ottawa maintained its 2 percent limit. These figures actually understate the extent of the problem, because the number of students in provincial schools was stagnating or dropping overall, but the number of Indigenous students was skyrocketing. This aggravated the disparity in per student funding between public schools and reserve schools. One factor that somewhat alleviated the gap was that Indigenous and Northern Affairs Canada was reallocating some infrastructure funding to invest more in services. This was likened to "robbing Peter to pay Paul." Steve Rennie, "Aboriginal Affairs short of cash for education, social programs: document," *CBC News*, 10 November 2014. This diversion of funding from infrastructure is one of the reasons why so many reserves are suffering from an infrastructure crisis.

12. Andrew Stobo Sniderman, "Aboriginal students: An education underclass," *Maclean's*, 8 August 2012.

13. Canada, Office of the Auditor General, *Report of the Auditor General on Indian and Northern Affairs Canada's Elementary and Secondary Education Programs* (Ottawa, 2004), 5.2, 5.27; Canada, Office of the Auditor General of Canada, June 2011 Status Report, "Chapter 4—Programs for First Nations on Reserves," 4.17.

14. For the full text of the motion, which was passed on 27 February, see Canada, House of Commons, *Debates,* 16 February 2012, 5359. The motion declares "that all First Nation children have an equal right to high-quality, culturally-relevant education."

15. Kate Hammer, "B.C. First Nations students to get equal funding," *The Globe and Mail,* 27 January 2012; Canada, "Agreement with Respect to Mi'kmaq Education in Nova Scotia," 1997; Bill Graveland, "Harper unveils retooled First Nations education plan," *Global News,* 7 February 2014. The major exception was in British Columbia, where the federal government committed over $15 million a year in funding for on-reserve education, in order to equalize funding with respect to provincial schools. In 2014, Stephen Harper also introduced legislation that would have committed the federal government to annual budget increases of 5 percent for the education of students on reserve, but the bill never became law.

16. Jody Porter, "First Nations students get 30 per cent less funding than other children, economist says," *CBC News,* 14 March 2016; Office of the Parliamentary Budget Officer, "Federal spending on Primary and Secondary Education on First Nations Reserves," 29. See also John Paul Tasker, "First Nations education a cash-strapped 'non-system,' bureaucrats tell Minister," *CBC News,* 5 October 2016.

15: "People Say We're Racists"

1. John S. Milloy, *A National Crime: The Canadian Government and the Residential School System, 1879 to 1986* (Winnipeg: University of Manitoba Press, 1999), xxxix; Sheila Carr Stewart, "First Nations Education: Financial Accountability and Educational Attainment," *Canadian Journal of Education* 29, no. 4 (2006): 998–1018. In residential schools, "chronic underfunding" was a "persistent flaw." As for the federal "day schools" on reserves—which many Indigenous students attended before the shift to integrated education—these schools were "notoriously under funded, poorly equipped and constructed, [and teachers were] paid less than their colleagues in neighboring public schools," according to evidence submitted to Parliament.

2. Canada, Department of Indian and Northern Affairs, *A Survey of the Contemporary Indians of Canada: Economic, Political, Educational Needs and Policies – Part 1 [The Hawthorn Report]* (Ottawa, 1967), 344.

3. See First Nations Child and Family Caring Society of Canada et al. v. Attorney General of Canada (Representing the Minister of Indigenous Affairs and

Northern Development Canada) 2016 CHRT 2, Canada (Canadian Human Rights Commission) v. Canada (Attorney General), 2012 FC 445, and other associated litigation.

4. Ipsos, "On Immigrants and Aboriginals: Majority (72%) of Canadians Disagree That Canada Should Admit More Immigrants than Current Levels, Split on Whether Immigration has Been Positive (40%) or Negative (34%)," 30 June 2012. "Nearly two in three (64%) 'agree' (27% strongly/36% somewhat) that 'Canada's Aboriginal peoples receive too much support from Canadian taxpayers.'"

5. Indigenous Peoples are the descendants of Canada's first inhabitants. "Status Indians," or "treaty Indians," are Indigenous Peoples deemed to be official "Indians" by the government. "Non-Status Indians" are Indigenous Peoples who lack the status designations, and are, therefore, not legally Indians.

6. Charlie Angus, *Children of the Broken Treaty: Canada's Promise and One Girl's Dream* (Regina: University of Regina Press, 2015), 56.

7. Angus Reid Institute, "Truths of reconciliation: Canadians are deeply divided on how best to address Indigenous issues," 7 June 2018.

8. Arlie Russell Hochschild, *Strangers in Their Own Land* (New York: The New Press, 2016), 52.

9. Chelsea Vowel, "The Myth of Taxation," in *Indigenous Writes: A Guide to First Nations, Métis and Inuit Issues in Canada* (Winnipeg: Portage and Main Press, 2016), 135–42; Aleksandra Sagan, "First Nations pay more tax than you think," *CBC News*, 24 April 2015.

10. Canada, Royal Commission on Aboriginal Peoples, *Report of the Royal Commission on Aboriginal Peoples, Volume 1: Looking Forward, Looking Back* (Ottawa, 1996), 248; John F. Leslie, "The Indian Act: An Historical Perspective," *Canadian Parliamentary Review* 25, no. 2 (2002), 23–7; John S. Milloy, "The Early Indian Acts: Developmental Strategy and Constitutional Change," in *As Long as the Sun Shines and Water Flows: A Reader in Canadian Native Studies*, ed. Ian A.L. Getty and Antoine S. Lussier (Vancouver: UBC Press, 1983), 56–64; John L. Tobias, "Protection, Civilization, Assimilation: An Outline History of Canada's Indian Policy," in Getty and Lussier, *As Long as the Sun Shines and Water Flows*, 39–55.

11. Dominion of Canada, *Annual Report of the Department of Indian Affairs for the Year Ended December 31st, 1899*. In 1899, David Laird, chief negotiator of Treaty 8, promised Indians the treaty would not lead to the imposition of taxes. He said: "We assured them that the treaty would not lead to any forced interference with their mode of life, that it did not open the way to the imposition of any tax."

12. Mitchell v. Peguis Indian Band, [1990] 2 S.C.R. 85.

16: "Kids Are Kids"

1. "Waywayseecappo First Nation LOU and Pilot Project with Park West School Division," Information for Deputy Minister, Originator: Derek Bradley, 22 November 2010, Unclassified – MB 13735. Accessed through Access to Information request.

2. Nick Martin, "Higher education: Funding puts reserve school on par with public system," *Winnipeg Free Press*, 19 May 2012.

3. "Waywayseecappo First Nation LOU."

4. Bruce Carson, *14 Days: Making the Conservative Movement in Canada* (Montreal: McGill-Queen's University Press, 2014), 170.

5. In 2016, the Paul Martin Initiative began to operate in the Waywayseecappo Community School, investing notably in literacy programs. Because of this additional intervention, we do not cite further data from the school after this date, because improvements in student outcomes could not be attributed as directly to the partnership with the Park West School Division that began in 2010.

6. Andrew Stobo Sniderman, "Aboriginal Students, an education underclass," *Maclean's*, 8 August 2012.

7. Andrew Stobo Sniderman, "Equal education funding gets big results on Manitoba reserve," *Maclean's*, 26 April 2016.

17: "Bury the Hatchet"

1. J.R. Miller, *Residential Schools and Reconciliation: Canada Confronts Its History* (Toronto: University of Toronto Press, 2017), 173, 172, 180–1.

2. This metaphor comes from the Iroquois Confederacy. At the founding of the Confederacy, once-hostile warriors were said to have buried their hatchets alongside the roots of the great Tree of Peace.

3. Statistics Canada, *Rossburn, Town, Census Profile*, 2016 Census; Statistics Canada, *Waywayseecappo First Nation, Indian Reserve, Census Profile*, 2016 Census.

4. Brian Brown, "Hockey players not the only people mistreated," *Crossroads This Week*, 13 December 2019.

5. Murray Clearsky, "Ignorance and misinformation," *Crossroads This Week*, 20 December 2019.

6. Kerry Lawless et al., "Rossburn council comments on letter," *Crossroads This Week*, 20 December 2019.

18: "A Grand Notion"

1. "Missing and Murdered: The Unsolved Cases of Indigenous Women and Girls," *CBC News*, n.d.

2. Guy Quenneville, "What happened on Gerald Stanley's farm the day Colten Boushie was shot, as told by witnesses," *CBC News*, 9 August 2016.

3. Benjamin Shingler, "Investigations launched after Atikamekw woman records Quebec hospital staff uttering slurs before her death," *CBC News*, 29 September 2020.

4. "More unmarked graves found near another school that housed Indigenous children in Canada," *CBC News*, 30 June 2021.

5. Clifford Sifton, "Natural Resources of Canada," Speech delivered to the Women's Art Association, Clifford Sifton fonds, vol. 313, Manuscript Group 27, series II D 15, LAC, Ottawa.

6. Jason Warick, "Trudeau not honouring $2.6B education promise, First Nations leaders say," *CBC News*, 13 September 2018.

7. Canada, Office of the Parliamentary Budget Officer, "Federal spending on Primary and Secondary Education on First Nations Reserves" (Ottawa, 2016), 29.

8. John Rawls, "Justice as Fairness," *The Philosophical Review* 67, no. 2 (April 1958). The philosopher John Rawls, in thinking about the idea of equality, once set out a list of basic items needed for citizens to flourish in a system of background equality. He termed these "the primary goods," and they include enough resources to adequately feed and house ourselves, and civil and political liberties, but Rawls called the most important of these goods "the social basis of self respect." Rawls understood that to flourish, each citizen must see their values reflected in social institutions lest we be forced to pursue a conception of the good different from our own. This is the reason that Indigenous schooling will look different from off-reserve schools: the reserve school curriculum is designed to affirm the dignity of Indigenous values and cultures.

9. Nunavut, Department of Education, "Educator Toolkit for Nunavut Schools" 2020–2021. In 2020, Nunavut issued an educator toolkit that focuses on core curriculum like reading and writing, but does so in the context of land-based learning. Curricular activities include berry picking, drying/smoking fish, hunting, carving, and skinning/cleaning caribou, to name just a few activities.

10. Canada, Royal Commission on Aboriginal Peoples, *Highlights from the Report of the Royal Commission on Aboriginal Peoples* (Ottawa, 1996).

11. Modern-day treaties like the Nisga'a or James Bay treaties remove those populations from the Indian Act and provide those treaty nations with a set of jurisdictional powers that is negotiated between the federal, provincial, and Indigenous governments.

12. The Indian Act and the First Nations Fiscal Management Act provide for property taxation, and this has been a boon for Indian reserves located in areas where

the real estate market is booming, such as near North Vancouver and Kelowna. The First Nations Sales Tax Act authorizes the taxing of alcohol, tobacco, and automobile purchases, while the First Nations Goods and Services Act authorizes a tax on retail transactions. Modern-day treaties can provide for the collection of personal income tax, and the First Nations Fiscal Management Act combined with the Indian Act authorize the collection of property taxes. For the most part, these various acts require reserve governments to enter into agreement with the federal government for the collection of these taxes.

13. First Nations reserves are almost wholly funded by transfers from the federal Crown, with the provinces doing all that they can to avoid spending on reserve communities. Nevertheless, most provinces do have some form of financial transfers ("Resource Revenue Sharing") paid to First Nations communities or provincially paid services that provide access for Indian people to provincial services (e.g., Native Child and Family Services, whose funders include several provincial ministries and the City of Toronto).

14. Indian reserves comprise just 11,000 square kilometres. Combined, the more than six hundred reserve communities equal about 0.2 percent of Canada's total land mass, or the size of two Prince Edward Islands.

15. In 2015, Ontario also brought in a further billion dollars in revenue from goods manufactured in the forestry and logging industry in Ontario. Statistics Canada, *CANSIM Table* 301-0009: *Logging Industries, Principal Statistics by North American Industry Classification System* (Ottawa, 2015).

16. Indeed, many of the forty-three northern communities are already bound together in a political territorial organization known as the Nishnawbe Aski Nation (NAN), and, at a still more local level, communities are also bound together in collectives known as tribal councils.

17. David Treuer, "Return the National Parks to the Tribes: The jewels of America's landscape should belong to America's original peoples," *The Atlantic*, May 2021. The main categories of federally held lands are national parks, military bases, airports, and Indian reserves. In the U.S., there has been recent discussion about the social, political, juridical, and economic benefits of handing back U.S. National Park lands to Indigenous Peoples. Given that the land mass of Canada's National Parks system is fifteen times the total area covered by Indian reserves (3.3 percent vs 0.6 percent), Treuer's suggestion might have relevance here in Canada as well.

18. Sidney B. Linden, *Report of the Ipperwash Inquiry* (Toronto: Ministry of the Attorney General, 2007). In addition to national parks, military bases may have a role to play as well.

19. Douglas Sanderson, "Against Supersession," *Canadian Journal of Law and Jurisprudence*, 24, no. 1 (January 2011), 155–82. In British Columbia, where no treaties were ever signed, Indigenous Peoples find it difficult to understand what is unjust about control over lands being returned to Indigenous Peoples, when those lands were never sold or ceded by the land's rightful owners. Returning the land is, on this view, simply righting a past wrong. Historic injustices do not simply go away.

20. There are, of course, more than public interests at stake. Even if urban citizens experienced no increase in taxes and received the same level of service, private investment in resource extraction may not be able to deliver the same level of returns when First Nations are the ones issuing permits. These losses could be felt not just by the resource companies but by the pension funds and other sources of private capital.

21. Confederation of Tomorrow, 2020 *Survey of Canadians, Report 2: The Division of Powers and Resources* (Toronto, 2020). Prince Edward Island and Quebec are perennial beneficiaries of the equalization formula, while Ontario, Alberta, and British Columbia are the funds' primary depositors. In October 2021, a referendum in Alberta suggested that most voters were dissatisfied with the existing practice of equalization.

22. McGirt v. Oklahoma, No. 18-9526, 591 U.S. __ (2020), 28.

23. *McGirt* does not transfer the property of Oklahomans to Creek Indians. Nevertheless, considerable confusion has arisen with respect to criminal prosecutions resulting from *McGirt*. By arguing that the original reservation boundaries remained intact, McGirt called into question the validity of his trial because it was conducted in state, not federal court. Federal criminal law, not state law, applies on an Indian reserve. McGirt was then tried in federal court and sentenced to three life counts.

24. Jamil Malakieh, Canadian Centre for Justice and Community Safety Statistics, *Adult and youth correctional statistics in Canada, 2017/2018* (Ottawa: Statistics Canada, 2019). Among the provinces in 2017/2018, Aboriginal adults represented three-quarters of admissions to custody in Manitoba (75 percent) and Saskatchewan (74 percent).

25. Robert A. Williams, *Linking Arms Together: American Indian Treaty Visions of Law and Peace,* 1600–1800 (New York, Routledge, 2000); Bruce Morito, *An Ethic of Mutual Respect* (Vancouver: UBC Press, 2012); William Fenton, *The Great Law and the Longhouse: A Political History of the Iroquois Confederacy* (Norman: University of Oklahoma Press, 2010).

26. "Ending long-term drinking water advisories," Indigenous Services Canada, accessed 16 June 2021. The number of communities under boil-water advisories

has diminished in recent years, following significant investments by successive governments.

27. Canada, Yukon Land Claims and Self-Government Agreements, 1994; Canada, The James Bay and Northern Quebec Agreement (JBNQA), 1975; Canada, The Northeastern Quebec Agreement, 1978. In addition to these agreements, there is the Nisga'a Final Agreement, as well as seven other comprehensive treaties finalized in British Columbia in the past twenty years.

INDEX

The Waterman's Song

Along Freedom Road: Hyde County, North Carolina,
and the Fate of Black Schools in the South (1994)

Democracy Betrayed: The Wilmington Race Riot of 1898 and Its Legacy,
co-edited with Timothy B. Tyson (1998)

William Henry Singleton's *Recollections of My Slavery Days,*
co-edited with Katherine Mellen Charron (1999)

A Historian's Coast: Adventures into the Tidewater Past (2000)

Waterman's Song

Slavery and Freedom
in Maritime North Carolina

DAVID S. CECELSKI

The University of North Carolina Press

Chapel Hill and London

Designed by April Leidig-Higgins
Set in Monotype Bell by Keystone Typesetting, Inc.
Manufactured in the United States of America

*Publication of this work was aided by a generous grant
from the Z. Smith Reynolds Foundation*

The paper in this book meets the guidelines for
permanence and durability of the Committee on
Production Guidelines for Book Longevity of the
Council on Library Resources.

Library of Congress Cataloging-in-Publication Data
Cecelski, David S. The waterman's song: slavery and
freedom in maritime North Carolina / by David S.
Cecelski. p. cm. Includes index.
ISBN 0-8078-2643-x (cloth: alk. paper)
ISBN 0-8078-4972-3 (pbk.: alk. paper)
1. Slaves—North Carolina. 2. Slavery—North Car-
olina—History. 3. African American ship pilots—
North Carolina—History—19th century. 4. African
American fishers—North Carolina—History—19th
century. 5. Inland water transportation—North Car-
olina—History—19th century. 6. North Carolina—
History—1775–1865. I. Title.
E444.N8 C43 2001 975.6'00496—dc21 2001027125

05 04 03 02 01 5 4 3 2 1

To Tim Tyson

Contents

Part Two. The Struggle for Freedom

Map & Illustrations

preface

The Waterman's Song

In October 1830 Moses Ashley Curtis arrived at the mouth of the Cape Fear River aboard a schooner from Boston. The North Carolina coast would be the young naturalist's first landfall of his first voyage into the American South. Emptying into the Atlantic, the Cape Fear was a tumult of heavy waves, strong currents, and dangerous shoals. Passage across the inlet's bar and outer shoals was folly without a local pilot. The schooner's master raised a signal flag and beckoned toward the village of Smithville for a pilot to guide him into the river. Curtis soon spied a pilot boat under sail, breaking through the waves toward him. Approaching the schooner, the fast, elegant craft turned into the wind and drifted alongside the larger vessel. "They boarded us," Curtis wrote in his diary that day, "And what saw I? *Slaves!*—the first I ever saw."[1]

Guided into Smithville by the slave pilots, Curtis "found the wharf and stores crowded with blacks, noisy and careless." After a brief stay, his schooner sailed toward Wilmington, a seaport 25 miles upriver. Unbeknownst to Curtis, this leg of his voyage was like a descent through the Cape Fear past. He sailed by Sugar Loaf, the high sand dune where colonial militia led by Colonel Roger Moore were said to have conquered the last of the Cape Fear Indians.[2] He passed under Fort Johnston, with its oyster-shell-and-pitch-pine walls built by slaves in 1802.[3] Along the western bank of the Cape Fear River, Curtis peered into cypress swamps draped with Spanish moss. Here and there, hundreds of black hands had hewn out great rice plantations along the water's edge.

Everywhere Curtis saw slave watermen: harbor pilots, oystermen, the entire crew of the federal revenue cutter, plantation boatmen. Among them was "a boat full of blacks [that] came rowing by us," chanting a song "repeated ad infinitum and accompanied with a trumpet obligato by the helmsman."[4] Curtis scribbled the lyrics and a line of music in his diary: "O Sally was a fine girl, O Sally was a fine girl, O!" It was the refrain of a popular sea chantey, called "Sally Brown," that spoke longingly of a beautiful Jamaican mulatto. Lonely mariners sang "Sally Brown" throughout the Atlantic and half a world away in the Pacific at the same time that these boatmen crooned it on the Cape Fear.[5] Other black maritime laborers crowded Wilmington on Curtis's arrival, and in his diary he noted that "a boat came along side with three negroes who offered an alligator for sale."[6] Curtis had discovered the maritime South—and the central role of African Americans within it.

When I began this study, I was no less surprised than Curtis at the degree to which slave watermen marked maritime life in North Carolina. His words— "And what saw I? *Slaves!*"—could have been my own. Until recently, few historians have recognized the prevalence of generations of African American maritime laborers along the Atlantic coastline. Scholars have tended to view the black South mainly in terms of agricultural slave labor—picking cotton, cutting sugar cane, winnowing rice, or priming tobacco, for example—not trimming sails or casting nets. But in recent years a new generation of scholars has begun to explore (from different angles, in a variety of locations, and in a number of eras) the complex and important roles played by black watermen and sailors in the Atlantic maritime world.[7]

While this research has only now begun to touch on the American South, rather than on New England and the Caribbean, nowhere was the magnitude of African American influence on maritime life greater than along the perilous seacoast and vast estuaries that stretch a hundred miles from the Outer Banks into the interior of North Carolina.[8] Slave and free black boatmen were ubiquitous on those broad waters, dominating most maritime trades and playing a major role in all of them. The intertidal marshes, blackwater creeks, and brackish rivers that flowed into the estuaries also teemed with black watermen. Between 1800 and the Civil War, African Americans composed approximately 45 percent of the total population in North Carolina's nineteen tidewater counties.[9] They made up nearly 60 percent of the total population in its largest seaports.[10] The percentage of black men working full-time as fisher-

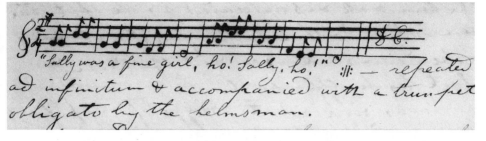

In 1830 Moses Ashley Curtis heard slave boatmen on the Cape Fear River singing this song and recorded its refrain in his diary. The piece is apparently a version of the sea chantey "Sally Brown," about a beautiful Jamaican mulatto, and sailors and boatmen spread the chantey across the globe. Courtesy Southern Historical Collection, University of North Carolina at Chapel Hill.

men or boatmen or in other maritime trades probably ranged from as little as 1 percent on the upper reaches of tidewater rivers to as much as 50 percent or more on the Outer Banks, but any firm estimate would be recklessly speculative and probably deceptive. Most coastal slaves worked on the water at least occasionally, whether it was rafting a master's timber to market once a year or fishing on the sly for their own suppers. Working on the water was a part of daily life for most tidewater slaves and their free brethren. Their preeminence in boating, fishing, and shipping can be seen again and again in contemporary newspapers, wills and estate records, plantation ledgers, ships' logs, court documents, and travel accounts.

I soon discovered that African American maritime laborers congregated in the wharf districts of every seaport, not merely Smithville and Wilmington, and their range and diversity far exceeded what Moses Ashley Curtis described in his diary. Along the Albemarle Sound, prodigious gangs of black fishermen wielded mile-and-a-half-long seines in what was the largest herring fishery in North America. Nearby, on the Roanoke River, slave bateaumen dared harrowing rapids and racing currents to transport tobacco from the foothills of the Blue Ridge Mountains all the way to seaports. Far to the east, at Portsmouth Island, slave crews piloted vessels through Ocracoke Inlet, lightered their cargoes, and then guided them to distant seaports on the other side of Albemarle and Pamlico Sounds. Their slave neighbors at Shell Castle Island, a shoal at Ocracoke Inlet, ranged up and down the Outer Banks with their nets in pursuit of jumping mullet and bottlenosed dolphins. In every port, slave stevedores trundled cargo on and off vessels, while shipyard

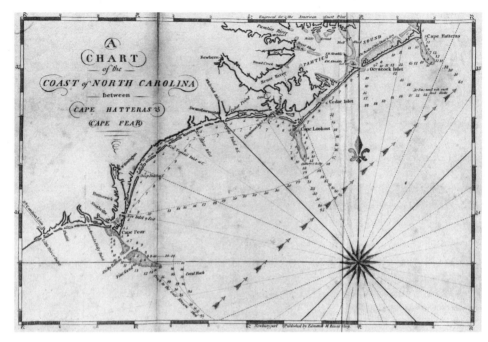

Edmund Blunt, "A Chart of the Coast of North Carolina between Cape Hatteras & Cape Fear," 1809. Courtesy North Carolina Collection, University of North Carolina at Chapel Hill.

workers in bondage built some of the sweetest-sailing cedar and white oak boats afloat. Still other slave watermen hawked firewood to steamers anchored in the Cape Fear at night, rafted lumber down the Lower Neuse River, guided duck hunting parties along the freshwater marshes of Currituck Sound, tonged for oysters on frigid winter days, poled shingle flats out of the Great Dismal Swamp, shoveled coal in the sweltering firerooms of steamboats, manned the sloops and schooners that traded both within and beyond North Carolina.

The breadth and complexity of this African American maritime culture stands out prominently in firsthand accounts of slavery. Of the seven authors of surviving narratives written by former slaves from tidewater North Carolina, four had been engaged in the maritime trades, another had a father who was a slave pilot, and maritime laborers played key roles in the escapes to freedom of the other two. The most compelling of these narratives are those of maritime laborers London Ferebee, Moses Grandy, and Thomas H. Jones.

Growing up by Currituck Sound in the 1850s, Ferebee learned boatmanship from his father, one of many slaves employed in local shipyards, and from the slave crewmen on his master's sloop. He had learned to sail that vessel over some of the most dangerous shoals along the Carolina coast before his twelfth birthday, as well as mastered the fundamentals of bluewater navigation. "Even at night," he wrote in *A Brief History of the Slave Life of Reverend London R. Ferebee* (1882), "I could steer by the compass, or by any star."[11]

Two generations earlier, Moses Grandy worked in several maritime trades that he described in his *Narrative of the Life of Moses Grandy, Late a Slave in the United States of America* (1843). Over three decades, he operated a river ferry in Camden County, captained barges between Elizabeth City and Norfolk, and crewed a schooner on Albemarle Sound. After purchasing his freedom, he served on packets that ran along the eastern seaboard and eventually on brigs and schooners that sailed the high seas.[12]

Far to the south of Grandy's haunts, a Wilmington stevedore named Thomas H. Jones was no less a part of maritime life. In *The Experience of Thomas H. Jones, Who Was a Slave for Forty-Three Years* (ca. 1854), he chronicled how loading and unloading seagoing vessels exposed him daily to sailors and boatmen from up and down the Atlantic coast. He eventually used his position to identify a sea captain willing to transport his wife, Mary, and their three children to New York and later negotiated his own escape with a black sailor bound for the same city.[13] None of the three maritime careers was exceptional in that era. All highlight a lost African American maritime culture whose vitality and significance still speak to us.

In Zora Neale Hurston's lyrical novel *Their Eyes Were Watching God*, her heroine Janie is comparing love to the sea when she says, "It takes its shape from de shore it meets, and it's different with every shore," but she could just as well have been speaking of the lives of African American maritime laborers. As I waded through archival records in my research for *The Waterman's Song*, I was first struck merely by the sheer magnitude of African American involvement in maritime society. I soon realized, however, how remarkably varied maritime life was within North Carolina waters. A bustling seaport like Wilmington, a quiet river town like Camden, a remote piloting village like Portsmouth, a mullet fishing camp at Core Banks, and a canal-digging outpost in the Great Dismal Swamp represented virtually different maritime worlds. In them, race relationships and the degrees of slaves' independence, mobility, and access to the political and cultural currents of Atlantic shipping varied enormously. Yet, for all their diversity, maritime trade and travel also united the state's beaches, wharves, and pilot camps, so that the lives of black watermen, like magician's hoops, were simultaneously held together and apart, distinctive but interconnected too.

I gradually recognized common patterns in African American maritime life. No pattern emerged more forcefully than that of black watermen serving as key agents of antislavery thought and militant resistance to slavery. The nature of their labors frequently meant that they could not be supervised closely, if at all, for days or even weeks. For all their grueling toil and severe hardships, many maritime black laborers traveled widely, grew acquainted with slaves and free blacks over a wide territory, and dealt with seamen who connected them to the revolutionary politics that coursed the black Atlantic. Almost invariably, black watermen appeared at the core of abolitionist activity, slave insurrections, and other antislavery activism in North Carolina.[14] When a slave insurrection spread across the coastal plain in 1775, a black waterman named Merrick was one of the two main conspirators.[15] When another slave revolt, later known as Gabriel's Rebellion, swept southside Virginia and the Albemarle Sound vicinity in 1800, and again in 1802, slave rivermen directed the rebels, passing secret plans for the uprising along waterways.[16] In the aftermath of Nat Turner's bloody revolt in southside Virginia in 1831, dozens of maritime slaves at Portsmouth Island, North Carolina, absconded with a schooner and disappeared into the Atlantic, their escape foiled only by an ill-timed nor'easter.[17] In antebellum Wilmington, a slave harbor pilot named Peter was at the heart of a far-reaching conspiracy to help fugitive slaves board seagoing vessels bound for New England and Canada.[18] At the outbreak of the Civil War, black watermen led a massive boatlift of slaves from the state's interior to freedom in Union-occupied seaports and islands. Liberated slave watermen piloted Union vessels and shared their knowledge of local navigation, undercutting one of the few advantages held by Confederate forces—their familiarity with local waters.

Most black maritime laborers never led a slave rebellion or escaped into the Atlantic, yet collectively they still had a powerful hand in building a culture of slave resistance that shaped African American freedom struggles before, during, and after the Civil War. Reinforced by strong linkages to black communities elsewhere in the Atlantic world, this maritime political culture was grounded in the egalitarian ideals of the Enlightenment, in an evangelical theology that stressed the "natural rights" of all peoples before God, and in a homegrown brand of abolitionism born of the African American experience of slavery in and around southern ports. Not surprisingly, this culture emphasized racial equality, political freedom, and the sort of expansive communitarian values upon which coastal slaves had long staked their survival. These predominately illiterate people preserved their political vision in song, sermon, and saying, which eventually made its way onto the written page at first flush of formal learning.[19]

It was no accident that David Walker, born a free black and raised in the seaport of Wilmington, North Carolina, became a celebrated abolitionist pamphleteer. After Walker settled in Boston in the 1820s, he recruited sailors at his secondhand clothes shop to carry copies of his *Appeal to the Coloured Citizens of the World*—one of the seminal treatises of American antislavery thought—throughout the South. As Peter Hinks has shown in his recent study of the *Appeal*, Walker arrived in Boston with his own abolitionist ideology in hand. He did not come under the spell of the more renowned white abolitionists of New England; he and his black colleagues, many of whom had roots in the maritime South, were the driving wedge of early abolitionism in the North. Walker's thoughtful, articulate, and militant call for armed resistance to slavery expressed the culture of slave resistance shaped by African Americans in the maritime districts of North Carolina and other southern states.

That spirit of militancy survived along the darkest edges of plantation society, but it burst into daylight during the Civil War. Beyond the African American watermen who boatlifted slaves out of Confederate territory, another revolutionary development unfolded within the Union-occupied seaports of the South. In these communities, maritime laborers, along with their families and neighbors, forged an African American politics that became decidedly independent of the Union cause by mid-1863 and projected a more expansive, democratic vision of the South's future into Reconstruction. That story will be told here through the mercurial life of Abraham H. Galloway (1837–70), who had been born a slave in the piloting village of Smithville. After escaping to Philadelphia aboard a schooner in 1857, Galloway returned to North Carolina at the outset of the Civil War as a Union spy and soon became an abolitionist leader in occupied New Bern. He played a leading role in organizing one of the first African American regiments in the South but refused to relinquish his recruits to the Union army until military commanders agreed to the soldiers' demands for racial justice and fair treatment. Determined that if the former slaves were denied political equality "at the ballot box, they would have it at the cartridge box," Galloway also organized chapters of the Equal Rights League in several Carolina ports in the last year of the war. In 1865, Galloway called one of the South's first political conventions of freedpeople. He later served as colonel of a black militia that fought the Ku Klux Klan, and he carried his "Jacobinical" politics and combative style into the state senate in North Carolina's first class of black legislators. In Galloway's life, we see the flowering, and ultimately the demise, of an insurgent political vision that emerged from the African American maritime society of the slave South.

The Waterman's Song explores African American maritime life in North Carolina over the course of a little less than a century, spanning the years from the consolidation of American slavery around 1800 to the last days of Reconstruction. This was the heyday of black maritime activity along the Atlantic seacoast and on the state's inland waters. My research looks mainly toward the shoreline, at slaves and free blacks who labored as boatmen, pilots, ferrymen, fishermen, sailors, and nautical artisans in ports and on the sounds, rivers, and creeks within maritime North Carolina, as well as in parts of the Atlantic accessible from shore by fishing boats and other small craft. Those maritime occupations, not deepwater sailing, were the mainstay of coastal life in North Carolina and, with the exception of a handful of seaports, all of the American South.

An exhilarating new wave of scholarship about black seafarers in the Atlantic also helped me to understand better how this local maritime culture was entangled with the Afro-Caribbean, with the work culture of seafaring men, and with revolutionary political tides that roiled the black Atlantic. Though I saw signs in the documentary record for every port that slaveholders feared the revolutionary ideology spread by black sailors, they would never have resonated for me if I had not read Julius Scott's powerful work on West Indian black sailors as agents of political communication during the Revolutionary era.[20] Similarly, I was able to put into historical context a distinctive strain of racial egalitarianism and antiauthoritarianism that I observed in some parts of the maritime culture of North Carolina because I was familiar with Jeffrey Bolster's groundbreaking research on the work culture of African American seafarers, mainly those sailing out of New England ports in the nineteenth century, as well as Marcus Rediker's compelling study of Anglo-American sailors in the seventeenth century.[21] Along with a number of other scholars who have recently examined elements of race and maritime society in New England ports, Scott, Bolster, and Rediker have revitalized American maritime history by viewing the staid old field anew through the lenses of race, class, and power. Their vision makes it possible for an almost literally provincial study like mine to carry expansive meanings, certainly for the American South and possibly for the Atlantic as a whole.[22]

While the historical events chronicled in these chapters occurred mostly in North Carolina, I intend to evoke the broader experience of the maritime South. The black maritime culture in seaports such as New Bern, Wilmington, and Beaufort was in many ways more similar to, and more in touch with, African American life in southern ports like Norfolk, Charleston, and Savannah than farm market towns only 30 miles inland. Antislavery militancy, for which North Carolina watermen were renowned, was certainly no less evident in Charleston, home of former cabin boy Denmark Vesey's famous revolt in 1822 and slave pilot Robert Small's commandeering of a Confederate vessel in 1862.[23] Similarly, slaveholders in other southern states felt no less threatened by black sailors and watermen than did those in North Carolina. Indeed, judging by the vigor with which they prosecuted black sailors under the Negro Seamen Acts, slaveholders in other parts of the South may have felt even more endangered by black salts.[24]

The watery pathway to freedom that I have chronicled in Chapter 5 ran through every port along the eastern seaboard, and a similar maritime escape route extended up and down the Mississippi River.[25] Likewise, canal labor varied little from the Great Dismal Swamp to the Louisiana bayous or the Georgia lowlands. The shad and herring fishery along the Albemarle Sound had only one comparable cousin, off the Chesapeake Bay, and the commercial mullet fishery between Bear Inlet and Ocracoke Inlet was unique. But slave fishing and boating were a deeply imbedded and important part of plantation life throughout the southern seacoast. There is obviously much more to learn about that vast seashore stretching from the Chesapeake Bay to the Texas Gulf, but the story of African American labor on North Carolina waters is at least a good starting point, and perhaps far more than that.

When I first began the research for this book, I had difficulty reconciling the enslaved status of African American watermen with what I knew of maritime labor in my childhood. I grew up among a seafaring and fishing people in a quiet tidewater community in North Carolina. A waterman's life was our greatest symbol of freedom and independence. As a child, I watched my elders cling tenaciously to their boats and their poverty rather than forsake their liberty for farming or factory jobs. I do not mean to draw a rigorous parallel between maritime life in the South in my day and before the Civil War, but this at least seemed clear to me from the outset: a waterman's life could exist only in a dynamic tension with a system of human bondage, at least in the tidal creeks, estuaries, and salt marshes within the Outer Banks and our other barrier islands. Navigating the region's shallow inlets and shifting shoals has always demanded a sharp mind and a free hand. A fisherman must rely on his own wits and intuition, not somebody else's orders, to guide the laying of a mullet net or a fish trap. And no boatman survives one of our nor'easters if he is not free to read weather and tide to his own reckoning. Above all, every waterman that I have ever known has a part of himself that is restless on land and belongs to the sea and its distant shores. If all this was no less true in an earlier era, then what, I wondered, did it mean for coastal slaves and their masters, for tidewater plantation society, and for the black struggle for freedom?

As I wrote *The Waterman's Song*, I often hummed the sea chantey sung by the black boatmen who passed Moses Ashley Curtis in 1830. Their version of "Sally Brown" reminded me of other, more recent chanteys that I heard when I was a child: the raucous songs hoisted by black menhaden fishermen as they hauled purse seines out of the Atlantic and the vibrant melodies sung by black women while they worked in Pamlico Sound crab canneries. Playful, reverent, or wistful, "Sally Brown" and these more recent songs helped pass the time and lighten the labor, but they also brought forth joy, hope, and a faith deepened by sorrow and affliction. Their singers' struggles, like the songs themselves, have deep roots in an African American maritime heritage that has nearly been forgotten. And no matter how much maritime life has changed from the slavery era to today, I will always suspect that African Americans, slave and free, found their hopes uplifted and their lives unbounded merely by the nearness of the sea, by working on the water, and by the vast horizon over Pamlico Sound and the Atlantic. I have never known a soul who did not.

The Waterman's Song

Thy way is in the sea, and thy paths
in the great waters, and thy footsteps
are not known.—PSALMS 77:19–20

The dreams of early sailors in the western Atlantic must have been haunted by the memory of the Outer Banks strewn with the broken ribs of shipwrecks. When the sailors returned to their home ports in Europe, colonial map-makers listened to their tales and embellished charts of the islands with ferocious dragons, sea monsters, and sunken ships.[1] The Outer Banks were, and are, a long ribbon of narrow, windswept islands rimming the North Carolina coastline and stretching 40 miles into the sea. Later known as "the Graveyard of the Atlantic," the islands saw so many vessels founder in their breakers that colonial Outer Bankers were renowned scavengers, accustomed to salvaging ships' masts, planking, and ironwork to build their cottages and boats. Gulf Stream currents and prevailing winds forced sailing vessels against unforgiving shoals, and all too many of their hands and passengers never lived to go back to sea again.

Disaster and cataclysm, not gradual evolution, was the nature of that coast-line: channels shifted precariously in every hurricane and nor'easter, and old inlets disappeared overnight while other inlets formed anew. The few inlets in the Outer Banks had shallow bars and narrow, uncertain channels that ren-dered them hopeless for even small brigs and sloops to navigate without lightering their cargo. No wonder that the Outer Banks loomed so ominously in sailors' minds: when the seafarers passed through Old Currituck or Ocra-coke Inlet, they viewed generations of wrecked hulls rising up out of the sands, some of them with a spar or a mast reaching heavenward.

The Outer Banks shoals may have posed the greatest danger to Atlantic shipping, but travel was also harrowing on the broad, shallow estuaries within the Outer Banks and the more southerly barrier islands that stretched down to Cape Fear. Their "continual shoals," as Virginia planter William Byrd declared in a 1719 account of a voyage down Currituck Sound, required "a Skillful Pilot to Steer even a Canoe over it." Byrd was hardly the first or last to discover that without a good pilot, "it was," as he said, "almost as hard to keep our Temper as to keep the Channel."[2] Winds and tides recarved channels, bars, and shoals so frequently that sailors found they could not trust charts, as a nautical surveyor declared, "no matter how accurate."[3] Riven with shoals, the two largest estuaries within the Outer Banks, Pamlico Sound and Albemarle Sound, were vast seas, passable in a dugout canoe in calm winds but a nightmare even for a seaworthy brig in a stiff nor'easter. Along the upper reaches of the estuaries, more reliably navigable blackwater rivers—"the color of Brandy or Madeira wine," as one traveler described them—flowed sluggishly out of uncharted wildernesses like the Great Dismal Swamp, but the colony had no deepwater harbor and scant bays where a seagoing vessel could take refuge in a storm. While the first English colonists landed at Roanoke Island, just within the Outer Banks, in 1584, North Carolina's harsh coastline discouraged seagoing trade, colonization, and plantation agriculture, particularly as compared to the tobacco and rice cultures that emerged in tidewater Virginia and South Carolina. A century after the Roanoke colonists vanished, the colony of North Carolina still had no English towns, boasted few roads or bridges, and relied on small boats and shallow-draft seagoing vessels for travel, trade, and communication.

As the colony's slave population swelled from but a few hundred souls in 1685 to more than 52,000 on the eve of the American Revolution, African American maritime slaves enjoyed a steady reputation, along with the Algonquian, Siouan, and Iroquoian peoples, as the coast's foremost boatmen, pilots, and fishermen.[4] References to their handiness on the water abound in documentary accounts of the day. In 1709, English surveyor John Lawson remarked that "some Negro's, and others, that can swim and dive well, go naked into the Water, with a Knife in their Hand, and fight the Shark, and very commonly killed him."[5] In 1738, Janet Schaw admired a tidewater planter's "very fine boat . . . and six stout Negroes in neat uniforms to row her" but was more intrigued by the African boatmen who were "very dexterous" at hunting alligators near Cape Fear.[6] And, in 1766, Governor Thomas Tryon remarked that piedmont rivers had "Rocky Stones so as to stop the navigation of any thing but Canoes, and those are not safe unless under the conduct of a dexterous Negroe."[7]

The early colonists relied heavily on the proficiency of their African slaves in building and handling dugout canoes, often called cooners (or kunners), 14–

to 28-foot-long boats usually hewn from one to three cypress logs. They also built larger dugouts, called periaugers or pettiaugers, that were fashioned out of two cypress logs fastened together with a third keel-log between them.[8] A large periauger was not a trifling craft; the boats were commonly 30 to 40 feet long and had a beam up to 8 feet in length, and they were capable of holding 20 persons or several tons of freight. Watermen usually fit both cooners and periaugers with one or two short masts that could be rigged quickly for sailing in open waters, though they often poled or rowed them in shallows.[9] Cooners and periaugers served especially well on the severe shoals of North Carolina's inland waters, like those on the west side of Hatteras Island or on practically all of Currituck and Core Sound. With their shallow draft, handiness in choppy waters, and strong log hulls, those boats stood up to the unavoidable collisions with shoals without requiring the steady caulking and repairs of plank-built vessels.[10] The cypress for making them was readily available by the seashore, and their plain construction did not require the tools, master boatbuilders, or expenses of a shipyard; slaves probably built most of them in backyards. Cooners and periaugers were the poor man's workboats for fishing, getting about, and hauling freight throughout the eighteenth century. Similar boats were used extensively in West Africa, and many colonial era slaves had had experience building and handling them in their native land.[11]

The Carolina tidewater may also have seemed comparatively familiar to many Africans in bondage. Many tidewater slaves came from sections of West Africa more closely resembling, and with maritime traditions better suited to, the shallow, marshy Carolina coastline than did their colonial masters, with their deepwater experience. "While some Africans had scarcely seen deep water before their forced passage to America," Peter Wood wrote in *Black Majority*, his classic portrait of the early colonial period in South Carolina, "many others had grown up along rivers or beside the ocean and were far more at home in this element than most Europeans."[12] While the inshore maritime heritage of the English, Scotch, Irish, and French Huguenot colonists should not be dismissed, Wood's point is compelling. As at Jamestown, where English colonists endured famine amid some of the most bountiful fishing grounds in North America, the early colonists in North Carolina looked to their African slaves and Indian neighbors both to man their boats and to supply them with food from the sea.[13]

By virtue of their shared status as servants and slaves, African Americans gleaned a great deal of maritime knowledge from coastal Indians. American

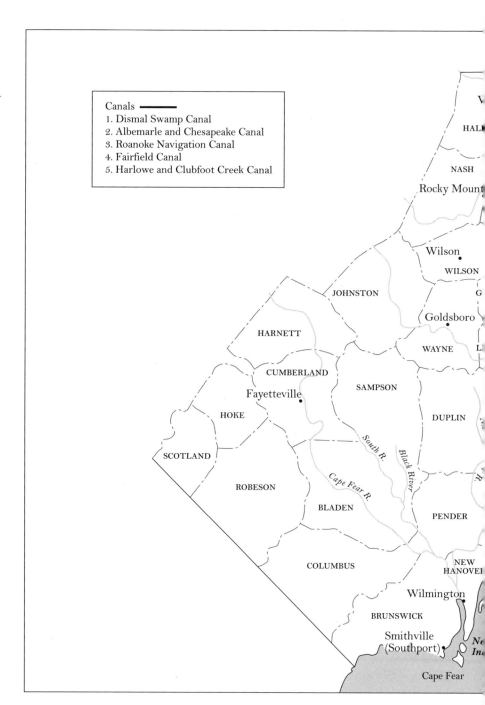

Canals ━━━━
1. Dismal Swamp Canal
2. Albemarle and Chesapeake Canal
3. Roanoke Navigation Canal
4. Fairfield Canal
5. Harlowe and Clubfoot Creek Canal

HAL▮

NASH

Rocky Mount▮

Wilson.

WILSON

JOHNSTON

G

Goldsboro

HARNETT

WAYNE   L▮

CUMBERLAND

SAMPSON

Fayetteville.

HOKE

DUPLIN

SCOTLAND

South R.

Black River

Cape Fear R.

ROBESON

BLADEN

PENDER

COLUMBUS

NEW
HANOVE▮

Wilmington.

BRUNSWICK

Smithville
(Southport).

N▮
In▮

Cape Fear

Maritime North Carolina on the Eve of the Civil War

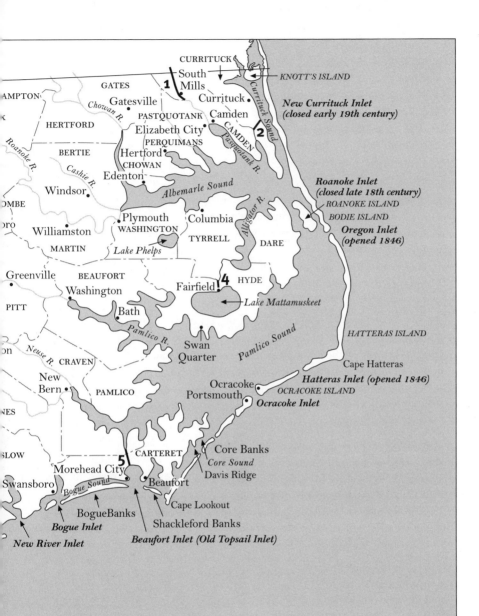

CURRITUCK

South
Mills   KNOTT'S ISLAND

1

GATES

AMPTON   Gatesville   Currituck
        Chowan R.   New Currituck Inlet
HERTFORD   PASQUOTANK   Camden   *(closed early 19th century)*

                Elizabeth City
                    PERQUIMANS
BERTIE   Hertford
        Cashie R.   CHOWAN   **2**

                Edenton   Roanoke Inlet
OMBE   *(closed late 18th century)*
                                              ROANOKE ISLAND
        Windsor   *Albemarle Sound*   BODIE ISLAND
bro   Oregon Inlet
    Williamston   Plymouth   Columbia   *(opened 1846)*
            WASHINGTON
    MARTIN   Lake Phelps   TYRRELL   DARE

Greenville   BEAUFORT   **4** HYDE
    Washington   Fairfield
PITT   Lake Mattamuskeet
            Bath

            Pamlico R.   HATTERAS ISLAND
        Neuse R. CRAVEN   Swan
on   Quarter   *Pamlico Sound*
    New   Cape Hatteras
    Bern   PAMLICO   Ocracoke   Hatteras Inlet (opened 1846)
ES   Portsmouth   OCRACOKE ISLAND
                                        Ocracoke Inlet

                                    Core Banks
LOW   CARTERET   *Core Sound*
    Morehead City   **5**   Davis Ridge
Swansboro   *Bogue Sound* Beaufort
        BogueBanks   Cape Lookout
    Bogue Inlet   Shackleford Banks
New River Inlet   Beaufort Inlet (Old Topsail Inlet)

0   25   50 miles

Indians had fished on the North Carolina coast since at least 8,000 B.C. The Algonquian, Iroquoian, and Siouan peoples built villages primarily on rivers and estuaries, but they also built seasonal fishing camps on the barrier islands and in a variety of swamp and marsh habitats. Over several hundred generations, they had adapted fishing techniques, gear, and watercraft uniquely well suited to all of those coastal waters.[14] They traded extensively by boat between Outer Banks villages and farming settlements along the sounds and rivers inland, bartered dried fish with piedmont tribes, and utilized shells for a variety of tools, weapons, and ceremonial and decorative arts.[15] As famine, epidemics, war, and the hardships of reservation life reduced piedmont and eastern North Carolina's Indian majority from a precontact population estimated at as high as 80,000 to only 10,000 in 1685, and a mere 300 out of a total population of 394,000 in 1790, it was the free blacks and slaves who intermarried with coastal Indians and worked local waters alongside them who most fully inherited their fishing skills and maritime traditions.[16] This had long-lasting ramifications for maritime culture.

Native boatmanship gained a singular reputation among the European colonists, who frequently found themselves at a loss on coastal salt marshes, rivers, and sounds. The colonists rather regretfully came to appreciate Indian small-craft skills first during the Tuscarora War of 1711–13, a monumental and very bloody conflict that ultimately forced all coastal Indians into political subjugation or exile. In 1713, when the Matchapunga remained one of only two tribes that had not fallen to the English, the colony's presiding governor cautioned that his Indian enemies would not be easy to defeat. "They have got . . . boats and canoes, being expert watermen," Thomas Pollock warned, and they would voyage into "lakes, quagmires, and cane swamps . . . where it is almost impossible for white men to follow them."[17]

Even more important than benefiting from adopting Indian watercraft and fishing technology, African Americans profited from gaining access to the native people's knowledge of coastal ecology and its seasonal cycles.[18] From the native fishermen, slaves learned what time of year to move onto the barrier islands to catch bluefish whose schools were so dense that they turned miles of ocean surface into a shimmering silver. They learned at what spring tide to scavenge salt marshes for the eggs of clapper rails and marsh hens, and at which midsummer moon to scour the Atlantic seashore for loggerhead turtle eggs. Ironically, as Algonquian society was forced to give way in the face of encroachment by the European colonists, it was the colonists' slaves who best watched and learned from the Indian fishermen. They discovered on

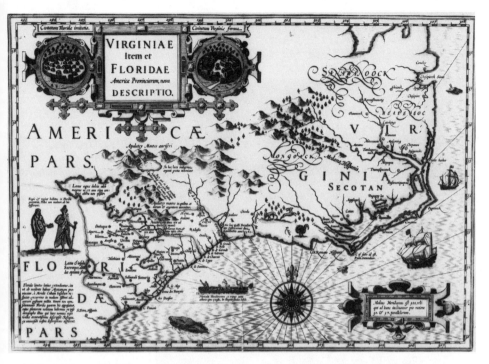

The earliest colonial maps of the North Carolina coast highlighted its navigational hazards and Indian boatmanship, as seen here in Gerardus Mercator, "Virginiae Item et Floridae Americae Provinciarum, nova descriptio," 1611. Courtesy North Carolina Collection, University of North Carolina at Chapel Hill.

what late winter day to abandon hunting camps to harvest the great waves of spawning shad that migrated out of the Atlantic into Pamlico and Albemarle Sounds. They learned what lunar tide beckoned bottlednosed dolphins into local inlets, in what current to erect a fishing weir, and what late summer wind shift marked the coming of the jumping mullet. "Being out of doors a great deal of the time," as a Chowan River slave named Allen Parker later wrote, the slaves "learned many things from the book of Nature, which were unknown to white folks."[19] Much of the "book of Nature" on boating and fishing had been written by the coastal Indians.

Beginning with an English assault on the Chowaneoic in 1679 and ending with the Tuscarora War three decades later, colonists and their slaves also took over the maritime infrastructure created by the coastal Indians. They adopted marsh canals excavated by Coree boatmen, confiscated trails worn

Theodor De Bry engraving after John White's drawing "Their manner of fishynge in Virginia," ca. 1590. During the Roanoke voyages of 1584–90, White drew the composite portrait of Algonquian fishing methods in the vicinity of the Outer Banks on which this later engraving is based. Courtesy North Carolina Collection, University of North Carolina at Chapel Hill.

down by Tuscarora autumnal migrations to the fishing beaches, pulled their seines by former Chowaneoic fish camps, placed fish impoundments where Moratuck weirs had stood. They may have even sought shelter from hurricanes on Algonquian shell mounds like those at Harkers Island and Core Point. The colonists also usurped the Tuscarora fish trade by carrying salted and smoked fish upriver every autumn to barter for corn, an ancient custom that had repeatedly proven its worth as a safeguard against famine.

The value of this accumulated knowledge to the colonists and their African slaves can scarcely be exaggerated. Unlike in New England and along many other deepwater coastlines, survival in the North Carolina tidewater never depended on mastery of a single fishery. Instead, tidewater people relied on having the knowledge, flexibility, and mobility to take advantage of a multitude of fish runs, seasonal cycles, and weather changes that could be read only with long experience and intimate familiarity with a host of coastal waters. Perhaps it is sufficient to note that for nearly three centuries, until after the

Theodor De Bry engraving after a John White drawing of the coastal Algonquins, "The broyling of their fish," ca. 1590. Courtesy North Carolina Collection, University of North Carolina at Chapel Hill.

Civil War, the fundamental character of fishing and boating on the coastal waters of North Carolina did not differ significantly from the practices found among the tidewater Algonquians when the first English colonists arrived at Roanoke in 1584.

Out of the ashes of the Tuscarora War emerged a maritime society in which the boating heritages of blacks, whites, and Indians gradually grew indistinguishable. The war-ravaged colony had only a few small English villages, all of them scraggly seaports with little traffic. The settlement was composed mainly of ruined or half-ruined Indian villages, most of them racked by disease and war, and small English plantations, lumbermill villages, and naval stores camps that were scattered along the sounds and the lower parts of the principal rivers. The ports and outlying plantations shared little commerce; most planters traded directly with English ports in the Bahamas, West Indies, or other southern colonies. Outer Banks shoals discouraged maritime trade and plantation agriculture but gained Carolina a reputation as a good place for harboring pirates and smugglers out of reach of the English navy and its deep-draft ships. Colonial outcasts—debtors, runaway servants, religious dissenters, women escaping unwanted marriages, free mulattoes, castaways, and deserters—gloried in being so far on the margins of the English empire, where they made sure that colonial agents with their ideas of good order and general decency felt entirely unwelcomed or, at the very least, were ignored as blithely as possible. "A nest of the most notorious profligates upon earth," Rev. John Urmstone called the colony in 1711. Frustrated at the paltry fruits of his own evangelical labors, the Anglican minister went on to disparage the Carolina colony as being "chiefly peopled by such as have been educated at some of the famous Colleges of Bridewell, Newgate or the Mint"—the most notorious English prisons of the time.[20]

For all their railing against outcasts, English evangelists insisted on the need for slave labor on local waterways. Immediately they discovered that they could not even reach the colony's "notorious profligates" if they did not have a slave and a boat. The villages, a Reverend Blair wrote in 1704, "are all bounded with two rivers, and those rivers at least twenty miles distant, without any inhabitants on the road, for they plant only on the rivers." He found traveling on the sounds and rivers disheartening and dangerous. "Any man that has tried it," recorded Blair, "would sooner undertake a voyage from this city to Holland than that, for beside a pond of five miles broad, and nothing to carry one over but a smal perryauger, there are about 50 miles desert to pass through, without any human creature inhabiting in it."[21] A few years later, Reverend Urmstone echoed the sentiment. In July 1711, he wrote his superiors in England that he could not possibly spread the Gospel effectively unless he could buy "a large boat and a couple of experienced Watermen."[22] He begged them for the price of "a couple of good Negro's."[23]

While the slowly rising number of Carolina colonists relied increasingly on slave labor to operate their boats and supply fish for their suppers, a more independent sort of society was developing along the region's remote tidal creeks and blackwater streams. Free and often mixed-race, those communities were destined to provide the spark for innovation in fishing and boatbuilding for generations to come. This society of outcasts included Indian refugees from the Tuscarora War, the mixed-race children of Indian women and English traders, runaway slaves, and a smattering of castaways and deserters who clung tenaciously to their new liberty. It also sheltered several clans of

"The Lightkeeper's Boat," by Edward Champney. This sketch of a sailing cooner, or possibly a small periauger, at Hatteras Island was not drawn until the Civil War, but it is a rare depiction of a kind of boat commonly built and used by African American watermen from the earliest colonial days. Courtesy Outer Banks History Center, Manteo, North Carolina.

mulatto refugees who sought asylum in North Carolina after the Virginia colony passed harsh laws against mixed-race marriages and their offspring in the 1710s.[24] Arising especially on the swampy fringes of Currituck, Albemarle, Pamlico, and Core Sounds, these communities held on dearly to their solitude and remained firmly attached to the sounds and creeks for their livelihood.

Racial boundaries were always less than certain along this watery frontier. The most notorious of the outlaws were pirates who took advantage of the Outer Banks and the colony's secluded bays to smuggle goods and resupply their vessels. The most celebrated of them was Edward Teach, better remembered as Blackbeard. In 1718 and 1719, Teach occasionally found refuge in North Carolina waters, where he conducted an illicit trade with some of the colony's highest officials, including the governor, Charles Eden. When he intentionally grounded his flagship, the *Queen Anne's Revenge*, on the sandy bottom off Beaufort Inlet in June 1718, Teach sailed away aboard a captured Spanish sloop manned by "40 whites and 60 negroes."[25] On marauding vessels like Teach's, African Americans lived amid the rough-hewn fraternity of maritime outcasts for whom the racial and caste boundaries ashore were not paramount, in some cases even sharing equitably in shipboard duties, prizes, and decision making.[26]

Not surprisingly, slaves found such pirate gangs enticing, especially given the dearth of other opportunities for a free life. Colonial leaders often dreaded, in fact, that their slaves might align with pirates. In 1718, the lieutenant governor of Bermuda, one of the Carolina colony's leading trading partners, warned that he could not rely on local slaves to defend against a pirate attack. "We can have no dependence on their assistance," he wrote, "but to the contrary . . . should fear their joining with the pirates."[27] Colonial leaders in North Carolina were far less anxious about pirate attacks; "their poverty is their security," Edward Randolph explained to the British Council of Trade and Plantations in 1701. Compared to the tobacco and rice plantation societies in Virginia and South Carolina, the early colonists of North Carolina had neither the inclination, financial wherewithal, nor strong central government to do battle with pirates. Therefore, as Randolph lamented, the colony was well known as "a place which receives Pirates, Runaways, and Illegal Traders."[28] Fearing that such rebelliousness might spread north, Virginia planters took the threat of piracy and slave rebellion far more seriously.[29] In 1719 Virginia's colonial governor directed a naval sloop into North Carolina waters in pursuit of Blackbeard. Five black sailors were among the pirate's 14-man crew when Lt. Edward Maynard of the British navy finally caught up with him and killed him in battle at Ocracoke Inlet. All five were captured and executed.[30]

By 1725, after English authorities had largely suppressed piracy, a new, more powerful generation of colonial leaders in North Carolina learned to view black sailors and watermen as a threat, though they too relied heavily on black maritime skills. In part, their fears arose out of incidents in which plantation slaves escaped into this unruly maritime society.[31] But even more threatening than slave runaways, the specter of slave insurrection and colonial war loomed over waterfront communities. In 1748, during the War of Jenkins' Ear, a group of black pirates sailing under the Spanish flag raided both Wilmington and Beaufort.[32] Five years later, during the French and Indian War, Wilmington authorities insisted that the armed sloop *Scorpion*

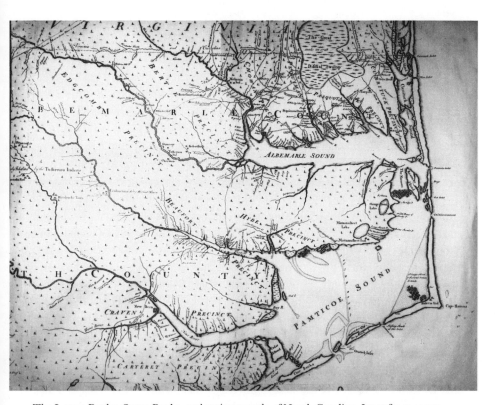

The Lower Banks, Outer Banks, and major sounds of North Carolina. Inset from a map by Edward Mosely, 1733. Courtesy North Carolina Collection, University of North Carolina at Chapel Hill.

stay on guard to allay, in Governor Mathew Rowan's words, the "inevitable disorder caused by sailors, contraband trade in various items, and likelihood of another attempted insurrection by Negroes."[33] He did not need to say what the *Scorpion*'s master knew full well, that the most serious threat to the English port was the possibility that Wilmington's slaves, three-fifths of the town's population, would throw their support to the French in the event of a naval attack. By that time, slave watermen had already earned a reputation as rebels and outlaws in the backcountry. In 1762, a group of Moravian immigrants traveling up the Cape Fear River watched their boats carefully at night for fear of slaves who, they had heard, "go about in small canoes, stealing where they can."[34] At the same time, black and white sailors alike had emerged in American ports as a radicalizing political force that, in the words of historians Peter Linebaugh and Marcus Rediker, provided "much of the spark, volatility, momentum and the sustained militance for the attack on British policy after 1765."[35]

The Revolutionary War only heightened the threat posed by black watermen. Fearful that their slaves might align with the British, coastal Carolina colonists lashed out harshly at a slave uprising whose leaders were said to be a white sea captain and a slave named Merrick, evidently a pilot, "who formerly belonged to Major Clark a Pilot at Okacock [Ocracoke] but now to Capt. Nath Blinn of Bath Town." After a posse captured more than 40 of the insurrection's "suspected heads," one of the arrested slaves confessed that their plan had been "to proceed from House to House (Burning as they went) until they arrived in the Back Country where they were to be received with open arms by a number of Persons there appointed and armed by the Government for their Protection, and as a further reward they were to be settled in a free government of their own." The confession and a cache of "considerable ammunition" lent credence to the colonists' worst fears of an alliance between their slaves and the royal forces. It also sharpened their distrust of black pilots, upon whom the British often relied for coastal navigation in southern waters.[36]

In November 1775, Lord Dunmore, the royal governor of Virginia, offered freedom to bondmen "able or willing to bear arms" who crossed to British lines. Word of the British gambit spread quickly through the maritime districts and watermen's camps of North Carolina, where it was also rumored that John Collet, the British commander at Fort Johnston, at the mouth of the Cape Fear River, had issued a similar pledge.[37] As Gary Nash has put it, "The belief now spread that the emancipation of slaves would be a part of the British war policy."[38] Thousands of slaves accepted Dunmore's invitation to fight for black liberty against the Americans. In the Great Dismal Swamp, slave shinglers rounded up their flatboats and lighters and fled to Virginia, among them "practically every slave belonging to the [Dismal Swamp Land] Company."[39] Political leaders cracked down hard on slaves in North Carolina ports, in Wilmington even banning the importation of new slaves, sending patrols to disarm slaves, and eventually imposing martial law.[40] Relatively few of the colony's slaves had the ability to infiltrate this dragnet to Dunmore's asylum, as Revolutionary troops moved toward Norfolk to cut off their escape and block Dunmore's regiment. An uncertain number of enslaved Carolinians, particularly boatmen, did, however, manage to reach British vessels whenever they raided coastal ports or blockaded local harbors.[41]

Not all maritime slaves fought with the British. Caesar, a slave pilot owned by Mary Torrant of Elizabeth City, guided American war vessels in and out of Virginia ports.[42] Local legend by Currituck Sound holds that a slave pilot known as Currituck Jack was a key agent in running the British blockade in 1779–80.[43] Other black Carolinians fought with the Revolutionary forces, hoping to hold their compatriots to their radical rhetoric of universal rights and political equality. Free black sailors could be found on the rosters of the Continental Navy, the state navies, privateers, and letters of marque.[44] Nevertheless, Revolutionary leaders repressed black aspirations for liberty with far too harsh a hand to have their egalitarian declarations taken seriously by most slaves. Into the 1780s, black sailors and watermen continued to see aligning with the British forces as their best hope for freedom. Few white Carolinians could have been surprised when, in September 1780, "pirates and Negroes" made a daring wartime raid into Edenton harbor to capture the schooner *Sally*.[45]

For all the perils of employing black watermen, coastal planters and shipping merchants continued to depend on them throughout the Revolutionary era. This was a powerful testament to the advantages of owning black maritime laborers. Most maritime jobs had the arduous and hazardous character customarily consigned to slave labor. But the masters of vessels also found it enormously advantageous to have skilled hands at the ready. Across the ages, shortages of free sailors and watermen plagued the maritime trades. Too often, recruiters believed that only the dregs of free society were willing to forsake home and hearth in exchange for measly wages, grueling duty, and severe discipline. Free laborers could also be lost at any wharf in favor of their own fields or fishing beaches or, at least as likely, a local tavern or county jail. Slave labor solved those recruiting hardships. Enslaved maritime workers gave planters and merchants far greater power to man their vessels at a moment's notice, to regulate their time in port, and to retain maritime skills honed under their employ.

African American maritime laborers did not let the masters of vessels forget that the profit of employing them usually outweighed the risks. Thomas and John Gray Blount, two of the tidewater's most avaricious planters and merchants, had this reality reinforced in the winter of 1794. After their sloop *Sally* (possibly the aforementioned vessel after re-rigging) ran aground, a succession of white pilots tried to refloat the vessel for three weeks. With winter's northeasterly gales rendering the inlet still more treacherous, Thomas Blount had given up on getting the *Sally* off the shoals till spring and had even suggested selling her for salvage, when a roving black pilot enticed by the reward of £60 finally succeeded where his white counterparts had failed. The Blounts showed an uncharacteristic generosity of spirit by rewarding the black waterman an extra £20 for his piloting feat.[46] The lesson was not lost on Carolina merchants, planters, or masters of vessels. For all the dangers involved, they continued to employ large numbers of black sailors, ferrymen, fishermen, pilots, and other boatmen.[47]

Other colonial slaves worked off the water, as shipbuilders, caulkers, sailmakers, cordswains, and other nautical tradesmen. These slaves were no less indispensable. In 1782, for instance, at "the most commodious, and . . . best shipyard in the providence [sic]," on Indiantown Creek, in Currituck County, Thomas MacKnight was said to own "the most valuable collection of Negroes in that Country—They were able to build a ship within themselves with no other assistance than a Master Builder."[48] Similarly, planter Josiah Collins employed several dozen of his slaves at a rope-making factory in Chowan County. And there were few tasks in maintaining his West Indian trading vessels for which Joseph Westmore of Edenton did not rely on black labor. In 1780, Westmore hired "Negro Jack" and "Negro Bob" to refit his schooner *Peggy*, and he paid a "Negro Carpenter" for 21 days work on her as well. He hired three other blacks to unload guns from his ship *Royal Exchange*, while his own slaves Ben, Sorrow, Paris, Phillis, and Doro helped outfit that vessel, the *Peggy*, and his two brigs and a sloop.[49] Clearly, many maritime jobs were performed almost exclusively by African American boatmen and tradesmen.[50]

Newspaper advertisements for runaway slaves suggest how thoroughly local African American maritime culture in North Carolina was entangled with the distant shores of the Atlantic. Particularly between the American Revolution and the War of 1812, tidewater slaves had frequently lived in or sailed to ports outside of the state. Typical was a 1793 advertisement by Joseph Pittman of New Bern, who was confident that his young runaway Jack (who "was brought up to the sea") would try to escape by ship to New England, "where he was born."[51] Somewhat earlier, John P. Williams believed that Cuffee, a ship's carpenter, would head to Nova Scotia or the Bahamas, two English colonies from which he had previously sailed.[52] Another local slave, a mulatto named Charles, fled home to Jamaica.[53] A runaway named John, in bondage in Onslow County, may have come from Puerto Rico or Cuba, for he spoke Spanish and only broken English.[54] Another Onslow County runaway, a sailor also named John, was originally from the Danish colony of St. Croix.[55] Many other advertisements referred to runaways who had come from the French West Indies.[56]

Many of the advertisements for runaway slaves hint at highly cosmopolitan lives whose details we can only imagine. Consider a French-speaking slave named Brandy who was captured by the Pamlico River in 1800. Born in the Guinea country of West Africa, Brandy had been taken by slavers to France during the early years of the French Revolution and was eventually brought to the United States in 1798 or 1799.[57] Then there is the mulatto Joe, who seems to capture the tenor of waterfront life as well as any slave of his time. When the 25-year-old escaped from the schooner *Endeavor* in New Bern in 1794, his master declared that he "was brought up to the sea business" and spoke French, Dutch, Spanish, and English.[58] Such tantalizing hints suggest the far-flung threads of connection that tied the slave communities of the North Carolina coast to larger worlds across the sea.

The African American maritime community also extended north and south along the eastern seaboard. By taking advantage of maritime shipping, North Carolina's coastal blacks, unlike their landlocked brethren, were sometimes able to keep in touch with distant family, friends, and religious and fraternal leaders. This was truest with respect to those in other southern ports, particularly ports between Baltimore and Savannah, but was sometimes the case for northern maritime communities as far away as New Bedford and Martha's Vineyard. United by coastal trading routes, the black communities of New Haven, Connecticut, and New Bern, North Carolina, are a case in point. By the end of the eighteenth century, slave runaways and free black migrants from New Bern already comprised a small but distinct exile community in New Haven. Destined to grow considerably in the nineteenth century, this community's members corresponded with their enslaved kindred, nourished abolitionist politics that transcended North or South, and welcomed new refugees from New Bern into their midst.[59] As Julius Scott has demonstrated in his landmark study of black mariners sailing out of West Indian ports, black seamen were especially important in uniting African American communities like New Haven and New Bern.[60] These distant ports were held together by black sailors such as Quacko, a slave who sailed out of Southport (then known as Smithville), North Carolina, who was said to be "acquainted along the sea coast from New Brunswick to the Virginia line." Those bonds would later play a decisive role in African American politics during the antebellum era and the Civil War.[61]

The colonial wars for European control of the Americas made for rapidly shifting political and racial lines that maritime black laborers at times navigated as skillfully as they did the shoals of the Outer Banks. In July 1793, Henry Toomer of New Bern advertised for a runaway slave Toby, a sailor and lighter captain. "It is likely he will endeavor to pass as free," Toomer asserted, "having remained as such with the British since they left this town until within these three years past."[62] Two years later, when local authorities in Wilmington captured a black fisherman named Jacob, he explained that he was seeking to return to Charleston, South Carolina, from where he had been "plundered" off a fishing boat by the British during the Revolutionary War.[63] True or not, blaming the British was a shrewd way of accounting for his disappearance and one that no doubt appealed to his captors' prejudices. Perhaps taking an overly optimistic view of North Carolina's comparatively liberal laws regarding the status of free blacks and hoping to pass as free, other runaways escaped from West Indian vessels in Wilmington, New Bern, and other local ports.[64]

The uncertain, shifting boundaries of slavery and freedom in Revolutionary America could just as easily sabotage a free black's fortunes. A slave in North Carolina might look to the sea with an eye toward freedom, but free blacks passing through the state's ports faced the constant risk of enslavement. In 1789, a black man in Wilmington named Josiah Peters contended that he was free when he arrived aboard a vessel from Princess-Ann-Town, Maryland. While Wilmington authorities inquired of Maryland officials as to his status, Peters was kept in the custody of a James Moore, who declared him his slave. By the time Wilmington officials confirmed Peters's freedom, it was a moot point: Moore had already sold him "as a Slave in foreign Countries."[65]

By the end of the eighteenth century, African American maritime life had gained a distinctive character in North Carolina waters. Slave watermen figured prominently as sailors, pilots, boatmen, fishermen, stevedores, and maritime tradesmen from the busiest seaports to the most remote fishing camps. On inland seas and rivers and on the Outer Banks, many were part of a creole society that relied heavily on boating and fishing traditions adapted from the Algonquian, Siouan, and Iroquoian Indians. Some of its "saltiest" communities were populated by free "blacks" who were, in reality, a mix of black, white, and often Indian lineage. Life in coastal seaports was deeply entangled with the Afro-Caribbean and black port communities up and down the Atlantic seaboard, as well as with a seafaring culture renowned for its disregard for the racial and caste orthodoxies that held sway ashore. Boat captains, masters of vessels, and planters had come to rely heavily on black laborers for their maritime skills and dependability, but they had been taught by eighteenth-century insurrections, escapes, and colonial wars that those watermen were to be feared as well. Those fears would be borne out in the next century.

part one

Working on the Water

chapter one

As Far as a Colored Man Can There Be Free

A Slave Waterman's Life

In 1808, a slave river pilot named Hews confronted his wife's master, Phillip McGuire, in the seaport of Edenton, North Carolina. Hews could no longer bear McGuire's claims on Dinah. The boatman threatened to steal her away. If he got the chance, the slave pilot declared, he would "keep his wife out eternally." Few bondmen had a realistic chance of making good on such a threat, but Hews was exceptional: he belonged to an elite fraternity of black watermen both irreplaceable to the plantation economy and subversive of the racial bondage that fueled it. He proved true to his word. That April, Hews and Dinah vanished from Edenton. Together they had seized at least a moment of freedom on the broad waters of the Albemarle Sound.[1]

The stories of slave watermen's lives usually have to be teased from the barest threads in the documentary record. Like the incident with Hews and Dinah, which comes from a single notice in an Edenton newspaper, they are found in tiny fragments throughout the journals, newspapers, and public documents of the day. Accounts rarely offer more than the briefest of glimpses into the daily lives of the individual black boatmen, fishermen, or sailors who plied the waters of the American South.

Fortunately, a striking number of the surviving American slave narratives describe African Americans fishing, boating, or going to sea. They are only one source for understanding coastal slavery, but even a partial list of the

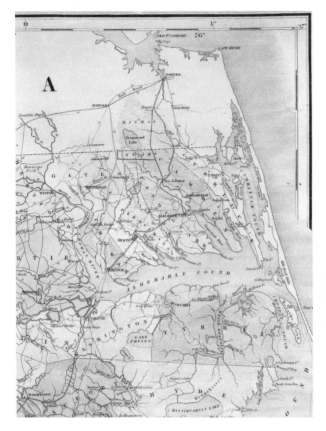

The Albemarle Sound vicinity of Moses Grandy's day. Inset from David H. Burr, "Map of North and South Carolina," 1839. Courtesy North Carolina Collection, University of North Carolina at Chapel Hill.

maritime slave laborers who later recorded their life stories conveys a powerful sense of the African American experience in the maritime South. A slave named Charles Ball, later the author of an influential narrative, served as a cook on a frigate at Washington Naval Yard and fished along the Patuxent River in Maryland and the Congaree River in South Carolina.[2] The most famous of all slave narrators, Frederick Douglass, was a ship's caulker in Baltimore. William Wells Brown hired himself out as an understeward on the *Patriot* and other steamboats on the Mississippi River.[3] Louis Hughes's master hired him to a canal boat that ran to Richmond, Virginia.[4] Anthony Burns hired his own time as a stevedore for "cargoes of coal, guano, and other lading" in Richmond; Thomas H. Jones unloaded ships in Wilmington, North Carolina, and John Andrew Jackson worked illicitly as a stevedore in Charleston, South Carolina.[5] Isaac Mason, a plantation slave in Maryland, manned his master's sloop and scow on trips to market and for wood.[6] Solomon Northup rafted lumber at Bayou Boeuf in Louisiana.[7] London Ferebee, a boatbuilder's son, navigated his master's sloop on the Currituck Sound of North Carolina.[8] And George Henry, a Virginia slave, rose from cook and deckhand to become master of the Chesapeake Bay schooners *Llewyllen* and *Susan Ellen*.[9]

The most far-ranging of the maritime slave narratives is the account of Moses Grandy, a slave waterman who may well have known the pilot Hews. From the 1790s to the 1830s, Grandy worked on watercraft in and around the Albemarle Sound. Few maritime trades eluded his hand. He labored as a river ferryman, canal boatman, schooner deckhand, and lighter captain while still in bondage. After purchasing his freedom, Grandy served on coasters, packets, and merchant ships. In 1843, Grandy stepped ashore long enough to collaborate with George Thompson, an English abolitionist, to publish his autobiography.[10] The *Narrative of the Life of Moses Grandy, Late a Slave in the United States of America* would prove to be the most comprehensive firsthand account ever written of slavery and African American maritime life in the South.[11]

Tracing Grandy's career from his youthful days working in small boats on the Pasquotank River to his later years sailing across the Atlantic helps us see more clearly a segment of African American life that shares little with conventional views of slavery. In his labors and in the lives of the African American watermen whom he encountered in coastal ports and remote maritime outposts, we can see the wide variety and complex character of maritime occupations performed by enslaved watermen. We can also begin to detect a dynamic tension between slavery and freedom throughout the maritime South, one that had important repercussions for American history.

Moses Grandy grew up in Camden, a small port on the banks of the Pasquotank River in the northeastern corner of North Carolina. Born into slavery about 1786, he grew up in a maritime society 40 miles west of the Outer Banks and the Atlantic Ocean. The seat of Camden County, a sparsely settled land of timber camps and modest plantations, Camden was bounded by blackwater rivers and the Great Dismal Swamp. Social and commercial life naturally centered on the Pasquotank, which flowed ten miles south of Camden into the Albemarle Sound. In 1790, African Americans made up 31 percent of the county's population.[12] Black sailors, boatmen, and fishermen were common sights, and as a youth Grandy moved among several generations of black watermen.[13]

Camden was the state's smallest port of call, but it had important shipping interests centered on the West Indies. In many respects, the Camden of Grandy's early years was one of the backwater crannies of what historian Julius Scott has termed the "Greater Caribbean."[14] Many of the early colonists who settled along the Albemarle Sound already had plantations in the West Indies, and their fortunes and those of their descendants rose and fell with the shifting political winds of the sugar islands of the Caribbean.[15] Albemarle planters had imported a large part of their slaves from the West Indies, usually via Charleston or Richmond. Signs of the Afro-Caribbean could be heard in the music and lilting speech of Albemarle settlers and seen in many other aspects of Carolina tidewater culture, ranging from the Atlantic creole architectural style to the raucous Jonkunnu festival that seems to have been uniquely celebrated by slaves in tidewater North Carolina, the Bahamas, and Jamaica.[16]

The West Indian trade boomed in Grandy's youth, when European wars broke the grip of British and French navigation laws on American trade. Vessels from Camden carried naval stores, lumber, shingles, staves, grains, and salted fish and pork to the West Indies and returned laden with molasses, rum, and sugar. It was a rough business. The shipping trade between North Carolina ports and the West Indies persisted at the mercy of storms and privateers, suffered from ill-built and ill-maintained vessels, and featured rampant smuggling. Drunken or mutinous crews were commonplace.[17] A gathering place for the rowdy sailors of the West Indian trade and the unruly swampers who cut lumber, shingles, and staves in the Great Dismal Swamp, Camden did not have a reputation for being a peaceful, churchgoing community. Despairing at the prospect of saving souls on a hard-drinking waterfront, an itinerant Methodist minister observed dourly that in Camden "most of the men are seafaring men."[18]

Demon rum was not the only West Indian import to Camden that intoxicated some and alarmed others. During the 1790s, every vessel also brought tidings of the slave revolution in Haiti. Slaveholders feared that the Haitian rebellion might spread to the Carolinas, and they took steps to prohibit vessels from Saint-Domingue, as the French called Haiti, from calling in local ports.[19] Nonetheless, sailors on West Indian trading vessels—Grandy's older brother, Benjamin, among them—kept the local slave community informed. After the War of 1812, the description of runaway slaves in newspaper advertisements rarely mentioned slave watermen with a country of origin beyond

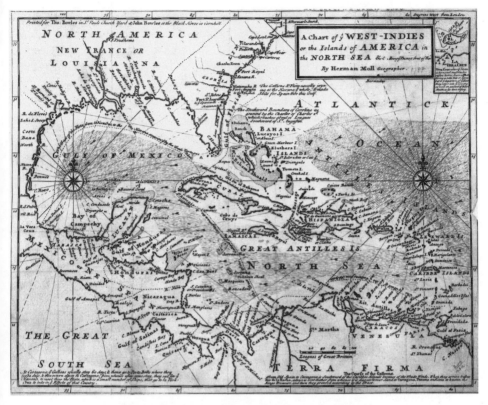

Eighteenth-century mapmakers often viewed the Albemarle Sound region as a fringe outpost of the colonial empires in the West Indies, as here in Herman Moll, "A Chart of ye West-Indies or the Islands of America in the North Sea &c," 1710. Courtesy North Carolina Collection, University of North Carolina at Chapel Hill.

the borders of North Carolina. In Grandy's youth, however, those black sailors were a worldly lot, a cosmopolitan, often multilingual class of maritime laborers. Not infrequently, they had been born in West Africa and shipped to the West Indies, and had followed the sea as far as New England and New Orleans. Many had served aboard merchant vessels and privateers and under more than one colonial power's flag. Inevitably, they quaffed the insurgent spirit of the Haitian Revolution in taverns, sailors' boarding houses, and ships' forecastles throughout the Atlantic. In 1802, the year that Touissant-Louverture's slave army finally crushed Napoleon's forces, Camden witnessed the public hanging of two slaves, allegedly part of a larger conspiracy to overthrow white planters. Black watermen had spread the revolt into Camden and other Albemarle ports via two waterborne routes, one out of Norfolk and the other down the Roanoke River. Sancho, a slave ferryman, and Salem, a shipyard worker, were among its insurrectionists. Twenty-five men overall were hanged for their involvement in the rebellion.[20] Observers traced the aborted uprising directly to revolutionary Haiti.[21]

The ghosts of another revolution also haunted ports like Camden. The Founding Fathers had clearly not meant African Americans when they said "all men are created equal," but the complex mix of freedom and slavery that had brought forth the new nation left an obvious moral conflict at its heart. This was the contradiction that Lord Dunmore, the royal governor of Virginia, had endeavored to exploit when he offered freedom to bondmen "able or willing to bear arms" for the British during the American Revolution.[22] As a youngster, Moses Grandy would certainly have been exposed to the radical ideologies and revolutionary rhetoric that his African American countrymen and -women had used to justify their own struggles for freedom during the conflict, no matter which side they joined in the war. He would have also been acquainted with slaves who had momentarily been free under British rule, as well as Africans who had fought for their freedom alongside the Americans. Indeed, black sailors who had fled the South and settled as far away as Canada occasionally tried to slip through North Carolina ports undetected while Grandy was still a lad.[23] The young Grandy had clearly been born into an age of revolution.

Camden would change a great deal in Grandy's lifetime. The last Africans who remembered their homelands passed away. Plantation slavery expanded dramatically. Nearby slave insurrections—from Gabriel's in 1800 to Denmark Vesey's in 1822 to Nat Turner's in 1831—and the circulation of incendiary abolitionist literature such as David Walker's *Appeal* provoked sharper restrictions on African Americans, and especially on black watermen. The center of the proslavery argument shifted from bondage being a "necessary evil" to a positive good. Even for the more privileged slaves who coursed the wide waters of the Albemarle, the horizon of freedom must have seemed terribly distant. Growing up in the 1790s, though, Grandy was not likely to forget the revolutionary visions of his youth.[24]

In 1790 Moses Grandy's first master, William "Billy" Grandy, owned more slaves than almost anyone in Camden County.[25] "My mother often hid us all in the woods, to prevent master selling us," his former slave recalled, but William Grandy eventually sold away most of Moses's brothers and sisters.[26] At his death, he deeded Moses to his young son, James, stipulating that his son's guardian hire Moses out to other masters until James reached his majority. Like many slaves in the Albemarle Sound vicinity, Moses Grandy thus moved annually from master to master.

Moses Grandy first worked on the water as a ferryman.[27] Hired from James Grandy's guardian by Enoch Sawyer, Grandy tended the ferry across the Narrows on the Pasquotank River. Three miles across at its nearby mouth on the Albemarle Sound, the river abruptly closed to a width of one-fifth of a mile at the Narrows, more recently remembered as Lamb's Ferry. First franchised to the Sawyer family during George Washington's administration, the ferry ran from the Sawyers' manor house in Camden to just north of Knobb's Creek.[28] It carried local traffic as well as travelers and goods passing down the main road between Norfolk and Edenton, the seat of Chowan County to the west and at that time the largest port on Albemarle Sound.

The daily traffic of tidewater life was in the hands of slave ferrymen like Grandy. They conducted wayfarers across the multitude of creeks, rivers, and lakes that had yet to be bridged. Slave ferrymen usually made short trips and suffered stiff oversight compared to other watermen, but a few were absent from their masters for a day or longer during every crossing. A slave ferryman carried passengers across Currituck Sound, a six-mile journey, and another slave transported passersby across Lake Mattamuskeet, approximately a ten-mile round-trip.[29] Their boats ranged from periaugers and dugout canoes to cable-drawn barges, but the preferred craft on a slow, blackwater river like the Pasquotank would have been a wide flatboat operated by at least two hands using fore and aft sweeps, or long oars.[30] Travelers contracted for ferry services with a local tavernkeeper or other merchant who had obtained a license to operate a toll ferry. In Grandy's case, they likely made arrangements at Sawyer's home. All ferry profits, of course, accrued to Sawyer.

Grandy tended Enoch Sawyer's ferry for three years. He later wrote that it was "a cruel living."[31] Sawyer was a planter, merchant, and, from 1791 to 1827, collector of the port of Camden. The scion of one of four families that dominated Camden County in the eighteenth century, and brother of U.S. congressman Lemuel Sawyer, he owned two plantations, ten slaves, a schooner, eight lots across the river in the new port of Elizabeth City, and approximately 10,000 acres of swamp forest in Camden and Pasquotank Counties.[32] Grandy acknowledged the decency of several of his other masters, but he recalled from his years on Sawyer's ferry only hunger, cold, and want. Grandy described being "half-starved" and his "naked feet being cracked and bleeding from extreme cold" while working for Sawyer. He rejoiced when finally George Furley hired him away from Sawyer, employing Grandy to haul lumber in the Great Dismal Swamp. There at least he had enough food and clothing. "I then thought I would not have left the [Dismal] to go to heaven," he wrote, a sentiment rarely shared by anybody who was not a slave.[33]

More than hunger and privation colored Grandy's contempt of Enoch Sawyer. Sawyer later owned Grandy's first wife, and, short on cash, he sold the woman away from the Albemarle. Grandy never saw her again.[34] "I loved her," he wrote in his *Narrative*, "as I loved my life."[35]

During the War of 1812, Grandy first ran boats on the Dismal Swamp Canal. Built by slave labor from 1793 to 1805, the canal ran 22 miles through cypress and juniper swamp, from Joyce's Creek, a Pasquotank tributary, to Deep Creek, a tributary of the southern branch of the Elizabeth River in Virginia. The narrow waterway linked Albemarle Sound to Norfolk's deepwater harbor, making it possible to reach other domestic and foreign markets without risking the dangerous shoals at Ocracoke Inlet.

Moses Grandy's master, James Grandy, had recently come of age and, taking possession of his slaves, allowed the slave waterman to "hire out" his own labor. This was a common arrangement for watermen and other slaves with a skilled trade; it left them free to solicit business with little oversight so long as sufficient profits accrued to their masters. Many planters worried about what slaves might do with this liberty and rued the precedent it set for other slaves. In hiring-out contracts, planters often singled out fishing and boating as the only work prohibited their slaves when they were outside of their custody.[36] Most planters, however, accepted hiring out as a fact of life. Free labor was costly, unreliable, and scarce; the handiness of slave boatmen was proverbial; and there was a rising demand for laborers in the building, craft, and shipping trades in every port. A planter might earn substantial profits if a skilled slave aggressively pursued employment. There was also an excessive supply of slave laborers on many Albemarle plantations, where, mainly due to soil exhaustion, planters were already moving away from tobacco cultivation to less soil damaging and labor intensive crops such as corn and wheat. Hiring out was especially alluring in a situation, such as James Grandy's seems to have been, in which a master did not have the ability or inclination to oversee slave labor closely.

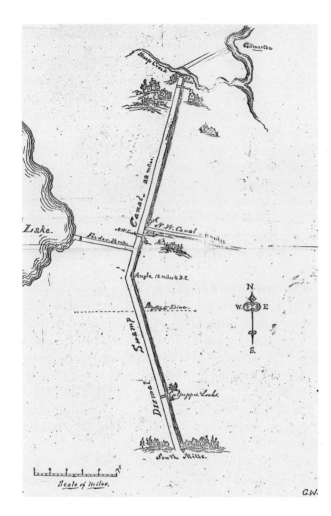

Drawing of the Dismal
Swamp Canal, ca.
1840, in the John Byrd
Papers. Courtesy
Southern Historical
Collection, University
of North Carolina at
Chapel Hill.

While James Grandy counted on methods of control more subtle than
chains to discourage his slave waterman from escaping, he also encouraged
Moses to stay by offering him privileges rarely available to other slaves.
His master allowed Grandy a high degree of independence and placed him
in a maritime trade in which it was possible to earn wages beyond the amount
that he was required to pay his master. The dream of one day buying his
freedom and that of his children and siblings may already have been with
Moses from his early days on the Dismal Swamp Canal. Such a plan certainly

entailed far less risk for Grandy and far more hope for his family than trying to escape by himself.

Recognizing that the British blockade of Chesapeake Bay diverted a portion of Norfolk's trade to Elizabeth City via the canal (and thence to sea through Ocracoke Inlet), Grandy arranged to work canal boats on shares. He captained boats owned by Charles Grice, a merchant and shipbuilder in Elizabeth City. Grice lived at Milford, one of Camden County's oldest estates, and he, and later his son James, did a sizable trade out of Elizabeth City to Norfolk, Baltimore, and Philadelphia.[37] Free to solicit business locally and in Norfolk, Grandy chartered his boats and paid Grice one-half of his freight charges. With the other half, he provisioned the vessels and hired slave crews. Grandy captained the vessel, maintained the boat, managed its crew, and kept basic commercial accounts. In return for his stewardship, he gained the exceptional privilege of free travel and the remarkable prospect of purchasing his freedom.

Out of his boating profits, Grandy paid his master, James Grandy, for his hire. Set every January, this fee probably ranged from $200 to $250 a year. Since slaveholders provided minimal, if any, rations or housing to a hired-out waterman, Grandy was a highly profitable investment for his master. Any money that he earned above the annual fee paid to his master, however, was his to keep. By diligent labor and through astute business sense, Grandy saved a considerable sum of money.

The Dismal Swamp Canal was hardly more than a ditch navigable by shingle flats when Grandy first worked on it. Those flats generally ranged from 30 to 40 feet in length and 4 to 6 feet in width, and they drew only 18 to 24 inches of water while carrying several thousand shingles. Even in the 1820s, when Grandy again captained boats there, shingle flats and barges formed the bulk of traffic through the Dismal Swamp Canal. Slave crews hauled most vessels through the canal by ropes while they walked alongside, then sailed into port.[38]

Guiding canal boats between Norfolk and the Pasquotank ports of Camden, Elizabeth City, and Weeksville, Grandy lived away from his master for weeks on end. He slept aboard his boat or among clusters of huts where "swampers," mainly slave lumbermen and shinglers, made their seasonal camps on the canal banks. Other than poachers and squatters, few whites ventured into this swamp society. It was a frequent refuge for slave runaways, and watermen like Grandy provided those fugitives with a link to the world beyond the swamp. One doubts that their company compensated for the long periods when the

Plan of the Port of Elizabeth City, on the Pasquotank River, ca. 1830. Courtesy Pasquotank County Register of Deeds Office, Elizabeth City, North Carolina.

slave waterman did not see his family in Camden, though among slaves, particularly sailors and boatmen, that hardship was hardly unique.

In contrast to the Great Dismal, the bustling city of Norfolk must have been eye-opening for the young canal boat captain. Boasting one of the finest deepwater harbors in the United States, the Virginia port had seagoing traffic and a maritime district that dwarfed the Albemarle Sound ports. There were exceptions in North Carolina—Wilmington, New Bern, Beaufort, Edenton— but most Carolina ports had only a single wharf, a ramshackle boardinghouse for sailors, a shipyard or two, and a dingy half-block of chandleries, taverns, and other businesses that catered to sailors' needs. In those ports, the arrival of any seagoing vessel was an occasion. But in Norfolk harbor, Grandy saw vessels far too heavy to cross the bars and shoals back home: naval frigates, ships of the line, huge merchant ships that plied the seven seas, as well as multitudes of the coastwise sloops and schooners that he was accustomed to seeing in Camden.

As in all southern harbors, African Americans crowded every wharf and shipyard in Norfolk.[39] The throng of black laborers included both free and slave, many of the latter living and working just as independently of their masters as Grandy. Indeed, maritime labor had a strong appeal to the growing pool of African American workers who resided in southern ports. Not much would have changed since 1794, when Virginia governor Richard Henry Lee complained that "laborers cannot be got by the Public Agents" because the black workers in Norfolk found that "working on board ships and about the wharves is more agreeable and less onerous."[40] Slavery always frayed at the sea's edge, where the uncertainty of wind, weather, and labor rendered unserviceable the sorts of work routines and constant oversight practiced on plantations.[41]

As Grandy settled accounts, bought provisions, and recruited business in the Norfolk harbor district, he became acquainted with a host of African American maritime laborers. Compared to what he knew from Albemarle ports, the much higher number of black skilled artisans in Norfolk may have struck him most forcibly. Norfolk's shipyards put many more, and far heavier, vessels to sea, and the port had a large shipbuilding industry.[42] Grandy mingled with African American ship's carpenters, painters, sailmakers, caulkers, blacksmiths, cordswainers, riggers, and plasterers.[43] By itself, the Norfolk Rope Works, which made the bulk of the city's cordage used in ship rigging, employed as many as 50 free blacks.[44]

As the slave captain of a canal boat, Grandy himself raised few eyebrows in the busy port. African Americans were common sights in command of all-black crews on canal boats, barges, flatboats, scows, and other small workboats. Black men were remarkable only when they served as masters of larger vessels, such as when the free black captain Paul Cuffe brought his 62-foot schooner *Ranger* into Norfolk harbor in 1797.[45] That was an event memorable mainly for its rarity. Several decades later, after Grandy had left the South, there was also a local slave waterman named George Henry who was promoted from cook and deckhand to master of the coasting schooner *Llewyllen*.[46] As a local slave, Henry provoked less controversy than Cuffe, with his free black crew, who had shipped out of Westport, Massachusetts.

As the only slave narrative other than Grandy's known to have been written by a former master of a vessel, Henry's *Life of George Henry* (1894) offers insights into aspects of a slave waterman's life on which Grandy is silent. Born in 1819, the retired sailor published his memoir long after the Civil War and evinced far less concern than Grandy for offending a white audience. He discussed explicitly both the coarser features of a black waterman's life and the struggle for manhood that every black waterman encountered ashore. Henry remembered his younger self as "a very profane man, uttering oaths at every word," and described himself at that time as "the king of the Devils." He was a sailor's sailor, he seems to be saying, and was not a man with whom one trifled. He boasted, too, of his dancing prowess, commonly a matter of great pride among sailors. Henry was, he said, "a great dancer, and continued dancing one night until Sunday morning dawned." He also recounted how, one night while docked in Richmond, he threatened a white watchman with "blood pudding" if he tried to report him for breaking curfew.[47]

Beyond frolics and fist fights, Henry aspired to prove his manhood through his seamanship and hard work. "I didn't know what sleep was day or night," he wrote, "for after I had charge of the vessel, I was determined to let them see that though black I was a man in every sense of the word."[48] For ten years, Henry was the very successful master of the *Llewyllen*, sailing out of Norfolk to Annapolis, Alexandria, Baltimore, and other Chesapeake ports. Later, he briefly commanded the schooner, *Susan Ellen*, just prior to escaping to Philadelphia and eventually to Providence, Rhode Island.[49] We cannot tell if the more guarded Grandy was as bold and saucy as Captain Henry, but no slave commanded a crew or made it in the shipping business if he did not somehow learn to stand his ground before the host of harbor agents, patrollers, and rummed-up sailors who might try to rob, cheat, or harass him, assuming that a slave would be an easy mark.

One doubts that Grandy, like Henry, visited frequently in Norfolk's grog shops, brothels, dance cellars, or gambling rooms, where so many sailors, black and white, invested their wages. Grandy was too adept at saving his hard-earned canal boat fees to indulge himself very often in the wharf district, any more than he did in its smaller, if no less rowdy, counterparts in every North Carolina port. Surely, though, he must have been drawn to them occasionally, if for no other reason than to recruit his crews. Such businesses catered to a sailor's most every craving and frequently did not discriminate against a black waterman as grossly as other white establishments, at least

African American ship's caulkers, detail from a shipbuilder's portrait, ca. 1790. Courtesy the Mariners' Museum, Newport News, Virginia.

not so long as he could pull a quarter eagle or a silver half-dollar out of his pocket. These haunts were infamous, as one merchant complained, "for the equality which reigned—all is hail fellow well met, no matter what the complexion."[50] The raucous, freewheeling nature of southern port life rankled planters, however.[51] Indeed, with the unbridled freedoms of harbor districts, the interracial mixing, and the hustling, independent nature of their slave labor force, southern seaports often proved to be flash points in political conflicts over slavery. Planters endured them with clinched teeth and only for the sake of sending their goods to market. At the other end of the social spectrum, white working men in Norfolk were also known to resent the predominance of black laborers in the city's shipyards, particularly during financial panics or depression years. At those times, a grog shop could become a center for racial uprisings of another sort.[52]

For all the proud manhood displayed by local black watermen like George Henry, Grandy must have been even more deeply impressed by the black seafarers in Norfolk. Not that he was unfamiliar with black "jack tars": vessels registered in New England ports dominated the coastwise trade throughout the South, and free blacks composed an estimated 10 to 20 percent of the registered seamen who served on them.[53] Many other free blacks—and an unknowable, but sizable number of slaves—sailed out of southern ports; at least 21 free black sailors called tiny Elizabeth City their home port as late as 1860.[54]

The sight of black hands on the worm-eaten old trading vessels that sailed out of Elizabeth City could be only so regal. But when Grandy visited Norfolk, he viewed black seamen working aboard great ships, foreign and American, and many of the black sailors handled themselves in a way that would have turned any slave's head. Since the colonial era, Atlantic shipping had been characterized by an unprecedented degree of racial equality in seamen's wages, social status, and duty assignments.[55] J. S. Buckingham, a British journalist who visited Norfolk harbor some years after Grandy, described the scope of racial equality aboard the naval frigate *Brandywine*. Some 40 to 50 free blacks were among the 470-man crew sailing the frigate.

In their arrangements and classification for duty, as forecastle-men, topmen, waisters, and after-guard, no distinction was made between black and white, but each were mingled indiscriminately, and classed only by their relative degrees of seamanship . . . the blacks were not at all inferior to the whites, either in their skill, readiness, or courage. Nor did the white seamen evince the slightest reluctance to be associated with them on terms of the most perfect equality in the discharge of their duties, or make their colour a subject of antipathy or reproach.

The *Brandywine*'s crew fell far short of a "perfect equality," of course. As was the universal custom, none of the frigate's officers was black. And though black enlisted seamen were not segregated by occupation aboard the *Brandywine*, black men composed the majority of cooks and stewards. Black sailors also dominated less desirable stations such as anchor duty and shore patrols for wood and water.[56] Nevertheless, black seaman like those aboard the

Brandywine enjoyed a measure of racial equality unimaginable for slaves or free blacks ashore. Grandy had to be impressed by their dignified bearing and the respect afforded them by their mates.

During a brief break from running his canal boat between Norfolk and the Pasquotank, Grandy also crewed a schooner on Albemarle Sound. A small fleet of schooners sailed regularly between Elizabeth City and smaller ports, such as Columbia and Hertford, located on rivers and creeks that flowed into the Albemarle. Grandy's vessel transported lumber; others carried corn, tobacco, naval stores, shingles, and staves. A number of other schooners maintained a more specialized, often seasonal trade with more remote hamlets. Along the Alligator River, a blackwater stream across the sound from Camden, an English traveler named Charles Janson observed that "a number of trading boats arrive from Edenton, Nixontown, Windsor, and the adjacent places, with merchandise, tobacco, and large supplies of rum, in order to exchange their commodities for honey and wax."[57] The internal trade of North Carolina depended on such vessels.[58] In the young canal town of Elizabeth City, which would soon eclipse Camden as the Pasquotank's leading port, black stevedores often transferred that cargo to oceangoing vessels for export.

On the Albemarle, Grandy likely shared the life of an ordinary sailor. With a crew that was most likely the proverbial "two men and a boy"—possibly slaves, possibly not—Grandy must have managed the sails and taken his turn at the helm like any schooner's hand. Though still relatively fast and handy, schooners evolved on North Carolina sounds into slower, heavier workboats with wide beams and a very shallow draft.[59] Matchless for carrying freight through shoal waters, they were also rarely intimidated by the open waters of Pamlico or Albemarle Sound and, with their fore-and-aft-rigged sails, were able to get in and out of narrow inlets and small bays more neatly than any square-rigged vessel. At anchor, Grandy caulked and scrubbed decks, mended sails, stripped masts, cooked meals, fished, washed clothes, made shore patrols for water, and stowed provisions.

On a coasting schooner, especially one that clung to inshore waters, Grandy's daily life shared little with the tradition-steeped, highly methodical routine of watches and bells that marked a sailor's every hour aboard a vessel in the open sea. Lunar and wind tides decreed when the schooner could navigate shoals, channels, and inlets or was forced to lay up and wait for

Schooner *Maggie Davis* in waters near Beaufort, ca. 1890. Although this schooner has the raking ends of a later era, most of her design indicates that she was built well before the Civil War. The schooner on which Moses Grandy served probably resembled this vessel in many respects. Courtesy North Carolina Maritime Museum, Beaufort.

higher water. Hurricanes and nor'easters altered the contours of channels so profoundly that Grandy and his crewmates had to make many a sounding. They had to be far too wary of shoals to sail after dark, except under the brightest moons; otherwise, they laid up in a harbor or a bay at sunset, as well as in rough weather. When they did sail at night, they rarely had the comfort of a lightship or lighthouse and had to rely on celestial navigation, dead reckoning, and the sorts of almost intuitive knowledge that local inshore sailors brought to their work—the saltiness of the water, the different smells of land, the color and contour of the waves. There was always work to be done, but waiting on sun, tide, or wind also left Grandy and his fellows with free time for fishing, telling yarns, or visiting ashore. Working on a coasting schooner was always hard duty, and, as a bondman, Grandy was saddled with the least desirable watches and chores.[60] He was away from his family a great deal, and he had to do without the fresh game that he might have caught and garden produce that he might have cultivated if he had been working on a plantation. But when he compared his lot to that of the enslaved men and women whom he sailed by in cotton, corn, or tobacco fields, he counted his blessings to work on the water. As Frederick Douglass wrote from his experience of his plantation by Chesapeake Bay, slave sailors like Grandy "were esteemed very highly by the other slaves, and looked upon as the privileged ones."[61]

On Albemarle Sound, a sailor's life placed Grandy among a host of other African American maritime laborers who opened up to him the inner workings of the ports where his schooner lay at anchor, as well as connected him both to distant seaports and to the southern upcountry. On a typical day out on Albemarle Sound, Grandy's schooner encountered black watermen fishing, piloting, or hauling freight.[62] A schooner always attracted a crowd, and many smaller craft would have tied up to Grandy's vessel at least briefly, especially while at anchor in the evening or when waiting out an ill wind or low tide. The crews gossiped and gambled, and slave boatmen often paddled dugouts out to see what they could get in exchange for fish, oysters, firewood, and wild game. Between the visiting and trading, a resonant, back-and-forth banter among the vessels that worked on the Albemarle was a part of daily life.

In port, Grandy mingled with African American tradesmen who worked in shipyards and chandleries, where they repaired bulwarks, mended sails, recaulked seams, and made other repairs.[63] In his account book of 1823–28, Thomas McLin chronicled his black craftsmen's work at his ship's chandlery in New Bern, south of the Albemarle. On the schooner *Rapid*, for instance, he indicates that slaves Bob, Tom, Henry, Elijah, America, and Aaron raised masts, fit rigging, and put in everything from mast hoops to hatch bars.[64] Other maritime artisans were free blacks, such as Hull Anderson, who owned a shipyard that occupied two lots in downtown Washington, North Carolina.[65] On such waterfronts, Grandy also met black mariners who hailed from every port on the eastern seaboard, as well as from the British, French, Spanish, Dutch, and Danish colonies in the Caribbean.[66] Blacks composed the large majority of deckhands on the local vessels that traded with the West Indies, and a white lady in Washington long recalled those "large, strong West Indies Negroes" with "their bright bandanas . . . and large golden rings that hung from their ears."[67] By working alongside such maritime laborers,

Ned, a sailor, drawn by David Hunter Strother during a visit to North Carolina. *Harper's New Monthly Magazine*, March 1857. Courtesy the Mariners' Museum, Newport News, Virginia.

slave watermen like Grandy helped local slave communities overcome their masters' attempts to keep them isolated from one another and uninformed about antislavery movements stretching from Boston to Port-au-Prince.

Grandy also encountered crowds of slave bateaumen, flatboat hands, and raftsmen when he was in Albemarle ports. Those stalwart souls carried tobacco, cotton, grains, timber, and other raw products from plantations upriver to coastal ports, thereby connecting Grandy's world with villages and fields hundreds of miles inland. Bateaux were square-ended, flat-bottomed scows 40 to 80 feet in length; they drew only 18 inches and held six tons of cargo or a dozen half-ton hogsheads of tobacco. Sometimes the crews worked in the open; at other times, the boat was covered with a hooped canopy.[68] Nearly always manned by slaves, who often signed their names on the cargo manifests, bateaux traversed white water with speed and deft steerage.[69] Bateaux were ill fitted for the sluggish blackwater rivers where Grandy grew up, but they handled ably in the fast currents of the rivers that descended precipitously out of the Appalachians onto the coastal plain—rivers like the Dan,

Staunton, and Roanoke, which flowed into the Albemarle Sound, or their more northerly cousins such as the James River.[70] The number of bateaumen working on most rivers is a matter of conjecture, but one river where we do have a firm estimate—the James River—gives a good idea of how heavily the river trade relied on them. In 1830, 1,500 slaves worked the 500 bateaux that carried tobacco into Richmond. The tobacco trade was not nearly as large into the Roanoke ports, but it was no less reliant on slave bateaumen.[71]

Slave bateaumen had a reputation as an especially proud, distinctive breed of watermen. "For if ever a man gloried in his calling," a Virginian named George Bagby recalled of the James River traffic in the 1830s, "the negro bateau-man was the man." He observed that the bateauman's "was a hardy calling, demanding skill, courage and strength in high degree."[72] Usually working in three-man crews, bateau hands carried written passes from their masters. Rarely did a master or overseer accompany them, even though their voyages downstream and back routinely took three to four weeks.[73] It was probably an impractical expense to provide an overseer for three slaves, but, more important, a bateau made it very difficult to keep a slave "in his place." Every bateau hand had to be highly skilled, and the difficulty of his task and the split-second decision making required for navigating river rapids left no room for standing over a boatman. That reality left masters in the untenable position of having to put a white man on inferior terms, or at best equal terms, with black boatmen—something that was not going to happen in the ante-bellum South. Planters chose to rely instead on all-black crews.

The boating itself was extremely demanding. Steering with long sweeps on the bow and stern, the slave watermen worked their way downstream through rushing currents, sometimes aided by sluices and wing dams (low stone walls, many of them built by pre-Columbian Indian boatmen) that channeled the cascading waters through openings in the rapids. Coming back upriver required less dexterity and fewer quick reflexes but was incredibly arduous.[74] George Bagby provides a description of slave bateaumen working their way upriver that is so vivid and well spoken, if more than a little romanticized, that it is worth quoting in detail. "I can see him now striding the plank that ran along the gunwale to afford his footing, his long iron-shod pole fixed in the water behind him," Bagby wrote.

Now he turns, and after one or two ineffectual efforts to get his pole fixed in the rocky bottom of the river, secures his purchase, adjusts the upper part of the pole to the pad at his shoulder, bends to his task, and the long, but not ungraceful bark mounts the rapids like a sea-bird breasting the storm. His companion on the other side plies the pole with equal ardor, and between the two the boat bravely surmounts every obstacle, be it rocks, rapids, quicksands, hammocks, what not. A third negro at the stern held the mighty oar that served as a rudder.[75]

In some rapids, the boatmen ascended "hauling walls," which were stone walls laid where they could get foothold enough to pull the bateau up through the white water.[76]

Bagby found the slave bateaumen "a stalwart, jolly, courageous set" who reveled in their independence. At night, he remembered, the bateaumen "haul[ed] into shore . . . under the friendly shade of a mighty sycamore, to rest, to eat, to play the banjo, and to snatch a few hours of profound, blissful sleep."[77] They dined in high fashion out of the river. They intermingled with plantation slaves, providing the locals with news from upriver and down and no doubt attracting a great deal of attention from the neighborhood slave patrols. Not without cause: just such bateaumen had been implicated among the main conspirators in both Gabriel's Rebellion in 1800 and even more so in the Easter Plot of 1802, when they had utilized the riverways to spread insurrectionary plans into much of southeastern Virginia and northeastern North Carolina.[78]

While bateaumen were more likely to work on the water, their flatboat and rafting cousins were usually plantation slaves who left their masters' fields to guide their craft to coastal ports. "Great quantities of products from the rich counties of Pitt, Edgecombe and Nash were freighted down on flatboats consigned to middlemen here," reminisced an antebellum resident of Washington, North Carolina. "The boats . . . were poled along by Negroes who walked along a plank footway along the side of the boat," she recalled. "These flatboats came down the river piled high with bales of cotton, barrels of tar, pitch and turpentine, bags of corn, sides of bacon and stacks of bricks, staves and shingles."[79]

Many rafts were only logs or barrels bound together with a jerry-rigged platform where the boatmen stood and steered with poles and a sweep. They relied mainly on the current to drift them downstream, though, in the words of a former slave waterman from another state, a boatman still had to be "perfectly familiar with the art and mysteries of rafting" to hold the channel and avoid shoals and downed trees.[80] Near the coast, in intertidal waters, boatmen often had to lash the raft or flatboat to the riverbank and wait out the incoming tide before they could continue downstream, an inconvenience that afforded a welcome respite for fishing, cooking a meal, or taking a nap. These boats were used mainly on lazy blackwater rivers or calmer stretches of other rivers, and most trips downriver were fairly peaceful.

Coming back upriver was another story. Many times, slave boatmen merely disassembled rafts, selling their logs and barrels in port and returning to their plantations by foot or in the company of draymen. If they had to bring a flatboat or raft home, the slaves had a grueling journey ahead of them. The hardships of poling and rowing a flatboat upstream for two or three weeks reminded all observers why it was slave duty. If the current was strong, the boatmen might even have to fasten ropes to trees on the riverbank and pull the boat forward one painstaking length of rope at a time. Then, when they encountered falls, they had to portage the boat around them, sometimes even having to take the flat apart and reassemble it. When slave boatmen took eleven days to carry a group of Moravians only 140 miles up the Cape Fear River, they were making good time, all things considered.[81]

Flatboating or rafting downstream, while usually relatively easy, did not always make for a tranquil idyll either. Many planters had to wait to float their cotton bales, naval stores, and livestock to market until they could count on the spring rains lifting flatboats and rafts over shoals, and those freshets made for an entirely different sort of boating. A former slave named Richard Jones never forgot the frightening thrill of running freshets while manning a flatboat on the Broad River. Years later, he told an interviewer how, during a freshet, the "water just tuck dat boat plumb smack out'n our hands. . . . We never had to hit a lick, but she went so fast dat we was all skeer'd to take a long breath."[82] A big freshet momentarily transformed even small blackwater rivers, like the upper reaches of the Waccamaw or the Northeast Cape Fear, into raging torrents that demanded a boatman's best if he and his boat were going to make it to port in one piece.[83] Storms, too, could pull rafts apart and scatter their logs or barrels across miles of shoreline.

In rough waters or calm, those flatboat and raft crews—like all slave watermen—played their own role in connecting slave communities upriver to the more cosmopolitan maritime world that was Moses Grandy's home. They were river people to the core: redolent of muddy waters, living off fish, and rarely straying far from their boats. But in slave quarters far upriver, among strangers to tides and saltwater, they attracted crowds of fieldhands to hear their songs of the river and the sea beyond.

Captain Grandy, as he was now known, next lightered shingles and lumber out of the Great Dismal Swamp. By that point, sometime in the mid-1810s, a series of unfortunate events had resulted in his sale to his old nemesis, Enoch Sawyer, the same man who had sold his wife away from him a few years earlier. His pathway back to Sawyer reveals the cruel and unpredictable exigencies of slave life. After the War of 1812, James Grandy had sold the slave boatman to a "Mr. Trewitt," in the process cheating Moses Grandy of $600 that he had already paid toward earning his freedom. James Grandy sold Moses Grandy, according to the latter, "because people had jeered him, by saying that I had more sense than he had." A "Mr. Mews" next acquired him when Trewitt, who had mortgaged Grandy to finance a brig's voyage to the West Indies, defaulted. Grandy lost another $600 that he had paid Trewitt in anticipation of eventually buying his freedom.[84] Trewitt cannot readily be traced in historical records, but "Mews" was almost assuredly William T. Muse, a Pasquotank land speculator who owned slaves and more than 20,000 acres of swamp forest.[85] Muse, who had not really wanted Grandy, sold him back to Sawyer. Grandy's second wife was also owned by Sawyer, who had prohibited the slave waterman from visiting his new wife unless he consented to work for him again.[86]

A decade earlier, in 1804, Enoch Sawyer had invested in a cross canal from the Dismal Swamp Canal just south of "the Angle," to the "headwoods in Camden County and to the White Oak Spring mark in Gates County."[87] Completed by 1816, the White Oak Spring Canal, also known as Goffs Cut or the Corapeake Lumber Canal, was likely where Grandy loaded shingles.[88] Grandy does not provide enough clues, however, to conclude what kind of lightering he did. He may only have poled a large flat to the wharf complex at South Mills, at the south end of the Dismal Swamp Canal. He may have guided a barge or sloop from the wharf complex down the Pasquotank River to Elizabeth City, where he rendezvoused with coastal schooners that conveyed the shingles to sea.[89] Or he may have commanded a schooner to Ocracoke Inlet, where stevedores at Shell Castle and Portsmouth Islands reloaded the shingles onto a more seaworthy vessel.[90] All those watercraft could be encompassed under the generic term "lighter"—and slave watermen manned them all.

Shingle getting, as the cutting and gathering of shingles was called, had long been one of the principal industries in the Great Dismal Swamp. Until replaced by creosote-treated pine shingles late in the nineteenth century, cypress and juniper shingles formed a staple in building construction, and the Albemarle region was a leading source for the United States' supply. Even in 1841, a depression year, lighter captains like Grandy sent approximately 36 million shingles over the Dismal Swamp Canal.[91] Shingling depended on adequate water transportation, and every new canal opened old-growth woodlands to exploitation.

The possibility that Grandy lightered shingles all the way to Ocracoke Inlet means that he may have had contact with a host of black maritime laborers who were among the most independent and worldly in the South. Located more than 25 miles out in the Atlantic at the Outer Banks, Ocracoke Inlet was bordered by the village of Ocracoke, at the southern end of Ocracoke Island, and the village of Portsmouth, on the northern point of Core Banks. Built out of the planks of shipwrecks and warmed by driftwood fires, these humble villages were home to a salty, weather-beaten people who rarely had much truck with the mainland. The island men had often been to sea when they were younger, and they fished and oystered when they were not piloting or lightering. In Grandy's lifetime, Ocracoke Inlet was the best entry into Albemarle and Pamlico Sounds, but the bar and a shoal known as "the Swash" frustrated larger vessels and forced them to anchor in a harbor by Core Banks and lighter their cargos across the shoals on more shallow-draft vessels. This lightering and piloting was the principal business of the inlet, besides that of supplying and entertaining the crews, who often lingered at the inlet for weeks awaiting fair winds, supplies, or repairs.[92]

Slaves figured prominently among the watermen's families at Ocracoke Inlet. In 1810 Portsmouth had a population of 225 whites, 115 slaves, and one free black. The same year, Shell Castle Island, a lightering outpost built up on a shoal in the inlet, had a population of 18 whites and 10 slaves. It was also a way station for a larger number of slave river pilots, sailors, and lighter crews who sailed back and forth between the inlet and ports inland.[93] The African Americans at Ocracoke Inlet were mainly skilled watermen and their families. The bar pilots guided seagoing vessels across the Swash and bar at Ocracoke Inlet and probably did not often abandon their home port; a slave who could dependably pilot at the Ocracoke bar was a treasure who would not be allowed to wander far. The other maritime slaves at Ocracoke Inlet had a great deal of mobility: river pilots navigated seagoing vessels "up the country,"[94] from the

Ceramic engraving of the piloting and light-erage outpost at Shell Castle Island, at Ocracoke Inlet, ca. 1790. Courtesy North Carolina Museum of History, Raleigh.

inlet into ports more than a hundred miles inland; lighter crews sailed in and out of seaports like New Bern and Edenton; some of Shell Castle's slaves ranged as far as 60 miles south to Cape Lookout hunting for jumping mullet and bottlenosed dolphins.[95]

The pilots were the most distinguished watermen among the African Americans at Ocracoke Inlet. Though long established in colonial North Carolina, their presence emerges dramatically from the records in 1773, when white pilots challenged their predominance. Local whites complained that "a considerable number" of unlicensed slaves and free blacks were piloting "vessels from [Ocracoke] Bar up the several Rivers to Bath, Edenton, and New Bern and back again."[96] Complaints of "stragling Negroes passing here piloting" were still coming from Ocracoke Inlet in 1810, when licensed blacks piloted there as well.[97] The prevalence of black pilots on the Cape Fear River was a bone of contention in Wilmington and Fayetteville during Grandy's lifetime, and the North Carolina General Assembly repeatedly debated the regulation of slave and free black pilots on the Cape Fear between 1800 and 1835.[98] Occurring so far out into the sea, where few planters might complain of their bad influence on local slaves, the controversies over the black pilots at Ocracoke Inlet did not receive nearly as much attention in the halls of government.

When a seagoing vessel arrived at Ocracoke Inlet, its master tacked back and forth until a pilot boat arrived and the pilot boarded and took the helm.[99] Much of the vessel's cargo would be off-loaded onto lighters for the journey across the bar. When the pilot judged that wind, tide, and currents were favorable for running the inlet, he steered the vessel over the bar and through the channel into a little harbor by Portsmouth. This was a harrowing passage. Coming in through the fierce breakers that bordered the narrow, shifting channel, a pilot had to have a steady hand and an instinctive knowledge of the local waters. Safe inside Core Banks, stevedores reloaded the vessel's cargo from the lighters for the journey into Albemarle or Pamlico Sound. A local river pilot would take the helm and guide the vessel into New Bern, Edenton, or another port. A slave river pilot could easily be away from the inlet for several weeks, during which time he usually remained with the vessel, away from his master, until he brought it back safely to the inlet.[100]

Racial boundaries had long been confused on the Outer Banks, where the islanders, including more than a few shipwreck survivors and deserters, heeded the less rigid racial mores of shipboard life more than those of tidewater plantations or inland ports. This lenience of the shoreline extended even to sexual relations. At Ocracoke Inlet, masters of vessels made few efforts to conceal black consorts who sailed with them and sometimes acknowledged the offspring of those illicit unions. Since the mid-eighteenth century, a few well-off sailors had freed their slave lovers, occasionally set them up in households that they could then visit at their pleasure, and more than once deeded significant parcels of Outer Banks land to their mixed-race children. A manumitted mulatto named Calvino Windsor inherited from his white father more than 60 acres at Shackleford Banks. Over the generations, Windsor's descendants intermarried with local blacks and coastal Indians and were renowned for their skill at handling fishing and whaling boats.[101] Neither Ocracoke Inlet nor the rest of the Outer Banks was a bastion of racial

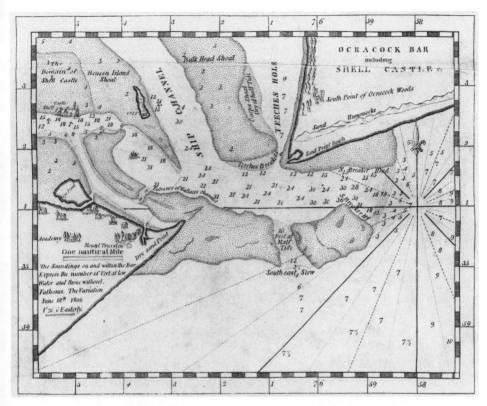

"Ocracock Bar including Shell Castle," 1806. This chart of Ocracoke Inlet shows the piloting village of Portsmouth, above the high dune known as Mount Truxston (extreme lower left), the piloting and lighterage outpost at Shell Castle Island (extreme upper left), and the far southern end of Ocracoke Island (upper right), as well as the daunting shoals that slave pilots had to navigate on a regular basis. Courtesy North Carolina Collection, University of North Carolina at Chapel Hill.

equality—planters and merchants inland would not have tolerated such a situation, even if it had been imaginable. Overall, however, black and white interactions were far more uncertain and egalitarian there than they were ashore.

For all the relaxation of racial boundaries on the Outer Banks, the island slaves still seem to have been a militant lot. In the spring of 1831, approximately 30 slaves, purportedly including the entire male slave population of Portsmouth village, confiscated a schooner and fled north into the Atlantic, their flight cut off only by an unseasonably late nor'easter that disabled their vessel.[102] If Grandy visited Ocracoke Inlet in his duties as a lighter captain, schooner hand, or sailor, he witnessed a side of the African American maritime world far removed from the restraints of plantation society. The inlet may have seemed to him at once foreign, dangerous, and enticing.

Twice frustrated in the attempt to buy his freedom, Grandy finally arranged in or around 1827 for Captain Edward Minner to purchase him from Enoch Sawyer. Minner, a former boating acquaintance at Deep Creek, held strong antislavery beliefs and may have been a Quaker. Minner could not afford to buy Grandy without compensation, but he agreed to let the slave waterman pay for his freedom. Grandy's experience in this regard was hardly typical; most bondmen and -women had neither the ability to earn sufficient wages to purchase their freedom nor a master willing to accept their money. (Feeling threatened by the free black population and leery of its alleged role in fostering slave revolts, the General Assembly made the practice illegal after 1831.)[103] After Minner paid Sawyer, Grandy returned to his canal boats for three years—broken up by a year at Lake Drummond, in the Great Dismal, to recover from severe rheumatism—until he had repaid Minner fully. He later recalled that the captain "made no claim whatever on my services. I was altogether on the footing of a free man, as far as a colored man can there be free."[104]

Working the water, Grandy had always enjoyed a high degree of freedom compared to the overwhelming majority of slaves. Nonetheless, he had always known that those privileges could be revoked at any time. Real freedom was different. "In my sleep," he wrote of his first days as a free man, "I was always dreaming of flying over woods and rivers. My gait was so altered by gladness, that people often stopped me, saying, 'Grandy, what is the matter?' I excused myself as well as I could; but many persons perceived the reason, and said, 'Oh, he is so pleased with having his freedom.' Slavery will teach any man to be glad when he gets freedom."[105]

After a two-month sojourn in Providence, Rhode Island, Grandy returned to his slave family in North Carolina.[106] Following in the footsteps of many other Albemarle slave boatmen, Grandy then went to sea. He worked for a year on the packets that had recently begun to sail from Elizabeth City to New York and Philadelphia. A number of free blacks from Elizabeth City served on those vessels, but Grandy also worked alongside free black sailors and hired-out slaves who hailed from other seaports both above and below the Mason-Dixon Line.[107] Sizable free black communities had sprouted and flourished in every northern port in the years since the American Revolution, and the maritime trades were a mainstay of them all.[108] Free black seamen like Grandy could be found on every sort of seagoing vessel sailing out of those ports, and they were conspicuous in the coastwise trade along the eastern seaboard and in the West Indies.[109] African Americans represented 18 percent of the able-bodied seamen on merchant ships sailing out of New York between 1800 and 1825, a time when more than half of the city's exports were southern products.[110] Between the Revolution and the Civil War, black sailors were probably a hefty majority of seafaring cooks and stewards,[111] 10 to 20 percent of all merchant American seamen, and as much as half of the native-born seamen in the merchant trade.[112] Dozens of vessels sailing out of ports from New Orleans to Boston were manned by crews that were three-quarters black, and more than a few had all-black crews.[113]

While the coastal trade offered free black sailors unprecedented pay and status, it also posed serious risks. In the 1820s, southern states had begun to clamp down on black sailors with Negro Seamen Acts that limited their mobility and rights. Those sanctions were then heightened amid the hysteria that followed in the wake of the circulation of David Walker's *Appeal to the Coloured Citizens of the World* by sailors in 1830 and Nat Turner's insurrection in 1831.[114] Walker, a free black born in Wilmington, North Carolina, at about the same time as Grandy, had become an abolitionist leader in Boston in the 1820s. Walker used the contacts among sailors that he made at his used-clothing shop on the Boston waterfront to disseminate his revolutionary call for abolition and armed struggle to southern ports, including at least New Bern and Wilmington in North Carolina.[115]

Coming in the aftermath of Walker's *Appeal*, the Turner revolt in nearby Southampton County, Virginia, caused widespread panic among slaveholders in the maritime districts of North Carolina. Even as far south as Southport, the piloting village at the mouth of the Cape Fear River, the entire white population feared a slave insurrection so much that they took shelter in the local garrison.[116] Wilmington authorities searched all black homes at least once every 20 days and banned night gatherings of slaves in the port. The state's adjutant general sent 200 muskets from a Raleigh arsenal to ward off a black revolt in New Bern, and the county court ordered all firearms confiscated from local slaves. Even inland, fear of a slave uprising grew into hysteria. Raleigh officials ordered all free blacks jailed. And in Duplin County, not far up the Northeast Cape Fear River from Wilmington, testimony induced by torture revealed plans for a slave rebellion, leading to a number of slaves being tried and put to death. Some were beheaded and their heads placed on posts as a warning to other blacks. At least one of the alleged slave conspirators was burned at the stake.[117]

A crackdown against both slaves and free blacks ensued throughout North Carolina, and from 1830 to 1835 the rights and liberties of all free blacks were drastically curtailed. This led to a broad exodus of the free black population, particularly the more successful tradesmen. Black shipbuilder Hull Anderson sold his shipyard in Washington, North Carolina, soon after the General Assembly took away his voting rights and limited his freedoms of speech, assembly, and movement.[118] Blamed for abolitionist activities, free black sailors such as Moses Grandy attracted more than their share of white enmity, including severe legal restrictions that went beyond those placed on other free blacks.[119] Fearful that he might be re-enslaved in Elizabeth City or another southern port, Grandy fled North Carolina.

Settling in Boston in late 1831 or 1832, Grandy did a variety of jobs, including stevedoring, but was soon at sea again. In his *Narrative*, he recounts two of his enlistments. On his first sea voyage, he sailed to the Spanish port of Puerto Rico under a Captain Cobb on the *New Packet*, a single-decked, 73-foot coastal schooner of 103 tons.[120] Grandy may have gotten acquainted with her master and crew as early as 1827, when a storm-battered *New Packet* came into Elizabeth City for a lengthy overhaul.[121] It is possible that her black sailors informed Grandy that their schooner was shorthanded after he moved north to their home port.

Grandy later sailed on the *James Maury*, a ship of 394 tons, to the East Indies and the Mediterranean. Originally a merchant vessel, she began whaling in the Pacific and Indian Ocean in 1833.[122] Grandy apparently sailed aboard her just prior to her whaling days.[123] With his experience, he could easily have been rated a seaman by then, possibly even first-class. Not every vessel's master allowed black sailors to rise in the ranks, but many did.[124]

Grandy may have experienced a rare sort of racial equality aboard those merchant ships, but he was still at sea in a day when shipboard life beat down hard on common sailors of all colors. Poor wages, harsh discipline, and high mortality rates were the norm for black and white alike in the merchant fleet of the day. William P. Powell, an African American who was a militant advocate for black sailors, wrote in 1846 that a sailor of any race was treated merely as "an article of merchandise. Imported and exported from one country to another, and bartered for, sold, transferred from his ship to a rum-selling boarding-house—to the brothel . . . , where he is exchanged for what he is worth, until, like a depreciated currency, he is shipped out at a discount to some foreign port, and passed off as current coin."[125] Powell was making an argument for reform, but his hard words were on the mark. Grandy, like many seamen, may have been attracted to the freedoms and excitement of a sailor's life, to say nothing of its relative degree of racial equality, but his years at sea also attest to the lack of opportunities for a black man in America, North or South, and the relative lure of any trade that might help to support or liberate his family.[126]

No matter what his status at sea, as a free black sailor Grandy was increasingly exiled from his native South. Many slaveholders believed that black sailors infected coastal slaves with a revolutionary spirit. They realized that seamen like Grandy—who had walked as free men in other nations, been exposed to slave revolutions in the Caribbean, and enjoyed aboard ship a degree of racial equality scarcely known in the United States—threatened the slave South.[127] Slaveholders went to great lengths to segregate local slaves from free black mariners. Grandy eventually did not dare to return to Elizabeth City. And in Norfolk he was once permitted to come ashore only because merchants who had previously chartered his canal boats vouched for him. When the mayor argued that Grandy "had been among the cursed Yankees too long," he was, despite being vouched for, nearly re-enslaved.[128]

Except for a year in Portland, Maine, Grandy made Boston his home port until he completed his *Narrative* in 1842. With his seaman's pay, he set about liberating his family. He bought his wife first, and then a son enslaved at Norfolk. Both joined him in Boston. Two daughters sold to owners in New Orleans purchased their own freedom.[129] Five other children remained slaves, however, and he could locate only one of them, a girl named Betsy. Grandy also sought to aid other enslaved relatives, especially those who he knew had been most severely abused. He seems to have written his *Narrative* mainly to raise funds to free a sister in Elizabeth City.[130] Though Grandy may not have appreciated it in his own day, his story would have a crucial and lasting importance to understanding slavery and freedom in the maritime South.

Whether poling a shingle flat or standing high in the rigging of a coastal schooner, Grandy could see only too well how much worse was the suffering of most slaves compared to that of the average slave waterman. Visiting Albemarle Sound ports, he witnessed slaves being tortured, starved, and worked to the point of death. He saw black families, including his own, torn apart. He recognized that black men and women often found innovative ways to confound the slave codes, but he also realized that, especially after David Walker's *Appeal* in 1829 and Nat Turner's revolt in 1831, slaveholders had taken away practically every right that could be denied a human being, including the rights to choose a mate, have a family, and worship God.

The stark contrast between working on the water and toiling ashore had also been drilled into Grandy during two brief interludes in his own maritime career. For at least one season, he had worked at a canal-digging camp; for another eight months, he did field work. Once he broke down in the fields from hunger and exhaustion, telling his overseer, who could not understand why Grandy found the work less bearable than did the other slaves, that "he knew well I had not been used to it . . . and that I could not stand it." That overseer increased his corn rations, but Grandy was not satisfied. "I wanted liberty," he insisted.[131]

African American watermen like Moses Grandy posed a constant danger to the power of slaveholders. They covertly linked slaves throughout the Albemarle Sound vicinity, even conveying news and messages to plantation fieldhands well up the Roanoke and Chowan Rivers. Familiar with distant ports, they spread political news and democratic ideologies from as far away as New England, France, and Haiti into local slave communities. It was no accident, then, that slave watermen had been among the leaders in Albemarle slave conspiracies in 1775, 1800, and 1802, or that slaveholders implicated them so frequently in aiding runaways to flee the South.[132] Perhaps most importantly, black watermen such as Grandy captured the imaginations of countless African Americans who observed their liberty and dreamed that they, too, might one day sail away from slavery.

chapter two

Common as Gar Broth

Slave Fishermen from Tidewater Plantations
to the Outer Banks

One eventide in about 1850, a young runaway slave faced an agonizing choice at Adams Creek, a wide tributary of the Lower Neuse River. Trapped on the creek's western bank, William Henry Singleton sought desperately to reach the other shore. His master had sold him a great distance from his family's plantation, but he had escaped and traveled to within five or six miles of his mother's cabin. Only that broad creek stood between him and his family, and twilight was upon him. He would soon be at the mercy of the slave patrol. Looking over the darkening horizon, Singleton spied a solitary fisherman so far away that he could not tell the man's race. Was he African American and hence a likely ally? Or white and a likely danger? Unable to say for certain, Singleton staked his life on the fact that he had rarely seen a white angler among the crowds of watermen who fished on the Lower Neuse. "I knew he must be a colored man," Singleton later remembered, "because the white people as a rule did not fish." Local whites "generally got their fish without taking that trouble," Singleton observed.[1] Hailing the fisherman, Singleton beckoned him near. The shadowy figure was indeed a black boatman, who not only ferried Singleton across Adams Creek, but also directed the young boy to his mother's home at John H. Nelson's Piney Point plantation on Garbacon Creek.

The slave fisherman who rescued Henry Singleton did not ply his maritime skills in a southern seaport as Moses Grandy did for so many years. His life did not revolve around the comings and goings of sloops and schooners, nor did he pick up political news from New England or West Indian ports at the local wharf. The chance of abolitionist writings such as David Walker's *Appeal* falling into his hands at Adams Creek, 40 miles from the closest seaport, was remote. This black angler watched seagoing vessels pass down the Neuse River between New Bern and Ocracoke Inlet, but he probably never met their crews or passengers. The Lower Neuse, a broad estuary, confined those vessels and the door that they represented into Atlantic seafaring culture to a main shipping channel, nearly a mile across the river from Adams Creek.

Singleton's unknown boatman also did not work in a commercial fishery. The great seine fishery for shad and herring on the Albemarle Sound, and a similar herring fishery and a burgeoning oyster industry on the Chesapeake Bay, were the only large commercial fisheries in the antebellum South. Among southern fishermen, only the black boatmen connected with these fisheries could be mentioned in the same breath with Yankee whalers and cod and halibut fishermen. Henry Singleton's co-conspirator was far more typical of southern fishermen—black, white, or Indian. He did not fish year round, but seasonally. He fished only after hoeing his master's cotton or cropping his master's tobacco. He fished by himself or with a few fellows for his own table, his master's family, or local barter, not for distant markets. At Adams Creek his life revolved around the annual cycle of plowing, planting, cultivating, and harvesting cotton and tobacco. He left the fields for any extended period two or three times at most a year, for a few weeks in the autumn for the mulleting beaches at the Atlantic seashore, 30 miles south, and to chase shad along the Lower Neuse for a few weeks in March and April. Once each winter, probably just before Christmas, his master may also have sent him 20 or 30 miles farther down the Neuse, into the saltier waters of Pamlico Sound, to the great oyster beds beyond Turnagain Bay. In his life we come as close as one can to the day-to-day experience of an ordinary slave fisherman in tidewater North Carolina.

Understanding how slave fishermen like the boatman on Adams Creek fit into, contributed to, or potentially undermined tidewater plantation society requires situating them in a maritime culture that has largely been forgotten. The historical literature on fishing in the early South has focused almost exclusively on the shad and herring fisheries of the Chesapeake Bay and the Albemarle Sound. Scholars have otherwise tended to open the history of southern fisheries with the commercial boom that began after the Civil War. Conventional notions of what is "traditional fishing" in North Carolina, as

William Henry Single-
ton, former slave on
the Neuse River. Cour-
tesy Leroy Fitch, New
Haven, Connecticut.

well as the maritime South generally, come roughly from the years 1870 to
1930, ironically a period when the state's fishing culture was influenced most
heavily by fishermen, boatbuilders, and cannery owners from New England,
Long Island, and the Chesapeake Bay.[2] A very different sort of fishing culture
flourished in coastal North Carolina before the Civil War, and one must turn
to it to understand slave fishermen and their work.

The coastal waters of North Carolina offered some of the most abundant fish
and shellfish grounds in North America. The source of this phenomenal

fecundity was the estuarine waters within the Outer Banks and the more southerly barrier islands. Estuaries, from the Latin *aestus*, meaning tide, are lagoons, bays, and sounds partially cut off from the sea, where fresh water flowing from rivers intermingles with salt water passing through ocean inlets. With more than 2.2 million brackish acres of estuary, North Carolina had more of these phenomenally prolific fishing grounds than any state besides Louisiana.[3]

All of North Carolina's estuaries are quite shallow. Currituck and Core Sounds range from only a few inches in depth to no more than seven feet. Even Pamlico Sound, approximately 80 miles long and 15 to 30 miles wide, is a mass of shoals in its northern part and never gets deeper than 22 feet in its southern waters. The shallow waters allow sunlight to reach the sea bottom, providing energy for the first rungs of the food chain: thick growths of sea grasses and rich broths of phytoplankton. Winds also make shallow waters more turbulent than deep waters, churning oxygen thoroughly into every layer of the estuaries, which also enhances fishery productivity. The Neuse, Tar, Roanoke, and Cape Fear Rivers provided marine life with a steady and ample stream of nutrients. The abundance of fresh- and saltwater marshlands, the convergence of the Western Atlantic's two great ocean currents (the Gulf Stream and the Labrador Current), and a large variety of bottom types—sand, mud, rock, and shell—also provided habitats suitable to a broad diversity of fish and shellfish. With these ecological factors creating a magnificently fertile marine food chain, it is no wonder that early Carolina watermen, like their Algonquian, Iroquoian, and Siouan predecessors, mainly employed small boats and looked to estuaries for nature's bounty, rather than using larger vessels and looking to the Atlantic.

Despite the fertility of coastal waters, only a small number of commercial fisheries had developed along the Carolina coast before the Civil War. That early fishing industry dealt mainly in salted fish and in seafoods that could be shipped alive in order to avoid spoilage, such as terrapins, oysters, and clams.[4] From Ocracoke Inlet to Cape Fear, haul seiners salted jumping mullet for a wagoneers' trade and for modest exports to the West Indies. The mullet fishery thrived best on the barrier islands off Beaufort, where fishermen also salted spot, hogfish, drum, and gray trout, as well as preserved mullet roe for a luxury export trade via Charleston to the West Indies.[5] To the north, between Hatteras Inlet and Cape Henry, several crews of Outer Banks fishermen caught bluefish with seines and gill nets. They sold them fresh or salted to steam-powered buyboats from Norfolk.[6] Those Virginia buyboats also purchased freshwater fish, mainly perch and chub, from Currituck Sound watermen.[7]

None of those fisheries was sizable. Not until after 1870, when New England and New York fishing grounds had deteriorated, market demand had risen, transportation had improved, and new preservation technologies (primarily steam canning and ice making) had been refined, did commercial fishing grow more significant in North Carolina.[8] Until then, coastal markets and peddlers sold a variety of fresh fish and shellfish, as well as a number of other seacoast creatures, such as diamondback terrapins, alligators, and waterfowl. Not even the port of New Bern, home to one of the largest fish markets in the South after the Civil War, had a wholesale fish trade or seafood cannery before 1860.

Up until the Civil War, the old practice of bartering fish and shellfish dwarfed the market trade. Carolina watermen traded salted fish for their year's supply of corn with merchants from Wilmington to Norfolk and with planters who lived up coastal rivers.[9] The practices of mullet crews near Beaufort exemplified the custom. Every autumn, after the last mullet had been salted and packed in barrels, the Beaufort fishing crews sent their captain up the Neuse River to trade for corn. "The captain," a visitor was later told, "was at liberty to make the exchange upon any basis that he might think proper, but as he was given a percentage—usually one-fifth of the corn received—for his services, he was apt to derive the best possible bargain."[10] News of a mullet trader's arrival spread quickly and spurred planters to send wagons laden with corn to the local wharf. Tidewater residents referred to the corn as their "bread" and to the heavy, broad-beamed sloops and schooners that transported the grain as "corn crackers."[11]

The fish trade meant little for coastal settlement. Even on the Outer Banks, fishing was rarely a serious vocation. The Bankers fished casually to meet their own needs and to salt enough fish to trade for corn and truck vegetables with planters inland. Once or twice a year, they also traded salt fish or raw oysters for coffee, sugar, and flour with furnishing merchants across the Pamlico Sound. Fishing was a subsistence enterprise, and only a few boatmen bothered to venture beyond local sounds into the Atlantic. Without access to markets to sell fresh fish, Outer Banks inhabitants relied instead on catching their own food and on a steady diet of corn pone and molasses, sweet potatoes and black-eyed peas.[12] During the Civil War, when Union soldier J. Waldo

Denny visited Bodie Island, he found "several hundred people . . . scattered along this bar, who get a living . . . by fishing, gathering oysters, picking up a [ship]wreck now and then, and doing a little piloting."

Piloting, salvage, or lighterage earned Bankers a little cash, but they could never rely on them. "They seldom see any money—indeed don't need it," observed Denny, "and are happy without it."[13] Their estrangement from a market economy was not the only part of Outer Banks life that separated the islanders from residents of the mainland. Like many of the secluded places that edged the Atlantic, the Outer Banks adhered less fixedly to the boundaries of race, class, and gender that held on the other side of the sounds. The unusual fluidity in race relations on the Outer Banks in the colonial era has already been discussed and will be looked at again for a later age, but here it is worth noting that island women were also renowned for their untraditional work roles. A woman who was married to a mariner or pilot had to learn to survive on her own, and many could handle a skiff as well as a frying pan. Dorcas E. Carter, an 88-year-old retired schoolteacher in New Bern, still recalls how her grandmother, born a slave at Portsmouth Island, owned her own boat, stitched her own nets, and went fishing or crabbing most days.[14] Outer Banks women, black and white, frequently tended nets and gathered oysters and also fished alongside husbands and brothers, as well as shucked oysters and scallops and cleaned and preserved their husbands' catches ashore.[15]

Life was harsh on the Outer Banks and the other barrier islands. Many of the islands were only narrow sand beaches without any forests. Lacking shelter, arable soil, or fresh water, they were simply too barren to make even a spartan homestead. Even when blessed with thick maritime forests of live oak, yaupon, wax myrtle, and scrub pine, the barrier islands were no match for hurricanes and nor'easters. An 1842 hurricane left only one home standing at Portsmouth village, and an 1846 nor'easter washed away the only two families who had dared to venture off Knotts Island to Currituck Banks.[16] Heat, sand, salt spray and insects made even the more hospitable barrier islands forbidding. A Union soldier later summed up what many early settlers must have felt about the barrier islands when he called Bogue Banks, one of the most heavily wooded of the islands, "a desolate place, inhabited by one or two poor families and thousands of alligators and venomous snakes."[17]

The Outer Banks and the more southerly barrier islands were nevertheless an important commons for tidewater residents of all races. Camping on the islands for the great mullet and bluefish runs was an autumn ritual that dated back thousands of years to the distant predecessors of the Algonquian and

Iroquoian tribes. Hunters sailed out to the islands to shoot small game, sea birds, and waterfowl, while townspeople scavenged bird and turtle eggs in their marshes and beaches. Mainlanders had also grazed cattle, sheep, horses, and hogs on the barrier islands since the earliest days of the colonial era. By the 1840s at the latest, pony pennings had become an annual festival that attracted crowds of tidewater onlookers.[18]

Fishing was also a daily part of life on the estuarine waters within the Outer Banks and the lower barrier islands. A later visitor's comments would have rung only truer before the Civil War: "Farmers, along the sounds and rivers, own boats as, in other places, they own horses, and a man must be poor, indeed, who has not even a 'cooner'—canoe dug from a solid log—in which he can carry his produce to market."[19] Most tidewater people spent at least a few days or weeks every year fishing, and several hundred small farmers who lived nearest the Atlantic placed fishing ahead of their gardens and fields, particularly in the vicinity of Roanoke Island and in the remote villages east of Beaufort. Local people later referred to those part-time fishermen, part-time cultivators as "saltwater farmers."[20]

Only on the marshy stretch of coastline by Core and Back Sounds, between Beaufort and Cedar Island, did the majority of household heads identify their main occupation as fishing by 1850. There daily life revolved primarily around the sea.[21] Unlike folks along Henry Singleton's stretch of the Lower Neuse, where farming came first, those coastal people had within their reach a phenomenal diversity of fishing grounds that allowed them to stay on the water most of the year. When the jumping mullet runs along Core Banks and Shackleford Banks ceased in late autumn, local watermen moved into the saltwater bays between Cedar Island and North River to harvest oysters and gun for ducks and geese. When the oyster season ended in late winter, they moved to the brackish waters of the Lower Neuse for the shad season. Then, after the shad had spawned in late April or early May, they sailed home to plant their gardens and till fields, slipping off now and then to rake clams, hunt terrapins, or tend fishing nets along Core Sound. They did not try to fit fishing into a hectic cycle of agricultural labor, but rather tended crops and gardens in between fishing seasons.[22]

Fishing was deeply entwined with slavery and tidewater plantation life. Even far inland, well up intertidal rivers or on the brackish reaches of Pamlico Sound, most planters employed slaves to catch fish and harvest shellfish. Slave watermen guided their masters on recreational fishing trips and wielded the nets that provided the salted fish rations that were standard fare in the tidewater slave diet. The largest planters often designated at least one slave to fish routinely, while their less prosperous neighbors diverted house servants or agricultural laborers more occasionally to the seashore or riverbank to catch fish for both the slave quarters and the big house. The vast majority of tidewater planters owned fishing nets, from small "set-nets" to massive seines, fishing gear of all descriptions, and several boats that could be used for fishing.[23]

The largest fishery for plantation slaves lay on the Lower Neuse, along the estuarine waters between New Bern and the Pamlico Sound. There shad fishing was a spring ritual for thousands of plantation slaves. Slave fishermen pursued flounder, bream, trout, bass, catfish, gar, and perch, but the spring runs of shad warranted their heaviest exertions; a good shad season could supply ample food and fertilizer for the entire year.[24] Coping with strong wind tides and three-foot swells, they chased the shad with small seines and dragnets that could quickly be moved to fit the weather and fishing conditions. Dragnetting, in particular, opened up the great broad waters of the Lower Neuse to the slave fishermen. Working two men in a skiff or other small boat, they "footed 'er up," as the expression went, by finding a shoal, with perhaps three or four feet of water, on the edge of a deeper channel. A fisherman jumped overboard and held one end of the net, while his captain "shot" the net in a semicircle across the channel in the skiff. When the net was completely out, the captain joined his partner in the water, and the two drew the ends of the net together and hauled in on the line until the net closed around the shad. Then, in one great heave, they raised the net out of the water and into the boat.[25] Dragnetting for shad, small gangs of slave fishermen moved up and down the Neuse, often staying in shoreside camps at night.

The relatively small, light dragnets did not confine the slave fishermen on the Lower Neuse to a single stretch of beachfront. Unlike the massive, heavy haul seines used on Albemarle Sound, the dragnets allowed them a great deal of mobility, as well as the flexibility necessary to adjust quickly to sudden changes in fishing conditions. As they chose where to spread their nets, the slave watermen could be guided by their own experience, by their own intuition, and by the wind, tide, currents, and weather. Their dominance of fishing on the Lower Neuse and of the retail fish trade in New Bern reached the point that, in 1831, 56 white residents of Craven County petitioned the General Assembly, claiming that they were harmed "by the large gangs of slaves" who came up from the Lower Neuse "in boats . . . to sell, buy, traffic, and fish."[26] Even a generation later, during and after the Civil War, the local fish trade in New Bern remained exclusively in black hands.[27] Before the war, those fishermen and fish hawkers were part of a far-ranging pool of black watermen that followed the shad, at once a part of plantation life and yet briefly on their own, moving up and down the Neuse and mingling at night with other black boatmen and plantation slaves.[28]

In his narrative of his life as a slave, Charles Ball described a common, more sedentary version of this sort of small shad fishery. He worked in the fishery while in bondage at a cotton plantation near the Congaree River, in South Carolina, but it would have resembled the smaller shad fisheries along the alluvial rivers of North Carolina as well. It was not his first time fishing. He had grown up in tidewater Maryland, where, as he said, "I had been employed at a fishery on the Patuxent [River], every spring, for several years; and . . . I understood fishing with a seine, as well as most people."[29]

On discovering that Ball was fishing successfully during his respites from the cotton fields, his master in South Carolina bid him prepare a shad fishery for the spring season. Ball knit a seine himself that was probably a few hundred yards in length, and he led slave crews in constructing "two good canoes" in "less than a week."[30] A local white fisherman supervised the seining crew during the day, but he was evidently a hook-and-line man wholly unfamiliar with the ways of a seine fishery. He soon learned to rely on Ball's knowledge of shad fishing and gradually began to leave the seining entirely in the slave's hands during the night shift. This gave Ball and the other slave hands the opportunity to feast on fried shad (which their master did not allow them), as well as to trade their master's fish for bacon with a keelboat captain on his way up and down the river. "We all lived well," Ball recalled, "and did not perform more work than we were able to bear." Indeed, he wrote, "I was in no fear of being punished by the fish-master, for he was now at least as much in my power as I was in his."[31] While few slave fishermen gained that sort of sway over their overseer, Ball's experience is typical of the ways in which a command over fishing skills and the relative freedoms of a fishing beach could alter the usual dynamics of power between slaves and their overseers.

Other planters sent slave gangs considerable distances to fish by the sea. The surviving records of slave life at John H. Nelson's plantation at Garbacon Creek, where the young runaway Henry Singleton was bound, indicate how slave fishermen expanded the horizons of even the most isolated tidewater plantations. The Nelsons and their 33 slaves lived a quiet, secluded life. The south shore of the Lower Neuse estuary, of which Garbacon Creek was a small tributary, a passerby would write in 1863, "seemed almost wholly unsettled, the wilderness appearance only here and there relieved by the small clearing of a turpentine plantation, fishing establishment, or the twenty-acre field of a 'poor white.' "[32] The nearest town, New Bern, was located a day's sail up the Neuse River. Even fewer signs of civilization could be found inland. Below the Nelson plantation lay a wide pocosin known as the Open Grounds, where a traveler would not find even a small village until the peat bog merged 20 miles south with the salt marshes along Core Sound.[33] Life at Garbacon Creek revolved around the plantation, a few neighbors, and the local Methodist church.

Yet even at Garbacon Creek, the presence in Nelson's household inventory of a pilot boat and a mullet seine suggests that he sent slave crews to work on saltwater fishing grounds, probably 20 miles south either on Core Sound or on the Atlantic. The sort of pilot boat Nelson owned was an elegant, double-ended craft designed solely to crash through ocean surf—and jumping mullet schooled in great multitudes along Core Sound, but not the Lower Neuse estuary. Nelson must have found the plantation's proximity to the mulleting beaches a special temptation, enticing him to send his slaves coastward either under the custody of an overseer or during his family's summer holiday to the seashore. Many planters who lived upriver of Garbacon Creek, farther from the Atlantic, also owned nets and gear designed for seacoast fishing.[34]

Those seasonal jaunts exposed plantation slaves to a maritime society far more cosmopolitan than that to which they were accustomed. On the seacoast, they rubbed shoulders with black maritime laborers who moved frequently in and out of seaports. Among them they found access to the news, politics, and culture of Atlantic maritime society, linking the tobacco fields of Garbacon Creek to ports from New England to the West Indies.[35] Indeed, John H. Nelson was continuously outraged by the abolitionist politics that percolated through his little backwater settlement. According to one of his former slaves, Nelson once even lost his temper at a church "dinner on the grounds" and whipped a slave minister for preaching what he considered an incendiary passage from the Bible. The roots of Nelson's fury may well have been the coastal fishing beaches that fed his family and slaves so well. Somewhat farther inland, other plantation slaves took advantage of the sea's bounty when sent east to shepherd livestock in marshes and pocosins or to collect peat, seaweed, oyster shells, marl, and "trash fish" for fertilizer.[36]

Fishing did more than join tidewater slave quarters to Atlantic maritime society. The pursuit of fish and shellfish afforded coastal slaves a foundation for at least a small degree of independence from their masters' households in a way that could rarely be imagined inland. Unlike forests or fields, coastal waters provided plantation slaves with access to a public realm, as common law grounded in ancient English custom decreed saltwater fishing grounds to be. Tidewater slaves did not have any right to fish on estuaries or the ocean, of course, but neither did their presence on those waters indicate necessarily that they were violating a white man's rights, as it would have on land. The only white man's right that they could be violating was their master's rights to control his slave property. On the agricultural plantations in the state's interior, slaves found that the lack of a commons reinforced their dependence on their masters. This reliance on the big house heightened the difficulty of protecting their families, resisting their masters' withholding of rations as a means of labor control, or "laying out" for any length of time. The quality and extent of slave rations was one of the many battlefields where slaves and masters wrestled over control of the slave's labor, which was one reason why so many inland plantation slaves went to great lengths to trap, fish, or garden in secret.[37] Coastal slaves had quite an advantage in this regard. One should not overestimate the ease with which slaves fished on estuarine waters, or the difference it made in their lives, but coastal waters did provide bondmen and -women with an opportunity to supplant rations and build a small but significant measure of independence from their masters.

Many plantation slaves never fished for their masters but only for their own sustenance and recreation. In most cases, field laborers, house servants, and skilled artisans might still fish on Sundays, customarily a day for slaves to tend to their own household affairs, or after they completed the work quotas assigned by their masters. Young slave children took a special delight in fishing, and their early childhood provided a chance to gain fishing experience that might serve them well later in life, when they no longer had as much time to test local fishing waters or experiment with gear, boats, and bait.[38]

Given the pervasiveness of slave fishing, most planters must have looked upon it in a favorable light, much like gardening, so long as it did not interfere with the master's profits. Even though it sometimes weakened their authority, planters benefited by such enterprise. Many bought surplus fish caught by slaves on their own time and also allowed slaves to sell fish, shellfish, and saltwater game to nearby markets. When an Englishman named Charles Janson met slaves near the Alligator River carrying loggerheads, terrapins, and snapping turtles to the Tyrrell County seat of Columbia, he was discovering a widespread trade conducted by slave watermen either after work or on the sly. "In summer," Janson wrote, "the slaves catch them in abundance, and bring them to market."[39] At other seasons, they would have been bringing wild bird eggs, shad and herring roe, or oysters. Hunting and fishing lessened the expense of slave rations, and many planters looked to the lure of fishing rights to motivate their bondmen and -women to complete other duties. Of course, most coastal slaves took advantage of their proximity to fishing grounds no matter what their masters intended. Even the slave boatmen who dredged sediment and grist out of rice canals, as at Charles Pettigrew's Bonarva plantation at Lake Phelps, fished during lunch breaks in the same channels where they dug the rest of the day in waist-deep muck.[40]

Not all planters or overseers viewed slave fishing with equanimity. A former slave from South Carolina, John Andrew Jackson, had built a fish trap and anchored it in a stream that ran through a local swamp. His overseer, a man named Anderson, "heard of it, and organized a party to proceed to the swamp, and search for it." Anderson finally found Jackson's fish trap, robbed him of his fish, and destroyed the trap. According to Jackson, Anderson explained only that "fish were too good for niggers."[41] Denying Jackson fresh fish was an important part of keeping him "in his place," while at the same time preventing him from achieving any degree of self-reliance.

Other planters may have limited their slaves' access to fish and saltwater game out of other motivations. Along the Back Bay of Virginia, and probably its southern neighbor, Currituck Sound, planters reportedly limited the number of diamondback terrapins that their slaves could catch to five a week. The terrapins were delectable and nutritious, and they were very common in shallow sea-grass beds and freshwater marshes. If many slaves were catching more than five of the terrapins a week, they may have been bartering them with slaves inland or selling them in local markets. Either way, tidewater planters apparently grew concerned that terrapin hunting on that scale was making their slaves too independent, or they may have been motivated by conservation concerns if the terrapin populations were decreasing precipitously. They may have been especially troubled if slave watermen were using a method of terrapin hunting popular along Pamlico Sound in the late antebellum era: the burning of entire salt marshes to kill terrapins by the score.[42]

As a practical matter, few coastal planters could keep their slaves off the water. A slave who earned, was granted, or stole even a half hour of his or her master's time could collect mussels in freshwater creeks, terrapin or bird's eggs in brackish marshes, or clams, conchs, crabs, and oysters on tidal mudflats. Those crabs and shellfish were far more abundant and accessible before the Civil War than they are today and could be gathered easily by hand, with or without a small boat. Even the briefest lull in their duties or their masters' vigilance afforded slaves the opportunity to tend trot-lines, fish traps, or set-nets once they had been laid out. Slave boatmen could camouflage illicit fish traps and trot-lines by covering them with branches and reeds or by securing them underwater rather than to overhanging tree limbs or by floats.[43] They could mark their homemade fishing gear with natural signs such as sticks and vines. Sanctioned or not, slaves needed to visit a shoreline or creekbank only for a moment to harvest the catch and bait and reset their gear.[44]

Many coastal slaves crafted their own fishing gear. Hooks and weights could be made out of fish bones, floats out of gourds, trap walls out of rushes, and nets out of Indian hemp. They manufactured fishing weirs with wooden splints and stays, jerry-rigged crude seines by interlacing pine tops, and made fishing poles out of cane.[45] Slaves did not always have to resort to nature, however, to create their fishing tools. Levi Branham, a Georgia slave, "secured dress pins and made them into fish hooks."[46] Henry Clay Bruce, a slave in Virginia and Missouri, "made lines of hemp grown on the farm" but also used "hooks of bent pins."[47]

The making of fishing nets was a craft practiced by many tidewater slave fishermen and -women. They may have used wild hemp as a last resort, but probably relied more frequently on cultivated jute or on appropriating the twine from manufactured nets. A runaway from Lenoir County, North Carolina, was said to have "a quick hand to knit, sein[e] or net."[48] Another Carolina slave, a ferryman, "made shad nets in his spare time."[49] The former slave Charles Ball recalled how he "made a small net of twine that I bought at the store" to use to fish for himself, and then later, under his master's orders, knitted a much larger seine.[50]

Frustrated by the meager rations allowed him by his master, the ingenious Ball "resolved to resort to the water for a living." Before being sold into South Carolina, he had grown up on the Patuxent River in Maryland and, as he put it, "had all my life been accustomed to fishing." One Sunday he surveyed the Congaree River with a practiced eye and set about preparing the gear necessary to fish it. "With the help of an axe that I had with me," he wrote many years later, "I had finished before night the frame-work of a weir of pine stocks, lashed together with white oak splints. I had no canoe, but made a raft of dry logs, upon which I went to a suitable place in the river and set my weir."[51] The slave left the weir—a fishing barrier built out of wooden splints or reeds that relies on tidal currents or a river's downstream flow to direct fish into it—and returned several days later to discover a half bushel of fish.

Other slaves employed fish traps. They constructed the traps much like the fine grass or reed baskets that tidewater bondmen and -women wove for their own kitchens and to sell in town markets. Sometimes called "fish baskets," the homemade devices were round or squarish baskets with a narrow opening and a funneled interior pathway that made it easy for a fish to enter in search of the bait but difficult to find its way out. Weighting the traps with a brick or stone, slaves laid them on a river or creek bottom, secured by a line or a grapevine attached to a float or to an overhanging limb.[52] The traps mainly captured bottom-dwelling scavengers—catfish, eels, and crabs—though a Georgia slave caught river trout in a fish basket. Fish traps suited the contours of slave life especially well because they did not harm their prey's gills; a slave who could visit a trap only every few days might still find his or her catch fresh and, often, still swimming.[53]

Little is known about what slaves used for bait, but it is doubtful that the availability of bait was a serious impediment to fishing in the Carolina tidewater, at least not in the warmer months. Slave fishermen and -women could collect crickets, grubs, worms, and minnows by hand, and they probably used pieces of herring and menhaden to lure larger fish and crabs. Having hewn cooners or punts out of cypress logs with a fire and adze, they concealed those small boats with brush, buried them under earth, or hid them in a canebrake. By avoiding open waters and retreating onto salt marsh creeks, isolated bays, or bottomland swamps, savvy slaves who did not have their master's approval might still improve their diet now and then by fishing. Even in a reclusive marsh, a patient soul could gig flounder, nab terrapins, pilfer marsh hen eggs, and trap eels and crabs.

Plantation slaves took to the water with a special vigor after dark. "Night was the slave's holiday," Allen Parker remembered of his days as a slave fieldhand along the Chowan River. His memory, if not his sentiment, was echoed by Ebenezer Pettigrew, an Albemarle Sound planter who grumbled of slaves in 1806 that "night is their day."[54] Indeed, fishermen and -women were not the only slaves who took advantage of night's respite from the fields to work on the water—Wilmington slaves, for instance, slipped canoes off their plantations after dark and hawked firewood to steamboats anchored on the Cape Fear River.[55] But fishing was a far more common occupation for "the slave's holiday." Just as nocturnal game such as opossum and raccoon became a mainstay of the slave diet and recreation, so too did slave fishermen embrace fish and fishing techniques that could be utilized at night: gigging flounder or sturgeon by moonlight, netting shad and herring, laying fishtraps, and checking weirs. Slave fishermen were renowned for catching jumping mullet by carrying torches at night "in their cypress canoes," a fishing method that was apparently borrowed from the Algonquians, and for catching song birds and waterfowl by blinding them with bonfires at night.[56]

Fishing at night also entailed a special familiarity with nature. "Being out of doors a great deal of time, and having no books," wrote ex-slave Parker, tidewater bondmen and -women "learned many things from the book of Nature, which were unknown to white people, notwithstanding their knowledge of books."[57] Nothing in this "book of Nature" was more essential than knowledge of fishing and boating at night. London Ferebee, a former slave boatman on Currituck Sound, observed that as a boy he had learned to navigate "by the compass, or by any star."[58] Parker, commenting on how his masters relied on clocks to tell the time, likewise observed that "the slaves were obliged to depend upon the sun, moon, and stars and other things in nature."[59] The secrets of nighttime fishing and boating were clearly the slave's special domain, though how they found the energy to fish at night remains a mystery.[60]

Especially for slaves who lived adjacent to an estuary, fish and shellfish grew deeply ingrained in their material culture and diet. Poor people have never refused many gifts from the sea, and bondmen and -women were no exception. Tidewater residents utilized oyster shells to build roads and paths, as vessel ballasts, to make lime for building, as wall plaster, and as cutting tools. In the Pamlico Sound vicinity, poor fishermen even harvested boatloads of smaller oysters and sold them unshucked for a few cents per bushel to lime kilns and to planters upriver to use for fertilizer.[61] The ingenuity of tidewater slaves coupled with their poverty to make determined parents of invention. Gar skins could be used as a coarse leather, fish skeletons for pins and combs, seaweed and marsh mud for fertilizing garden plots in the slave quarters, sea bird feathers for pillows and blankets, turtle carapaces for bowls, oyster shells for fashioning carving tools or, burnt down and mixed with sand, for caulking cabins. Other seashells made good kitchen implements and garden tools.[62] Archaeological excavations of eighteenth-century coastal sites have revealed that some American slaves used sea shells in religious ceremonies, and this practice may well have continued into the nineteenth century. Shells played a central role in Igbo and Mande ancestral shrines in the South, including shrines to water deities such as the Igbo spirit Idemili.[63] Slaves of Kongo ancestry in tidewater North Carolina used sea shells to adorn graves.[64]

African Americans and poorer whites realized that nearly all marine and estuarine life was nutritious and could be prepared and consumed safely. Accustomed to making do, slaves showed little finickiness and a great deal of creativity when they combed the waterfront or seashore for fish and shellfish. Their willingness to consume fish not esteemed by their masters was especially important for it lessened the risk of potential conflicts over stealing from their catch. Around New Bern, a popular saying, "common as gar broth," referred to one abundant fish spurned by whites and relished by African Americans. A "trash fish" (a notion always in the eye, or taste buds, of the beholder) caught incidentally in river seines and gill nets, gar often reached 50 pounds and 5 feet in length. Other abundant coastal prey consumed only by blacks and the lowest classes of whites included menhaden, eels, saltwater catfish, conchs, blue crabs, snapping turtles, sliders, and some other turtle species.[65] A variety of sea birds, such as loons and herons, also fit this category. No documentary evidence confirms it, but one suspects that shrimp may have likewise fallen into this dietary realm. Local whites, including even the poorest white fishermen, rarely ate the little crustaceans until the 1930s, but slaves may not have been so squeamish. The slave quarter's competition for all such "trash fish" came not from the Big House, where they might be used in the kitchen, but from the fields, where they would be used as fertilizer.[66]

Archaeologists have not yet excavated slave sites adjacent to North Carolina estuaries. But if estuarine sites in Georgia, Florida, Virginia, and South Carolina can serve as a reliable guide, then coastal slaves enjoyed a comparatively diverse diet that featured other seafood rarely if ever eaten by their masters. An archaeological dig at a coastal plantation in South Carolina found evidence that slaves consumed 32 different marine species, including such unconventional delicacies as horseshoe crabs and sting rays, nearly three times the diversity eaten by their masters.[67] Moreover, such archaeological studies provide insight only into marine fauna with bones, cartilage, or shells durable enough to survive since the slavery era. They rarely find the fragile bones of probably the most widely eaten fish, herring and shad, and they say little, if anything, about whether coastal slaves indulged in more ephemeral, soft-bodied marine invertebrates, such as jellyfish, octopus, and squid, or if they found culinary uses for sea lettuce and other edible seaweeds. Slave consumption of none of these would be surprising; aside from the wealth of

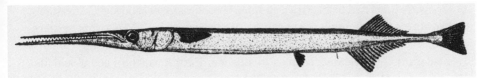

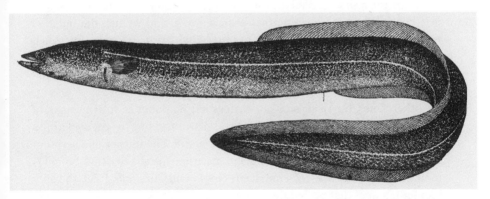

Gar (top), menhaden (middle) and common eel (bottom). These were among the "trash fish" disdained by most coastal whites, who often fertilized fields with them, but they were a staple in the diets of many coastal slaves. From Hugh M. Smith, *Fishes of North Carolina* (Raleigh: North Carolina Geological and Economic Survey, 1907).

foodways inherited from Africa and the Algonquians, coastal slaves inevitably had access to the knowledge of sailors, castaways, and other maritime settlers, of all races, who had explored the world's oceans and shared in the culinary wisdom of sea-oriented peoples in Europe, East Asia, the Pacific, and the Americas at large.

The sea's bounty afforded coastal slaves opportunities to improve their diets never found in upland parts of the South. Yet there were also dangers in relying so heavily on fish and shellfish. Neither slave nor free knew what the sea might provide or deny. An Atlantic storm could abruptly throw 10,000 stone crabs or a herd of pilot whales onto a beach without warning. Schools of bluefish, a voracious predator, drove multitudes of menhaden ashore. Other "freak accidents" of nature seemed no less a blessing to hungry souls. For instance, local people had long credited sudden, dramatic swings in temperature with paralyzing gray trout by the tens of thousands. The coastal poor rushed to the scene of such "trout numbs" to catch the stunned fish with dip nets or their bare hands before the fish recovered.[68] Fairly often, haul seiners also brought ashore catches of mullet, bluefish, or spot so large that they could not possibly find markets for them; they abandoned tons of the fish on the beach for sea gulls and the poor. Extant records do not say how coastal planters or their slaves reacted to such exaggerated signs of nature's beneficence, but it is hard to imagine that enslaved men and women did not find ways to partake of them. At the same time, the great fish runs on which coastal people had grown to depend occasionally failed to appear at all. Sometimes the fish simply vanished for a year—or five years—for reasons beyond the ken of even the old-timers.

At other times, hurricanes or nor'easters left no doubt as to the causes of scarcity: they devastated shellfish beds and drove fish out to sea, sometimes destroying the local maritime economy in a night. The impact of a series of hurricanes and nor'easters on fishing and maritime life at Currituck Sound is a good case in point. In 1828, a hurricane closed Old Currituck Inlet, the only navigable channel that passed through Currituck Banks and the sound's only entry for saltwater from the Atlantic. Cut off from the Atlantic, Currituck Sound was suddenly no longer a bountiful estuary rich in sea life; the great oyster beds died off, the salt marshes withered, and the famous mullet runs vanished. Over a period of a few years, Currituck Sound became a freshwater sea. Local fishing families, free and slave, haltingly began to find consolation in the thick growths of freshwater grasses that gradually took root in the new environment, turning the edges and shallows of the sound into one of America's great hunting grounds for migratory waterfowl. Market waterfowling, not commercial fishing or maritime trade, became the foundation of the Currituck Sound economy.

Then, in 1846, a March nor'easter raged out of the North Atlantic and buried Currituck Banks, briefly restoring saltwater to Currituck Sound. The saltwater killed off the freshwater fish and the freshwater grasses on which the migratory birds fed. The nor'easter drove salt spray over Currituck Banks and all the way across Knotts Island into Great Marsh Bay. The storm drowned livestock, contaminated fields with salt, and, perhaps most harmfully, dealt a fatal blow to longleaf pine forests that had been the islanders' most important source of wood for fuel and building. "From this loss the island to this day has not recovered, nor can it ever recover," wrote Knotts Islander Henry Ansell, more than 60 years later.[69]

As if Currituck Sound families had not suffered enough, in September 1846, another hurricane hit Currituck Banks, decimating crops at harvest time and blowing open two new Outer Banks inlets to the south—Oregon Inlet and Hatteras Inlet—that assured the marginality of Currituck Sound to maritime commerce for perhaps centuries to come.[70] Those storms were another powerful reminder that sudden, jolting cataclysms, not gradual change, marked the nature of coastal life. Slave and free shared the brunt of that reality and struggled to adapt to its harshest edges as best they could. Combined with the wind damage and saltwater contamination of fields and gardens, the loss of seafood in such calamities often led to food scarcity or famine.[71] On those occasions, if no other, both slave and free coastal residents must have looked enviously at the agricultural communities inland.

Reliance on fish and shellfish varied enormously, however. An average slave on the Outer Banks probably ate fish or shellfish nearly every day, a great deal of it fresh and procured while he or she was engaged in other maritime trades. In the brief moments during which some slaves inland could tend a garden on their own time, Outer Banks slaves combed the beaches for fish and shellfish or wandered onto the sound side of the islands to catch salt marsh game and waterfowl. Slaves who lived by estuaries probably partook of saltwater fish and game nearly as much. Excavation of estuarine plantation sites elsewhere in the coastal South indicates that slaves at those sites procured 40 to 70 percent of their total meat diet from the wild, a vastly higher percentage than slaves in uplands, and a powerful testament to their self-sufficiency.[72] At the Cannon Point plantation, on St. Simons Island, Georgia, 70 percent of that edible meat was fish.[73] Other slaves had much less access to fishing grounds.

For slaves on plantations upstream of estuaries, but with access to rivers or creeks, fishing was usually a Sunday pastime or a surreptitious vocation pursued only in the dark of night.

For all slaves who fished, whether for their masters' table or their own households, the rhythm of daily life was far different from that on a plantation in the upcountry. Along the tidewater, a slave fisherman or fisherwoman had to be attentive to the cadence of tides and currents. An awareness of the tidal flow, lunar cycles, wind shifts, and seasonal cycles of fishing—when the fish ran, where they spawned, what they ate, what their diurnal habits were, what wind and tide they favored—had to be second nature if a slave was going to take advantage of the sea's proximity, and more so than for their white masters and neighbors who did not have to fish around the confines of bondage. Along the Outer Banks and the sea-oriented villages by estuaries, coastal society moved to the sea's rhythms in ways that had little resemblance to conventional notions of daily bells and strict order on southern plantations. Along the plantation districts of tidewater North Carolina, the ring of the big house's bell still punctuated the daily routine of slave labor in the fields, but underneath that outward, workaday division of time, slaves moved to other, very different rhythms.

Fishing united plantation slave fishermen with both other African American maritime laborers and the handful of commercial fisheries that emerged prior to the Civil War. A slave who had made a name for himself as a capable fisherman might command or crew his master's other vessels, including flatboats, sloops, and other freight craft that sailed from the local wharf to seaports. He became acquainted with a host of maritime laborers in port and at the watermen's camps scattered along coastal waterways. In slack agricultural seasons, a planter was also prone to send a slave waterman to one of the seashore fisheries, where he might make a profit or at least catch fish and shellfish for the plantation. If a plantation household was disrupted by the master's death or illness, such that he could no longer supervise his bondmen, a slave fisherman had a marketable skill and could be hired out. The slave could make a profit either in a fishery or by hawking fish and oysters in town. Similarly, if a commercial fishery failed because of bad weather or ill luck, as often happened, a slave waterman likely found himself laboring at least temporarily back in his master's fields, with fishing reduced to a sideline.

Black watermen worked seasonally in all of the small commercial fisheries that existed before the Civil War. The pilots, stevedores, and boatmen employed at Shell Castle Island, the lighterage outpost at Ocracoke Inlet, exemplified this facet of maritime life. In 1789, David Wallace and John Gray Blount bought the shoal, formerly known as Old Rock, and built it up with sand and oyster shells into a 25-acre island. The Shell Castle complex eventually included a wharf, several warehouses, a gristmill, a lumberyard, a general store, a ship chandlery, and a tavern. Blount and Wallace employed approximately 20 slaves to unload cargo from seagoing vessels onto 35- to 75-ton lighters. The outpost also housed pilots and their boat crews, an unknown number of whom were African Americans.[74] Wallace managed Shell Castle, but the outpost was part of Blount's burgeoning empire. Blount was a reckless and fabulously wealthy speculator in swamplands, plantations, and slaves, eventually accumulating more than a million acres of land. He used Shell Castle to ensure a strong trading presence at the state's busiest inlet and also as a way station for his vessels that engaged in the West Indian trade. Fishing was a minor part of his Shell Castle enterprise but helped to balance his commerce with the West Indies and occupied his maritime slaves in slack seasons.

As early as 1803, the slaves at Shell Castle Island were already operating a dolphin fishery. A tremendous number of the sea mammals fed between Bogue Inlet and Hatteras Inlet every winter. In small boats, black watermen surrounded the dolphin pods and snared them by the score in long, heavy, wide-meshed seines. The seiners were known to have caught 200 or more in a single haul. They deployed several nets independently and fastened them together after the dolphins had been surrounded. That typically required four boats and a total of 15 to 18 crewmen. The rest was a grisly business. Once they had trapped them in the surf, the slave boatmen waded into the water and knifed the dolphins that had not already drowned. Then they gaffed the animals and dragged them ashore. Cutting off the flippers and dorsal fins, the men stripped off the skin and blubber and rendered their oil by fire. Each dolphin yielded on average 6 to 8 gallons of oil that was sold as an illuminant or lubricant.[75]

Though not as dramatic as the bloody fracas of wrestling dolphins in the surf, catching mullet also tested boatmanship and ingenuity. As early as 1793, the slave crews at Shell Castle Island sailed 90 miles south in the autumn to harvest striped, or "jumping," mullet for several weeks at Cape Lookout, at the western point of Core Banks.[76] Starting in late summer, mullet gathered in tremendous schools for a southward migration along the shoreline between

New River and Ocracoke Inlet. Out at Cape Lookout, the slave boatmen caught the delectably sweet fish in long, shallow nets and hauled them ashore on a beach or shoal, where they salted them and packed them in barrels, while no doubt putting more than a few aside to roast for their suppers. Mulleting demanded able boatmen who knew their way around local waters but also required an intimacy with the barrier islands to tolerate the camp life. A hardy, seasoned waterman who had grown up around the islands could find a cornucopia of fish, shellfish, and small game. To strangers, the banks usually seemed only a weary desert: hot in summer, cold in winter, arid, buggy, and exposed to vicious storms.[77]

For shelter in these harsh conditions, mullet fishermen drew on building practices and an architectural style that West African slaves had originally brought to the North Carolina coast. Grasping for words to describe one of the mullet camps on Ocracoke Island, a surprised traveler called it "a Robinson Crusoe looking structure," but of course he had never seen a West African roundhouse before.[78] He was by no means the only coastal visitor intrigued and mystified by the mullet camps.[79] Mullet fishermen built their shelters with vertical round walls and conical or hemispherical roofs. They left a small hole near the apex of the roof to release fire smoke, and, for access, they provided a rectangular opening, often only large enough to crawl through, facing away from the cold northeasterly winds that prevailed all winter. The men constructed the framework of juniper (red cedar) or live oak limbs brought from the maritime forests or from "ghost forests" overrun by migrating sand dunes. They covered the frame top to bottom with layers of thatching, apparently salt-marsh cordgrass (*Spartina alterniflora*) and possibly black needlerush (*Juncus roemerianus*), both extremely resistant to fire and salt spray. The fishermen bound the layers to the framework with strands of bear grass (yucca). Documented immediately after the Civil War along a hundred-mile stretch of coastline from Bogue Banks to Ocracoke Island, this African American mullet camp design was ideally suited to enduring the salt spray, high winds, and intense summertime heat on the Outer Banks and other barrier islands.[80]

Near Cape Lookout, other African American boatmen worked seasonally at a whaling fishery. From February to May, two or three crews pursued pilot, humpback, and sperm whales from camps at Shackleford Banks. A typical camp had three boat crews of six men each. Lookouts searched the horizon for whales while the other men seined along the shore for whatever fish could be caught and salted. When the lookouts spotted a whale, the crews dashed their

Mullet fishermen's camp, nets, and skiff, Shackleford Banks, ca. 1900. From Hugh M. Smith, *Fishes of North Carolina* (Raleigh: North Carolina Geological and Economic Survey, 1907).

pilot boats through the surf and pursued the great cetacean until they could harpoon it. The whale was allowed to "have its run" while a wooden drag attached to the harpoon by a long line gradually wore it down. When the boats caught up to the whale, a gunner killed it with an explosive cartridge. Ashore, the whalers stripped off the blubber and "tried out" its oil. Whalers were a poor class of men who made meager livings almost entirely from the sea, and the capture of even one or two whales made for a profitable season.[81]

Far more than they chased whales, slave watermen plied oyster beds so vast that modern observers might find their size beyond belief. Even 20 years after the Civil War, the state's first oyster survey charted more than 10,000 acres of natural oyster beds. The surveyor, Lt. Francis Winslow, found places such as Core Creek, near Beaufort, that had so many oysters he found it "easier to locate the spots where they were not, than those where they were."[82] Not until 1890 did Chesapeake Bay oysters decline enough to inspire Baltimore packing companies to open branch plants in North Carolina.[83] Before the Civil War, local watermen mainly worked oyster beds near coastal villages,

Shad fishermen's camp, Lower Neuse River, ca. 1900. Courtesy North Carolina State Archives, Raleigh.

particularly in the vicinity of Sladesville, Portsmouth, Bay River, Hunting Quarters, Beaufort, and Southport.[84] Their labors supplied salty oysters to taverns and hotels from Wilmington to Elizabeth City, and, once the first railroads had been built in the 1840s, to towns as far inland as Charlotte. In river towns, black vendors hawked fish and oysters through neighborhood streets every day at dawn.

Tonging for oysters was the coldest, dirtiest, and most hazardous fishery in North Carolina waters. To harvest the shellfish at their most flavorful and when they could be kept alive longest, oystermen worked during the dead of winter. Sailing dugout canoes, skiffs, or small, flat-bottomed scows (called "flatties") over the oyster rocks, they harvested the shellfish with short-handled, wood-headed tongs.[85] Wrestling the oysters from the rocks was drenching wet, icy cold labor that wore down body and soul. A coastal visitor observed of local oystermen after the Civil War that "the injury to health from exposure is so great that few ever reach old age."[86] Oystering was always a perilous vocation. The people who owned slave oystermen employed them instead of free labor in large part because of their fishing experience, knowledge of local waters, and boating skills. But oystering exemplifies the reasons why commercial fishing has always been even more dangerous than mining and logging. That African Americans played so dominant a role in those early fisheries had at least as much to do with the trade's perils as it did their prowess.

Together, the character of the coastal landscape and the nature of antebellum fishing loomed as a steady threat to plantation society in North Carolina. Fishing required flexibility to adjust quickly to changing currents, winds, and tides, as well as unfettered mobility to take advantage of a wide variety of different coastal environments. It relied on proficiency with small boats and an individual waterman's skill and knowledge, not things readily managed by a master or overseer. The lack of large commercial fisheries likewise curtailed the possibility of supervising slave fishermen adequately. To be effective, the fishermen worked alone or in small gangs, often in very remote locales. In the absence of large commercial operations, coastal fisheries also could not support processing centers that would have congregated slave laborers and made their supervision more realistic. A fisherman's life was hard, dangerous, and showed little profit, but it was also a relatively independent calling throughout the slavery era.

The necessity of conceding mobility to slave fishermen entailed trade-offs for their masters. Strict oversight of slave fishermen not employed in large crews or on open waters was difficult, counterproductive, and usually impractical. A planter, overseer, or driver might feasibly supervise slave gangs diverted from the fields to haul nets—but the mullet crews at Shackleford Banks? the oystermen at Southport Bay? the lone angler on Adams Creek who helped Henry Singleton to escape? So long as coastal planters relied on slaves to fish and boat, they would never have total control over them. The sea could not be shackled in that way. The twilight moment when a solitary fisherman aided Henry Singleton to cross Adams Creek is one shaft of light shed on an African American maritime culture deeply entwined with coastal plantation society, but we can be assured that much else moved within its shadows.

chapter three

Like Sailors at Sea

Slaves and Free Blacks in the Shad, Rockfish, and Herring Fishery

In 1840 William Valentine visited a seine fishery by the Albemarle Sound. The small-town lawyer was awestruck. Great crowds gathered to watch African American fishermen catching hundreds of thousands of shad, rockfish, and herring. The black boatmen wielded seines massive enough to span whole inlets and river mouths. They fished around the clock seven days a week, working at night in the flickering glow of torches, bonfires, and lanterns. The fishermen's chanteys, the great clouds of gull and osprey, and the thousands of writhing fish leaping in the surf all heightened the drama. Valentine was virtually overcome, he wrote in his diary, by the "throbbing, pulsating pleasure" that he felt when watching the fishermen make a big haul of herring or shad.[1]

Thriving along the Albemarle Sound from late in the eighteenth century until the Civil War, the shad, rockfish, and herring fishery that Valentine had witnessed was like no other in North Carolina.[2] The size of the catches dwarfed the state's other fishing industries. It was also gang labor, closely supervised, market driven, and export oriented. The work routines had little in common with those of other fisheries or maritime trades in local waters, reminding onlookers instead partly of life aboard seagoing vessels, partly of plantation life at cotton picking or tobacco harvest time. When colonial or antebellum residents looked east and referred to "the fisheries," they invariably meant those seine fishing camps that crowded the shores of Albemarle Sound and its tributaries. Along with their cousins by the Chesapeake Bay, the Albemarle seiners comprised by far the largest commercial fishery in the South prior to the Civil War. It was also the only major commercial fishery in North America that relied exclusively on slave and free black labor.[3] Looking at the watermen and -women who charted a path of survival through this unique blend of plantation slavery and shipboard work routines opens a distinctive chapter in the history of African American maritime life, one that provides insight into the intersection of slavery, the environment, and industry in the maritime South.

Shad and river herring share the taxonomic family of *Clupeidae* with sardines, menhaden, and other small, silvery fishes.[4] The members of that family have long included the most abundant and important food fishes in the world. Readily preserved by smoking or salting, they provided an inexpensive, high-protein (if rather bony) staple in early American diets. Harvested all along the Atlantic coast, the fish grew proverbial as the ration of soldiers, sailors, slaves, and slum dwellers. Rockfish, or "striped bass," on the other hand, belong to the bass family. While herring grow on average to a foot in length and half a pound in weight, and shad are only somewhat larger, a mature rockfish often weighed 50 pounds and, at lengths of up to 6 feet, had been known to tip the scales at 125 pounds.[5]

Rockfish, shad, and river herring are anadromous fish, which is to say that they usually live in salt water but spawn in fresh water. Along the rivers and sounds of North Carolina, their spawning runs extended from mid-February to early May. Huge schools annually migrated out of the Atlantic Ocean, entered Outer Banks inlets, and swam through Albemarle and Pamlico Sounds to lay their eggs in the rivers that flow into them. Albemarle Sound, which was more of a freshwater sea during most of the nineteenth century than the salty Pamlico, attracted numbers of fish that appeared infinite and inexhaustible.

The coastal Indians fished for herring, shad, and rockfish long before English colonization. Along the Albemarle, Iroquoian and Algonquian fishermen set up seasonal camps on the banks of rivers and creeks and used a variety of dip nets, gigs, weirs, and traps to catch the fish. The timing of the fish runs must have seemed a godsend. By the day that the herring reached Albemarle Sound, winter meat stores were often depleted; the fish's arrival was always a celebrated event.[6] English colonists who began to trickle into the Albemarle Sound vicinity from the Chesapeake in the 1650s quickly adopted Indian fishing techniques and fishing lore. A barrel or two of pickled herring became a customary part of every local family's winter storehouse from early colonial days well into the twentieth century.[7]

Commercial herring fisheries did not appear on North Carolina shores until late in the colonial era. In the 1740s, John Campbell and his son-in-law Richard Brownrigg established a fishery at Colerain, Campbell's plantation on the Chowan River in Bertie County.[8] Brownrigg later founded his own fishery, named Wingfield after a family estate on the Irish coast, on a Chowan River bay near the former site of a Chowaneoic Indian village. Brownrigg's son Thomas and an English minister named Daniel Earl—the "herring fishing parson" of a famous local doggerel—are credited with popularizing seine fishing along the Chowan, a wide blackwater river whose gentle flow made a good starting point for the fishery's development.[9] The Chowan River fisheries had grown sufficiently by 1764 to warrant laws protecting them, and shipments of pickled herring were soon playing a role in the busy mercantile trade between Albemarle ports and the West Indies.[10] The fish runs transformed life along the Albemarle tributaries: "You will see Roanoke in all its glory—cover'd with Seines," wrote planter James Cathcart Johnston in 1807, "its bank strewed with fish carts—fish and fish guts—more fragrant than the roses & lilies with which poets and romance writers have decorated their streams & rivulets."[11]

Whatever their real assessment of the aroma, Chowan County planters began establishing the first seine fisheries on the Albemarle Sound between 1800 and 1810.[12] They patterned their "beaches" on fledgling fisheries along the Chowan River and on older herring fisheries on Long Island and Chesapeake Bay, but moving out onto the sound allowed for a dramatic upsurge in the fishery's size.[13] Soon other merchants and planters invested in fisheries as well. The wealthiest planters around Albemarle Sound joined the ranks of the fishing entrepreneurs, including the Capeharts, Blounts, Pettigrews, Johnstons, Benburys, Littlejohns, and Collinses.[14] Those families all owned at least one plantation with river or sound frontage, as well as the sizable stocks of mules and oxen necessary to drag the seines ashore and cart the fish away.[15] They also owned considerable numbers of slaves and the capital or credit necessary to purchase boats, capstans, salt, barrels, and haul seines.[16] Many already had shipping interests in the West Indies or the Chesapeake Bay, so they could export salt fish directly from their wharves along with tobacco,

"Landward Boat," Belvidere fishery, 1856, by David Hunter Strother. Courtesy West Virginia and Regional History Collection, West Virginia University, Morgantown.

grain, cotton, pork, shingles, and staves. They also wielded the political clout to avoid undue restrictions on the size and extent of seining operations.[17] These planters revolutionized the local fishery by introducing seines a mile and a half in length and powerful, mule-driven windlasses to haul in the seines. They also employed tremendous numbers of free and enslaved African Americans to handle the giant seines and preserve the fish.

Moving beyond Albemarle Sound, other enterprising planters founded seine fisheries on its main tributaries and also on rivers flowing into Pamlico Sound, until more than 70 seine fisheries were operating by the late 1840s.[18] The seine fisheries made North Carolina waters the largest herring ground in the United States. Coastal merchants annually shipped out more than 90,000 barrels of salted herring and an unknown but "considerable quantity of shad and rockfish."[19] They sold primarily to merchants in Norfolk, Philadelphia, and Baltimore but also did business in other southern ports, the Bahamas, and the West Indies. There was also a sizable local business in shad and herring. Wagons crowded remote coastal roads during the spring season, bringing customers many miles to purchase the fish directly on the beaches.

State political leaders recognized the fishery as one of North Carolina's most important industries. An 1852 report by the General Assembly claimed,

"Seaward Boat," Belvidere fishery, 1856, by David Hunter Strother. Courtesy West Virginia and Regional History Collection, West Virginia University, Morgantown.

with a zeal typical of descriptions of the seine fishery, that it was "one of the most highly benefactious bestowed by the Great Creator, on mankind."[20] A Raleigh editor was no less impressed with the shad and herring fisheries, declaring that "for the very brief season they exist, they are decidedly the most important interest in the State."[21] Anticipating savory meals and a rare influx of cash, Albemarle residents of all races welcomed the spawning runs with a cheerful banter of market prices, haul sizes, and watercraft heroics. Shopkeepers closed stores, students vacated school, and judges excused fishermen from jury duty.[22] Educators and social reformers complained that they could accomplish nothing during the fishing season, one observing that the "public mind is occupied with the subject to the exclusion even of politics."[23] Another contemporary referred to his neighbors in springtime as being victims of "the fishery distemper."[24]

The removal of bald cypress stumps from river and sound bottoms was the crucial first step in building a seine fishery. With their wide, shallow waters, level sand bottoms, and placid currents, Albemarle Sound and its tributaries otherwise presented an ideal and nearly unique locale for using the seines. But the ubiquitous stumps, vestiges of swampy bottomlands overtaken over thousands of years by erosion and gradually rising sea levels, snagged and tore the valuable nets. "No prudent man will spend a dollar upon the shore," advised an Edenton fishery owner, "until he is satisfied that the water can be cleared of all obstructions."[25] Fishery managers consequently employed teams of African American divers to clear away the underwater stumps during the summer months.

Dislodging the stumps required great ingenuity, deft boatmanship, and diving skill. Bald cypresses have tenacious root systems and a resolute unwillingness to succumb to water rot and decay. Often referred to as the "wood eternal," cypress was the local wood of choice for shingles, canoes, and grave markers.[26] Their stumps did not give way without a fight. At smaller fisheries, slaves simply waded into the river, in one former slave fisherman's words, "and wrench[ed] them from their places with long hand-spikes"; this often required them, as he recalled, "to wade up to our shoulders, and often to dip our very heads under water."[27] Among the large seine fisheries along the Albemarle, the slave watermen employed what Frederick Law Olmsted called a "titanic dentistry." The famous landscape architect toured the Albemarle in the 1850s and described what he saw in *A Journey in the Seaboard Slave States*:

> The position of the stump having been ascertained by the divers, two large seine-boats are moored over it, alongside each other, and a log is laid across them, to which is attached, perpendicularly, between the boats, a spar, fifteen feet long. The end of a chain is hooked to the log, between the boats, the other end of which is fastened by the divers to the stump which it is wished to raise. A double-purchase tackle leads from the end of the spar to a ring-bolt in the bows of one of the boats, with the fall leading aft, to be bowsed upon by the crews. The mechanical advantages of the windlass, the lever, and the pulley being thus combined, the chain is wound on to the log, until either the stump yields, and is brought to the surface, or the boats' gunwales are brought to the water's edge.[28]

When this strategy failed to remove a stump, black divers resorted to more drastic methods. They first carved a deep cavity in the recalcitrant stump with a long, iron-tipped spike. After a diver had situated the spike on the stump, the crews erected a platform between two seine boats in order to gain enough leverage to drive the spike into the stump with sledgehammers. Then they inserted a long iron tube with a detonation cap into a cylindrical tin box filled with gunpowder, and they waterproofed the joint with soap or tallow.

Submerging again, the diver guided the end of this tube connected to the tin box carefully into the hole in the cypress stump, the other end remaining above water. Then:

> The diver . . . is drawn into one of the boats—an iron rod is inserted in the mouth of the tube—all hands crouch low, and hold hard—the rod is let go—crack!—whoo—oosch! The sea wells, boils, and breaks upward. If the boats do not rise with it, they must sink; if they rise, and the chain does not break, the stump must rise with them. At the same moment the heart of cypress is riven; its furthest rootlets quiver: the very earth trembles, and loses courage to hold it![29]

The method was as dangerous as it was dramatic. The divers had to adjust the placement of the spike, the amount of gunpowder, and the depth of the tube to fit exactly the size of the stump and the water depth. A miscalculation could overturn the seine boats or prove fatal. Despite the dangers, African American divers removed as many as a thousand cypress stumps off a single fishing beach. Fishery owners customarily used rewards of brandy, tobacco, or special privileges to motivate the divers to work their hardest.[30]

When the herring began their run into Albemarle Sound, approximately 3,500 African Americans labored in the seine fishery.[31] Thousands more independent fishermen of all races used bow nets, stake nets, and gill nets to harvest the spawning fish. Indeed, during peak season it is likely that few able-bodied souls did not fish. Even men and women so downtrodden that they could not build a dugout canoe could still fashion an ash bow net and a jerry-rigged stand that leaned far enough over a small creek to fish successfully. While most documentary records refer to seine fisheries owned by large planters, an 1857 petition from Martin County acknowledged the importance of the shad, rockfish, and herring runs to poor Carolinians, calling coastal waterways "a great public blessing . . . that a great many persons in indigent circumstances . . . [use] to supply their families with fish, and other necessaries of life."[32]

Seine fishery managers ritually recruited their black workers every year soon after Christmas. Enlisting the fishermen, fish cutters, and tradesmen necessary to work a seine often proved difficult. Few planters owned enough male slaves of the right age to handle the great seines, much less the women and children necessary to clean the fish. Even the most prosperous slaveholders were reluctant to divert so many laborers from agricultural duties to staff a fishery. As a result, fishery operators augmented their own slaves with other African American laborers, often both free people of color and slaves hired for the fishing season.

Many fishery owners preferred to employ free blacks rather than slaves. That would not have been a realistic choice elsewhere in North Carolina, but a large class of free blacks resided in the counties north of the Albemarle Sound, where they scratched out a living by hunting, trapping, fishing, and farming. A high percentage descended from free people of color who had migrated out of southeastern Virginia early in the eighteenth century in order to evade that colony's stricter legislation against free blacks and mixed-race marriages. Many of the original emigrants had apparently been the progeny of marriages between black men who were slaves and white women who were indentured servants.[33] Free blacks had comparatively higher civil status in North Carolina, where they even enjoyed voting rights from the American Revolution until 1835.[34]

In 1840, Pasquotank County had a free black population of nearly 2,000, which represented 15 percent of the county's residents. More than 900 free blacks lived in Camden and Hertford Counties, and sizable free black populations also resided in Gates, Chowan, Perquimans, and Bertie Counties.[35] An uncertain number of free blacks journeyed coastward from as far away as Halifax and Northampton Counties, 90 miles and more to the west. There is not enough documentary evidence to estimate the ratio of slaves to free blacks who fished along the Albemarle, but it is clear that significant numbers of free men and women worked alongside their enslaved brethren. The reasons behind the preference for free black laborers seem apparent. Planters required the bulk of their slave labor to till and sow their fields, especially toward the end of the fishing season in the late spring. Fearful of giving slaves a taste of life off the plantation and uneasy at the freewheeling character of a fishing beach, many slaveholders were also reluctant to hire their enslaved laborers to the shad and herring fisheries. Local hiring-out contracts often specifically prohibited slaves from fishing, usually the only occupational prohibition in the contracts.[36] At the same time, fishery managers never hired free white labor except as superintendents. Free blacks could be paid less and worked harder, and it is doubtful that fishery operators could have enticed white yeomen to abandon their own fields, gardens, or woodlots for so long in order to answer at all hours to the demands of a seine fishery. In addition, employing black laborers was an opportunity to take advantage of African American fishing, boating, and diving skills that had been proverbial in North Carolina since the colonial era.[37]

To facilitate recruitment, fishery owners attended annual "fishermen's courts" to hire black workers. Held during the first circuit court session of the year in county seats near the Albemarle Sound, fishermen's courts were quite a spectacle. All court sessions combined elements of high drama, county fairs, and livestock auctions. "In those days," the Reverend Reuben Ross recalled of his youth along the Roanoke River in the early 1800s, "court days were a kind of Saturnalia."[38] Hawkers, cockfights, boxing matches, minstrel acts, and medicine shows were standard fare. The festive atmosphere was only heightened by the addition of several dozen recruiters competing to find fishermen, fish cutters, and tradesmen. Fishermen's courts also involved plenty of drinking and carousing for both free and slave. "Everybody would seem to be there buying or selling rum, beer, cider, oysters, or gingerbread," Reverend Ross remembered.[39]

Behind the frivolity, fishermen's court was serious business. Like ship recruiters of the era, fishery managers needed to find a good number of experienced workers; they did not expect every hand to know how to lay a seine or handle a shad galley, but they required a critical mass of seasoned workers, perhaps a quarter of the total, in order to have a successful season. The other workers performed jobs that required mainly brawn and perseverance or were expected to master finer aspects of the trade with practice. Several duty stations, however, absolutely required highly skilled and experienced workers, much as did vessels at sea. In the late 1840s, for instance, Edenton fishery owner Edward Wood traveled a day's journey to attend fisherman's court in Gatesville because he desperately needed to recruit a seine mender.[40]

Similarly, for African Americans the court presented a crucial and dicey set of negotiations. It determined their living conditions, their personal safety, and, for free blacks, the vast preponderance of their wages for the year. Slaveholders seem to have perfunctorily auctioned off unskilled hands to the highest bidder.[41] Skilled fishery workers were so valuable, however, that they had more say in what fishery they joined and commanded special status and pay. Fishery superintendents had to understand that they could buy a slave's labor, but without proper inducements they could not assure themselves the full fruits of that labor. Skilled slave fishermen could get the job done in a satisfactory manner without exerting the extra effort required to make a truly great haul, and a skilled fish cutter had no reason to cut more than a passable, but unexceptional, 10,000 herring a day unless a fishery superintendent found

"Going Out," Montpelier fishery, 1856, by David Hunter Strother. Courtesy West Virginia and Regional History Collection, West Virginia University, Morgantown.

proper incentives. Those inducements—store credit, West Indian rum, a share of the catch to take home—may seem modest, but Albemarle slaves found them inspiring. For free blacks, and for skilled slaves left by their masters to haggle on their own behalf, fishermen's court was even more important. Because they were often paid in shares based on the fishery's catch, they had to consider both the reputation of its superintendent and the relative merits of its location.

The crowds of slaves and free blacks headed coastward in late February or early March, sometimes walking several days to reach a fishing beach. On the shore, they lived in weather-beaten camps that were a jumble of barracks, warehouses, sheds, stables, and salting houses.[42] In addition to 1 or 2 white superintendents, a typical fishery employed 30 to 40 black fishermen and 10 to 20 fish cutters, as well as coopers, seine menders, cooks, and hostlers.[43]

The fishermen combed the water with gigantic seines that averaged approximately 2,500 yards in length and ranged from 12 to 24 feet in depth. Those nets spanned entire river mouths, channels, and inlets. Typically having a two-inch mesh in the center and 3-inch mesh in the wings, they were woven in New England from imported hemp. The fishermen waterproofed the nets locally by soaking them in a tar and water mixture and sun drying them for several days.[44] In crews of eight to twenty, they laid out the seines in two long rowing boats, known as shad galleys, usually 40 to 60 feet long, 8 to

"A Night Haul," by David Hunter Strother, from *Harper's Weekly*, September 28, 1861. Courtesy North Carolina State Archives, Raleigh.

10 feet wide, and a little less than 4 feet deep. Built out of white oak and cedar, with flat bottoms, a sharp bow, and a wide transom stern, the boats had the stability to support the heavy seines and to maneuver easily over their lines.[45]

Laying the seines around schools of a hundred thousand fish required an orchestra's sense of timing and teamwork. The fishermen first packed the seine on the stern platforms of their two boats. They rowed together approximately a mile directly off the landing, and then the helmsmen steered the boats in opposite directions, parallel to the shore, as the two crews slowly laid out the seine between them. Hundreds of large corks attached to a top line kept the seine afloat. "When the seine is all played out," observed a journalist visiting Albemarle Sound in the 1850s, "heavy ropes, made fast to the staves securing either end, are carried to the great four-mule windlasses at the extremities of the beach, from eight to twelve hundred yards apart." The combined length of the two ropes and the seine reached nearly two and a half miles. "As the circumference of this vast sweep is diminished," the writer continued, lines are attached to inner windlasses of less power, until the center pair, of one-mule power and not more than a hundred yards apart, are put in motion. The circle of the net has now become so small that the inclosed shoals may be seen leaping, swimming with their back fins out, and churning the water in their affrighted movements. Presently the mules are discharged, and all hands called to handle the ropes. Fifty stalwart men rush into the water, waist-deep. . . . A few minutes of heavy dragging and the flashing, wriggling mass is rolled upon the beach [and] a line of wide planks is hastily staked up behind.[46]

The size of their catches confounds the imagination. The black fishermen often caught 100,000 herring in a single haul and occasionally more than half a million.[47] As a general rule, fishery owners estimated that their workers caught one-tenth to one-twentieth the number of shad as herring, but that was still a phenomenal quantity. Fishing crews caught far fewer rockfish, but at rare moments rockfish runs sometimes rivaled the harvest of the smaller fish. Though they averaged catches of 20,000 to 40,000 pounds of rockfish a season, in 1858 slave fishermen at W. R. Capehart's Black Walnut Point fishery in Bertie County purportedly caught 30,000 pounds in one haul.[48]

There was a quality of epic drama in the struggle to land a large catch. Both fishermen and bystanders felt it, and many people visited the fisheries simply for the amusement. Rev. Reuben Ross, of Williamston, long recalled the "animated crowds along the fishing shores" of the Roanoke River.[49] Fishery owners invited guests from the state's interior to watch the black fishermen work, and their children frequently asked boarding school chums to join them at the fishing beaches.[50] William Valentine, the local lawyer who seemed to find an erotic edge to the Albemarle fisheries, was not the only observer to find himself entranced by the carefully choreographed dance of the haul seiners.[51]

A number of coastal visitors believed that the African American fishermen shared this enthusiasm for the seine fishery. British journalist William Howard Russell encountered a group of North Carolina plantation slaves headed toward a distant fishery. He later wrote that they were exceptional among the slaves that he met in the United States. "The only evidence of the good spirits and happiness of [slaves] which I saw was on the part of a number of men who were going off from a plantation for the fishing on the coast. They and their wives and sisters, arranged in their best—which means their brightest colors—were grinning ear to ear as they bade good-by."[52]

Another journalist, David Hunter Strother, who wrote under the name Porte Crayon, found similar excitement among African Americans en route to the fisheries. He described black laborers traveling coastward to join the fishery "as to an annual festival."[53]

While such claims from white observers must always be taken with more than a grain of salt, one can imagine several reasons why African Americans would look forward to the seine fishery. Few could deny the pleasures of fishing compared to most other occupations held by free or enslaved blacks. One writer, in fact, claimed that the black fishermen were "passionately fond of the sport and excitement."[54] They must also have appreciated the financial rewards. Free black fishermen earned comparatively good wages—and *any* wage was comparatively good in that time and place—and both they and their slave brethren earned bonuses in cash, scrip, tobacco, or spirits for catching or cleaning extraordinarily large quantities of fish. Fishery managers offered similar incentives to compensate black laborers for giving up customary privileges. In a fictional but generally reliable account of daily life while he was a tutor at Scotch Hall plantation, in Bertie County, George Higby Throop described the Capehart family paying $1.00 bonuses to fishery slaves for working on Sundays.[55]

The former slave Charles Ball's account of shad fishing along the Patuxent River in Maryland also mentions the fishery's festive nature, but concentrates more on the luxury of having enough food to eat. "In Maryland," Ball wrote, "the fishing season was always one of hard labor, it is true, but also a time of joy and hilarity. We then had . . . plenty of bread, and at least enough bacon to fry our fish with . . . [as well as] a daily allowance of whiskey, or brandy."[56] After he was sold to a cotton planter in South Carolina, Ball chose to fish on his own mainly because he was deprived otherwise of an adequate diet. He stressed the availability of fresh fish again when he described the small shad fishery that he founded on the Congaree River, near his new master's plantation. His master allowed slave fishermen to dine only on the "trash fish"— pike, perch, eels—that they caught and cooked over coals and ate without seasoning. Ball rejoiced when he was left with the responsibility of overseeing the fishery during its night shift, while the superintendent slept, because he and the other slave fishermen began to dine secretly on the far more delectable shad. They even bartered shad for bacon with which to fry their fish. "We at the fishery lived sumptuously, although our master certainly believed that our fare consisted of corn-bread and river-fish, cooked without lard or butter," he wrote.[57]

Slaves like Ball must also have welcomed the camaraderie of the fishing camps. Few slaves had so good an opportunity to come out from under the shadow of the big house. In their waterfront camps they mingled with black neighbors and made the acquaintance of black fishermen and fish cutters from more distant parts. Surviving records have little to say about what the black fishermen and fish packers did at these seasonal camps when they were not working, but we can be sure that they took advantage of the chance to renew old ties, forge new friendships, and share the last year's news from up and down Albemarle Sound. If the few moments of leisure at fish camps resembled seagoing life in this aspect, as in so much else, then the fishermen and -women also indulged in music, gambling, storytelling, dancing, and other ribaldry, particularly after a big haul. William Howard Russell, the British journalist, went so far as to say that the slave fishermen felt "for the moment free."[58]

Historical documents tell us very little about how the shad and herring fishermen and -women participated in the slave revolts, runaway camps, and other antislavery activities of the day. Because the fishery was seasonal, even when court records or other documents list a rebellious slave's occupation, they indicate "fieldhand," "blacksmith," or "boatman," rather than "fisherman." What we do know is that at various times, from Gabriel's Rebellion in 1800 to the black boatlift of slaves to freedom during the Civil War (see Chapter 6), slaves in the Albemarle Sound vicinity conspired with one another quickly, methodically, and over large distances. Better cover for the far-flung plotters to convene is hard to imagine. One has to suspect that the shad and herring fishery played a central role in building a regional African American culture and in holding together the antislavery movements that percolated through the Albemarle.

No matter how enlivening, the fishery was still a Herculean test of endurance and perseverance. One observer described the ardor and stamina required of the laborers as "equal to that of a brisk military campaign in the face of an enemy."[59] The fish ran so bountifully during the six- to eight-week peak season that the fishermen worked the seines every day of the week, all day and all night. Every haul lasted on average from four to seven hours, making three or four hauls daily an accomplishment.

The log books kept by Edward Wood offer a unique look at the working conditions experienced at a seine fishery. Beginning in 1844, Wood recorded

"Repose of Fishermen," 1856, by David Hunter Strother. Courtesy West Virginia and Regional History Collection, West Virginia University, Morgantown.

daily weather and fish hauls at his Montpelier fishery on Albemarle Sound. Though his log entries are blunt and brief, the daily reality of the fishery can still be culled from them. Take typical entries from the relatively warm, windy spring of 1844: March 19, "Strong SW wind, attempt to shoot [seine] at 10 o'clock but could not get out"; March 23, "North wind Rope broke, came near loosing seine"; April 9, "Light SW wind—dead line broke four times"; April 27, "strong E wind rope broke and did not get the seine till night." Even a mild spring obviously exacted a heavy price on the seine fishery's equipment and workers; a bad year, like 1847, could be disastrous. That year not only did the fish run unevenly, but unusually strong currents and high winds slowly tore apart Wood's seine. Consider March 13, "Wind N and moderate—have torn the seine every haul at upper end"; March 16, "Wind west and N.W. very hard—hung in the mud all day & tore to pieces"; March 19, "Wind light E. & N.E.—hung in mud all night & 12 hours to make a haul."[60]

Wood's log reveals that winds, currents, and weather made conditions on the water highly unpredictable. The cadence of the work shifted abruptly from almost unbearably intense labor to extended periods of tedium while waiting for clear weather or equipment repairs. At times, the seine seemed to take on a life of its own, writhing and turning until it risked sinking the boats. The fishermen continually had to adapt to new water conditions and improvise on the spur of the moment to recover ripped, mired, or drifting seines and ropes while losing as few fish as possible. Surrendering an entire seine, the product of six or more hour's sweat, was an unthinkable loss. However, the logs do confirm that the coastal travelers who described the fishery in such mythic prose had not exaggerated its exertions. Behind terse log entries such as "12 hours to make a haul" and "hung in the mud all day" lay endless hours of backbreaking toil in miserable weather simply to preserve the seine, to say nothing of hauling in tons of fish.

March was the most trying month. Often the coldest days of Albemarle Sound winters occurred in March. Those days left seines and lines frozen stiff and boatmen hacking their way through ice. Entries like that for March 13, 1846—"Wind North, Rainy and disagreeable"—appear frequently in Wood's log.[61] The winters of 1831, 1848, and 1859 were especially cold for fishing; in 1859, the fishing grounds froze so hard that carriages crossed the ice over Albemarle Sound from Edenton to Plymouth. Yet the Montpelier fishermen rarely missed a haul, even when catching only a paltry few thousand fish daily. Wood cut his losses due to bad weather by tying wages to the size of the catch. But bearing in mind the short fishing season and the enormous fixed capital investment in seines, salt, barrels, and provisions, it is still no wonder that fishery owners insisted that weather not interfere with "making a seine." For their black workers, though, this meant enduring remarkably difficult and dangerous water conditions.[62] By mid-April the weather grew warmer, but seine fishing was never easy.

If unpredictable fish and bad weather gave the fishermen occasional breaks from their toil, they needed careful planning and good fortune to take even a catnap on many days. At times the shad and herring seemed to overawe the mere mortals struggling to rein them in. A correspondent to the *Albemarle Enquirer* long recalled the fishing season of 1845. "The streams were literally alive with the fish," he wrote. "The water everywhere swarmed with them. So thick were they that considerable quantities were dipped up at bridges over the creeks in common farm baskets, and they were actually swimming about in many of the ditches on farms, contiguous to the sounds."[63] Edmund Ruffin, the famed Virginia agriculturalist, visited several seine fisheries in the hectic midst of such fish runs during the late 1850s. He observed that "the hands, like sailors at sea, work and rest . . . not by day and by night, but by shorter 'watches.'"[64] William Valentine likewise marveled at "what regularity and system they manage so as to allow time for all to rest," yet he acknowledged, too, that the fishermen sometimes "have almost to banish sleep."[65]

Because they needed to complete their labors between hauls, the cutters, washers, and salters—mostly African American women and children—maintained a pace that rivaled that of the haul seiners. When the fishermen loaded their net for the next haul, the women and children had already begun their work on the beach. They first sorted out the herring, shad, and rockfish and separated the prized roe herring from the "buck" herring. They also culled from the "trash" or "offal" fish the few species, such as trout, perch, and sturgeon, that might have local markets if sold fresh. The trash fish would eventually manure coastal farmlands.[66] The shore workers next headed and gutted the shad and herring. An average fish cutter cleaned several shad or an astounding 25 to 30 herring every minute, or well over a thousand an hour. It was cold, wet, arduous toil, requiring rapid, repetitive hand motions. Yet pay or premiums based on piece-rate production (so many cents per 1,000 herring headed, for example) often spurred the most skilled cutters to a blinding pace. At the Montpelier fishery, top cutters Elvy Speight, Anna Holland, and Edy Howell headed tens of thousands of herring a day.[67]

The laborers next washed the blood and grime off the fish by dipping handbarrows full of them into water. They carried the shad and rockfish directly to a packinghouse and emptied wheelbarrow loads into the salting trays for "first salting." Using six-foot paddles that resembled narrow oars, two workers stirred approximately a peck of salt into every herring batch. Finally, they scooped the herring into vats next to the salting trays to allow the salt to permeate the fish for several days. Other hands, often older black men, later packed the herring, shad, and rockfish into barrels, layering them with roughly two pecks per barrel of a finer quality salt. An experienced packer loaded 15 to 20 barrels a day.[68]

While the seine fisheries shipped the large majority of their salted herring and shad to northern markets, they also sold a significant quantity of fish directly on the beach. The first fresh fish of the season commanded high prices locally, but the fish could soon be had for only a few cents.[69] Farmers

April 8th 1856.

"Heading Herring," 1856, by David Hunter Strother. Courtesy West Virginia and Regional History Collection, West Virginia University, Morgantown.

descended upon the coast to buy trash fish by the cart load and many planters bought herring for a price as low as 75 cents a thousand to supply their slaves for the year.[70] Fishery owners tried to arrange for bulk purchases of fresh fish well before the season, but they often had so large a surfeit that no sale could be overlooked.[71] At the company store by his wharf, Edward Wood sold fresh perch, rockfish, and catfish, as well as briny kegs brimming with salted sturgeon and herring.[72] The scene at the fishing beach was doubly lively for its haggling over fish prices. Fish hawkers and merchants from towns upriver

"Betsy Sweat," fish cutter and cleaner, 1856, by David Hunter Strother. Courtesy West Virginia and Regional History Collection, West Virginia University, Morgantown.

were always among the buyers, and companies like R. & J. Dunn of Halifax regularly advertised consignments of herring and shad "put up this season at one of the most celebrated fisheries on the Roanoke."[73]

The great seine fisheries thrived for a mere half-century. Only a scattered few, mostly on the Chowan River, survived the Civil War.[74] Fishermen had already observed large declines in catches by the early 1840s.[75] Blaming overfishing, a group of fishery owners petitioned the North Carolina General Assembly for government regulation of the use of seines, especially for restrictions against Sunday fishing and seining across the entire width of channels and inlets.[76] A special report by the General Assembly concluded in 1852 that "where plenty abounded, there is now scarcity and disappointed hopes."[77]

Though a marked decline in fish stocks occurred in the mid-nineteenth century, shad and herring fishing still flourished in the Albemarle Sound vicinity after the Civil War.[78] Without the availability of slave labor, however, fishery owners scaled back their aspirations and relied on technology. "Dutch nets," a type of pound net requiring less labor, replaced most of the giant seines by the 1870s. Steam-powered winches and boats enabled fishery managers to employ fewer laborers for the handful of remaining seines. Shad and herring catches continued to decline, and by 1892 an Elizabeth City editor observed that the "Chowan River fishery has . . . been virtually abandoned."[79] Local people soon began to point to the Capehart seine fishery in Bertie County as a historical curiosity.[80] The arrival of the diminished schools of shad, herring, and rockfish nevertheless remained a festive event and an important source of food and income along the Albemarle. Not until after World War II did coastal development, pollution, and oceanic factory trawlers destroy the commercial fishery altogether. By the time that sunny assertions about the inexhaustibility of the fish were proven wrong, the great seines, their spectacular catches, and the African American laborers whose skill, banter, and song had sparked the annual ritual had long been forgotten.

chapter four

A March Down into the Water

Canal Building and Maritime Slave Labor

In 1786 the brig *Camden* arrived in Edenton harbor with a cargo of 80 West African slaves. This was not an everyday occurrence. Few slaving ships entered the harbors of North Carolina directly from Africa. Most new slaves arrived via a more circuitous path leading through Charleston, the Chesapeake Bay ports, or, less often, the West Indies. The slave trade had evolved toward southern ports with better deepwater harbors, more lucrative exports, and larger plantations.[1] This had made slavery only marginally less integral to the state's economy; when the *Camden*'s crew lowered her sails off Edenton, the slave population of North Carolina already exceeded 100,000, 35 percent of the state's total population. Slaves were concentrated in far higher numbers in the plantation belt counties of the tidewater and coastal plain than in the piedmont counties, where small, mixed-crop farms were more the rule.[2] But the vessel's cargo of unseasoned Africans—all male, unfamiliar with the Americas, speaking no English except what they might have picked up on the transatlantic voyage—reflected the fact that their importers had a special fate in mind for them.

Josiah Collins and his two Edenton business partners had formed the Lake Company to transform a large pocosin on the south side of Albemarle Sound into an agricultural plantation. This vast tract, located by Lake Phelps, in Washington County, lay in the remote heart of a swamp that stretched 60 miles along the Albemarle and 30 miles to the south. That great wilderness had been the last holdout of the native forces in the Tuscarora War of 1711–13 and remained, long after the American Revolution, a soggy thicket with scarcely any roads, no towns, and few inhabitants. It was a mosquito-infested land of vipers, panthers, bears, malaria, and lawlessness. If it was going to be developed, Collins and his partners knew, they needed slave labor to construct the canals that would drain it. They anticipated the feelings of another planter who later resided on the shores of Lake Phelps: "Negroes are a troublesome property," William S. Pettigrew wrote in 1847, "and unless well managed, an expensive one, but they are indispensable in this unhealthy and laborious country; for these long canals, that are all important in rendering our swamplands valuable, must be dug by them, or not at all."[3]

The Lake Company set the "new negroes" from the *Camden* to digging the canals that eventually turned the pocosins around Lake Phelps into one of the largest plantations in North Carolina. The Lake Company directors believed that unseasoned West Africans could best dig the canals. The pocosins were isolated and the African workers had no family in the Albemarle vicinity; Collins and the other Lake Company investors would not have to risk reprisals from or escapes to the slave communities nearby. The Africans had acquired neither the knowledge of coastal geography nor the familiarity with the slave underground necessary to have any hope of escaping.

The African slaves at Lake Phelps toiled in waist-deep muck, sunup to sundown, day in and day out. They suffered steadily from malaria and other fevers. They endured the hottest, most humid summer days and clouds of insects. They came to know a system of discipline and punishment brutal even by the usual standards of slavery, one almost unique to canal sites. With the slaves working in those conditions, one wonders if Dorothy Redford, a descendant of the slaves at Somerset Place, was right when she wrote in her moving memoir that the physical suffering was not the worst of it. Worse, Redford concluded after reviewing the Lake Company's records, "was the emotional shock of being ripped from their tradition-soaked homeland and the unspeakable anguish of ending up in a completely unrecognizable land."[4] The life of slave canal workers was so excruciating that some preferred death. "At night," wrote William Trotter, the Lake Company's overseer, the Africans "would begin to sing their native songs. . . . In a short while they would become so wrought up that, utterly oblivious to the danger involved, they would grasp their bundles of personal effects, swing them on their shoulders, and setting their faces toward Africa, would march down into the water singing as they [were] recalled to their senses only by the drowning of some of their party."[5]

To understand fully the despair of the newly imported Africans, we must turn from broad estuaries and crowded ports to remote, sun-baked marshes and humid swamp forests, where avaricious masters worked men literally to death. These isolated camps reflect a grisly but important aspect of slavery and maritime life. Though it hardly makes for a popular image of maritime or plantation society, the work of canal builders played a crucial role in coastal North Carolina for four generations, roughly from 1785 to 1860. Laborers— most, but not all, of them slaves; most, but not all, of them black—built canals essential to maritime commerce, circumventing dangerous shoals and inlets along the Outer Banks and joining the sounds of North Carolina with the Chesapeake Bay. They dug canals that bypassed river falls, opening the commercial traffic of the piedmont to coastal ports. When slave laborers dug smaller canals for swamp drainage, water power, or rice cultivation, those narrow channels doubled as local waterways: for rafting goods to market, for floating timber and shingles out of swamp forests, for gaining access to fishing grounds, for visiting neighbors and going to town. The building of canals involved at least a variety of small workboats and as much as a modest flotilla of barges, houseboats, and dredges. No boat, however, could permit canal diggers or river dredgers to share in the independence enjoyed by so many other African American watermen; building canals was the nightmare of maritime slave life. Contemporary descriptions of canal construction—and not just accounts of the circumstances of the *Camden*'s African laborers—read like cantos from the deepest circles of Dante's *Inferno*.

Canal digging was as much a part of tidewater Carolina life as salting herring or roasting mullet. Between the American Revolution and the Civil War, canals shaped the nation's commerce and determined which places would boom and which would wither, much as railroads and highways did in later generations.[6] North Carolina's political leaders viewed canals as the only way to overcome the state's natural barriers to a prosperous market economy. Shifting inlets, shallow harbors, and broad shoals hindered seaborne trade. As the nation's shipyards turned out heavier, deeper-draft sailing vessels in the late eighteenth and early nineteenth centuries, the state's ports grew even less competitive with deepwater harbors like Norfolk and Charleston. Alarmed by declining maritime trade, a stagnant economy, and a high rate of out-migration, North Carolina progressives pinned their hopes for the future on improving what they called "internal navigation": building ship canals to sidestep the dangers of navigating the Outer Banks, dredging rivers and digging canals around their falls to extend shipping farther into the state's interior, and draining swamps to open them to agriculture and forest industries.[7] All these enterprises hinged on slave labor.

The Dismal Swamp Canal was the longest, most ambitious canal constructed in North Carolina before the Civil War. Financed by private investors and built by hundreds of slave laborers between 1794 and 1805, the canal cut through 22 miles of pocosin and swamp forest. Connecting the Elizabeth River, a branch of the Chesapeake Bay, to the Pasquotank River, a tributary of the Albemarle Sound, the canal was navigable only for shingle flats and small lighters until the late 1820s when slaves widened and deepened its channel for safe passage of vessels with a 5 ½-foot draft.[8] In 1829, the Dismal Swamp Canal Company's slaves also opened a navigable route to Currituck Sound by digging a 6-mile canal to the Northwest River. Not long thereafter, they dug a 5-mile feeder canal to Lake Drummond in order to raise water levels in the main canal. Slave laborers also built several smaller canals to float shingles and staves out of the old-growth swamp forests.[9]

Other canals opened distant parts of the coastal plain to boating traffic. Slave laborers built a second ship canal, the Harlowe and Clubfoot Creek Canal, on and off from 1795 to 1828. Silting up at its two ends almost immediately, the canal served principally as a route for small workboats between the ports of New Bern and Beaufort.[10] A later generation of slaves dug the Albemarle and Chesapeake Canal, a 14-mile shortcut between North River and Currituck Sound, from 1855 to 1859.[11] Along the Roanoke River, slaves carved a nine-mile series of canals and an aqueduct around the Great Falls, a drop of 90 feet between Rock Landing and what became the town of Weldon, much of it through solid rock.[12] Another canal extended from Fairfield, a lumbermill camp on Lake Mattamuskeet, to the Alligator River, tying the lake's commerce to the Albemarle Sound.[13] Other canals were begun but never finished. In 1818, slave laborers dug large portions of the Fayetteville Canal and Buckhorn Canal at falls on the Cape Fear River, but excavation and digging ended with the financial collapse of the Cape Fear Navigation Company.[14] Spurred by dreams of opening a stable channel from Pamlico Sound into the Atlantic, investors also launched a canal at Roanoke Inlet. Sand refilled the channel so quickly that the canal was abandoned in 1855.[15]

Canals were vital for coastal agriculture as well as commerce. Much of the coastal plain was too soggy for farming or settlement without draining swamps.[16] When the General Assembly made a public giveaway of unclaimed swamplands in 1794, a few dozen land speculators purchased at least 5 million acres and spurred a drainage boom in the state's lowlands.[17] After slaves dug drainage canals by Lake Mattamuskeet, Edmund Ruffin visited the lakeside plantations and exclaimed that he had "never seen such magnificent growths of corn, upon such large spaces."[18] Those fields and the fertile lands created out of pocosins at Somerset Place, by Lake Phelps, seemed to confirm the worth of drained swamplands for agriculture. Canals dug in pocosins also descended naturally toward sea level, enabling the flow to power grist- and sawmills. Many new drainage canals opened a fresh territory of old-growth swamp forest for shingling, lumbering, and stave making.

The canals dug by the Lake Company's African slaves at Lake Phelps are indicative of what it took to drain pocosin swamplands effectively. Excavating a bed 20 feet wide and 6 feet deep, the diggers first forged a canal from the lake six miles to the Scuppernong River, a lazy blackwater stream that flowed into the Albemarle Sound.[19] Collins and his neighbors, Ebenezer and Charles Pettigrew, later drove their slaves to construct three other sizable canals in order to drain several thousand more acres of swampland. To draw the water out of the pocosins into those main canals, the slaves also dug an elaborate network of smaller canals, ditches, and cross-furrows.[20] Of course, only slave-holders as wealthy as Collins, who kept 350 slaves at Lake Phelps by 1860, could contemplate canal-digging projects of such colossal magnitude.

Slave laborers on the great swamp plantations at Lake Phelps and Lake Mattamuskeet carried out the largest drainage projects, but several other projects proved nearly as bold. The most ambitious were launched by the State Literary Fund, which set aside $200,000 to drain swamplands given to it by the General Assembly to develop and sell for the benefit of public education. Between 1838 and 1842, the Literary Fund financed canal-digging projects at Lake Mattamuskeet, Alligator Lake, and Pungo Lake. Hired from their masters for $90 to $150 per year, approximately 250 slaves built the canals through some of the state's densest swamps and marshlands. The Mattamus-keet canal ran seven miles from Lake Landing to Wysocking Bay and ranged from 40 to 60 feet in width. The state also financed a smaller canal to provide earth for a roadbed that gave Hyde County its first land bridge to the mainland proper.[21] From 1852 to 1855, the Literary Fund's slaves dug a canal from Ward's Creek, a branch of the South River, into the Open Grounds, a 70,000-acre pocosin near the Lower Neuse. Slaves dug other, smaller canals for swamp drainage throughout the coast, particularly in the East Dismal Swamp, the White Oak Pocosin, Goshen Swamp, and the Holly Shelter Pocosin.[22]

Even the rice planters of the Lower Cape Fear relied on a system of canals, ditches, levees, and dams similar to, if rather less grand than, the drainage projects at Lake Phelps and Lake Mattamuskeet. Growing rice required periodically flooding the fields, and bondmen and -women readied the wetlands by digging feeder canals and ditches, much as other slaves built canals for boat traffic or swamp drainage. Also like canal building, rice cultivation depended on slave labor. Only the largest planters could muster the work force necessary to make a successful crop.[23] Planters considered 30 slaves a minimum for raising rice; in the 1850s, when the "golden grain" ruled the Lower Cape Fear, the average rice planter there owned nearly twice that number.[24] Those slaves made digging agricultural canals and planting rice their own unique part of maritime culture. They worked with a variety of small craft, and they created important local waterways. Poling or paddling canoes, rafts, and punts along rice canals, they visited other plantations and found their way into natural streams, where they were bound to encounter slave fishermen and boathands who had strayed from the main channels of the Cape Fear. Here, as in so much of tidewater Carolina, the boundary between maritime labor and plantation labor could rarely be drawn with any precision.

From the point of view of the state's progressive leadership, the canal-digging era was a mixed success. The Dismal Swamp Canal and the Albemarle and Chesapeake Canal succeeded in making the state's commerce far more accessible to Chesapeake Bay ports. Canals also opened many swamp forests to loggers, shinglers, and stave makers. A few plantations, most notably those by Lake Phelps and Lake Mattamuskeet, fulfilled the promise of swamp drainage for agriculture, but their success was not repeated widely. None of the canals financed by the State Literary Fund, for example, proved to be a financial success. The canal from Lake Mattamuskeet lessened the threat of floods by lowering the lake's water level, and the Pungo Lake and Alligator Lake canals drained 60,000 to 70,000 acres. But the difficulty of achieving anything more than partial drainage, land title disputes, the prohibitive costs of additional ditching, and the lack of access roads all discouraged land buyers.[25]

Canal digging also had unexpected ecological consequences. The drainage of pocosins, in particular, made them vulnerable to wildfires. Periodic wildfires are a fundamental part of pocosin ecology, necessary for the dispersal of the seeds of several native pine species and essential to recycling key nutrients. The brushfires that swept through pocosins usually were not very hot, relatively speaking, and caused little damage to evergreen thickets or mature swamp forests.[26] After canals drained the pocosins, however, the wildfires blazed through the dryer, upper layers of organic soils with an unquenchable intensity, often burning several feet into the ground. The peaty soils acted like so much prime kindling, and fire soon exploded into the forest canopy, generating a heat that no forest could withstand. Just prior to the Civil War, those wildfires prompted Edmund Ruffin to observe of the Great Dismal that "there is no large or beautiful forest growth left anywhere."[27] Hundreds of thousands of acres of juniper, sweet gum, oak, and cypress forest may have vanished before shinglers and lumbermen ever reached them.[28] For political leaders in North Carolina, then, the legacy of canal digging was one of partial progress, unrealized hopes for profit and development, and unintended ecological outcomes.

For African Americans, however, the state's canals did not have such a mixed legacy. Canal digging was the cruelest, most dangerous, unhealthy, and exhausting labor in the American South. Even above the Mason-Dixon Line, where slave labor was rarely employed, canal builders faced working conditions nothing short of gruesome. Only the North's most desperate souls, often Irish immigrants, worked as canal diggers; many were worn down by exhaustion, suffered fatal accidents, or succumbed to malaria and influenza. The grave conditions grew so alarming that churches and fraternal orders organized special relief missions to canal-digging projects in several states, including New York and Pennsylvania.[29]

Building canals in southern swamps was harder yet. Even the first stage of canal building, when laborers excavated a pathway for the canal bed, often seemed unendurable. Cutting a course through thick tangles of vines, scrub, cane, and trees was a disheartening task.[30] "The earth," Edmund Ruffin found at a canal-digging site in the Great Dismal Swamp, "is . . . a quagmire of peat, . . . full of dead roots and buried logs, under the water, and of living trees and roots over and at the surface."[31] Canal workers wielded axes and spades to cut through thickly matted juniper roots. Ruffin described how "stumps were exposed thickly everywhere, and those below the surface were still thicker. I could from that, well appreciate the enormous labor of digging a canal for navigation through such a mass of solid wood—or even of cutting small ditches for drainage." The president of the Dismal Swamp Land Company told Ruffin that the canal had been cut, "not by the spade, but principally by the axe, the saw and the mattock."[32] Yard by yard, canal workers jerry-rigged tree- and stump-pulling devices. All of this work was done standing in waist-deep water. "The Negroes are up to the middle or much deeper in mud and water, cutting away roots and baling [*sic*] out mud," remembered Moses Grandy of the canal diggers in the vicinity of the Great Dismal Swamp. "If they can keep their heads above water, they work on."[33] The sun was ex-cruciatingly hot during humid summer days. Steel-gray cottonmouths lurked by the score in the canal waters, and slave laborers could scarcely walk on dry land without encountering a copperhead or rattler. Worse than venomous snakes were the insects. The mosquitoes, ticks, yellow flies, and chiggers tortured all who dared—or in this case, were compelled—to trespass in their swampy homelands.[34]

The living conditions in the canal-digging camps astounded even invete-rate travelers of the South, who, one might imagine, would have been inured to the sight of slavery's hardships. Just after 1800, when a gale forced his sailboat off Pamlico Sound into Juniper Bay, an Englishman named Charles Janson took shelter at a slave labor camp owned by John Gray Blount. Janson found there approximately 60 slaves who in two years had dug a mile-long canal into a remote juniper swamp. They worked, he said, "in water, often up to the middle, and constantly knee-deep." They lived in log or thatch huts, probably like ones described in the Great Dismal Swamp as being "secured from inundation on high stumps."[35] Most canal work camps were all male, the separation from families being one of their enduring afflictions, but at Juniper Bay the slave inhabitants included at least a few women and children. Janson does not say whether the slave women dug in the canal or had other duties. Either way, they were more vulnerable to sexual exploitation from the white overseer than were female slaves on most plantations, where the gaze of white women may have placed some curb on potential rapists.[36] At Juniper Bay, the overseer lived in a small log cabin a few hundred yards from the slave huts. The slaves presumably had built walking and cart paths by felling trees, the first task in shingling and lumbering in any swamp. Janson described their rations as salted herring and a peck of Indian corn, on the cob, per week, with a few pieces of salted beef or pork when supply vessels arrived every few months. Observing how dense swamp and the open waters of Pamlico Sound surrounded the slave laborers, Janson believed that "there was no chance of them escaping."[37]

Janson was more right than not. Slaves escaped fairly often from canal-building camps located in uplands, as at the canal and aqueduct around the falls of the Roanoke River, but flight from a canal-digging camp in a swamp was highly unlikely.[38] The terrain was not as much a barrier to escaping as the harsh system of labor management. Cut off from plantation society's more orderly ways of slave control—the slave patrol, the sheriff, the local militia, the courts, ties to family, privileges that could be extended or taken away— canal-digging overseers relied almost exclusively on savage force and violent retribution. The slaves who dug canals suffered work routines, living conditions, and diets that caused psychological as well as physical torment; many stayed in chains day and night. One also has to suspect that canal overseers, like torturers who live intimately with their victims, found themselves distorted by their lot, leading them and the slaves to discover the worst of their humanity.

One can scarcely imagine the enmity and fear that festered under these circumstances between canal overseers and slave laborers. To preserve his own life, much less assure the canal's completion, the overseer asserted a total discipline over his slave workers rarely practical in plantation life. He did not have as many incentives to offer as at a plantation, where "privileges" that an overseer could dispense or withhold ranged from permission to have a garden plot or a few hours to go fishing to the right to marry one's beloved or keep one's own children. The few incentives available show how desperate things were in a swamp. One slave, for instance, recalled the canal diggers at the Dismal Swamp getting blankets only if they exceeded their work quotas; otherwise, they slept on the mud.[39] Nor did an overseer have Christmas holidays or laying-by festivals to soften slavery's harshest edges. He was contracted to accomplish one task, digging a canal; every day meant a greater expense to the canal's owner, and overseers presumably sought to spend as few months as possible in the fetid confines of a swamp.

Neither did the overseer need to cultivate the goodwill of his slaves in order to gain the use of skills that might otherwise be withheld, as a planter might do with a slave blacksmith or fisherman. This left the canal overseer even fewer reasons to treat his workers decently. He scarcely needed their minds, only their muscles.[40] Thus Josiah Collins was willing to send more than 80 West African laborers, knowing little or no English, to dig his canals. Collins understood that canal digging would "season"—a colonial term—his workers or kill them. Indeed, large tidewater planters often sent new Africans to work in swamplands in order to "break" them the way a wrangler might a wild mustang. Having worked at a canal-digging camp, a fieldhand—or, for that matter, a sailor like Moses Grandy—never forgot that life could get even worse if he or she was caught not working hard enough or engaging in an act of rebellion. Certainly Grandy never forgot the hardships of his own season at a canal-digging camp near the Albemarle Sound.[41]

Discipline was absolute. Willis Augustus Hodges, a free black who worked on the Dismal Swamp Canal, later remembered his overseer as "a very cruel and hard master in all his ways."[42] In order to repay a debt, in or about 1827 Hodges and his brother-in-law joined a work gang of 500 men, all but a dozen of them slaves, who were deepening the canal. Two crews, one of masons, another of laborers, were based outside of South Mills, a rough little lumber camp town just south of the Virginia line. Slave patrols from South Mills intimidated the black laborers nightly, sometimes firing shots across the canal into their camp, and Hubbard, the overseer, "flogged the men often." In his autobiography, Hodges recounts an incident in which a slave named Frank was unjustly accused of stealing one of the overseer's pigs. Hubbard and two other white men "struck him with a hickory stick several times in the face and across the head . . . , then kicked poor Frank several times." They tied Frank to a tree and gave him at least a hundred lashes. "I would hear poor Frank hollow [sic] for mercy at every blow until his voice failed him," Hodges said; then they "brought him back and threw him upon a pile of straw in one of the huts." When the pig came home of its own accord that night, Hubbard seemed to have no regrets, telling the slaves that the punishment was still a good lesson for them all to remember. For his part, Hodges began to have dreams of ruthlessly murdering Hubbard and the other white guards.[43]

Also in the Dismal Swamp vicinity, Moses Grandy recalled an overseer named McPherson tying up slaves and whipping them because they had not completed their previous day's work. "After they were flogged," he wrote, "pork or beef brine was put on their bleeding backs to increase the pain." According to Grandy, McPherson often left the whipped slave tied up. "Thus exposed and helpless," he continued, "the yellow flies and musquitoes [sic] in great numbers would settle on the bleeding and smarting back, and put the sufferer to extreme torture. This continued all day, for they were not taken down till night." At night, Grandy recorded, the canal slaves boiled a bitter weed called "Oak of Jerusalem" to drive the "creepers or maggots" out of the whipped slave's wounds, while trying to relieve the pain by rubbing the slave's back with their rations of fatback meat.[44]

Similarly, Charles Janson described John Gray Blount's overseer taking an entire day to whip every canal worker at Juniper Bay because none would point out the slave who stole his fowl.[45] That none confessed or informed on his comrades might suggest that canal laborers mustered a measure of solidarity in the bleakest circumstances. But it was never easy. The willingness of Collins's slaves to drown themselves rather than endure canal digging speaks volumes about their own sense of alternatives and reveals clearly the depth of their determination to resist their treatment.

Maintaining canals was also a trial without end. Spring freshets often washed out dams. Locks and dams made of wood decayed and required constant repairs, work that was regularly performed by slave carpenters.[46] If fallen trees and other debris were not removed from the channel, they blocked boat traffic and damaged dams and locks. Muskrat tunnels undermined canal banks, and the hogs that grazed so uninhibitedly in coastal forests caused the banks to erode and crumble. Maintenance chores generally fell to slaves engaged in other swamp industries; the shinglers employed by the Dismal Swamp Land Company, for instance, also helped to maintain the Dismal Swamp Canal.[47] If a sawmill was located on a canal, then laborers also had to dredge the channel periodically to remove accumulations of sawdust.[48] At Lake Phelps, Ebenezer Pettigrew's slaves annually lowered the water level on the Bonarva Canal at the sluice gates and then waded into the canal's channel with shovels and hoes to load the debris onto flatboats. The Pettigrews found this duty so burdensome and debilitating to their slaves that they came to doubt the efficacy of their whole system of agricultural drainage.[49]

If digging and maintaining canals was horrible, maritime life was significantly better for slave laborers making improvements in river navigation. They dynamited shoals, dredged channels, removed stumps, and constructed dams, locks, and small canals. Many of the tasks, such as removing cypress stumps by underwater diving, required considerable skill.[50] Generally, this work was not one major project, like a ship canal, but a series of smaller undertakings over at least several miles of waterway. The laborers might work on the edges of swamp bottomlands, but rarely in them. Instead, they tended to live on vessels and move up and down the waterway from work site to work site. The Cape Fear Navigation Company, as a prime example, maintained a virtual flotilla. The company's vessels included barges, two steamers, and a shanty boat that housed slave quarters and a workshop.[51] The laboring conditions could have been only somewhat better than those of canal digging, but they did offer certain advantages: less strict oversight, somewhat more independence, a much healthier environment, and more contact via slave boatmen with the outside world. Given how widely they traveled, these maritime laborers probably had their own role in spreading news, political intelligence, and folkways among riverside slave communities.

For all its rigors, canal digging was not always considered exclusively slave labor or black labor. Canal building companies preferred to hire slaves, but they were rarely able to find an adequate supply because most planters did not want their property treated so poorly.[52] At the same time, canal companies in North Carolina never seem to have hired local white laborers. That would have been a breach of the fundamental racial code that made some jobs exclusively black, others white. The recruitment of immigrant white labor sidestepped that issue. Canal companies often went to great lengths to import free laborers, mainly Irish and Slavic immigrants, from ghettos in the northern states. This probably reflected the high costs of buying slaves and the reluctance of an adequate number of slaveholders to hire out their bondmen for such dangerous work.

Free labor never took hold, however. Free men, white and black, widely recognized the health risks of canal building. Without exception, canal-digging projects that depended on free workers sooner or later faced labor shortages. Even if they could be recruited initially, free laborers quickly abandoned canals and dredging projects. Canal-digging companies learned that they had to depend on slave labor. Their reliance on African American workers may have stemmed to some extent on people of African descent's greater genetic resistance to malaria.[53] Certainly planters attributed to their slaves a natural capacity to withstand swamp diseases. In 1842, Ebenezer Pettigrew reported a dreadful series of illnesses and deaths among the poorer whites who lived adjacent to his canal and indicated that they "are literally starving" and willing to work "to procure bread." Yet he also reported that his slaves, including canal diggers, had had "no serious sickness . . . since the fall."[54] Charles Janson made similar observations earlier in the century. "The swamps and low lands are so unhealthy, that they cannot be cultivated by white persons . . . [for whom] such an occupation would, in a few days, prove certain death."[55] Sorting out the elements of truth and self-deception in such comments is not necessary in this context. Canal overseers, just like rice planters, rationalized their exploitative use of slave laborers in terms of a racially bred stamina, but the reality was that canal building was a dangerous, brutal, and unhealthy occupation that few human beings, whatever their origins, endured voluntarily.

Even the use of slaves did not resolve the labor shortages that plagued the

Cape Fear Navigation Company. Between 1851 and 1860, company agents never succeeded in recruiting sufficient labor to complete 19 dams and 22 locks on an 87-mile stretch of the Cape Fear and Deep Rivers. Faced with severe labor shortages in 1851, the company imported 180 German and Hungarian immigrants from New York. Most apparently fled North Carolina posthaste. Two years later, the Company still reported that "Hands could not be procured to work upon the lower works [from Fayetteville to Smiley's Falls], on account of its alleged unhealthiness. Laborers . . . absolutely refuse to work . . . and hundreds have returned home sooner than work there." At Jones' Falls, seven miles above Fayetteville, a construction superintendent reported that hands "come and commence work, but quit and leave in a few days."[56] Approximately 40 slaves owned and another 15 slaves hired by the company proved to be the only steady labor supply in a work force that often reached 200 but should have been twice that number.[57] The labor shortage delayed construction, made it impossible to maintain completed locks and dams adequately, and contributed to the company's downward financial spiral. The Cape Fear Navigation Company went bankrupt in 1860; most of its slaves were sold at auction in Cumberland County.

The Roanoke River Navigation Company also attempted to employ both slave and free laborers. Chartered in 1817, the company immediately arranged to buy slaves and build housing for them. Several enslaved laborers escaped right away, probably all too familiar with the hazards of canal digging. By October 1819, the company employed approximately 30 white laborers, evidently recent immigrants recruited in the North, and 98 blacks. From the beginning, the free laborers found the working conditions unbearable. The company had responsibility for navigation all the way from the juncture of the Dan and Staunton Rivers to the Albemarle Sound. Workers blasted away navigational obstacles and constructed two minor canals and a variety of wing and side dams. The glory of this huge enterprise was the Roanoke Canal, which entailed a nine-mile series of canals and an aqueduct around the Great Falls. It was a vast and arduous undertaking that required canal hands to cut a course estimated at 2,235 yards, including 420 through solid rock.[58] Cadwaller Jones, the company president, reported that his free workers "entertain the greatest fears from the effects of our climate during the summer and fall; it is with utmost difficulty, that we have been enabled at any time to retain them here longer than the commencement of winter to the last of June."[59] Jones had to plan all the canal digging to finish before what he called "the sickly season." After stonemasons brought from New York fled in 1822 when a few grew ill, the company gave up on free labor. The 42 slaves owned by the company would bear the brunt of the work and disease.[60]

The construction of the Albemarle and Chesapeake Canal signaled the end of that harrowing age of canal building in North Carolina. Dredged by slave labor between 1855 and 1859, the Albemarle and Chesapeake—known locally as the Juniper Canal—ran 14 miles from the North River, a tributary of Chesapeake Bay, to Currituck Sound, opening a better passageway than the Dismal Swamp Canal between Chesapeake Bay and Albemarle Sound.[61] Building the Juniper Canal, however, slave laborers worked not with axe and mattock but with seven robust steam dredges capable of cutting deep channels through the thickest mud and swampland. Powered by 16-horsepower engines, the dredge boats were 50 to 60 feet in length, and their shovels carried away as much as 40 cubic feet of soil every minute. "Nothing," Edmund Ruffin exclaimed, "can effectively resist, or defeat, the monster ditcher."[62] The steam dredges revolutionized canal digging and probably saved many a slave's life. Sixty-one feet wide and roughly eight feet deep, the new waterway overshadowed the Dismal Swamp Canal. One thousand vessels passed through the Juniper Canal annually by 1860 and more than 2,500 in 1861.[63]

In a mere decade or two, the arrival of steam railroads rendered most ship canals obsolete. The channels dug at such enormous human expense quickly fell into disuse and disrepair. Railroads, not canals, determined how America grew for the next century. The fate of the Roanoke Canal was typical. As early as 1836, the completion of the Wilmington & Weldon Railroad began to siphon the commerce of the Upper Roanoke Valley away from the small seaports of the Albemarle Sound to Wilmington. Two decades later, in 1856, the Wilmington & Weldon and the Gaston Railroad together skirted the Great Falls, ending the Roanoke Canal's commercial value altogether.[64] Other railroads made canals outdated across the South.

At the same time, a decline in land prices undermined the profitability of canals built for agricultural and timbering purposes. The expansion of the United States west of the Appalachians, the forced removal of the native population, and the opening of former Indian lands for colonization undercut the profitability of buying unreclaimed swamplands and draining them. The costs had always been high, and only the most affluent slaveholders had ever been able to command the manpower to develop swamplands. Now the westward frontier made it unprofitable even for them. In 1831, Eli Smallwood of New Bern, one of John Gray Blount's partners in the Juniper Bay canal, wrote to Blount that "I do not think any unrecovered swamp land worth reclaiming."[65] The western lands proved a daunting temptation. In the 1830s, half of North Carolina counties had population losses. For three generations, however, from roughly 1790 to 1860, canals shaped the American continent—and left a deep scar in the annals of slavery and maritime life in North Carolina.

part two

The Struggle for Freedom

chapter five

All of Them Abolitionists

Black Watermen and the Maritime
Passage to Freedom

Far from both the canal-digging camps of the East Dismal Swamp and the fishing beaches of Albemarle Sound, a slave named Peter guided vessels in and out of the harbor at Wilmington, North Carolina. Merchants and planters depended on local pilots and skilled engineers like him to guide their vessels safely around the serpentine shoals on the Cape Fear River and across the narrow channel into the Atlantic.[1] But Peter navigated more than freight through those treacherous passages. He also steered fugitive slaves toward freedom along maritime escape routes that endured throughout the slavery era. In a little-known autobiography, his son, a former slave named William H. Robinson, remembered that Peter "enjoyed the friendship of two very distinguished Quakers, Mr. Fuller and Mr. Elliot, who owned oyster sloops and stood at the head of what is known in our country as the underground railroad. . . . Father was with Messrs Fuller and Elliot every day towing them in and out from the oyster bay. This gave them an opportunity to lay and devise plans for getting many [slaves] into Canada . . . and my father was an important factor in this line."[2] The success of the slave-smuggling conspiracy was evident in October 1849, when a correspondent to the *Wilmington Journal* complained that "it is almost an every day occurrence for our negro slaves to take passage [aboard a vessel] and go North."[3] Echoing a long-standing

Rev. William Robinson, son of the slave pilot Peter. From William H. Robinson, *From Log Cabin to the Pulpit; or, Fifteen Years in Slavery*, 3rd ed. (Eau Claire, Wis.: James H. Tifft, 1913).

grievance against sailors and watermen, the newspaper's editors lamented this maritime escape route as "an evil which is getting to be intolerable."[4] Alert to the landscape of opportunity, runaway slaves regularly headed to the coast instead of attempting overland paths out of bondage.[5]

Charting that clandestine corridor up the eastern seaboard offers a rare glimpse at slave runaways and African American maritime culture. This perspective also speaks poignantly to the fundamental character of coastal society in nineteenth-century North Carolina. Black watermen such as Peter may have been the most critical link in this oceangoing route to freedom, but many other tidewater people, black and white, helped runaway slaves to survive as fugitives and arrange passage to free territory. Their stories reveal a complex, tumultuous, and dissident undercurrent to coastal life in the slavery era. Wealthy planters and merchants held the reins of power, drafting and enforcing the state's punitive laws, but lowly watermen, slave stevedores, piney woods squatters, reclusive swampers, and sometimes even slaveholders' wives and children defied those laws and sustained tenuous pathways by which fugitives might pass from land to sea.[6]

We are fortunate to know anything at all about this maritime passage to freedom. It was, after all, an illicit undertaking, participating in it a potentially capital crime that necessarily occurred only on the fringes of society. Few former slaves dared to leave written accounts of their involvement; most who were apprehended had no day in court, where their daring might have entered the documentary record. Historical documents understandably yield only oblique references to these ocean-bound slave runaways and their sympathizers. ("I was to escape in a vessel," wrote one former slave who had succeeded in escaping in a schooner's hold, "but I forebear to mention any further particulars.")[7] Or, like William Robinson, they disclosed only enough details about what he called the "Underground Railroad" to hint at its breadth and vitality, while they maintained a habitual caution against discussing specific names, routes, or vessels.

Documentary sources provide several dozen accounts of specific runaway slaves who reached vessels sailing out of North Carolina ports between 1800 and the Civil War. Given the degree of secrecy that enveloped this path of flight, and a sizable body of corroborating evidence, one may safely conclude that they represent only a small portion of those who fled the South by sea. The presence of a coastal escape route was widely known in tidewater slave communities, among merchants and planters who went to great lengths to control it, and among northern abolitionists who frequently assisted fugitive slaves after their voyage from the South. From a wide assortment of contemporary newspapers, slave narratives, personal diaries, court records, and travel accounts, it is possible to reconstruct much of the character and scope of this watery path toward freedom that passed through North Carolina ports.

Most slaves who endeavored to escape aboard seagoing vessels traveled to the busy harbors at Wilmington, New Bern, and Washington. Relying on their own watercraft skills or on the ubiquitous black boatmen who plied the waters, fugitive slaves often followed rivers to those ports. The majority could not risk a long canoe or flatboat trip, even traveling only at night. But slaves escaped frequently enough by boat that when a Slocumb Creek man discovered a cypress dugout deserted near his home on Christmas Day 1828, he simply assumed that the craft "must have been last in the possession of a runaway negro."[8] If they could not commandeer a boat or make their own, runaways had to depend on sympathetic watermen, usually slaves, to transport them across rivers, creeks, and bays.

Wilmington, the largest port in antebellum North Carolina, had a special reputation, in the words of a Rocky Point planter, as "an asylum for Runaways" because of its location near the mouth of the Cape Fear River, its steady sea traffic, its strong ties to New England, and its black-majority population.[9] Fugitive slaves followed the Cape Fear to Wilmington from rice and turpentine plantations throughout southeastern North Carolina. They fled to New Bern along the Neuse and Trent Rivers from cotton and tobacco fields as far inland as Goldsboro.[10] And they trailed the Tar River toward Washington, and the Roanoke to Plymouth, from timber camps and herring fisheries stretching to the Virginia border. Slaves confined in the remote wetlands east of those major ports—in soggy Hyde and Tyrrell Counties, for instance—often fled west to their wharves.[11] Men and women who escaped from the Albemarle Sound vicinity usually headed north through the Great Dismal Swamp to rendezvous with seagoing vessels in Norfolk or Portsmouth, Virginia.[12]

The larger ports were not the only destinations for fugitive slaves. Runaways and race rebels extended this maritime escape route into fishing hamlets and seafaring villages up and down the North Carolina coast. Henry Anderson, for example, escaped from a slave trader in Beaufort by ship.[13] Miles White, only twenty-one years old, stowed away on a vessel carrying shingles from Elizabeth City to Philadelphia after convincing the captain to take the risk of letting him aboard.[14] Harriet Jacobs escaped by sea from Edenton in 1842. And in July 1856 Peter Heines, Mathew Bodams, and James Morris all escaped on a schooner captained by a man named Fountain who apparently met them at one of the rough-hewn villages along the Roanoke River or Albemarle Sound.[15] Other runaway slaves fled from the landings at larger plantations and timber camps, where vessels that combined shallow

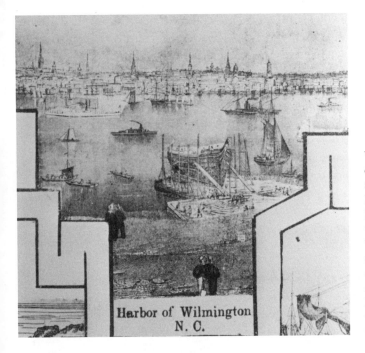

Harbor of Wilmington
N. C.

Wilmington harbor, ca. 1860, where the slave pilot Peter and his co-conspirators helped runaways board vessels headed north. The engraving shows schooners, a flatboat, a canoe, steamboats, and a shipyard. Courtesy Museum of the Lower Cape Fear, Wilmington, North Carolina.

drafts and ocean worthiness loaded crops, fish, or timber and sailed for New England and the West Indies.

No matter which ports runaway slaves sought out, they faced many dangers before reaching the open sea. Bloodhounds, bounty hunters, and port inspectors stood between them and the Gulf Stream's warm, northward currents.[16] Escaping slaves risked their lives around every turn. Slave catchers and patrol squads pursued them, and anyone could turn them in for a substantial bounty. Inspectors searched many seagoing vessels and, at points, regularly fumigated ships to drive hidden runaways up onto the deck. The chance of betrayal or discovery always existed, and an extraordinarily high proportion of fugitives never reached a wharf. The exceptional ones who did, like a slave named Anthony on board the schooner *Butler* in 1836, occasionally were caught before departure.[17] Punishments included re-enslavement, public whipping, hard duty, deportation into the Deep South, and death.

Confronted by so many pitfalls and deterrents, most slaves could only dream of the sea. Like the young Frederick Douglass, himself once a slave in a port town, they may have mused about the "beautiful vessels, robed in white" that might "yet bear [them] into freedom."[18] But throughout the plantation belt of eastern North Carolina, slaves tried to fulfill that dream frequently enough that their owners viewed the ocean as a serious threat and regularly suspected that runaways would try to sail away. Slaveholders' preoccupation with the ocean's proximity often bordered on obsession. Reward posters and newspaper advertisements routinely warned masters of seagoing vessels not to harbor, employ, or carry away their departed workers.[19] State penalties for protecting fugitive slaves were harsh; ship captains after 1793 risked hanging for carrying a runaway out of North Carolina.[20] Slaveholders also threatened seamen with civil prosecution for carrying away their slaves and offered extravagant rewards for information that would identify sailors who helped a slave to flee. In February 1838, to mention only one of many instances, Edward Dudley, the state's governor, offered up to $500 to anyone who would inform him what mariner had allowed his runaway slave to sail from Wilmington to Boston.[21]

Coastal geography and the willingness of some local inhabitants to protect runaways compounded the threat of the open sea for slaveholders and its allure for their slaves. Remote swamps and dense forests offered havens for runaway slaves who needed a long-term refuge, a point for hasty reconnaissance, or a momentary way station en route to a port.[22] Blackwater swamps, pocosins, pine savannas, or tidal marshes encroached on every settlement in coastal North Carolina. Towns were few, scattered, and small. Before the advent of steam navigation and the completion of the coast's first railroad in the 1840s, Wilmington still had well under 5,000 residents.[23] Small harbors, menacing shoals, and unpredictable inlets dampened mercantile prospects and inhibited growth in the state's plantation economy.[24] While the coastal region was no longer quite the lawless refuge for runaways, debtors, and dissidents that Virginia and South Carolina planters had complained about so vociferously in the eighteenth century, visitors still remembered best the lonely stretches of forest, the impassable roads, and the backwoods poverty. A village of any size seemed a welcome relief from the monotony of pines and bogs.[25] Blackwater swamps and vast pocosins covered more than 3 million acres, and a dense longleaf pine forest blanketed the upland stretches of the coastal plain, in what later became the tobacco belt. Though drainage and foresting of the wetlands were well under way by the early nineteenth century, those areas promised a haven for fugitive slaves, many of whom had at least some schooling in how to survive in the wild.[26]

But to reach the sea, fugitive slaves could not simply vanish into coastal swamps and the backwoods. Even for those who had the skills necessary for wilderness survival, a hermit's life did not provide access to crucial information about sea traffic or expose them to the kinds of contacts necessary to reach a seagoing vessel. As a result, runaways usually had to rely on the complicity of men and women prepared to disregard the slave laws. All runaways, but especially those who planned to board a vessel, looked to clandestine networks of both slaves and free persons. From the vantage point of the state's political leaders, those networks remained a dangerous and ephemeral world beyond the edges of their towns and plantations. One cannot underestimate the power of the slaveholding class; it was unquestionably far-reaching. Beyond the firm grasp of its authority, however, runaway slaves often discovered support for their journey to the sea.

Whether or not they aspired to reach a seagoing vessel, fugitive slaves received their most important backing from other slaves. "The slaves generally know where the runaway is secreted," remembered Nehemiah Caulkins, a white carpenter who closely observed daily life on several rice plantations near Wilmington between 1824 and 1835, "and visit him at night and on Sundays."[27] The former slave William Robinson, himself a onetime runaway, remembered the assistance that slaves gave to their fugitive brethren in the Wilmington vicinity. In his autobiography, he recalled that during his youth in the 1850s, "there was always an understanding between the slaves, that if one ran away they would put something to eat at a certain place; also a mowing scythe, with the crooked handle replaced with a straight stick with which to fight the bloodhounds."[28] Over weeks, months, and even years, slaves supplied refugees with provisions and intelligence that might help them to elude their pursuers. Fugitive slaves looked most often for this sort of help among family members who remained with their masters or who had been sold in the vicinity. The concentration of slave markets in port towns meant that runaways often had enslaved relatives at several locations on a river flowing into a port; it was a side effect of the otherwise tragic separation of black families on the auction block.[29]

Behind individual acts of solidarity lay broader networks within the enslaved population of coastal North Carolina. Slave watermen, couriers, and draymen traveled widely and conveyed news and goods over long distances. African Americans also took advantage of limited free time to create cultural and social webs, out of sight of their owners, that linked slaves over a wide territory. Though discovery meant severe punishment, slaves often slipped about surreptitiously in the evening hours, visiting friends and family on other plantations, worshiping, courting, hunting, fishing, and trading illicitly.[30] Those nocturnal forays not only sharpened their ability to dodge slave patrols but also stretched the boundaries of their bondage by identifying blind spots in the vigilance of their owners. Maintaining a liaison between the slave quarters and a swamp hideout entailed the utmost caution and great risks, but those who colluded with runaways maneuvered along well-worn cracks in slavery's walls.

Runaway slaves also depended on kindred souls concealed in blackwater swamps and pocosins. Slaveholders went to great and brutal lengths to dislodge those defiant individuals, but "maroons" continued to inhabit the North Carolina coast to a degree that scholars may never fully know. It can be concluded, however, that runaway slaves counted heavily on maroons to assure a successful flight. When William Robinson escaped from an abusive master in 1858, he immediately sought out a group of fugitive slaves living in the nearby swamps to protect him. His knowledge of their hideout dated from his early childhood. Robinson explained that "I had often heard ex-runaway slaves, men and women, tell the adventures of when they were in the woods and about their hiding places or rendezvous. I had heard it so often at my father's fireside that I knew almost directly where they were, for I had passed close by them many times."[31] The young Robinson fled at once to the "three mile farm" on the edge of a swamp near Wilmington, where he asked an elderly slave woman for the precise location of the refugee camp. This woman—Robinson reverently called her "mother"—gave him food, a blessing, and directions to the fugitive encampment. He found 18 people hidden that night on a rock outcrop shielded by a large canebrake deep within the swamp. Robinson and his companions foraged for food and relied on friendly slaves to help them.[32]

Black men and women on the run found similar support in coastal areas beyond Wilmington. In 1830, 30 to 40 fugitive slaves had established a base in Dover Swamp, in western Craven County, and they evidently had opened lines of communication extending to several other runaway camps as far away as the Newport River, more than 35 miles to the east.[33] Similarly, in the mid-1850s runaway slaves enjoyed what petitioners to the governor called a "very secure retreat" in Brunswick County's Green Swamp, then one of the largest bottomland swamps in North America. They built at least eleven cabins and carved out a garden and grazing area in the midst of the swamp. White raiders tried but failed to overrun the camp's battlements in the summer of 1856. Afterward, local whites were unable to recruit slave hunters willing to make another foray into the swamp.[34] Runaways must have found a rare welcome in such company.

The immense, boggy wilderness that extended from the Albemarle Sound and the Chowan River into the Great Dismal Swamp was notorious for its maroon encampments.[35] One sea captain who sailed the Albemarle called it "a slave territory that defies all the laws."[36] The documentary record supports his observation. By 1802 a runaway named Tom Copper had established a swamp hideout near Elizabeth City, from which he led raids on local plantations. Relying on slave boatmen who worked the Albemarle waterways, Copper reportedly conspired with runaways and other slaves more than 100 miles away.[37] In the 1820s slave renegades near Edenton even united, one said, "for mutual defense," thwarting all attempts to recapture them for two years.[38] The outlaw Manuel earned great notoriety among Pasquotank River planters in the 1830s for helping slaves escape and for harboring them.[39] When Manuel and his band assisted two fugitive slaves to rescue their wives from John Wood in Hertford in 1833, the renegades not only hid the runaways but apparently supplied them with forged travel documents as well.[40] Visiting the Great Dismal in 1853, Frederick Law Olmsted heard of phantom colonies of fugitive slaves whose children had been "born, lived, and died" in the swamp.[41] To ocean-bound fugitives, maroon camps provided temporary shelters and opportunities to learn from experienced fugitives how to navigate the many obstacles to a port.[42]

Fugitive slaves with an eye to going asea sometimes found allies among free men and women.[43] Resorting to free collaborators was a dangerous choice, but one that could not always be avoided. When Allen Parker ran away from a harsh master in the Chowan River vicinity, he could find shelter only with an impoverished white woman whom his mother had befriended years before. While runaways sought asylum most often among the poor and dispossessed, the historical record suggests a rather more varied picture of their free sympathizers. Thomas H. Jones conspired with free worshipers at his Methodist church to arrange his family's escape from Wilmington.[44] In Chowan County, an upper-class white woman who had long been a family friend concealed Harriet Jacobs.[45] In 1848 a Wilmington merchant named Zebulon Latimer even contrived his own slave's escape to New York.[46] Reviewing most such accounts today, we can usually only guess at motivations. But clearly runaways recognized and exploited a variety of forbidden bonds— including romantic love, friendship, family, and faith—that connected the

This drawing of slaves poling timber on the Dismal Swamp Canal appeared in *Harper's New Monthly Magazine* in 1860. The Great Dismal and its waterways often provided employment and a means of communication and mobility for refugee slaves. Courtesy North Carolina State Archives, Raleigh.

slave community and free citizens of both races. While proslavery militants drove nearly all public expression of abolitionist viewpoints underground after about 1830, it was far more difficult to pluck out the slender threads of collusion that remained woven into the fabric of coastal society.

Blacks who aspired to flee by sea had a special need to interact with free persons in order to earn money for their ship's fare. There were good Quaker salts and militant abolitionists who would not deign to charge to stow away a slave, but most seamen demanded compensation; it was also necessary in many cases to bribe port officials and harbor guards. Though obtaining money must often have seemed an insurmountable obstacle, some runaway slaves nevertheless found ways to finance their passage northward.[47] Even in slavery, many African Americans secretly sold products that they grew, traded for, or made after completing their assigned duties.[48] They also traded stolen goods to poor whites and to black market brokers.[49] Port slaves, in particular, earned money by "hiring out" when their masters did not require their labor. Sometimes the master gave permission and shared the proceeds; at other times such work was done clandestinely, increasing both the risk and the reward. This hidden economy flourished despite the threat of repercussions ranging from sizable fines to "Judge Lynch" for slaves, their trading partners, and illicit employers.

When slaves ran away, the hidden economy helped assure their survival. Though William Kinnegay did not attempt to escape by sea, his case is a good illustration. Kinnegay, a slave said to have a "meditative" air, ran away in 1857 after being sold apart from his wife and children in Jones County. Concealed in the piney woods and swamplands south of New Bern, Kinnegay bargained with poor whites. He killed and dressed hogs and cattle grazing in the woods and traded the meat to his piney woods allies for a gun, powder and shot, and other supplies.[50] He certainly might have obtained currency as well. Other fugitives identified poor widows, plantation tenants, and other social outcasts willing to provide food or shelter in exchange for fresh game, woodcutting, or farm chores.[51]

North Carolina's extensive forest products industry had a special reputation for hiring runaway slaves "no questions asked" to cut shingles and to extract submerged timber out of swamps. Those shadowy laborers were legendary in the vicinity of Lake Phelps and the Great Alligator Swamp, and the Dismal Swamp Land Company was constantly tempted to hire runaways.[52] Frederick Law Olmsted reported that both "the poor white men" and slave woodsmen in the Great Dismal routinely hired fugitives to work for them in exchange for "enough to eat, and some clothes, and perhaps two dollars a month in money."[53] Shinglers and other slave woodsmen labored for months at a time in deep swamp forests, where they cut great tracts of cypress, juniper, oak, and gum for absentee land speculators. Often they also hired runaways to work on lighters and flatboats that carried the shingles and lumber out of the swamp. In 1811 a planter named Joseph Banks, for instance, discovered that his runaway slave Frank was working in "the Shingle Swamp" and manning a flatboat on the Dismal Swamp Canal.[54]

Fugitive slaves often found work in the naval stores industry. The heart of coastal North Carolina pumped pine sap: its longleaf pine forests generated the great majority of the United States' production of turpentine, tar, pitch, and rosin.[55] Maintenance of forest plantations required enormous numbers of slave laborers working in isolated locales, where crew bosses were often tempted to hire runaways to meet their labor needs. Supervising naval stores operations was also difficult. Black laborers often spent weeks at a time in far-flung forest camps. As in the shingling business, slave overseers in the naval stores industry recognized that they could not control slave woodsmen solely by coercion and punishment—not that there was not plenty of that too. Consequently, they offered slaves financial bonuses, special privileges, and greater liberties to exceed work quotas.[56] That incentive system proved a great inducement for slave woodsmen to earn money or free time by subcontracting with fugitives.[57]

Shingling, lumbering, and the naval stores industry all employed large numbers of slave laborers in remote locales, where crew leaders or their enslaved workers could develop surreptitious and symbiotic relationships with refugee slaves. The jobs available to refugees were exploitative and risky, built around the vulnerability of desperate men and women. Nevertheless, for those who would try to board a seagoing vessel, they provided one of the best sources of income for their fare and access to people who might help them to arrange contacts in coastal ports.

Political leaders recognized the subversive nature of illicit collusion between fugitive slaves and free persons. The North Carolina General Assembly warned in its 1846–47 session that the number of free men and women sheltering and employing runaway slaves posed a serious danger, especially near the Great Dismal Swamp. "Many slaves belong[ing] to persons residing or having plantations in the neighborhood of the great dismal swamp, and by the aid of free persons of color and of white men, have been and are enabled to elude all attempts to secure their persons. . . . Consorting with such white men and free persons of color, they remain setting at defiance the powers of their masters, corrupting and reducing their slaves, and by their evil example and evil practices, lessening the due subordination."[58] State legislators responded to the crisis by requiring Dismal Swamp employers to register the names and descriptions of their black workers with local clerks of court. They also obligated company officials to verify with owners the fact that their slaves had permission to work in the swamp. The legislators penalized white and "certified" black laborers if they could be shown to "consort with, or work, or be employed in company with any runaway slave." The General Assembly soon amended the act to include large sections of the Great Alligator and East Dismal Swamps.[59] Legislative mandates, however, could not confer upon local authorities the willingness or capability to enforce laws. Fugitive slaves, many of them dreaming of the sea, continued to find asylum among the free citizenry of these elusive worlds apart.

Despite the help of other slaves and free persons, a large majority of the African Americans who dared to flee bondage never made it to the shore. Those who did faced the formidable task of finding sympathetic seamen who could help them obtain a secret berth to freedom. Finding passage on a vessel to free territory proved a difficult, risk-laden endeavor that sometimes required months or years. A single wrong step, misplaced trust, or a rash inquiry doomed a runaway. Success depended as much on patience and prudence as on daring and courage. Henry Gorham, a 34-year-old slave carpenter, remained in forests for 11 months before he found a way to board a schooner sailing out of a North Carolina port in 1856.[60] The slave Ben Dickenson waited and eavesdropped on harbor conversations for three years until he discovered the right opportunity to stow away.[61] Harriet Jacobs hid in an attic in Edenton for seven years before friends and family arranged her passage to Philadelphia.[62] And Harry Grimes lived in swamp forests for 18 months before contacting a ship in November 1857. "While in the woods," he later recalled, "all my thoughts [were on] how to get away to a free country."[63]

Word of a vessel's master who harbored runaways spread quickly along the docks and from ports into the hinterlands.[64] Gossip, vain hopes, and reality mingled in precarious measure. Approaching the master of a vessel who was rumored to assist slave runaways always posed special dangers, and African Americans who had already escaped or who were planning to flee could rarely afford total confidence in any stranger. The experience of two young slaves in Wilmington illustrates the dilemma. In 1857 Abraham Galloway and Richard Eden approached with considerable trepidation the captain of a schooner bound for Philadelphia. According to William Still, a black leader of the Underground Railroad in Philadelphia who later helped the two men reach Canada, their conversation "had to be done in such a way, that even the captain would not really understand what they were up to, should he be found untrue."[65] By sly indirection, Galloway and Eden had succeeded in finding a captain willing to conceal them amid barrels of turpentine, tar, and rosin for the northward passage—but they were fortunate. He could just as easily have collected a reward on them or sold them back into slavery in another southern port.

William Still. From
William Still, *The
Underground Railroad:
A Record of Facts, Au-
thentic Narratives, Let-
ters, etc., Narrating
the Hardships, Hair-
Breadth Escapes, and
Death Struggles of the
Slaves in their Efforts
for Freedom* (Phila-
delphia: Porter &
Coates, 1872).

The dangers of soliciting a shipboard berth loomed too great for most
runaways, and especially for fugitives unfamiliar with the waterfront. Slaveholders posted descriptions of their runaway slaves in harbor towns and
advertised in local newspapers. An unfamiliar black making inquiries or lin-
gering by the wharves quickly attracted attention. Wilmington and other
ports required hired-out slaves and all free black laborers to wear badges
obtained for a fee from the town commissioners, and the absence of the proper
badge alerted town guards. Several ports, including Wilmington, enforced
evening curfews on all blacks within the town limits.[66] Local authorities
imprisoned black strangers on the slightest suspicion. To avert capture,
slaves relied heavily on intermediaries to establish contact with masters of
vessels or other sailors.

In 1842 a free black man named Peter helped Harriet Jacobs make her
escape by schooner from Edenton. During the years when Jacobs was con-

cealed in town, Peter continually kept in touch with her. Probably with the help of black sailors, Peter finally identified a sea captain who would provide Jacobs passage to Philadelphia aboard his vessel. Jacobs later admitted that the obligatory bribe would have "paid for a voyage to England," but her family and Peter somehow raised enough to pay off the captain.[67] Peter had made meticulous arrangements in all respects. He met Jacobs under cover of dusk at her hideaway and escorted her through the streets of Edenton. He had a rowboat and two oarsmen waiting for her when she arrived at the wharf, and lookouts had been posted to detect any intruders. The captain set sail immediately, and after a short voyage Jacobs found herself safely in Philadelphia.[68]

In 1855 another escaped slave, William Jordan, survived in a Cape Fear forest by eating wild plants and animals and pilfering local plantations. Jordan also depended on a trusted ally to find a seaman sympathetic or mercenary enough to secret him away on his vessel. According to William Still, "William had a true friend, with whom he could communicate; one who was wide awake, and was on the alert to find a reliable captain from the North, who would consent to take this 'property,' or 'freight,' for a consideration. He heard at last of a certain Captain, who was then doing quite a successful business in an Underground way. This good news was conveyed to William, and afforded him a ray of hope in the wilderness."[69] Jordan escaped by sea after hiding in forests for ten months.

Jordan's accomplice knew the Wilmington waterfront. In order to identify the "certain Captain," he must have met with sailors, watermen, or dockworkers known to be abolitionists. While it is impossible to know precisely who those contacts were, it is reasonable to surmise that they may have come from a sizable contingent of seafaring men and shipping merchants who had recently emigrated from New York and New England, inspired by the city's cotton and naval stores boom. Those men and their families continued to have personal ties and trading interests in the North. The fact that they had moved south to share in a prosperity built on slave labor does not necessarily mean that they all embraced slavery. Some held abolitionist sympathies, and others, homesick for the North and resentful of unfamiliar folkways, came to detest the peculiar institution.[70]

Few runaways had intermediaries between land and sea situated as advantageously as did New Bern slaves in the 1830s. According to a letter written in 1838 by a Quaker society president, the son of a local slaveholder regularly concealed slaves in timber vessels bound for Philadelphia. Described as a "most effective worker," the unnamed conspirator also provided northbound slaves with the address of the Vigilance Committee of Philadelphia or had them accompanied by its undercover agents.[71] The slaveholder's son may have been the final contact in a spur of the Underground Railroad that followed the Neuse and Trent Rivers to New Bern, or he may have operated alone. The surviving correspondence is understandably silent on that question. Either way, this homegrown dissident affirms the unpredictable backgrounds of the men and women who supported runaway slaves bent on reaching the sea.[72]

To cross the dangerous divide between land and sea, slaves depended most heavily on maritime blacks. Their maritime culture provided runaways with a complex web of informants, messengers, go-betweens, and other potential collaborators. Having one foot in the local shoreline culture and the other on board the vessels that sailed the Atlantic, slave watermen lay like a gangplank between the two worlds. All the clandestine pathways funneled into seafaring villages, and only watermen could provide the final portage that fugitive slaves needed.

When runaways sought watermen's help, they entered a distinctive maritime society that existed on the outskirts of the plantation world. African Americans stood at its center. A steady traffic of slave boatmen converged on North Carolina ports aboard river and sound boats laden with cotton bales, cedar shingles, and turpentine barrels.[73] Awaiting fair winds or new cargo, black seamen crowded the wharf districts. They worked as stewards and cooks on most ships that sailed out of or visited the state, held skilled crew stations on many vessels, and constituted a majority of hands on more than a few vessels.[74] Slave fishermen arrived in skiffs loaded with shad and mullet destined for their masters' supper tables.[75] Other slaves brought alligators, waterfowl, and small game killed in nearby salt marshes to the waterfront to sell. Still other black boatmen passed by on foraging excursions in search of crabs and marsh birds' eggs for their own consumption.[76] Ferrymen, nearly always slaves, departed from local docks to convey passengers and goods across rivers and to remote island villages. Even slave artisans moved in the harbor traffic, doing the caulking, refitting, rigging, and rebuilding necessary to keep wooden vessels at sea.

At the wharves, slave women peddled fish and oysters, hawked stew and cornbread to hungry sailors, and found a ready market for laundry services. Draymen waited by the score to load their masters' carts with West Indian molasses and rum, Bahamian salt, English cloth, and New England manufactures.[77] Black stevedores trundled freight on and off ships, a profitable and

Thomas H. Jones, a slave stevedore in Wilmington, arranged his flight to New York with a black sailor on the brig *Bell*. Engraving from Thomas H. Jones, *The Experience of Thomas H. Jones, Who Was a Slave for Forty-three Years* (Boston: Bazin and Chandler, 1862).

popular day-labor job.[78] From those wharf laborers, shipping agents hired crews for dredge boats, lighters, and other local workboats.[79]

The breadth and complexity of this African American maritime culture stands out in all seven autobiographies known to have been written by former coastal slaves. This is especially true in the memoirs of former slave watermen London Ferebee, Moses Grandy, and Thomas H. Jones. Raised beside Currituck Sound in the 1850s, Ferebee learned the principles of boatmanship and navigation from his father, who worked in a local shipyard, and from the slave crewmen on his master's sloop.[80] Grandy, as already noted, was indeed a maritime jack of all trades. He operated a river ferry in Camden County, captained canal boats between Elizabeth City and Norfolk, crewed an Albemarle Sound schooner, worked on coastwise packets, and served on brigs and schooners that sailed as far as the Mediterranean.[81] Thomas H. Jones loaded and unloaded cargo on the Wilmington waterfront, where he encountered sailors and boatmen from places far and wide. Jones ultimately found a master of a vessel who was prepared to carry his wife, Mary, and their three children to New York and later negotiated his own escape with a black sailor bound for the same city.[82]

Another firsthand account of slavery, the diary of William Gould I, reveals how far into tidewater plantation society this black maritime culture reached. A New Hanover County planter owned Gould, a slave mason, but Gould worked at least occasionally in Wilmington, ten miles south of his plantation, where he had some liberty and was exposed to a relatively urbane seafaring culture. There Gould apparently picked up more than a passing familiarity with boats. In 1862, early in the Civil War, Gould escaped his plantation by sailing a sloop to a Union blockader. On his second day aboard the Union vessel, he made his first entry in an extraordinary diary and soon wrote a letter to his wife's family in Massachusetts. His highly literate diary and his close ties to New England relatives were possible only in a tidewater plantation society, like that along the Lower Cape Fear, that was entwined with seafaring culture. Union officers welcomed his enlistment into the navy because of his handiness at sea, and Gould served aboard Union vessels that coursed the Atlantic from Cape Fear to France.[83]

While Ferebee, Grandy, Jones, and Gould all indicate slave watermen's potential for assisting runaways, another North Carolina memoirist—William H. Robinson, whose father, Peter, was a slave pilot—provided the greatest insight into how slaves drew upon contacts in the black maritime culture to escape by sea. The experience of Peter and the two Quaker oystermen who were his accomplices also illustrates the intricate planning required to reach a seagoing vessel. Piloting oyster sloops and other vessels in and out of Wilmington harbor around 1850, Peter belonged to the elite corps of black pilots on whom much of coastal transport had relied since the colonial era.[84] His master, a prominent merchant in town, allowed Peter to work by himself, to manage his own affairs within bounds, and to solicit jobs freely in the harbor in exchange for most, if not all, of his piloting fees.

Despite the risks, Peter put his watercraft skills and independence at the disposal of slaves who hoped to escape north. He worked closely with two Quaker abolitionists, Samuel Fuller and "Mr. Elliot," piloting their oyster sloop through local bays and sounds.[85] Deeply enmeshed in harbor life, the three watermen were well positioned to identify mariners who might convey escaping slaves away from Wilmington. Those sailors also kept them in touch with potential benefactors in New England and Canada. Runaways contacted them through Peter, who was well known among local blacks and was readily approached in the wharf district, or through other black watermen, stevedores, tradesmen, or hawkers with whom they dealt in their oyster business. Even from plantations well inland and remote swamps, fugitive slaves may have communicated with Peter and his colleagues with the aid of slave boatmen and draymen who delivered inland products into port towns.

Their regular interaction in the far reaches of coastal waters, well distant from public scrutiny, gave the three conspirators an "opportunity to lay and devise plans" for helping slaves to secure passage on seagoing vessels.[86] They also knew many seamen, observed efforts to catch slaves headed to sea, and cultivated local abolitionists on whom they might call to hide fugitive slaves temporarily or to raise funds for their passage. Aspiring runaways must have found their collective knowledge indispensable. The trio even may have carried black Carolinians from the wharf to seagoing vessels waiting on the Cape Fear River or further south beyond the bar at the two local inlets into the Atlantic.

The success of Peter and his collaborators hinged less on their own unique skills than on the general characteristics of maritime slavery. The harsh restrictions enforced on plantation labor gangs broke down in a maritime economy that was thoroughly reliant on slave watermen for travel, trade, and communication.[87] Regular surveillance proved impractical: too many slave watermen performed too many important jobs over too wide and remote a coastline. Marshy shores and poor roads meant that the simplest chores, such as communicating with neighbors or sending produce to market, revolved around slave boatmen. Work routines used to exact slave productivity and regulate slave behavior on plantations did not stand up well before the forces of wind and tide. Even charting the length of a slave waterman's journey could not be done reliably. Except on steamers, which began appearing locally only about 1840, traveling from Beaufort to Currituck could take one day or two weeks. Poling a Cape Fear flatboat between Hallsville and Wilmington could require two weeks or a month.[88] Inlets and shoals changed constantly and could delay a vessel further. Storm damage and fallen trees rendered smaller creeks and rivers impassable for months. Confronted with that uncertainty, and dependent on African American maritime skills, merchants and planters generally conceded slave watermen the mobility and independence that was necessary to conduct their business.

Most significant to runaways headed to sea, many slave boatmen enjoyed an exceptional amount of privacy and autonomy. Many traveled for days and weeks without overseers on board their vessels. Even those obligated to return to their masters' households every evening had uncommon liberty during the day. They cooked, slept, and socialized in boatmen's camps that sprang up nightly on isolated beaches and remote riverbanks.[89] They mingled with black stevedores and other slaves in busy seaports, and they fraternized with the solitary residents, free and enslaved, at fishing camps and piloting stations. Their work afforded slave watermen the best opportunity to meet runaways, to glean information useful to them, and to connect them with seagoing vessels.

Black watermen also had opportunities to build relationships with white boatmen and sailors who might assist runaways. That was truest on remote islands like the Outer Banks. In small windswept settlements on marshy atolls and sandbanks, slaves associated with their white counterparts, within bounds, on far more equal terms than on the mainland. Certainly the high proportion of watermen in the slave population, their autonomy, and the premium placed on their maritime skills stretched the conventional boundaries of slavery. Many of the Outer Banks slaves were also mulattoes, descended from slave mothers and free white sailors, or from Indian watermen, and their mixed-race heritage and extended family lines contributed in some cases to a certain ambiguity in race relations.[90] Their distance from the seats of power must also have been significant. Not having plantation owners or slave patrols looking over their shoulders, white islanders seem to have taken a greater latitude in their public relationships with bondmen and -women.

No less important, the islanders lived on the edge of an Atlantic seafaring culture renowned for a crude egalitarianism among black and white seamen.[91] Since the colonial era, Atlantic shipping had been characterized by an unusual degree of racial equality in seamen's wages, social status, and duty assignments.[92] In port towns, slaveholders might viably confine such heresies to the taverns and boardinghouses in the wharf district, but at isolated outposts like Ocracoke, Portsmouth, or Davis Ridge those shipboard customs eroded the stricter racial barriers ashore. Island residents had more contact with northern and foreign sailors than with mainland slave patrols. Oftentimes, in fact, they seemed to have deeper commercial and cultural ties to the ports of New England than to mainland North Carolina. They crewed, piloted, provisioned, and lightered Yankee ships and drank with, hunted with, and married "jack tars" from the Northeast. It was no wonder that, at the outbreak of the

Civil War, the state's planters so quickly suspected the loyalties of coastal watermen of both races.[93]

Race relations in seaports were not as wide open as on some of the state's more remote islands, but black and white maritime laborers there still lived and worked together in ways quite different from the ways that pertained in towns inland. A snapshot of New Bern's wharf district in 1850, for instance, would have revealed a veritable melting pot. The waterfront district was majority-black. In two of the district's three boardinghouses free blacks shared living quarters with white sailors. "Black" space and "white" space were all jumbled. A white fisherman boarded with Mary Richardson, a free black woman of some means, while a shipping merchant named Alonzo Perkins had three white boatmen and three free black boatmen living with him. A successful ship's carpenter, Thomas Howard, lived with a young free black woman, his clerk, plus six slaves who presumably helped him in the shipyard. Moses Jarvis, a white merchant, had 3 free black sailors living in his household, as well as 19 slaves. Most of the sailors, black and white, were young and very poor, and many of the white sailors staying in the wharf district had come from New York or foreign ports—in the West Indies, Ireland, the Netherlands, Wales, England, and Germany, among other places.[94] This was obviously not the plantation South, and for slaves determined to reach a ship, it presented one of their most promising chances to escape.

Whether or not they sheltered fugitive slaves, African American seamen had regular contact with a broader world and were fonts of information for blacks confined to shore. Coastal ports like Bath, Ocracoke, and even New Bern may have outwardly resembled backwater outposts on minor trade routes, but a tour of those harbor districts would have belied any notion of provincialism. There a visitor would have met black sailors from many nations, swapping the latest scuttlebutt from Boston, San Juan, and Port-au-Prince in a half dozen languages.[95] The scope of their maritime fraternity could be glimpsed in 1859, when one plot to assist a single Wilmington slave to escape by sea involved black seamen from the West Indies, Sierra Leone, the Sandwich (later Hawaiian) Islands, and New England.[96] Even if black sailors refused such risks, they still kept coastal slaves informed about the political climate beyond the South and offered practical details about coastal geography, sea traffic, and sympathetic captains. Black seamen were also known to carry letters between Carolina slaves and family, friends, and church leaders in the North.[97] Planters inland may have had more success, but at the

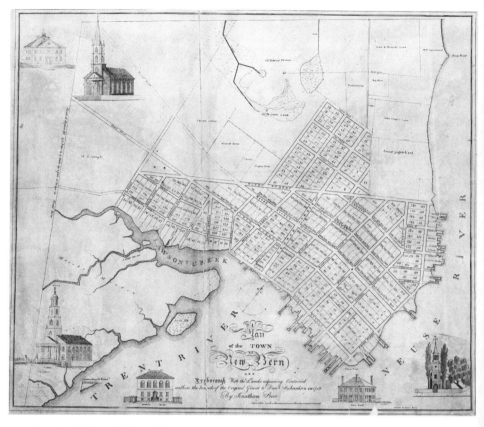

Jonathan Price, "A Plan of the Town of New Bern," 1806. Facing both the Neuse and Trent Rivers, the waterfront district of New Bern presented a mélange of maritime laborers of many different races, ethnicities, and nationalities. Free and slave sailors, shipyard workers, and boatmen mingled there in a way that often threatened planters in the countryside nearby. Courtesy North Carolina Collection, University of North Carolina at Chapel Hill.

coast slaveholders tried in vain to dam a torrent of forbidden knowledge, from which even the smallest droplets could prove invaluable to slaves trying to flee.

The attributes of maritime work also gave slave watermen their own opportunities to escape.[98] Not surprisingly, enslaved sailors most readily fled during voyages to ports outside the South.[99] However, slaveholders routinely anticipated that all fugitive slaves in maritime industries, even those confined to North Carolina, would employ their skills and contacts to escape by sea. Reward announcements published in port newspapers reflected that suspicion.[100] In 1803 Benjamin Smith warned that his slave Bristol, who had briefly been a stevedore in Wilmington, would surely try to reach a ship. (Outraged that Bristol enticed two other slaves to go with him, Smith offered $50 for "his head, severed from his body.")[101] In 1820 the seaman Sam allegedly masqueraded as a free sailor and, his owner lamented, "has, no doubt, already gone or will attempt to go to some of the Northern seaports."[102] When the slave Jim escaped in 1832, his master warned that "he was raised to the water" and would likely to try to board a ship for the North.[103] Captain James Wallace believed in 1838 that Rodney, a slave "accustomed to a seafaring life," would naturally try to flee by ship.[104] And in the spring of that year, Sam Potter of Wilmington also expressed confidence that Caesar, whom he described as "well acquainted with all sorts of vessel work," would seek employment on a northbound vessel.[105] Slaveholders recognized that runaways had to be intercepted before they headed out to sea or they could disappear without a trace into the maritime underworld.

To thwart runaways, political leaders tried to circumscribe black watermen's duties and influence. The maritime economy depended so extensively on black laborers, however, that many shipping agents and business leaders were reluctant even to restrict their activities, much less ban them from working on the water altogether. In 1800 the General Assembly did compel merchants who owned slave pilots to apply for licenses and post bonds of $500 to assure their good conduct.[106] But when state legislators introduced a bill outlawing slave pilots completely in 1816, merchants in Wilmington and Fayetteville defeated the measure.[107] The persistence of escape by sea finally prompted the state legislature to prohibit slaves from piloting vessels over bars or inlets and to ban slaves from traveling on steamboats or schooners without written permission.[108] But even if it had been possible to enforce such laws, which it was not, those restrictions left slave pilots and other black watermen a very strong presence on the North Carolina coast.

Port authorities tried similarly to control black shore workers. Stevedoring, in particular, provided blacks with openings to conceal their escaping brethren on vessels and to prevent the detection of slaves already stowed away. Because black stevedores had regular contact with seamen, they also heard about persons with reputations for aiding runaways and could intro-

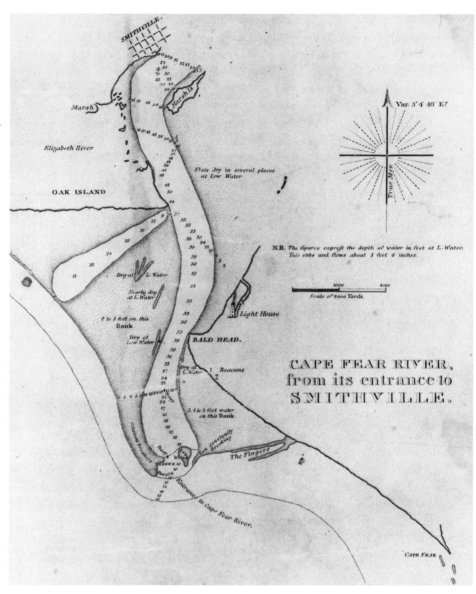

"Cape Fear River, from Its Entrance to Smithville," 1806. The dominance of slave pilots on the Cape River River often provoked controversy. Bar pilots guided seagoing vessels from the ocean into Smithville (later Southport), while river pilots guided vessels from Smithville upriver to Wilmington and beyond. Courtesy North Carolina Collection, University of North Carolina at Chapel Hill.

Turpentine barrels at the Wilmington docks, ca. 1880. The port's waterfront would have looked very similar during the naval stores boom of the antebellum era. Courtesy North Carolina State Archives, Raleigh.

duce them to slaves hoping to reach the North. A citizen writing in the *Wilmington Journal* echoed a popular white sentiment when he argued that "we must have *White* men in the place of *negroes* engaged in that business," because they "shall be under the obligations to inspect the stowage [of] vessels."[109] Shipping agents and harbor authorities found it impractical to outlaw black stevedores, but concerns over slave smuggling eventually led the commissioners of navigation and pilotage on the Cape Fear to contract with private agents to board, search, and fumigate ships in order to force hidden runaways above deck.[110]

If Cape Fear slaveholders could not persuade the masters or owners of private vessels to lessen their reliance on African American laborers, they could exert political pressure on the government to forsake its custom of hiring slaves to work on lightships, revenue cutters, and other federal vessels. Early in 1851, a United States Treasury Department official, C. W. Rockwell, received a complaint that slaves were still employed as sailors in the revenue service despite a federal naval policy against employing slave labor that had been in effect since 1839. Rockwell disapproved of the practice and noted that "Southern gentlemen" seemed universally against it as well. Responding to an inquiry from Rockwell, Robert G. Rankin, the port collector in Wilmington, argued that "white labor cannot be obtained at the hourly rate of compensation allowed." He also suggested that slave boatmen were less prone to fraud and smuggling than white laborers. "It has been the practice [to hire slaves as boatmen] ever since the Revenue Boats has been established in this district, through *all* administrations," Rankin insisted to Rockwell. He relented to his superior's order to hire white boatmen only after he was budgeted extra funds to pay them.[111]

Political leaders viewed black sailors with the greatest wariness. "They are of course," wrote the *Wilmington Aurora*'s editor, "all of them, from the very nature of their position, abolitionists, and have the best opportunity to inculcate the slaves with their notions."[112] Slaveholders went to great lengths to limit the influence of black sailors. The General Assembly passed a law in 1830 that quarantined ships employing free black sailors and prohibited, under penalty of up to 39 lashes, all African Americans from visiting those vessels. The law also made it illegal for black sailors even to "communicat[e] with the coloured people" of North Carolina. The reliance of commerce on black watermen and sailors, however, again conflicted with the spirit of restriction. Coastal merchants harmed by the penalties against northern vessels and local boats with black crewmen had the measure overturned during the next legislative session.[113] When the General Assembly considered prohibitions against free black sailors in later years, warnings that such laws would seriously harm foreign trade also assumed a great deal of importance in rejecting them. The state's ports were already at a comparative disadvantage relative to the deepwater harbors and larger markets at Norfolk, Charleston, and other southern seaports.[114]

Recognizing their critical link in aiding slave runaways, political leaders also sought through municipal ordinances to separate black sailors and slaves. Wilmington, for instance, finally outlawed its slaves from piloting or stevedoring on seagoing vessels manned by free blacks.[115] White citizens also discouraged free black sailors from coming ashore by harassing them in a number of ways. Slave patrols were known to flog and jail black seamen for the most minor infractions of racial decorum.[116] Sheriffs quickly jailed any black sailor whose seaman's papers had been lost or were of questionable

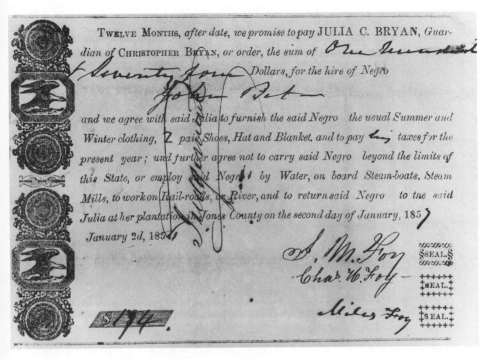

Hiring-out bond prohibiting a slave from working on the water, Jones County, North Carolina, 1857. Courtesy North Carolina State Archives, Raleigh.

authenticity, and sailors who failed to prove their free status were sold into slavery.[117] Ports also took the firmest stands in requiring all free blacks to register with town clerks and wear badges emblazoned with the word "free" on their shoulders.[118]

As a further deterrent, white authorities severely punished free black sailors caught aiding runaways, as illustrated by three cases from the 1850s. In 1855 the Bertie County Superior Court sentenced Alfred Wooby to hang for concealing a slave on a schooner headed down the Roanoke River. In rejecting a petition for pardon, Governor Thomas Bragg reminded Wooby's former employer that "our lawmakers . . . have deemed such punishment necessary to put a stop if possible to the practice of enticing away slaves to the northern states."[119] By then, in the growing racial turmoil just prior to the Civil War, slaveholders had become even more suspicious of black sailors. Also in 1855, Dawson Wiggins faced the hangman's noose for stowing away a slave named Bill on a voyage from New Bern to New York City. His attorney,

Thomas Sparrow, worried that "the public appetite is whetted for the sacrifice of a victim" because so many slaves had recently escaped by sea. Sparrow argued that Wiggins had been blamed solely because he was the only black hand on the vessel, and that any crewman could have been the culprit.[120] No wonder that, in 1859, Wilmington abolitionists frantically raised funds to secure a prominent lawyer for black seamen accused of concealing slaves aboard a ship. They not only secretly financed legal counsel for the four sailors but also somehow arranged for a sympathetic judge to preside over the trial. The stakes were incontestable. "There would be but little danger of hanging if they were slaves," wrote a Quaker ally to a colleague, for "it would be an unjustifiable waste of *property* [but] it is none too good for a free negro in Carolina."[121]

Despite reprisals and regulations, slave watermen provided the best hope for runaway slaves who struggled to reach the sea. Their complex networks somehow persisted beyond the command of slaveholders. Nonetheless, the historical evidence never lets one forget how fragile that network was. The fate that would befall the pilot Peter and his co-conspirators demonstrated that it could collapse at any time. Suspected of abusing his privileged status by planning his and other slaves' escape, Peter was eventually sold into the Deep South. According to his son, he never saw his wife or children again. Suspicious slaveholders also pointedly threatened Fuller and Elliot and warned local overseers not to allow the two oystermen to speak with slaves. Soon after discovering a skull and crossbones painted on the door of his home, Sam Fuller vanished from Wilmington. His family assumed that vigilantes had murdered him for his activities on behalf of fugitive slaves.[122]

Even after they had successfully embarked on the sea voyage for the North, runaway slaves encountered many dangers. Betrayal lurked constantly. A schooner is a small vessel, and fugitives who had hidden themselves or had only the protection of a single seaman crouched in abiding fear. A slave stowaway from North Carolina was captured after 12 days at sea at the mouth of the Mystic River in September 1859 but escaped by jumping ship and swimming to New London, Connecticut.[123] Similarly, in 1849 the master of the *Bell* discovered Thomas Jones where a black sailor had hidden him. Jones avoided re-enslavement in Wilmington only by building a makeshift raft and escaping from the brig while it rested in New York harbor.[124] Other stowaways were not so lucky. On a voyage from New Bern to New York in 1847, sailors discovered the slave Ned hidden in the forecastle of the schooner *Dolphin*. He had apparently been sheltered by two black seamen, Thomas Fortune and Furney Moore.[125] None of the three made it out of the South.[126] Two years later, while sailing to New York City, Captain Smith of the schooner *Minerva Wright* found two Wilmington slaves concealed on board. He abandoned the two men in port at Norfolk, where the sheriff oversaw their return to North Carolina.[127]

A sudden storm, a damaged rudder, or any unexpected delay exposed the frailty of this maritime passage out of bondage. One can scarcely imagine the disappointment of Mary Smith, a stowaway captured only because the *Mary of Duxbury* wrecked on Ocracoke Island.[128] Of course, the threat of shipwreck loomed in the back of every mind when passing the Outer Banks. The skeletons of wrecked vessels littered the beaches from Cape Lookout to Currituck Banks, a constant reminder to all, regardless of race, of one's mortality and the precariousness of sea travel. But for a runaway slave or a free black, a shipwreck meant something more immediate as well: slave castaways such as Mary Smith might be re-enslaved, while free black sailors might find themselves in bondage for the first time. When the schooner *Friend* wrecked in 1804, Wilmington authorities imprisoned a black man named John Read, who spoke French and English and said he "followed the sea," rejecting his claim that he had lost his seaman's papers in the wreck.[129] Two decades later, when the sloop *Falcon* wrecked on Cape Lookout shoals on July 14, 1827, the rescued crewmen included Joseph Raymond, a black seaman; Benjamin Ross, a black cook; and George, a "black boy." They were taken to New Bern, where their fate was to be decided by local leaders.[130]

Other stowaways found that a seagoing vessel did not always afford true asylum, even on the threshold of freedom. After passage of the Fugitive Slave Act in 1850, inspectors searched arriving vessels for runaways in several northern seaports.[131] Antislavery sentiment often prevented the law's strict enforcement, but local officials did capture fugitive slaves from Wilmington in Boston harbor on board the brigantine *Florence* in July 1853 and on the schooner *Sally Ann* in September 1854.[132] Once exposed, stowaways could expect little aid from the maritime underworld that had sheltered them.

Wise slave parents taught their children from an early age never to trust any white folks, especially strangers, and their vulnerability on the seaward passage made fugitive slaves even more fearful of white sailors. Harriet Jacobs could not overcome her deep distrust of the sea captain who had hidden her aboard his schooner, even after they had sailed from Edenton. Having been a domestic servant to an upper-class family, Jacobs admitted that she "was an entire stranger to that class of people." She wrote: "I had heard that sailors were rough, and sometimes cruel. We were so completely in their power, that if they were bad men, our situation would be dreadful. Now that the captain was paid for our passage, might he not be tempted to make more money by giving us up to those who claimed us as property?"[133] In reality, many sailors merited the worst suspicions. While some white sailors held slavery in no high esteem, they also displayed a mercenary inclination that could work to the advantage or disadvantage of runaways like Jacobs. The story was told, for example, of a master of a vessel who informed his crew that he would auction off a stowaway discovered near the Outer Banks to the highest bidder, whether an abolitionist or a slave trader.[134] True or not, the story was quite believable.

William Still would have sympathized with Harriet Jacobs. Two decades later, he responded similarly to a sea captain who, for a price, often carried fugitive slaves out of Virginia and North Carolina. The captain, named Fountain, hardly resembled the refined gentlemen with whom Still worked at the Pennsylvania Anti-Slavery Society. According to Still, his coarse behavior and rugged appearance were "not calculated to inspire the belief that he was fitted to be entrusted with the lives of unprotected females, and helpless children [or] that he could take pleasure in risking his own life to rescue them from the hell of Slavery."[135] He nevertheless proved to be as good as his word. Though Captain Fountain's motives beyond his own financial gain are unclear, he was, in Still's view one of the genuine heroes of the Underground Railroad. Though always rare exceptions, sailors like Fountain could complete the long, difficult channel by which black Carolinians passed from slavery ashore to freedom at sea.

From colonial days onward, the shores of North Carolina had frustrated slaveholders. Small, ill-protected harbors had prevented the development of a major port and stunted growth of the state's plantation economy. Outer Banks inlets posed a constant threat to shipping. Frying Pan Shoals and Diamond Shoals inspired fear in sailors throughout the world. The coastline that seemed so inhospitable to slaveholding merchants and planters, however, provided their black workers with hope of a passage to freedom. It was a tenuous hope, dampened by what must have seemed an endless number of futile attempts and bitter reprisals for every triumph. Yet coastal slaves still dreamed of freedom and continued to dare the high seas all the way up to the Civil War. When war broke out, a few who had braved the sea's escape route returned to guide Union vessels through those dangerous waters. Beyond teaching us about their unquenchable thirst for freedom, their struggles compel us to look past the relatively few slaves who managed to escape by sea, to the broader aspects of maritime and tidewater culture that sustained their clandestine path out of the South. The boundaries of slavery and freedom may have been more complicated than we have ever imagined.

chapter six

The Best and Most Trustworthy Pilots

Slave Watermen in Civil War Beaufort

Slave watermen brought the Civil War to Beaufort, North Carolina, on the night of April 22, 1862. The old seaport's citizens were sleeping peacefully, confidant that the guns of Fort Macon stood between them and a Union assault for at least several more days. Unbeknownst to them, local slave fishermen stood ready to launch rowboats carrying Federal troops from a secluded wharf three miles west. George Allen, a corporal in the Fourth Rhode Island Volunteers, later recalled that the fishermen were "thoroughly conversant with these waters, and were faithful guides." Hidden from the Fort Macon lookouts by darkness, they snaked the boats through the labyrinthine shoals of Bogue Sound and navigated a narrow channel across the mouth of the Newport River. Then, without a word spoken or a torch to light the way, they slipped the craft beneath Fort Macon's ten-inch cannons at pistol-shot range. As they reached Beaufort Inlet, the fishermen let the incoming tide drift the Union troops into the harbor, so that not even the splash of oars alerted the town guards. At sunrise on April 23, Beaufort citizens awoke to find bluecoat pickets patrolling their sand-and-oyster-shell streets. The seaport had passed into Union hands without a shot being fired. Fort Macon, still in Confederate hands, now guarded a port occupied by the Union army.[1]

The use of slave fishermen to pilot the seaport's invading force was only the beginning of Union reliance on maritime black laborers in Beaufort. One of

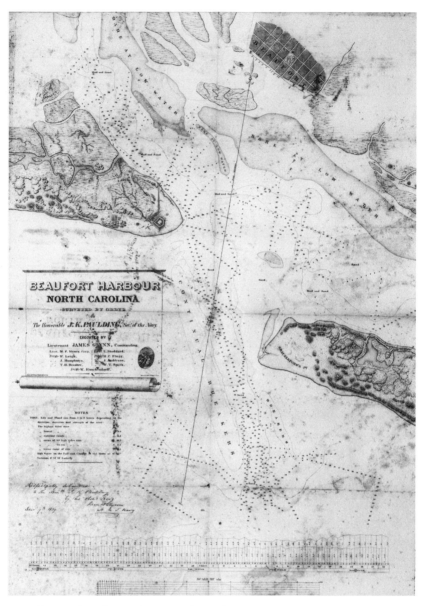

James Glynn, "Beaufort Harbour, North Carolina," 1839. In 1862, recently liberated slave watermen guided Union rowboats along these tricky shoals and narrow channels and made a surprise capture of the port of Beaufort. Courtesy North Carolina Collection, University of North Carolina at Chapel Hill.

Union general Ambrose E. Burnside's first acts in the captured seaport, a Confederate sympathizer named James Rumley groused in his diary, "was to press into service, chiefly as boatmen[,] fifteen or twenty slaves."[2] With black men at the helm, Union vessels quickly took possession of most of the barrier islands in the Beaufort vicinity. Then Burnside's officers looked to the Confederate stronghold at Fort Macon. The imposing fort overlooked Beaufort Harbor from high dunes on the eastern tip of Bogue Banks, a long, narrow barrier island separating Bogue Sound and the Atlantic. Union army planners intended to bombard the fort from gunships, but they also believed that an assault from island batteries was necessary.[3] To establish the batteries, they needed a local pilot to guide a vessel carrying heavy mortars and munitions across Bogue Sound. This was potentially more dangerous than the midnight capture of Beaufort. Instead of rowboats, a larger craft, a steamer probably of 30 or 40 tons, had to navigate the maze of shoals in the sound. Worse, the crossing again had to occur at night in order to elude Fort Macon's guns and, as luck would have it, during a flood tide. If a pilot ran aground, the steamer would founder overnight in the receding tide and Confederate gunners would blast the vessel into splinters at dawn.

The Union forces again recruited a slave pilot. Under cover of darkness, the slave—anonymous to this day—guided the steamer successfully across Bogue Sound. "The man who did take her through without an accident," wrote a New York journalist, "has never received a cent for his service; nor did he expect anything but his freedom."[4] Fort Macon fell after a three-day artillery barrage from land and sea.

The nighttime captures of this small seaport and Confederate fort highlight an important and usually neglected aspect of Civil War history: the role that maritime slaves played in the war and in their own struggle for freedom. Slave watermen and sailors had long played a central part in spreading abolitionist politics and insurrectionary plans in the South, as well as in assisting other African Americans to escape bondage by sea. Prior to the Civil War, they acted covertly, as far as possible from prying eyes. This changed with the Federal occupation of the North Carolina coast. Union and Confederate troops saw a subterranean world of maritime black activity emerge into public view, as African American sailors, boatmen, pilots, fishermen, and stevedores pressed forward their struggle for liberation. In the port of Beaufort, the Union army found itself immersed in this maritime society.

The Union forces could not have found a better place to recruit African American watermen. With a population of approximately 2,000, Beaufort was by far the most sea oriented port on the North Carolina coast. Founded in 1715 on the site of an Indian village called Wareiock that was said to have meant "Fish Town" or "Fishing Village," Beaufort sat on a broad peninsula bordered by Core Sound and two marshy, estuarine rivers, the Newport and North.[5] In 1860 the heads of 570 free families in Carteret County, of which Beaufort was the county seat, earned a living primarily by fishing, piloting, or going to sea, more than the combined total of all other North Carolina counties. Most of the county's men worked on the water at least seasonally.[6] "Farmers, along the sounds and rivers," a later visitor commented, "own boats, as in other places, they own horses."[7] The port was not located on a navigable river or railroad line connecting its harbor to inland markets, however. Beaufort consequently had only a modest shipping traffic compared to New Bern and Wilmington, despite having a finer harbor and closer proximity to the sea. Beaufort's people were tied far more closely to lands beyond the sea than to the state's interior.

"The fact is," recalled an antebellum visitor, "Beaufort in those days, was as nearly out of the world as a town could well be. Communication with New York, Boston, Philadelphia, and Baltimore was more direct and frequent than with New Bern."[8] The town's connection to Caribbean ports was apparent in a creolized air in the lilt in local people's voices and in the styles of their homes, music, and street festivals.[9] Beaufort's prosperity rose and fell with shipping, upheld by a small fleet of local schooners, and with the fortunes of a number of newly emerging fisheries for salted mullet, oysters, and terrapin. The town also had a few shipbuilding yards, which, while small, had long enjoyed "a considerable reputation" for their workmanship, innovation, and high-quality cedar and live oak materials.[10] African American slaves figured prominently in every aspect of maritime commerce in antebellum Beaufort. With less arable land and fewer plantations, Carteret County had a lower percentage of slaves in its total population than did other tidewater counties, only 28 percent as of 1860, but those slaves had always figured heavily in fishing, piloting, sailing, boatbuilding, and other nautical trades.[11]

By the time slave fishermen helped capture Beaufort, Union officers realized that they could not afford to overlook African American watermen. From the first days of the North Carolina invasion in November 1861, when General Burnside's flotilla launched one of the war's earliest campaigns by capturing Hatteras Island, the Union forces had learned to depend on black watermen's piloting skills and knowledge of local waters.[12] On November 17, 1861, at a time when Burnside's men had secured only Hatteras Inlet, astonished bluecoats watched a lone black man named Ben sail a leaky cooner—a long cypress dugout rigged with a mainsail and probably a jib—from a Rebel stronghold on Roanoke Island across a stormy sea to the Federal encampment on Hatteras Island.[13] None would have dared the voyage himself. Soon the renegade sailor provided Burnside with insights into the numbers, morale, and defenses of the Confederate troops at Roanoke Island. Another bondman who had fled from Roanoke Island, a 16-year-old named Thomas Robinson, provided the invading fleet with critical intelligence. He identified Ashby's Harbor as the safest way onto the island and escorted a topographical engineer ashore to survey the landing site. Soon 7,500 bluecoats had successfully come ashore at Ashby's Harbor, setting up a grim surprise for outmanned Confederate troops who had staked their defense of the island on the enemy's ignorance of local waters.[14]

After the Union victory at Roanoke Island, Burnside's forces rapidly captured the coastal towns on the interior of the Outer Banks. The Carolina coast between Currituck Sound and Beaufort Inlet would remain in Union hands for the final three years of the war. With one swift blow, Burnside's fleet had captured the Pamlico and Albemarle Sounds, including the ports of Washington, Plymouth, New Bern, and, finally, Beaufort. The campaign opened a strategic back door to the Confederate capital in Richmond, eliminated a base for privateers, and deprived the Confederacy of much of North Carolina's agricultural wealth. Beaufort became a vital supply depot for Union vessels blockading Confederate shipping on the North Carolina coast. It was also the main point of entry into the state for Union troops and a launching ground for major naval operations further south, especially for the siege of Charleston, South Carolina, in 1863 and the long siege of Fort Fisher, near Wilmington, in 1864 and 1865.[15] To an important extent, black pilots made all of this possible.[16]

As Burnside's armada secured a narrow stretch of coastline, runaway slaves staged a massive boatlift. Bondmen and -women who had previously piloted their masters' vessels or fished for the big house now used their maritime skills to gain their freedom. They commandeered makeshift rafts, cooners, periaugers, and flatboats, as well as the finest sloops and schooners, and guided them to Federal territory. Watching this extraordinary boatlift, Union soldiers could not help but be impressed by the seamanship displayed by the black refugees. A crowd of slaves, their clothes "patched until their patches themselves were rags," sailed 75 miles from the Roanoke River port of Plymouth down the Albemarle Sound, across the Croatan Sound, and then past rebel forts to Roanoke Island. "How they succeeded," a bluecoat exclaimed, "is a wonder to us all."[17] A dingy loaded with fleeing "contrabands," as slaves who escaped behind Union lines were called, sailed down the Chowan River while a frustrated owner took potshots at the boat from shore. A slave woman named Juno escaped with her children by paddling a canoe down the Neuse River at night. A slave waterman known as "Big Bob" carried 16 runaways to a Union navy vessel at Washington, North Carolina, and then headed back upriver into Rebel territory for more.[18] Another slave pilot slipped 24 runaways aboard his master's schooner at Columbia, on the Scuppernong River, and sailed to freedom at Roanoke Island.[19] By mid-1862, more than 10,000 contrabands had converged on the North Carolina coast.

The scene in Beaufort was one of unrivaled bedlam and joyous homecoming. Slaves inland thronged to the town's wharves, most of them arriving by boat. "Our town is crowded with runaway negroes," James Rumley scribbled in his diary in December 1862. "Not only the able bodied, but the lame, the halt, the blind and crazy, have poured in upon us, until every habitation has been filled with them." Already in stunned disbelief that Burnside's forces actually paid wages to slave pilots, Rumley grew even more disdainful as he watched runaway slaves pouring into Beaufort. "Even the Methodist Parsonage and the Odd Fellows Lodge have been desecrated in this way," he wrote, "and are now filled with gangs of these black traitors."[20] Scenes like one that occurred on August 20, 1862, when at least two boatloads of slave families sailed jubilantly down Bogue Sound into Beaufort, grew commonplace.[21] The county's black sailors, fishermen, and boatbuilders appeared at the Beaufort waterfront almost immediately. Eventually, as the Union troops occupying Beaufort began to conduct coastal raids and reconnaissance missions further south, slaves who did not have access to boats fled to meet Union vessels. On one occasion, a Union reconnaissance party to Bogue and Bear Inlets returned to Beaufort with 43 runaways.[22] Such newcomers left their bondage behind for good, but many still did not consider the seaport a satisfactory refuge and sought to distance themselves further from their former masters. Some attempted to flee Beaufort on Union vessels, as was the case, for example, on July 6, 1862, when an aghast Rumley noted that "some negroes went voluntarily and boldly on board [the *Empire City*] before the eyes of their owners." Other slaves boarded the northbound steamer stowed away in boxes and casks.[23]

The mass flight of slaves to Federally occupied ports such as Beaufort sent a powerful signal to African American slave families far inland. Long vital agents of communication between coastal ports and the state's interior, black boatmen now spread word of the Union invasion into the plantation districts of eastern North Carolina. The details of how to reach Federal territory— what towns were in Union hands, where Confederate power was weakest, what routes to freedom were safest—flashed through slave communities. In some cases, black soldiers and intelligence agents recruited contrabands to return to Confederate territory as spies and messengers to spread this news. In other cases, word spread along time-worn routes that slaves and their free allies had crafted to protect slave runaways before the war. This exodus revealed to coastal planters for the first time the particulars of long-standing patterns of slave organization that had remained clandestine until then. Kate Edmondston, a Roanoke River planter, witnessed the daily departure of slaves from her neighborhood. "Nearly a hundred crossed the river last night and went into Bertie [County] on their way to Yankee lines," she wrote in her diary. "So much method do they seem to observe and so well are they piloted that the idea of its being a panic seems to lose ground."[24]

Many coastal planters wisely relocated their slaves inland as soon as word of the invasion force reached them. Those who tarried paid a heavy price. Henry Jones, an overseer for the Donnell family's two plantations near Lake Mattamuskeet, a few miles inland from Pamlico Sound, wrote John R. Donnell as early as September 12, 1862, to inform him that control over his slaves was eroding. Any illusions about the slaves' fidelity to him shattered as soon as word of the Union invasion reached the remote plantation; so, too, did any notion of his benevolent paternalism. Jones reported that the slaves were growing "restless, careless, & don't want to work." A few of Donnell's slaves had already escaped, and Jones had shot "old Pompey" for disobedience and threatening him.[25] Ten days later, Jones wrote that "something like 100 [slaves had] gone off in the last month," 35 on a single night.[26] The rest of Donnell's slaves departed when Yankee troops raided Lake Mattamuskeet in 1863.[27]

African American watermen spread knowledge of the Federal invasion far beyond Union lines. In November 1862, a journalist reported that near Goldsboro, sixty miles up the Neuse River west of Union territory, "the negroes are beginning to manifest . . . a general spirit of insubordination. . . . Almost every day negroes are shot . . . for attempting to run away."[28] William Loftin, a Goldsboro planter, was among slaveholders hit hardest. His letters to his mother describe a succession of slave uprisings that amounted to personal tragedies for him. Even before Beaufort fell in 1862, he informed his mother that "a good many negroes are running away . . . [and] all of mine are gone to [the Yankees] from the oldest to the youngest." Six months later, he reported that the last of his aunt's slaves had also departed, "even old Rose and David." Loftin may have felt that his low point had been reached that year—on October 2, 1862, he wrote "all that I ever had is gone"—but the final affront occurred during a Union raid in January 1863: "My boy Tony came up with the Yankees in full uniform saying he was a U.S. soldier. He went to J. H. Bryan's and took his gun away from him. He says he has killed four damned rebels. . . . He had a rifle strapped to his back."[29]

While the boatlift of runaway slaves wreaked havoc on plantation society across North Carolina, the use of runaway slave watermen to capture Beaufort and Fort Macon had been only the beginning of their service to the Union. There was a general shortage of pilots along the North Carolina coast, and Union efforts to impress local white pilots faltered.[30] In Beaufort, Union commanders discovered, according to one journalist, that "the negroes were altogether the best and most trustworthy pilots"—and, he added, "few harbors were more difficult of navigation than that of Beaufort."[31] When the Reverend Horace James, the occupying army's superintendent of Negro affairs, visited the seaport in 1864, he witnessed no fewer than 100 black watermen ferrying troops and supplies to Federal camps and lookout posts. "This whole business [is] wholly in the hands of the negroes," Reverend James reported, and he observed that they "take to the water almost as readily as the sea fowl that abound in this vicinity."[32]

The advantage of employing local pilots was incalculable. Prior to the battle of Roanoke Island, Union pilots had grounded countless vessels and had sunk at least five others. The Federal flotilla had taken almost a month to enter Hatteras Inlet and nearly had to return north for fresh stores of food and water. The unfamiliarity with Carteret County waters made passing through Beaufort Inlet a risky business and made every raiding party and reconnaissance mission a potential disaster. Shattered rudders, grounded vessels, missed rendezvous, stranded scouting parties, and similar mishaps occurred so frequently as to be almost comical.[33] Union pilots found the shallow, shifting inlets and channels unnerving, nautical charts useless, and virtually all of the coastline near Beaufort nightmarish.[34] A bluecoat infantryman quickly saw the difference when a local pilot—of unnamed race—took over the helm on a transport entering Beaufort Inlet. "Before we went carefully and slowly along," he wrote home in November 1862, and "now we went full speed winding, turning, straight—right—left and so on, till we entered More-head City."[35] Confederate patriots were galled that their advantage of fighting in familiar territory was undercut by the knowledge and experience that black watermen supplied Union troops. "The negroes . . . in that region are mere nomads," complained Kate Edmondston in her diary, "owing allegiance to Neptune and Boreas only"—a reference to classical gods of the sea and wind.[36]

A slave pilot was a valuable asset for the Union forces even if he never took the helm. Many fugitives from the Confederacy brought with them a knowl-edge of local geography and intelligence about Rebel troops that was useful to Union commanders, but slave pilots contributed a specialized understanding of coastal waters that had a unique value.[37] The planning of scouting parties, reconnaissance missions, and military raids always benefited from intimacy with local waters. In 1862, for instance, Union navy officers consulted with a black pilot named Washington Newton about the feasibility of a surprise attack on Wilmington, the state's only major port still held by the Con-federacy. They were contemplating a ruse in which the uss *Brewster* and *Spaulding* would have masqueraded as blockade runners in order to sneak past Fort Fisher into the state's largest port. Newton must have been a Cape Fear river pilot or one of the Southport pilots who guided seagoing vessels across the river's bar, for he was conversant with both the Cape Fear River and Wilmington's Rebel fortifications. The black pilot explained to the navy plan-ners why the proposed attack could not succeed, and it was not attempted.[38]

African American watermen did far more than piloting during the Federal campaign. They had been involved in every maritime trade in antebellum ports and seemed to be everywhere on the water in wartime Beaufort. The Union quartermaster hired black watermen to man the boats that enforced the Union blockade along the state's smaller inlets. In the occupied ports, including Beaufort, other "contrabands," reported Vincent Colyer, "served regularly as crews on about forty steamers . . . [and] a number of men were good carpenters . . . and did effective work at . . . ship joining."[39] Black stevedores loaded and unloaded Union vessels and also used their boating skills to refloat sunken vessels.[40] Yet other contrabands employed dugout canoes to catch logs and raft them to sawmills.[41] Others earned their living by ferrying off-duty troops. Among them was a boatman named Cuff, who showed up every morning at Fort Macon in case any of the Union soldiers wanted to sail to Beaufort.[42] Other boatmen took off-duty soldiers across the Newport River between Beaufort and Morehead City.[43]

Black fishermen also helped to make the port's contraband community more self-reliant and to enable the fugitive slaves to earn money by selling seafood to Union troops. Their enterprise kept food aid from becoming quite so important a bargaining chip in the Union's negotiations with black leaders over the status of the contrabands, and it contributed to making Beaufort a duty station coveted throughout the Union army. While Federal soldiers inland subsisted on jerky and beans, the servicemen in Beaufort enjoyed abundant seafood, most of it provided by black fishermen. Wartime conditions kept most provisions in short supply, but oysters, drum, gray trout, sheepshead, shad, and mullet could always be purchased from the former slaves for a few cents. Black fishermen hawked their catches around Union camps, and black women sold fish dinners from their homes and roadside stands.[44] Guided by black watermen, other soldiers ventured onto Bogue, Back, and Core Sounds, where the fishing, as a Vermonter put it, was "glorious."[45] "Fish is to be found everywhere," opined a New Bern editor in 1864, "in the market, on the table of every Carolinian, as well as the 'hated Yankee.' It is the staple article of diet, fish in the morning, fish at noon, fish at night, fish for lunch, and fish all the time."[46] Massachusetts militiaman D. E. Dunlop, who relished the local oysters, expressed a common sentiment among the men fortunate enough to be stationed in Beaufort. "It is very pleasant and cozy here," he wrote home, and added, "it does not seem much like soldiering."[47]

The former slaves found occupied Beaufort rather less comfortable than did Union soldiers. Navigating an ever-shifting race line was frequently more difficult than steering a ship across Diamond Shoals. The clearly demarcated etiquette that governed every encounter between a black person and a white person before the Civil War had been erased, but new lines of racial conduct had not yet been drawn. Black and white seemed to meet on trembling earth, the experience fraught with a foretaste of the uncertainty that greeted freedpeople throughout the South during Reconstruction. To some whites, the old order had dissolved that fateful night when black watermen slipped Union troops into the seaport. They no longer expected utter deference from blacks at every turn. For maritime people who had dealt on at least somewhat more equal footing with blacks at sea or in foreign ports, this may not have been quite as large a step as for whites raised on a southern plantation. To other whites in Beaufort, even the most minor breeches of Old South racial etiquette, such as a black man refusing to yield the sidewalk, provoked seething rages. Inevitably, the seaport's blacks tested the boundaries of their new freedoms in these and other ways. When an African American woman demanded that a Mr. Davis relinquish his ownership of her daughter, Davis and another Beaufort white man "tied [her] to a tree[,] her arms over her head and then whipped her severely." A Union captain reported that, when he saw her, "the flesh on her arms was badly lacerated and her arms covered with blood."[48]

Only the power of the occupying army and the contrabands' own insistence on self-defense curbed this sort of fierce retaliation against the former slaves. Of course, black racial attitudes shaped these uncertain encounters no less than did white attitudes. Not surprisingly, some of the former slaves were more prepared psychologically than others to relate to white people as equals, or even as somewhat more equal. Many continued to be called by their first names only, to give ground on a sidewalk, to sit apart on ferries, or to cast their eyes downward when speaking to a white person. Others did not.

In gauging their new leeway, the seaport's black residents likewise had to consider both the Union's erratic support for black civil rights and its no less reliable fortunes in battle. At the same time, Beaufort was the scene of a remarkable experiment in race relations. While many Union troops stationed in the seaport regarded blacks with prejudices indistinguishable from those of the slaveholding class in the South, others brought ardent abolitionist feelings that they articulated both politically and personally. As can be seen in a variety of Union soldiers' diaries, as well as in wonderful drawings of wartime life in Beaufort by bluecoat Edward Champney, Union soldiers attended worship services at black churches, roomed and boarded with black families, played with black children, and made enduring friendships with black men and women.[49]

Race relations in occupied Beaufort inevitably shifted in response to black political actions, but they were also affected by class and political divisions within the town's white population. Overall, Beaufort's white residents had not been strong supporters of secession, and the occupying troops were surprised initially at the extent of white sympathy for the Union. In 1862 J. Madison Drake, a New Jersey volunteer, noted how enthusiastically local white people supplied his company with seafood and produce. He described Carteret County citizens—"especially the poor classes"—as sympathetic to the "old flag."[50] A large number of white residents showed little enthusiasm for the Confederate cause. Many had longstanding family or shipping ties to New

York and New England, and the bonds of dependency and paternalism that existed inland between wealthy planters and poor whites had little meaning in a maritime economy dominated by fishing and shipping.[51] Many local shipping merchants, boatbuilders, and fishermen had emigrated from the maritime districts of New England, in fact, and Yankee fishermen and sailors had always been welcomed in the port. On the other hand, a few (but only a few) Beaufort families lost loved ones during Burnside's siege of Fort Macon, personal tragedies that no doubt shaped their feelings toward the Union.[52]

Still, many adapted rather comfortably to the Federal occupation. Local white watermen's families—described by an American Missionary Association (AMA) worker as "more abject than the contrabands"—could not afford to relinquish the fish and oyster trade entirely to their black neighbors and took advantage of the chance to sell both fish and produce to the occupying army.[53] Even James Rumley acknowledged, with more than a little disgust, that "the people of this County find here a ready market for their agricultural products, fish, and every living thing from beneath the water."[54]

The seaport's use as a coaling, supplying, and refitting depot for Union vessels sparked a financial boom along its waterfront, and few local businessmen, no matter where their political loyalties lay, allowed the profits to pass them by. Pro-Union sentiment was not always a matter of convenience, however, and Unionist meetings had occurred publicly in Carteret County into the middle of 1862, until a series of Confederate kidnappings and assaults on Union sympathizers compelled Unionists into a more reticent posture.[55] Guerrilla attacks did not deter some of Carteret's ladies from entertaining the bluecoats. The first marriage between the enemies, that of a New Jersey private and a "Miss Bell," occurred barely six weeks into the Federal occupation, on May 29, 1862.[56] The comparatively warm hospitality shown the Union soldiers by the white women of Beaufort contributed to the seaport's idyllic reputation among northern soldiers. Referring to Mercy Hospital, a Union clinic built directly over Taylor Creek, a New Bern soldier wrote rather longingly that "the patients ride in sail boats, eat strawberries, and disport with the fair secesh of Beaufort."[57]

If most white citizens indulged the Union occupation, the seaport still had a significant number of Confederate partisans. They refused to cooperate with Union officials, reported local Union sympathizers to Confederate guerrillas, and quietly smuggled military intelligence and imported goods out of the port. The seaport's citizens who were kin to the large slaveholding planters residing north and west of Beaufort embraced the Confederate cause most ardently. James Rumley's diary forcefully conveys their bitterness toward the Union occupation in general and the liberation of local slaves in particular. At first, Rumley and many of the town's other leading citizens did not assume that the Federal occupation would end slavery. Soon after the capture of Beaufort, in fact, Rumley was among a local group that optimistically petitioned Burnside to ban slaves from crossing Union lines in order, as he put it, "to avoid the difficulty created by a late act of the Federal Congress prohibiting the surrender of fugitive slaves after they have entered the lines of the army."[58]

At first consenting to their plea, Burnside did not, as it turned out, have the ability to stop the great boatlift carrying runaways to Federal territory. As the contrabands forced the issue of slavery into the war's forefront, men such as Rumley grew more hostile to the Union occupation.[59] Rumley saw the slave code's decay as a harbinger of doom and chaos. He abhorred that Union officers took advantage of slave pilots to defeat Confederate defenses, but he seems scarcely to have comprehended that they would hire the pilots for wages. He likewise saw black schools as seditious. He called the Union enlistment center in Beaufort "the house of Satan and the very gate of hell."[60] He blanched at white Union troops fraternizing openly with black women. He complained that former slaves could legally accuse white citizens of crimes and testify against them at military tribunals. On a certain level, Rumley simply could not envision a world that treated African Americans as his peers—and he could not imagine a world without slave labor. "Drudgeries, to which they have never been accustomed, have now to be performed by delicate women and aged men, while the negroes," he wrote in scorn and despair, "look on with indifference."[61]

The lack of white support for the Confederacy stung Rebel loyalists such as James Rumley at least as much as the disaffection of their slaves. Even as early as the fall of 1863, Confederate deserters had begun to crowd Beaufort's streets. Rumley alleged rightly that the deserters flocked to the seaport because, in his words, "they find a safe asylum in a place farther beyond the reach of Confederate Power than any other in the state."[62] By this point in the war, Rumley had seen so much of his world turned upside down that his diary's reflections seem drained of feeling. Words that in 1862 would have been written in furious indignation now came out matter-of-factly. "Our town is crowded with refugees," he scrawled without comment in December 1863, "most of them are young men who have fled from conscription. They . . . speak very contemptuously of 'Old Jeff' and the 'rebel Confederacy.'"[63]

After the Civil War, Elizabeth Oakes, a local congressman's wife, wrote a friend that in the Beaufort vicinity "they were for the Union mostly"; "but," she added, tellingly, "an army is an army."[64] Indeed, even for Beaufort's most fervent Unionists the Federal occupation soon grew troublesome. The sight of former slaves exercising new freedoms disenchanted some white residents. To what extent the Union's growing support for abolition affected local white attitudes toward the Federal occupation is unclear. Without a doubt, however, the restrictions imposed by the occupying army exasperated white residents. Military edicts regulated nearly every aspect of daily life. Federal officers set prices for food and most other goods and services, down to the cost of a haircut, and they required permits for everything from traveling beyond the town limits to purchasing a coffin. They also decided all judicial matters in a manner that local whites found capricious.[65] White watermen resented the commandeering of their boats for Union duty, sometimes, no doubt, to be piloted by former slaves. Union forces claimed many public buildings for military uses.[66] Some of these actions might have been dismissed by fairer-minded souls as unavoidable aspects of wartime occupation, but Union troops also subjected Beaufort's white citizenry to measures that southern whites considered unforgivable indignities. At one point, a Union captain impressed, in the words of an AMA missionary, "all or many of the secech" to labor on Fort Macon's defenses. The sight of black refugees "in ecstasy upon seeing them pressed into service" did little to lessen local white resentment against the Union occupation.[67] Furthermore, the fact that at least a few Union officers seemed bent on exploiting their military powers for financial gain by exporting every local product from turpentine to Outer Banks ponies did not help.[68] These battles in what historian Wayne Durrill has referred to as the state's "Inner Civil War" shaped the political geography in which African Americans had to maneuver during the war.[69]

During the Civil War, African American culture and society blossomed openly in Beaufort in a way that had been impossible during slavery. None of the contrabands could know how long their moment of freedom would last, yet old women sang hymns of praise and jubilation late into the nights. Families once separated by the auction block celebrated joyful reunions, while other ex-slaves searched fruitlessly for sons and daughters, husbands and wives, mothers and fathers.[70] Taking advantage of the Union army's initial confusion about their legal status, an unknown number of African Americans managed to slip out of Beaufort on Union transports. Others chose to remain in Beaufort and support the Union as pilots, spies, or, eventually, soldiers and sailors. Many black men and women found jobs in Beaufort as launderers, wood cutters, cooks, nurses, turpentiners, stewards, laborers, or servants, many of them working for the Federal army. Other refugees later moved to near New Bern, site of the Union army's largest contraband camp, or, weary of abuse by both sides in the war, leased Federally occupied lands from the U.S. Treasury Department to raise cotton or produce naval stores for their own gain.

Many of the Union soldiers in Beaufort found the everyday life of the former slaves fascinating. Their letters and journals refer frequently to ordinary aspects of African American culture about which a native southerner probably would not have bothered to comment: the Mande-influenced textiles, with their bright red stripes, so favored by many coastal bondmen, for example, or the habit of decorating huts with gourds and feathers.[71] But if the seaport's bluecoats felt such customs lent an exotic air to their duty station, they found other elements of slave culture more disquieting—and a first sign that the former slaves would not simply embrace Yankee culture or politics as their own. Expressions of the communion of the living and the dead, a central tenet in Ba-Kongo and Yoruba religion, in which art and ritual mediated a spiritual relationship between the current generation and its ancestors, seemed most troubling, especially because those African-rooted beliefs had entwined with—and, in the soldiers' eyes, distorted—Christian doctrine.

Union soldiers observed with curiosity the mass baptisms that took place in Taylor Creek, right off Front Street, but seemed almost haunted by the funeral celebrations that, in one's words, "render night so hideous by their songs and shoutings."[72] Similarly, the drama, fervor, and ecstasy of the ex-slaves' unbounded worship rattled white missionaries. For northern soldiers accustomed to Puritan hymns and solemn prayers, those religious practices must have been disconcerting.[73] For the liberated slaves, though, the open expression of their religious faith was exhilarating. Before the Civil War, planters had restricted slave religion severely, forcing African Americans to observe their own rituals in swamps and forests. Not surprisingly, liberated Beaufort became the scene of an extraordinary African American cultural renaissance and religious revival between 1862 and 1865.

In those fearful and intoxicating years, the contrabands filled summer nights with music. Then, as now, the appeal of African American music subverted cultural barriers and racial prejudices. A few of the white Union sol-

Black boys on the beach near Beaufort, 1862, by Edward Champney. Courtesy Outer Banks History Center, Manteo, North Carolina.

diers appreciated the sacred music sung in Beaufort's black churches, but more reveled in black secular music. At a freedpeople's camp near New Bern, large crowds attended performances of what one soldier called "'jigging'—a species of vocal and pantomime music," he went on to say, "almost peculiar to the African race." Jigging involved several performers building a rapid, syncopated rhythm by clapping and hitting their palms on their thighs, legs, and chest and accenting that beat with singing. "The time thus beat could be followed by the dancer as precisely as if played upon a full band."[74] Similar performances must have also occurred in Beaufort, and the liberated slaves quickly made both vocal and instrumental music a part of their parades on the Fourth of July and Emancipation Day.

Strong underground currents of African American spirituality had flowed beneath slavery's bedrock prior to the Civil War. That coastal slaves had worshiped in covert congregations seems certain considering how quickly

Gingerbread vender on the beach, Beaufort, 1862, by Edward Champney. Courtesy Outer Banks History Center, Manteo, North Carolina.

their churches appeared in occupied Beaufort. The refugees immediately made churches a centerpiece of wartime life. Many of the former slaves crowded into Purvis Chapel, founded by free black Methodists in 1854, and soon transformed it into one of the first southern congregations affiliated with the African Methodist Episcopal Zion (AME Zion) Church.[75] A black Baptist church sprang up seemingly out of nowhere, while a significant number of Beaufort contrabands worshiped at Washburn Seminary, a church and school founded by the AMA and governed jointly by its missionaries and contrabands.

The Methodist Church's Benevolent Society, organized before the Civil War, showed itself ready to aid runaway slaves from the first days of the Federal invasion, as did other mutual-aid societies that had existed clandestinely during slavery. They came out of the shadows to assist the black refugees and, at least as important, to serve as foundations for organizing self-help and political groups among the former slaves. The black congregations distributed food and clothes to new refugees and to the families of black recruits. They helped contrabands locate family members, many of them still in Confederate territory. They helped to recruit Union soldiers and undercover agents. And they became a center of black political activity, hosting pro-Union meetings and inviting Union leaders, black and white, to address them.

Education was always a central concern within the African American congregations. Wherever black churches arose, schools soon followed. Having been forbidden to read or write before the Civil War, the former slaves now passionately embraced book learning. By the fall of 1863, the Baptist church, the Methodist church, and Washburn Seminary all housed both day schools for children and night classes for adults. African Americans' ardor for learning impressed many Union soldiers. One observed that a group of black watermen "had each his spelling book which was speedily whipped out and zealously studied at every break."[76] With support from the New England Freedmen's Aid Society and the National Freedmen's Relief Association, the AMA first founded the Whipple School in Beaufort in 1863 and eventually supplied a number of teachers for other local schools.[77] The contrabands at Washburn Seminary, who were constantly wrestling with AMA missionaries for control of its church and school, soon began to help recruit new teachers. Somewhat to the consternation of the missionaries, they showed a special preference for hiring black Union soldiers stationed at Beaufort or Morehead City.[78] They also persuaded private tutors, again usually black Union soldiers, to organize new schools whenever the church schools grew overcrowded. By 1864, several hundred contrabands attended Beaufort schools, including more than 100 children at a school on Market Street.[79]

The contrabands spearheaded the organization and support of the Beaufort schools. They outfitted school buildings with furniture and supplies, though hardly lavishly. Generally, they were able, in a teacher's words, to "pay their way." At one school, students paid $5 in tuition, $1 for classroom rent, and 30 cents for light.[80] Such fees were a substantial sum under the circumstances, and AMA instructor George Greene acknowledged that "some who pay for books really have to deny themselves most severely."[81] To most of the black refugees, however, schooling was well worth the price. Hundreds of contrabands paid hard-earned wages to send themselves or their children to Beaufort schools. In 1864, they even found a few extra dollars to thank their teachers with a gift of a Thanksgiving supper, one they could not afford for themselves.[82] They seem to have shared the sentiments of Beaufort freedman George Jenkins, who wrote his former teacher, a Miss Sarah, "We never will forget the kind teachers for bringing light to our land, when she was dark as night."[83]

Despite the earnest efforts of the northern missionaries and the seriousness of their students, black efforts to gain an education remained difficult throughout the Federal occupation. Few of the black teachers from the Union army remained long in Beaufort before being transferred. Sometimes white missionaries grew frustrated and quit because of overcrowded classrooms, lack of heat, and shortages of school equipment. Some seemed disappointed that former slaves who so desperately sought the three R's proved less interested in their moral, political, or spiritual guidance.

Other obstacles to black schooling abounded. Many of the contrabands could not find money enough for decent clothes to wear to school, much less to pay for tuition or books. Older students left at midterm to enlist in the Union army or found themselves impressed to serve as stevedores at the Federal docks in Morehead City or to build fortifications as far away as New Bern.[84] More than once, the Union army commandeered school buildings to serve as hospitals.[85] Most disruptive was the yellow fever epidemic of 1864; it killed many students and several teachers and led eventually to the temporary cancellation of classes as too great a risk to public health. A schoolteacher later recalled the epidemic as "a time of heat, languor, sickness and death."[86] In addition, while not a problem within the safety of Beaufort's town limits, in the surrounding countryside Confederate guerrillas targeted black schools for military raids. They succeeded in making school attendance an insurrectionary activity, one that threatened harmful repercussions for black students after the war. Confronted by so many obstacles, the seaport's black residents frequently had to seek out more informal schooling. On December 9, 1864, Aunty Southwhite, a former slave who lived in Beaufort, offered Corporal Edmund J. Cleveland a quilt if, in his diary's words, "'I learn her how to read.'"[87]

Few wartime visitors shaped the overcrowded seaport's complex racial politics more than the black sailors serving in the Union navy. Black navy sailors first arrived in Beaufort aboard Burnside's invasion fleet. Their numbers grew steadily as the vessels from the North Atlantic Blockading Squadron began to use Beaufort Harbor for coaling and refitting, and later as Union vessels crowded into the harbor in preparation for the sieges of Charleston and Fort Fisher. News of an independent black regiment forming in New Bern, instigated by former slaves without the Union's approval, reached the seaport late in 1862. Its black soldiers would eventually be incorporated into the 35th, 36th, and 37th Regiments, United States Colored Troops, made up mainly of ex-slaves from eastern North Carolina.[88] The black regiments boarding Union transports at Morehead City were a remarkable sight for local blacks, who closely followed their campaigns in South Carolina, Georgia, and Florida. Many of the soldiers' families, in fact, remained encamped at a local contraband settlement at the "Hammocks."[89] And although the sight of black soldiers in Union blue did not stir souls in Beaufort until 1863, black sailors had stood out from the war's first days as a powerful symbol of the African American struggle for freedom.

The navy's willingness to enlist African Americans had strong historical antecedents. Blacks had long composed a large part of the maritime labor force in the Americas, and ship recruiters perpetually faced chronic shortages of skilled hands. The United States Navy often looked to black sailors, especially in times of crisis. Blacks had served in the American navy from 1775 to 1798 and composed approximately 10 percent of sailors during the Revolutionary War. The United States also enlisted black sailors during the War of 1812, when they again made up about 10 percent of the enlisted naval force. Blacks continued to serve aboard U.S. Navy vessels up to the Civil War, though after 1839, under pressure from southern leaders, naval policymakers set a quota on black enlistments of roughly 5 percent.[90] As a result, the Union navy began the Civil War with black sailors and racially integrated crews, the latter a step in keeping with maritime custom but one never adopted by the Union army. Just prior to the invasion of the North Carolina coast, the Union sanctioned the employment of runaway slaves and other contrabands as "boys"—the lowest ratings—on ships of war.[91] By the end of 1862, as they faced a shortage of sailors, naval leaders had opened higher ratings to the contrabands, including seaman, ordinary seaman, fireman, and coal heaver.[92] Black sailors composed just under 5 percent of the Union's 18,447 sailors in 1861, but their numbers eventually grew to as high as one in four of Union enlisted seamen. Out of a total of 12,144 sailors serving aboard the 139 vessels making up the North Atlantic Blockading Squadron, headquartered in New Bern, 1,824 were black.[93] During the siege of Fort Fisher, blacks composed approximately 11 percent of Union sailors. One of them, Clement Dees, a black seaman who hailed from the Cape Verde Islands, earned the Medal of Honor.[94]

While many of the navy's black sailors arrived in Beaufort from distant ports, former slaves from North Carolina also served on Union vessels. At least 721 black North Carolinians enlisted in the Union navy.[95] Handy and Isaiah Rhodes escaped from a plantation at Catharine Lake, in Onslow County, joined the Union navy at Beaufort on December 2, 1863, and served together on the USS *William Badger*.[96] John Griffin, a slave waterman in Currituck County, sailed to the USS *Brandywine*, where he enrolled in the Union navy.[97]

William Gould, the slave mason, escaped from Rich Inlet aboard a sloop in 1862 and then served with the blockading squadron between Beaufort and Cape Fear.[98] Prior to the Civil War, most of the black recruits had been farmhands, ditchers, and other hard laborers in coastal counties, though a sizable percentage—just over 16 percent of those whose military records listed an occupation—had worked in the maritime trades: Anderson Burrows, of Hyde County, as a fisherman; Obid Nelson, of Beaufort, as a "lighter man"; Mills Reddick, of Perquimans County, as a steamer's engineer; Scipio Spicer, of Chowan County, as a sailmaker and shipjoiner, to name just a few.[99]

One hundred and fourteen of those 721 blacks from North Carolina joined the U.S. Navy at northern ports, many of them apparently because merchant vessels on which they were serving had been caught out of the South at the war's outset.[100] Andrew Roberts, for instance, hailed from Gates County, North Carolina, but he joined the navy in Philadelphia in 1862 and was immediately rated a seaman. Nelson Ward sailed out of New Bern but joined the navy in Boston as an ordinary seaman. Richard Green of New Bern enlisted in New Bedford; Alfred Bettoncort, of Wilmington, in Philadelphia; James Brundage, of Beaufort, in New York City.[101]

Other former slaves served aboard Union vessels without being officially enrolled in the navy. Chronically shorthanded and rarely averse to exploiting black labor, many Union captains looked the other way as contrabands came aboard their vessels. While some Union naval officers confined contrabands to the drudgery of the coal room or mess hall, others placed more value on their maritime skills. In the summer of 1862, a Union captain in New Bern sponsored a rowing race between two crews of his seamen, one white and the other contraband. A correspondent for *The Liberator* commented on the six former slaves "beautifully attired in man-of-war costume." They won the race by three rods. "The captain said his contrabands could not only pull a small boat faster and with more steadiness than the same number of white seamen," wrote the journalist, "but that they, with the others he had on board, could man his guns with more agility and skill in time of action than any white seamen he had ever seen."[102] Most pilots, in particular, were not enrolled in the navy. In 1863, for instance, the commander of the uss *Ceres* found a contraband named Nicolas Dixon "a good pilot in the Neuse and Pamlico rivers and Pamlico Sounds," but Dixon never appeared on any official enrollment list.[103]

Black sailors in Union blue may have been a powerful inspiration for the former slaves in Beaufort, but few sights could have galled Confederate pa-

Black crewmen sewing and relaxing on the forecastle of the uss *Miami*, ca. 1864–65. Nearly 19,000 African Americans served aboard Union naval vessels during the Civil War. Courtesy Naval Historical Center, Washington, D.C.

triots more. James Rumley observed that by August 1862 it was common "to see a gang of black negroes, dressed in naval uniform, walking our streets." He recognized many of the black sailors as men who had escaped slavery in Beaufort, and he blamed the Union navy for having "stolen them from the coast, or harbored them as runaways." The black sailors came ashore to socialize in town, to attend worship services and political rallies, and simply to escape the monotony of shipboard routine. Eyeing the black sailors, some of them carrying rifles, Rumley fumed at their officers: "The scoundrels who send them ashore deserve to be shot for thus insulting a southern community whom, for the present, they have in their power."[104]

The life of a black sailor aboard a naval vessel anchored in Beaufort Harbor entailed its own struggle for dignity and equality. On the one hand, black sailors in the Union navy experienced a status far superior to any they could find in the American South. Aboard Union vessels, they served side by side with white sailors. Naval regulations permitted black hands to rise in the ranks as high as seaman, and many earned ratings by virtue of their seamanship that put them in duty stations over white sailors, an unimaginable breach of racial orthodoxy on shore. Caesar Burns, a black sailor from Beaufort, even became captain of the hold—a petty officer's rank—on the uss *Fort Morgan*.[105] The relatively high status of black sailors aboard Union vessels had not, of course, started during the Civil War. A strong current of racial egalitarianism had persisted in Atlantic maritime culture since at least the seventeenth century. Marcus Rediker argues convincingly that this derived from the primacy of naval regulations required to maintain strict discipline and orderliness among crews drawn from the lowest classes of many nations, races, and ethnicities. Given the chronic shortages of skilled sailors, it assured that a vessel's master could take full advantage of a crewman's talents and maritime experience, no matter his caste or background. This tradition had long overruled the unwritten edicts of racial oppression ashore, and for generations the high status of black sailors had been a thorny issue for southern leaders, who felt that racial conditions aboard naval vessels set a dangerous example for slaves.[106]

On the other hand, while the navy's black sailors enjoyed relatively high status and often served with distinction aboard Union vessels, they still suffered discrimination at sea and in port. Free blacks and foreign-born black sailors in the Union navy faced relatively little discrimination in terms of enlistment or ratings, at least up to the rank of petty officer. Contraband sailors, however, encountered very different working conditions. Naval officers put the former slaves, perhaps three-fourths of all black Union sailors, disproportionately in the toughest, dirtiest, and lowest-paying duty stations aboard ship. They formed the preponderance of firemen and coal heavers and dominated the menial duties traditionally assigned to "boy"-rated hands. Their chores ranged from cleaning the bilge to going on shore patrols for wood and water. Naval rules reinforced their second-class status. Naval regulations did not permit contrabands to rise above seaman's rating, and Union officers often compelled freedpeople to perform duties appropriate to higher ratings without receiving the commensurate rating or pay. By military edict, they also could not transfer among Union vessels and retain a rating higher than that of a lowly "landsman." The former slaves also made up a disproportionately high number of the crew complement on supply ships and storeships.[107] Moreover, they had to endure a steady banter of racist remarks, a stream of menial tasks, and often a measure of racial segregation at the mess table.[108]

White supremacy was all too evident among the Union vessels at anchor in Beaufort Harbor. The shipboard routines and naval regulations that constrained a crew's disorderly conduct at sea frayed while lying for weeks or months at harbor. A Maine sailor aboard the uss *Nansemond*, a steamer chasing blockade runners and reconnoitering Bogue Sound, quickly grew weary of life aboard ship. On May 15, 1864, he wrote his cousin that, "I long to be my own master again" and "to go where I like & to do as I like." He bemoaned his duty in the steamer's boiler room, and he bristled with indignation that he served under black sailors. "If I had my way," he wrote, "I would cut every nigers throat in the united states."[109] Union troop transports, crowded with Federal soldiers unaccustomed to the ways of a ship, were the most unruly. While waiting for the siege of Fort Fisher, white sailors and soldiers grew more reckless daily. "The animal spirits . . . must find vent," one white infantryman at Beaufort declared, "and, in a ship crowded like the *Morton*, that vent is apt to be in mischief." The white soldier listed "flourishing the niggers" along with wrestling, smoking, fighting, dancing, gambling, and reading as among the "occupations" by which his bored crewmates amused themselves.[110]

Other Union sailors in Beaufort vented their frustrations in no less racist antics. The Maine sailor aboard the *Nansemond* expressed only contempt for the seaport's black community. "Most all of the fellows are ashore today," the sailor wrote on April 10, 1864; "I would not [go with them] for there is nobody but nigars ashore here."[111] Other sailors who evidently had a similar racial outlook did venture into Beaufort. In 1863, James Rumley chortled at the thinness of the Union commitment to racial equality as he observed that 500 Rhode Island conscripts "drove the negroes from their presence whenever they encounter them."[112] And in August 1864, navy sailors who had no doubt been partaking of some of the locally brewed rum broke up a black church meeting, stampeding into the sanctuary crying, "The rebels are coming!"[113] Presumably alcohol had not deprived the white sailors of all their survival instincts; they knew to direct such hooliganism at targets well away from the armed African American sentinels who patrolled Beaufort's streets.

The Civil War legacy of these African American maritime laborers continued to shape politics and race in North Carolina long after Appomattox. The occupied seaports, especially Beaufort and New Bern, saw the rise of a black political culture that would dominate African American politics during Reconstruction. Espousing universal suffrage, women's rights, state-supported public education, civil rights, and even armed self-defense, postwar black radicalism reflected political currents that had survived for generations amid the black maritime culture of the Atlantic world. Moses Grandy, David Walker, and the maritime rebels in the age of revolution would have recognized their principles immediately, even if they did not live to see such a revolutionary vision expressed so openly in the South. The Federal occupation also gave black leaders a three-year head start on other North Carolina blacks, time they used to organize political groups, churches, schools, and self-help societies. These self-organized groups held political beliefs far more revolutionary than those of either the Union army or all but the most ardent Yankee abolitionists. Not surprisingly, they dominated the freedpeople's conventions of North Carolina after the Civil War. Similarly, covert ties had long existed between African Americans in southern seaports such as Beaufort and the free black communities of New England. During and after the Civil War, these relationships, too, came out into the open, with free blacks from the North returning as teachers, missionaries, soldiers, and Union spies. It was no accident that the first southern congregations affiliated with the AME Zion Church were formed in the New Bern and Beaufort vicinities. Much as seamen had linked the antebellum black communities of the eastern seaboard, they also forged a basis for a national black politics after the Civil War. In these ways African American maritime laborers played a major role in infusing into American politics a powerful vision of a more just society.

chapter seven

A Radical and Jacobinical Spirit

Abraham Galloway and the Struggle for Freedom in the Maritime South

In the spring of 1863, a recruiting agent for the Union army walked the streets of New Bern, North Carolina, looking for Abraham H. Galloway. The seaport was usually a town of 5,500 inhabitants, but at that moment it was overflowing with thousands of fugitive slaves who had escaped from the Confederacy. The setting was one of excess in all things: hardship, disarray, fear, heartbreak, joy. Federal troops crowded into colonial homes and antebellum manors. Downtown buildings lay in charred ruins: retreating Confederates had burned some of them, and a Union general torched the others after snipers shot at his sentries. The Confederates had fled so quickly that they left doors banging in the wind, family portraits in front yards, a piano in the middle of a street. The murmur of sawmills could be heard across the Trent River, the sound of the former slaves building a new city. The days clattered noisily by, and even the stillness of evening was broken by short bursts of ecstasy: slave sisters reunited after a lifetime apart or a slave family that had survived a journey of 150 miles. But no one breathed easy. New Bern was a sliver of sanctuary for African Americans in the slave South, and the Confederate army could recapture the city at any time.[1]

Edward W. Kinsley, the recruiting agent, did not originally come to New Bern looking for Galloway. He had arrived there as an emissary of Governor

John Albion Andrew of Massachusetts, an abolitionist leader seeking to recruit an African American regiment. Kinsley had expected the former slaves
to throng into the army's ranks—instead, they avoided him nearly to a man.
"Something was wrong," he realized, "and it did not take [me] long to find
out the trouble." All pointed him to one individual, the man that the slave
refugees considered their leader. "Among the blacks," he learned, "was a man
of more than ordinary ability, a coal black negro named Abraham Galloway."[2]

In 1863 Galloway was only 26 years old, a prodigy who had already lived
three men's lives. Born into enslavement beside the Cape Fear River, Galloway had grown up in Wilmington. He had become a fugitive slave, an abolitionist leader, a Union spy. He was tall, strong, and handsome, with long wavy
hair and flashing eyes. He was not, as Kinsley remembered, "coal black," but
light-skinned. He consented to see Kinsley but even after several meetings
refused to help recruit former slaves into the Union army. Then, for unknown
reasons, Galloway changed his mind. He sent a message to Kinsley to meet
him at the home of a black leader named Mary Ann Starkey. When the New
England abolitionist arrived at midnight, somebody blindfolded him and led
him into an attic room. When the blindfold came off, Kinsley "could see by the
dim light of the candle that the room was nearly filled with blacks, and right in
front of him stood Abraham Galloway and another huge negro, both armed
with revolvers."[3]

That night the convocation of liberated slaves did not mince words. If the
Union intended to make this war a crusade for black liberation, then Kinsley
would find no shortage of recruits in New Bern. But if the Federal army
planned to use black men like chattel and wage a war merely for the preservation of the Union, that was another story. Kinsley had to know that Galloway
was serving the Union army—wild rumors of his exploits as a Union spy were
whispered on every street corner—and must have wondered: was Galloway
really willing to hurt the Union cause by withholding black troops or was this
merely a negotiating tactic to improve the lot of black soldiers and their
families? Galloway and his lieutenants did not let Kinsley know, and we will
probably never know either. Instead, they bluntly listed their demands: equal
pay, provisions for black soldiers' families, schooling for their children, and
assurances that the Union would force the Confederacy to treat captured
blacks as prisoners of war, not to be executed like traitors.

Kinsley later described the next few moments as the most harrowing of his
life. Galloway had not brought him to that dark attic to negotiate terms but to
guarantee them. Holding a revolver to Kinsley's head, he compelled the

Union recruiter to swear a personal oath that the Federal army would meet these conditions. After Kinsley did so, the former slaves released him into the night air. "The next day," he remembered later, "the word went forth, and the blacks came to the recruiting station by [the] hundreds and a brigade was soon formed."[4] The more than 5,000 African Americans eventually recruited in New Bern, most of them former slaves, became the core of the 35th, 36th, and 37th Regiments, United States Colored Troops, known originally as the African Brigade.[5]

Few stories have described as vividly what the black southerners who found asylum in Federal territory during the Civil War did with their new freedom. Despite several recent studies that highlight black initiative during the Civil War, we still tend either to view the freedpeople, or "contrabands," as if through the eyes of so many New England missionaries, as downtrodden, helpless souls entirely reliant on white goodwill, or, just as misleading, to see them exclusively as patriotic "good soldiers" blindly devoted to the Union cause and serving unquestionably under the terms and conditions that Federal commanders offered them. This scene in New Bern hints at a different story: instead of docility, we see militancy. Instead of unquestioning loyalty to the Union cause, we see former slaves attempting to shape the Union cause. Instead of imbibing the politics of white abolitionists or Republicans, we see black Carolinians charting their own political course. Instead of the contrabands looking to northern blacks for political guidance, we glimpse a new politics emerging from the struggle against slavery in the South.

For all of the story's broader implications about the former slaves and the Civil War, the center of its intrigue is Kinsley's portrayal of that "man of more than ordinary ability . . . named Abraham Galloway." Galloway was arguably the most important African American leader in North Carolina during the Civil War and Reconstruction. Beyond being a vocal abolitionist and important Union spy, he was a visionary contraband leader, a key Union recruiter, a political leader of the freedpeople after the Civil War, the colonel of a black militia that fought the Ku Klux Klan, and one of the state's first black senators.[6] But during the reactionary era of the 1890s and early 1900s, white historians replaced thoughtful, heroic black figures such as Galloway with images of corrupted, deferential blacks so unable to recognize their own best interests that they needed white guidance at every step.[7] Galloway and like-minded black insurgents were purged from the southern past, and so too was any understanding of the maritime slave culture that had produced them. They can be put in their proper historical context only by understanding their roots in the African American maritime society of the slave South and its revolutionary course through the Civil War. Galloway's story traces in miniature the emergence of a subversive politics out of a black maritime culture that was generations old. In his mercurial life, we see the revolutionary ideas of freedom and equality espoused by the likes of David Walker and Nat Turner collide with an oppressive politics that was born and bred in the white supremacy of the Old South. The contest between the two visions would rip the South apart and tear men's and women's souls to shreds.

Galloway was born on February 13, 1837, in the tiny port of Smithville (later Southport), the seat of Brunswick County, 25 miles south of Wilmington at the mouth of the Cape Fear River.[8] His mother was Hester Hankins, a slave woman born in 1820.[9] His father was a free white man named John Wesley Galloway, the son of a local planter.[10] Relatively little is known about Abraham's mother; she was probably, but not certainly, owned by planter William Hankins of Town Creek, and she married Amos Galloway, one of John Wesley Galloway's slaves, in or about 1846.[11] As we will see later, she and her son Abraham remained close throughout his life. Not surprisingly, the life of Abraham's father is better documented. The Galloways included some of the wealthiest planters and merchants in Brunswick County, but John Wesley was only a small farmer, later a ship's pilot, and, sometime after 1850, captain of the Federal lightship off Frying Pan Shoals. He seems to have shared the aristocratic values of his wealthier cousins, but he never owned much property beyond four African Americans.[12] The circumstances of his relationship with Abraham's mother are altogether murky. We know only that Abraham later recalled that John Wesley "recognized me as his son and protected me as far as he was allowed so to do."[13]

A well-off railroad mechanic in Wilmington named Marsden Milton Hankins owned Galloway from infancy.[14] How the mulatto child came into the Hankins household is not clear; Hankins may have owned Abraham's mother or, if she was owned by John Wesley Galloway, Abraham may have been sold for discretion's sake when John Wesley first married in 1839. Galloway later recalled that Hankins "was a man of very good disposition who always said he would sell before he would use a whip." His wife Mary Ann evidently was not so even-tempered; Galloway remembered her as a "very mean woman" who "would whip contrary to his orders."[15] Trained as a brickmason, young Galloway was hiring out his own time before his twentieth birthday. Hankins, a skilled laborer himself, could not supervise a slave closely. He left Galloway to seek out brickmasonry jobs when, where, and how he pleased so long as the slave continued to bring into the Hankins household a steady $15 a month.[16]

In 1857 Galloway escaped from Wilmington. He later explained that he fled the port city because he could no longer earn the $15 a month that Hankins required of him. This may seem a rather uncompelling motivation for such a risky undertaking, especially if we take his word that Hankins was not a malicious master. But if the failure to earn money might lead to Galloway's sale in the local slave market—a fate that could have marooned him on one of the rice fields or turpentine orchards of the Lower Cape Fear—then his flight is not surprising. No matter Hankins's gentle nature, he clearly saw Galloway primarily as a financial investment—and every investor sometimes has to cut his losses. At any rate, Galloway and a friend, a slave named Richard Eden, found a schooner captain willing to conceal them among the turpentine barrels in his cargo hold.[17]

An abolitionist underground of free and slave residents of Wilmington helped fugitive slaves to escape by ship throughout the 1850s.[18] Reluctant to acknowledge subversive ideas originating within the local slave community, the seaport's political leaders seemed to find solace in blaming free black sailors from ports outside the South for such antislavery activity.[19] Typically, when copies of David Walker's landmark *Appeal to the Coloured Citizens of the World* appeared in Wilmington in 1830, the town's leaders struck out brutally at black sailors but apparently did not consider the fact that Walker had been born and raised a free black in Wilmington.[20] Though Walker had traveled extensively after leaving the South, his call for armed resistance to slavery had its roots in a culture of slave resistance that African Americans had managed to create in southern ports like Wilmington. This intellectual culture had been most deeply shaped by the experience of slavery along the Carolina coast, but it was also influenced by the democratic ideals of the Enlightenment, an evangelical faith that emphasized the "natural rights" of all peoples before God, and the abolitionist politics that arrived in Wilmington aboard every vessel that had called in New England or the West Indies. Slave literacy was illegal in North Carolina after 1830, but local bondmen and -women found ways to refine and convey this political vision by word of mouth, in hymns, and, to a surprising degree, through the written word. Walker's *Appeal*, as Peter Hinks has shown, was fundamentally an expression of a collective vision of African American struggle that arose out of southern ports.[21] So it was that Galloway left Wilmington, as Walker had, with a

Abraham H. Galloway. From William Still, *The Underground Railroad: A Record of Facts, Authentic Narratives, Letters, etc., Narrating the Hardships, Hair-Breadth Escapes, and Death Struggles of the Slaves in their Efforts for Freedom* (Philadelphia: Porter & Coates, 1872).

political vision far more defiantly egalitarian than most of the abolitionists that he met north of the Mason-Dixon Line.

Galloway arrived in Philadelphia in June 1857. Perhaps with the help of black sailors, he and Eden reached the Vigilance Committee of Philadelphia. They met with William Still, an African American coal merchant who was the committee's executive secretary, and they were soon forwarded to its contacts in Canada in order to evade the fugitive slave laws of the United States. On July 20, 1857, Eden wrote one of the committee's directors that he and Galloway had arrived in Kingston, Ontario, in "good health" and that Galloway had found employment, presumably as a brickmason, at $1.75 a day.[22] Over the next four years, Galloway immersed himself in the abolitionist movement and quite likely in aiding other African Americans to flee the South. As the nearest part of Canada for most fugitive slaves who fled the South, Ontario had a large African American community with a strong stake in the abolitionist cause. The black fugitives founded relief societies, newspapers, political groups, and even secret militias that supported the Underground Railroad in the United

States and helped black refugees get established in Canada.[23] Galloway seems to have devoted himself to the abolitionist cause in a serious way. Several newspaper reports later indicated that he left Canada and gave antislavery speeches in the United States and was especially active in the abolitionist movement in Ohio, which, if true, he did at the risk of being prosecuted under the Fugitive Slave Act of 1850.[24] During those years, Galloway built extensive ties among the abolitionist leaders of Boston, though the exact character of his relationship with the Bird Club and other Boston antislavery groups remains uncertain.

Whatever else Galloway accomplished in the abolitionist movement or the Underground Railroad, he convinced George L. Stearns, the Boston financier who backed John Brown's military raids in Kansas and sponsored the 54th Regiment, Massachusetts Volunteers (the black regiment featured in the 1989 movie *Glory*), that he would serve the Union army well as a spy. This is the single most compelling reason for believing that Galloway was involved in the most covert, and probably most militant, activities in the abolitionist movement. Stearns was a serious man who recruited thousands of black soldiers from Maine to Texas, and Galloway would have made a fine Union enlistee. By the outbreak of the Civil War, however, Stearns had seen something in Galloway that suggested a far more decisive role.[25]

Galloway returned south at the beginning of the Civil War. Stearns had brought the young mulatto to the attention of a Boston acquaintance, Col. Edward A. Wild, who evidently introduced Galloway to Gen. Benjamin F. Butler at Fortress Monroe, Virginia. Galloway was soon recruited into the Union's secret service under Butler. Working out of Fortress Monroe, Galloway undertook special missions in the coastal portions of Virginia and North Carolina that had been captured by Federal troops during Gen. Ambrose B. Burnside's campaign of 1861–62.[26] We will probably never know more than a hint of what Galloway did in his capacity as an intelligence agent for the Union army. Mystery shrouds much of his life, none of it more than his service under Butler.[27] He reportedly answered directly to Butler and was said to "possess the fullest confidence of the commanding General."[28] It is likely that Galloway returned to North Carolina even prior to the Federal occupation; a Union corporal stationed in occupied Beaufort later noted in his diary that Galloway was "in the detective service of Gen. Butler" and had scouted marine landings for Union troops, presumably during the Burnside campaign.[29] That is quite plausible. Union commanders depended heavily on local slaves to identify landing sites during the Burnside expedition. Somebody had to recruit the slave pilots or somehow elicit the necessary piloting knowledge from African American watermen. One report indicated that Galloway also investigated claims of Union sympathy among Confederate prisoners of war near Norfolk and recruited white Unionists into a military regiment.[30]

Galloway began working out of New Bern soon after its capture by Federal forces in March 1862. That colonial era river port became headquarters for the Federal regiments in North Carolina and for the Union blockading fleet. During the remainder of the war, the Union kept a precarious hold on the city, using it as a base for military raids into eastern North Carolina and for a nasty war with Confederate guerrillas. Thousands of runaway slaves poured into the city. One can only imagine the different ways that Galloway might have been, as a northern journalist later wrote of him, "of some service to the Union army." The slaves who assembled in New Bern brought with them a wealth of information about the Confederacy that had to be culled. Guides for reconnaissance missions and raids into the state's interior had to be recruited, as well as spies willing to move across Confederate lines on espionage and intelligence-gathering missions. Familiar with the terrain, Confederate defenses, and local slave communities, the former slaves were especially well situated to perform these challenging tasks. "Upwards of fifty volunteers of the best and most courageous," wrote Vincent Colyer, superintendent of Negro affairs in New Bern in 1862–63, "were kept constantly employed on the perilous but important duty of spies, scouts, and guides." Colyer reported that the black operatives "were invaluable and almost indispensable. They frequently went from thirty to three hundred miles within the enemy's lines; visiting his principal camps and most important posts, and bringing us back important and reliable information."[31] More than likely, Galloway was the chief intelligence agent working among the fugitive slaves in North Carolina—in effect, what we would call today a spymaster. He worked closely with the Union commanding officers in New Bern, including Brig. Gen. Edward A. Wild (promoted from colonel in 1863), Brig. Gen. John J. Peck, and Maj. Gen. John C. Foster.[32]

Whatever duties Galloway carried out as a spy for the Union army, they gave him a unique vantage point from which to organize among the great crowds of former slaves congregating behind Federal lines. As soon as New Bern had fallen in March 1862, the city was, in Burnside's words, "overrun with fugitives from the surrounding towns and plantations." Hundreds, then thousands, of African American men, women, and children fled from bondage in Confederate territory to freedom in New Bern. "It would be utterly impossible . . . to keep them outside of our lines," an overwrought Burnside reported to the secretary of war, "as they find their way to us through woods and swamps from every side."[33] Situated in New Bern, Galloway built strong contacts among the fugitives there as well in the smaller, outlying freedpeople's camps in Beaufort, Plymouth, Washington, and Roanoke Island. In these camps congregated the most ardent radicals, the most incorrigible troublemakers, the most militant artisans, the most defiant slave preachers—in short, the black Carolinians who had most boldly dared to defy or deceive slavery. Inevitably, these insurgents saw the nature of power in the slave South with the clarity characteristic of outlaws. They saw its inherent violence, its paternalist veneer, its grim foundations in ideas of racial purity, sexual domination, and social hierarchy. They bore scars that they had acquired the hard way as they negotiated plantation discipline and eluded slave patrols and the Home Guard. It was no accident that Galloway emerged a leader among this self-selected assembly of liberated slaves. Many, including Galloway himself, moved back and forth into Confederate territory, acting as Union agents or searching for family and friends still in bondage. Out of New Bern's freedpeople's camps, those black men and women cast lifelines deep into Confederate territory, expanding and informing the radical political culture that was emerging in New Bern.

By the spring of 1863, Galloway had become more than a Union spy. He had become the most important political leader among the more than 10,000 former slaves who resided in the freedpeople's camps and seaports occupied by the Federal army. The liberated slaves had erected their largest shanty towns along the outskirts of New Bern. Out of those rough-hewn villages arose a great revival of African American political culture, a ferment comparable in ways to the black freedom movement that would come a century later. Unfettered by slavery, the black multitude exulted in the free expression of worship, family life, even music. Moreover, they looked to politics both as a weapon against their outlandishly racist treatment by the Union occupying forces and as a tool to shape their destiny after the Civil War.[34] They organized schools, relief societies, self-help associations, and churches, including St. Peter's, the first AME Zion church in the South.[35] These institutions became cornerstones of black political life.

Confronted by the dangers of Confederate guerrillas and the depredations

of Union soldiers, they also organized a black militia. William Henry Singleton, the only black veteran who wrote a memoir of the New Bern occupation,
indicated that the refugees had been drilling on their own during the early
spring of 1862, well before President Lincoln permitted African Americans to
serve in the army. Singleton suggests that this militia formed the heart of the
black brigades recruited in New Bern in the summer of 1863. If that is true,
then on the night that Galloway negotiated the terms of black enlistment, he
had a stronger hand than merely the revolver aimed at Edward Kinsley's
head; he had a fighting force of at least several hundred black soldiers waiting
to join the fray.[36] The fact that hundreds of black men showed up almost
instantly at a word from their leader certainly suggests a high degree of
existing organization. Galloway had also clearly begun to mark an independent political course that placed his first loyalty to the former slaves, not the
Union army.

This was the milieu in which Galloway grew into political prominence. No
matter how much his radical politics had been shaped by his own life in
slavery, in the abolitionist movement, or as a Union spy, Galloway was home.
He was of this society, knew its people, knew its horrors. He could scarcely
help but play a leadership role in the black political movement emerging
within New Bern, and he developed a close relationship to the black women
organizing support for the slave refugees. He worked especially closely with
Mary Ann Starkey, at whose home Edward Kinsley met Galloway. Starkey
had turned her home into a meeting place for a small adult "reading school"
and a Bible school class. She also led a black women's relief society that
solicited funds and supplies among both the former slaves and northern
abolitionists for refugee families and, later, for black soldiers.[37]

Working with black groups like Mary Ann Starkey's relief society and
William Singleton's militia, Galloway seems to have discovered a new matu-
rity. Prior to this moment, the 26-year-old youth had lived the kind of rebel's
life that required talents for subterfuge: guile, restraint, dissemblance, patience, the ability to act boldly but carefully under pressure and in solitude.
These gifts served Galloway well as a fugitive, an abolitionist, and a spy. Now
Galloway developed a genius for politics. He became a grassroots organizer, a
coalition builder, an inspiring orator. As a secret agent and political leader, he
seemed to pop up everywhere in Federal territory—and he struck quite a
figure. He was already renowned for a severe sense of honor and a fearless
readiness to defend it, a trait that could only have endeared him to former
slaves, for whom honor had always been a white man's prerogative. Galloway

may have already gotten into the habit that he developed later of always carrying a pistol where people could see it in his belt. Yet he could not have seemed reckless or foolhardy. For all his bravado, there was a disarming quiet about Galloway; patience, tact, and wariness had helped him to survive too many dangers not to be a part of him. Yet he laughed loud and often, and he must have had a sweet side, for everywhere the young man went the black Carolinians crowded around him as if he were a prophet.[38]

The recruitment of North Carolina's former slaves into the Union army began in May 1863. In Beaufort, 35 miles east of New Bern, James Rumley complained in his diary that "the black traitors are gathering in considerable numbers" to join the army. Rumley described the "horror, or the fiery indignation that burns in [the Rebels'] bosoms . . . when they think of their husbands and brothers and sons who may fall at the hands of the black savages."[39] Galloway did nothing to allay such Confederate hostility. Prior to President Lincoln's approval for former slaves to join the Union army, Galloway had made black military service the issue about which he was most outspoken. He not only recruited black soldiers when the time came, but he also articulated a political rationale for armed struggle that unnerved die-hard Rebels such as Rumley. At black political rallies held during the Federal occupation, Galloway argued that the former slaves would fight harder and better than white Union soldiers. At one point, he was quoted as saying that although McClellan "failed to take Richmond with 200,000 white soldiers, Butler would soon take it *with twenty thousand negroes.*"[40]

More fervently, Galloway contended that the black regiments would compel a victorious Union to grant the former slaves both freedom and political equality—that is, the right to vote, to serve on juries, and to run for elected office, all issues about which no political consensus had yet been reached even in the North. Galloway's linkage of military service and political equality reflected a growing accord among African American leaders. "Once let the black man get upon his person the brass letters U.S., let him get an eagle on his button and a musket on his shoulder and bullets in his pocket," Frederick Douglass had said, "and there is no power on earth which can deny that he has earned the right to citizenship in the United States."[41] Galloway shared Douglass's conviction. During a speech at a rally celebrating the first anniversary of the Emancipation Proclamation, Galloway told Beaufort's freedmen and -women, as James Rumley remembered it, "that their race would have not only their personal freedom, but political equality, and if this should be refused them at the ballot box[,] they would have it at the cartridge box!"[42]

With more than 50,000 blacks fighting in the Union army by the end of 1863, Galloway shifted his priorities toward the achievement of black political equality after the Civil War.[43] He was still seen frequently among the liberated slaves in North Carolina. Moving to Beaufort, he married Martha Ann Dixon, the 18-year-old daughter of two former slaves, on December 29, 1863.[44] He was active with pro-Union political groups and local organizations that defended the rights of black soldiers in Beaufort and New Bern. He spoke frequently at the black churches that had become the heart of political education and community organizing in the freedpeople's camps, as well as at the mass rallies held by the former slaves on Independence Day and Emancipation Day. He assisted Union officers to recruit black soldiers in Beaufort and New Bern, and probably over a much wider area.[45] Brigadier General Wild referred to him at this point not as a Union spy but as his "confidential recruiting agent," a term that suggests that Galloway was recruiting former slaves for special missions, presumably in Confederate territory. Galloway's contacts among slaves within the Confederacy were extensive by the fall of 1863. Their extent can be measured by his success that November at, in Wild's words, "manag[ing] to get his *mother* sent out of Wilmington, N.C." Wilmington was one of the most heavily guarded cities in the Confederacy, yet Galloway somehow arranged for his slave mother to escape to New Bern. Three Union generals—Wild, Peck, and Foster—felt so beholden to Galloway that they promised their former spy and "confidential recruiting agent" that they would play a part in getting his mother from New Bern to the home of one of Galloway's contacts in Boston. "I would like to do all I can for Galloway, who has served his country well," Wild wrote Edward Kinsley on November 30, 1863.[46]

The scope of Galloway's political leadership grew as he represented the freedpeople's communities of North Carolina at the national level. In May 1864, he was part of a five-man delegation of black leaders who met with President Lincoln to urge the Union commander to endorse suffrage for all African Americans. He also began to travel extensively to Boston and New York, where he met with abolitionist leaders to discuss the political fate of the former slaves after the war.[47] In addition, Galloway was one of 144 black leaders who answered the call to "the strong men of our people" and attended the National Convention of Colored Citizens of the United States, on October 4, 1864, in Syracuse, New York. Presided over by Frederick Douglass, the convention was the most important gathering of American black leaders during the Civil War. Skeptical of the commitment to racial equality of both the Democratic and Republican Parties, the convention delegates articulated a black political agenda that called for the abolition of slavery, the end of racial discrimination, and the realization of political equality.[48] They also founded the National Equal Rights League and pledged themselves to organize state chapters to advocate for political equality. Though his political organizing in the freedpeople's camps must have tailed off at the end of 1864—many of his most militant lieutenants were fighting with Grant in Virginia and a yellow fever epidemic had swept New Bern and Beaufort—Galloway had organized a state chapter and five local chapters of the Equal Rights League in North Carolina by January 1865.[49]

New Bern and Beaufort remained the central points for black political organizing in North Carolina immediately after the Civil War. New Bern and its adjacent freedpeople's camp, James City, were especially important. The Federal forces had compelled the state's other refugee camps to disband, returning the lands to their antebellum owners, but the former slaves in James City had refused to surrender their new homes. They and other black residents of the Federal occupation had developed political, educational, and religious institutions that gave them a long head start in confronting postwar life. For all its hardships (or perhaps because of its hardships), the Federal occupation had been a very effective "rehearsal for Reconstruction," to borrow the title of Willie Lee Rose's landmark study of black freedpeople in South Carolina.[50] While former slaves elsewhere struggled to disentangle themselves from the web of slavery, fitfully trying out new rights and testing their new limits for the first time, the freedmen and -women whom Galloway had helped to politicize during the Federal occupation of the North Carolina coast moved steadfastly to make an impact on Reconstruction politics. Galloway remained in the thick of this political ferment, exhibiting, as one journalist said of him, an "exceedingly radical and Jacobinical spirit" that resonated deeply among African Americans.[51] When, in 1865, more than 2,000 former slaves celebrated the Fourth of July in a Beaufort rally and parade organized by the Salmon P. Chase Equal Rights League, Galloway delivered the keynote address, calling for "all equal rights before the law, and nothing more."[52]

Not surprisingly, a few weeks later, on August 28, Galloway emerged, as a correspondent for the *New York Times* put it, as the "leading spirit" of a mass meeting of New Bern's black citizens to shape a political agenda for the postwar era. It was one of the earliest such gatherings of former slaves held in the South. In a long keynote address, Galloway called for voting rights and public schooling. "We want to be an educated people and an intelligent people," he told the crowd. In a double-edged declaration that echoed his words of two years before, he also declared that "if the negro knows how to use the cartridge box, he knows how to use the ballot box."[53]

Beyond endorsing black suffrage, the mass meeting in New Bern addressed the white backlash against freedpeople and the violent, undemocratic nature of the postwar society that had emerged during Presidential Reconstruction. The black New Bernians, led by Galloway, resolved that "the many atrocities committed upon our people in almost every section of our country . . . clearly demonstrate the immense prejudice and hatred on the part of our former owners toward us." They protested "the enforcement of the old code of slave laws that prohibits us from the privileges of schools, that deny us the right to control our families, that reject our testimony in courts of justice, that after keeping us at work without pay till their crops are laid by and then driving us off, [refuse] longer to give us food and shelter." In great detail, the delegates described white terrorism—"whipping, thumb-screwing and not infrequently murdering us in cold blood"—against blacks who challenged the antebellum racial code. "In our judgement," they concluded, with something more than a measure of understatement, North Carolina "comes far short of being a republican form of government and needs to be remodeled."[54]

The New Bern assembly appointed Galloway and two other men, John Randolph and George W. Price, to call for a statewide freedpeople's convention in Raleigh on September 29. The organizers appealed to the state's black citizens soon thereafter in newspapers under the banner: "Freedmen of North Carolina, Arouse!" The three New Bern leaders instructed black North Carolinians to assemble in every township to "speak their views" and to organize district meetings where delegates would be nominated to the freedpeople's convention in Raleigh.[55] On the same day that Governor William Holden called to order a state constitutional convention dominated by the antebellum aristocracy, Galloway called to order 117 black delegates representing 42 counties at an African Methodist Episcopal church in Raleigh. Few dressed so finely as their white counterparts across town, some had passed the collection plate to obtain a railroad ticket, and many had slipped out of their hometowns quietly in order to avoid violence at the hands of local white conservatives.[56] While the white conservatives drafted the so-called Black Codes to bar African Americans from political life, the black delegates articulated a profoundly more democratic vision of southern society. They demanded the full rights of citizenship, public schools, equal protection under the law, regulation of working hours, and the abolition of all laws "which make unjust discriminations on account of race or color."[57]

The black delegates represented a wide range of political views, from strident nationalists to fearful accommodationists, but the more radical delegates from New Bern and Beaufort dominated the convention, in large part because they had refined their political ideology and gained practical experience in political argument and strategy during the years of Federal occupation. Several black leaders from the Federal occupation shown with special brilliance in Raleigh. The Reverend James W. Hood, an AME Zion leader in New Bern, was elected chairman of the convocation. His willingness to appeal to white goodwill and his cautious advice for the freedpeople to move slowly carried a great deal of influence. But none of the delegates made a deeper impression on the black participants or white observers than Galloway. "Perhaps the most remarkable person among the delegates," a northern journalist, John Richard Dennett, observed, was "a light-yellow man whose features seemed to indicate that there was a cross of Indian blood in his veins."

In Dennett's description of Galloway one can imagine why white conservatives found the former slave so unsettling and why he held so powerful an appeal for so many freedmen and -women. The ex-slaves had been born into a southern society that upheld white supremacy and tried to deny the existence of interracial sex, that associated blackness with ugliness, that compelled black men to carry themselves with great deference, and that punished any black who dared to challenge a white man's superior intelligence. Politically and personally, Galloway would have none of it. "His hair was long and black and very curly," Dennett wrote.

> He appeared to be vain of its beauty as he tossed it carelessly off his forehead, or suffered it to fall heavily and half conceal his eyes. These were twinkly and slippery, and nearly always half shut, for he laughed much, and then they partly closed of themselves, and at other times he had a way of watching from under his dropped lids. He was a well-shaped man, but it was hardly to be discovered as he lolled in his seat, or from the insufferably lazy manner of his walking. When he spoke, however, he stood erect, using forcible and graceful gestures. His voice was powerful, and, though an illiterate man, his speaking was effective.

We can hear Dennett trying to fit Galloway into an antebellum racial stereo-type—the insufferably lazy manner of his walking, the slippery eyes—but neither Galloway's force of will nor Dennett's grudging admiration allows him to do it. "His power of sarcasm and brutal invective," Dennett conceded, "and the personal influence given him by his fearlessness and audacity, always secured him a hearing."[58] Galloway's defiance of white authority alarmed more cautious black delegates, and the freedpeople's convention as a whole struck a more conciliatory posture than Galloway's own when they presented their demands to the white convention. But few would forget Galloway or fail to tell stories about him when they returned to homes besieged by white terror. He may have frightened them, for they knew how white conservatives might react to such an insurgent, but he also gave voice to the vision of freedom born in bondage.

Galloway left New Bern for Wilmington late in 1866 or early in 1867. He may have moved to rejoin his mother—she probably returned to Wilmington soon after the Civil War (she was definitely there by 1870)—or he may have re-turned home because he recognized that Wilmington would again become the capital of African American political life in North Carolina.[59] Wilmington was the state's largest city, it had a majority-black population, and its large number of black artisans and maritime laborers formed the core of a politically militant class that would have attracted Galloway. By January 3, 1866, the North Carolina office of the Equal Rights League had also conspicuously opened in downtown Wilmington. Galloway's relocation to Wilmington and the open-ing of the Equal Rights League's office may not have been coincidental.[60]

Galloway tried to give his life a semblance of normalcy in Wilmington. He and his wife went about raising their two sons, they attended St. Paul's Episcopal Church, and he joined the Masons. Reconstruction was not an ordinary time, however, and a quiet life was hardly his destiny. The Wilming-ton that Galloway returned to was in the throes of a violent conflict over the shape of postwar society. Nothing was guaranteed—certainly not the freed-people's right to vote, to own land, to have access to schooling, to earn decent wages, to exercise their civil rights, or to enjoy equal protection under the law. These issues were all being worked out on the streets of towns like Wilmington just as surely as in the halls of the U.S. Congress. Every encoun-ter between a black person and a white person was fraught with danger. "They perceive insolence in a tone, a glance, a gesture, or failure to yield enough by two or three inches in meeting on the sidewalk," a visitor noted of Wilmington's white citizens.[61] Cape Fear conservatives sought to reestablish their antebellum power at the same time that blacks sought to assert their new rights of freedom and citizenship. The talents for covert organizing and self-defense that Galloway had honed as a runaway slave, a fugitive abolitionist, and a Union spy would be put to good use in Reconstruction Wilmington.

By the beginning of 1866, the conservatives had regained power in Wilmington, largely thanks to Union military commanders who sympathized more with Cape Fear aristocrats than with former slaves. "The true soldiers, whether they wore the gray or the blue are now united in their opposition . . . to negro government and negro equality," gloated a local newspaper, adding, "Blood is thicker than water."[62] Night riders and white militias beat, killed, and otherwise terrorized African Americans who dared to act like free citizens, and they strove to reimpose control over freedpeople's lives—including control over whom they worked for, what wages they commanded, where they lived, and how they raised their children. The presence of black troops among the Federal occupying force in Wilmington had momentarily restrained conservative violence, but Union commanders showed a lack of resolve in supporting the black troops, even refusing to intervene when Confederate militia groups targeted them. Increasingly, the black troops realized that they were on their own in postwar Wilmington. They mutinied against their white officers in September 1865, and they laid siege to the city jail in February 1866 in order to halt the public whipping of black prisoners convicted in a trial in which the conservative judge had not allowed testimony by African Americans. After that, Union commanders withdrew all black troops from the Lower Cape Fear and replaced them with white soldiers.[63] White terror reigned throughout the Cape Fear. "The fact is," a freedman reported, "it's the first notion with a great many of these people, [that] if a Negro says anything or does anything that they don't like, [they] take a gun and put a bullet into him."[64] Not far from Wilmington, in Duplin County, a police captain named J. N. Stallings gave orders to shoot without trial blacks who had been accused of minor theft.[65]

With passage of the Reconstruction Acts of 1867 by the Republican Congress, Wilmington blacks gained a crucial new political opportunity. The Reconstruction Acts restored Federal military authority in the South and required states in the former Confederacy to pass a constitution that guaranteed universal male suffrage before they could be readmitted to the Union. The acts also opened the polls to black voters while banning from political life any antebellum officeholder who had taken an oath to uphold the U.S. Constitution but then sided with the Confederacy. Galloway was soon looking toward the constitutional convention that would occur in Raleigh early in 1868. On September 4, 1867, he addressed a mass meeting of the state's Republican Party at Tucker Hall in Raleigh, delivering a conciliatory address aimed at building broad, biracial support for the Republicans. He exhorted his audience to "go everywhere there is a black man or a poor white man and tell him the true condition of the Republican Party."[66] Later that month, "after loud calls for 'Galloway,'" he addressed a torchlit procession of black citizens from the top of Wilmington's market house. "My people stand here tonight fettered, bound hand [and] foot by a Constitution that recognizes them as chattel," Galloway exclaimed.[67] That fall he was elected one of thirteen delegates from seven Cape Fear counties to serve at the constitutional convention.

Galloway was, in the words of historian W. McKee Evans, one of "a small group of active delegates who largely dominated the life of the convention."[68] During the constitutional convention, which ran from January to March 1868, Galloway served on the judiciary committee, and alongside white reformer Albion Tourgée on the committee for local government. As one of only 13 blacks out of 120 persons elected to the constitutional convention, he felt a special responsibility to represent the political concerns of the state's African American population. At one point, on February 20, Galloway explained his support for the popular election of the judiciary by saying, in a reporter's paraphrase, that "the Judiciary in New Hanover was a bastard, born in sin and secession. In their eyes," he continued, "it was a crime to be a black or a loyal man," and he denounced conservative judges who had allegedly imprisoned blacks solely to keep them from voting.[69] At another point, Galloway vehemently opposed public support of a railroad that, in his words, "did not employ a single colored man," and he refused to support a Young Men's Christian Association request to use the convention hall unless "no distinction be made between the races."[70]

Galloway routinely endured arguments about black inferiority from conservative delegates and their newspaper editors, as he would do again later in the state senate. Every day that he spent in Raleigh, he heard comments such as the *Sentinel*'s contention that true North Carolinians would blush "that a set of apes and hybrids should be holding a brutal carnival in her halls of legislation."[71] Much to their dismay, conservative delegates discovered that such remarks inspired Galloway's most cutting rhetoric. At the end of one harangue on the unfitness of blacks for suffrage, Galloway responded by saying, "The best blood in Brunswick County flowed in [my] veins," a reference to his own mixed-race heritage, "and if [I] could do it, in justice to the African race, [I] would lance [my]self and let it out."[72] Despite the rancor, conservatives were a small minority at the constitutional convention. On March 16, 1868, the delegates signed a new state constitution that introduced universal male suffrage, removed all property qualifications for officeholding, endorsed the popular election of county officials, increased public school support, and made the state's penal code more humane.[73]

When he returned to Wilmington, Galloway discovered that conservatives had launched a vicious campaign to intimidate black voters from ratifying the new constitution or electing Radical Republican leaders in the upcoming April election. Galloway himself was running for the state senate, in the first election in which blacks were eligible to hold state office. Under the leadership of Col. Roger Moore, one of the Cape Fear's most celebrated aristocrats, the Ku Klux Klan attempted to frighten blacks away from the polls. Klan terrorism prevailed in other parts of North Carolina but collided with a stubborn militancy among African Americans in Wilmington. Black men patrolled the city's streets, firing their guns in the air and wielding fence rails to intimidate Klansmen. Shots and scuffles shattered the evening quiet on the downtown streets repeatedly on the nights from April 18 to 21, 1868, and, while exactly what happened in that darkness is unknown, the Ku Klux Klan was never a force in Wilmington again during Reconstruction.[74] One can feel confidant that Galloway was not sitting quietly at home with his family. In the spring 1868 election, the Republicans carried two-thirds of the electorate in New Hanover County, and voters chose Galloway to represent New Hanover and Brunswick Counties in the state senate. That fall, he was also voted the first black elector to a presidential convention in North Carolina history.[75]

Galloway realized that armed self-defense was crucial to political survival in Wilmington. Conservative leaders held him in contempt, Democratic editors parodied him mercilessly, and the threat of assassination dogged his every step. Wherever he went in the port city, Galloway conspicuously wore a pistol in his belt, a noteworthy symbol of defiance only a couple years after Wilmington conservatives had organized house searches to disarm the black population. The rise of the Republican Party helped to back up Galloway's lone firearm. Later in 1868, a local militia, one of several organized by Wilmington blacks to defend themselves against white terrorists, elected Galloway their commander. Led most commonly by Union veterans, the black militias—like their ubiquitous white counterparts—supposedly existed to fight off foreign invasion or to quell insurrections, but in fact they acted during Reconstruction as a military wing of the Republican Party.[76] Nobody understood better than former slaves and Union veterans that a constitution was only as strong as the military power available to defend it. The Klan would rage out of control in the Carolina piedmont from 1868 to 1870 but remained prudently quiet in Wilmington.[77]

Galloway was one of three black senators and seventeen black representatives in the North Carolina General Assembly of 1868. He was only 31 years old, was poor, and still could not read or write.[78] He was, however, an extraordinary orator and an influential legislator. He was an intelligent, ferocious debater, the kind of man whose biting sense of humor and sharp eye for hypocrisy inspired most of the senate conservatives to steer away from a direct argument with him. Few of his fellow senators had ever been compelled to confront a black man as an equal, much less a black man as fearless and battle-tested as Galloway. The *Wilmington Daily Journal*, a Democratic newspaper that was apparently still squeamish about Galloway's mixed-race parentage, once referred to him as "the pugilistic 'Indian Senator.'"[79] On one occasion, after a white senator from Craven County had insulted him in the midst of a floor debate over the racial makeup of New Bern's city council, Galloway declared "that he would hold the Senator from Craven responsible for his language, outside of this Hall; and . . . that, if hereafter, the Senator from Craven insulted him, he would prove to him the blood of a true Southron."[80] That was hardly the only incident in which Galloway reminded conservative Democrats that he was at least as aristocratic by birth as they. He not only claimed to be "a true Southron," but he also brazenly touted his parentage by a black woman and a white man.[81] No senate floor debate could examine the "color line" or antiblack laws without Galloway taunting his Democratic colleagues for their hypocrisy in language that reminded them that they were ultimately talking about family. Repeatedly, when a conservative called black men sexual predators posing threats to "white womanhood," Galloway reminded the senators how commonly white men pursued black women—and, knowing Galloway, he was probably well enough acquainted with the conservative Democrats' private lives to make more than a few of them nervous with a wink or a whisper. No wonder Galloway attracted such venomous editorials in Democratic newspapers. The *Wilmington Journal* referred to Galloway's flaunting of his "bastardy" as "disgusting vulgarity [that] . . . was a disgrace to any civilized community." Another time, the *Daily Journal's* editors could barely bring themselves to comment on Galloway's mentioning his parentage and interracial sex, referring obliquely to "some indelicate remarks [by Galloway] in regard to . . . white men mingling with negroes which we omit for the sake of decency."[82]

The codifying of a new color line occupied the senate repeatedly during Galloway's first term. This was true even with respect to the conduct of the General Assembly. On July 8, 1868, as a typical example, Galloway successfully amended a proposal to segregate the senate galleries by race to allow for a middle section that could be occupied voluntarily by blacks and whites.[83] Such a racial "middle ground" would become unthinkable after the Wilmington "race riot" of 1898, but for a generation black activists such as Galloway drew a more fluid boundary between black and white North Carolinians. Maintenance of that line required constant diligence, however, as can be seen from a floor debate over racial segregation in public schools on February 26, 1869. When a Senator Love introduced an amendment requiring that no black teacher be employed in a school that had white students, a Senator Hayes, with Galloway's support, moved to amend Love's amendment to say, "or employ white teachers to serve in any school wherein colored children are to be instructed." This second amendment unnerved conservatives who feared the political implications of black control over black schooling. To make the point stronger, Galloway moved next to amend Love and Hayes's amendment, facetiously adding a provision "that no white Democrat should teach any colored girl." Ruled out of order, Galloway had won the day if not the war. The full senate rejected Love's amendment and later created a state board of education and North Carolina's first statewide system of public schooling. Yet not even white Republicans supported the call by Galloway and his fellow black legislators for racially integrated public schools or for equal funding of black schools.[84]

Much of Galloway's brief senate career addressed the most fundamental rights of the freedmen and -women. He voted for the Fourteenth and Fifteenth Amendments to the U.S. Constitution, introduced a successful bill to help former slaves hold onto land and homes given them while in bondage, and supported several measures to curtail the activities of the Ku Klux Klan, including a bill to create a state militia to combat white terrorism. Galloway strongly supported Governor Holden's ill-fated attempts to crack down on the Ku Klux Klan in the piedmont, where by mid-1870 at least 260 terrorist acts had been documented. He also pushed to guarantee that blacks serve on juries, a right granted by the 1868 constitution, but one that Galloway contended was often ignored by county commissioners.[85]

More than any other elected leader in North Carolina, Galloway also fought for women's rights. The rights of women had become an important political issue in the Reconstruction South, with blacks and white suffragists briefly finding common cause in an advocacy of universal suffrage. Black southerners supported women's suffrage far more strongly than white southerners, perhaps a sign of the relatively higher status that black women had held in slave families and of a more collective sensibility toward voting among the ex-slaves.[86] Twice Galloway introduced bills to amend the state's constitution to allow women's suffrage, once in 1868 and again in 1869. Outraged by an 1868 state supreme court ruling that men had a right to beat their wives, he sought unsuccessfully to force the senate judiciary committee to report a bill against domestic violence. He also supported a bill that gave women a greater right to sign deeds and another to protect married women from willful abandonment or neglect by their husbands.[87] Women's suffrage and many of the other pioneering women's rights measures advocated by Galloway would not become law in North Carolina for half a century.

With respect to his support for women's suffrage, as for most issues for which he fought, Galloway should not be seen as ahead of his time. The fiery young activist had emerged out of an African American intellectual culture that was deeply committed to egalitarian values and a revolutionary struggle for freedom. That culture of slave resistance had arisen over many generations in the maritime districts of North Carolina and, in spirit at least, Galloway and his supporters were the true heirs of David Walker, Denmark Vesey, and other black radicals raised in southern seaports in the age of revolution. Galloway's years as a fugitive slave, northern abolitionist, and Union spy had honed his political vision and strengthened his commitment to the African American men and women among whom he had grown up. He must also have been deeply influenced by his experience of community and politics in the freedpeople's camps along the Carolina coast. But if Galloway embodied the black radicalism that emerged onto the public stage in the seaports of North Carolina during Reconstruction, he certainly did not invent it; this tradition grew from a collective experience. To his credit, he found within himself the strength of will and the raw courage to carry that collective vision of racial justice and political equality out into a world that was not ready for it.

Galloway died unexpectedly of fever and jaundice on September 1, 1870, at his mother's home in Wilmington.[88] He was only 33 years old. He had just been reelected to the state senate, still held together a fragile biracial coalition in the local Republican Party, and had recently survived an assassination attempt.[89] He died on the cusp of a conservative resurgence that between 1870 and 1877 prevailed across North Carolina. Racial violence, official corruption, and the Republican Party's own internal divisions paved the way for the Democratic triumph. Compared to the rest of North Carolina, however, Wilmington remained a stronghold of African American political power and working-class militancy. W. McKee Evans has argued, in fact, that the unique ability of Wilmington Republicans to maintain significant numbers of black policemen and militia units preserved the relative peace of Cape Fear society from 1868 to 1877. At one point, in 1875, the *Wilmington Journal* even alleged that "there are now nearly, or quite as many negro [militia] companies in this city, as there are white companies throughout the limits of North Carolina."[90] This was an exaggeration, but it does suggest that Wilmington blacks continued to embrace the political militancy personified by Galloway long after his death.

Though he died a pauper, an estimated 6,000 mourners gathered at Galloway's funeral on September 3, 1870. They came from every Wilmington neighborhood and from the countryside for many miles around. The funeral procession stretched half a mile through a downtown Wilmington decorated with American flags at half-mast. The Masons in their finery, the black firemen's brigades, the political and fraternal societies, a hundred carriages, and throngs of people on horseback and on foot marched down Market Street to St. Paul's Episcopal Church. The multitude could not fit into the church and crowded the streets nearby. One newspaper called it the largest funeral in the state's history.[91] As the mass of black men, women, and children accompanied his coffin to the cemetery, they could not possibly have imagined that his life would so quickly seem like a half-forgotten dream. Indeed, Galloway's story is a familiar saga, and one that cuts across the ages. It is the oft-told story of the rebel hero who lives a life so deeply unreconciled to tyranny that even the most downtrodden and despised are moved to believe, at least for a brief instant, that freedom and justice may not be just a dream.

The Last Daughter of Davis Ridge

Whenever I pass the old clam house between Smyrna and Williston, I glance east across Jarrett Bay to Davis Ridge. You will go that way if you drive Highway 70 across the broad salt marshes of Carteret County to catch the Cedar Island ferry to the Outer Banks. Most passersby admire the beautiful vistas across Core Sound and look for the wild ponies grazing in the Cape Lookout National Seashore and the Cedar Island National Wildlife Refuge. Some travelers wander through the old seaside villages, such as Harkers Island, that are renowned for their boatbuilding, fishing, and seafaring heritages. Few coastal visitors know that the secluded hammock of Davis Ridge was once home to an extraordinary fishing community founded by liberated slaves. Nobody has lived at "the Ridge" since 1933, yet the legend of those African American fishermen, whalers, and boatbuilders still echoes among the elderly people in the maritime communities between North River and Cedar Island that locals call "Downeast."

I had heard of Davis Ridge when I was growing up 25 miles to the west. When I became a historian, I searched for the history of those black Downeasterners with much ardor and little success. For a long time, I assumed all record of them had been lost. I found no trace of Davis Ridge in history books. Exploring the Ridge by boat and on foot, I uncovered only an old cemetery in a live oak grove surrounded by salt marsh and, only a few yards away, Core Sound and Jarrett Bay. All the documents that I examined in research libraries, archives, and museums yielded only tantalizing clues to the community's past. The best sources I could find were a few mostly secondhand recollections from elderly people who had grown up in fishing villages not far from Davis Ridge. At last, after I had given up, I stumbled upon a tape-recorded interview with Nannie Davis Ward in a storage pantry at the North Carolina Maritime Museum in Beaufort. Most success in historical research comes from persistence and hard work; finding Ward's interview was an undeserved act of grace.

Folklorists Michael and Debbie Luster had interviewed Ward in 1988 only a few years before her death. At that time, Ward was apparently the last living soul to have grown up at Davis Ridge. A retired seamstress and cook, she was born at the Ridge in 1911. Ward was blind by the time the Lusters interviewed her, but she had a strong memory and a firm voice. Listening to her eloquent words, I found a vivid portrait of her childhood home taking shape in my mind. Her story fills in an important part of the history of the African American maritime people who inhabited the coastal villages and fishing camps of North Carolina before the Civil War. It is the story of only one community, Davis Ridge, but it speaks to the broader experience of the black watermen and -women who came out of slavery and continued to work on the water.

When Nannie Davis Ward was a child, Davis Ridge was an all-black community on a wooded knoll, or small island, on the eastern shore of Jarrett Bay, not far from Core Sound and Cape Lookout. A great salt marsh separated the Ridge from the mainland to the north, which was known as Davis Shore. Davis Island was just to the south. A hurricane cut a channel between Davis Ridge and Davis Island in 1899, but in her grandparents' day it had been possible to walk from one to the other.

The founders of Davis Ridge had been among many slave watermen at Core Sound before the Civil War. Ward's family was in many ways typical of the African American families along the Lower Banks. They were skilled maritime laborers with a seafaring heritage. They had eighteenth-century family roots in the West Indies and had black, white, and Native American ancestry. They moved seasonally from fishery to fishery, working on inshore waters, rarely the open sea. They also had a history of slave resistance. Nannie Davis Ward's mother, who identified herself as Native American, had grown up on Bogue Banks, a 26-mile-long barrier island west of Beaufort, and her mother's grandfather had evidently been a slave aboard a French sailing vessel. According to Ward, that great-grandfather had escaped from his French master while in port at New Bern and had been raised free in the family of a white waterman at Harkers Island, ten miles west of Davis Ridge.

It was Sutton Davis, Ward's paternal grandfather, who first settled Davis Ridge. As a slave, Sutton Davis had belonged to a small planter and shipbuilder named Nathan Davis at Davis Island. Sutton Davis had been a master boatbuilder and carpenter. According to his granddaughter, he had learned the boatbuilding trade at a Wilmington shipyard owned by a member of the white Davis family and then moved back to Davis Island. Family lore on one side of the white Davis family holds that Nathan was Sutton's father. Nannie Davis Ward did not address that question in her interview, except to note that Sutton and his children were very light skinned.

When Union troops captured Beaufort and New Bern in 1862, Sutton Davis led the Davis Island slaves to freedom. They rowed a small boat across Jarrett Bay to the fishing village of Smyrna, from where they fled to Union-occupied territory on the outskirts of New Bern. After the war, some of those former slaves founded the North River community, a few miles outside of Beaufort, but Sutton Davis bought four acres at Davis Ridge in 1865. Nathan Davis sold him the property for the sort of low price usually reserved for family. Sutton Davis and his children eventually acquired 220 more acres at Davis Ridge.

The number of black Downeasterners declined sharply after the Civil War, but Davis Ridge remained a stronghold of the African American maritime culture that had thrived along Core Sound. Nearly all of Nannie Davis Ward's relatives worked on the water. Her grandfather Sutton, of course, was a fisherman and boatbuilder. Her mother's father, a free black named Samuel Windsor, became a legendary fisherman and whaler at Shackleford Banks, the nine-mile-long barrier island just east of Beaufort. (Sam Windsor's Lump is still marked on nautical charts of Shackleford.) Her father, Elijah, owned a fish house. Her great-uncle Palmer was a seafarer and sharpie captain. Her great-uncle Adrian was captain of the fishing boat *Belford*. Another great-uncle, Proctor, was a waterman who lived at Quinine Point, the northwest corner of Davis Ridge. Many other kinsmen became stalwarts in the Beaufort menhaden fleet, which rose in the late nineteenth and early twentieth centuries to become the state's most important saltwater fishery. During its heyday, black watermen dominated the menhaden fishery, which had black leadership earlier than any other local industry. Out of Nannie Davis Ward's family came the menhaden industry's first African American captains.

Sutton Davis and his thirteen children operated one of the first successful menhaden factories in North Carolina, long before the industry's boom in Beaufort. Sutton built two fishing schooners, the *Mary E. Reeves* and the

Purse seining for menhaden (top) and a menhaden scrap and oil factory, Beaufort vicinity, ca. 1880–1900. This menhaden boat and factory likely resembled those run by Nannie Davis Ward's ancestors at Davis Ridge. Courtesy North Carolina Maritime Museum, Beaufort.

Shamrock. His sons worked the boats while his daughters dried and pressed the menhaden—known locally as "shad" or "pogie"—to sell as fertilizer and oil. "Men should have been doing it," Ward explained, "but he didn't have them there, so the girls had to fill in for them." In fact, Ward pointed out, at Davis Ridge, "the girls did a lot of farm working, factory work too."

The black families at Davis Ridge were what local historian Norman Gillikin in Smyrna calls "saltwater farmers": the old-time Downeasterners who lived by both fishing and farming. They hawked oysters across Jarrett Bay and raised hogs, sheep, and cattle. They grew corn for the animals and sweet "roasting ears" for themselves. At night they spun homegrown cotton into cloth. Their gardens were full of collard greens and, as Ward recalled vividly, "sweet potatoes as big as your head." They worked hard and prospered.

Sometimes Sutton Davis augmented his children's labor by hiring fishing hands from Craven Corner, an African American community 30 miles west. Craven Corner had been settled in the eighteenth century by free blacks who were granted land and freedom as a reward for their service in the Revolutionary War. According to local oral tradition, many had intermarried with the descendants of the Native American survivors of the Tuscarora War of 1711–13. Over the generations, African Americans at Craven Corner had earned a strong reputation for a fierce independence and for being excellent watermen and artisans. One does not have to stretch one's imagination to see them fitting into the fishing life at Davis Ridge.

Davis Ridge was a proud, independent community. When Nannie Ward was growing up there in the 1910s and 1920s, seven families—all kin to Sutton Davis—still lived at the Ridge. They sailed across Jarrett Bay to a Smyrna gristmill to grind their corn and to a Williston grocery to barter fish for coffee and sugar, but mainly they relied on their own land and labor. They conducted business with their white neighbors at Davis Shore or across Jarrett Bay by barter and by trading chores. "You didn't know what it was to pay bills," Ward reminisced.

While the Davis Ridge men worked away at Core Banks mullet camps or chased menhaden into Virginia waters, the island women cared for farms and homes. They gathered tansy, sassafras, and other wild herbs for medicines and seasoning. They collected yaupon leaves in February, chopped them into small pieces, and dried them to make tea. In May, they sheared the sheep. Nannie Ward's grandmother spun and wove the wool. They produced, Ward explained, "everything they used."

Davis Ridge was a remote hammock, but Ward could not remember a day of loneliness or boredom. She told how two Beaufort menhadenmen, William Henry Fulcher and John Henry, used to visit and play music on her front porch. "We enjoyed ourselves on the island," Ward said. "There wasn't a whole lot of things to do, but we enjoyed people. We visited each other."

The camaraderie of black and white neighbors around Davis Ridge was still striking to Nannie Ward half a century later. For most blacks in coastal North Carolina, the 1910s and 1920s were years of hardship and fear. White citizens enforced racial segregation at gunpoint. Blacks who tried to climb above "their place" invited harsh reprisals. The Ku Klux Klan marched by the hundreds in coastal communities as nearby as Morehead City, and word went out in several fishing communities—including Knotts Island, Stumpy Point, and Atlantic—that a black man might not live long if he lingered after dark.

Davis Ridge was somehow different. Black and white families often worked, socialized, and worshiped together. "The people from Williston would come over to our island," Ward said of school recitals and plays, "and we'd go over to their place." Sutton Davis's home, in particular, was a popular meeting place. Hymn singers of both races visited his home at Davis Ridge to enjoy good company and the finest pipe organ around Jarrett Bay.

Ward even recalled a white midwife staying with black families at Davis Ridge when a child was about to be born, a simple act of kindness and duty that turned racial conventions of the day upside down. This may seem a trivial thing, but it was quite the opposite. A coastal midwife had to move into an expectant mother's home well before her due date or risk not being in attendance at the birth because of the time required to travel to and from the islands. The midwife stayed for the child's birth and then tended to mother and child—and sometimes the cooking and housework—until the mother was recovered fully. Taking care of those duties, a midwife could easily spend two or three weeks living in the mother's household. In the American South during the era of Jim Crow, it was not unusual at all for a black midwife to serve a white family in that capacity; the arrangement was entirely consistent with a traditional role of black women serving as maids and nannies in white homes. But to reverse the arrangement was unheard of. The white South simply did not allow one of its own to serve a black woman. Even more fundamental to the complex racial landscape of the day, a white woman could never stay the night under a black man's roof, that being a breech of the sexual code that was at the heart of Jim Crow. The daily conduct of blacks and whites at Davis Ridge would have caused riots, lynching, or banishment in most southern places, including coastal towns 20 miles away.

Similarly, in the 1950s and 1960s, many white ministers across the American South lost their jobs for inviting black choirs to sing at a church revival. Yet the Davis Ridge choir sang at revivals at the Missionary Baptist church at Davis Shore two generations before the civil rights movement. An old legend even tells how, in 1871, black and white worshipers rushed from a prayer meeting and together made a daring rescue of the crew and cargo of a ship, the *Pontiac*, wrecked at Cape Lookout.

The work culture of mullet fishing on the barrier islands near Davis Ridge both reflected and reinforced this blurring of conventional racial lines. Every autumn all or most of the Davis Ridge men joined interracial mulleting gangs of 4 to 30 men tending seines, gill nets, and dragnets along the beaches between Ocracoke Island and Bogue Banks. During the 1870s and 1880s, that stretch of coastline had supported the largest mullet fishery in the United States. More than 30 vessels carried the salted fish out of Beaufort and Morehead City, and the Atlantic and North Carolina Railroad transported such large quantities that for generations local people referred to it as the "Old Mullet Road."

Out on those remote islands, black and white mullet fishermen lived, dined, and worked together all autumn, temporarily sharing a life beyond the pale of the stricter racial barriers ashore. They worked side by side, handling sails and hauling nets, and every man's gain depended on his crew's collective sailing and fishing skills. For most, a lot was riding on the mullet season. Local fishermen were a hand-to-mouth lot, and mulleting was one of the few fisheries that promised barter for the flour, cornmeal, and other staples necessary to fill a winter pantry, to say nothing of putting aside a little for Christmas or for a bolt of calico that might save their wives a fortnight of late-night weaving. Every fisherman hoped for the strongest crew possible, and nobody worked the mullet nets or knew how to survive the vicious storms on the barrier islands better than the men from Davis Ridge. On those secluded islands, away from the prying eyes of the magistrates of Jim Crow, a man's race might start to seem a little less important. Work customs reflected this camaraderie and interdependence. Mullet fishermen traditionally worked on a "share system," granting equal parts of their catch's profits to every hand, no matter his race. (Owners of boats and nets earned extra shares.) Often they also voted by shares to settle work-related decisions. These were the sort of working conditions that might attract even the independent-minded souls of Davis Ridge to work alongside their white counterparts.

This fraternity of black and white fishermen on the islands off Davis Ridge

Engraving of mullet fishermen at their camp, Shackleford Banks, circa 1880. From George Brown Goode, ed., *The Fisheries and Fishery Industries of the United States*, 5 secs. (Washington, D.C.: Commission of Fish and Fisheries, 1884–1887), sec. 5, vol. 2.

comes across clearly in a stunning engraving of a mulleting gang at Shackleford Banks. The original photograph on which the engraving was based was taken in about 1880 by R. Edward Earll, a fishery biologist who visited the local mulleting beaches as part of the United States Fish Commission's monumental survey of all of the nation's fisheries. Look closely at the engraving and what stands out immediately are the equal numbers of black and white fishermen, their intermingled pose, their close quarters, their obvious familiarity—one might even say chuminess—and the unclear lines of authority. All were entirely foreign to the standard racial attitudes of the American South in that day. I find it one of the most extraordinary images ever made of life in the Jim Crow era. One never sees anything close to that intimacy and equality in the portraits of black and white workers in cotton mills, lumber camps, coal mines, or agricultural fields, much less in the trades or professions. The notion of blacks and whites sharing a fish camp whose design was inspired by a West African architectural tradition stretches the imagination even farther. A mullet fisherman from Davis Ridge may, in fact, have built the camp in this engraving. Sallie Salter, a white woman who lived near the Ridge from 1805 to 1903, recalled for her grandson that Proctor Davis "lived in a rush camp" at Davis Ridge and later moved closer to her family at Salter Creek "and built another rush camp, and lived in it for a long time."

One must be careful not to exaggerate the racial harmony around Davis Ridge. Not a crossroads in the American South escaped the reality of racial oppression. Certainly Davis Ridge did not. After the statewide white supremacy campaigns of 1898 and 1900, local whites fostered an atmosphere of racial intimidation that increasingly drove African Americans out of other parts of Downeast, as well as discouraged any new black settlement in the fishing villages east of North River. For years, a hand-scrawled sign at the town limits of Atlantic, 15 nautical miles from Davis Ridge, read: "No Niggers After Dark." Even when I was a young boy, no blacks lived anywhere Downeast, and I often heard the admonition that African Americans could work in the Downeast clam houses or oyster shucking sheds during the day but could never spend the night safely. Once, on a club field trip to one of my teachers' homes at Harkers Island, the teacher—a native of Downeast—had the one African American girl in the club lay on the floor of her car as soon as she drove across the North River Bridge. My teacher did not have to explain why. Seen in this light, Davis Ridge was an island in more than one sense; as the rest of Downeast grew whiter and whiter after the Civil War, this remote knoll was increasingly seen as a last redoubt of African American independence and self-sufficiency. White fishermen could look across Jarrett Bay and refer to the *Mary E. Reeves* or the *Shamrock* as "the nigger boats," as I have heard Downeast old-timers call them, but Sutton Davis's clan still had two of the only menhaden boats Downeast and the skills to make good money with them.

That was the heart of the matter. Sutton Davis and his descendants could not remove themselves from the white supremacy pervasive in the American South, but they had at least two advantages that most black southerners could only dream of: land and a fair chance to make a living. And, unlike the rest of the Jim Crow South, the broad waters of Core Sound could not so easily be segregated into separate and unequal sections. Self-reliant, in peonage to no one, the African Americans at Davis Ridge joined their white neighbors as rough equals in a common struggle to make a living from the sea.

Ward left Davis Ridge in 1925. She first went to Beaufort to attend high school; then she moved to South Carolina and New York. While she was gone, the great 1933 hurricane laid waste to the island's homes and fields. The Ridge was deserted when she returned in 1951. No African Americans resided anywhere Downeast by that time.

"I still loved the island," Ward told the Lusters only a few years before she died in Beaufort. "When you grow up there from a child, you learn all the things in the island, you learn how to survive. You learn everything."

I heard a low, wistful sigh and a deep yearning in her voice. "We were surrounded by so many good things that I don't get anymore, that I never did get again." I knew that she was not speaking merely of roasted mullet and fresh figs.

She was silent a moment. Then, with a laugh, she exclaimed, "I'd like to be there right now."

Glossary of North Carolina Watercraft, 1790–1865

BATEAU: a narrow, flat-bottomed craft up to 80 feet long, drawing 18 inches or less; sometimes with one or both ends square, sometimes double-ended (i.e., with two pointed ends). Bateaux were used on middle and upper reaches of rivers; steered downstream by sweeps; and rowed, poled, or towed upstream. Boatmen paddled or poled smaller versions, 12 to 20 feet long, on creeks.

BRIG: a two-masted, oceangoing sailing vessel, square-rigged on both masts, carrying two or more headsails and a gaff sail or spanker aft of the mizzenmast. It was small in comparison to most seagoing merchant vessels. Locally supplanted by schooners early in the nineteenth century, some brigs were of sufficiently shallow draft that they could handle the shoals of North Carolina.

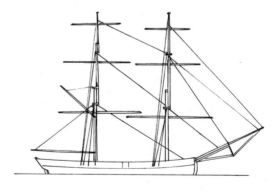

The glossary was compiled with the assistance of Mike Alford, retired curator of watercraft, North Carolina Maritime Museum, Beaufort, North Carolina, who also did all of the drawings. The cooner, periauger, schooner, shad galley, skiff, sloop, and steamer drawings are reproduced from Michael B. Alford, *Traditional Work Boats of North Carolina* (Beaufort: North Carolina Maritime Museum, 1990).

Terms used in historical documents to describe or define boat types present peculiar problems for researchers. The tendency is to presume each term applies to a very specific type of boat. In truth, boats

COONER (also *kunner, canoe,* etc.):
a dugout log boat fashioned from
one to three logs, typically
cypress. Fourteen to 28 feet long,
cooners were propelled by paddle, oar, push pole, or small sails,
or some combination of these.
They were usually open, not
decked and were a very common
form of transport from earliest
colonial times through the Civil
War. They could be narrow and
pointed at each end, especially on
smaller rivers. In larger bodies
of water, such as Pamlico Sound,
they were often very "boatlike,"
exhibiting sophisticated construction such as interior framing and partial decks.

FERRY: any boat engaged in the
act of ferrying. Ferries moved
people, animals, or vehicles back
and forth across narrow bodies
of water like rivers or creeks, or,
occasionally, large bodies of
water such as Lake Mattamuskeet. On rivers and creeks, they
were typically very simple and
moved by means of a system of
ropes or cables. In colonial times,
county courts administered ferries, an indication of their
importance.

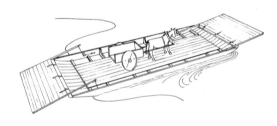

varied in form and construction from one locality to another, reflecting cultural traditions, materials
available for construction, and environmental conditions in which the completed boat would have to
function. Often, the terms that appear in documents apply to the function that a boat was put to (for
example, lighters and pilot boats), not to a boat of specific form and construction. The job to be done was
uppermost in the user's mind, not the proper name of the craft doing the job. Additionally, writers of
early documents sometimes used names of European types that resembled what they saw in America,
while the local population may have had a completely different name for the boat. Those "new" terms
present another kind of problem in that disparate spellings (for example, "periauger" and "kunner") were
invented by almost every author, based on his phonetic interpretation.

FLAT AND FLATBOAT: a low-sided, flat-bottomed boat of shallow draft and large capacity. Square at both ends, flatboats were used on protected or slow-moving waters, especially as ferries and for carrying livestock, produce, and other plantation products.

FLATTIE: any small, flat-bottomed utility skiff (usage varied locally).

LIGHTER: any vessel, large or small, that is used in lightering (i.e., the act of loading or off-loading from one vessel to another and transporting the load ashore or to another vessel). In a harbor, lightering might be done with barges or even a fleet of skiffs, if the cargo permitted. Lightering was sometimes done with vessels lying offshore, as at Portsmouth and Ocracoke, and in those instances lighters were usually small sailing vessels rigged as sloops or schooners. Those boats were maintained as "lighters" but would not appear very different from any another sloop or schooner of the day.

LIGHTSHIP: any manned boat or vessel kept offshore, at anchor, carrying a lighted beacon to warn shipping traffic away from shoals. Not commonly in use until the 1850s, and then only erratically, they were placed principally on inshore waters, such as the Lower Neuse River, though a lightship was also on station at Frying Pan Shoals, beyond the mouth of the Cape Fear River.

PERIAUGER (also *pettiauger* and
various other spellings): a very
popular workboat fashioned out
of two logs (usually cypress) fastened together with a third keel-
log between them, often rigged
with one or two masts. It could
be 30 to 40 feet long and up to 8
feet wide. The periauger served
as the "sloop" and "schooner" of
remote and isolated communities
from the colonial era into the
early part of the nineteenth century, being much more easily
built and maintained than plank-
built boats.

PILOT BOAT: generally, a boat
that ferried pilots to and from
vessels entering or leaving ports.
Most ports maintained a large
pilot boat, usually a schooner,
"on station" out from the harbor
entrance, from which a small
boat would transfer the pilot to
or from the arriving or departing vessel. Colonial ports such as
Ocracoke, however, maintained
seaworthy, double-ended boats
that were based on shore and
rowed through the inlet to deliver or retrieve pilots. These
boats were probably 24 to 30 feet
long, lightly but strongly built,
and manned by six to ten oarsmen. This method of transporting pilots was used only when
the distance to the pickup point
was not great.

PUNT: an open, flat-bottomed boat used on creeks and small rivers, typically by one person, for hunting, fishing, basic transportation, etc. It was usually square-ended and propelled by a paddle or pole. In England, a punt is a boat that is poled, and "punting" is the act of pushing a boat by pole. However, if there is any association between the English usage and "punt" as applied in North Carolina, it is weak indeed.

RAFT: a watercraft made by bundling together material that is naturally buoyant, as opposed to boats or vessels that are built like a shell to create buoyancy. On North Carolina waters, rafting was a popular means of transporting sawn lumber from where it was cut and sawn into planks. When logs were floated down a river to a sawmill, several were bundled together into a raft, called a bateau, on which the crews rode.

REVENUE CUTTER: a fast-sailing schooner, lightly armed and used for enforcing United States Treasury customs laws.

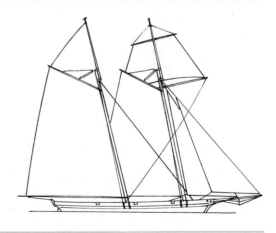

SCHOONER: a two-masted, fore-
and-aft-rigged sailing vessel. It
was fast and handy and a favorite
of the coastwise trade along the
eastern seaboard. By the early
1800s, Chesapeake Bay and
North Carolina schooners generally had wide beams and very
shallow drafts, making them
ideal freight and fishing vessels
where large capacity was
desired. Schooners were also
capable of making offshore passages, and sometimes those from
North Carolina traded in other
U.S. and West Indies ports.
Throughout this era, local
shipyards turned out more
schooners than any other vessel.

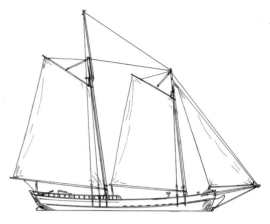

SCOW: a burdensome carrier,
square-ended on deck but with
raking or curved bottoms at the
ends to improve maneuvering
and sailing ability. Sloop- or
schooner-rigged, scows were
used for carrying freight and
livestock. Beginning in the mid-
nineteenth century, they were a
popular freight boat and lighter
on Albemarle and Pamlico
Sounds.

SHAD GALLEY: a very long rowing boat propelled by 8 to perhaps 16 oarsmen. Ubiquitous for seine hauling in the shad and herring fishery on Albemarle Sound and its tributaries, the craft had a long, sharp bow and a wide transom stern.

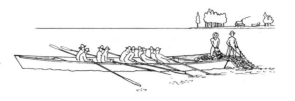

SKIFF: any small, open boat, rowed and often fitted with a small sail, usually a spritsail, and sometimes a jib. It paralleled and replaced the cooner. Skiffs were usually further described by use, such as oyster skiff, pole skiff, sail skiff.

SLOOP: a single-masted, fore-and-aft-rigged seagoing sailing vessel with a bowsprit and a single headsail set from the forestay. Sloops and schooners were the two largest seagoing vessels that commonly visited North Carolina waters or were built at local shipyards.

STEAMER: any relatively small, steam-powered decked vessel, usually confined to rivers and other inland waters. Steamers were first used for river transport in North Carolina in the 1820s but were still uncommon at the advent of the Civil War.

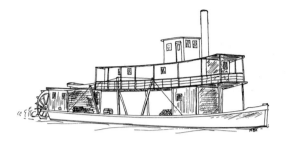

STEAM SHIP: a steam-powered, oceangoing vessel. Steam ships made regular runs from New York City to southern deepwater ports such as Charleston and Norfolk after 1820, though no port in North Carolina was a regular stop.

Notes

ABBREVIATIONS

AMAA   American Missionary Association Archives, Dillard University, New Orleans, La.

CRNC   William L. Saunders, ed., *Colonial Records of North Carolina*, 10 vols. (Raleigh: State of North Carolina, 1886–90).

DU   Special Collections Department, Perkins Library, Duke University, Durham, N.C.

JNH   *Journal of Negro History*

NA   National Archives, Washington, D.C.

NCHR   *North Carolina Historical Review*

NCSA   North Carolina State Archives, Raleigh

RG   Record Group

SHC   Southern Historical Collection, Wilson Library, University of North Carolina, Chapel Hill

WMQ   *William and Mary Quarterly*

PREFACE

1. October 5, 1830, entry, personal diary, 1830–36, Moses Ashley Curtis Papers, SHC.

2. *Our Living and Our Dead* (New Bern, N.C.), September 17, 1873.

3. Gen. Joseph Swift, memoirs, in James Sprunt, "Notes on Cape Fear History," article 86, in *Southport Leader*, October 10, 1895.

4. October 5, 1830, entry, personal diary, 1830–36, Moses Ashley Curtis Papers, SHC.

5. William Main Doerflinger, *Songs of the Sailor and Lumberman* (New York: Macmillan, 1951), 73–76, 97–101. For several versions of this chantey, see references in Minnie Earl Sears, *Song Index* (New York: H. W. Wilson, 1926), 485.

6. October 23 and October 24, 1830, entries, personal diary, 1830–36, Moses Ashley Curtis Papers, SHC.

7. A number of valuable works on black mariners in the Americas have appeared in the last few decades, most of them with an emphasis on black sailors in the northern states. See Philip S. Foner, "William P. Powell: Militant Champion of Black Seaman," in *Essays in Afro-American History*, ed. Philip S. Foner (Philadelphia: Temple University Press, 1978), 88–111; W. Jeffrey Bolster, " 'To Feel Like a Man': Black Seamen in the Northern States, 1800–1860," *Journal of American History* 76 (March 1990): 1173–99; Gaddis Smith, "Black

Seamen and the Federal Courts, 1789–1860," in *Ships, Seafaring and Society: Essays in Maritime History*, ed. Timothy J. Runyan (Detroit: Wayne State University Press for the Great Lakes Historical Society, 1987), 321–38; Martha S. Putney, "Black Seamen of Newport, 1803–1865: A Case Study in Foreign Commerce," *JNH* 57 (1972): 156–68; Martha S. Putney, *Black Sailors: Afro-American Seamen and Whalemen prior to the Civil War* (New York: Greenwood Press, 1987); James Barker Farr, *Black Odyssey: The Seafaring Tradition of Afro-Americans* (New York: Peter Lang, 1989); Lamont D. Thomas, *Rise to Be a People: A Biography of Paul Cuffe* (Urbana: University of Illinois Press, 1986); Rosalind Cobb Wiggins, *Captain Paul Cuffe's Logs and Letters, 1808–1817: A Black Quaker's "Voice from within the Veil"* (Washington, D.C.: Howard University Press, 1996); and—for an excellent bibliography—Mary Malloy, *African-Americans in the Maritime Trades: A Guide to Resources in New England* (Sharon, Mass.: Kendall Whaling Museum, 1990). For a broader view of black seafarers throughout the Atlantic, see Peter Linebaugh and Marcus Rediker, "The Many-Headed Hydra: Sailors, Slaves and the Atlantic Working Class in the Eighteenth Century," *Journal of Historical Sociology* 3 (September 1990): 225–52; Marcus Rediker, *Between the Devil and the Deep Blue Sea: Merchant Seamen, Pirates, and the Anglo-American Maritime World, 1700–1750* (Cambridge: Cambridge University Press, 1987); Julius S. Scott, "Afro-American Sailors and the International Communication Network: The Case of Newport Bowers," in *Jack Tar in History: Essays in the History of Maritime Life and Labour*, ed. Colin Howell and Richard Twomey (Fredericton, N.B.: Acadiensis Press, 1991), 37–52; and W. Jeffrey Bolster, *Black Jacks: African American Seamen in the Age of Sail* (Cambridge: Harvard University Press, 1997).

Among the most interesting of a somewhat earlier generation of pioneering works that address the history of black seafarers in the Americas, see Rayford W. Logan, "The Negro in the Quasi-War, 1798–1800," *Negro History Bulletin* 14 (March 1951): 128–32; Peter Olsen, "The Negro Maritime Worker and the Sea," *Negro History Bulletin* 19 (January 1956): 80; Jesse Lemisch, "Jack Tar in the Streets: Merchant Seamen in the Politics of Revolutionary America," *WMQ*, 3rd ser., 25 (1968), 371–407; Harold D. Langley, "The Negro in the Navy and Merchant Service, 1798–1860," *JNH* 52 (October 1967): 273–86; and Lorenzo Johnston Greene, *The Negro in Colonial New England* (New York: Atheneum, 1974), 113–18.

8. Only a handful of articles have focused on the experience of black watermen within the American South before 1865. An article by Douglas R. Egerton discusses in a new light the role of black boatmen, ferrymen, and sailors in a slave revolt along the Roanoke River in Virginia and North Carolina. See "'Fly across the River': The Easter Slave Conspiracy of 1802," *NCHR* 68 (April 1991): 87–110. And for further details, see Egerton's *Gabriel's Rebellion: The Virginia Slave Conspiracies of 1800 and 1802* (Chapel Hill: University of North Carolina Press, 1993), esp. 129–31, 164–65. Mark T. Taylor has briefly described the leading role played by slaves and free blacks in the tremendous shad, rockfish, and herring fishery in antebellum North Carolina. See "Seiners and Tongers: North Carolina Fisheries in the Old and New South," *NCHR* 69 (January 1992): 4–10. In a fascinating account, John Herbon Moore has chronicled the life of a slave waterman who was in charge of log rafts and lumber flatboats on the Yazoo River and other Mississippi riverways. See "Simon Gray, Riverman: A Slave Who Was Almost Free," in *The Other Slaves: Mechanics, Artisans, and Craftsmen*, ed. James E. Newton and Ronald L. Lewis (Boston: G. K. Hall, 1978), 157–

67. For an interesting look at black watermen on the Outer Banks in a somewhat later era, see David Wright and David Zoby, "Ignoring Jim Crow: The Turbulent Appointment of Richard Etheridge and the Pea Island Lifesavers," *JNH* 80, no. 2 (Spring 1995): 66–80.

For a useful synthesis on slave boating in the territories north and south of North Carolina during the eighteenth century, see Philip D. Morgan, *Slave Counterpoint: Black Culture in the Eighteenth-Century Chesapeake and Lowcountry* (Chapel Hill: University of North Carolina Press, 1998), 236–44, 337–42.

9. Second–Eighth Censuses of the United States, 1800–1860, North Carolina Population and Slave Schedules, NA.

10. Second–Eighth Censuses of the United States, 1800–1860, Craven County, Chowan County, and New Hanover County, N.C.: Population Schedules, NA.

11. London R. Ferebee, *A Brief History of the Slave Life of Reverend London R. Ferebee* (Raleigh: Edwards, Broughton, 1882), 8–9.

12. Moses Grandy, *Narrative of the Life of Moses Grandy, Late a Slave in the United States of America* (London: Gilpin, 1843), 14, 18–19, 21–22, 41–42.

13. Thomas H. Jones, *The Experience of Thomas H. Jones, Who Was a Slave for Forty-Three Years* (Boston: Bazin and Chandler, 1862), 35–36. The narrative was first published ca. 1854.

14. A similar observation could well be made for the American South as a whole. While Denmark Vesey had, of course, been a cabin boy and was deeply enmeshed in maritime society in Charleston at the time of his insurrection of 1822, black maritime laborers often appear at the heart of less well known slave revolts as well. Even the far more obscure slave conspiracy in Adams Creek, Mississippi, so brilliantly pieced together by Winthrop D. Jordan, was hatched, tellingly, "on the fishing creek." See Winthrop D. Jordan, *Tumult and Silence at Second Creek: An Inquiry into a Civil War Conspiracy* (Baton Rouge: Louisiana State University Press, 1993), 100. The rebellious reputation of slave watermen is emphasized more broadly in two important studies of Virginia and South Carolina in the eighteenth century. Peter H. Wood examines with a careful eye the presence and skills of slave watermen in colonial South Carolina. See Peter H. Wood, *Black Majority: Negroes in Colonial South Carolina from 1670 through the Stono Rebellion* (New York: W. W. Norton, 1974), 123–24, 200–205. Gerald Mullin emphasizes the significance and rebelliousness of black watermen in early Virginia throughout his *Flight and Rebellion: Slave Resistance in Eighteenth-Century Virginia* (New York: Oxford University Press, 1972).

15. Jeffrey J. Crow, *The Black Experience in Revolutionary North Carolina* (Raleigh: North Carolina Department of Cultural Resources, Division of Archives and History, 1977), 58.

16. Egerton, *Gabriel's Rebellion*, esp. 28–30, 39–40, 61, 119–20, 129–31.

17. *American Beacon* (Norfolk, Va.), April 12, 1831.

18. William H. Robinson, *From Log Cabin to the Pulpit; or, Fifteen Years in Slavery*, 3rd ed. (Eau Claire, Wis.: James H. Tifft, 1913).

19. Peter P. Hinks, *To Awaken My Afflicted Brethren: David Walker and the Problem of Antebellum Slave Resistance* (University Park: Pennsylvania State University Press, 1997), 1–21, 173–236; Julius S. Scott, "The Common Wind: Currents of Afro-American Communication in the Era of the Haitian Revolution" (Ph.D. diss., Duke University, 1986); Bolster, *Black Jacks*, esp. 190–214; David Walker, *David Walker's Appeal to the Coloured*

Citizens of the World, ed. Peter P. Hinks (University Park: Pennsylvania State University Press, 2000).

20. Scott, "The Common Wind." See also Scott's "Afro-American Sailors."

21. See Rediker, *Between the Devil and the Deep Blue Sea*; Linebaugh and Rediker, "The Many-Headed Hydra"; and Bolster, *Black Jacks*.

22. Historians have shown a growing appreciation for the cultural and political connections that bound black communities in the Americas, Africa, and Europe together in what is often referred to as "the black Atlantic." Among the many excellent works that have framed the black Atlantic conceptually and emphasized the importance of taking a transnational perspective in early American history, see especially Paul Gilroy, *The Black Atlantic: Modernity and Double Consciousness* (Cambridge: Harvard University Press, 1993); Philip D. Morgan, "The Cultural Implications of the Atlantic Slave Trade: African Regional Origins, American Destinations and New World Developments," *Slavery and Abolition* 18, no. 1 (April 1997): 122–45; Henry Louis Gates Jr. and William L. Andrews, *Pioneers of the Black Atlantic: Five Slave Narratives from the Enlightenment, 1772–1815* (Washington, D.C.: Civitas, 1998), esp. vii–xi; Ira Berlin, "From Creole to African: Atlantic Creoles and the Origins of African-American Society in Mainland North America," *WMQ*, 3rd ser., 53 (April 1996): 251–88; and Daniel Vickers, "Beyond Jack Tar," *WMQ*, 3rd ser., 50, no. 2 (April 1993): 418–24. For the role of black sailors in creating a diasporic identity in the eighteenth-century Atlantic, see Bolster, *Black Jacks*, esp. 19–41.

23. On Vesey's revolt, among many other sources, see especially Michael A. Gomez, *Exchanging Our Country Marks: The Transformation of African Identities in the Colonial and Antebellum South* (Chapel Hill: University of North Carolina Press, 1998), 1–4; Edward A. Pearson, ed., *Designs against Charleston: The Trial Record of the Denmark Vesey Slave Conspiracy of 1822* (Chapel Hill: University of North Carolina Press, 1999); John Lofton, *Denmark Vesey's Revolt: The Slave Plot That Lit the Fuse to Fort Sumter* (Kent, Ohio: Kent State University Press, 1983); and Robert S. Starobin, ed., *Denmark Vesey: The Slave Conspiracy of 1822* (Englewood Cliffs, N.J.: Prentice-Hall, 1970).

24. Bolster, *Black Jacks*, 199–211. See also chap. 6, n. 90, below.

25. For references to slaves escaping by sea from other southern states and the Caribbean, see chap. 5, n. 5, below.

PROLOGUE

1. Paul Hulton, *America 1585: The Complete Drawings of John White* (Chapel Hill: University of North Carolina Press and British Museum Publications, 1984), esp. 108.

2. William Byrd, *William Byrd's Histories of the Dividing Line Betwixt Virginia and North Carolina*, introduction and notes by William K. Boyd (Raleigh: North Carolina Historical Commission, 1929), 48.

3. William Tatham, "Survey on the Coast of North Carolina from Cape Hatteras to Cape Fear" (1806), North Carolina Collection, Wilson Library, University of North Carolina, Chapel Hill.

4. Peter H. Wood, "The Changing Population of the Colonial South: An Overview by Race and Region, 1685–1790," in Peter H. Wood, Gregory A. Waselkov, and M. Thomas Hatley, *Powhatan's Mantle: Indians in the Colonial Southeast* (Lincoln: University of Nebraska

Press, 1989), p. 38. Because of the colony's lack of a deepwater harbor, relatively few slave ships crossed the Atlantic directly to North Carolina ports. Statistics on slave shipping are incomplete, but most slaves in colonial North Carolina seem to have been shipped into Charleston, South Carolina, though presumably many of the slaves in the Albemarle region had first entered at Norfolk or Richmond. See Walter E. Minchinton, "The Seaborne Slave Trade of North Carolina," *NCHR* 71, no. 1 (January 1994): 1–61, and Michael A. Gomez, *Exchanging Our Country Marks: The Transformation of African Identities in the Colonial and Antebellum South* (Chapel Hill: University of North Carolina Press, 1998), 23.

5. John Lawson, *New Voyage to Carolina* (London: n.p., 1709), 158.

6. Janet Schaw, *Journal of a Lady of Quality*, ed. Evangeline W. Andrews and Charles M. Andrews (New Haven: Yale University Press, 1922), 149–51, 171.

7. William S. Powell, ed., "Tryon's Book on North Carolina," *NCHR* 34, no. 3 (July 1957): 406–15. See also William S. Price Jr., "North Carolina and the First British Empire: Economy and Society in an Eighteenth-Century Colony," in *The North Carolina Experience: An Interpretive and Documentary History*, ed. Lindley Butler and Alan Watson (Chapel Hill: University of North Carolina Press, 1984), 92.

8. Eugene P. Odum, ed., *A North Carolina Naturalist: H. H. Brimley, Selections from His Writings* (Chapel Hill: University of North Carolina Press, 1949), 17–18.

9. Peter H. Wood, *Black Majority: Negroes in Colonial South Carolina from 1670 through the Stono Rebellion* (New York: W. W. Norton, 1974), 124; W. Jeffrey Bolster, *Black Jacks: African American Seamen in the Age of Sail* (Cambridge: Harvard University Press, 1997), 60–61.

10. Nathaniel H. Bishop, *Voyage of the Paper Canoe: A Geographical Journey of 2,500 Miles from Quebec to the Gulf of Mexico, During the Years 1874–5* (Edinburgh: David Douglass, 1878), 178.

11. Arna Alexander Bontemps, "A Social History of Black Culture in Colonial North Carolina" (Ph.D. diss., University of Illinois at Urbana-Champaign, 1989), 151–57. On the African roots of periaugers, see Bolster, *Black Jacks*, 60–61.

12. Wood, *Black Majority*, 122–24, 200–205. Gwendolyn Midlo Hall also observes that Senegambians built vessels for deepwater fishing. See her *Africans in Colonial Louisiana: The Development of Afro-Creole Culture in the Eighteenth Century* (Baton Rouge: Louisiana State University Press, 1992), 32.

13. Edmund S. Morgan, *American Slavery, American Freedom: The Ordeal of Colonial Virginia* (New York: W. W. Norton, 1975), 102, 104. For a good overview of the African roots of black seafaring in the Americas, see Bolster, *Black Jacks*, 44–67.

14. On native boatbuilding, see Mark Joseph Hartman, "The Development of Watercraft in the Prehistoric Southeastern United States" (Ph.D. diss., Texas A&M University, 1996), esp. 182–84, 218–22, and Kenneth G. Roberts and Philip Shackleton, *The Canoe: A History of the Craft from Panama to the Arctic* (Camden, Maine: International Marine Pub. Co., 1983), 74–80.

15. Thomas C. Loftfield, "Prehistoric Oystermen of the Central North Carolina Coast," in *Sea and Land: Cultural and Biological Adaptations in the Southern Coastal Plain*, Southern Anthropological Society Proceedings No. 21, ed. James L. Peacock and James C. Sabella (Athens: University of Georgia Press, 1988), 106–21; David S. Phelps, "Archaeology of the

North Carolina Coast and Coastal Plain: Problems and Hypotheses," in *The Prehistory of North Carolina: An Archaeological Symposium*, ed. Mark A. Mathis and Jeffrey J. Crow (Raleigh: North Carolina Department of Cultural Resources, Division of Archives and History, 1983), 39–44; Christian F. Frest, "North Carolina Algonquians," in ibid., esp. 273–76; Douglass W. Boyce, "Iroquoian Tribes of the Virginia–North Carolina Coastal Plain," in *Handbook of North American Indians*, vol. 15, ed. G. B. Trigger (Washington, D.C.: Smithsonian Institution, 1978), 284. The better-documented fishing culture of Algonquian Indians in tidewater Virginia offers much insight into fishing among their southern kindred. See especially Helen C. Rountree, *The Powhatan Indians of Virginia: Their Traditional Culture* (Norman: University of Oklahoma Press, 1989), 34–38, 44.

The early colonists commented on the fishing skills of the Indians throughout the coastal Americas. In about 1604, in what is now southern Maine, Samuel Champlain, for instance, regretted that the coastal Indians were not better hunters, as he was looking to trade furs, but he noted that they were "good fishermen and tillers of the soil." Quoted in James Axtell, *The Invasion Within: The Contrast of Cultures in Colonial North America* (New York: Oxford University Press, 1985), 35.

16. Wood, "The Changing Population of the Colonial South," 38. The larger estimate of the native population is based on unpublished archaeological research by David Phelps at East Carolina University. I would like to thank Dr. Phelps for sharing the results of his data with me.

17. *CRNC*, 2:45.

18. Charles M. Hudson, *The Southeastern Indians* (Knoxville: University of Tennessee Press, 1976), 281–84; Charles C. Jones Jr., *Antiquities of the Southern Indians* (New York: D. Appleton, 1873), 327.

19. Allen Parker, *Recollections of Slavery Times* (Worcester, Mass.: Charles W. Burbank & Co., 1895), 63.

20. John Urmstone to the Society for the Propagation of the Gospel, July 17, 1711, *CRNC*, 1:772.

21. "Mr. Blair's mission to North Carolina" (1704), *CRNC*, 1:600–603.

22. John Urmstone to the Society for the Propagation of the Gospel, July 7, 1711, *CRNC*, 1:763.

23. Ibid., 772.

24. Paul Heinegg, "Free African Americans of Virginia and North Carolina," *North Carolina Genealogical Society Journal* 20, no. 3 (August 1994): 177–93; David Cecelski, *A Historian's Coast: Adventures into the Tidewater Past* (Winston-Salem, N.C.: John F. Blair, 2000), 9–14.

25. Benjamin Cowse, *The Tryals of Major Stede Bonnet, and Other Pirates . . . To which is Prefix'd, An Account of the Taking of the said Major Bonnet, and the rest of the Pirates* (London: n.p., 1719), 45–46. For a good discussion of black pirates, see K. J. Kinkor, "Black Men under the Black Flag," unpublished draft, March 1995, in the possession of the North Carolina Maritime Museum, Beaufort, N.C. Based on 14 crew lists that demarcate racial makeups, Kinkor estimates that blacks composed just under 30 percent of the average crew serving on pirating vessels between 1715 and 1725 (14–15).

26. Marcus Rediker, "Under the Banner of King Death: The Social World of Anglo-American Pirates, 1716–1726," *WMQ*, 3rd ser., 38, no. 2 (April 1981): 210–11; Marcus

Rediker, *Between the Devil and the Deep Blue Sea: Merchant Seamen, Pirates, and the Anglo-American Maritime World, 1700–1750* (Cambridge: Cambridge University Press), 107–11. While acknowledging a maritime fraternity among Atlantic pirates that included black sailors, W. Jeffrey Bolster casts a warier eye on the extent of racial equality among buccaneers. See Bolster, *Black Jacks*, 13–16.

K. J. Kinkor has pointed out several factors that might have reinforced the softening of racism's edges among Atlantic pirates: their own marginality, a constant short supply on pirating vessels of seamen of any race, and the overbearing preeminence of the Articles of Piracy, a compact signed by many pirate gangs to restrain the captain's powers and spread the risks and prizes of piracy equitably among outlaws renowned for their fierce independence and diversity. See Kinkor, "Black Men under the Black Flag," 5–7.

27. Lt. Governor Bennett to the Council of Trade and Plantations (1718), in Great Britain, Public Record Office, *Calendar of the State Papers, Colonial Series: America and the West Indies, 1574–1738* (London: Her Majesty's Stationery Office).

28. Edward Randolph to the Council of Trade and Plantations, March 24, 1700, *CRNC*, 1:527.

29. Great Britain, Public Record Office, *Calendar of State Papers, Colonial Series: America and the West Indies, 1574–1738*, 1701, p. 105.

30. Robert E. Lee, *Blackbeard the Pirate: A Reappraisal of His Life and Times* (Winston-Salem, N.C.: John F. Blair, 1974), 136.

31. The flight of a Coromantee slave, who in 1759 traveled from Rowan County 200 miles to Wilmington, may have been unusually long, but neither his escape nor his destination was exceptional. More common, perhaps, was the escape in 1769 of Frank and Jerry, two of Richard Quince's slaves, from a periauger on the Cape Fear River. See Marvin L. Michael Kay and Lorin Lee Cary, *Slavery in North Carolina, 1748–1775* (Chapel Hill: University of North Carolina Press, 1995), 130, and *Cape-Fear Mercury* (Wilmington), December 8, 1769.

32. The Publick to William Moore, September 6, 1748, *State Records of North Carolina*, ed. Walter Clark, 26 vols. (Raleigh: P. M. Hale, 1896–1907), 22:268.

33. Mathew Rowan to William Wilkins, February 1, 1753, Colonial Governor's Papers: Mathew Rowan, NCSA.

34. A. L. Fries et al., *Records of the Moravians in North Carolina,* 12 vols. (Raleigh: Edwards & Broughton, 1922–69), 1:261.

35. Peter Linebaugh and Marcus Rediker, "The Many-Headed Hydra: Sailors, Slaves and the Atlantic Working Class in the Eighteenth Century," *Journal of Historical Sociology* 3 (September 1990): 225–52. See also Jesse Lemisch, "Jack Tar in the Streets: Merchant Seamen in the Politics of Revolutionary America," *WMQ*, 3rd ser., 25 (1968): 371–407.

36. John Simpson to Richard Cogdell, July 15, 1775, Richard Cogdell Papers, NCSA. On Merrick's rebellion, see the excellent discussion in Jeffrey J. Crow, *The Black Experience in Revolutionary North Carolina* (Raleigh: North Carolina Department of Cultural Resources, Division of Archives and History, 1977), 57–59.

37. Proceedings of the Safety Committee at Wilmington, July 20, 1775, *CRNC*, 10:112. See also Crow, *The Black Experience in Revolutionary North Carolina*, 57–59.

38. Gary B. Nash, "Thomas Peters: Millwright and Deliverer," in *Struggle and Survival*

in Colonial America, ed. David G. Sweet and Gary B. Nash (Berkeley: University of California Press, 1981), 73–74.

39. Dismal Swamp Land Company Papers, DU.

40. Proceedings of the Safety Committee at Wilmington, July 20, 1775, *CRNC*, 10:112.

41. Gov. Alexander Martin to Gen. Greene, May 7, 1782, Clark, *State Records of North Carolina*, 16:319–20. On Dunmore's regiment and the black experience in the American Revolution, see Ira Berlin, *Many Thousands Gone: The First Two Centuries of Slavery in North America* (Cambridge: Belknap Press of Harvard University Press, 1998), 256–89; Crow, *The Black Experience in Revolutionary North Carolina*, 59–61; Benjamin Quarles, *The Negro in the American Revolution* (Chapel Hill: University of North Carolina Press, 1961), 19–31; Philip S. Foner, *Blacks in the American Revolution* (Westport, Conn.: Greenwood Press, 1975), 69–70; Peter H. Wood, "'The Dream Deferred': Black Freedom Struggles on the Eve of White Independence," in *In Resistance: Studies in African, Caribbean, and Afro-American History*, ed. G. Y. Okihiro (Amherst: University of Massachusetts Press, 1986), 170–75; Sylvia R. Frey, *Water from the Rock: Black Resistance in a Revolutionary Age* (Princeton: Princeton University Press, 1991), 76–80, 162–65, 190–205; and John B. Boles, *Black Southerners, 1619–1869* (Lexington: University Press of Kentucky, 1983), 54–55.

42. Foner, *Blacks in the American Revolution*, 70.

43. Charles H. Whedbee, *Outer Banks Mysteries and Seaside Stories* (Winston-Salem, N.C.: John F. Blair, 1978), 44–66.

44. Many Cape Fear runaways fought the remainder of the war in a British company known as the Black Guides and Pioneers. See Nash, "Thomas Peters," 74–75. On black sailors on American vessels, see Foner, *Blacks in the American Revolution*, 69–70.

45. John Holloway to Cursor and Governor St. Eustatius, September 25, 1780, English Records Collection, NCSA.

46. Thomas Blount to John Gray Blount, December 21, 1794, John Gray Blount Papers, NCSA. Though the use of slave pilots was still legal in 1794, the General Assembly had regulated these pilots as early as 1783, requiring their masters to post £100 in specie and the slaves to undergo an examination by the local port commissioners. The unknown man who piloted the *Sally* off the shoals could have been a free black, a licensed slave, or a slave pilot working illegally. See "An Act for facilitating the navigation, and regulating the pilotage of the several ports of this State," Laws of North Carolina, 1783, Clark, *State Records of North Carolina* 24:502–3.

47. Advertisements of slave runaways, in particular, redound with stories such as that of Cuffee, a ship's carpenter; Frank, a stevedore; Andrew, a riverboatman; and Toby, a lighter captain. See *Wilmington Centinel and General Advertiser*, February 12, 1789, and *Hall's Wilmington Gazette*, February 9, 1797, April 1797, and April 20, 1797.

48. Loyalist Claims Papers 1782, Audit Office 13, Bundle 121, NCSA, and Treasurer's and Comptroller's Papers, 1760–1775, *Ports, Port of Roanoke*, Custom House Papers, NCSA, both cited in Sheridan R. Jones, "Historical and Archaeological Investigation of the MacKnight Shipyard Wreck" (M.A. thesis, East Carolina University, 1996), 14, 18–20. Jones points out that many of the vessels listed as "Currituck built" in the Treasurer's and Comptroller's Papers of 1760–1775 would have been built by MacKnight's slaves. In that period, the MacKnight shipyard workers turned out mainly sloops and schooners but also

produced vessels as large as the 80-ton snow *Hope* and the 100-ton brig *Peggy*, both registered in 1775.

49. William S. Tarlton, "Somerset and Its Restoration," report prepared for the Department of Conservation, Division of State Parks, August 1, 1954, 119–20; January 18, March 4, May 1, and May 13, 1780, Joseph Westmore Journal, DU.

50. For travel accounts describing slave watermen, particularly ferrymen, in colonial North Carolina, see chap. 1, n. 29, below.

51. *North-Carolina Gazette* (New Bern), March 23, 1793. Many tidewater slaves fled on seagoing vessels; others fled the immediate vicinity in their masters' canoes, periaugers, flatboats, and sloops, an act of resistance that happened often enough for John West, when he discovered a 25-foot-long "pettyauger" abandoned near New Bern, to assume that "she was brought there by runaway negroes." See the *North-Carolina Gazette*, July 4, 1795; Alice Barnwell Keith, ed., *John Gray Blount Papers*, 4 vols. (Raleigh: North Carolina State Department of Archives and History, 1952–82), 2:288; and Crow, *The Black Experience in Revolutionary North Carolina*, 43.

52. *Wilmington Centinel and General Advertiser*, February 12, 1789.

53. Ibid., June 18, 1788.

54. *Newbern Herald*, May 13, 1809.

55. *The True Republican or American Whig* (Wilmington), May 16, 1809.

56. See *North-Carolina Gazette* (New Bern), May 14, 1796; *Fayetteville Gazette*, July 23, 1793; and *Hall's Wilmington Gazette*, August 30, 1798.

57. *Post Angel, or Universal Entertainment* (Edenton), November 12, 1800. African-born slaves appear frequently in runaway slave advertisements, especially in the period roughly prior to the War of 1812. For example, when a ship's carpenter named Bob escaped from Wilmington in 1807, his master, Captain Thomas Hunter, announced that was "a Guinea born negroe with marked African accent." *Wilmington Gazette*, July 28, 1807.

58. *North-Carolina Gazette* (New Bern), April 5, 1794.

59. Kinship and church seem to have been at the heart of this enduring bond. See William Henry Singleton, *Recollections of My Slavery Days*, ed. Katherine Mellen Charron and David S. Cecelski (Raleigh: North Carolina Department of Cultural Resources, Division of Archives and History, 1999), 26–27, 69, 100–101.

60. Scott, "A Common Wind."

61. *Newbern Herald*, November 27, 1809. See also *Wilmington Centinel and General Advertiser*, January 29, 1789, and *Wilmington Gazette*, June 23, 1805, and January 3, 1804.

62. *North-Carolina Gazette* (New Bern), August 31, 1793. Toby was apparently caught, but then escaped again four years later. *Hall's Wilmington Gazette*, February 9, 1797.

63. *Wilmington Chronicle and North-Carolina Weekly Advertiser*, September 24, 1795.

64. The state's comparatively high, if still very limited, degree of racial tolerance was evident in its voting laws. The North Carolina constitution of 1776 did not prohibit free blacks from voting, and state laws did not take away their right to vote until 1835. Free blacks never had the right to vote in Virginia, South Carolina, Florida, Alabama, Mississippi, and Louisiana, and held it only briefly in Georgia and Kentucky. Even Connecticut, New Jersey, and Pennsylvania disfranchised free blacks before North Carolina. John Hope Franklin, *The Free Negro in North Carolina, 1790–1860* (New York: W. W. Norton, 1943), 12–13, 116. For instances of West Indian slaves escaping into North Carolina, see

North-Carolina Gazette, June 4, 1791, and March 8, 1794, and *Hall's Wilmington Gazette*, February 9, 1797.

65. *New Hanover County Court Minutes*, ed. Alexander McDonald Walker (Wilmington, N.C.: n.p., 1991), vol. 3, October 6, 1778, and July 9, 1789.

CHAPTER ONE

1. *Edenton Gazette and North Carolina Advertiser*, April 27, 1808.

2. Charles Ball, *Fifty Years in Chains; or The Life of an American Slave* (New York: H. Dayton, 1859).

3. Frederick Douglass, *Narrative of the Life of Frederick Douglass, an American Slave* (Boston: Anti-Slavery Office, 1845). William Wells Brown, *The Black Man: His Antecedents, His Genius, and His Achievements* (New York: T. Hamilton, 1863), 20, 23.

4. Louis Hughes, *Thirty Years a Slave: From Bondage to Freedom* (Milwaukee: South Side Printing Co., 1897), 5–6.

5. Charles Emery Stevens, *Anthony Burns: A History* (Boston: John P. Jewett, 1856), 173–79; Thomas H. Jones, *The Experience of Thomas H. Jones, Who Was a Slave for Forty-Three Years* (Boston: Bazin and Chandler, 1862); John Andrew Jackson, *The Experience of a Slave in South Carolina* (London: Passmore & Alabaster, 1862), 24–28.

6. Isaac Mason, *Life of Isaac Mason as a Slave* (Worcester, Mass.: n.p., 1893), 22–23, 32.

7. Solomon Northup, *Twelve Years a Slave: Narrative of Solomon Northup, a Citizen of New-York, Kidnapped in Washington City in 1841 . . .* (Auburn, N.Y.: Derby and Miller, 1853), 22–23, 98–100.

8. London R. Ferebee, *A Brief History of the Slave Life of Reverend London R. Ferebee* (Raleigh: Edwards, Broughton, 1882), 8–9.

9. George Henry, *Life of George Henry: Together with a Brief History of the Colored People in America* (Providence, R.I.: n.p., 1894), 12–37.

10. See *Letters and Addresses by George Thompson, during his mission in the United States, from October 1, 1834, to November 27, 1835* (Boston: I. Knapp, 1837).

11. Moses Grandy, *Narrative of the Life of Moses Grandy, Late a Slave in the United States of America* (London: Gilpin, 1843). A U.S. edition was first published in 1844.

12. In 1790 Camden County had 5,497 residents: 3,795 whites, 1,623 slaves, and 79 free blacks. First Census of the United States, 1790, North Carolina Population Schedules, NA.

13. *Wilmington Centinel and General Advertiser*, February 12, 1789; *North-Carolina Gazette* (New Bern), March 23, 1793, and April 5, 1794; *Wilmington Chronicle and North-Carolina Weekly Advertiser*, September 24, 1795; *Hall's Wilmington Gazette*, February 9, 1797, and April 20, 1797. See also Thomas Blount to John Gray Blount, December 21, 1794, John Gray Blount Papers, NCSA, and Alice Barnwell Keith, ed., *John Gray Blount Papers*, 4 vols. (Raleigh: North Carolina State Department of Archives and History, 1952–82), 3:92–93.

14. Julius S. Scott, "Afro-American Sailors and the International Communication Network: The Case of Newport Bowers," in *Jack Tar in History: Essays in the History of Maritime Life and Labour*, ed. Colin Howell and Richard Twomey (Fredericton, N.B.: Acadiensis Press, 1991), 38.

15. Political winds were not the only gales that influenced Carolina trade with the West

Indies. Shipping merchants also closely followed the hurricane season in the South Atlantic. In 1793 John Gray Blount and Thomas Blount lamented that a hurricane that hit St. Kitts, St. Thomas, St. Croix, and St. Martins did not damage many buildings and thus did not create more demand for the Blounts' lumber business to the islands. Cox Coart to John Gray Blount and Thomas Blount, September 14, 1793, Keith, *John Gray Blount Papers*, 2:307–8.

16. Catherine W. Bishir, *North Carolina Architecture* (Chapel Hill: University of North Carolina Press, 1990), esp. 26–27, 114–16; Jay D. Edwards, "The Origins of Creole Architecture," *Winterthur Portfolio* 29, nos. 2–3 (Summer–Autumn 1994): 183–88; Elizabeth Fenn, "'A Perfect Equality Seemed to Reign': Slave Society and Jonkonnu," *NCHR* 65 (1988): 127–53; Marvin L. Michael Kay and Lorin Lee Cary, *Slavery in North Carolina, 1748–1775* (Chapel Hill: University of North Carolina Press, 1995), 183–86.

17. See, in toto, Craven County, Records of Ships and Merchants, 1770–1816, NCSA. This diverse collection is the best source with which I am familiar that describes the unruly character and pitfalls of the maritime trade in North Carolina during the Revolutionary and Early National periods. See also Alice Barnwell Keith, "Three North Carolina Blount Brothers in Business and Politics, 1783–1812" (Ph.D. diss., University of North Carolina at Chapel Hill, 1940), esp. 178–81, 191–201, and Burton Spivak, *Jefferson's English Crisis: Commerce, Embargo, and the Republican Revolution* (Charlottesville: University Press of Virginia, 1979), 167–72.

18. August 1, 1808, entry, John Early diary, SHC.

19. On black sailors and the Haitian Revolution's impact on American ports, see Julius S. Scott, "The Common Wind: Currents of Afro-American Communication in the Era of the Haitian Revolution" (Ph.D. diss., Duke University, 1986); Scott, "Afro-American Sailors," 42–51; and W. Jeffrey Bolster, *Black Jacks: African American Seamen in the Age of Sail* (Cambridge: Harvard University Press, 1997), 144–53.

20. Douglas R. Egerton, *Gabriel's Rebellion: The Virginia Slave Conspiracies of 1800 and 1802* (Chapel Hill: University of North Carolina Press, 1993), 119–23, 127–31, 145.

21. Jeffrey J. Crow, *The Black Experience in Revolutionary North Carolina* (Raleigh: North Carolina Department of Cultural Resources, Division of Archives and History, 1977), 87–94.

22. Gary B. Nash, "Thomas Peters: Millwright and Deliverer," in *Struggle and Survival in Colonial America*, ed. David G. Sweet and Gary B. Nash (Berkeley: University of California Press, 1981), 73–74.

23. North Carolina House Minutes, December 22, 1795, *State Records of North Carolina*, ed. Walter Clark, 26 vols. (Raleigh: P. M. Hale, 1896–1907), 17:385; *North-Carolina Gazette* (New Bern), August 31, 1793; *Wilmington Chronicle*, September 24, 1795.

24. For an especially insightful discussion of antislavery politics and ideology in the black Atlantic during the Revolutionary era, see Ira Berlin, *Many Thousands Gone: The First Two Centuries of Slavery in North America* (Cambridge: Belknap Press of Harvard University Press, 1998), 220–28.

25. First Census of the United States, 1790, Camden County, N.C., NA.

26. Grandy, *Narrative*, 5–6.

27. Tending a ferry was not a far leap for most of the plantation slaves who lived near Albemarle Sound. The lines between plantation toil and maritime labor were dimly drawn,

and most fieldhands regularly worked on the water. Billy Grandy did not leave a journal describing his slaves' work routines, but several decades later, John N. Benners, a planter in Craven County, did. From 1857 to 1860, Benners managed approximately 20 slaves at Wilkinson's Point, on the Lower Neuse River estuary, and tracked their every task and job. None of his slaves worked primarily on the water; instead, they joined him in tending hogs, cutting lumber, scraping turpentine, and grubbing potatoes. Yet Benners's diary indicates that his slaves were constantly engaged in maritime activities. They served as deckhands on his canoe and flatboat when he carried turpentine barrels to New Bern. The slaves Willis and Ben were gone for two weeks one spring, rafting timber up the Neuse River. Willis and another slave, Henry, helped to salvage a neighbor's "flat boat that was sunk in the river." A slave named Will made oars for a new canoe. Will also helped to build a wharf, and he, Henry, and even the slave women Eliza, Charity, and Sarah built a "bulkhead to prevent the bank at landing from washing [away]." All the slaves contributed to Benners's "accounts of shad caught" listed in the back of his journal. These were fieldhands, but fieldhands clearly intimate with coastal waters. Though separated from those slaves by 50 years and 50 miles, the young Moses Grandy would have had no less salt in his veins than John N. Benners's plantation slaves at Wilkinson Point when he was first set to ferry work. July 25, 1857, August 18, 1857, January 5, 1858, August 6, 1858, and April 25–May 10, 1859, entries, John N. Benners plantation diary, as well as "Account of shad caught, 1848, 1849, 1851," John N. Benners Papers, NCSA.

28. William Griffin, *Ante-Bellum Elizabeth City: The History of a Canal Town* (Elizabeth City, N.C.: Roanoke Press, 1970), 23.

29. October 2, 1808, entry, John Early diary, SHC, and Samuel Huntington Perkins journal, May 12, 1818, cited in Robert C. McLean, ed., "A Yankee Tutor in the Old South," *NCHR* 47, no. 1 (1970): 71. Judging from late eighteenth- and early nineteenth-century travel accounts, slaves dominated the ferrying profession. See J. F. D. Smyth, *A Tour in the United States of America*, 2 vols. (Dublin, 1784), 1:73; Louis B. Wright and Marion Tinling, eds., *Quebec to Carolina in 1785–1786, Being the Travel Diary and Observations of Robert Hunter, Jr., A Young Merchant of London* (San Marino, Calif.: Huntington Library, 1943), 269–70; Winslow Watson, ed., *Men and Times of the Revolution, or Memories of Elkanah Watson* (New York: n.p., 1856), 47; Lida Rodman, ed., *Journal of a Tour to North Carolina by William Attmore* (Chapel Hill: University of North Carolina Press, 1922), 44–45; H. B. Johnston, ed., "The Journal of Ebenezer Hazard in North Carolina, 1777 and 1778," *NCHR* 36 (1959): 368–69. See also two cases cited in Michael H. Goodman, "The Black Tar: Negro Seamen in the Union Navy, 1861–1865" (Ph.D. diss., University of Nottingham, 1975): 51: Helen Tunicliff Catteral, *Judicial Cases Concerning American Slavery and the Negro*, 5 vols. (Washington, D.C.: n.p., 1926–37), 2:304, and James Stuart, *Three Years in North America*, 2 vols. (Edinburgh and London: n.p., 1833), 2:79.

30. Michael B. Alford, "The Ferry from Trent: Researching Colonial River Ferries," *Tributaries* 1, no. 1 (October 1991): 10–16.

31. Grandy, *Narrative*, 7.

32. Lemuel Sawyer, *Autobiography of Lemuel Sawyer* (New York: n.p., 1844), 3–5, 13; Jesse Forbes Pugh, *Three Hundred Years along the Pasquotank: A Biographical History of Camden County* (Durham, N.C.: Seeman Printery, 1957), 129–32; Griffin, *Ante-bellum Elizabeth City*, 38.

33. Grandy, *Narrative*, 7–11.

34. For a moving and insightful view of slave sales in the antebellum South, see Walter Johnson, *Soul by Soul: Inside the New Orleans Slave Market* (Cambridge: Harvard University Press, 2000).

35. Grandy, *Narrative*, 11.

36. See especially the array of slave contracts in the Roberts Papers, 1806–14, and in the Miscellaneous Papers, 1729–1869, Cupola House Papers, Shepherd-Pruden Memorial Library, Edenton, N.C. For an example away from the Albemarle, see Charles H. Foy (1856), Jones County Estate Records, NCSA.

37. Account Book of Charles Grice & Co., 1800–1828, NCSA.

38. Not until 1829, after slaves dredged the channel to 5 ½ feet, did the canal regularly accommodate vessels as large as sloops and schooners. Alexander Crosby Brown, "The Dismal Swamp Canal," *The American Neptune* 5, no. 3 (July 1945): 213–17; Thomas Wertenbaker, *Norfolk: Historic Southern Port* (Durham, N.C.: Duke University Press, 1931), 178–79; Samuel Huntington Perkins journal, October 24, 1817, cited in McLean, "A Yankee Tutor in the Old South," 56.

39. On black maritime culture in other southern seaports, see Bernard Edward Powers, *Black Charlestonians: A Social History, 1822–1885* (Fayetteville: University of Arkansas Press, 1994), 11; Philip D. Morgan, "Black Life in Eighteenth-Century Charleston," *Perspectives in American History* 1 (1984): 199; Barbara Jeanne Fields, *Slavery and Freedom in the Middle Ground: Maryland during the Nineteenth Century* (New Haven: Yale University Press, 1985), 40–62; T. Stephen Whitman, *The Price of Freedom: Slavery and Manumission in Baltimore and Early National Maryland* (Lexington: University Press of Kentucky, 1997), 19–21, 25; Julia Floyd Smith, *Slavery and Rice Culture in Low Country Georgia, 1750–1860* (Knoxville: University of Tennessee Press, 1985), 118, 166–68; Martha S. Putney, *Black Sailors: Afro-American Merchant Seamen and Whalemen prior to the Civil War* (New York: Greenwood Press, 1987), 12–14; and Bolster, *Black Jacks*, esp. 131–57. See also the references in nn. 50 and 51 below.

40. Scott, "Afro-American Sailors," 41.

41. For thought-provoking discussions of slavery's conflicts with and adaptations to maritime life in the South, see Fields, *Slavery and Freedom in the Middle Ground*, esp. 49, and Scott, "Afro-American Sailors," 38.

42. For slaves and shipbuilding in other southern ports, see Whitman, *The Price of Freedom*, 19–21, 25.

43. Wertenbaker, *Norfolk*, 143; Raymond B. Pinchbeck, *The Virginia Negro Artisan and Tradesman* (Richmond: William Byrd Press, 1926), 31; Duke de le Rochefoucault Liancourt, *Travels Through the United States of North America, The Country of the Iroquois and Upper Canada, in the Years 1795–1797*, 2nd ed., 3 vols. (London: T. Gillet, 1800), 3:35. For an outstanding discussion of black maritime culture in Norfolk, see Tommy Bogger, "The Slave and Free Black Community in Norfolk, 1775–1865" (Ph.D. diss., University of Virginia, 1976), 163–65.

44. Tommy Bogger, *Free Blacks in Norfolk, Virginia, 1790–1860: The Dark Side of Freedom* (Charlottesville: University Press of Virginia, 1997), 86.

45. Sailing with an all-black crew, Cuffe was one of the few black captains in New England. Although he made a highly profitable voyage up the Nanticoke River of Virginia

to pick up a load of corn, the controversy caused by his command discouraged him from making other voyages into the South. Lamont D. Thomas, *Rise to Be a People: A Biography of Paul Cuffe* (Urbana: University of Illinois Press, 1986), 15–18.

46. Henry, *Life of George Henry*, 12–21.

47. Ibid., 20, 35.

48. Ibid., 35.

49. Ibid., 37–62. For efforts by Norfolk leaders to curtail the ownership of larger vessels by free blacks in the 1820s, see Bolster, *Black Jacks*, 172–73.

50. Egerton, *Gabriel's Rebellion*, 29. For a fascinating discussion of race relations in Norfolk's wharf district, see 28–40, 60.

51. This open, freewheeling society, with elements of quasi-free slave labor and interracial activity, could be found to a significant degree in every southern port. For Baltimore, see Christopher Phillips, *Freedom's Port: The African American Community of Baltimore, 1790–1860* (Urbana: University of Illinois Press, 1997), 30–113; Fields, *Slavery and Freedom in the Middle Ground*, 40–62; and Whitman, *The Price of Freedom*, 8–32. For Charleston, see Bernard E. Powers Jr., "Black Charleston: A Social History, 1822–1885" (Ph.D. diss., Northwestern University, 1985), 20–22. For Savannah, see Whittington Bernard Johnson, *Black Savannah, 1788–1864* (Fayetteville: University of Arkansas Press, 1996), 85–132, and Betty Wood, *Women's Work, Men's Work: The Informal Slave Economies of Lowcountry Georgia* (Athens: University of Georgia Press, 1995), 81–121. See also Richard C. Wade, *Slavery in the Cities: The South, 1820–1860* (New York: Oxford University Press, 1964), 149–60, and Graham Russell Hodges, *Slavery, Freedom and Culture among Early American Workers* (Armorik, N.Y.: M. E. Sharpe, 1998), 127–44.

52. Bogger, *Free Blacks in Norfolk*, 62–66.

53. See nn. 106–14 below.

54. Eighth Census of the United States, Population Schedule, Pasquotank County, N.C. (1860), NA. On free black seamen registered in southern ports, see Putney, *Black Sailors*, 12–14.

55. For a seminal interpretation of the egalitarian ethic that persisted among mariners in the nineteenth century, see W. Jeffrey Bolster, " 'To Feel Like a Man': Black Seamen in the Northern States, 1800–1860," *Journal of American History* 76 (March 1990): 1173–99. See also Harold Langley, "The Negro in the Navy and Merchant Service, 1798–1860," *JNH* 52 (October 1967): 282–83; and Philip S. Foner, "William P. Powell: Militant Champion of Black Seamen," in *Essays in Afro-American History*, ed. Philip S. Foner (Philadelphia: Temple University Press, 1978), 91. The shipboard conditions and patterns of resistance that shaped a similar impulse and a collective identity among Atlantic seamen in an earlier era are explored in Marcus Rediker, *Between the Devil and the Deep Blue Sea: Merchant Seamen, Pirates, and the Anglo-American Maritime World, 1700–1750* (Cambridge: Cambridge University Press, 1987), esp. 92–111, 161–62, 243–49.

56. J. S. Buckingham, *The Slave States of America*, 2 vols. (London: Fisher and Son, 1842), 2:471–72.

57. Charles Janson, *A Stranger in America: Containing the Observations made during a long residence in that country. . . .* (London: Albion Press, 1807), 308.

58. Records of the Bureau of Marine Inspection and Navigation, Certificates of Enrollment issued at North Carolina Ports, 1815–1911, RG 41, NA. For a good sense of the

shipping traffic in North Carolina sounds a bit later, see also Logbook, 1845–49, Neuse River Lightship off Marsh Point, Pamlico Sound, N.C., Joseph S. Fowler Papers, DU. For an interesting sense of sailing conditions on those sounds, see journal of the schooner *Bancroft* (1852–53), vol. 16, William Francis Martin Papers, SHC.

59. For a splendid study of the schooner's history in North Carolina waters, see Ann M. Merriman, "North Carolina Schooners, 1815–1901, and the S. R. Fowle and Son Company of Washington, North Carolina" (M.A. thesis, East Carolina University, 1996), esp. 14–65. See also Joseph A. Goldenberg, *Shipbuilding in Colonial America* (Charlottesville: University Press of Virginia, 1976), 79–81, 120–21; Hugh Lefler and William S. Powell, *Colonial North Carolina: A History* (New York: Charles Scribner's Sons, 1973), 165; and, for an important, updated study on schooners and shipbuilding in North Carolina ca. 1760–1810, Sheridan R. Jones, "Historical and Archaeological Investigation of the MacKnight Shipyard Wreck" (M.A. thesis, East Carolina University, 1996), 11–14.

60. For two interesting looks at life aboard coastal schooners sailing out of North Carolina ports, including those sailing to the West Indies, see William Henry von Eberstein memoir, William Henry von Eberstein Papers, and William Augustus Pavin memoir, William Augustus Parvin Papers, both in Manuscript Collection, J. Y. Joyner Library, East Carolina University, Greenville, N.C.

61. Douglass remembered that the slaves Peter, Isaac, Rich, and Janke formed the crew of his master's sloop *Sally Lloyd*. See Douglass, *Narrative*, 9.

62. *Albemarle Enquirer* (Edenton), August 5, 1886; Pay roll of captain and hands of steamboat *Newbern*, State Literary Fund: Minutes, Reports, Deeds, Etc., 1827–1868, State Board of Education Papers, NCSA. A few free blacks in North Carolina even owned their own larger vessels; among them was Silas Moore, master and half-owner of the schooner *Susan*. Moore hauled lumber up the Neuse River into New Bern. Bolster, *Black Jacks*, 173–74.

63. Schooner *Franklin* logbook, 1788, NCSA; *Wilmington Gazette*, July 23, 1807; Thomas McLin to Thomas Sparrow, Account Book (1823–28), Craven County: Records of Ships and Merchants, 1830–58, NCSA; Merriman, "North Carolina Schooners" 69–70; *North Carolina Freedmen's Savings and Trust Company Records*, abstracted by Bill Reaves (Raleigh: N.C. Genealogical Society, 1992), New Bern branch; Goodman, "The Black Tar," 88–89.

64. Sometimes blacks and whites worked side by side in southern shipyards, as Frederick Douglass reported of the yard where he learned caulking, "and no one seemed to see any impropriety in it." At other times, competition for shipyard jobs led to labor disputes, resentments, and whites lashing out against black tradesmen. Douglass, *Narrative*, 95–99.

65. C. Wingate Reed, *Beaufort County: Two Centuries of Its History* (Raleigh: n.p., 1962), 172; Gale Farlow, "Black Craftsmen in North Carolina," *North Carolina Genealogical Society Journal*, pt. 1: 6, no. 1 (February 1985): 2–13; pt. 2: 6, no. 2 (May 1985): 91–103. For other references to black shipbuilders in a somewhat later period in antebellum North Carolina, see George P. Rawick, ed. *The American Slave: A Composite Autobiography*, 19 vols. (Westport, Conn.: Greenwood, 1972–76), 14:450–52, and Nannie Davis Ward interview, by Michael and Debbie Luster, Beaufort, N.C., 1988, North Carolina Coastal Folklife Collection, North Carolina Maritime Museum, Beaufort. For background on slaves and the shipbuilding industry in another southern port, see Bogger, "The Slave and Free Black Community in Norfolk," 163–65.

66. References to slave sailors from North Carolina are scattered in court records, the personal papers of merchants and planters, slave narratives, and many other documentary sources but are not listed in any single registry or other source. One collected source that by inference indicates the large number of slave sailors before the Civil War is the lists of occupations of the black North Carolinians who enlisted in the Union army in 1863 and 1864. See *Descriptive Books of the 35th, 36th, and 37th Regiments of the United States Colored Troops*, RG 20, NA (microfilm, NCSA). For references to free black sailors, see the Seventh and Eighth Censuses of the United States, 1850 and 1860, Brunswick, Chowan, Perquimans, Camden, Carteret, Craven, New Hanover, and Beaufort Counties, N.C., Population Schedules, NA. See also Craven County Apprentice Bonds, 1748–1835, NCSA.

67. Mary McIlhenny Toler, "Reminiscences: Memories of Pattie Baughham McMullan," in *Washington and the Pamlico*, ed. Ursula Fogleman Loy and Pauline Marion Worthy (Washington, N.C.: Washington–Beaufort County Bicentennial Commission, 1976), 109.

68. Lindley S. Butler, "The Forgotten Boatmen: Navigation on the Dan River, 1792–1892," *Tributaries* 3 (October 1993): 13–14, is a pathbreaking article on slave bateaumen and their trade. See also Frederick Tilp, *The Chesapeake Bay of Yore: Mainly about the Rowing and Sailing Craft* (Annapolis and Richmond: Chesapeake Bay Foundation, 1982), 26–27.

69. Butler, "The Forgotten Boatmen," 14. A collection of such bateaux cargo manifests can be found in the Robert Wilson Papers, SHC. On the large number of slave bateaumen on the James River, see James H. Brewer, *The Confederate Negro: Virginia's Craftsmen and Military Laborers, 1861–1865* (Durham, N.C.: Duke University Press, 1969), 18, 23, 27.

70. Butler, "The Forgotten Boatmen," 13; Tilp, *The Chesapeake Bay of Yore*, 26–27; Bruce Terrell, "The James River Batteau: Tobacco Transport in Upland Virginia, 1745–1840" (M.A. thesis, East Carolina University, 1988).

71. Tilp, *The Chesapeake Bay of Yore*, 26–27.

72. George Bagby, *Canal Reminiscences: Recollections of Travel in the Old Days on the James River and Kanawha Canal* (Richmond: West, Johnston & Co., 1879), 9.

73. Butler, "The Forgotten Boatmen," 14.

74. Ibid., 11–13.

75. Bagby, *Canal Reminiscences*, 9–11.

76. Butler, "The Forgotten Boatmen," 11–13.

77. Bagby, *Canal Reminiscences*, 8–11.

78. Egerton, *Gabriel's Rebellion*, 61, 119–23, 127–31. On the autonomy of slave boatmen in neighboring states during the eighteenth century, see Philip D. Morgan, *Slave Counterpoint: Black Culture in the Eighteenth-Century Chesapeake and Lowcountry* (Chapel Hill: University of North Carolina Press, 1998), 337–42.

79. Lucy Wheelock Warren Myers, "By-Gone Days," in Loy and Worthy, *Washington and the Pamlico*, 35.

80. Northup, *Twelve Years a Slave*, 22–23.

81. Charles C. Crittenden, "Inland Navigation in North Carolina, 1763–1789," *NCHR* 8 (April 1931): 151.

82. Rawick, *The American Slave*, 3(pt. 3): 68–69.

83. Later, after the rise of steam travel in the 1840s, other slave boatmen manned steamers that traveled regularly between the Albemarle and ports upriver. A slave steward named Henry, for instance, was a fixture on the *Fox*, an Edenton steamer that carried mail

and passengers up and down the Chowan River. Work aboard a steamer tended to be segregated by race more than work on other vessels, with blacks often confined to being stewards, coal heavers, and engineers. Black hands endured greater oversight and enjoyed less independence than the more skilled watermen who guided bateaux, rafts, and flatboats. Steamers would not replace those other river craft until well after the Civil War, however. See *Albemarle Enquirer*, August 5, 1886 (for reference to steamer *Fox*); *North Carolina Sentinel*, March 23, 1836; Schooner *Polly* log, February 5–27, 1827, Peabody Essex Museum, Salem, Mass.; May 1811 entry, schooner *Amphibious* letter book, Munson Institute, Mystic Seaport, Mystic, Conn.; *North Carolina Freedmen's Savings and Trust Company Records*, New Bern branch; F. Roy Johnson, *Riverboating in Lower North Carolina* (Murfreesboro, N.C.: Johnson Publishing Co., 1977), 12–13.

84. Grandy, *Narrative*, 20–24.

85. Griffin, *Ante-Bellum Elizabeth City*, 41–42.

86. Grandy, *Narrative*, 24–25.

87. Camden County Historical Society, *Historical Highlights of Camden County, 1776–1976* (Camden, N.C.: n.p., 1976), 23.

88. In this period, the Dismal Swamp Land Company and other shingling businesses continually experienced shortages of shinglers and lighter captains. The Dismal Swamp Land Company often recruited independent contractors like Grandy to lighter shingles out of the swamp, paying them $1.00 per thousand shingles. A lighter generally carried 9–10,000 shingles per load in deep water. See series of letters from Frederick Hall to James Henderson, March 15, April 17, and June 30, 1817, January 20, October 27, and December 5, 1818, and January 22, 1819, Dismal Swamp Land Company Papers, DU.

89. Brown, "Dismal Swamp Canal," 215–16.

90. Enrollments from the Port of Ocracoke, RG 41, Records of the Bureau of Marine Inspection and Navigation, 1815–29, NA.

91. Peter Stewart, "The Shingle and Lumber Industries in the Great Dismal," *Journal of Forest History* 25, no. 2 (April 1981): 99–102.

92. Alan D. Watson, "Pilotage and Pilots in Colonial North Carolina: The Case of Ocracoke Inlet," *Tributaries* 3 (October 1993): 20–25.

93. Kenneth E. Burke Jr., "The History of Portsmouth, North Carolina, from Its Founding in 1753 to Its Evacuation in the Face of Federal Forces in 1861" (senior thesis, University of Richmond, 1958), 24–25, 34–39. For background on John Gray Blount and his involvement in Shell Castle Island, see Keith, "Three North Carolina Blount Brothers," esp. 69–74, 80–88, 91–92.

94. The reliance on black watermen for pilotage and stevedoring on the passage "up the country" can often be seen in ships' logs. During an 1811 voyage into an unnamed North Carolina port, the master of the *Amphibious* rented a "flat and negro" for $10.00. The log also lists two charges for pilotage: the first, through Ocracoke Inlet, and the second, for "pilotage up the country," that is, from Ocracoke Inlet to an Albemarle port such as Camden. Black pilots frequently performed both jobs. Schooner *Amphibious* letter book, May 1811 (Thomas Hall, master), Munson Institute, Mystic Seaport, Mystic, Conn.

95. See chap. 2 below for a more detailed discussion of African Americans in the mullet fishery and bottlenosed dolphin fishery.

96. *CRNC*, 9:803–4.

97. See Josiah Bradley to John Gray Blount, November 30, 1810, Keith, *John Gray Blount Papers*, 4:136, as well as William Blount to John Gray Blount, August 30, 1813, John Gray Blount Correspondence, William Blount Rodman Papers, Manuscript Collection, J. Y. Joyner Library, East Carolina University, Greenville, N.C.

98. See the discussions in James Howard Brewer, "Legislation Designed to Control Slavery in Wilmington and Fayetteville," *NCHR* 30 (April 1953): 163–64, and in John Hope Franklin, "The Free Negro in the Economic Life of Ante-bellum North Carolina, Part I," *NCHR* 19 (July 1942): 253–54.

99. The pilots relied on some of the fastest crafts asea: fast, shallow-draught schooners with raking masts that gave them the ability to sail close to the wind and come about quickly as they maneuvered through the inlet's shoals on the way to a vessel waiting beyond the bar for a pilot. See Graham Blackburn, *The Illustrated Encyclopedia of Ships, Boats, Vessels and Other Watercraft* (Woodstock, N.Y.: Overlook Press, 1978), 112, 254, 303.

100. Edmund Ruffin, *Agricultural, Geological, and Descriptive Sketches of Lower North Carolina* (Raleigh: State of North Carolina, 1861), 123–24.

101. Likewise, as early as 1763 a free black named William Meekins owned 50 acres on "Chicknacomack Banks" in Currituck County. His children intermarried with white families and owned 140 acres at Cape Hatteras and 50 acres at Kinnakeet Banks at the time that Moses Grandy would have visited the Outer Banks. See Abner Neale to John Gray Blount, September 28, 1793, John Gray Blount Papers, NCSA; Keith, "Three North Carolina Blount Brothers," 80; Michael Luster, " 'Help to Raise Them': The Menhaden Chanteymen of Beaufort, North Carolina" (Ph.D. diss., University of Pennsylvania, 1993), 3–11; Paul Heinegg, *Free African Americans in North Carolina*, 2nd ed. (Abqaiq, Saudia Arabia: n.p., 1991).

102. *American Beacon* (Norfolk, Va.), April 9, 1831, and April 12, 1831; *Elizabeth City Star*, March 28, 1831.

103. John Hope Franklin, *The Free Negro in North Carolina, 1790–1860* (New York: W. W. Norton, 1943), 28–29.

104. Grandy, *Narrative*, 25.

105. Ibid.

106. The black community in Providence was heavily reliant on maritime labor and the sea. In 1832 one out of four black household heads listed in Providence's *City Directory* was a seaman. See Rhode Island Black Heritage Society, *Creative Survival: The Providence Black Community in the 19th Century* (Providence: Rhode Island Black Heritage Society, 1985), 43.

107. The 1860 federal census, the first to detail occupations, listed 24 free black mariners sailing out of Elizabeth City. Though evidence is sparse, historians generally believe that the number of black sailors was then at a low point for the century, due to anti–free black legislation and the Negro Seamen Acts that had been passed by southern legislators in the 1820s and 1830s. Seventh Census of the United States, 1860, Population and Slave Schedules, Pasquotank County, N.C., NA.

108. Gary B. Nash has estimated that, during the Federalist era, one-fourth of Philadelphia's young black men made their living at sea at some point in their lives. Philadelphia, much like other northern ports, was a "city of refuge" for many black southerners in both the Revolutionary and Federalist eras, and maritime labor was central to the black community. In the 1830s, those northern blacks encountered growing racial hostility from

new European immigrants and increasingly found the maritime trades less welcoming. See Nash's *Forging Freedom: The Formation of Philadelphia's Black Community, 1720–1840* (Cambridge: Harvard University Press, 1988), esp. 134–71, 246–79 (estimate, 146). For maritime black laborers in other northern seaports, see Shane White, *Somewhat More Independent: The End of Slavery in New York City, 1770–1810* (Athens: University of Georgia Press, 1991), 159; Rhoda Golden Treeman, *The Free Negro in New York City in the Era before the Civil War* (New York: Garland, 1994), 175, 336–39; Rhode Island Black Heritage Society, *Creative Survival*, 28–31, 40–43; Graham Russell Hodges, *Root and Branch: African Americans in New York and East Jersey, 1613–1863* (Chapel Hill: University of North Carolina Press, 1999), esp. 206–7; James Oliver Horton and Lois E. Horton, *Black Bostonians: Family Life and Community Struggle in the Antebellum North* (New York: Holmes & Meier, 1979), 97–114; and Thomas H. O'Connor, *Civil War Boston: Homefront and Battlefield* (Boston: Northeastern University Press, 1997), 15–18. For a recent, excellent overview of maritime black life in the North in the nineteenth century, see Bolster, *Black Jacks*, 158–89.

109. For another former slave's perspective on a sailor's life during this period, see Robert Voorhis, *Life and Adventures of Robert Voorhis, the hermit of Massachusetts, who has lived 14 years in a cave....* (Providence, R.I.: H. Trumball, 1829), esp. 21–25. Voorhis, who had escaped bondage in Charleston aboard a brig, sailed for nine years aboard merchant ships out of Boston and Salem, Massachusetts, to ports in Europe, India, and China. For another eight or nine years he served on packets between Providence and New York, and on at least one occasion he visited southern ports. He retired in Providence as something of a recluse and was likely known, by reputation at least, to Grandy.

110. Bolster, " 'To Feel Like a Man,' " 1185.

111. A steward was equal parts janitor, butler, personal attendant to a vessel's officers, and sailor; stewards were very frequently black men. An African American man named William Brown had the duties of a steward defined for him as he was undertaking the post aboard the sloop *Venus* on a run from Boston to New York. "John Smith, the cook," Brown later wrote, "showed me how to perform the duty of a steward. He took me in the cabin and showed me how to make up the beds (there being thirty two berths), clean the cabin, etc., set the tables . . . and put things in good order, then went on deck and helped to get in readiness to sail." William J. Brown, *The Life of William J. Brown, of Providence, R.I., with Personal Recollections of Incidents in Rhode Island* (Providence, R.I.: Angell & Co., 1883), 57.

112. Gaddis Smith, "Black Seamen and the Federal Courts, 1789–1860," in *Ships, Seafaring and Society: Essays in Maritime Culture*, ed. Timothy J. Runyan (Detroit: Wayne State University Press for the Great Lakes Historical Society, 1987), 322. Based on War of 1812 prisoner of war records and protection certificates issued to Philadelphia seamen for the years 1812–15, Ira Dye concluded that blacks made up 17.6 percent of merchant seamen in that port—half being cooks and stewards, half being seamen. See Ira Dye, "Early American Merchant Seafarers," *Proceedings of the American Philosophical Society* 120, no. 5 (October 1976): 331–60. Martha Putney found that 90 percent of all vessels in foreign commerce sailing out of Newport, Rhode Island, had at least one black crewman. More than half the sailors were black in some crews, and a few vessels had all-black crews. Martha S. Putney, "Black Seamen of Newport, 1803–1865: A Case Study in Foreign Commerce," *JNH* 57 (1972): 156–68.

113. Putney, *Black Sailors*, 12–16; Hodges, *Root and Branch*, 206–7.

114. On the Negro Seamen Acts and their impact on black sailors in southern ports, see Smith, "Black Seamen and the Federal Courts," 325–28; Philip M. Hamer, "Great Britain, the United States, and the Negro Seamen Acts, 1822–1848," *Journal of Southern History* 1 (1935): 5; Putney, *Black Sailors*, 12–13, 30–31; and Bolster, *Black Jacks*, 199–211.

115. On David Walker and the southern roots of his radicalism, see especially Peter P. Hinks, *To Awaken My Afflicted Brethren: David Walker and the Problem of Antebellum Slave Resistance* (University Park: Pennsylvania State University Press, 1997), 1–21, 173–236. See also Sterling Stuckey, *Slave Culture: Nationalist Theory and the Foundations of Black America* (New York: Oxford University Press, 1987), 98–137.

116. September 9–13 and 21, 1831, entries, personal diary, 1830–36, Moses Ashley Curtis Papers, SHC.

117. Charles Edward Morris, "Panic and Reprisal: Reaction in North Carolina to the Nat Turner Insurrection, 1831," *NCHR* 62, no. 1 (January 1985): 35–48.

118. Franklin, *The Free Negro in North Carolina*, 64–74.

119. *American Beacon* (Norfolk, Va.), April 12, 1831.

120. Boston Ship Register, 1816, Peabody Essex Museum, Salem, Mass. The author is indebted to the late Richard D. Martin at the Peabody Essex Museum for identifying both the *New Packet* and *James Maury* in New England maritime records.

121. Hit hard by a storm en route from Grenada, the *New Packet* arrived in Elizabeth City with its bowsprit broke in three places, its sheathing badly cut, and its inner planks "considerably injured." The repairs required three months; she sailed for Boston on April 25, 1827. *Elizabeth-City and North-Carolina Eastern Intelligencer*, January 27, 1827, and April 28, 1827.

122. Boston Ship Register, 1827, 1833, Peabody Essex Museum, Salem, Mass. Grandy incorrectly identifies this ship as the *James Murray*. Because he lists the ship's master and owner, it is clear that he meant the *James Maury*. The mistake was presumably made by his interlocutor, George Thompson.

123. Many free blacks did sail on New England whalers. On cooperation and tensions among the whalers' diverse crews, see Margaret Creighton, *Rites and Passages: The Experience of American Whaling, 1830–1870* (Cambridge: Cambridge University Press, 1995), 116–38. On the diversity of whaling crews and the conditions of labor aboard their ships in an earlier era, see Daniel Vickers, "Nantucket Whalemen in the Deep-Sea Fishery: The Changing Anatomy of an Early American Labor Force," *Journal of American History* 22, no. 2 (September 1985): 277–96, and Daniel Vickers, "The First Whalemen of Nantucket," *WMQ*, 3rd ser., 40, no. 4 (October 1983): 560–83. See also James Barker Farr, *Black Odyssey: The Seafaring Tradition of Afro-Americans* (New York: Peter Lang, 1989), 77–104.

124. For background on the egalitarian ethic among sailors, see Bolster, " 'To Feel like a Man,' " 1173–99.

125. Foner, "William P. Powell," 91–93. Beyond advocating for the rights of black sailors, Powell founded the Colored Seaman's Home in New York City and, in 1863, played an important role in organizing the American Seaman's Protective Association, the first organization of black seamen in the United States. A devoted admirer of David Walker, he was also a founder of the Manhattan Anti-Slavery Society.

126. Bolster, *Black Jacks*, esp. 68–101, 178–82. Bolster makes just this point when he

writes that "seafaring . . . meant something very different for black men and white men," in large part because black sailors were "more likely to define themselves with dignity as respectable men because seafaring enabled at least some of them to provide for their families" (170).

127. The impact of visiting foreign ports on free black sailors from America, like Grandy, can scarcely be exaggerated. Herman Melville, who had himself served before the mast as a young man, pointed out how transforming the experience could be in the words of the protagonist of his novel *Redburn* (Boston, 1849), 203:

> In Liverpool indeed the negro steps with a prouder pace, and holds his head like a man; for there no such exaggerated feeling exists in respect to him, as here in America. Three or four times, I encountered our black steward, dressed very handsomely and walking arm in arm with a good-looking English woman. In New York, such a couple would have been mobbed in three minutes; and the steward would have been lucky to escape with whole limbs. After visiting ports like Liverpool, a black sailor no doubt found it rather more difficult to accept the southern arguments for the naturalness of his racial inferiority.

The images of black sailors in the novels of Melville and other early American writers are often historically quite sound, and they can be a good source of insight into the sailors' lives. For a first-rate review of black sailors in the novels of the writer who perhaps featured them most centrally, see Harold D. Langley, "Images of the Sailor in the Novels of James Fenimore Cooper," *The American Neptune* 57, no. 4 (Fall 1997): 359–78.

128. Grandy, *Narrative*, 27. On the imprisonment and enslavement of free black sailors under the Negro Seamen Acts, see Carol Wilson, *Freedom at Risk: The Kidnapping of Free Blacks in America, 1780–1865* (Lexington: University Press of Kentucky, 1994), 40–41, 57–63, 105–6, 110–11.

129. One of the two sisters, Catherine, earned the money by working as a stewardess on a Mississippi steamboat, where "she was hired for the place at thirty dollars a-month" and "had the liberty to sell apples and oranges on board; and commonly, the passengers gave her from twenty-five cents to a dollar, to a stewardess who attends them well." Grandy, *Narrative*, 47–48.

130. Ibid., 26–36.

131. Ibid., 19–20, 22–24.

132. See Egerton, *Gabriel's Rebellion*; Jeffrey J. Crow, "Slave Rebelliousness and Social Conflict in North Carolina, 1775 to 1802," *WMQ*, 3rd ser., 37, no. 1 (January 1980): 84–86; and the discussion in chap. 5 below.

CHAPTER TWO

1. William Henry Singleton, *Recollections of My Slavery Days*, ed. Katherine Mellen Charron and David S. Cecelski (Raleigh: North Carolina Department of Cultural Resources, Division of Archives and History, 1999), 37.

2. David S. Cecelski, "A World of Fisher Folks," *North Carolina Literary Review* 2, no. 2 (Summer 1995): 183–99.

3. See Thomas J. Schoenbaum, *Islands, Capes, and Sounds: The North Carolina Coast*

(Winston-Salem, N.C.: John F. Blair, 1982), 7; Gary Dunbar, *Historical Geography of the North Carolina Outer Banks* (Baton Rouge: Louisiana State University Press, 1958); and, for an excellent contemporary study, Edmund Ruffin, *Agricultural, Geological, and Descriptive Sketches of Lower North Carolina* (Raleigh: State of North Carolina, 1861), 113–54.

4. Fishermen harvested terrapins in several ways. Most commonly, they caught them by dragging iron dredges across mud bottoms or by baiting traps that resembled lobster pots, but they also were known to burn salt marshes to drive them out of their burrows with heat. Reports of hunting terrapins with dogs also came from the Beaufort vicinity. R. Edward Earll, "North Carolina and Its Fisheries," in *The Fisheries and Fishing Industries of the United States*, ed. George Brown Goode, 5 secs. (Washington, D.C.: Commission of Fish and Fisheries, 1884–87), sec. 2, 482.

5. Beaufort was the only seaport in the state near saltwater fisheries and, after 1858, the only saltwater fishing grounds in proximity to a railroad. See R. Edward Earll, "The Mullet Fishery," in Goode, ed., *Fisheries and Fishing Industries*, sec. 5, 1:575.

6. Earll, "North Carolina and Its Fisheries," 497; Hugh M. Smith, *Fishes of North Carolina* (Raleigh: North Carolina Geological and Economic Survey, 1907), 218.

7. Henry Beasley Ansell, "Recollections of a Life Time and More," 54–55, in Henry Beasley Ansell Papers, SHC.

8. See especially Ernest Ingersoll, "The Oyster, Scallop, Clam, Mussel, and Abalone Industries," in Goode, *Fisheries and Fishing Industries*, sec. 5, 2:507–19.

9. Earll, "North Carolina and Its Fisheries," 483, 486.

10. Earll, "Mullet Fishery," 578.

11. Earll, "North Carolina and Its Fisheries," 483, 487; Earll, "Mullet Fishery," 578; Ansell, "Recollections," 5–6, SHC; Nell Wise Wechter, *Some Whisper of our Name* . . . (Manteo, N.C.: Times Printing Co., 1975), 30–32.

12. See especially William D. Valentine diary, SHC; Ansell, "Recollections," SHC; Ruffin, *Sketches*, 113–54; and George Higby Throop, *Nag's Head, or Two Months among the "Bankers": A Story of Seashore Life and Manners* (Philadelphia: n.p., 1850). So few descriptions of Outer Banks life prior to the Civil War are available that scholars must, to a large degree, rely on extrapolating carefully backward from somewhat later sources. Several oral history collections are invaluable: the North Carolina Coastal Folklife Project, North Carolina Maritime Museum, Beaufort; the Cape Hatteras National Seashore Papers, the David Stick Papers, and the Ben MacNeill Papers, all at the Outer Banks History Center, Manteo, N.C.; the Cape Lookout National Seashore Collection, Cape Lookout National Seashore Headquarters, Harkers Island, N.C.; and the "Behind the Veil Project," Craven County interviews, DU. See also E. E. Buckman, "Our Trip from Beaufort, N.C., to Baltimore, Md. on Schooner *Ogeeche*," December 12, 1873, Beaufort Historical Association, Beaufort, N.C.; *New Berne Weekly Times*, July 24, 1873, and August 21, 1873; *New Bern Weekly Journal of Commerce*, December 4, 1866; Nathaniel H. Bishop, *Voyage of the Paper Canoe: A Geographical Journey of 2,500 Miles from Quebec to the Gulf of Mexico, During the Years 1874–5* (Edinburgh: David Douglass, 1878), 162–215; and Theodore S. Meekins interview, Federal Writers' Project (ca. 1939), Thad S. Feree Papers, Private Collections, NCSA. Several published sources, based on local reminiscences, are also valuable. For a survey of more recent published sources, see Cecelski, "A World of Fisher Folks," 183–99.

13. J. Waldo Denny, *Wearing the Blue in the 25th Mass. Volunteer Infantry* (Worcester, Mass.: Putnam & Davis, 1879), 58–59.

14. Dorcas E. Carter interview, August 5, 1993, by Karen Ferguson, Behind the Veil Collection, DU; Dorcas E. Carter interview, July 1999, by David Cecelski, Southern Oral History Program Collection, SHC.

15. Clarence L. Robinson, *The Core Sounder* (Norfolk, Va.: C. L. Robinson, 1970), 4, 29.

16. Ansell, "Recollections," SHC.

17. J. Madison Drake, *The History of the Ninth New Jersey Veteran Vols.* (Elizabeth, N.J.: Journal Printing House, 1889), 253.

18. Cecelski, "A World of Fisher Folks," 186–89; November 8 and 10, 1853, entries, William D. Valentine diary, SHC; Ansell, "Recollections," 5–6, SHC. See also the primary sources cited in n. 12 above.

19. G. F. Stanton reminiscence (1901), 4–5, Alida F. Fales Papers, NCSA.

20. Norman Gillikin interview (Smyrna, N.C.), July 1996, by David S. Cecelski, Southern Oral History Program Collection, SHC.

21. Sixth, Seventh, and Eighth Censuses of the United States, 1840–60, Population Schedules, Carteret County, N.C., NA.

22. "General Review of the Fishery Interests of the State," pt. A of Earll, "North Carolina and Its Fisheries," 486.

23. Nearly all coastal and tidewater planters owned fishing nets, usually several different types, and the more slaves planters owned, the greater the number and variety of their nets. Their surviving wills and estate records indicate that masters and slaves hauled nets from beaches (the two principal types referred to in their inventories being "drum nets," evidently a large-meshed seine, and "herring nets," a longer, smaller-meshed seine); floated them behind sailboats ("tow nets," or trawls); staked them in estuary or river shallows ("set-nets," apparently a simpler precursor to the more sophisticated pound nets introduced after the Civil War); and "footed them up," as the expression went, standing waist deep in shoals ("drag-nets"). Fish gigs, oyster tongs, fish hooks, fishing poles, dip nets, net corks, and lead weights also appear frequently in plantation inventories. Other, more improvised fishing gear, such as weirs, fish traps, and trot-lines, were mainly the providence of slaves; they had no real monetary value and did not appear in plantation inventories. Fishing vessels included canoes, periaugers, punts, flatties, and pilot boats, as well as freight craft such as schooners and sloops that doubled as fishing boats. Even scows and barges, unwieldly vessels used primarily for canal and river transport, served capably as net boats for haul seining. Based on a survey of vessels and fishing gear listed in the household and estate inventories of all slaveholders with ten or more slaves at the time of their deaths in ten coastal and tidewater counties. Wills and estate records, 1783–1861, Brunswick, New Hanover, Carteret, Craven, Beaufort, Hyde, Dare, Chowan, Perquimans, and Currituck Counties, NCSA.

24. After the Civil War, the Lower Neuse's shad fishery surpassed the Albemarle Sound's herring industry as the state's largest fishery and was for several decades the largest shad grounds in the United States. At the time, shad fishing made New Bern probably the largest fish market between Norfolk and New Orleans. While a paucity of railroads, steamships, and preservation methods stunted New Bern's fish trade before the war, limiting it mainly to the brokering of oysters and salted fish between Carteret

County's fishermen and towns up the Neuse and Trent Rivers, the origins of the town's great postwar fish trade can be traced to the enslaved fishermen and fish cutters who resided at Garbacon Creek and similar plantations along the Neuse River. As early as 1866, a directory of New Bern businesses listed 40 fish dealers, more than any other type of business. *Newbern Weekly Journal of Commerce*, October 30, 1866. To gain a sense of New Bern's postwar fish trade, see Marshall McDonald, "The River Fisheries of the Atlantic States: The Rivers and Sounds of North Carolina," in Goode, *Fisheries and Fishing Industries*, sec. 5, 1:628; Smith, *Fishes of North Carolina*, 128–29; *Newbern Journal of Commerce*, April 11, 1874; *Newbernian*, July 14, 1877; and *New Berne Weekly Journal*, April 26, 1883.

25. Earll, "North Carolina and Its Fisheries," 488.

26. Alan D. Watson, *A History of New Bern and Craven County* (New Bern, N.C.: Tryon Palace Commission, 1987), 313.

27. Earll, "North Carolina and Its Fisheries," 485.

28. Watson, *A History of New Bern and Craven County*, 313.

29. Charles Ball, *Fifty Years in Chains; or The Life of an American Slave* (New York: H. Dayton, 1859), 205.

30. Ibid., 206, 211.

31. Ibid., 215–23.

32. Thomas Kirwan, *Soldiering in North Carolina* (Boston: n.p., 1864), 14.

33. Ruffin, *Sketches*, 244–51.

34. Based on a survey of vessels listed in the household and estate inventories of all slaveholders with ten or more slaves at the time of their deaths in seven coastal and tidewater counties. Wills and estate records, 1783–1861, New Hanover, Craven, Beaufort, Hyde, Chowan, Perquimans, and Currituck Counties, NCSA.

35. Singleton, *Recollections*, 6–10.

36. By 1800, tidewater planters already suffered from a shortage of forage for their cattle, sheep, and horses and increasingly pastured them in pocosins and fresh- and saltwater marshes. The need for good forage compelled larger planters to invest in such lands even at a considerable distance, and the responsibility for shepherding the livestock usually fell to their slaves. At the same time, a serious decline in soil fertility in tidewater lands worked for several generations by plantation agriculture required slaveholders to take soil improvement more seriously by the 1820s. They sent slaves coastward to collect peat, seaweed, oyster shells, "trash fish," and marl with which to fertilizer their crops. Collecting and carting tons of fertilizer to distant fields was an arduous, time-consuming job but one that granted more inland plantation slaves at least some access to the fruits of the sea. Petition from Jesse Fulcher to Gov. David Settle Reid, March 14, 1853, Governors Papers 132, NCSA; Ruffin, *Sketches*, 127.

37. On illicit gardening and livestock raising by coastal slaves, see Hattie Brown and Leora Murray interview (Goshen, N.C.), November 17 and 24, 1994, by David S. Cecelski, Southern Oral History Program, SHC. Other slaves had sanctioned garden plots. See also the discussion in chap. 5 below.

38. For good, if brief, discussions of plantation slaves, recreational fishing, and the role of fish in the slave diet in the antebellum South, see Guion Griffis Johnson, *A Social History of the Sea Islands* (Chapel Hill: University of North Carolina Press, 1930), 142; L. C. Gray, *History of Agriculture in the Southern United States to 1860*, 2 vols. (Washington, D.C.:

Carnegie Institution of Washington, 1933), 1:564 and 2:836; Theodore Rosengarten, *Tombee: Portrait of a Cotton Planter* (New York: Morrow, 1986), 130–31; David K. Wiggins, "Good Times on the Old Plantation: Popular Recreation of the Black Slave in the Antebellum South, 1810–1860," *Journal of Sport History* 4, no. 3 (1977): 260–84; Betty Wood, *Women's Work, Men's Work: The Informal Slave Economies of Lowcountry Georgia* (Athens: University of Georgia Press, 1995), 20, 41; Brenda E. Stevenson, *Life in Black and White: Family and Community in the Slave South* (New York: Oxford University Press, 1976), 189; Norrece T. Jones Jr., *Born a Child of Freedom, Yet a Slave: Mechanisms of Control and Strategies of Resistance in Antebellum South Carolina* (Hanover, N.H.: Wesleyan University Press, University Press of New England, 1990), 52; and especially Charles Joyner, *Down by the Riverside: A South Carolina Slave Community* (Urbana: University of Illinois Press, 1984), 99–101, 130, 133, and Ball, *Fifty Years in Chains*, 11–12, 17.

39. Charles Janson, *A Stranger in America: Containing the Observations made during a long residence in that country.* . . . (London: Albion Press, 1807), 312.

40. Bennett H. Wall, "The Founding of the Pettigrew Plantations," *NCHR* 27 (1950): 395–418.

41. John Andrew Jackson, *The Experience of a Slave in South Carolina* (London: Passmore & Alabaster, 1862), 30.

42. Harry M. Walsh, *The Outlaw Gunner* (Cambridge, Md.: Tidewater Publishers, 1971), 101.

43. Fish traps were so common that they were sometimes considered a major impediment to navigation on smaller rivers and creeks. Alan D. Watson, " 'Sailing Under Steam': The Advent of Steam Navigation in North Carolina to the Civil War," *NCHR* 75, no. 1 (January 1998): 63.

44. Runaway slaves could also take advantage of fish traps, trot-lines, and weirs to help sustain themselves. A former Georgia slave named John Brown discovered a trot-line as he was escaping by raft down the Tennessee River. "One night," he wrote, "my raft ran foul of a line stretched across the water. I traced it with my paddle and pole, and found it had a good many other smaller lines attached to it, each having a hook at the end. On one of them was a catfish, which I appropriated, and of which I made a famous feast." John Brown, *Slave Life in Georgia: A Narrative of the Life, Sufferings, and Escape of John Brown, a Fugitive Slave*, ed. F. N. Boney (Savannah, Ga.: Beehive Press, 1991), 83.

45. Levi Branham, *My Life and Travels* (Dalton, Ga.: A. J. Showalter, 1929), 1; Ball, *Fifty Years in Chains*, 203–4; Solomon Northup, *Twelve Years a Slave: Narrative of Solomon Northup, a Citizen of New-York, Kidnapped in Washington City in 1841* . . . (Auburn, N.Y.: Derby and Miller, 1853), 153.

46. Branham, *My Life and Travels*, 6–7.

47. Henry Clay Bruce, *The New Man: Twenty-Nine Years a Slave, Twenty-Nine Years a Free Man* (York, Pa.: Anstadt & Sons, 1893), 17–18, 24, 51.

48. *Raleigh Register & North Carolina State Gazette*, November 30, 1802, cited in Arna Alexander Bontemps, "A Social History of Black Culture in Colonial North Carolina" (Ph.D. diss., University of Illinois at Urbana-Champaign, 1989), 139.

49. Bontemps, "A Social History of Black Culture," 138.

50. Ball, *Fifty Years in Chains*, 203–6.

51. Ibid., 203–4.

52. Fish traps probably deteriorated too rapidly in very salty waters to be used near the ocean, though the author recalls them being used in brackish waters near his family's homeplace in the 1960s.

53. Bontemps, "A Social History of Black Culture," 139–40; Branham, *My Life and Travels*, 6–7; Jackson, *The Experience of a Slave in South Carolina*, 30.

54. Allen Parker, *Recollections of Slavery Times* (Worcester, Mass.: Charles W. Burbank & Co., 1895); Ebenezer Pettigrew to James Iredell Jr., December 31, 1806, in Sarah Mc-Culloh Lemmon, ed., *The Pettigrew Papers*, 2 vols. (Raleigh: North Carolina State Department of Archives and History, 1971), 1:398.

55. "Narrative of Mr. Caulkins," in Theodore Weld, *American Slavery as It Is: Testimony of a Thousand Witnesses* (New York: American Anti-Slavery Society 1839; reprint, New York: Arno Press and New York Times, 1968), 13.

56. Charles C. Jones Jr., *Antiquities of the Southern Indians* (New York: D. Appleton, 1873), 327; S. Marks, *Southern Hunting in Black and White: Nature, History, and Ritual in a Carolina Community* (Princeton: Princeton University Press, 1991), 36–37.

57. Parker, *Recollections*, 63.

58. London R. Ferebee, *A Brief History of the Slave Life of Reverend London R. Ferebee* (Raleigh: Edwards, Broughton, 1882), 8–9.

59. See "The Book of Nature," 37–47, in David Cecelski, *A Historian's Coast: Adventures into the Tidewater Past* (Winston-Salem, N.C.: John F. Blair, 2000).

60. Both day and night, slave watermen also found an opportunity for waterfowl hunting in the great *spartina* marshes, especially on Currituck Sound. Even without a gun, slaves could catch migratory ducks and geese in small skiffs and punts by baiting the birds with corn and trapping them or by blinding the birds at night with torchlight and spearing or clubbing them. Few documents describe waterfowl hunting before the Civil War, but those hunting techniques were among the favorites of poachers determined to shirk the first wave of waterfowl conservation laws later in the nineteenth century. One cannot help but suspect that slave watermen had pioneered those waterfowling methods: slave laws had encouraged innovation in their lives long before conservation laws. Walsh, *The Outlaw Gunner*, 51–57, 77, 101.

61. Ingersoll, "Oyster, Scallop, Clam, Mussel, and Abalone Industries," 563–64.

62. Bontemps, "A Social History of Black Culture," 140; Smith, *Fishes of North Carolina*, 59.

63. Patricia M. Samford, "Power Runs in Many Channels: West African–Style Ancestor Veneration in Eighteenth-Century Virginia," in *Archaeology of Colonialism*, ed. Claire Lyons, Richard Lindstrom, and John Papadopoulos (Getty Research Institute), forthcoming. See also Loretta Lautzenheiser, Patricia M. Samford, Jaquelin Drane Nash, Mary Ann Holm, and Thomas Hargrove, " 'I Was Moved of the Lord to Go to Carolina': Data Recovery at Eden House Site 31BR52 Bertie County, North Carolina," report prepared by Coastal Carolina Research for the North Carolina Department of Transportation, 1998. On water in slave folklore, see Bontemps, "A Social History of Black Culture," 121–28. For a consideration of water and its ritual uses in African cultures, see Michael A. Gomez, *Exchanging Our Country Marks: The Transformation of African Identities in the Colonial and Antebellum South* (Chapel Hill: University of North Carolina Press, 1998), 272–74. On the

sea in Bambara, Ibo, and Kongolese cosmology, see W. Jeffrey Bolster, *Black Jacks: African American Seamen in the Age of Sail* (Cambridge: Harvard University Press, 1997), 62–66.

64. Elizabeth A. Fenn, "Honoring the Ancestors: Kongo-American Graves in the American South," *Southern Exposure* 13, no. 5 (September–October 1985): 42–47. Arna Bontemps describes slaves at Roanoke Island decorating graves with sea shells. See Bontemps, "A Social History of Black Culture," 140.

65. Richard Rathbun, "The Crab, Lobster, Crayfish, Rock Lobster, Shrimp, and Prawn Fisheries," in Goode, *Fisheries and Fishing Industries*, sec. 5, 2:642–43; Elliot Coues, "Fort Macon, North Carolina," in *A Report on Barracks and Hospitals with Descriptions of Military Posts*, ed. John Shaw Billings, circular no. 4, War Department, Surgeon General's Office (Washington, D.C.: Government Printing Office, 1870), 86.

66. Rathbun, "The Crab, Lobster, Crayfish, Rock Lobster, Shrimp, and Prawn Fisheries," 642–43.

67. Elizabeth J. Reitz, Tyson Gibbs, and Ted A. Rathbun, "Archaeological Evidence for Subsistence on Coastal Plantations," in *The Archaeology of Slavery and Plantation Life*, ed. Theresa E. Singleton (Orlando, Fla.: Academic Press, 1985), 163–91. See also Robert Ascher and Charles H. Fairbanks, "Excavation of a Slave Cabin: Georgia, U.S.A.," *Historical Archaeology* 5 (1971): 3–17; Stephen Charles Atkins, "An Archaeological Perspective on the African-American Slave Diet at Mount Vernon's House for Families" (M.A. thesis, College of William and Mary, 1994), 45–48, 63–71; and Stephen Charles Atkins, "Rich Neck Slave Quarter, Root Cellar 5: Taxa Identified," research memo provided to the author by Atkins, a staff archaeologist at Colonial Williamsburg.

68. Smith, *Fishes of North Carolina*, 311–12.

69. Ansell, "Recollections," SHC.

70. For a fuller discussion of the ecological impacts of these storms on Currituck Banks and Knotts Island, see Cecelski, *A Historian's Coast*, 21–27.

71. On the serious aftermath of hurricanes in Carteret County, for instance, see Sam Leffers to John Leffers, April 16, 1804, and September 10, 1815, Personal Correspondence, Samuel Leffers Papers, Frank Salisbury Collection, J. Y. Joyner Library, East Carolina University, Greenville, N.C.

72. K. Walker, "Kingsley Plantation and Subsistence Patterns of the Southeastern Coastal Slave," *Florida Journal of Anthropology* 4 (1985): 35–56; John Solomon Otto, *Cannon's Point Plantation, 1794–1860: Living Conditions and Status Patterns in the Old South* (New York: Academic Press, 1984), esp. 47–61; Reitz, Gibbs, and Rathbun, "Archaeological Evidence for Subsistence on Coastal Plantations," 163–91. For an excellent summary of archaeological work on fish and coastal game in the slave diet, see Atkins, " Archaeological Perspective on the African-American Slave Diet," 45–48.

73. Otto, *Cannon's Point Plantation*, 47–56.

74. Jonathan Price, "A Description of Occacock Inlet" (New Bern, 1795), republished in *NCHR* 3 (October 1926): 624–35; Doren A. Padgett, *William Howard: Last Colonial Owner of Ocracoke Inlet, North Carolina: His Family and Descendants* (Washington, D.C.: published by the author, 1974); Wilson Angley, "A History of Ocracoke Inlet and the Adjacent Areas," research report (June 1984), North Carolina Division of Archives and History, 26–27.

75. A. Howard Clark, "The Blackfish and Porpoise Fisheries," in Goode, *Fisheries and*

Fishing Industries, sec. 5, 2:297–310, and Earll, "North Carolina and Its Fisheries," in ibid., sec. 2, 490. Much of our understanding of dolphin fisheries in antebellum North Carolina must be gleaned carefully from documents describing similar fisheries soon after the Civil War. See especially George L. Sparks, "Porpoise Products," *Bulletin of the United States Fish Commission* 5 (1885): 415–16; F. W. True, "The Porpoise Fishery of Hatteras, N.C.," ibid. 5 (1885): 3–6; "John W. Rolinson Book, Cape Hatteras, 1845–1905," in John W. Rolinson Papers, SHC; and *The Weekly Record* (Beaufort), April 21, May 26, and June 16, 1887.

76. John Wallace to John Gray Blount, August 14, 1793, Alice Barnwell Keith, ed., *John Gray Blount Papers*, 4 vols. (Raleigh: North Carolina State Department of Archives and History, 1952–82), 2:297. The slaves owned by Wallace and Blount also visited the cape in the spring at least occasionally, for in April 1795 their fishery superintendent reported a catch of 75 barrels of "Large Mullets" and the expectation of 70 to 80 barrels of smaller mullets. John Wallace to John Gray Blount [from Shell Castle Island], April 14, 1795, ibid., 2:531–32.

77. For background on the natural history and ecology of the barrier islands, particularly along the mulleting beaches of Carteret County, see Paul J. Godfrey and Melinda M. Godfrey, *Barrier Island Ecology of Cape Lookout National Seashore and Vicinity, North Carolina* (Washington: National Park Service, 1976), as well as Shu-fun Au, *Vegetation and Ecological Processes on Shackleford Bank, North Carolina* (Washington: National Park Service, 1974), which includes an excellent literature review. Several older studies are also interesting, especially D. S. Johnson, "Notes on the Flora of the Banks and Sounds at Beaufort, N.C.," *Botanical Gazette* 30 (December 1900): 405–10, and I. F. Lewis, *The Vegetation of Shackleford Banks*, North Carolina Geological and Economic Survey, Economic Paper No. 46 (Raleigh: Edwards & Broughton, 1917).

78. Bishop, *Voyage of the Paper Canoe*, 191, 206.

79. Four written accounts clearly refer to the mullet camps. In 1878, an adventurer named Nathaniel Bishop first described one of the rush huts, referring to a "Robinson Crusoe looking structure" at Ocracoke Island, five miles south of Hatteras Inlet. Midway on a kayak voyage from Canada to the Gulf of Mexico in 1874, Bishop stayed one night in an abandoned rush hut on Ocracoke Island, and he later seems to have seen another hut when he passed by Bogue Banks. A few years later, sometime around 1880, Edward Earll, employed as a field biologist with the United States Fish Commission, wrote more fully about these "strange-looking pieces of architecture." He encountered the fish camps on Shackleford Banks and other Carteret County islands, as well as more than 60 miles south in the Cape Fear vicinity. Three decades later, in 1908, a University of North Carolina geologist, Collier Cobb, reported "hemispherical huts of woven rushes" on several remote islands in Carteret County. Cobb visited that type of mullet camp on Cedar Island, Core Banks, Shackleford Banks, Carrot Island, and at Tar Landing and the Rice Path on Bogue Banks. See Bishop, *Voyage of the Paper Canoe*, 191, 206; Earll, "Mullet Fishery," 563–64; and Collier Cobb, "Some Human Habitations," *National Geographic* 19 (July 1908): 509–15.

James Salter, a native of the Down East section of Carteret County, mentioned the fish camps in a personal reminiscence. In the 1960s, the elderly Salter described the life of his grandmother, Sallie Salter, who lived near the small fishing community of Davis, in eastern Carteret County, from 1805 to 1903. Salter reported that a black man named Proctor Davis "lived in a rush camp" at Quinine Point, the northwest corner of the African American community known as Davis Ridge. Later, his grandmother had told him, Proctor Davis moved closer to her family at Salter Creek "and built another rush camp, and lived in it for a long time." Davis Ridge and Salter Creek are both located near Core Sound, roughly seven nautical miles from Shackleford Banks. James W. Salter, "Memories of Oyster Creek," in Mabel Murphey Piner, *Once Upon a Time: Stories of Davis, N.C.* (Davis, N.C.: n.p., 1987), 65–69.

Two other sources may refer to similar fish camps, even though they are too vague to be identified with confidence and have little descriptive value. First, an oral tradition on Ocracoke Island holds that a black man named Quork settled there in a rush hut, having come from the West Indies sometime in the mid-nineteenth century, possibly before the Civil War. No documentary record of "Old Quork" is known, though a geographical landmark at Ocracoke Island is still called "Quork Hammock." Second, in 1916 Frank Speck, an anthropologist, reported that the coastal people who lived along the mainland of Hyde and Dare Counties—he identified them as a mix of Indian, black, and white— "construct camps of palmetto leaves supported on cross poles" when "they resort to the outlying sandbanks where numbers of wild ponies are still maintained as a source of supply for the settlers." Hyde County Bicentennial Committee, *Hyde County History: A Hyde County Bicentennial Project* (N.p.: Hyde County Historical Society, 1976), 27; Frank Speck, "Remnants of the Matchapunga Indians in North Carolina," *American Anthropologist* 18, no. 2 (1916): 271–76.

Five surviving illustrations also depict the fish camps. Cobb and Earll both published illustrations of the mullet camps. (Earll's is reproduced here on p. 210.) In 1907 Hugh M. Smith, a fishery biologist, published a photograph of the same kind of mullet camp on Shackleford Banks (see p. 79) but did not write about it. In addition, there are two previously unpublished photographs of the fish camps in the photographic files of the North Carolina State Archives. They were found in a rather scattered assortment of landscapes and rural scenes taken in the vicinity of New Bern. (One of the two is reproduced here on p. 80.) The photographer is not identified, and the photographs are labeled only "New Bern, N.C., early 1900s." See Smith, *Fishes of North Carolina*, plate 20.

All of the documentary and photographic sources describing the mullet camps are from the half-century after the Civil War, and particularly from the period 1870–85, but one has to conclude that they reveal only the final years of an African American architectural tradition that had been sustained by maritime slaves and free blacks for many generations. It seems very unlikely that an architectural form so well defined over so broad a territory was suddenly introduced into the region after Appomattox, or even in the antebellum era. Instead, in the 1870s and 1880s the mullet fishery boom spurred fishermen to draw on that tradition more frequently in order to live and work for extended periods on the barrier islands, but its roots must extend much deeper into the past. For a fuller discussion of the mullet camps, see David S. Cecelski, "The Hidden World of Mullet Camps: African-American Architecture on the North Carolina Coast," *NCHR* 70, no. 1 (January 1993): 1–13.

80. Cecelski, "Hidden World of Mullet Camps," 1–13.

81. Earll, "North Carolina and Its Fisheries," 490; Marcus B. Simpson Jr. and Sallie W. Simpson, "The Pursuit of Leviathan: A History of Whaling on the North Carolina Coast," *NCHR* 65, no. 1 (January 1988): 1–51.

82. Francis Winslow, "Report on the Waters of North Carolina, with reference to their possibilities for Oyster Culture" (Raleigh: P. M. Hale, 1886), 96–97, 107–12; "Third Biennial Report of S. G. Worth, Superintendent of Fish and Fisheries, to the Board of Agriculture," *Senate Document #16* (Raleigh, 1885).

83. David S. Cecelski, "Shuckers and Peelers," *Southern Exposure* 20, no. 1 (Spring 1992): 61–63.

84. The fishing village of Hunting Quarters, on Core Sound in eastern Carteret County, is now known as Atlantic.

85. Caswell Grave, "Investigations for the Promotion of the Oyster Industry in North Carolina," *Report of the Commissioners*, U.S. Commission of Fish and Fisheries, Part 29, for 1903 (Washington, D.C.: Government Printing Office, 1905), 276.

86. Ingersoll, "The Oyster, Scallop, Clam, Mussel, and Abalone Industries," 519.

CHAPTER THREE

1. April 23, 1840, entry, William D. Valentine diary, SHC.

2. An overview of the nineteenth-century fisheries, including the shad and herring fishery, can be found in Mark T. Taylor, "Seiners and Tongers: North Carolina Fisheries in the Old and New South," *NCHR* 69, no. 1 (January 1992): 1–36. For an intriguing analysis of the political conflict between piedmont shad fishermen and dam builders, one that touches on questions central both to understanding the formation of democratic thought and to the uses of the environment, see Harry L. Watson, " 'The Common Rights of Mankind': Subsistence, Shad, and Commerce in the Early Republican South," *Journal of American History* 83, no. 1 (June 1996): 13–43.

3. For the best general review of the fisheries in nineteenth-century North Carolina, refer to George Brown Goode, ed., *The Fisheries and Fishing Industries of the United States* (Washington, D.C.: Government Printing Office, 1884–87), esp. sec. 2, 475–97, and sec. 5, 1:419–39, 625–37. See also Marcus B. Simpson Jr. and Sallie W. Simpson, "The Pursuit of Leviathan: A History of Whaling on the North Carolina Coast," *NCHR* 65, no. 1 (January 1988): 1–51; William N. Still Jr., "A Nickel a Bucket: A History of the North Carolina Shrimping Industry," *The American Neptune* 47, no. 3 (Fall 1987): 257–74; Taylor, "Seiners and Tongers," 87–110; and David S. Cecelski, "A World of Fisher Folks," *North Carolina Literary Review* 2, no. 2 (Summer 1995): 183–99.

4. The herring caught in the Albemarle Sound vicinity were actually two different fish in the herring family: alewives (*Alosa pseudoharengus*), which were known as "big-eyed herring" or "wall-eyed herring" to the haul seiners of early North Carolina, and blueback herrings (*Alosa aestivalis*), locally known as "glut herrings." Likewise, the shad caught there included the American shad (*Alosa sapidissima*) and the Hickory shad (*Alosa mediocris*). The seine fishermen did not treat the two shad or the two herring species differently, packing them together and selling them for an identical price, and I do not distinguish between them in discussing them here. See C. Richard Robins and G. Carleton Ray, *A Field Guide to the Atlantic Coast Fishes of North America* (Boston: Houghton-Mifflin Co., 1986), 66–72, and George Brown Goode, *American Fishes* (Boston: Estes & Lauriat, 1887), 394.

5. Robins and Ray, *Atlantic Coast Fishes*, 66–72, 130.

6. On native fishing in North Carolina, see David S. Phelps, "Archaeology of the North

Carolina Coast and Coastal Plain: Problems and Hypotheses," in *The Prehistory of North Carolina: An Archaeological Symposium*, ed. Mark A. Mathis and Jeffrey J. Crow (Raleigh: North Carolina Department of Cultural Resources, Division of Archives and History, 1983), esp. 39–44; Christian F. Frest, "North Carolina Algonquians," in *Handbook of North American Indians*, vol. 15, ed. G. B. Trigger (Washington, D.C.: Smithsonian Institution, 1978), 273–76; Douglass W. Boyce, "Iroquoian Tribes of the Virginia–North Carolina Coastal Plain," in ibid., 284; Charles M. Hudson, *The Southeastern Indians* (Knoxville: University of Tennessee Press, 1976), 281–84; and Timothy Silver, *A New Face on the Countryside: Indians, Colonists, and Slaves in South Atlantic Forests, 1500–1800* (Cambridge: Cambridge University Press, 1990), 44–46.

7. Benjamin Nathan Basnight memoir (1969), copy in the Mariners' Museum, Newport News, Va.

8. Alan D. Watson, *Bertie County: A Brief History* (Raleigh: North Carolina Department of Cultural Resources, Division of Archives and History, 1982), 57.

9. *Economist-Falcon* (Elizabeth City), April 7, 1891; Don Higginbotham, ed., *The Papers of James Iredell*, 2 vols. (Raleigh: North Carolina Department of Cultural Resources, Division of Archives and History, 1976) 1:138n; Richard Dillard, "The Brownriggs of Wingfield," in *Economist-Falcon* (Elizabeth City), June 8, 1894.

10. Thomas Iredell to James Iredell, July 2, 1770, Higginbotham, *Papers of James Iredell*, 1:33, 53–54; January 18, 1780, entry, Joseph Westmore journal, 4, DU; series of letters from John Brownrigg Jr. to Thomas Brownrigg, September 18, 1789, October 29, 1791, and November 24, 1792, Brownrigg Family Papers, SHC.

11. James Cathcart Johnston to James Iredell Jr., April 12, 1807, Charles E. Johnston Collection, NCSA.

12. J. B. Skinner to W. A. Blount, January 18, 1841, Correspondence, 1837–58, John Gray Blount Papers, NCSA; Jos. B. Skinner, "Letter on the Subject of the Albemarle Fisheries" (1846), typescript, North Carolina Collection, Wilson Library, University of North Carolina, Chapel Hill; Watson, *Bertie County*, 46–47; *Economist-Falcon* (Elizabeth City), April 7, 1891.

13. Marshall McDonald, "The River Fisheries of the Atlantic States: The Rivers and Sounds of North Carolina," in Goode, *Fisheries and Fishing Industries*, sec. 5, 1:625–37; William H. Leary, "The Fisheries of Eastern North Carolina," *North Carolina Booklet* 14 (April 1915): 176–81; James Wharton, *The Bounty of the Chesapeake: Fishing in Colonial Virginia* (Williamsburg: Virginia 350th Anniversary Celebration Corp., 1957), 23–70.

14. Leary, "Fisheries of Eastern North Carolina," 176–81.

15. Fishery operators not situated quite so advantageously often leased beaches and/or seine outfits from other planters for amounts that seem to have ranged from $200 to $500 a season plus, often, a proportion of the "trash fish" to use for fertilizer. See accounts of Mrs. Sarah C. Skinner and inventory and account of sales, Jos. H. Skinner (1837), Chowan County Estate Records, NCSA; Leary, "Fisheries of Eastern North Carolina."

16. This was no mean sum; in 1837 even Joseph Skinner's well-used seine was appraised at $1,500. See inventory & account of sales, Jos. H. Skinner (1837), Chowan County Estate Records, NCSA.

17. This was an important consideration, as haul seines soon drew the ire of more

subsistence oriented piedmont fishermen who discovered their own stocks of shad and herring depleted. See Watson, "'The Common Rights of Mankind,'" 34–39.

18. North Carolina General Assembly, "Report of the Select Committee on Fisheries," *North Carolina Senate Document #22* (Raleigh, 1852), 181. This trend was heightened as soil exhaustion prompted Albemarle planters to shift from cotton and tobacco production to less labor intensive row crops in the 1820s and 1830s, increasing pressure on them to find new employments for slave workers. The agricultural depression of the 1840s also compelled planters to diversify beyond row crops. L. C. Gray, *History of Agriculture in the Southern United States to 1860*, 2 vols. (Washington, D.C.: Carnegie Institution of Washington, 1933), 2:908–11, 921–40.

19. James De Bow, *The Industrial Resources, Statistics, Etc., of the United States*, 2 vols. (London: D. Appleton, 1854), 1:182.

20. North Carolina General Assembly, "Report on Fisheries," 181.

21. *Wilmington Journal*, August 13, 1874.

22. Kenneth Rayner et al. to Gov. Morehead, October 23, 1842, Governors Papers 102, NCSA.

23. April 23, 1840, entry, William D. Valentine diary, SHC.

24. Tho. Trotter to Ebenezer Pettigrew, March 28, 1817, in Sarah McCulloh Lemmon, ed., *The Pettigrew Papers*, 2 vols. (Raleigh: North Carolina State Department of Archives and History, 1971), 1:559.

25. Edward Wood, "Letter to the President of the State Agricultural Society of North Carolina, October 10, 1871," Wood Family Series, Hayes Collection, SHC.

26. M. A. Curtis, *Botany; Containing a Catalogue of the Plants of the State . . .*, Geological and Natural History Survey of North Carolina, Part 3 (Raleigh: W. W. Holden, 1860), 29–30; Silver, *A New Face on the Countryside*, 119–20; Albert E. Radford, Harry E. Ahles, and C. Ritchie Bell, *Manual of the Vascular Flora of the Carolinas* (Chapel Hill: University of North Carolina Press, 1968), 40.

27. Charles Ball, *Fifty Years in Chains; or The Life of an American Slave* (New York: H. Dayton, 1859), 213.

28. Frederick Law Olmsted, *A Journey in the Seaboard Slave States* (New York: Dix & Edwards, 1856), 353–54.

29. Ibid., 354.

30. Ibid., 354–55. The gunpowder-blasting method of removing underwater stumps is also described in Edmund Ruffin, *Agricultural, Geological, and Descriptive Sketches of Lower North Carolina* (Raleigh: State of North Carolina, 1861), 143–45. Removing cypress stumps was a one-time task, but other preparations for the spring runs kept a fishery manager and several workers busy through much of every winter. Simply amassing the supplies to outfit a fishery was a considerable chore. An 1859 inventory of fishing supplies at Edward Wood's Montpelier Fishery listed large quantities of seven different mesh twines, eight dozen copper thimbles, several boats, and 500 corks. Local merchants knew that a fishery required much more than seines and boats, and every fall and winter they stocked plenty of Bahamian salt, workers' shoes, construction supplies, and barrel staves, as well as heady amounts of indulgences long precious to fishermen, such as apple brandy and tobacco. When they had purchased all the equipment and provisions and conveyed them to shore, fishery managers and their black laborers turned their attentions to a final

handful of rituals: they had to coat the seine with tar to protect its fibers from water rot, and no fisherman would last the season without his boots having a good waterproofing. See 1857–60 memorandum of fishery management, vol. 10, Wood Family Series, Hayes Collection, SHC; *Edenton Gazette,* December 2, 1828; *Plymouth News,* October 12, 1849; and L. B.(?) Capehart to William R. Capehart, February 12, 1859, William R. Capehart Papers, SHC. Ebenezer Pettigrew swore that a concoction of linseed oil, mutton suet, beeswax, and rosin permitted his fishermen "to stand in their boats hour after hour, without inconvenience." See "Ebenezer Pettigrew's Method of Making Leather Impervious to Water," December 20, 1818, in Lemmon, *Pettigrew Papers,* 1:660.

31. De Bow, *Industrial Resources* 2:182; *Wilmington Journal,* August 13, 1847.

32. Legislative Papers, North Carolina Senate, January 9, 1857, NCSA, cited in Guion Griffis Johnson, *Ante-Bellum North Carolina: A Social History* (Chapel Hill: University of North Carolina Press, 1937), 95.

33. Paul Heinegg, "Free African Americans of Virginia and North Carolina," *North Carolina Genealogical Society Journal* 20, no. 3 (August 1994): 177–93; Barnetta McGhee White, *Somebody Knows My Name: Marriages of Freed People in North Carolina County by County* (Athens, Ga.: Iberian Pub. Co., 1995). The North Carolina General Assembly complained in 1723, in fact, "of great numbers of Free Negroes, Mulattos, and other persons of mixt Blood that have lately removed themselves into this Government, and that several of them have intermarried with the white Inhabitants of this Province." Walter Clark, ed., *The State Records of North Carolina,* 26 vols. (Raleigh: P. M. Hale, 1886–1907), 13:106–7.

34. John Hope Franklin, *The Free Negro in North Carolina, 1790–1860* (New York: W. W. Norton, 1943), 12–13, 35, 42–46.

35. Ibid., 14–19, 35.

36. See especially the array of slave contracts in the Roberts Papers, 1806–14, and in the Miscellaneous Papers, 1729–1868, Cupola House Papers, Shepherd-Pruden Memorial Library, Edenton, N.C.

37. See John Lawson, *New Voyage to Carolina* (London: n.p., 1709), 158; Janet Schaw, *Journal of a Lady of Quality,* ed. Evangeline W. Andrews and Charles M. Andrews (New Haven: Yale University Press, 1922), 149–51; William S. Powell, ed., "Tryon's Book on North Carolina," *NCHR* 34, no. 3 (July 1957): 412; Marvin L. Michael Kay and Lorin Lee Cary, *Slavery in North Carolina, 1748–1765* (Chapel Hill: University of North Carolina Press, 1995), 144–45.

38. James Ross, *Memories of the Life of Elder Ruben Ross* (Philadelphia: n.p., 1882), 86.

39. Ibid., 86. For a later view of fishermen's courts along Albemarle Sound, one that certainly suggests what the antebellum spectacle must have been like, see Federal Writers' Project, *North Carolina: The WPA Guide to the Old North State* (Chapel Hill: University of North Carolina Press, 1939), 277.

40. Fishery Memorandum Books, 1849–53, Wood Family Series, vol. 6, Hayes Collection, SHC.

41. Mary Benbury in account with Samuel B. Halsey, Guardian, Edward Benbury Sr. Estate Record (1824), Chowan County Estate Records, NCSA.

42. George L. Ryan to Ebenezer Pettigrew, September 25, 1818, and October 17, 1818, in Lemmon, *Pettigrew Papers,* 1:642–43, 645.

43. The size of the fisheries varied considerably but stayed within certain limits. The difference in two of Edward Wood's fisheries is instructive. In 1848, his Skinner Point fishery hired what was probably a minimum to operate a seine fishery: 22 boat hands, 8 beach hands, 2 hostlers, 1 cooper, 2 seine menders, 8 fish cutters, and a cook. Ten seasons later, in 1857, his Montpelier fishery was among the largest on Albemarle Sound and probably worked the local shore as close to its potential as possible with the technology available. At Montpelier, he hired 30 boat hands, 11 beach hands, and 19 cutters, not including seine menders, hostlers, cooks, and coopers. Memorandum of Fishery Management, Wood Family Series, 1857–60 (vol. 10) and Fishery Memorandum Book: Spring 1848, Wood Family Series: 1848–52 (vol. 5), Hayes Collection, SHC.

44. *Plymouth News*, October 12, 1849; Wood, "Letter to the President," SHC; Charles H. Stevenson, *The Shad Fisheries of the Atlantic Coast of the United States* (Washington, D.C.: Government Printing Office, 1899), 172.

45. Frederick Tilp, *The Chesapeake Bay of Yore: Mainly about the Rowing and Sailing Craft* (Annapolis and Richmond: Chesapeake Bay Foundation, 1982), 36–37.

46. Porte Crayon, "The Fisheries of Albemarle and Pamlico Sounds, North Carolina," *Harper's Weekly* 5 (September 28, 1861): 620–22.

47. Goode, *Fisheries and Fishing Industries*, 1:583.

48. Goode, *American Fishes*, 25–26.

49. Ross, *The Life and Times of Elder Reuben Ross*, 29.

50. Robert Philip Howell Memoirs, p. 2, SHC; L. B.(?) Capehart to William R. Capehart, March 13, 1849, 1846–57 File, William R. Capehart Papers, SHC; George Higby Throop, *Bertie: Or, Life in the Old Field* (Philadelphia: A. Hart, Late Carey, and Hart, 1851), 72–85, 198–99.

51. April 23, 1840, entry, William D. Valentine diary, SHC.

52. William Howard Russell, *My Diary North and South* (New York: Harper and Brothers, 1863), 41.

53. Porte Crayon, "North Carolina Illustrated—the Fisheries," *Harper's New Monthly Magazine* 14 (March 1857): 442.

54. Crayon, "North Carolina Illustrated," 442.

55. Throop, *Bertie*, 198–99.

56. Ball, *Fifty Years in Chains*, 206.

57. Ironically, Ball believed that the shad fishery was ultimately "a losing affair" for him. "Although I lived better at the landing than I usually did at the plantation, yet I had been compelled to work all the time, by day and by night, including Sunday, for my master." This left him without the time to hunt, garden, or otherwise provide for himself on his own time. Ibid., 223, 240–41.

58. Russell, *My Diary North and South*, 41.

59. Crayon, "Fisheries of Albemarle and Pamlico Sounds," 621.

60. Montpelier Fishery Account Book, 1844–51, Wood Family Series, Hayes Collection, SHC.

61. Ibid.

62. Sudden heavy squalls also endangered the slave boatmen who ferried kegs of salt, fish, and other supplies between market towns and fishing beaches. See *Edenton Gazette*, March 31, 1809, and April 13, 1831.

63. "Recollections of an Old Man," in *Albemarle Enquirer* (Edenton), July 29, 1886.

64. Ruffin, *Sketches*, 147.

65. April 23, 1840, entry, William D. Valentine diary, SHC.

66. According to Edward Wood, a typical shad and herring fishery provided enough "trash fish" to fertilize approximately 150 acres a year, a significant contribution to plantation fields suffering from soil exhaustion. See Wood, "Letter to the President," SHC, and Ruffin, *Sketches*, 149.

67. Montpelier fishery account book, 1844–51 (vol. 4), Wood Family Series, Hayes Collection, SHC.

68. Joseph B. Skinner to W. A. Blount, January 18, 1841, John Gray Blount Papers, Correspondence, 1837–58, NCSA; S. E. Ammistand (writing for her father, C. Capehart) to W. A. Blount, February 9, 1846, ibid.

69. *Edenton Gazette*, February 17, 1829.

70. Ibid., November 13, 1820.

71. Ibid., November 29, 1819.

72. A company store at a seine fishery was at once a grocery, bank, and recruiting depot. The proprietor sold fishing supplies, hired day laborers, paid wages, extended loans, and supplied food, tobacco, and liquor. Greenfield fishery records, 1842–58 (vol. S-2), Wood Family Series, Hayes Collection, SHC; *Edenton Gazette*, March 26, 1821. These waterfront buyers must have been stocking up for the year, and Wood was willing to receive payment in cash or tobacco, a common medium of exchange on the Albemarle Sound. Indeed, since half of Montpelier's local customers regularly paid on credit, tobacco was a better deal than most. Account book of fish sales, 1859–61 (vol. 11), and Greenfield fishery records, 1842–58 (vol. S-2), ibid.; Montpelier fishery account book, 1844–51, ibid.

73. *Halifax Minerva*, May 14, 1829.

74. North Carolina General Assembly, "Report on Fisheries."

75. Overfishing on Albemarle Sound was noted by Olmsted, Strother, and Ruffin in the 1850s. See especially Ruffin, *Sketches*, 146.

76. "A Bill to prevent fishing with seines, at certain times, in rivers emptying into Albemarle Sound," *House Document* #67 (Raleigh, 1850). For an alternative view, see Skinner, "Letter on the Subject of the Albemarle Fisheries," (1846), 4–5, North Carolina Collection.

77. North Carolina General Assembly, "Report on Fisheries."

78. See J. W. Milner, "Summary of fishing records for shad and alewives kept at Willow Branch fishery, North Carolina, from 1835 to 1874," *Bulletin of the U.S. Fish Commission* 1 (1881): 396–400. See also descriptions of the shad and herring fishery's decline in the *North Carolinian* (Elizabeth City), April 16, 1873, and the *Albemarle Times* (Windsor), July 31, 1874. For a close examination of how the fishery's decline affected piedmont fishermen, see Watson, " 'The Common Rights of Mankind,' " 38–43.

79. By the 1890s, shad had replaced herring as the state's most profitable fish, but the rise of the shad fishery resulted principally from the enormous number of small fishing crews who employed pound nets along the Lower Neuse River, 75 miles south of Albemarle Sound. *New Berne Weekly Times*, May 1, 1873; McDonald, "The River Fisheries of the Atlantic States," 628; Hugh M. Smith, *Fishes of North Carolina* (Raleigh: North Carolina Economic and Geological Survey, 1907), 128–29.

80. *Economist-Falcon* (Elizabeth City), March 8, 1892; *The Orient* (Windsor), September 19, 1896.

CHAPTER FOUR

1. On the slave trade to North Carolina, refer to the prologue, n. 4, above.

2. First Census of the United States, 1790, North Carolina, NA. See also Peter H. Wood, "The Changing Population of the Colonial South: An Overview by Race and Region, 1685–1790," in *Powhatan's Mantle: Indians in the Colonial Southeast*, ed. Peter H. Wood, Gregory A. Waselkov, and M. Thomas Hatley (Lincoln: University of Nebraska Press, 1989), 38.

3. William S. Pettigrew to James C. Johnston, January 6, 1847, Pettigrew Family Papers, SHC. For a moving account of the importation of the *Camden*'s slaves and their work at Lake Phelps, see Dorothy Spruill Redford, *Somerset Homecoming: Recovering a Lost Heritage* (New York: Doubleday, 1988), 128–37.

4. Redford, *Somerset Homecoming*, 131–32.

5. Quote in ibid., 131. Michael Gomez speculates that this incident at Lake Phelps may reflect an Igbo protest tradition in which group suicide was an escape from slavery. See Michael A. Gomez, *Exchanging Our Country Marks: The Transformation of African Identities in the Colonial and Antebellum South* (Chapel Hill: University of North Carolina Press, 1998), 119–20.

6. Peter Way, *Common Labour: Workers and the Digging of North American Canals, 1780–1860* (Cambridge: Cambridge University Press, 1993), 78.

7. Some of the canal-building schemes were truly magnificent. One canal route that seized the General Assembly's imagination in varying guises for several decades would have linked the Chesapeake Bay with Old Topsail Inlet near Beaufort, a route that bypassed Cape Hatteras and Cape Lookout altogether. Variations of this plan called for as many as five canals spanning 90 miles. Unrealistic for financial and technological reasons, the ambitious plan was a testament to how profoundly the state's boosters placed their hopes in canal building. The proposed route ran roughly from Plymouth and Williamston, on the Roanoke River, to Washington, on the Tar River, and then from Washington 35 miles to New Bern, on the Neuse River, from where it continued via Clubfoot Creek into the Newport River and Beaufort. Another, less-discussed version of the proposal would have gone a step farther south and connected New Bern with the seaport of Swansboro, at the mouth of the White Oak River. Though the scheme was seemingly far-fetched, a century later, after the advent of hydraulic dredges, the construction of the Inland Waterway did allow shipping traffic to run approximately on that path from the Chesapeake Bay to Beaufort. See John Allen to John Gray Blount, November 28, 1796, in Alice Barnwell Keith, ed., *John Gray Blount Papers*, 4 vols. (Raleigh: North Carolina State Department of Archives and History, 1952–82), 3:116; John Roulhac to John Gray Blount, November 12, 1803, ibid., 4:42–43, 408; Albert Gallatin, *Report of the Secretary of the Treasury on the Subject of Public Lands and Canals* (Washington, D.C.: R. C. Weightman, 1808); Hamilton Fulton, *Report of Sundry Surveys, made by Hamilton Fulton, . . . submitted to the General Assembly, at this session in 1819* (Raleigh: Thomas Henderson, 1819); North Carolina General Assembly, *Report of the Convention Committee to the Legislature of North Carolina, 1816* (Raleigh: Tho.

Henderson, Jr., 1816); North Carolina General Assembly, *Report of the Committee on Inland Navigation* (Raleigh: Tho. Henderson, 1815); Charles Clinton Weaver, *Internal Improvements in North Carolina Previous to 1860* (Baltimore: Johns Hopkins University Press, 1903); William Henry Hoyt, ed., *The Papers of Archibald D. Murphey*, 2 vols. (Raleigh: E. M. Uzzell & Co., 1914), 2:32, 34; and Clifford R. Shaw, "North Carolina Canals before 1860," *NCHR* 25, no. 1 (January 1948): 4–5.

8. The canal saw a dramatic rise in vessel traffic by June 1829, as, in a two-week period, 50 sloops, schooners, rafts and lighters made their way through it. By the late 1830s, approximately 350 vessels a year used the waterway. Ronald E. Shaw, *Canals for a Nation: The Canal Era in the United States, 1790–1860* (Lexington: University Press of Kentucky, 1990), 117–18.

9. Clifford Hinshaw, "North Carolina Canals Before 1860," *NCHR* 26, no. 1 (January 1948): 25–26. See also Thomas Parramore with Peter C. Stewart and Tommy L. Bogger, *Norfolk: The First Four Centuries* (Charlottesville: University Press of Virginia, 1994), 147–60.

10. The Harlowe and Clubfoot Creek Canal, the state's second ship canal, ran between Clubfoot Creek, a small tributary of the Neuse River, and Harlowe Creek, a tributary of the Newport River. The canal was only 3.5 miles in length, but its construction limped along from 1795 to 1828. Designed to join the Lower Neuse River estuary—and hence all of Pamlico Sound—with Old Topsail Inlet at Beaufort, the canal never fulfilled its promise. From the beginning, the canal had difficulties holding water and had a tendency to shoal up at both ends, making passage too suspect for sloops and schooners. Steamship owners as far away as Norfolk and Philadelphia had announced ambitious plans to introduce new lines to take advantage of the canal, but only a small traffic of canoes, periaugers, barges, and flatties actually used the canal, mainly as a shortcut between Beaufort and New Bern. See Hinshaw, "North Carolina Canals Before 1860," 9–15.

11. Shaw, *Canals for a Nation*, 118–20.

12. Peggy Jo Cobb Braswell, *The Roanoke Canal: A History of the Old Navigation and Water Power Canal of Halifax County, North Carolina* (Roanoke Rapids, N.C.: Roanoke Canal Commission, 1987), 19, 28–29.

13. Edmund Ruffin, *Agricultural, Geological, and Descriptive Sketches of Lower North Carolina* (Raleigh: State of North Carolina, 1861), 214–22.

14. *Report of the Cape Fear Navigation Company to the Board of Internal Improvements* (Fayetteville, N.C.: n.p., 1838), 7–8.

15. Ruffin, *Sketches*, 120.

16. Archibald Murphey to Thomas Ruffin, April 8, 1819, Hoyt, *Papers of Archibald D. Murphey*, 1:135–36.

17. Two speculators, John Gray Blount of Washington, North Carolina, and his brother William, governor of the Indian lands south of the Ohio River, accumulated by themselves more than a million acres. See Kenneth Pomeroy and James G. Yoho, *North Carolina Lands: Ownership, Use, and Management of Forest and Related Lands* (Washington, D.C.: American Forestry Association, 1964), 81–82.

18. A large drainage project in Washington County also was cited often as showing the potential for agriculture in drained swamplands. Ruffin, *Sketches*, 225–27.

19. Bennett H. Wall, "The Founding of the Pettigrew Plantations," *NCHR* 27 (1950): 164–65.

20. The four central canals dug by the bondmen owned by Collins and Pettigrew did not begin to reflect the slave labor necessary to drain swamplands like the East Dismal. Edmund Ruffin visited Lake Phelps in 1857 and described the network of smaller canals and ditches that had made Somerset Place so renowned for its crops. He wrote:

> The general system of drainage for all these lands is similar to what is in use in all this low country. . . . The great canals receive the drainage water collected by the largest ditches, which enter the canal at right-angles, and a quarter of a mile apart. Into these larger ditches enter smaller ones, parallel with the canal and 110 yards apart when the land is new and most open, and at 55 yards when it becomes close. The rectangular pieces, surrounded by these larger and smaller crossing ditches, are ploughed in 5 feet beds, parallel with the smaller ditches; and these beds are crossed, at intervals, by cross-furrows, or grips, which are deeper by a few inches than the alleys of the narrow beds.

Ruffin's comments underscored the difficulty of draining swamps. Digging the main canals demanded the hardest exertions, but construction of the web of smaller canals and ditches that drained into the main canal required nearly as much backbreaking toil. Ruffin, *Sketches*, 236–37.

21. Ibid., 227. See also minutes and stockholders accounts, 1837–47, Rose Bay and Swan Quarter Turnpike Company, NCSA.

22. John Stuart James, *Two Centuries at Sycamore Springs Plantation* (N.p.: n.p., 1990), 119–21; Tom Byrd, "Navigation on Goshen Swamp, Duplin County, N.C.—1785," *North Carolina Genealogical Society Journal* 8, no. 1 (February 1982): 2–7.

23. On the culture and hardships of rice cultivation, see William Dusinberre, *Them Dark Days: Slavery in the American Rice Swamps* (New York: Oxford University Press, 1996).

24. James M. Clifton, "Golden Grains of White: Rice Planting on the Lower Cape Fear," *NCHR* 50, no. 4 (October 1973): 368–69, 371–73, 381.

25. See Ruffin, *Sketches*, 214–22; Pomeroy and Yoho, *North Carolina Lands*, 99–101; and J. Paul Lilly, "History of Swamp Land Development," in *Pocosin Wetlands: An Integrated Analysis of Coastal Plain Freshwater Bogs in North Carolina*, ed. Curtis R. Richardson (Stroudsburg, Pa.: Hutchinson Ross, 1981), 26–29.

26. On the complex role of fire in pocosin ecology, and for other references to the subject, see Norman Christensen, Rebecca Burchell, Annette Liggett, and Ellen Simms, "The Structure and Development of Pocosin Vegetation," in Richardson, *Pocosin Wetlands*, 43–61.

27. Ruffin, *Sketches*, 211–13, 221.

28. The worst fires occurred in what ecologists call "deep pocosins," where the layer of peat soil was four or more feet deep. In deep pocosins, severe rains were known to drive flames underground, where they might smolder unobtrusively, like banked coals, for weeks or even months until another dry spell led them to erupt again to the surface. See Christensen et al., "Structure and Development of Pocosin Vegetation."

29. Shaw, *Canals for a Nation*, 170–72, 196–97.

30. Way, *Common Labour*, 136–43.

31. Ruffin, *Sketches*, 143.

32. Ibid., 211.

33. Moses Grandy, *Narrative of the Life of Moses Grandy, Late a Slave in the United States of America* (London: Gilpin, 1843), 35.

34. Ibid., 35.

35. Samuel Huntington Perkins journal, October 24, 1817, cited in Robert C. McLean, ed., "A Yankee Tutor in the Old South," *NCHR* 47, no. 1 (1970): 56–58; Grandy, *Narrative*, 35. Canal builders erected other huts in a barracks or small-cabin style. See, for example, the building of huts for slave workers at the Harlowe and Clubfoot Creek Canal described in James Manney to William Bell, February 22, 1825, Correspondence File, 1825–1958, George Holland Collection, NCSA.

36. See James M. Clifton, "The Rice Driver: His Role in Slave Management," *South Carolina Historical Magazine* 82, no. 4 (October 1981): 348.

37. Charles Janson, *A Stranger in America: Containing the Observations made during a long residence in that country. . . .* (London: Albion Press, 1807), 373–75.

38. *Carolina Observer* (Fayetteville), February 27, 1817; *Edenton Gazette*, May 12, 1818; *Halifax Minerva*, March 26, 1829.

39. Grandy, *Narrative*, 35.

40. Canal digging was fundamentally a menial job that demanded far more muscle than ingenuity, but canal builders could not totally neglect engineering. They had to take special pains to ensure that the channel would hold water and retain its shape and depth, not an easy task when digging in thick organic soils with little clay or rock. Water supply was always an issue. Slave laborers had to slope the canal so that water filled the channel and fell by gravity into the canal. At the same time, they had to pitch the bed of the canal carefully so that water did not flow too quickly and delay boats going upstream. The canal overseer had responsibility for meeting these building requirements, but black workers still had to carry them out. See Alvin F. Harlow, *Old Towpaths: The Story of the American Canal Era* (New York: D. Appleton, 1926), 298, 303.

41. Janson, *A Stranger in America*, 373–75.

42. Willis Augustus Hodges, *Free Man of Color: The Autobiography of Willis Augustus Hodges*, ed. Willard B. Gatewood Jr. (Knoxville: University of Tennessee Press, 1982), 40.

43. Ibid., 40–42.

44. Grandy, *Narrative*, 36–37.

45. Janson, *A Stranger in America*, 373–75.

46. Thomas Richards to John Gray Blount, May 4, 1805, in Keith, *John Gray Blount Papers*, 4:63.

47. Frederick Hall to James Henderson, January 18, 1817, Dismal Swamp Land Company Papers, DU.

48. Letter by Charles Pettigrew Pertaining to a Civil Suit, March 27, 1796, in Sarah McCulloh Lemmon, ed., *The Pettigrew Papers*, 2 vols. (Raleigh: North Carolina State Department of Archives and History, 1971), 1:180; Ruffin, *Sketches*, 229; Wade H. Hadley Jr., *The Story of the Cape Fear and Deep River Navigation Company* (N.p.: Chatham County Historical Society, 1980), 34; Braswell, *The Roanoke Canal*, 23; Shaw, *Canals for a Nation*, 173.

49. Wall, "The Founding of the Pettigrew Plantations," 180.

50. See especially Hamilton Fulton, State Engineer, "Report of Sundry Surveys," in *Edenton Gazette*, January 13, 1820. See also *Edenton Gazette*, December 10, 1821.

51. Hadley, *The Story of the Cape Fear and Deep River Navigation Company*, 55.

52. "Willoughby Dozier's Account of Work Done on the Dismal Swamp Canal, 1816," Camden County Miscellaneous Records: Apprentice-County, 1786–1928, NCSA; *Elizabeth City Star & North-Carolina Eastern Intelligencer*, September 8, 1827.

53. Coastal planters certainly recognized the health dangers of living in swampy areas during the summer months. Many, including Josiah Collins and John Gray Blount, kept homes in breezy seaports and rarely visited their swamp plantations. Other coastal planters fled lowlands during the summer months, either to plantations located in healthier climates, to summer homes in sea resorts such as Beaufort and Smithville, or to popular watering holes such as Shocco Springs in Warren County and Greenbriar Springs in what was then Virginia. See Clifton, "Golden Grains," 377–78.

54. Ebenezer Pettigrew to James Cathcart Johnston, January 17, 1843, in Lemmon, *Pettigrew Papers*, 2:548; Ebenezer Pettigrew to James Johnston Pettigrew, November 1, 1843, ibid., 600–601.

55. Janson, *A Stranger in America*, 358.

56. 1852 report from the board of directors of the Cape Fear Navigation Company to Gov. David S. Reid, David S. Reid, Governors Papers, 24, NCSA. See also Hadley, *The Story of the Cape Fear and Deep River Navigation Company*.

57. Hadley, *The Story of the Cape Fear and Deep River Navigation Company*, 35–38.

58. Braswell, *The Roanoke Canal*, 19, 28–29.

59. Virginia Board of Public Works, 1822, Report to Stockholders, 38–40, Norfolk Public Library, Norfolk, Va.

60. Braswell, *The Roanoke Canal*, 22–23.

61. The decision to build the Juniper Canal underscored a growing frustration among merchants and sailors with the older waterway. The canal through the Dismal Swamp had proven too narrow for sloops, which were capable of passing one another only at a handful of recesses built into the channel, and the two ends of the canal twisted in a way that slowed boat traffic. Most exasperating, masters of vessels could not rely on adequate water in the Dismal Swamp Canal during droughts. They often waited for several days at the canal's south end for towage or higher water. Shaw, *Canals for a Nation*, 118–20.

62. Ruffin, *Sketches*, 145.

63. Another innovation, the "reversible-head" guard lock, was also an important factor in the ability of engineers to excavate the path of the Juniper Canal. It overcame the tidal effect in the Elizabeth River at Great Bridge by adjusting canal water depths for the lunar and wind tides. Shaw, *Canals for a Nation*, 118–20.

64. Braswell, *The Roanoke Canal*, 42–44.

65. Eli Smallwood to John Gray Blount, January 23, 1831, Keith, *John Gray Blount Papers*, 4:556–58.

CHAPTER FIVE

1. A nautical surveyor in 1806 concluded that seamen could never trust charts or quadrants of the area, "no matter how accurate," because severe winds and tides altered the

coastline so frequently. Under such conditions, local pilots proved indispensable. William Tatham, "Survey on the Coast of North Carolina from Cape Hatteras to Cape Fear" (1806), North Carolina Collection, Wilson Library, University of North Carolina, Chapel Hill.

2. William H. Robinson, *From Log Cabin to the Pulpit; or, Fifteen Years in Slavery*, 3rd ed. (Eau Claire, Wis.: James H. Tifft, 1913), 13. The autobiography was first published in 1904.

3. *Wilmington Journal*, October 19, 1849.

4. Ibid., November 9, 1849.

5. Slaves used waterways to escape not only in North Carolina but throughout the South. The steamboats and barges that plowed the Mississippi and Ohio Rivers were always highly suspect in slaveholders' eyes, and slaves frequently sought to hire out or stow away on those vessels as a means to escape upriver to the North or more indirectly to New Orleans and a vessel bound for the northern states or another free country. See John Hope Franklin and Loren Schweninger, *Runaway Slaves: Rebels on the Plantation, 1790–1860* (New York: Oxford University Press, 1999), 26–27, 143–44; William Wells Brown, *The Black Man: His Antecedents, His Genius, and His Achievements* (New York: T. Hamilton, 1863), 23–26; and especially Thomas C. Buchanan, "The Slave Mississippi: African American Steamboat Workers, Networks of Resistance, and the Commercial World of the Western Rivers, 1811–1880" (Ph.D. diss., Carnegie Mellon University, 1998). Similarly, all ports in the South, not merely those in North Carolina, were notorious for their role in this maritime route out of slavery. On Charleston, see Franklin and Schweninger, *Runaway Slaves*, 127–28; on Norfolk, see Tommy Bogger, "The Slave and Free Black Community in Norfolk, 1775–1865" (Ph.D. diss., University of Virginia, 1976), 247–74.

On slaves escaping by sea from the Caribbean, see N. A. T. Hall, "Maritime Maroons: Grand *Marronage* from the Danish West Indies," *WMQ*, 3rd ser., 42 (October 1985): 476–98, and, for an earlier era, Hilary Beckles, "From Land to Sea: Runaway Barbados Slaves and Servants, 1630–1700," in *Out of the House of Bondage: Runaways, Resistance, and Marronage in Africa and the New World*, ed. Gad Heuman (London: Frank Cass, 1986), 79–94.

6. The quoted phrase is borrowed from Loren Schweninger, "The Underside of Slavery: The Internal Economy, Self-Hire, and Quasi-Freedom in Virginia, 1780–1865," *Slavery and Abolition* 12 (September 1991): 1–22.

7. Harriet Jacobs, *Incidents in the Life of a Slave Girl, Written by Herself*, ed. L. Maria Child, annotated ed., Jean Fagan Yellin (Cambridge: Harvard University Press, 1987), 151.

8. *New Bern Carolina Sentinel*, January 17, 1829.

9. *Wilmington True Republican*, May 23, 1809.

10. In the spring of 1818, New Bern authorities captured runaway slaves from at least five inland counties. See *New Bern Carolina Centinel*, April 4, May 16 and 30, and June 13, 1818.

11. Advertisements for runaway slaves from Hyde, Tyrrell, and Beaufort Counties regularly appeared in Washington, N.C., newspapers. See, for example, the *American Recorder*, May 4 and September 7, 1821.

12. In 1854, for instance, the slave Daniel Carr escaped from Plymouth and hid in the Dismal Swamp for three months before he boarded a schooner in Virginia. William Still, *The Underground Railroad: A Record of Facts, Authentic Narratives, Letters, etc., Narrating the*

Hardships, Hair-Breadth Escapes, and Death Struggles of the Slaves in their Efforts for Freedom (Philadelphia: Porter & Coates, 1872), 137–38.

13. Ibid.

14. Ibid., 234.

15. Ibid., 316–17.

16. The rigorous steps taken to inspect slave passes, enforce curfews, and otherwise monitor the activity of coastal slaves are described in Sir Charles Lyell, *A Second Visit to the United States of North America*, vol. 1 (New York: Harper and Bros., 1849), esp. 219, and in Rufus Bunnell, untitled manuscript, 1858, Manuscript and Archives Department, Yale University Library, New Haven, Conn.

17. *Wilmington Advertiser*, March 25, 1836.

18. Douglass, a ship's caulker by trade, escaped from slavery in Baltimore disguised as a sailor and carrying forged seaman's protection papers. Though he fled by train, Douglass had dreamed as a young man that he would one day escape by ship. Frederick Douglass, *Life and Times of Frederick Douglass* (Hartford, Conn.: Park, 1881), 125, 196.

19. In a typical advertisement, a planter near Windsor announced in December 1818 that his slave Caesar would likely "ship on board the first vessel whose Captain can be deceived, or is villainous enough to secret him away." *Edenton Gazette*, January 19, 1819. No less representative, in 1851 J. Ballard of Wilmington was confident that his slave Mary and her twelve-year-old daughter, "both very intelligent, and calculated to deceive unless closely scrutinized," would escape by sea. *Wilmington Journal*, October 24, 1851.

20. For two still-useful overviews of laws related to runaway slaves, see Marion Gleason McDougall, *Fugitive Slaves (1619–1865)* (Boston: Ginn and Co., 1891), esp. 102, and John Spencer Bassett, *Slavery in the State of North Carolina* (Baltimore: Johns Hopkins University Press, 1899), 15.

21. *Wilmington Advertiser*, February 2, 1838.

22. In 1831, despite the massive manhunt that followed his unsuccessful revolt in southside Virginia, Nat Turner managed to elude authorities for several months by hiding in the swamps. See Peter H. Wood, "Nat Turner: The Unknown Slave as Visionary Leader," in *Black Leaders of the Nineteenth Century*, ed. Leon Litwack and August Meier (Urbana: University of Illinois Press, 1988), 21–40.

23. For background on the boom years in antebellum Wilmington, see Guion Griffis Johnson, *Ante-Bellum North Carolina: A Social History* (Chapel Hill: University of North Carolina Press, 1937), esp. 117; Alan D. Watson, *Wilmington: Port of North Carolina* (Columbia: University of South Carolina Press, 1992), 46–52; and David S. Cecelski, "Oldest Living Confederate Chaplain Tells All?: Or, James B. Avirett and the Rise and Fall of the Rich Lands," *Southern Cultures* 3, no. 4 (Winter 1997–98): 5–24.

24. For historical background on the impact of coastal geography on North Carolina's development, see Edmund Ruffin, *Agricultural, Geological, and Descriptive Sketches of Lower North Carolina* (Raleigh: State of North Carolina, 1861), 113–54. For a good modern study, see Gary Dunbar, *Historical Geography of the North Carolina Outer Banks* (Baton Rouge: Louisiana State University Press, 1958).

25. Among many similar travel accounts, see especially "Diary of the Hon. Jonathan Mason," *Proceedings of the Massachusetts Historical Society*, 2nd ser., 2 (1885–86): 22; Anne Royall, *Mrs. Royall's Southern Tour*, vol. 1 (Washington, D.C.: n.p., 1830), 154; and Rev.

Philo Tower, *Slavery Unmasked: Being a Truthful Narrative of a Three Years' Residence and Journey in Eleven Southern States* (Rochester, N.Y.: Darrow and Bro., 1856), 73–74.

26. A former slave from Chowan County provided the most detailed account of the hunting and foraging skills developed by North Carolina slaves to supplement meager diets and to survive in hiding. Accustomed to working outdoors, Allen Parker wrote, he and other slaves learned "many things from the book of Nature which were unknown to white people." Their knowledge ranged from maneuvers for eluding bloodhounds to recognizing a subtle change in an owl's call that signaled the approach of a stranger. Allen Parker, *Recollections of Slavery Times* (Worcester, Mass.: Chas. W. Burbank & Co., 1895), 43–62.

27. "Narrative of Mr. Caulkins," in Theodore Weld, *American Slavery as It Is: Testimony of a Thousand Witnesses* (New York: American Anti-Slavery Society, 1839; reprint, New York: Arno Press and New York Times, 1968), 11.

28. Robinson, *Log Cabin to the Pulpit*, 30–32.

29. Runaways so often sought out family members from whom they had been separated that slaveholders anticipated their attempts at reunion. When a group of young men and women escaped from Josiah Howard in Jones County in 1821, for instance, their owner advertised that Jack and Kesiah would likely seek protection from their fathers at a nearby plantation, and he expected Anica and Elias to find refuge with their fathers in New Bern. He realized, however, that the group had other relatives at "Trent, White Oak, New River, and up [the] Neuse" who would likely shelter them as well. *Carolina Centinel* (New Bern), December 1, 1821.

30. See especially Parker, *Recollections*, 58.

31. Robinson, *Log Cabin to the Pulpit*, 29.

32. The presence, if not the location, of fugitive slaves in the swamps that border the Cape Fear was well known among Wilmington's white population as well. See Mortimer DeMott, "Sojourn in Wilmington and the Lower Cape Fear, 1837," *Lower Cape Fear Historical Society Bulletin* 22 (May 1979).

33. J. Burgwyn to Governor Owen, November 15, 1830, John Owen, Governors Letter Books, and J. I. Pasteur to Governor Owen, November 15, 1830, John Owen, Governor's Papers, NCSA.

34. Petition from Richard A. Lewis et al. to Governor Bragg, August 25, 1856, Thomas Bragg, Governors Letter Books, NCSA.

35. See *Edenton Gazette*, May 8, 1827; Edmund Ruffin, "Observations Made during an Expedition to the Dismal Swamp," *Farmer's Register* 4 (January 1, 1837): 515; and Robert Arnold, *The Dismal Swamp and Lake Drummond: Early Recollections* (Norfolk, Va.: Evening Telegram Print, 1888), 7. Dismal Swamp fugitives inspired a sizable body of folklore and fiction, most notably Harriet Beecher Stowe's novel *Dred: A Tale of the Great Dismal Swamp* (Boston: Houghton, Mifflin, and Co., 1884). Drawing on interviews with elderly Carolinians, Chowan County folklorist F. Roy Johnson recorded many of the Dismal Swamp legends about fugitive slaves, especially in *Tales from Old Carolina* (Murfreesboro, N.C.: Johnson Publishing Co., 1965) and *From Slavery and Other Folksy Tales* (Murfreesboro, N.C.: Johnson Publishing Co., 1982). Bland Simpson has lyrically rendered the history and lore of the Great Dismal fugitives, and much else worth knowing about the swamp, in *The Great Dismal: A Swamp Memoir* (Chapel Hill: University of North Carolina Press, 1990).

36. Jacobs, *Incidents*, 158.

37. With the assistance of black watermen who used their mobility to communicate with slaves through much of the Roanoke River valley and Albemarle region, Copper helped to organize a widespread but unsuccessful slave insurrection in the spring of 1802. The definitive work on the Easter Slave Revolt, as it has become known, is Douglas R. Egerton's *Gabriel's Rebellion: The Virginia Slave Conspiracies of 1800 and 1802* (Chapel Hill: University of North Carolina Press, 1993). For briefer discussions of that slave insurrection and its implications, see Douglas R. Egerton, "'Fly Across the River': The Easter Slave Conspiracy of 1802," *NCHR* 68 (April 1991): 87–110, and Jeffrey J. Crow, *The Black Experience in Revolutionary North Carolina* (Raleigh: North Carolina Department of Cultural Resources, Division of Archives and History, 1977), 87–94.

38. "Dictated autobiography of an unnamed fugitive slave from Georgia and North Carolina," n.d., Pennsylvania Abolition Society Papers, Historical Society of Pennsylvania, Philadelphia.

39. *Edenton Gazette*, March 2, 1819, May 2, 1820; *Elizabeth City Star and Eastern Intelligencer*, April 1, 1826, and August 10, 1833.

40. *Elizabeth City Star and Eastern Intelligencer*, August 10, 1833. Fortunate runaways could take advantage of their own or an ally's literacy to help assure a successful escape by sea. They were known to forge documents granting permission to travel in the vicinity of a port or certifying that the holder was a free black with the legal right to seek employment aboard seagoing vessels ("seaman's papers"). Though slaveholders discouraged slave literacy and eventually enforced laws to prohibit it in antebellum North Carolina, they warned in reward posters and newspaper advertisements that many fugitive slaves could read and write. In August 1852, a Perquimans County slaveholder described runaway Charles Powell as "a very intelligent negro [who] will no doubt show papers written by himself" in order to escape by sea. *Elizabeth City Old North State*, August 21, 1852. In his autobiography, Thomas H. Jones described vividly the dangers and obstructions encountered by himself and other Cape Fear slaves who tried to learn to read and write. See Thomas H. Jones, *The Experience of Thomas H. Jones, Who Was a Slave for Forty-Three Years* (Boston: Bazin and Chandler, 1862), 13–23.

41. Frederick Law Olmsted, *A Journey in the Seaboard Slave States* (New York: Dix & Edwards, 1856), 159; Frederick Street, "In the Dismal Swamp," *Frank Leslie's Popular Monthly*, March 1903, 530.

42. Contemporary newspapers periodically mentioned black men and women caught after as many as five, six, or seven years concealed in coastal swamps. See, among many others, the *Carolina Sentinel*, April 8, 1826; *New Bern Spectator*, March 7 and May 2, 1829; and *Newbernian*, May 16, 1848. When Union troops occupied the North Carolina coast in 1862, they were greeted by refugee slaves who also testified that they had survived in swamps for several years. See Vincent Colyer, *Report of the Services Rendered by the Freed People to the United States Army in North Carolina in the Spring of 1862, after the Battle of Newbern* (New York: Vincent Colyer, 1864).

43. The willingness of North Carolina's yeoman farmers, free laborers, and social outcasts, from swampers to smugglers, to consort with fugitive slaves had been proverbial in neighboring Virginia and South Carolina since early in the colonial era. See especially Gerald Mullin, *Flight and Rebellion: Slave Resistance in Eighteenth-Century Virginia* (New

York: Oxford University Press, 1972), 110–13. For three instructive works on the breadth and limits of slave/free relations in antebellum North Carolina, see Bill Cecil-Fronsman, *Common Whites: Class and Culture in Antebellum North Carolina* (Lexington: University Press of Kentucky, 1992), esp. 32–38, 80–92; Wayne Durrill, *War of Another Kind: A Southern Community in the Great Rebellion* (New York: Oxford University Press, 1990); and Victoria E. Bynum, *Unruly Women: The Politics of Social and Sexual Control in the Old South* (Chapel Hill: University of North Carolina Press, 1992). Cecil-Fronsman and Bynum focus on the piedmont; Durrill, on coastal Washington County.

44. Jones, *Experience of Thomas H. Jones*, 17–35. By the 1830s, Methodist congregations had gained a strong reputation for fostering slave unrest in the Cape Fear region. See especially the December 3, 1831, entry, personal diary, 1830–36, Moses Ashley Curtis Papers, SHC.

45. Jacobs, *Incidents*, 99–100.

46. "Juble Cain" to Zebulon Latimer, October 13, 1848, Lower Cape Fear Historical Society Archives, Wilmington.

47. An extensive hidden economy, involving slaves and free persons alike, operated beneath the formal economy controlled by wealthy planters and merchants. The best overview of the prominence and complexity of this underground slave economy may still be a special journal issue—*Slavery and Abolition* 12 (May 1991): 1–208. It includes articles on South Carolina and Virginia in the nineteenth century by John Campbell, John J. Schlotterbeck, and Roderick A. McDonald, as well as an overview by Ira Berlin and Philip D. Morgan. Readers interested in this subject might also refer to Loren Schweninger's "Underside of Slavery." For the best firsthand account of the hidden economy of coastal North Carolina, see Parker, *Recollections*, 56–59, 76–77.

48. Concerning ways that coastal slaves earned money, see Robinson, *Log Cabin to the Pulpit*, 12; James Battle Avirett, *The Old Plantation: How We Lived in Great House and Cabin before the War* (New York: F. Tennyson Neely, 1901), 88; and Jones, *Experience of Thomas H. Jones*, 33.

49. Coastal slaveholders continually guarded against poor whites who traded with their slaves. For example, John Avirett, who owned an Onslow County turpentine plantation, realized that slaves surreptitiously met white traders at night to barter goods. Though he and his neighbors considered this trading bearable at low levels, they periodically took harsh steps to suppress it. Court records indicate that such illicit business was one of the crimes prosecuted most commonly in antebellum North Carolina, yet these unsanctioned meetings still helped establish ties that persisted when slaves escaped. See Avirett, *Old Plantation*, 118–19; Johnson, *Ante-Bellum North Carolina*, 670.

50. Planters and smaller farmers allowed hogs and cattle to forage freely in antebellum North Carolina. According to Vincent Colyer's account of Kinnegay's fugitive years, "the poor people about, frequently kill them, and the owners seem not to be aware of it, or do not care for it." Colyer, *Report of the Services Rendered by the Freed People*, 19–20.

51. Herbert Aptheker, "Maroons in the Present Limits of the United States," *JNH* 24 (1939): 161.

52. C. H. Wiley, *Roanoke; or "Where is Utopia?"* (Philadelphia: T. B. Peterson and Bros., 1866), 77; Porte Crayon [David Hunter Strother], *The Old South Illustrated*, ed. Cecil D. Eby Jr. (Chapel Hill: University of North Carolina Press, 1959), 145–50; *Edenton Gazette*,

January 7, 1822. On the Dismal Swamp Land Company's labor shortages, see John Driver to —, May 2, 1790, Letters and Papers, 1783–91, Dismal Swamp Land Company Papers, DU; December 31, 1810, memorandum from Thomas Swepson, ibid.; and Frederick Hall to James Henderson, June 10, 1817, and January 20, 1818, ibid.

53. Olmsted, *Journey in the Seaboard Slave States*, 160. For a detailed description of the lumber trade in North Carolina and the role of runaway slaves in it, see 153–63.

54. *Edenton Gazette*, February 1, 1811. A few years later, when Adam, Patience, and their three children escaped from Farmville, their frustrated owner went out of his way to threaten any person who employed any of them, "but him in particular, in getting shingles." *Carolina Centinel*, June 13, 1818.

55. In 1840, 96.2 percent of the 507,275 barrels of tar, turpentine, and pitch produced in the United States originated in North Carolina, virtually all of it in twelve coastal counties with navigable rivers. They dominated the naval stores industry until the Civil War. See Michael Williams, *Americans and Their Forests: A Historical Geography* (Cambridge: Cambridge University Press, 1989), 83–90, 157–60, and Cecelski, "Oldest Living Confederate Chaplain Tells All?," 5–24.

56. In his autobiography, James Avirett of Onslow County recalled the greatest disadvantage to producing naval stores: "The laborers . . . are employed in large, wooded tracts of country, out of range of anything like close oversight and must be stimulated to their best work, as well by premiums for the best crops as by so regulating their work that a portion of each week is their own to do as they please with. It is very different on the cotton, sugar, tobacco, and rice plantations." Avirett, *Old Plantation*, 70.

57. Though a controversial practice finally prohibited by law, if not always in practice, blacks also managed some turpentining crews without white supervision. That independence heightened their ability to hire or shelter fugitive slaves. Ibid., 62–70, 117–18.

58. North Carolina General Assembly, *Laws of North Carolina* (serial), 1846–47 (Raleigh: Thomas J. Lemay), chap. 46.

59. Ibid., 1848–49, chap. 46.

60. Still, *Underground Railroad*, 381.

61. Ibid., 332.

62. Jacobs, *Incidents*, 95–155.

63. Still, *Underground Railroad*, 422–27.

64. Wrote Capt. David Drayton of his encounters with slaves in Chesapeake Bay ports: "No sooner, indeed, does a vessel, known to come from the North, anchor in any of these waters—and the slaves are pretty adroit in ascertaining from what state a vessel comes— then [*sic*] she is boarded . . . by more or less of them, in hopes of obtaining a passage to a land of freedom." Drayton only reluctantly accepted slaves aboard his schooner, *Pearl*, after a single incident of sympathy for a slave family led his name to spread in slave communities. He was captured and jailed for four years, until President Millard Fillmore pardoned him. See *Personal Memoir of David Drayton . . . Including a Narrative of the Voyage and Capture of the Schooner Pearl* (Boston: Bela Marsh, 1855).

65. Still, *Underground Railroad*, 150–52. Larry Gara has pointed out that in their historical accounts many northern leaders of the Underground Railroad misleadingly downplayed the initiative and heroism of fugitive slaves in order to highlight their own accomplishments. Gara argues that William Still was "markedly different" because he

emphasized the fugitive slaves' own daring and skill in reaching the North. Still's Philadelphia Vigilance Committee, like other branches of the Underground Railroad based in the northern states, generally did not assist runaway slaves until they had already completed the most dangerous part of their journey, escaping from the South. See Larry Gara, *The Liberty Line: The Legend of the Underground Railroad* (Lexington: University Press of Kentucky, 1961), 175–78. This is not to say that northern abolitionists did not aid fugitive slaves to flee the South. When they offered bounties to sea captains who brought runaway slaves out of the South, they doubtless spurred a stronger traffic along the Underground Railroad's maritime routes.

66. Bunnell, untitled manuscript, Yale University Library.

67. Jacobs, *Incidents*, 230.

68. Ibid., 236–38.

69. Still, *Underground Railroad*, 129–31.

70. See especially Bunnell, untitled manuscript, Yale University Library.

71. Letter from Robert Purvis, 1838, quoted in R. C. Smedley, *History of the Underground Railroad in Chester and the Neighboring Counties of Pennsylvania* (Lancaster, Pa.: Office of the Journal, 1883), 335–36. See also *Wilmington Advertiser*, October 19, 1838, and January 18, 1839.

72. D. Worth to Lewis Tappan, October 2, 1859, and George Mendenhall to Lewis Tappan, December 20, 1859, AMAA.

73. The prevalence of African Americans in river transport and ferrying has never been fully appreciated. In North Carolina, as in other southern states, in the nineteenth century, black watermen were ever-present sights crewing flatboats, scows, periaugers, steamers, and other cargo boats on tidewater rivers and sounds. References to black boatmen appeared frequently in contemporary newspapers and travel accounts. See, for instance, *Fayetteville Carolina Observer*, February 27, 1817, and April 30, 1818; *Carolina Centinel*, October 3, 1818; *New Bern North Carolina Sentinel*, March 23, 1836; *New Bern Spectator*, December 18, 1830; *Tarboro Free Press*, August 27, 1824; and *Wilmington's Weekly Chronicle*, December 9, 1840. Though referring to the early postwar years, the occupation listings in Freedmen's Bureau documents also indicate the prevalence of black watermen prior to the Civil War. See "Registers of Signatures of Depositors in Branches of the Freedman's Saving and Trust Company, 1865–1874," Office of the Controller of the Currency, RG 101, NA (microfilm, New Hanover County Public Library, Wilmington).

74. John Hope Franklin, "The Free Negro in the Economic Life of Ante-bellum North Carolina, Part I," *NCHR* 19 (July 1942): 254; *Newbern Herald*, November 17, 1809.

75. William Henry Singleton, *Recollections of My Slavery Days*, ed. Katherine Mellen Charron and David S. Cecelski (Raleigh: Department of Cultural Resources, Division of Archives and History, 1999), 37. See also Mark T. Taylor, "Seiners and Tongers: North Carolina Fisheries in the Old and New South," *NCHR* 69, no. 1 (January 1992): 4–10.

76. October 5 and October 24, 1830, entries, personal diary, 1830–36, Moses Ashley Curtis Papers, SHC. For an insightful discussion of black whalers and fishermen in antebellum Carteret County, see Michael Luster, "'Help to Raise Them': The Menhaden Chanteymen of Beaufort, North Carolina" (Ph.D. diss., University of Pennsylvania, 1993), esp. 3–6.

77. See especially the description of the Wilmington wharf district in Bunnell, untitled manuscript, Yale University Library.

78. Johnson, *Ante-Bellum North Carolina*, 606.

79. Abraham Rencher, Report of Meeting of Cape Fear and Deep River Navigation Co. to Governor Bragg, April 24, 1855, Thomas Bragg, Governors Papers, NCSA; Edward B. Dudley to Governor Graham, February 23, 1846, William A. Graham, Governors Letter Books, NCSA; "Rates of Lighterage for the Port of Wilmington," *Wilmington Gazette*, February 26, 1801.

80. London R. Ferebee, *A Brief History of the Slave Life of Reverend London R. Ferebee* (Raleigh: Edwards, Broughton, 1882), 8–9. Though Ferebee and most other slaves learned watercraft skills by observation and informal training, merchants and planters also entered young slaves into formal apprenticeships to learn maritime trades. Court records indicate that slaves and free blacks were apprenticed to boatbuilders and ship's carpenters. See James H. Craig, *The Arts and Crafts in North Carolina, 1699–1840* (Winston-Salem, N.C.: Museum of Early Southern Decorative Arts, 1965), 251–66.

81. Moses Grandy, *Narrative of the Life of Moses Grandy, Late a Slave in the United States of America* (London: Gilpin, 1843), 14, 18–19, 21–22, 41–42.

82. Jones, *Experience of Thomas H. Jones*, 35–36. A similar experience of stevedoring was shared by John Andrew Jackson, who escaped to the Charleston wharves from a South Carolina cotton plantation 150 miles upriver. "I joined a gang of negroes working on the wharfs," Jackson wrote, "and received a dollar-and-a-quarter a day, without arousing suspicion. Those negroes have to maintain themselves, and clothe themselves, and pay their masters two-and-a-half dollars per week out of this, which, if they fail to do, they receive a severe castigation with a cat-o-nine tails." Jackson went into hiding after being asked to show his badge (required of slaves in Charleston to hire out their own time) and eventually stowed away on a schooner bound for Boston. John Andrew Jackson, *The Experience of a Slave in South Carolina* (London: Passmore & Alabaster, 1862), 24–28.

83. William H. Gould IV, "The Unwinding Trail: Some Reflections on the Life and Times of William Benjamin Gould," presentation at the New Hanover County Public Library, Wilmington, N.C., December 15, 1998. The Gould diary is the pride of William Gould's great-grandson, Professor William Gould IV, a Stanford law scholar and former chairman of the National Labor Relations Board. Gould is currently editing the diary for publication.

84. See *CRNC*, 9:803–4; J. Gilpin to John Gray Blount, August 18, 1802, in Alice Barnwell Keith, ed., *John Gray Blount Papers*, 4 vols. (Raleigh: North Carolina State Department of Archives and History, 1952–82), 3:532–33; Josiah Bradley to John Gray Blount, November 30, 1810, ibid., 4:136; William Blount to John Gray Blount, August 30, 1813, John Gray Blount Correspondence, William Blount Rodman Papers, Manuscript Collection, J. Y. Joyner Library, East Carolina University, Greenville, N.C.; James Howard Brewer, "Legislation Designed to Control Slavery in Wilmington and Fayetteville," *NCHR* 30 (April 1953): 163–64, and Franklin, "Free Negro," 253–54.

85. While North Carolina Quakers had officially opposed slavery in the late eighteenth and early nineteenth centuries, their certitude had seriously weakened by the 1840s. The Yearly Meeting in 1843 declared its "long established practice and utter despisal of such interference [abetting runaways] anyway whatever." The priority of individual conscience

remained a central tenet in Quaker belief, however, and the fact that Fuller and Elliot counted themselves among the Friends would have directed suspicion at them. See Stephen B. Weeks, *Southern Quakers and Slavery* (Baltimore: Johns Hopkins University Press, 1896), 224–44.

86. Robinson, *Log Cabin to the Pulpit*, 13.

87. As discussed in chap. 1 above, Moses Grandy, who was forced to do field work for eight months in mid-career, graphically described the contrasts between the relative freedom of working on the water and the far harsher restrictions of agricultural labor. See Grandy, *Narrative*, 26–31.

88. Benjamin F. Hall Paper, 13–15, Private Collections, NCSA.

89. Olmsted, *Journey in the Seaboard Slave States*, 359–60.

90. Nannie Davis Ward interview by Michael and Debbie Luster, Beaufort, N.C., 1988, North Carolina Coastal Folklife Collection, North Carolina Maritime Museum, Beaufort.

91. See especially W. Jeffrey Bolster, " 'To Feel Like a Man': Black Seamen in the Northern States, 1800–1860," *Journal of American History* 76 (March 1990): 1173–99.

92. See J. S. Buckingham, *The Slave States of America*, 2 vols. (London: Fisher and Son, 1842), 2:471–72.

93. Because white watermen mingled so extensively with northern seamen, owned few slaves, and dealt so often with black boatmen, their loyalties had long been suspect in the eyes of North Carolina slaveholders. This was most apparent during the Civil War. Frustrated by reports of watermen's assisting both fugitive slaves and the Union navy on North Carolina sounds, a Halifax County diarist wrote in 1862 that "the negroes and [white] fishermen in that region are mere nomads, owing allegiance to Neptune and Boreas only." Beth Gilbert Crabtree and James W. Patton, eds., *Journal of a Secesh Lady: The Diary of Catherine Ann Devereux Edmondston, 1860–1866* (Raleigh: North Carolina Department of Cultural Resources, Division of Archives and History, 1979), 86–87.

94. Seventh Census of the United States, 1850, Craven County, N.C., Population and Slave Schedule, NA.

95. The landmark study of black seafarers as agents of communication in the Atlantic is Julius S. Scott, "The Common Wind: Currents of Afro-American Communication in the Era of the Haitian Revolution" (Ph.D. diss., Duke University, 1986).

96. George Mendenhall to Lewis Tappan, December 20, 1859, AMAA.

97. Jacobs, *Incidents*, 128; Jones, *Experience of Thomas H. Jones*, 36–43; Letter from Daniel Williams to Amos Wade, August 16, 1857, John W. Blassingame, ed., *Slave Testimony: Two Centuries of Letters, Speeches, Interviews, and Autobiographies* (Baton Rouge: Louisiana State University Press, 1977), 110–11. These covert messages could even have helped to arrange escapes with northern sailors traveling into the South. The extent of communication between port slaves and northerners is unknown but was probably extensive. The slave community in New Bern had long-standing contacts with free blacks in New York and New Haven who had fled or, in the case of free blacks, migrated away from the South and established exile communities late in the eighteenth century and early in the nineteenth. Black religious leaders in New Bern and these northern towns maintained a regular correspondence. This is why, when Union troops occupied New Bern in 1863, the AME Zion church in New Haven sent a missionary to the town and established the first AME Zion congregation in the southern states. James W. Hood, *One Hundred Years of the*

African Methodist Episcopal Zion Church (New York: AME Zion Book Concern, 1895), 290–93. See also the discussion in Singleton, *Recollections*, 26–27, 69.

98. This trend had emerged in the colonial era. A study of runaways in North Carolina from 1748 to 1775 concluded that slave watermen were the skilled occupational group most likely to run away. See Marvin L. Michael Kay and Lorin Lee Cary, "Slave Runaways in Colonial North Carolina," *NCHR* 63 (January 1986): 18–19.

99. For a good illustration of the ties that bound slave sailors to their southern homes, and of their propensity to escape in distant ports when those ties had been severed, see Jacobs, *Incidents*, 276.

100. See slave hiring contracts in the Roberts Papers, 1806–14, and in the Miscellaneous Papers, 1729–1868, Cupola House Papers, Shepherd-Pruden Memorial Library, Edenton, N.C.

101. *Wilmington Gazette*, May 4, 1803.

102. *Carolina Sentinel*, June 3, 1820.

103. *North Carolina Sentinel* (New Bern), October 5, 1832.

104. *New Bern Spectator*, January 23, 1838.

105. *Wilmington Advertiser*, May 25, 1838.

106. Brewer, "Legislation Designed to Control Slavery," 163.

107. Ibid., 163–64. Balancing their desire to give slave watermen enough freedom to perform vital jobs with the need to control subversive behavior led state legislators to pass laws that at times encouraged and at other times limited bondmen's professional activities. For example, as late as 1828 a state law restricting the issuance of travel passes to most Wilmington slaves specifically exempted laborers "on board a vessel lying in the river, or on some wharf opposite the town." In 1817, on the other hand, the General Assembly passed a law prohibiting Craven County slaves from navigating decked boats without a white person on board. See North Carolina General Assembly, *Laws of North Carolina*, 1828–29, chap. 112, and 1817, chap. 135. Evidence indicates that Craven County authorities enforced the law at least occasionally during the antebellum era, as in 1845 Thomas Fenner faced a $20 fine for "employing a decked boat [without a] white man forming a part of the crew thereof." See petition of B. E. Thorpe, April 5, 1845, Civil Action Papers concerning Slaves and Free Persons of Color, Craven County Miscellaneous Records, NCSA.

108. North Carolina General Assembly, *Laws of North Carolina*, 1836–37, chap. 35, and 1840–41, chap. 58.

109. *Wilmington Journal*, October 19, 1849.

110. "List of Vessels Searched and Fumigated, 1858–1862" and "Account Records with Wm. J. Love," Board of Commissioners of Navigation and Pilotage for the Cape Fear River and Bar Papers, DU. The practice continued well into the Civil War. See Captain Roberts [C. Augustus Hobart-Hampden], *Never Caught: Personal Adventures Connected with Twelve Successful Trips in Blockade-Running during the American Civil War, 1863–1864* (Carolina Beach, N.C.: Blockade Runner Museum, 1967), 13–14, 28.

111. Robert G. Rankin to C. W. Rockwell, March 15, 1851, and Rockwell to Rankin, March 22, 1851, *Papers of William A. Graham*, ed. J. G. De Roulhac Hamilton, 5 vols. (Raleigh: North Carolina State Department of Archives and History, 1961), 4:137–39; C. W. Rockwell to Thomas Corurin, March 29, 1851, ibid., 61–64.

112. Johnson, *Ante-Bellum North Carolina*, 577–78.

113. The effect of the law was evident immediately to some citizens. John Hope Franklin cites a letter to the *Wilmington Cape-Fear Recorder* in 1831 observing that, because of the prohibition on free black labor, "the merchants of Wilmington are in want of vessels to carry away the produce lying on their wharves." The General Assembly also prohibited free blacks not employed on a ship from visiting a vessel at night or on a Sunday, presumably after the quarantine period of 30 days. See North Carolina General Assembly, *Laws of North Carolina*, 1830–31, chap. 30; Franklin, "Free Negro," 253–54; and Bassett, *Slavery in North Carolina*, 35. According to W. Jeffrey Bolster, the presence of black mariners in southern seaports had prompted other state legislatures to pass similar Negro Seamen Acts as early as 1822. Southern laws restricting black sailors also contributed to a large decline in the number of seafaring blacks on northern ships after 1840. See Bolster, "'To Feel Like a Man,'" 1192–99.

114. George W. Mathews to Governor Reid, January 7, 1851, David S. Reid, Governors Letter Books, NCSA.

115. March 6, 1847, Minutes of the Town Commissioners of Wilmington, Museum of the Lower Cape Fear Archives, Wilmington.

116. Johnson, *Ante-Bellum North Carolina*, 577–78.

117. Many blacks arrested for failing to have proper seaman's papers were runaway slaves; others were simply black sailors without clear documentation of their free status. Abraham Carpenter, for example, a sailor on a brig carrying limestone from New York to Fort Macon (under construction on Bogue Banks) in 1829, languished at least "six long and weary months" in the New Bern jail before obtaining adequate proof that he was a free man. "Plea for a writ of *Habeas Corpus* by Abraham Carpenter," February 4, 1830, Slaves and Free Negroes, Craven County Miscellaneous Records, NCSA. For other cases, see *Wilmington Gazette*, April 17 and 24, 1804; John Kollock to Henry Vanneter, October 19, 1815, Henry Vanneter Papers, Historical Society of Pennsylvania, Philadelphia; *Carolina Sentinel*, October 11, 1823; *First Annual Report of the New York Committee of Vigilance* (New York: Piercy and Reed, 1837), 50; "Plea for a writ of *Habeas Corpus* by Francis A. Golding," 1835, Slaves and Free Negroes, Craven County Miscellaneous Records, NCSA; *Wilmington Journal*, January 10 and August 22, 1851; George Aaron to Governor Reid, October 22, 1851, David S. Reid, Governors Papers, NCSA.

118. Johnson, *Ante-Bellum North Carolina*, 128.

119. Governor Bragg to J. H. Crowdrey, April 5, 1855, Thomas Bragg, Governors Letter Books, NCSA. See also related correspondence for April 9 and June 25, 1855, ibid. This is not to say that sailors who concealed runaways in an earlier era did not also risk the severest reprisals. Especially since 1825, when the General Assembly made it a capital crime to conceal a slave aboard a vessel with the intent of carrying him or her out of the state, courts showed little leniency in the matter. See especially the controversy around the slave sailor Edmund, who in 1833 concealed a slave named Polly aboard the brig *Fisher*. Refer to Supreme Court Original Files no. 2141: State vs. Edmund (a slave), 1833, NCSA, and Thomas P. Devereux, *Cases Argued and Determined in the Supreme Court of North Carolina, From December Term, 1833, to June Term, 1834*, vol. 4 (Raleigh: Edwards and Broughton, 1892), 290–95.

120. Thomas Sparrow, "State v. Dawson Wiggins," 1853–56 file, Thomas Sparrow Papers, SHC.

121. D. Worth to Lewis Tappan, October 2, 1859, and George Mendenhall to Lewis Tappan, December 20, 1859, AMAA.

122. Robinson, *Log Cabin to the Pulpit*, 15.

123. Horatio Strother, *The Underground Railroad in Connecticut* (Middleton, Conn.: Wesleyan University Press, 1962), 183.

124. Jones, *Experience of Thomas H. Jones*, 46.

125. Thomas S. Singleton to John S. Hawks, July 18, 1847, and Samuel Salyer and Caldwell Jones to Governor Graham, July 23, 1847, William A. Graham, Governors Papers, NCSA.

126. Governor Graham to the governor of Virginia, August 5, 1847, William A. Graham, Governors Letter Books, NCSA.

127. January 9, 1850, Minutes of the Town Commissioners of Wilmington, Museum of the Lower Cape Fear Archives.

128. Edward Everett, governor of Massachusetts, to Governor Spaight, February 22, 1836; John Pike to Governor Spaight, April 30, 1836; and Governor Spaight to Edward Everett, May 24, 1836, all in Richard Dobbs Spaight Jr., Governors Letter Books, NCSA.

129. *Wilmington Gazette*, April 24, 1804.

130. *Carolina Sentinel*, July 28, 1827.

131. See Stanley Campbell, *The Slave Catchers: Enforcement of the Fugitive Slave Law, 1850–1860* (Chapel Hill: University of North Carolina Press, 1968), 110–69.

132. Austin Bearse, *Reminiscences of Fugitive-Slave Law Days in Boston* (Boston: Warren Richardson, 1880), 34–39.

133. Jacobs, *Incidents*, 157.

134. Sparrow, "State v. Dawson Wiggins," SHC.

135. Still, *Underground Railroad*, 165.

CHAPTER SIX

1. George H. Allen, *Forty-Six Months with the Fourth R.I. Volunteers* (Providence, R.I.: J. A. & R. A. Reid, 1887), 101–2.

2. James Rumley diary, 1–2, Levi W. Pigott Collection, NCSA.

3. Union military strategy may have also relied heavily on intelligence reports from local slave watermen. More than 175 slaves and free blacks had been employed the previous year to strengthen Fort Macon's walls and reinforce its guns, so many local blacks would have been familiar with the smallest details of its gun placements and guard posts. See Fort Macon records, vol. 2 (April–October 1861), Alexander Justice Papers, SHC.

4. *Douglass' Monthly* (June 1862); *The Liberator*, July 11, 1862; and John Edward Bruce, *Defense of the Colored Soldiers Who Fought in the War of the Rebellion* (Yonkers, N.Y.: n.p., 1919), 5–6, cited in Michael H. Goodman, "The Black Tar: Negro Seamen in the Union Navy, 1861–1865" (Ph.D. diss., University of Nottingham, 1975), 360.

5. William S. Powell, *The North Carolina Gazeteer* (Chapel Hill: University of North Carolina Press, 1968), 32.

6. Eighth Census of the United States, 1860, Carteret County, N.C., Population and Slave Schedules, NA.

7. G. F. Stanton reminiscence (1901), 4–5, Alida F. Fales Papers, NCSA.

8. John E. Edwards, "Reminiscences of Beaufort in 1839," in *Raleigh Christian Advocate*, July 19, 1882.

9. The presence of West Indian roots in Beaufort folk culture is a steady theme in local oral histories. See the North Carolina Coastal Project interviews (Carteret County), Southern Oral History Program Collection, SHC; the North Carolina Coastal Folklife Project interviews, North Carolina Maritime Museum, Beaufort; and the New Bern, N.C., interviews in the Behind the Veil Collection, DU.

10. A. R. Newsome, "A Miscellany from the Thomas Henderson Letter Book, 1810–1811," *NCHR* 6, no. 3 (October 1929): 398–401.

11. See Wills and Estate Records, Carteret County, N.C., NCSA; David S. Cecelski, "The Shores of Freedom: The Maritime Underground Railroad in North Carolina, 1850–1861," *NCHR* 71, no. 2 (April 1994): 174–206, esp. 193–96; Michael Luster, "'Help to Raise Them': The Menhaden Chanteymen of Beaufort, North Carolina" (Ph.D. diss., University of Pennsylvania, 1995), esp. 3–6. A variety of Civil War and Reconstruction records listing occupations held by former Carteret County slaves are also highly suggestive of black involvement in maritime activities during slavery. See *Descriptive Books of the 35th, 36th, and 37th Regiments of the United States Colored Troops*, RG 20, NA (microfilm, NCSA); "Registers of Signatures of Depositors in Branches of the Freedman's Savings and Trust Company, 1865–1874," Office of the Comptroller of the Currency, RG 101, NA (microfilm, New Hanover County Public Library, Wilmington); and Ninth Census of the United States, 1870, Carteret County, N.C., Population Schedule, NA.

12. On the military role of slave pilots in another part of the occupied South, see Clarence L. Mohr, *On the Threshhold of Freedom: Masters and Slaves in Civil War Georgia* (Athens: University of Georgia Press, 1986), 83–84, 289–90.

13. Charles F. Johnson, *The Long Roll: Being a journal of the Civil War, as set down during the years 1861–1863* (East Aurora, N.Y.: Roycrofters, 1911), 70–71.

14. Ambrose E. Burnside, "The Burnside Expedition," p. 24 in *Personal Narratives of Events in the War of the Rebellion*, no. 6, 2nd ser. (Providence, R.I.: Soldiers and Sailors Historical Society of Rhode Island, 1882); John K. Burlingame, *History of the Fifth Regiment of Rhode Island Heavy Artillery* (Providence, R.I.: Snow & Farnham, 1892), 20–22.

15. On the Civil War and the Federal occupation of the North Carolina coast, see especially Ira Berlin, Steven F. Miller, Joseph P. Reidy, and Leslie S. Rowland, eds., *Freedom: A Documentary History of Emancipation, 1861–1867*, ser. 1, vol. 2, *The Wartime Genesis of Free Labor in the Upper South* (Cambridge Cambridge University Press, 1993), 85–240.

16. Not all black pilots remained with the Union for the duration of the war. As early as June 1862 the *Worcester Spy*, in Worcester, Massachusetts, reported the "arrival of a 'contraband'" who had "rendered important services to Gen. Burnside, in the capacity of a pilot." Janette Greenwood concludes that this pilot was probably William Bryant. See Janette Thomas Greenwood, "Southern Black Migration and Community Building in the Era of the Civil War: Worcester County as a Case Study," 1–5, presented at "Immigrant Massachusetts, 1840–2000," Massachusetts Historical Society, May 19, 2000.

17. David Cecelski, "A Thousand Aspirations," *Southern Exposure* 18, no. 1 (Spring 1990): 22–25.

18. William Wells Brown, *The Negro in the American Rebellion* (Boston: n.p., 1867), 212–16.

19. J. Waldo Denny, *Wearing the Blue in the 25th Mass. Volunteer Infantry* (Worcester, Mass.: Putnam & Davis, 1879), xx.

20. James Rumley diary, December 1862, Levi W. Pigott Collection, NCSA.

21. J. Madison Drake, *The History of the Ninth New Jersey Veteran Vols.* (Elizabeth, N.J.: Journal Printing House, 1889), 84–85.

22. *North Carolina Times* (New Bern), April 16, 1864.

23. James Rumley diary, July 1862, Levi W. Pigott Collection, NCSA.

24. Beth Gilbert Crabtree and James W. Patton, eds., *Journal of a Secesh Lady: The Diary of Catherine Ann Devereux Edmondston, 1860–1866* (Raleigh: North Carolina Department of Cultural Resources, Division of Archives and History, 1979), 670.

25. Henry Jones to John R. Donnell, September 12, 1862, Bryan Family Papers, DU.

26. H. Jones to J. R. Donnell, September 22, 1862, Bryan Family Papers, DU.

27. H. Jones to J. R. Donnell, December 1863, Bryan Family Papers, DU.

28. *New York Herald*, November 17, 1862.

29. Series of letters from William Loftin to his mother, March 18, September 5, and October 2, 1862, and January 22, 1863, William F. Loftin Papers, SHC. For an important discussion of slave runaways and the Civil War in the Tar River vicinity, north of Goldsboro, see Robert Hinton, "Cotton Culture on the Tar River: The Politics of Agricultural Labor in the Coastal Plain of North Carolina, 1862–1902" (Ph.D. diss., Yale University, 1993), 54–68.

30. *New Bern Progress*, January 27, 1862; *New York Herald*, February 2, 1862; Goodman, "The Black Tar," 358–60. Many white watermen eventually overcame their reluctance to pilot Union vessels, probably because they grew tired of losing piloting fees to black competitors. When one such vessel, the *Haze*, called for a pilot at Hatteras Inlet in 1863, the old steamer's crew was regaled with a race among 15 local pilot boats for the chance to guide her through the inlet. Thomas Kirwan, *Soldiering in North Carolina* (Boston: n.p., 1864), 12–13.

31. Goodman, "The Black Tar," 360.

32. Hired by the Union forces, the black watermen connected Beaufort with the railroad depot at Morehead City and with outlying military posts such as those at Cape Lookout and Fort Macon. They also guided Union forays along the seacoast and up the White Oak, Trent, and Neuse Rivers. Horace James, *Annual Report of the Superintendent of Negro Affairs in North Carolina, 1864, with an appendix containing the history and management of the freedmen in this department up to June 1st, 1865, by Rev. Horace James* (Boston: W. F. Brown, [ca. 1865]).

33. Frank T. Robinson, *History of the Fifth Regiment, M.V.M.* (Boston: W. F. Brown & Co., 1879), 196–97; Burlingame, *History of the Fifth Regiment*, 74; Drake, *History of the Ninth New Jersey Veteran Vols.*, 26–39, 83–85, 145.

34. Kirwan, *Soldiering in North Carolina*, 14; W. P. Derby, *Bearing Arms in the Twenty-Seventh Massachusetts Regiment of Volunteers Infantry during the Civil War, 1861–1865* (Boston: Wright & Potter, 1883), 128–29; John J. Wyeth, *Leaves from a Diary, Written While*

Serving in Co. #44 Mass. From September, 1862, to June, 1863 (Boston: L. F. Lawrence, 1878), 15; J. H. E. Whitney, *The Hawkins Zouaves (Ninth N.Y.V.): Their Battles and Marches* (New York: n.p., 1866), 62; Drake, *History of the Ninth New Jersey Veteran Vols.*, 253; *New York Herald*, May 4, 1862.

35. Anonymous soldier, Company G, 44th Regiment Massachusetts Volunteers, to his family, November 16, 1862, Federal Soldiers' Letters, SHC.

36. Crabtree and Patton, *Journal of a Secesh Lady*, 86–87.

37. Herbert E. Valentine, *Story of Co. F, 23d Massachusetts Volunteers in the War for the Union, 1861–1865* (Boston: W. B. Clarke, 1896), 88; Burlingame, *History of the Fifth Regiment*, 208–9; Drake, *History of the Ninth New Jersey Veteran Vols.*, 57–58, 81, 260.

38. *Official Records of the Union and Confederate Navies in the War of the Rebellion* (Washington, D.C.: Government Printing Office, 1894–1922), 9:251, cited in Goodman, "The Black Tar," 358–59.

39. Vincent Colyer to Hon. Rob. Dale Owen, 25 May 1863, filed with O-328 1863, Letters Received, ser. 12, RG 94, in Berlin et al., *Freedom: A Documentary History*, 124.

40. *New York Herald*, November 1, 1862; *North Carolina Times* (New Bern), April 7, 1865.

41. James A. Emmerton, *A Record of the Twenty-Third Regiment, Mass. Vol. Infantry, in the War of the Rebellion, 1861–1865* (Boston: William Ware, 1886), 97.

42. Albert W. Mann, *History of the Forty-Fifth Regiment Massachusetts Volunteer Militia* (Jamaica Plain, Mass., 1908), 202.

43. November 18 and November 27, 1864, entries, Edmund J. Cleveland diary, SHC.

44. Denny, *Wearing the Blue*, 92; Drake, *History of the Ninth New Jersey Veteran Vols.*, 67.

45. Otto Eisenschiml, ed., *Vermont General: The Unusual Experiences of Edward Hastings Ripley, 1862–1865* (New York: Devin-Adair, 1960), 164.

46. *North Carolina Times* (New Bern), May 28, 1864.

47. C. F. Pierce, *History and Camp Life of Company C, Fifty-First Regiment, Massachusetts Volunteer Militia, 1862–1863* (Worcester, Mass.: Charles Hamilton, 1886), 100–104.

48. Capt. Wm. B. Fowle Jr. to Maj. Southard Hoffman, [14 January 1863], F-6 1863, Letters Received, ser. 3238, Dept. of N.C., RG 393 pt. 1, pp. 86–87, in Ira Berlin, Barbara J. Fields, Thavolia Glymph, Joseph P. Reidy, and Leslie S. Rowland, eds., *Freedom: A Documentary History of Emancipation, 1861–1867* ser. 1, vol. 1, *The Destruction of Slavery* (Cambridge: Cambridge University Press, 1985).

49. Edward Champney drawings, Outer Banks History Center, Manteo, N.C.

50. Drake, *History of the Ninth New Jersey Veteran Vols.*, 71.

51. For an excellent study of the internal divisions within Washington County, a hundred miles north of Beaufort, see Wayne K. Durrill, *War of Another Kind: A Southern Community in the Great Rebellion* (New York: Oxford University Press, 1990).

52. Drucilla Davis Potter Willis, "My Life's History as Remembered at Eighty-Five Years of Age" (1928), unpublished typescript, Beaufort Historical Association, Beaufort, N.C.

53. George Greene to Geo. Whipple, April 25, 1864, AMAA, cited in Maxine D. Jones, "'A Glorious Work': The American Missionary Association and Black North Carolinians, 1863–1880" (Ph.D. diss., Florida State University, 1982), 260–63.

54. James Rumley diary, October 17, 1863, Levi W. Pigott Collection, NCSA.

55. Most notoriously, on June 11, 1862, Confederate guerrillas eluded bluecoat pickets and kidnapped Rev. Thomas Mann for having addressed a Union meeting. See Drake, *History of the Ninth New Jersey Veteran Vols.*, 75. See also *New York Herald*, May 22, 1862.

56. Drake, *History of the Ninth New Jersey Veteran Vols.*, 75.

57. "Corporal" [Z. T. Haines], *Letters from the Forty-fourth Regiment M.V.M.: A Record of the Experience of a Nine Months' Regiment in the Department of North Carolina in 1862–3* (Boston: Herald Job Office, 1863), 112–13.

58. James Rumley diary, April 26, 1862, Levi W. Pigott Collection, NCSA.

59. *New York Herald*, June 15, 1862.

60. James Rumley diary, October 1862, Levi W. Pigott Collection, NCSA.

61. Ibid., January 1, 1863.

62. Ibid., November 21, 1863.

63. Ibid., December 1, 1864.

64. Elizabeth Oakes to Mr. and Mrs. William J. Spence, June 30, 1874, Appleton Oaksmith Papers, SHC.

65. December 12 and 18, 1864, and March 13, 1865, entries, Edmund J. Cleveland diary, SHC.

66. Drake, *History of the Ninth New Jersey Veteran Vols.*, 84.

67. George N. Greene to Rev. Geo. Whipple, February 5, 1864, AMAA.

68. See especially. Eisenschiml, *Vermont General*, 179–81, 188–89, 191–92, 206.

69. See Durrill, *War of Another Kind*.

70. H. Clay Trumball, *The Knightly Soldier: A Biography of Maj. Henry Ward Camp* (Philadelphia: John D. Wattles, 1892), 75–76.

71. D. L. Day, *My Diary of Rambles with the 25 Mass. Volunteer Infantry, with Burnside's Coast Division; 18th Army Corps, and Army of the James* (Milford, Mass., 1884), 51; October 30 and November 6, 1864, entries, Edmund J. Cleveland diary, SHC.

72. A Union soldier wrote from New Bern on June 1, 1863: "The negroes here honor the Hibernian custom of 'waking' their dead . . . they sometimes render night so hideous by their songs and shoutings that the guard is attracted to the scene of the spiritual orgies, to enforce order. At midnight, the revelers solemnly refresh themselves with coffee, and then resume their howling, reciting and chanting simple hymns." Haines, *Letters from the Forty-Fourth Regiment M.V.M.*, 14.

73. This was particularly so during the mass burials that accompanied a yellow fever epidemic in Beaufort in 1864. F. Lyman to Geo. Whipple, December 19, 1864, and February 1, 1865, AMAA. The AMA missionaries' frustrations at black resistance to what Lyman called "a truer, more reasoned, less emotional Christianity" is a central theme in Jones, "'A Glorious Work.'"

74. Kirwan, *Soldiering in North Carolina*, 54.

75. Thomas A. Jordan, "A Church Examines Its Self-Concept," *The Providence American* (Providence, R.I.), May 8, 1993.

76. Emmerton, *A Record of the Twenty-Third Regiment*, 97.

77. Jones, "'A Glorious Work,'" 35–36.

78. F. Lyman to Geo. Whipple, December 19, 1864, and February 1, 1865, AMAA.

79. November 16 and 17, 1864, entries, Edmund J. Cleveland diary, SHC.

80. November 16, 17, and 30, and December 16 and 18, 1864, entries, Edmund J. Cleveland diary, SHC.

81. George N. Greene to Brother Whiting, February 8, 1864, AMAA.

82. November 22, 1864, entry, Edmund J. Cleveland diary, SHC.

83. George W. Jenkins to Miss Sarah, June 29, 1864, AMAA.

84. March 7, 1865, entry, Edmund J. Cleveland diary, SHC.

85. Jones, "'A Glorious Work,'" 46–50.

86. Rev. T. Lyman to Geo. Whipple, February 1, 1865, AMAA.

87. December 9, 1864, entry, Edmund J. Cleveland diary, SHC.

88. William Henry Singleton, *Recollections of My Slavery Days*, ed. Katherine Mellen Charron and David S. Cecelski (Raleigh: North Carolina Department of Cultural Resources, Division of Archives and History, 1999), 48–49, 95–97; *North Carolina Times* (New Bern), December 24, 1864.

89. James Rumley diary, October 1862, Levi W. Pigott Collection, NCSA.

90. David Lawrence Valuska, "The Negro in the Union Navy, 1861–1865" (Ph.D. diss., Lehigh University, 1973), 4–8. See also Harold D. Langley, "The Negro in the Navy and Merchant Service, 1798–1860," *JNH* 52 (October 1967): 273–86; James Barker Farr, *Black Odyssey: The Seafaring Traditions of Afro-Americans* (New York: P. Lang, 1989), 105–44; James Oliver Horton and Lois E. Horton, *In Hope of Liberty: Culture, Community, and Protest among Northern Free Blacks, 1700–1860* (New York: Oxford University Press, 1997), 69–70; Gary B. Nash, *Forging Freedom: The Formation of Philadelphia's Black Community, 1720–1840* (Cambridge: Harvard University Press, 1988), 51–53; Herbert Aptheker, "The Negro in the Union Navy," *JNH* 32 (1947): 161–200.

91. Valuska, "The Negro in the Union Navy," 29.

92. Ibid., 54–55.

93. See Goodman, "The Black Tar," 273; Valuska, "The Negro in the Union Navy," 30–31; and, for a crucial new assessment of black sailors in the Union navy based on the first thorough review of their pension and service records, Joseph P. Reidy, "The African-American Sailors' Project: The Hidden History of the Civil War," *CRM: Cultural Resource Management* 20, no. 2 (1997): 31–33, 43. I would like to thank Dr. Reidy for sharing the early fruits of the Black Civil War Sailors Research Project with me.

94. Goodman, "The Black Tar," 300, 331–32.

95. Data on Black Union navy sailors claiming North Carolina nativity is from the database of the Black Civil War Sailors Research Project, Howard University. This number includes blacks who enlisted either in a northern seaport, at a recruitment center in one of the Union-occupied ports in Virginia or North Carolina, or on board a vessel serving in the North Atlantic Blockading Squadron.

96. Thomas A. Jordan, "A Black Civil War Navy Veteran and His Times," *The Providence American* (Providence, R.I.), February 1, 1992, 8. See also Thomas A. Jordan, "The Men Who Could Not Wait Around for Liberation" (unpublished manuscript, 1992), copy at North Carolina Maritime Museum, Beaufort. Jordan does a splendid job of using pension and disability claims to document the participation of Beaufort watermen in the Union navy.

97. Valuska, "The Negro in the Union Navy," 181–522.

98. William H. Gould IV, "The Unwinding Trail: Some Reflections on the Life and

Times of William Benjamin Gould," presentation at the New Hanover County Public Library, Wilmington, N.C., December 15, 1998.

99. Of the 721 enrollment and pension records for black Union sailors from North Carolina, only 519 listed an occupation (other than "slave") for the enlistee. Eighty-seven of those 519 listed at least one maritime occupation prior to enlistment: cook and/or steward, 54; mariner, 17; fireman, 8; seaman, 5; boatman, 3; waterman, 2; fisherman, 2; caulker, 1; sailor, 1; coal heaver, 1; ship carpenter, 1; "lighter man," 1; engineer, 1; sail-maker/shipjoiner, 1. Data from the Black Civil War Sailors Research Project, Howard University.

100. Data base of the Black Civil War Sailors Research Project, Howard University.

101. Valuska, "The Negro in the Union Navy," 181–522.

102. *The Liberator*, August 8, 1862. Cited in Goodman, "The Black Tar," 314–15. For a good description of a black sailor's life aboard the USS *Nereus*, which chased blockade runners off North and South Carolina, see Testimony by Alex Huggins, in George P. Rawick, ed., *The American Slave: A Composite Autobiography*, 19 vols. (Westport, Conn.: Greenwood, 1972–76), 14:450–52.

103. "List of Pilots submitted by Fleet Captain Pierce Crosby to Acting Rear Admiral S. P. Lee, Flag Ship *Minnesota*," 25 August 1863, RG 45, Subject Files, NP Pilots, U.S. Navy 1861–1865, box 348, folder 5, NA; Lt. Cmdr. H. N. T. Arnold to Comdr. W. H. Macomb (commanding 3rd Division, N.A.B. Squad), USS *Oswego*, New Bern, N.C., 16 August 1864, ibid. I would like to thank Joseph Reidy and his colleagues at the Black Civil War Sailors Project, Howard University, for sharing these references to Nicholas Dixon with me.

104. James Rumley diary, August 1862, Levi W. Pigott Collection, NCSA.

105. Goodman, "The Black Tar," 433. See also Langley, "The Negro in the Navy and Merchant Service," 282–83.

106. Marcus Rediker, *Between the Devil and the Deep Blue Sea: Merchant Seamen, Pirates, and the Anglo-American Maritime World, 1700–1750* (Cambridge: Cambridge University Press, 1987).

107. See Reidy, "The African-American Sailors' Project," 32–33; Goodman, "The Black Tar," 245–55, 263–64.

108. Valuska, "The Negro in the Union Navy," 130–34.

109. Anonymous to his cousin, May 15, 1864, in Arthur M. Schlesinger, ed., "A Blue Bluejacket's Letters Home, 1863–1864," *New England Quarterly* 1, no. 4 (October 1928): 565.

110. Emmerton, *A Record of the Twenty-Third Regiment*, 135–36.

111. Anonymous letter, April 10, 1864, in Schlesinger, "A Blue Bluejacket's Letters Home," 562.

112. James Rumley diary, August 15, 1863, Levi W. Pigott Collection, NCSA.

113. Ibid., August 17, 1864.

CHAPTER SEVEN

1. The broad picture that I have drawn of occupied New Bern and the specific incidents that I have mentioned are derived from a variety of primary and secondary sources. See John Barrett, *The Civil War in North Carolina* (Chapel Hill: University of North Carolina

Press, 1963), 93–113; Joe A. Mobley, *James City: A Black Community in North Carolina, 1863–1900* (Raleigh: North Carolina Department of Cultural Resources, Division of Archives and History, 1981), 1–25; and David Cecelski, "A Thousand Aspirations," *Southern Exposure* 18, no. 1 (Spring 1990): 22–25. Among the most interesting of the many published reminiscences and diaries written by Union soldiers in New Bern, see W. P. Derby, *Bearing Arms in the Twenty-Seventh Massachusetts Regiment of Volunteers Infantry during the Civil War, 1861–1865* (Boston: Wright & Potter, 1883), esp. 94–95; James A. Emmerton, *A Record of the Twenty-Third Regiment, Mass. Vol. Infantry, in the War of the Rebellion, 1861– 1865* (Boston: William Ware, 1886); "Corporal" [Z. T. Haines], *Letters from the Forty- fourth Regiment M.V.M.: A Record of the Experience of a Nine Months' Regiment in the Depart- ment of North Carolina in 1862–3* (Boston: Herald Job Office, 1863); Vincent Colyer, *Report of the Services Rendered by the Freed People to the United States Army in North Carolina in the Spring of 1862, after the Battle of Newbern* (New York: Vincent Colyer, 1864); J. Waldo Denny, *Wearing the Blue in the 25th Mass. Volunteer Infantry* (Worcester, Mass.: Putnam & Davis, 1879); Thomas Kirwan, *Soldiering in North Carolina* (Boston: n.p., 1864); John J. Wyeth, *Leaves from a Diary, Written While Serving in Co. #44 Mass. From September, 1862, to June, 1863* (Boston: L. F. Lawrence, 1878); J. Madison Drake, *The History of the Ninth New Jersey Veteran Vols.* (Elizabeth, N.J.: Journal Printing House, 1889); Herbert E. Valentine, *Story of Co. F, 23d Massachusetts Volunteers in the War for the Union, 1861–1865* (Boston: W. B. Clarke, 1896); D. L. Day, *My Diary of Rambles with the 25 Mass. Volunteer Infantry, with Burnside's Coast Division, 18th Army Corps, and Army of the James* (Milford, Mass., 1884); and Albert W. Mann, *History of the Forty-Fifth Regiment Massachusetts Volunteer Militia* (Jamaica Plain, Mass., 1908).

2. Mann, *History of the Forty-Fifth Regiment*, 446–49.

3. Ibid.

4. Ibid. Kinsley later related this story to a reunion of the Forty-Fifth Regiment, Massachusetts Volunteer Infantry, which had been stationed in New Bern in 1863. The essential parts of Kinsley's story—including his role in the recruitment of African American soldiers in New Bern, his acquaintance with Galloway and Starkey, Galloway's involvement in Union recruitment yet his devotion to independent black organizing, and Starkey and Galloway's having worked together—are confirmed in a series of letters between Kinsley, Brig. Gen. Edward A. Wild, and Mary Ann Starkey in the Edward W. Kinsley Papers, 1862–89, DU.

5. For an excellent overview of the recruitment of the African Brigade in New Bern, and for references to more general works on the recruitment of black soldiers into the Union army, see Richard Reid, "Raising the African Brigade: Early Black Recruitment in Civil War North Carolina," *NCHR* 70, no. 3 (July 1993): 266–97.

6. Except for brief entries in a few biographical dictionaries and short passages in broader scholarly works about Reconstruction, Galloway had never been the subject of a book, a journal article, or a magazine feature until an earlier version of this chapter was published in David S. Cecelski and Timothy B. Tyson, eds., *Democracy Betrayed: The Wil- mington Race Riot of 1898 and Its Legacy* (Chapel Hill: University of North Carolina Press, 1998). The few other published works that discuss Galloway refer mainly to his political life during Reconstruction. See W. McKee Evans, *Ballots and Fence Rails: Reconstruction on the Lower Cape Fear* (Chapel Hill: University of North Carolina Press, 1966), 87–91;

Leonard Bernstein, "The Participation of Negro Delegates in the Constitutional Convention of 1868 in North Carolina," *JNH* 34, no. 4 (October 1949): 391–409; Elizabeth Balanoff, "Negro Legislators in the North Carolina General Assembly, July, 1868–February, 1872," *NCHR* 49, no. 1 (January 1972): 23–24, 27; William S. Powell, ed. *Dictionary of North Carolina Biography*, 6 vols. (Chapel Hill: University of North Carolina Press, 1979–96), 2:271–72; and Eric Foner, *Freedom's Lawmakers: A Directory of Black Officeholders during Reconstruction* (New York: Oxford University Press, 1993), 81–82.

7. For background on this literature of the "Age of Reaction" in North Carolina, see David S. Cecelski, "Oldest Living Confederate Chaplain Tells All?: Or, James B. Avirett and the Rise and Fall of the Rich Lands," *Southern Cultures* 3, no. 4 (Winter 1997–98): 5–24.

8. *New National Era* (Washington, D.C.), September 4, 1870.

9. Martha A. Little deposition, September 22, 1927, Celie Galloway Pension Application File (1927), U.S. Department of the Interior, Bureau of Pensions, Veterans Administration Hospital, Winston-Salem, N.C. (hereafter, Celie Galloway pension file, VA); October 15, 1866, entry, New Hanover County, Record of Cohabitation, 1866–68, NCSA; Ninth Federal Census of the United States, 1870, New Hanover County, N.C., Population Schedule, NA. In 1927 Celie Galloway, the widow of another Abraham (or Abram) Galloway, also of Brunswick County, applied for veterans benefits based on her husband's military service in the Union army. To establish that her husband was not the better-known Abraham H. Galloway, the subject of this chapter, her attorney visited Beaufort, North Carolina, to take depositions from the surviving family of Abraham H. Galloway that might indicate details about his personal appearance, military career, and death and thus distinguish the two men, justifying the widow's claims for pension benefits. The attorney interviewed Abraham H. Galloway's widow, Martha Ann Little, who still lived in her native Beaufort; she had remarried in 1887.

10. William Still, *The Underground Railroad: A Record of Facts, Authentic Narratives, Letters, etc., Narrating the Hardships, Hair-Breadth Escapes, and Death Struggles of the Slaves in their Efforts for Freedom* (Philadelphia: Porter & Coates, 1872), 150–52; Petition of Lewis A. Galloway for Division of Negroes (March 1837), Lewis A. Galloway Estate Record, Brunswick County Estate Records, NCSA; Lewis Galloway Will (1826), Brunswick County Wills, 1765–1912, NCSA.

11. William Hankins is the only member of the Hankins family in Brunswick County or New Hanover County who owned slaves in 1850. In that year, he owned 24 slaves, including 2 female slaves of Hester's age. The 1850 census does not list slaves by name, only age and gender. Seventh Census of the United States, 1850, Brunswick County and New Hanover County, N.C., Population and Slave Schedules, NA.

Amos Galloway belonged to Lewis Galloway at the time of his death in 1826 and was apportioned to his son John Wesley legally by 1837 and in practice some time before that date. Amos and Hester Hankins considered themselves married as of April 1846, though it is doubtful that they shared a household at that time. They were living together in Wilmington as of the 1870 federal census. See Petition of Lewis A. Galloway for Division of Negroes (March 1837), Lewis A. Galloway Estate Record, Brunswick County Estate Records, NCSA; October 15, 1866, entry, New Hanover County Record of Cohabitation,

1866–68, NCSA; Ninth Census of the United States, 1870, New Hanover County, N.C., Population Schedule, NCSA.

12. Sixth, Seventh, and Eighth Censuses of the United States, 1840–60, Brunswick County, N.C., Population and Slave Schedules, NA; Seventh and Eighth Censuses of the United States, 1850 and 1860, New Hanover County, N.C., Population and Slave Schedules, NA; John W. Galloway (1864), Brunswick County Estate Records, NCSA. John W. Galloway died at the age of 53 of yellow fever, evidently while serving in the Confederate coast guard in Bermuda on September 27, 1864. See *Wilmington Daily Journal*, October 15, 1864, cited in Helen Moore Sammons, *Marriage and Death Notices from Wilmington, North Carolina Newspapers, 1860–1865* (Wilmington, N.C.: North Carolina Room, New Hanover County Public Library, 1987), 76.

13. Quote is from Still, *Underground Railroad*, 150–52.

14. William Still indicates that a Milton Hawkins owned Galloway, but the deposition of Galloway's wife and the listings of a locomotive mechanic named Milton Hankins in the 1860 and 1870 federal censuses confirm his owner as Milton Hankins. The mistake was presumably a typographical error. See Martha A. Little deposition, Celie Galloway pension file, VA; Still, *Underground Railroad*, 150–52; Eighth and Ninth Censuses of the United States, 1860 and 1870, New Hanover County, N.C., Population Schedules, NA.

15. Still, *Underground Railroad*, 150–52; Fugitive Slave Ledger, William Still Papers, Historical Society of Pennsylvania, Philadelphia; *Wilmington Daily Journal*, July 20, 1869.

16. Still, *Underground Railroad*, 150–52. For background on slave life in antebellum Wilmington, see chap. 5 above and Peter P. Hinks, *To Awaken My Afflicted Brethren: David Walker and the Problem of Antebellum Slave Resistance* (University Park: Pennsylvania State University Press, 1997), 1–21; Alan D. Watson, *Wilmington: Port of North Carolina* (Columbia: University of South Carolina Press, 1992), 46–52; and James Howard Brewer, "Legislation Designed to Control Slavery in Wilmington and Fayetteville," *NCHR* 30, no. 2 (April 1953): 155–66. There are also two indispensable autobiographies written by former slaves who grew up in Wilmington. See William H. Robinson, *From Log Cabin to the Pulpit; or, Fifteen Years in Slavery*, 3rd ed. (Eau Claire, Wis.: James H. Tifft, 1913), and Thomas H. Jones, *The Experience of Thomas H. Jones, Who Was a Slave for Forty-Three Years* (Boston: Bazin and Chandler, 1862).

17. Still, *Underground Railroad*, 150–52.

18. See chap. 5 above for a detailed study of this maritime route to freedom.

19. Guion Griffis Johnson, *Ante-Bellum North Carolina: A Social History* (Chapel Hill: University of North Carolina Press, 1937), 577–78.

20. David Walker, *David Walker's Appeal to the Coloured Citizens of the World*, ed. Peter P. Hinks (University Park: Pennsylvania State University Press, 2000).

21. Hinks, *To Awaken My Afflicted Brethren*, 1–21, 173–236. On the emergence of this radical ideology out of the black Atlantic, see also Julius S. Scott, "The Common Wind: Currents of Afro-American Communication in the Era of the Haitian Revolution" (Ph.D. diss., Duke University, 1986); W. Jeffrey Bolster, *Black Jacks: African American Seamen in the Age of Sail* (Cambridge, Mass.: Harvard University Press, 1997), esp. 190–214; Elizabeth Raul Bethel, *The Roots of African-American Identity: Memory and History in the Antebellum Free Communities* (New York: St. Martin's Press, 1997), 53–79; Sterling Stuckey, *Slave*

Culture: Nationalist Theory and the Foundations of Black America (New York: Oxford University Press, 1987), 98–137.

22. Still, *Underground Railroad*, 151–52.

23. David G. Hill, *The Freedom-Seekers: Blacks in Early Canada* (Agincourt, Ont.: Book Society of Canada, 1981), 24–61; Ken Alexander and Aris Glaze, *Towards Freedom: The African-Canadian Experience* (Toronto: Umbrella Press, 1996), 51.

24. The abolitionist movement in Ohio seems a likely field for Galloway's labors. Secret, militant black abolitionist groups with strong ties to Canada operated out of Ohio throughout the 1850s, among them a military group known as the Liberators that had close ties to John Brown. There is some evidence that these clandestine groups served the Union army in an intelligence capacity in the early stages of the Civil War, which, if true, makes it an enticing possibility that it was from one of these groups that Galloway was recruited into the spy service. See Richard Hinton, *John Brown and His Men* (New York: Funk & Wagnalls, 1894), 171–75, and William Cheek and Aimee Cheek, *John Mercer Langston and the Fight for Black Freedom, 1829–65* (Urbana: University of Illinois Press, 1989), 350–52.

25. Edward A. Wild to Edward W. Kinsley, November 30, 1863, Edward W. Kinsley Papers, DU; *National Cyclopaedia of American Biography*, 63 vols. (New York: James T. White, 1898), 8:231; Frank P. Stearns, *The Life and Times of George Luther Stearns* (Philadelphia: J. B. Lippincott, 1907), esp. 276–320; Charles E. Heller, *Portrait of an Abolitionist: A Biography of George Luther Stearns, 1809–1867* (Westport, Conn.: Greenwood Press, 1996), 123–59.

26. Edward A. Wild to Edward W. Kinsley, November 30, 1863, Edward W. Kinsley Papers, DU; *New National Era*, September 4, 1870.

27. Union military records occasionally refer to spying activities, but no official records have yet been found that discuss Galloway's duties as an intelligence agent. The following National Archives records have been consulted for mention of Galloway without success: RG 110, Scouts, Guides, Spies, and Detectives; Secret Service Accounts; RG 109, Union Provost Marshal's Files of Papers Relating to Citizens or Business Firms (M345); RG 92, index to scouts in Reports of Persons and Articles Hired and the index to Quartermaster Claims; RG 59, Letters of Application and Recommendation During the Administrations of Abraham Lincoln and Andrew Johnson; RG 94, indexes to Letters Received by the Adjutant General's Office, 1861–65 (M725) and General Information Index.

28. *Raleigh Weekly Standard*, September 7, 1870.

29. November 24, 1864, entry, Edmund Cleveland diary, SHC.

30. *New National Era*, September 22, 1870.

31. Colyer, *Report of the Services Rendered by the Freed People*, 9–10. Colyer describes (10–22) a number of intelligence missions conducted by former slaves in Confederate territory.

32. Edward A. Wild to Edward W. Kinsley, November 30, 1863, Edward W. Kinsley Papers, DU.

33. Gen. Ambrose E. Burnside to Hon. E. M. Stanton, Secretary of War, March 21, 1862, U.S. War Department, *The War of the Rebellion: A Compilation of the Official Records of the Union and Confederate Armies*, 128 vols. (Washington, D.C.: Government Printing Office, 1880–1901), ser. 1, 9:199–200.

34. The racist conduct of the Union army is one of the strongest themes in both the

private papers and published works of Federal soldiers stationed in North Carolina during the Civil War. See, among many others, Arthur M. Shlesinger, ed., "A Blue Bluejacket's Letters Home, 1863–1864," *New England Quarterly* 1, no. 4 (October 1928): 562, 565; Emmerton, *A Record of the Twenty-Third Regiment*, 135–36; James Rumley diary, August 15, 1863, and August 17, 1864, Levi W. Pigott Collection, NCSA; and John David Smith, *Black Voices during Reconstruction, 1865–1877* (Gainesville: University Press of Florida, 1997), 34–39.

35. See especially Colyer, *Report of Services Rendered by the Freed People*, 29–51; Mobley, *James City*, 5–13, 29–46; and Cecelski, "A Thousand Aspirations," 22–25.

36. William Henry Singleton, *Recollections of My Slavery Days*, ed. by Katherine Mellen Charron and David S. Cecelski (Raleigh: North Carolina Department of Cultural Resources, Division of Archives and History, 1999), 48–49, 95–97. Singleton's claim of black soldiers' drilling on their own, to the dismay and ire of Union officers, is confirmed in Lt. George F. Woodman to Lt. Col. Hoffman, 19 February 1863, W-31 1863, Letters Received, ser. 3238, Dept. of N.C. and 18th A.C., RG 393 Pt. 1, NA, published in Ira Berlin, Joseph P. Reidy, and Leslie Rowland, eds., *Freedom: A Documentary History of Emancipation, 1861–1867*, ser. 2, *The Black Military Experience* (Cambridge: Cambridge University Press, 1982), 129.

37. Andrew J. Wolbrook to Edward W. Kinsley, September 3, 1863, and Wolbrook to Kinsley, September 12, 1863, Edward W. Kinsley Papers, DU. Starkey and Galloway worked closely throughout the Civil War, and Starkey clearly held Galloway in great esteem. After the war, however, the two seem to have had at least a momentary falling out over financial matters. See Mary Ann Starkey to Edward W. Kinsley, July 27, 1865, ibid.

38. Evans, *Ballots and Fence Rails*, 111–12; John Richard Dennett, *The South As It Is: 1865–1866*, ed. Henry M. Christman (New York: Viking, 1965), 151–53.

39. Rumley diary, May 30, June 1, and June 18, 1863, Levi W. Pigott Collection, NCSA.

40. Ibid., January 1, 1864; *Proceedings of the National Convention of the Colored Citizens of the United States, 1864*, reprinted in Herbert Aptheker, *A Documentary History of the Negro People in the United States*, vol. 1 (New York: Citadel Press, 1951), 511–13.

41. Aptheker, *Documentary History*, 522–23.

42. Rumley diary, January 1, 1864, Levi W. Pigott Collection, NCSA.

43. The Lincoln administration first contemplated the use of black troops in mid-1862. "Limited and unauthorized" use of black troops had actually occurred in at least Kansas, Louisiana, and South Carolina before August 1862, when the War Department finally authorized the recruitment of the first slave regiment—the 1st South Carolina Volunteers, recruited from the occupied portion of the Sea Islands—into the Union army. In September 1862, Lincoln issued a "Preliminary Proclamation of Emancipation" that stated that as of January 1, 1863, slaves in the Confederate states would be "forever free." Once the proclamation went into effect, the recruitment of blacks began on a mass scale. Six months later, 30 black regiments had been organized. More than 186,000 blacks enlisted in the Union army, and roughly one-third of them would eventually be listed as dead and missing. See Leon F. Litwack, *Been in the Storm So Long: The Aftermath of Slavery* (New York: Knopf, 1979), 69–71, 98.

44. Galloway married Martha Ann Dixon at the Beaufort home of her parents, Napoleon and Massie Dixon. Martha A. Little deposition, Celie Galloway pension file, VA; Marriage

Register, Carteret County, N.C., 1850–1981, NCSA; Eighth Census of the United States, 1860, Carteret County, N.C., Population and Slave Schedules, NA.

45. Rumley diary, August 4, 1863, Levi W. Pigott Collection, NCSA; November 24, 1864, entry, Edmund J. Cleveland diary, SHC.

46. Edward A. Wild to Edward W. Kinsley, November 30, 1863, Edward W. Kinsley Papers, DU. In this letter, Wild refers to Galloway's Boston contact as a "Mr. Stevenson of 7 Hull St." This was presumably John Hubbard Stephenson (1820–88) of 9 Hull Street, of the millinery firm of Stephenson & Plympton. He is not known to have been a part of the city's abolitionist movement. See *Boston Directory* (Boston: George Adams, 1862) and *Boston Evening Transcript*, December 22, 1888.

47. *North Carolina Times* (New Bern), May 21, 1864; Mary Ann Starkey to Edward W. Kinsley, May 21, 1864, Edward W. Kinsley Papers, DU.

48. *The Liberator*, September 9, 1864. Reprinted in Aptheker, *Documentary History* 511, 516.

49. Horace James, *Annual Report of the Superintendent of Negro Affairs in North Carolina, 1864, with an appendix containing the history and management of the freedmen in this department up to June 1st, 1865, by Rev. Horace James* (Boston: W. F. Brown, [ca. 1865]), 6–18; *Old North State* (Beaufort), January 7, 1865; John Niven, ed., *The Salmon P. Chase Papers*, vol. 1, *Journals, 1829–1872* (Kent, Ohio: Kent State University Press, 1993), 542–44.

50. Willie Lee Rose, *Rehearsal for Reconstruction: The Port Royal Experiment* (Indianapolis: Bobbs-Merrill, 1964).

51. Sidney Andrews, *The South Since the War; As Shown by Fourteen Weeks of Travel and Observation in Georgia and the Carolinas* (Boston: Ticknor & Fields, 1866), 125.

52. Roberta Sue Alexander, *North Carolina Faces the Freedmen: Race Relations during Presidential Reconstruction, 1865–67* (Durham, N.C.: Duke University Press, 1985), 16; Rumley diary, July 4, 1865, Levi W. Pigott Collection, NCSA.

53. *New York Times*, September 17, 1865.

54. Ibid.

55. *Wilmington Herald*, September 8, 1865.

56. Evans, *Ballots and Fence Rails*, 87–91.

57. Aptheker, *Documentary History*, 546.

58. Dennett, *The South As It Is*, 151–53.

59. *New National Era*, September 22, 1870. Galloway is not listed in the city directories of New Bern or Wilmington in 1865–66. See Frank D. Smaw Jr., *Smaw's Wilmington Directory* (Wilmington, N.C.: Frank D. Smaw Jr., ca. 1866), and R. A. Shotwell, *New Bern Mercantile and Manufacturers' Business Directory and North Carolina Farmers Reference Book* (New Bern, N.C.: W. I. Vestal, 1866).

60. Evans, *Ballots and Fence Rails*, 93.

61. Dennett, *The South As It Is*, 42.

62. Quoted in Litwack, *Been in the Storm So Long*, 271.

63. Evans, *Ballots and Fence Rails*, 64–81; Litwack, *Been in the Storm So Long*, 289.

64. Dennett, *The South As It Is*, 110.

65. Evans, *Ballots and Fence Rails*, 83–85.

66. *Tri-Weekly Standard* (Raleigh), September 7, 1867.

67. Wilmington *Evening Star*, September 25, 1867; *New National Era*, September 22, 1870.

68. Evans, *Ballots and Fence Rails*, 95–97.

69. *Wilmington Journal*, February 21, 1868.

70. *The Standard* (Raleigh), January 25, 1868, and February 17, 1868, cited in Bernstein, "The Participation of Negro Delegates," 399, 407.

71. Quoted in Evans, *Ballots and Fence Rails*, 98.

72. *Wilmington Weekly Journal*, February 28, 1868.

73. Evans, *Ballots and Fence Rails*, 95–97.

74. Ibid., 98–102.

75. Linda Gunter, "Abraham H. Galloway: First Black Elector," *North Carolina African-American Historical and Genealogical Society Quarterly* (Fall 1990): 9–10.

76. *The Christian Recorder* (Philadelphia), September 24, 1870. For background on black militias in the Reconstruction South, see Otis A. Singletary, *Negro Militia and Reconstruction* (Austin: University of Texas Press, 1957).

77. Allen W. Trelease, *White Terror: The Ku Klux Klan Conspiracy and Southern Reconstruction* (Baton Rouge: Louisiana State University Press, 1971), 189–225; Evans, *Ballots and Fence Rails*, 101–2, 145–48; William C. Harris, *William Woods Holden: Firebrand of North Carolina Politics* (Baton Rouge: Louisiana State University Press, 1987), 287–307.

78. Balanoff, "Negro Legislators," 23–24, 27.

79. *Wilmington Daily Journal*, July 20, 1869.

80. *Wilmington Weekly Journal*, April 2, 1869.

81. See, for example, *New York Times*, September 17, 1865.

82. *Wilmington Daily Journal*, July 20, 1869; *Wilmington Journal*, August 4, 1870, Bill Reaves Collection, New Hanover County Public Library, Wilmington.

83. North Carolina General Assembly, Senate, *Journal of the Senate of the General Assembly of the State of North Carolina . . .* (serial), 1868 (Raleigh: The Senate), 41–42.

84. Ibid., 1869 (Raleigh: The Senate), 360–61; Balanoff, "Negro Legislators," 34–36.

85. Balanoff, "Negro Legislators," 41–42, 44–48; *North Carolina Standard*, January 21, 1868, and February 10, 1870; North Carolina General Assembly, *Laws of North Carolina* (serial), 1868–69–70 (Raleigh: Thomas J. Lemay), chap. 77; letter from A. H. Galloway, George Z. French, and J. S. W. Eagles to Governor Holden, August 10, 1869, William Woods Holden, Governors Letter Book 60, NCSA.

86. For an informative discussion of the collective outlook toward voting held by Reconstruction blacks, see Elsa Barkley Brown, "Negotiating and Transforming the Public Sphere: African American Political Life in the Transition from Slavery to Freedom," *Public Culture* 7, no. 1 (Fall 1994): 107–46.

87. North Carolina General Assembly, Senate, *Journal of the Senate*, 1868–69, 209, 223, 648; ibid., 1869–70, 466; *Wilmington Journal*, February 1869, in Bill Reaves Collection, New Hanover County Public Library; Balanoff, "Negro Legislators," 42–44.

88. Galloway grew ill so suddenly that his wife and two young sons, John L. and Abraham Jr., were not able to return from a trip to New Bern before his death. "Widow's Declaration of Pension for Martha A. Little," January 29, 1894, Celie Galloway pension file, VA.

89. *Raleigh Weekly Standard*, September 7, 1870; *Wilmington Daily Journal*, September

2–4 and 10, 1870, and April 23, 1871, Bill Reaves Collection, New Hanover County Public Library; *The Christian Recorder* (Philadelphia), September 24, 1870.

90. Evans, *Ballots and Fence Rails*, 137–41.

91. *The Christian Recorder*, September 24, 1870; *Wilmington Journal*, September 2–4, 1870, Bill Reaves Collection, New Hanover County Public Library; *Raleigh Weekly Standard*, September 17, 1870.

Acknowledgments

I would like to thank my friends, colleagues, and family for all their help with *The Waterman's Song*. Tim Tyson was the book's godfather, reading and editing every page of every draft, and he and his family took raucously good care of me during my long writing retreats to their home. Kat Charron, Bland Simpson, Peter Wood, Jeff Crow, Steve Kantrowitz, and Cathy Lutz also read the entire manuscript and improved it immeasurably. Lu Ann Jones, Glenda Gilmore, Tera Hunter, Laura Edwards, Chuck Eppinette, Tim Borstelman, Richard Ward, Kay Wyche, Catherine Bishir, Robert Hinton, John David Smith, Kirsten Fisher, Rod Barfield, and Joe Mobley all read at least parts of early drafts and offered sage counsel. At the University of North Carolina Press, David Perry supported my work with equally strong parts intellect and faith. Douglas Egerton and Joseph Reidy, who read the manuscript for the Press, offered many helpful suggestions. And I could never have finished the book without the support of Jacquelyn Hall and my other colleagues at the Southern Oral History Program at the University of North Carolina at Chapel Hill. The history department at East Carolina University also gave a tremendous boost to my final revisions when it extended me its Whichard Chair in the Humanities.

My friend Maruja García Padilla was a wonderful guide on my tour of the maritime archives of New England. Patricia Samford at Tryon Palace Historic Sites, Stephen Atkins at Colonial Williamsburg, and David Phelps and Larry Babits at East Carolina University introduced me to gold mines of unpublished archaeological findings on Native American and slave life along southern estuaries. Michael and Debbie Luster generously shared their earliest discoveries on the black maritime community of Davis Ridge. Joseph Reidy and his graduate students at Howard University volunteered their remarkable database of black sailors in the Union navy. Without the technical expertise of Mike Alford, the retired curator of watercraft at the North Carolina Maritime Museum, I would never have pieced together the historical use, construction, or design of the types of boats and vessels that I found listed in eighteenth- and nineteenth-century documents. His knowledge of those craft is remarkable, and unique. In addition, at two conferences, the staff at Mystic Seaport in Connecticut provided a marvelously rich intellectual climate in which to study race, power, and maritime society in America.

I am also indebted to a number of archivists and curators who were deeply committed to this project. I would particularly like to thank George Stevenson at the North Carolina State Archives, who directed me to a host of diaries, private papers, and other manuscripts that I would never have found otherwise. I am also grateful for the help of Connie Mason and David Moore at the North Carolina Maritime Museum, Harry Warren at the Museum of the Lower Cape Fear, Beverly Tetterton at the New Hanover County Public Library, Merle Chamberlain at the Lower Cape Fear Historical Society Archives, Bill Erwin of the Special Collections Department at Duke University, Alice Cotten and Bob Anthony of the North Carolina Collection at the University of North Carolina at Chapel Hill, Ben Trask at the Mariners' Museum in Newport News, and the late Richard D. Martin at the Peabody Essex Museum.

Finally, I would like to thank my family—siblings, parents, in-laws, nieces and nephews, and cousins all—and especially my wife Laura and my children, Vera and Guy. They have accompanied me on research trips from Ocracoke to Mystic, and a few places maybe less enthralling, and they always seem to understand why I go back, again and again, into the lost past of my native land.

Index

sels, 39–40, 140–41, 172–76; on Albemarle Sound schooners, 40–43; in coastwise trade, 52–54; legal restrictions on and harassment of, 53–54, 146–49, 175–76, 271 (nn. 113, 119); and conditions at sea, 54–55; subversive reputation of, 55, 146, 183; aid runaway slaves, 138–39, 140–43, 146–50, 183; escape by sea, 142–43; during Civil War, 167, 171–76, 278 (n. 99); at Davis Ridge, 205; with uncertain papers, 271 (n. 117)

African American schools, 165, 170–71, 187, 192, 199

African American soldiers, 170, 171–72, 176, 189–90, 283 (n. 43); and struggle for equal rights, 180–81; as militant veterans, 197–98

African Brigade, 181

African Methodist Episcopal Zion Church, 169, 177, 187, 193

Afro-Caribbean, xviii, 28

Albemarle and Chesapeake Canal, 106, 108, 116

Albemarle Enquirer (newspaper), 98

Albemarle Sound: shad and herring fishery near, xiii, xix, 9, 58, 64, 83–102; Moses Grandy on or in vicinity of, xv, 27–56 passim, 137; slave revolts in vicinity of, xvi; navigation and shipping on, 4, 42, 48, 115; maritime culture of, 13; slave watermen on, 25, 50, 83–102; early colonists of, 28; free blacks in vicinity of, 90–91; canals near or to, 103, 106, 107, 112, 116; and runaway slaves, 124, 129, 158; and Civil War, 157, 158

Alexandria, Va., 37

Allen, George, 153

Alligator Lake, 107, 108

Alligator River, 40, 67, 106

Algonquians, 4, 8–11, 20, 60, 63, 71, 74, 84–85

America (slave shipwright), 42

American Missionary Association, 164, 166, 170

American Revolution, 4, 18, 30, 90, 207;

era of, xviii, 15–21; black watermen and sailors in, 16–17, 20, 172

Amphibious (schooner), 237 (n. 57)

Anderson (overseer), 68

Anderson, Henry, 124

Anderson, Hull, 42, 54

Andrew, John Albion, 180

Annapolis, Md., 37

Ansell, Henry, 75

Appeal to the Coloured Citizens of the World, xvii, 30, 53, 55, 58, 183

Ashby's Harbor, 157

Atlantic, N.C., 208, 211

Atlantic and North Carolina Railroad, 209

Back Bay (Va.), 68

Back Sound, 63, 162

Bagby, George, 44–45

Bahamas, 11, 18, 28, 86, 136

Ba-Kongo religion, 167

Ball, Charles, 26, 65, 69–70, 95–96

Baltimore, Md., 19, 26, 34, 37, 79, 86, 156

Banks, Joseph, 131

Baptists, 169–70

Bateaumen (slave) and bateaux, 43–45, 213

Bath, N.C., 16, 49, 141

Bayou Boeuf, La., 27

Bay River, 80

Bear Inlet, xix, 158

Beaufort, N.C., 14, 35, 106, 204, 208, 212; mullet fishery at, 60, 61, 209; other fisheries in, 63, 79, 80, 156; and runaway slaves, 124; and shipping trade, 139; Civil War in, 153–77, 185, 189, 205; maritime culture of, 156; Abraham Galloway in, 185, 187, 189–91; freedpeople in or from, 189–91, 193; menhaden industry in, 205

Beaufort Harbor, 155, 171, 174–76

Beaufort Inlet, 14, 153, 157, 161

Belford (fishing boat), 205

Bell (bride), 164

Bell (brig), 148

Ben (slave sailor), 157

Ben (Westmore slave), 18

Cannon Point (plantation), 75
Cape Fear, xi, 3, 4, 60, 135, 145, 173, 195
Cape Fear Indians, xi
Cape Fear Navigation Company, 106, 113, 115
Cape Fear River, xi, xii, 16, 53, 180, 182; slave boatmen and pilots on, xi–xii, xiv, 15, 46, 50, 70, 108, 121, 138–39, 161; fishing on, 60; canals on, 106, 108, 115; and runaway slaves, 124, 139, 145
Capehart, W. R., 94
Capehart family (fishery owners), 85, 95
Cape Hatteras, 238 (n. 101)
Cape Henry, 60
Cape Lookout, 49, 77–78, 149, 204, 209
Cape Lookout National Seashore, 203
Cape Verde Islands, 172
Caribbean, xii, 28, 42, 55, 156. *See also* Afro-Caribbean; West Indies
Carrot Island, 248 (n. 79)
Carter, Dorcas E., 62
Carteret County, N.C., 156, 160, 163, 164, 203, 248 (n. 79)
Catharine Lake, 172
Catherine (slave stewardess), 241 (n. 129)
Caulkins, Nehemiah, 127
Cedar Island, 63, 203, 248 (n. 79)
Cedar Island National Wildlife Refuge, 203
Ceres (vessel), 173
Champney, Edward, 163
Chanteys, xii, xx, 83
Charles (slave), 18
Charleston, S.C., xix, 20, 26, 28, 60, 103, 105, 146, 157, 171, 268 (n. 82)
Chesapeake Bay, xix, 34, 37, 42, 58, 59, 79, 84, 85, 103, 106, 108, 116, 266 (n. 64)
Chowan County, N.C., 18, 31, 85, 90, 129, 173
Chowaneoic Indians, 9, 10, 85
Chowan River, 9, 56, 70, 85, 101–2, 129, 158, 237 (n. 83)
Civil War: role of slave watermen in, xvi, xvii, 96, 153–77, 273 (n. 16); reliance on fish during, 61–62; fish trade during, 65; slaves escape by boat during, 138;

Unionist sympathies on coast during, 140–41; Union invasion of coast during, 153–58; race relations during, 162–66; black soldiers in, 179–81; freedpeople organizing during, 179–81, 185–91. *See also* Federal occupation
Clamming, 60, 203, 211
Clark (pilot), 16
Cleveland, Edmund J., 171
Cobb (sea captain), 54
Cobb, Collier, 248 (n. 79)
Colerain (plantation), 85
Collet, John, 16
Collins, Josiah, 18, 85, 103–4, 107, 111, 113
Columbia, N.C., 40, 67, 158
Colyer, Vincent, 161, 186
Confederacy, xvii, 161, 165, 169, 179, 180, 186–88, 190, 195, 196; forces of, xvi, 153, 155, 157, 165, 179; vessels of, xix, 157; partisans of, 164–65, 189; deserters from, 165; guerrillas for, 171, 186, 195
Congaree River, 26, 65, 69, 95
Continental Navy, 17, 172
Contrabands. *See* Freedpeople
Cooks, on vessels (slave and free black), 39, 53, 136
Cooners (boats), 4–5, 124, 157, 214
Copper, Tom, 129
Corapeake Lumber Canal, 47
Core Banks, xv, 48, 50, 63, 77, 207, 249 (n. 79)
Core Creek, 79
Coree Indians, 9
Core Point, 10
Core Sound, 5, 60, 63, 66, 156, 162, 203; maritime culture of, 13, 204–12
Crabbing industry, xx
Craven Corner, N.C., 207
Craven County, N.C., 64, 128, 198
Crayon, Porte. *See* Strother, David Hunter
Croatan Sound, 158
Cuba, 18
Cuff (ferryman), 161–62
Cuffe, Paul, 36

Evans, W. McKee, 196, 201
Experience of Thomas H. Jones, The, xv

Fairfield, N.C., 106
Falcon (sloop), 149
Fayetteville, N.C., 50, 115
Fayetteville Canal, 106
Federal occupation: roles of slave watermen in, 153, 155, 160–62; slave boatlift during, 157–60; race relations under, 162–66; Unionist sentiment during, 163–64; Confederate partisans in, 164–65; Confederate deserters flock to, 165; black culture and society under, 167–71; recruitment of black spies and agents during, 185–90; black militia formed under, 187–88; emergence of black political movement under, 187–91; recruitment of black soldiers in areas of, 189–90
Ferebee, London R., xiv–xv, 27, 71, 137–38
Ferrying and ferrymen (slave), 31–32, 69, 136, 160, 161–62, 214, 231–32 (n. 27)
Fish: as fertilizer, 66, 72, 207; in slave diet, 67, 72–76, 84, 95; "trash" species of, 72, 95; in Civil War diet, 162
Fish camps, 78, 209–11
Fisher (brig), 271 (n. 119)
Fishermen and -women (slave), xii–xiii, 57–81, 83–102, 136, 173; rhythms of daily life of, 76; recruitment of, 89–92; in Civil War, 153, 162, 173; at Davis Ridge, 203–12
Fishermen's court, 91
Fish hawkers, 80
Fishing: by Indians, 5, 8–10; by slaves in general, 8–11, 57–81, 83–102; annual cycle of, 8–11, 63; commercial, 60, 61, 76–81, 83–102; for barter, 61–62; by plantation slaves, 63–76, 94; conflicts over, 64–65; at night, 70–71; dangers of, 80–81; during Civil War, 162; by black fishermen at Davis Ridge, 203–12; share system in, 209; racial egalitarianism in,

209–11; boats used for, 243 (n. 23). *See also* specific fisheries and forms of fishing
Fishing gear, 68–71, 243 (n. 23), 245 (n. 44). *See also* Nets
Fish trade, 10, 60–61, 67–68, 207
Fish traps, 68, 69, 70, 245 (n. 43), 245 (n. 44)
Flatboating (by slaves): for shingling, xi; on rivers, 45–47; boats for, 215
Florence (brigantine), 149
Florida, 72, 172
Fort Fisher, 157, 161, 171, 172, 176
Fort Johnston, xi, 16
Fort Macon, 153, 155, 160, 161, 164, 166, 272 (n. 3)
Fort Morgan (vessel), 175
Fortress Monroe, 185
Fortune, Thomas, 149
Foster, John C., 186, 190
Fountain (sea captain), 124, 150
Fourth Rhode Island Volunteers, 153
Fox (steamer), 236–37 (n. 83)
France, 15, 19, 56, 138, 204; Huguenots from, 5; colonies of, 19
Frank (slave canal digger), 112
Frank (slave flatboat hand), 131
Free blacks: as pilots, 50; as sailors, 52–55, 141, 146–48, 149, 183; exodus of, 54; as fishermen, 86, 90–92, 205, 207; voting rights of, 90, 229 (n. 64); as canal diggers, 112, 114; restrictions on, 134, 146–48, 271 (n. 113); as boatmen, 141
Freedpeople (contrabands), 158, 162–72, 176–77; as Union pilots, 153, 155, 160–61; as Union spies and intelligence agents, 159; as ferrymen, 160, 161–62; raft lumber, 161; as ship's carpenters and joiners, 161; as steamer hands, 161; as fishermen, 162; culture of, 167–71; churches of, 168–70; schools of, 170–71; as Union sailors, 171–76; Abraham Galloway as leader of, 187–201; struggle for political and civil rights by, 191–201
Free grazing of livestock, 63, 265 (n. 50)

French and Indian War, 14
French Revolution, 19
Friend (schooner), 149
Frying Pan Shoals, 150, 182
Fugitive Slave Act of 1850, 149, 185
Fulcher, William Henry, 208
Fuller, Samuel, 121, 138, 148
Furley, George, 32

Gabriel's Rebellion, xvi, 30, 45, 96
Galloway, Abraham H., xvii–xviii; escapes
   by sea, 133, 183; as leader of freedpeople
   in North Carolina, 179–81, 187–90;
   early life of, 182–83; as militant abolitionist, 183–85, 282 (n. 24); as Union spy,
   185–87, 190; meets with Lincoln, 190; at
   National Convention of Colored Citizens,
   190–91; organizes chapters of Equal
   Rights League, 191; calls freedpeople's
   convention in New Bern, 192–93; calls
   statewide freedpeople's convention in
   Raleigh, 192–94; helps found state
   Republican Party, 196; as delegate to con-
   stitutional convention of 1868, 196–97;
   as leader of black militia, 197–98; in state
   senate, 197–201; death of, 201
Galloway, Amos, 182
Galloway, John Wesley, 182
Garbacon Creek, 57, 65–66
Gaston Railroad, 116
Gates County, N.C., 47, 90, 173
Gatesville, N.C., 91
George (black sailor), 149
Georgia, xix, 69, 70, 72, 171
Germany, 141; immigrants from, 115
Gillikin, Norman, 207
Glory (movie), 185
Goffs Cut, 47
Goldsboro, N.C., 124, 159
Gorham, Henry, 133
Goshen Swamp, 108
Gould, William, I, 138, 173
Grandy, James, 31–32, 47
Grandy, Moses, xiv–xv, 58, 137–38, 177;
   as ferryman, 31–32; as canal boat cap-

tain, 33–40, 52; as schooner deckhand,
   40–47; as lighter captain, 47–52; as
   sailor, 52–55; as stevedore, 54; as canal
   hand, 56, 110, 112
Grandy, William, 30–31
Grant, Ulysses S., 191
Great Alligator Swamp, 131, 132
Great Dismal Swamp, 27; shingle flats in,
   xiv, 131; slaves dig canals in, xv, xix,
   110–13; geography of, 4; slave shinglers
   in, 16, 48, 131; unruly swampers from,
   28; slave lumbermen in, 32; as refuge for
   slave runaways and outcasts, 52, 124,
   131, 132; ecological impact of canals on,
   108–9
Great Marsh Bay, 75
Green, Richard, 173
Greene, George, 170
Green Swamp, 128
Grice, Charles, 34
Grice, James, 34
Griffin, John, 172
Grimes, Harry, 133

Haiti, 28–30, 56
Haitian Revolution, 28–30
Halifax, N.C., 101
Halifax County, N.C., 90
Hallsville, N.C., 139
Hankins, Hester, 182
Hankins, Marsden Milton, 182–83
Hankins, Mary Ann, 182
Hankins, William, 182
Harkers Island, 10, 203, 204, 211
Harlowe and Clubfoot Creek Canal, 106,
   257 (n. 10)
Hatteras Inlet, 60, 75, 77, 157, 160
Hatteras Island, 5, 156, 157
Haze (steamer), 274 (n. 30)
Heines, Peter, 124
Henry (slave shipwright), 42
Henry (slave steward), 236–37 (n. 83)
Henry, George, 27, 36–39
Henry, John, 208
Herring, rockfish, and shad fishery, xiii, ix,

Kongo, 72
Ku Klux Klan, xviii, 181, 197–98, 199–200, 208

Lake Company, 103, 107
Lake Drummond, 52, 106
Lake Landing, N.C., 107
Lake Mattamuskeet, 31, 106, 107, 108, 159
Lake Phelps, 68, 103–4, 107, 108, 113, 131
Lamb's Ferry, 31
Latimer, Zebulon, 129
Lawson, John, 4
Lee, Richard Henry, 36
Lenoir County, N.C., 69
Liberator, The (newspaper), 173
Life of George Henry, 37
Lighters and lightering (by slaves): at Ocracoke Inlet, 47–48, 77; out of Great Dismal Swamp, 47–48, 237 (n. 88); in ports, 137, 173; defined, 215
Lincoln, Abraham, 188, 190, 283 (n. 43)
Linebaugh, Peter, 16
Littlejohn family (fishery owners), 85
Llewyllen (schooner), 27, 36–37
Loftin, William, 159
Long Island, 59, 85
Louisiana, xix, 27, 60
Lower Banks, 204. *See also* Outer Banks
Lower Cape Fear (region), 108, 138, 183, 195
Lower Neuse River (estuary), xiv, 57–58, 63, 66, 107, 232 (n. 27); shad fishery at, 64–65, 243–44 (n. 24)
Luster, Debbie, 204
Luster, Michael, 204

McClellan, George, 189
McGuire, Phillip, 25
MacKnight, Thomas, 18
MacKnight shipyard, 18, 228–29 (n. 48)
McLin, Thomas, 42
McPherson (overseer), 112
Maine, 176, 185
Mande, 72, 167

Manuel (slave outlaw), 129
Martha's Vineyard, 19
Martin County, N.C., 89
Mary (free black), xv, 138
Mary E. Reeves (schooner), 205, 211
Maryland, 26, 65, 69, 95
Mary of Duxbury (vessel), 149
Mason, Isaac, 26
Masons, 194, 201
Massachusetts, 138, 180, 185
Matchapunga Indians, 8
Maynard, Edward, 14
Mediterranean Sea, 54, 137
Meekins, William, 238 (n. 101)
Melville, Herman, 241 (n. 127)
Menhaden fishery, 205, 207, 208, 211
Mercy Hospital (Beaufort, N.C.), 164
Merrick (slave pilot), xvi, 16
Methodists, 169–70
Midwives, 208
Milford (estate), 34
Minerva Wright (schooner), 149
Minner, Edward, 52
Missionary Baptist church (Davis Shore), 209
Mississippi River, xix, 26, 261 (n. 5)
Missouri, 69
Montpelier fishery, 97–98, 99, 252–53 (n. 30)
Moore, Furney, 149
Moore, James, 20
Moore, Roger (18th century), xi
Moore, Roger (19th century), 197
Moratuck Indians, 10
Moravians, 15, 46
Morehead City, N.C., 161, 162, 170, 171, 208, 209
Morris, James, 124
Morton (vessel), 176
Mullet camps, 78, 248–49 (n. 79)
Mullet fishery, xix, 58, 60–63, 77–78, 207, 209–11, 248–49 (n. 79)
Muse, William T., 47
Mutual-aid societies, 169
Mystic River, 148

Windsor, Calvino, 50
Windsor, Samuel, 205
Windsor, N.C., 40
Wingfield fishery, 85
Winslow, Francis, 79
Women: nontraditional work roles of, 62; as fish cleaners and cutters, 99; at canal-digging camps, 110; as fish hawkers and cooks, 136, 162; and Civil War, 162, 164, 188; schools and relief societies run by, 169–71, 188; rights of, 200; in men-haden fishery, 207; at Davis Ridge, 207–8; as midwives, 208

Wooby, Alfred, 147
Wood, Edward, 91, 96–98, 100, 252–53 (n. 30), 254 (n. 43)
Wood, John, 129
Wood, Peter, 5
Wysocking Bay, 107

Yoruba religion, 167
Young Men's Christian Association, 196